ALBERT,

IT HAS BEEN A PLEASURE

TO WORK WITH YOU OVER

THE YEARS.

Regards,

Geoff Cunningham

JANUARY 2002

PINKERTON

*High-Rise Security
and Fire Life Safety*

High-Rise Security and Fire Life Safety

Geoff Craighead, CPP, MII Sec

*Certified Protection Professional by the American Society
for Industrial Security*

*Certified High-Rise Fire Life Safety Consultant
by the Los Angeles City Fire Department*

Member of the International Institute of Security

Butterworth–Heinemann

Boston   Oxford   Melbourne   Singapore   Toronto   Munich   New Delhi   Tokyo

Library of Congress Cataloging-in-Publication Data
Craighead, Geoff.
    High-rise security and fire life safety / by Geoff Craighead.
        p.   cm.
    Includes bibliographical references and index.
    ISBN 0-7506-9576-5 (hc)
    1. Skyscrapers—Security measures.   2. Skyscrapers—Fires and fire prevention.   I. Title.
TH9745.S59C73   1995
658.4'73--dc20   95-34538
                                                        CIP

British Library Cataloguing-in-Publication Data
A catalogue record for this book is available from the British Library.

The publisher offers discounts on bulk orders of this book.
For information, please write:

Manager of Special Sales
Butterworth–Heinemann
313 Washington Street
Newton, MA 02158–1626

10 9 8 7 6 5 4 3 2 1

Printed in the United States of America

To my wife, Sarah, for encouraging and helping me,
to Pip and Searcy for being so very patient,

and

to American Protective Services, Inc.,
for giving me the opportunity
to work in high-rise buildings

Contents

Foreword

Vertical cities—or high-rise buildings, as they are called—pose unique problems for security and safety professionals charged with the responsibility of protecting life and property. High-rise buildings, such as the Sears Tower in Chicago, the World Trade Center in New York, and thousands of others across the United States, are virtually cities within themselves. Just as the architecture within each varies, so do the regulations governing security and fire life safety programs for each building.

Every year, we see, hear, and read about the terrible tragedies caused by fires, earthquakes, tornadoes, bombings, disgruntled employees, terrorists, and the like. Every possible scenario must be accounted for. There is no substitute for an effective security and fire life safety program. Thousands of lives are dependent on it. Awareness and training are essential. Security and safety personnel must be trained for any and all eventualities.

The author includes here the terminology, the functions, the procedures, the equipment, and the standards for an effective program. *High-Rise Security and Fire Life Safety* is a comprehensive resource for everyone who manages, works in, or visits high-rise commercial office buildings.

> Robert G. Lee, CPP, CFE, CDRP
> *Vice President and Corporate Security Director*
> *Great Western Financial Corporation*
>
> *Chairman of the National Standing Committee*
> *on Disaster Management*
> *American Society for Industrial Security*

Preface

I have been associated with the operation of high-rise commercial office buildings for the past fifteen years. During this time, I have seen the increased need for comprehensive documentation of security and fire life safety programs in these unique facilities. Reference materials for today's building owners and managers, security directors, fire safety directors, maintenance departments, and contract security firms need to include the following:

- The meaning of the terms *security* and *fire life safety*
- The types of security and fire life safety systems and equipment found in high-rise buildings
- How to conduct security and fire life safety surveys
- What comprises a security program and how it can be managed effectively
- How to manage security investigations
- The types of emergencies likely to occur, and how to establish, implement, and maintain a Building Emergency Plan to effectively handle them
- How to write security instructions for building security staff and a Building Emergency Procedures Manual for all building emergency staff, including tenants and occupants.
- How to communicate the security and fire life safety program effectively to building tenants
- The laws, codes, and standards that are the framework of security and fire life safety
- How to interact effectively with law enforcement and fire authorities

This book supplies these materials, which can be adapted, modified, rejected, or used for the reader's own purposes. I have endeavored to avoid errors, both of ommission and commission. I will be glad to correct in future editions any inaccuracies that are brought to my attention.

In conclusion, I commend this book to the kind consideration of building owners and managers in general, and security and fire life safety professionals in particular, with the hope that it will be of material benefit to the high-rise community. Only when knowledge is applied specifically to the needs of a particular facility will it become of real value. Therein lies the reader's part.

Geoff Craighead

Acknowledgments

There are many people who have contributed to the field of security and fire life safety during the century that high-rise buildings have existed. I am personally indebted to those who took the time to document their thoughts so that others, such as myself, could learn and benefit.

The following have all contributed in part to my experience, learning, and understanding the world of security and fire life safety: Hong Kong, with its myriad of high-rise structures; the International Institute of Security, with its certification program for security professionals throughout the world; the United States of America, with its thousands of well-designed and well-operated buildings; the American Society for Industrial Security and its Certified Protection Professional program; and the National Fire Protection Association, with its sound standards and training materials for fire life safety professionals. In addition, there have been many wise building managers, tenants, security and life safety professionals, law enforcement and fire department personnel, and friends from whom I have had the privilege of learning over the years.

In particular, I would like to acknowledge:

Sarah Craighead, who reviewed all my work, was a great sounding board for ideas, and is my constant helpmate.

Tom Keating for his thorough proofing and sound advice on how to manage the security function.

Sam D'Amico for his professional counsel and constant support.

Dwight Pedersen, Rodger Cramer, Art Bloomer, Spike Speicher, Tom Sutak, Rich Michau, Tannis Watson, Victor Polek, Larry Goebel, Roy Rahn, Bob Smith, Dick Keatley, Inky Surh, Milton Lin, Dan Cossarek, George Lee, Lynne Cooper, Dolores Bender, Pat Neal, and Shelley Olsen, for their valuable assistance.

Mike Brunning, Stewart Kidd, and Mike Clewes, for getting me started in the world of security and fire life safety.

Maguire Thomas Partners; Gerald D. Hines Interests; The Koll Company; Toyota Motor Sales; Stephen Lo; Roger Flores; the Los Angeles City Fire Department; the Department of Alcohol, Tobacco and Firearms; Dames & Moore; and the many vendors, for providing photographs.

Dan Gifford, Sue Doyle, Les Schaeffer, Diane Kroeker, Tom Kruggel, Rob Perkins, Rand Dixon, Brian Plymell, Jeff Needs, Eddie Edmiston, Betty Grove, Deborah Hysen, Cory Kristoff, Birgit De Geere, Jeff Cowgill, Hal Justice, Cliff Dow, Bill Forman, Craig Kramer, Robin Riso, and Don Rugee, from whom I have learned about managing facilities. Also, Steve Achorn, Jeff Bell, Glen Berryhill, Ed Beluin,

Bill Roedell, and Keith Omsberg, Esq., who gave much of their time and expertise in painstakingly reviewing material.

Dr. Wilbur Rykert of the National Crime Prevention Institute, for his expertise.

Bill Hopple, Bill Webb, Roy Fewell, Kevin Hensel, Mel Harris, Mike Jordan-Reilly,
Mark Gleckman, and Richard Geringer, for their extensive proofing of the text.
Likewise, Larry Ricksen, Pat Olmstead, Sue Niemiec, Charlie Pierce, Dondi
Albritton, Larry Cornelison, Gail Simonton, Mary Perry, Mark Gorman, Hugh
Jagger, and Scott Serani, for their assistance.

Tim Gilmore, Fred Werno, Fred Dickey, and Dennis Lang, for introducing me to
contract security.

Fernando Villicana of the Los Angeles City Fire Department for his professional
counsel and friendship.

Joanne Cameron, Philip Favro, Nancy Karl, Bernie Brent, Dave Dusenbury, Cap-
tain Anderson, Bill Corrigan, Susan Ben-David, Ron Smith, Ken Samuelsen,
Chris Edmonson, Bill Peden, Bill Wren, Tim Banker, Terry Gardner, Tim Cole-
man, Myron Davis, Albert DeLeon, August Spillers, Dave Stewart, Joel Wein-
stein, Scott Gimple, Aubrey Weldon, Said Abubakar, Mark Stokhaug, Chuck
Cone, Vinnie Esposito, Jeanne Arneson, Terry Machian, and Larry Legind, for
helping me understand how fire life safety programs should be administered.

Dr. Lynn and David Beedle of the Council on Tall Buildings and Urban Habitat,
for providing information on high-rises.

Martin Hickey, John Sprengelmeyer, Jerry Adair, Chuck Scroggins, Jim Bigelow,
Jim Bacon, "Ski" Nowowiejski, Cappy Carlson, Steve Barnett, Jim Turner, Dave
Edwards, Jeff Kazmark, Harvey Hlista, Bryan Meurer, and Mike Wilson, for tak-
ing the time to explain how high-rise building systems and equipment work.

Dale S. Brown of the President's Committee on the Employment of Persons with
Disabilities and Eva Giercuszkiewicz of ASIS, for their input. Dennis Berry and
Robert Miller, for paving the way for me to use NFPA material extensively, and
Juan Hovey for his similar assistance at The Merritt Company.

Francis Brannigan, S.F.P.E., and the late John O'Hagan, for their invaluable contributions to the high-rise fire protection community; and Allan Apo and Randall
Atlas for their contribution to security education.

Murrie Alcorn and Al Cadena, for their architectural drawings.

Lela Gilbert and Geoff Geiger, for their literary advice and encouragement.

My family: Bill and Lyn Craighead; Peter and Barbara; Ian and Trisha; Darren and
Megan; Mark and Diane; and Elizabeth Searcy, Harriet, Gilles and Livvy, and
Lulu.

My pastors: Rick and Jean Willans; and John and Joan, Allen and Lorraine, Mei
and Stephen, Chak Siu Ming, Alfred and Peggy, Nina, Loraine, and Virginia.

Kevin Cassidy, and the tremendous staff at Butterworth–Heinemann who have
worked with me on this project—namely, Karen Speerstra, Elizabeth McCarthy,
Stephanie Aronson, Eileen Anderson, and Mary-Kate Bourn—and their free-
lance experts: Sherri Dietrich (indexer), Katherine Harvey (interior design),
Ruth Maassen (typesetter), Anne Miller (proofreader), and MaryEllen Oliver
(copyeditor). Also, Marilyn Rash of Ocean Publication Services, my production
manager, and Laurel DeWolf, my professional, and very supportive Butterworth–
Heinemann editor, warrant very special thanks.

Come, let us build for ourselves a city, and a tower whose top will reach into heaven.

—GENESIS 11:4

1 What Is Security and Fire Life Safety?

For the purposes of discussion, and to address issues in a systematic way, this book treats *security* and *fire life safety* in a high-rise structure as two different subjects. However, at times these disciplines are so closely interwoven that they appear to be one and the same. Before we begin, it is important to understand what these terms mean.

What Is Security?

Security is a noun derived from the Latin word *securus*, which means "free from danger" or "safe." The *New Webster Dictionary* defines security as "the state of being secure; confidence of safety; freedom from danger or risk; that which secures or makes safe; something that secures against pecuniary loss." Fischer and Green (1992, p.3) write, "Security implies a stable, relatively predictable environment in which an individual or group may pursue its ends without disruption or harm and without fear of such disturbance or injury."

Public security involves the protection of the lives, property, and general welfare of people living in the public community. This protection is largely achieved by the enforcement of laws by police funded by public monies. *Private security*, on the other hand, involves the protection of the lives and property of people living and working within the private sector. The primary responsibility for achieving this rests on an individual, the proprietor of a business employing an individual, the owner or agent of the owner of the facility where a business is conducted, or an agent of the aforementioned who specializes in providing protective services. As Post and Kingsbury state: "In providing security for specific applications, the purpose of private security may be described as providing protection for materials, equipment, information, personnel, physical facilities, and preventing influences that are undesirable, unauthorized, or detrimental to the goals of the particular organization being secured" (1991, p. 1).

In the high-rise setting, threats to security come in many forms. Threats to persons include:

- *Murder*—the unlawful killing of a human by another with malice aforethought, either express or implied.

1

- *Manslaughter*—the unjustifiable, inexcusable, and intentional killing of a human without deliberation, premeditation, and malice.
- *Robbery*—felonious taking of money, personal property, or any other article of value in the possession of another, from his or her person or immediate presence, and against his or her will, accomplished by means of force or fear.
- *Assault*—any willful attempt or threat to inflict injury on the person of another. An assault may be committed without actually touching, striking, or doing bodily harm to another.
- *Assault and Battery*—any unlawful touching of another that is without justification or excuse.
- *Mayhem*—*Webster's College Dictionary* defines mayhem as: "the crime of willfully inflicting an injury on another so as to cripple or mutilate. Random or deliberate violence or damage." In many states the crime of mayhem is treated as aggravated assault.
- *Sex Offenses* (including rape, sexual harassment, and lewd behavior)—*rape* is unlawful sexual intercourse with a female without her consent. Under some statutes, this crime may now include intercourse between two males. *Sexual harassment* is a type of employment discrimination that includes sexual advances, request for sexual favors, and other verbal or physical conduct of a sexual nature prohibited by federal law (Title VII of 1964 Civil Rights Act) and commonly by state statutes. *Lewd behavior* relates to morally impure or wanton conduct; indecent exposure is included.

Threats to property include:

- *Vandalism*—willful or malicious acts intended to damage or destroy property. Included among these acts is the use of graffiti. Often a sharp instrument, such as a key or pocket knife, is used to scratch initials, logos, or drawings, or graffiti is written using color markers, crayons, pencils, lipstick, or spray paint. In buildings, graffiti is commonly found in rest rooms, on lockers, and on walls of elevator lobbies (particularly those of service or freight elevators), elevator cars, rest areas, and walls immediately adjacent to public pay phones.
- *Trespass*—any unauthorized intrusion or invasion of private premises or land of another. Criminal trespass is entering or remaining on or in any land, structure, or vehicle by one who knows he or she is not authorized or privileged to do so. This includes remaining on property after permission to do so has been revoked.
- *Burglary*—entering a vehicle or building or occupied structure (or separately secured or occupied portion thereof) with purpose to commit a crime therein, at a time when the premises are not open to the public and the perpetrator is not licensed or privileged to enter.
- *Larceny*—the unlawful taking and carrying away of property of another with the intent to appropriate it to use inconsistently with the owner's rights. Theft is a popular name for larceny. Larceny-theft includes offenses such as shoplifting, pocket-picking, auto theft, and other types of stealing where no violence occurs.
- *Sabotage*—in commerce, sabotage includes the willful and malicious destruction of employer's property or interfering with the employer's normal operations such as during a labor dispute. This act could also be perpetrated by a disgruntled employee or ex-employee seeking revenge, or by a business competitor.
- *Espionage*—the crime of "gathering, transmitting or losing" information regarding the national defense with intent or reason to believe that the information is to be used to injure the United States, or to the advantage of any foreign nation; could also be perpetrated by a business competitor engaging in industrial espionage.
- *Arson*—the malicious burning of another's house. This definition has been broadened by some state statutes and criminal codes to include starting a fire or caus-

ing an explosion with the purpose of: (a) destroying a building or occupied structure of another; or (b) destroying or damaging any property, whether one's own or another's, to collect insurance for such loss. Other statutes include the destruction of property by other means (e.g., an explosion).

- *Disorderly conduct* can be considered a threat to people or property depending on the nature of the offense.

Threats to both persons and property include: fire, explosions, bombs, power failure, natural disasters, water leaks, chemical and hazardous materials, strikes and labor disturbances, demonstrations, riots and civil disorder, hostage taking and barricade situations.

What Is Fire Life Safety?

Safety is a noun derived from the Latin word *salvus*, which means safe (salvation is also from this root). The *New Webster Dictionary* defines *safety* as "the state or quality of being safe; freedom from danger." Obviously, there is very little distinction between the terms security and safety. *Fire life safety, fire safety, life safety,* and *fire and life safety* are four synonymous terms commonly in use in high-rise structures. In the high-rise setting, threats to life safety include:

- Fire
- Explosions
- Violence in the workplace
- Medical emergency
- Elevator entrapment
- Natural disasters
- Accidents (including slip-and-falls and traffic accidents)
- Chemical and hazardous materials
- Strikes and labor disturbances, demonstrations, riots, and civil disorder.
- Aircraft collision
- Hostage taking and barricade situations
- *Terrorism*—"act of terrorism" means an activity that involves a violent act or an act dangerous to human life, or the threat to commit any crime of violence with the purpose to terrorize another or to cause evacuation of a building, place of assembly, or facility of public transportation, or otherwise to cause serious public inconvenience, or in reckless disregard of the risk of causing such terror or inconvenience.

In addition to the above, an individual may exhibit *aberrant behavior* such as that caused by substance abuse. Such conduct may be a threat not only to the personal safety of the individual involved, but also to other persons. There is the chance that some people may attempt to deliberately injure themselves or take their own lives. Because high-rise buildings are such tall structures, the possibility exists that people may attempt to jump from the uppermost heights, particularly if they are successful in reaching the roof.

According to The Merritt Company: "The most critical exposures in high-rise structures include fire, explosion, and contamination of life-support systems such as the air and potable water supply. These threats can be actuated accidentally or intentionally and can quickly develop into catastrophic proportions because of the rapid propagation of fire, smoke, and contaminants" (1991, p. 19-101).

The property at risk to security and fire life safety threats in the high-rise setting includes not only things but also information. The *things* can be the building itself and the fittings, furnishings, and equipment it contains. The equipment may consist of the lighting, power, gas, electrical, mechanical, heating, ventilating, air conditioning, elevator, escalator, communication, security, and fire life safety systems. In addition, within tenant offices there will be office equipment such as telephones, computers, word processors, printers, typewriters, fax machines, photocopiers, audio-visual equipment, and general-use items—coffee machines, vending machines, refrigerators, microwaves, ovens, and often antiques and works of art. The *information* can be stored in files, reference books, photographs, microfilm, x-rays, or within computer systems. Accidental or deliberate loss of such information could have a devastating effect on the tenant businesses or building operations.

Summary

In high-rise buildings there are many threats to the individuals who use these facilities on a daily basis and to the business, personal property, and information that is contained within them. The terms *security* and *fire life safety* are synonymous but can be separated into different subjects for the purposes of systematic analysis and discussion. The primary objective of a security and fire life safety program is to identify threats to security and life safety and attempt to prevent them or mitigate their effects should they occur. In developing a program a useful rule of thumb is to "define problems with two basic assumptions: (1) If something is not secured, it will be stolen. (2) If an accident can happen, it will" (Building Owners and Managers Association 1986, p. 14-6).

References

Building Owners and Managers Association, "Security and safety," The Design, Operation and Maintenance of Building Systems (Part II), RPA Course 2 (BOMA 1986).

Fischer, Robert J., and Gion Green, "Origins and development of security," *Introduction to Security*, 5th ed. (Butterworth–Heinemann, Stoneham, 1992).

Merritt Company, The, "High-rise structures—Section A: Life safety considerations," *Protection of Assets Manual*, vol. III, 9th printing. Editor, Timothy J. Walsh (Used with permission from The Merritt Company, Santa Monica, CA, 800/638-7597. Copyright 1991).

New Webster Encyclopedic Dictionary of the English Language, 1980 Edition, Editor-in-Chief, Virginia S. Thatcher (Consolidated Book Publishers, Chicago).

Post, Richard S., and Arthur A. Kingsbury, "What is security?" *Security Administration: An Introduction to the Protective Services*, 4th ed. (Butterworth–Heinemann, Boston, 1991).

Webster's College Dictionary, 1992 Edition (From *Random House Webster's College Dictionary* by Random House, Inc. Copyright © 1995, 1992, 1991 by Random House, Inc. Reprinted by permission of Random House, Inc., New York, 1992).

Note: The definitions of security and fire life safety threats were largely derived from *Black's Law Dictionary*, 6th ed., by The Publisher's Editorial Staff. Co-authors Joseph R. Nolan and Jacqueline M. Nolan-Haley (Used with permission of West Publishing, St. Paul, 1990).

2 *High-Rise Building Development and Utilization*

The Development of High-Rise Buildings

Over one hundred and fifty years ago, cities looked very different from the way they look today. The buildings that housed people and their businesses were rarely over the height of a flagpole. Urban landscapes tended to be flat and uniform in pattern. Three major developments led to the massive skyscrapers that dominate many city skylines today:

1. In 1853 an American, Elisha Graves Otis, invented the world's first safety elevator. This new form of transportation enabled people to travel safely upward at a much greater speed, and with considerably less effort than by walking.
2. In the 1870s steel frames became available, replacing the weaker combination of cast iron and wood previously used in construction. Until then, the walls had to be very thick to carry the weight of each floor.

   It usually was agreed that a 12-inch wall was needed to support the first story, and four inches had to be added to the thickness of the base to support each additional story. The depth-to-height ratio precluded building structures above 10 stories. (An exception was the 16-story Monadnock Building in Chicago, built in 1889 to 1891. Still standing, it is the last great monument to the age of load-bearing walls. At their base, the Monadnock Building's walls are six feet thick.) (Institute of Real Estate Management [IREM] 1985, p. 3)

   Steel frames were able to carry the weight of more floors, so walls became simply cladding for the purpose of insulating and adorning the building. This development, which included applying hollow clay tiles to the steel supports, resulted in a fireproof steel skeleton and "also permitted movable interior partitioning, which allowed office suites to be reconstructed to meet the demands of new tenants" (IREM 1985, p. 3).
3. The invention of air conditioning by Willis H. Carrier, in 1902, addressed the issue of providing ventilation in large buildings.

According to the Institute of Real Estate Management (1985, pp. 2, 15),

The modern office building was created in response to rapid population increases and industrialization that occurred during the late nineteenth century. Between 1870 and 1920, the nation's population doubled, and demand for office

5

space increased fivefold. The first commercial structures were in the East, but with railroads and a dynamic economy spurring national expansion, office buildings soon appeared in the Midwest, particularly in Chicago. In 1871, a fire destroyed this city. The disaster, combined with increased urban land values, the invention of the elevator, and the development of structural steel, gave rise to the skyscraper.

At the turn of the century tall buildings began to spring up in New York City—in 1909, the 50-story Metropolitan Life Insurance Building, 700 feet high; and in 1913, the 57-story Woolworth Building, 792 feet high. In 1930 and 1931 two of the tallest buildings in the world were constructed in New York City: the Chrysler Building (77 floors, 1,046 feet) and the Empire State Building (102 floors, 1,250 feet). Also, in 1931, the 55-story Citibank Building (also known as 20 Exchange Place), 741 feet high, was built. After these were erected, 40-, 50-, and 60-story structures were built all over the United States. In 1969, the John Hancock Center (100 floors, 1,127 feet) was built in Chicago.

From 1970 to 1990, there has been a combined total of 2,273 new construction starts of buildings eight stories or more in the major metropolitan areas of New York, Chicago, and Los Angeles (Dodge 1991, p.1). Two of these buildings were the 110-story twin towers of the New York World Trade Center (NYWTC), which were completed in 1973; the South Tower is 1,362 feet in height, and the North Tower is 1,368 feet. This means the NYWTC towers were the tallest buildings in the world. Today the world's tallest building is the Sears Tower (constructed in 1974). Located in Chicago, it has 110 floors, beginning at street level and ending 1,454 feet in the air.

Outside the United States, the tallest building is the 78-story Central Plaza Building located in Hong Kong (1,227 feet). At present, according to the Council on Tall Buildings and Urban Habitat, the United States has 60 of the 100 tallest buildings in the world. Petronas Tower in Kuala Lumpur, Malaysia, currently under construction and expected to be completed in 1996, will, at 1,476 feet, become the world's tallest building (Council on Tall Buildings and Urban Habitat 1995).

The tallest building in the world on the drawing board is Illinois Tower, a 528-story, 5,280-foot office building. In 1956, Frank Lloyd Wright conceived this "mile-high" office building that was to have been constructed on Chicago's lakefront (Fortune 1992, p. 87).

Three Generations of High-Rise Buildings

Since the appearance of the first high-rises around 1870 there has been a transformation in their design and construction. This has culminated in glass, steel, and concrete structures in the International (or Miesian) and postmodernistic styles of architecture prevalent today.

Before proceeding any further, it is appropriate to define what is considered a high-rise building. A *building* is an enclosed structure that has walls, floors, a roof, and usually windows. "Generally, a *high-rise structure* is considered to be one that extends higher than the maximum reach of available fire-fighting equipment. In absolute numbers, this has been set variously between 75 and 100 feet"

(Merritt 1991, p. 19-103), or about seven to ten stories. According to the Council on Tall Buildings and Urban Habitat (1995), the height of a building is measured from the sidewalk level of the main entrance to the structural top of the building. (Television and radio antennas and flag poles are not included.)

The following information, adapted largely from *High Rise/Fire and Life Safety* by the late John T. O'Hagan, former fire commissioner and chief of the New York City Fire Department (O'Hagan 1977, pp. 145 and 146), establishes that since the 1880s there have been three generations of high-rise buildings in the United States. (The approximate dates for each broad classification were obtained from *Building Construction for the Fire Service* by Francis L. Brannigan, 1993.)

First Generation (1870 to 1930)

The exterior walls of these buildings consisted of stone or brick, although sometimes cast iron was added for decorative purposes. The columns were constructed of cast iron, often unprotected, while steel and wrought iron were used for the beams, and the floors were made of wood. Elevator shafts were often unenclosed. The only means of escape from a floor was through a single stairway usually protected at each level by a metal-plated wooden door. There were no standards for the protection of steel used in the construction of these high-rises.

Second Generation (1920 to 1940)

As Brannigan (1993, pp. 458–459) describes them, these

> pre-World-War II buildings were universally of steel-framed construction. Floor construction and fireproofing of steel were often of concrete or tile, both good heat sinks and slow to transmit heat to the floor above. The construction was heavy but no feasible alternative existed. Relatively small floor areas were dictated by the need for natural light and air. Advertisements for the RCA Building in New York proclaimed, "no desk any farther than 35 feet from a window." This limited both the fire load and the number of occupants. . . . The typical office was quite spartan, though executive suites and eating clubs often were paneled with huge quantities of wood. Nevertheless, most fire loads were low.

(*Fire load* or *fuel load* is defined by the Fire Safety Institute as: "the amount of material that is contained in a building, including both contents and combustible parts of the structure" [Abbott 1994, p. 3-59]. Included in the contents are office furniture and furnishings such as draperies, curtains, carpets, and mats.) The windows provided a means for ventilation and escape of smoke from a fire because usually they could be opened and were not sealed air-tight.

In this generation of buildings, developments such as the following occurred:

- The use of noncombustible construction materials that reduced the possibility of the collapse of structural members during a fire
- The inclusion of assemblies rated for a particular fire resistance (*Assemblies* are barriers that separate areas and provide a degree of fire resistance determined by the specific fire resistance rating of the assembly itself. An assembly may consist of a floor, ceiling, wall, or door.)

- The enclosure of vertical shafts with protected openings
- The use of compartmentation (*Compartmentation* involves the use of walls, floors, and ceilings to create barriers against the spread of smoke and fire.)

Third Generation (Post–World War II to Present)

Buildings constructed after World War II up until today make up the most recent generation of high-rise buildings. They are constructed of lightweight steel or reinforced concrete frames, with exterior curtain walls, as Salvadori (1980) describes: "The so-called *curtain walls* of our high-rise buildings consist of thin, vertical metal struts or *mullions*, which encase the large glass panels constituting most of the wall surface. The curtain wall, built for lighting and temperature-conditioning purposes, does not have the strength to stand by itself and is supported by a frame of steel or concrete, which constitutes the structure of the building" (p. 22). The majority of modern high-rise commercial office buildings are steel framed. Interspersed among steel-frame high-rises are those of reinforced concrete construction, or a mixture of steel and concrete. Two Prudential Plaza of Chicago has been recognized by the Council on Tall Buildings and Urban Habitat as being, at 978 feet, the tallest concrete building in North America.

In the center of these buildings, or infrequently to the side, there is an inner core constructed of reinforced concrete. Most building services—stairwells, elevator shafts, air-conditioning supply and return shafts, power, water, and gas utilities, and rest rooms—are enclosed in this central core. Extending out from this core are steel beams that connect to vertical columns located in the exterior walls. This type of construction means that there is no longer a requirement for interior vertical columns. Hence these buildings have floor spaces free of such obstructions.

Francis L. Brannigan, in *Building Construction for the Fire Service*, asserts that modern high-rise buildings are lighter than previous generation high-rises: "The Empire State Building [a second-generation building] weighs about 23 pounds per cubic foot. A typical modern high-rise weighs approximately eight pounds per cubic foot" (Brannigan 1993, p. 462). Brannigan also states: "The development of fluorescent lights and air conditioning helped to remove limits to the floor area. Thus, building populations could be enormously increased. As a result, many floors have substantial areas beyond the reach of hand hose streams" (Brannigan 1993, p. 462).

Fire Life Safety of High-Rise Buildings versus Low-Rise Buildings

From a fire life safety perspective, high-rise buildings differ from lower-height buildings in the following ways:

1. The existence of multiple, occupied floors, one on top of another, means a greater concentration of occupants and therefore a greater concentration of personal and business property, hence, a greater potential fuel load of the building. Also, the

probability of a large uncontrolled fire moving upward is an ever-present danger in a high-rise building because it is a vertical structure.

2. The more individuals assembled in one location at any one time, the more likely it is that some of these people could be injured or killed, particularly by an incident occurring close to them. Depending on the location of the incident, there may be a delay in reaching the area to provide assistance. For example, a medical emergency that occurs on the uppermost floor of a skyscraper will require considerably more travel time for the responding medical team than a similar incident occurring in a building lobby.

3. Evacuation of occupants, when an emergency occurs, is hampered by the fact that large numbers of people (sometimes hundreds, but possibly thousands) cannot all leave the structure at once via elevators and emergency exit stairwells.

4. Access by the fire department—from both without and within the building—may be restricted. According to the International Fire Service Training Association (IFTA) (1976, pp. 57–60), external access may be limited by the following:

    • Setback of the building from public access roads and driveways, landscaping, berms, fountains, and surfaces covering subterranean parking structures that will not support the weight of fire fighting vehicles. These may restrict the proximity to the building that fire department aerial ladder apparatus can attain.

    • External features of the structure such as decorative walls, sunscreens and building offsets (where an upper floor is set back from the floors beneath it) may inhibit the use of aerial ladders.

    • The limited reach of fire department aerial ladders. (In New York, fires above the 10th floor are beyond the reach of fire department ladders and exterior streams, while in Los Angeles, it is fires above the 7th floor.)

Internal access may be restricted to the use of stairwells and elevators that are approached through the building lobby or lower levels such as basements. Internal access may also be complicated by the time required for fire department personnel to reach, and equipment to be transported to, an incident occurring in the upper levels of a structure.

The effectiveness of the response to an incident, such as a fire, may be affected by the availability of fire department personnel and equipment—hoses, forcible entry tools, breathing apparatus, lights, and power supplies. In the case of an advanced high-rise fire, only the largest fire departments are able to provide the several hundred fire fighters that may be necessary to control such an incident. The number of fire department staff required for response will depend on the type of tenancy and pattern of use of the building, the size and type of fire, its location within the structure, and whether an extensive search of the building needs to be conducted. Much of this information will be ascertained on-site, when fire department personnel have had an opportunity to evaluate the incident. "Also, the delivery of personnel and equipment to the fire may be blocked by very hazardous falling glass which may cut hose lines and injure personnel. The glass hazard may make evacuation from the building impossible" (Brannigan and Brannigan 1995). Because modern high-rise building floor areas are frequently very large, interior hose lines run from stairwells by fire fighters may not reach every part of a floor.

5. According to Boyce (1991, p. 8-186):

    The high-rise building often has natural forces affecting fire and smoke movement that are not normally significant in lower buildings. Stack effect and the impact of winds can be very significant, and very different, in high-rise buildings. *Stack effect* is the result of the temperature differential between two areas, which creates a pressure differential that results in natural air movements within a building. In high-rise buildings, this effect is increased due to the height of the building. Many high-rise buildings have a significant stack effect, capable of moving large volumes of heat and smoke uncontrolled through the building.

Are Modern High-Rise Buildings Safe When Fire Occurs?

Third-generation steel-frame buildings, particularly those constructed during the past 25 years, may be distinguished by the following features:

- Fire-resistant insulation is sprayed directly onto steel columns, floor beams, and girders to protect these structural members from distortion. It is applied in accordance with the requirements of the local building code. If the insulation is not correctly applied (for example, if the steel is rusted and the surface has not been properly prepared or if the insulation has not been applied at the specified thickness or density) or if the insulation has been dislodged during construction, heating an exposed steel floor beam to high temperatures can cause vertical deflection (because the secured beam has no space to move horizontally when it elongates) and failure of the connection used to secure the beam to other beams or to the main girders. The floor beams and girders are often covered with corrugated steel panels or plates and are then covered with a 2- to 3-inch layer of concrete to form the floor itself. These lightweight floors are commonly called *metal decks* (see Figure 2.1).
- The exterior skin–type curtain walls do not support any of the weight of the building. They frequently consist of glass windows and a lightweight metal framework; stone pre-cast concrete panels may also be attached to the exterior. The windows provide some resistance to heat and are often made of tempered glass; they usually cannot be opened and are well insulated. The exterior skin–type curtain walls are attached to the exterior wall columns, sometimes creating an empty space (of width varying from 6 to 12 inches) between the interior of these walls and the outer edges of the floors. If there is such a gap, it is usually filled with fire-resistant material to restrict the vertical spread of fire. However, according to Brannigan and Brannigan (1995), "the reliability of much perimeter firestopping is open to serious question" (see Figure 2.2).
- A concealed space is located above the suspended ceiling on each floor, and often extends throughout an entire floor area (apart from mandatory fire walls extending from a base floor slab to the floor slab of the next story). This uninterrupted space is usually about 30 inches in depth and is created when noncombustible acoustical ceiling tiles are hung from metal hangers attached to the floor above. It often is used to house electrical, plumbing, and ducting systems, as well as telephone wiring conduits and computer wiring for that particular floor. In some buildings it is also used as a return *plenum* for the heating, ventilating, and air-conditioning (HVAC) systems. (See the diagram of a typical building in Figure 2.3 on page 13.)
- Multiple stairwells provide primary and secondary means of egress and are often equipped with automatic stairshaft pressurization and smoke evacuation systems. Because these stairwells are located in the central core, they are less remote from each other than those in pre–World War II buildings.
- Stair and elevator shaft openings are equipped with protective assemblies.
- Horizontal openings are protected.

Figure 2.1
This photograph depicts the floors of a steel-frame high-rise building exposed during construction. Note the metal decks, sprayed-on fire-resistant insulation, and beam-to-column connections.
Photograph by Stephen Lo.

- Floor areas tend to be larger and generally open-plan design, with little compartmentation using floor-to-ceiling walls and barriers. Aluminum-framed, cloth-covered foam partitioning is often used to construct cubicles to be used as individual offices. This partitioning is cheaper than the hardwood partitioning used in the past, and just as effective as a sound barrier. However, it is more combustible.
- The number of occupants tends to be high and this results in a high concentration of business and personal property and hence a high fire or fuel load. Much of this property (including office supplies, plastic wastepaper baskets, files, paper, computer diskettes, and the personal computer systems that now equip most workstations) is made of synthetic materials that are flammable and, in a fire, produce toxic gases that become components in the resulting smoke and gas. "Smoke is defined as the total airborne effluent from heating or burning a material. Thus, expressions such as 'smoke and toxic gases' are, by this definition, redundant" (Clarke 1991, p. 3-19). As Bathurst writes, "Over the past several years, there have been many changes in the furnishings put into buildings. At one time, desks and chairs were routinely made of wood. Then metal became popular. Now, any combination of wood, metal, thermoplastics, and foamed plastics can be found" (1991, p. 8-146). To mitigate this threat to life safety, office furniture and interior furnish-

Figure 2.2
This photograph depicts
the exterior skin–type curtain wall of a steel-frame
high-rise building exposed
during construction.
Photograph by Roger Flores.

ings in all offices, conference and waiting rooms, and reception and assembly
areas should be of fire-resistive quality and treated to reduce combustibility.

• There is the potential during fires for the stack effect described earlier in this
chapter. Brannigan notes of pre–World War II buildings: "Windows could be
opened in buildings of this era. This provided local ventilation and relief from
smoke migrating from the fire. The windows leaked, often like sieves, therefore
there was no substantial stack effect" (1993, p. 459). "There are no manual fire
fighting techniques known to counter stack effect or to mitigate its effect during a
fire" (Boyce 1991, p. 8-187). Boyce goes on to say that, due to building height and
the temperature differential that exists between areas, the only way to reduce the
potential of stack effect is to change building design and construction techniques
to those that minimize the effect.

• Automatic fire detection systems and automatic fire suppression systems are often
incorporated into building design. As Brannigan and Brannigan (1995) state:

> Most new high-rise office buildings are sprinklered. The huge losses suffered in
> such fires as Philadelphia's One Meridian Plaza and Los Angeles' First Interstate

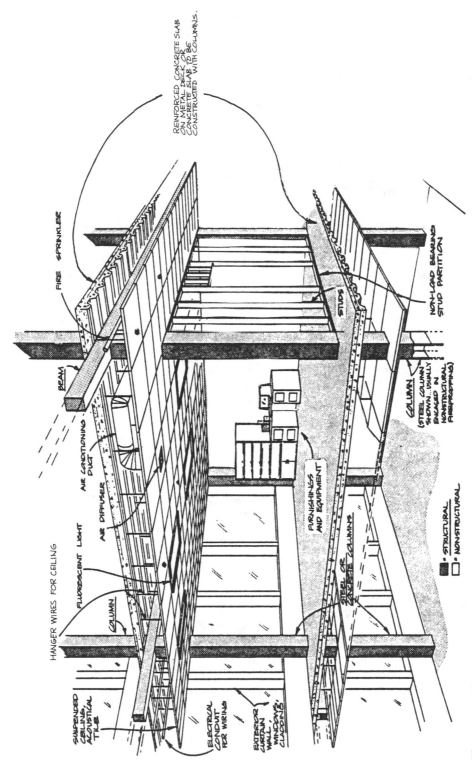

Figure 2.3 Nonstructural portions (including every part of a building and all its contents except the structure) and structural portions of a typical building. Courtesy of The Southern California Earthquake Preparedness Project (SCEPP), revised for the second edition by the Bay Area Regional Earthquake Preparedness Project, *Reducing the Risks of Nonstructural Earthquake Damage: A Practical Guide* (Los Angeles: SCEPP, 2nd ed., 1983), p. 2. A Federal Emergency Management Agency-sponsored project.

Tower leave little room for argument. But there is still much opposition to any requirement for retroactive installation of sprinklers in existing buildings. While much of the opposition is financial, the specious argument that such requirements are unconstitutional has found some favor. This argument is without merit with respect to United States law. Much of the cost, particularly of a retroactive installation, is caused by hiding the sprinkler system. If the argument of overall sprinkler cost is an issue, the opposing argument is that safety requires only the cost of a bare bones system. Aesthetic costs such as hiding the sprinklers and the piping, are the option of the owner, not a fire protection requirement.

Both Francis L. Brannigan, in *Building Construction for the Fire Service*, and John T. O'Hagan, in *High-Rise/Fire and Life Safety*, put forth the opinion that modern steel-frame buildings are less fire-resistant than those of the previous generation. Brannigan defines a fire-resistive building as one "that to some degree will resist fire-caused collapse" (Brannigan 1993, p. 11). He further defines the limits of fire resistance by stating: "Fire resistance is intended to provide, within limits, resistance to collapse by structural members and floors, and resistance to the passage of fire through floors and horizontal barriers" (Brannigan 1993, p. 452). He goes on to say that buildings built after World War II have poorer fire protection features (Brannigan 1993, p. 458).

O'Hagan (1977, p. 28) believes modern steel-frame high-rise buildings are less fire resistive than the previous generation because of their lightweight type of construction, they have a greater potential for bigger fires because of open-floor design, and greater heat retention because of better insulation. Add to this greater fuel loads caused by a higher concentrations of business and personal property, and it may look as if modern high-rise buildings should be considered high-risk occupancies.

Although, from a fire resistance standpoint, modern high-rise buildings may not appear to be as safe as those of the previous generation, nevertheless, one has to take into consideration what is being discussed here. Brannigan makes the issue clear when he says: "Note, however, that fire resistance standards are not directly concerned with life safety, the control of the movement of toxic combustion products, or with the limitation of dollar loss" (1993, p. 452).

In other words, modern high-rise buildings may be considered not as fire-resistant as previous generation buildings, but from a life safety standpoint the picture may be different. Modern steel-frame buildings that have properly designed, installed, operated, tested, and maintained automatic fire detection and suppression systems, and other fire protection features—automatic closing fire doors for compartmentation and maintenance of the integrity of occupant escape routes and automatic smoke control systems—do have the necessary early warning systems to quickly detect fires and warn occupants of their presence, and the necessary automated sprinkler systems to quickly extinguish a fire in its early stages.

Fire detection systems can trace their origin to the middle of the nineteenth century. Since then, the performance and reliability of the "number of mechanical, electrical, and electronic devices [that] have been developed to mimic human senses in detecting the environmental changes created by fire" (Moore 1991, p. 4-42) has constantly improved. Also, "since they were introduced in the latter part of the nineteenth century, the performance and reliability of automatic sprinklers have been improved continually through the experience and the efforts of manufacturer and testing organizations" (Fleming 1991, p. 5-174).

One of the key issues here is the *presence or absence of sprinklers*. "The probability of a serious fire in any given office building or other building with many occupants is extremely low. It is also a fact, however, that in the typical unsprinklered glass-enclosed office building with interior stairways and a substantial fire load, the consequences of a serious fire during working hours could be very severe—with multiple fatalities" (Brannigan 1993, p. 570).

A study by Dr. John Hall, Jr., of the National Fire Protection Association's (NFPA) Fire Analysis and Research Division, using statistics from the U.S. Fire Administration's National Fire Incident Reporting System, stated that from 1987 to 1991, office buildings, hotels and motels, apartment buildings, and facilities that care for the sick, averaged 13,800 high-rise building fires per year and associated annual losses of 74 civilian deaths, nearly 720 civilian injuries, and $79 million in direct property damage. However, most of these high-rise building fires and associated losses occurred in apartment buildings (Hall 1994, pp. 47–53).

Dr. Hall added that for this period:

- More than half of the high-rise office building fires occurred in buildings that were not equipped with sprinklers or any other automatic suppression equipment.
- High-rise buildings generally tend to have a larger share of fires that start in halls and corridors than other types of buildings.
- Only a small proportion of high-rise building fires spread beyond the room of origin, let alone the floor of origin.
- The causes of high-rise building fires are not very different from the causes of fires in other buildings. In high-rise office buildings, electrical distribution system fires rank first in causes of fire-related property damage.

This study used the NFPA's definition of a high-rise building, as found in Section 3-2 of the 1994 edition of NFPA 101 *Life Safety Code*, as "a building more than 75 feet (23m) in height. Building height shall be measured from the lowest level of fire department vehicle access to the floor of the highest occupiable story" (NFPA 101 1994, p. 101-21).

The Institute of Real Estate Management (1990, p. 111) states:

Two of the leading causes of office building fires are electrical problems and arson, with a third major cause being careless workers. In office buildings, fires originate in tenant spaces 28 percent of the time, usually occurring between 7:00 A.M. and 6:00 P.M. on weekdays when the building is full. Another 21 percent of building fires occur in electrical and mechanical rooms, with a similar proportion of fires starting in common areas and other building areas.

The Concrete and Masonry Industry's Firesafety Committee (1991, p. 1) states:

The number of lives lost in high-rise building fires has historically been lower than for other types of structures. Each year approximately 5,000 people die in building fires in the United States. Over the last three decades, however, based on fire incidents reported to the NFPA, an average of fewer than 28 fire-related deaths per year have occurred in high-rise building fires (excluding those involving grain elevators and silos). If the MGM Grand and DuPont Plaza hotel fires are excluded, the death toll is approximately 22 per year.

In modern high-rise buildings the type of fire protection equipment and how it should be designed, installed, operated, tested, and maintained is specifically subject to the strict laws, codes and standards laid down by the authority having jurisdiction. Building fire life safety systems and equipment that allow adequate time for occupants to escape, furthermore, are not in themselves sufficient: *the life safety of occupants depends critically on how ready they are to react appropriately at the time of an incident.* If building management has provided a sound fire life safety program, then a building can be considered safe. The fire life safety program will assist all building emergency staff and occupants to be in a constant state of readiness to react to an emergency, particularly one that involves fire, in a way that will help provide for everyone's safety.

The preceding review has centered on fire protection as the underlying factor in the transformation in design and construction of high-rise buildings. This is warranted because fire in these structures poses such a serious threat to persons and property. Having considered fire life safety, we can now address security within the high-rise structure.

Security of High-Rise Buildings versus Low-Rise Buildings

From a security perspective high-rise buildings differ from lower-height buildings in two ways. First, the existence of multiple, occupied floors, one on top of another, means a greater concentration of occupants and therefore a greater concentration of personal and business property; hence, there is an increased likelihood that property may be damaged or stolen. The potential for theft is increased by the fact that the concentration of property makes the site more attractive to a criminal; also, the greater the concentration of people, the better are the chances for a thief's anonymity. Second, the more individuals assembled in one location at any one time, the higher the possibility is of one of these persons committing a crime against another.

Security of Modern High-Rise Buildings

The changes in the design and construction of high-rises since their appearance around 1880 have impacted the security risks of these facilities. Modern high-rise buildings have inherent security hazards different from those of the earliest high-rises because of the following:

• Open-style floors with little compartmentation and fewer individual offices that can be secured have made it easier for a potential thief to gain access to business and personal property. The advent of answering machines and services has meant that the presence of a tenant receptionist to screen persons entering the office is now not always the standard. The open-style floor has also made it easier for an unauthorized person, having once gained access, to move unchallenged throughout the entire floor.

- The concealed space located above the suspended ceiling on each floor has provided a possible means of ingress to a tenant office. This space could also be used to hide unauthorized listening or viewing devices such as microphones or cameras. The central HVAC has provided a similar means for unauthorized listening and viewing.
- The larger number of occupants per floor in a modern high-rise means a greater concentration of business equipment and personal items and therefore a more desirable target for a potential thief.
- The greater number of occupants per floor means the greater potential for these individuals to be perpetrators or targets of a crime, and an increased likelihood that some of these people could be injured or killed, particularly by an incident occurring close to them.

In addition to these changes, other factors have added to the security risks of modern high-rise buildings. For one thing, the tenant offices in modern high-rises are often the headquarters of highly successful corporations that have designed and furnished their places of business in a style to reflect their status. This has resulted in very high-quality furnishings and expensive state-of-the-art business equipment and tools. The tenant employees themselves are generally well paid, often carry cash and valuables, and tend to drive and park expensive vehicles in the building parking garage. This, in conjunction with the upsurge of crimes against people and property that has occurred in society since the 1960s, has made the modern high-rise, which constitutes both a high concentration of people and property and a perceived seat of corporate power, a very desirable target for criminal or terrorist activity.

Next, the computer revolution with its proliferation of compact business machines (such as lightweight personal, laptop, and notebook computers) has resulted in equipment and proprietary information that can be carried away relatively easily by a potential thief. The computer, in itself, has presented a unique set of risks, because crimes can now be committed without the perpetrator ever setting foot on the premises where the information is stored.

Finally, the development in the mid-1950s of completely automatic control systems for the operation of elevators eliminated the need for elevator attendants and, in effect, did away with an important access control and screening measure for high-rise buildings. With the elevator attendant gone, it is possible for people to travel unchecked throughout a structure once they have entered an elevator. Such unchecked travel can be curtailed by the use of other security measures such as security personnel, locking off certain "secured" floors from elevator access, and the installation of modern electronic access control systems in elevator cars and lobbies.

Some of the aforementioned security risks have been mitigated by the technological advances that have occurred in the security field, particularly over the past 30 years. Centralized, microcomputer-based, control of security and elevator systems has considerably extended and improved the application of basic security measures such as the following:

- Locks and locking systems
- Access control devices—electronic keypads, cards, and biometric readers
- Lighting systems

- Communication systems—intercoms, hand-held radios, pagers, and portable cellular telephones
- Closed-circuit television systems and audio/video recording equipment
- Intrusion alarm systems
- Patrol monitoring devices
- Better-trained security officers to oversee the operation of these systems and equipment

These changes have all contributed to improved and better-designed security programs.

Tenancy and Pattern of High-Rise Building Use

In considering security and fire life safety programs in high-rises, it is vital to consider the way the buildings themselves are occupied and utilized. "The types of building tenancy and the pattern of use are important factors to consider when we plan and carry out a security [and fire life safety] program. A building can be (1) single-tenant/single-use, (2) single-tenant/multiple-use, (3) multiple-tenant/single-use, or (4) multiple-tenant/multiple-use" (American Protective Services 1980, p. 3).

A *single-tenant/single-use* building is occupied by one particular tenant and is used solely for one type of business—for example, a bank building where the business of that bank alone is conducted. A *single-tenant/multiple-use* building, however, is occupied by one particular tenant who uses the building not only for one type of business but also for other purposes. An example would be a bank building that has parking facilities, restaurants, or retail outlets open for use by the public.

A *multiple-tenant/single-use* building is occupied by more than one tenant, each of whom uses the building to conduct a similar type of business—for example, a medical office building where tenants conduct medical-related business. A *multiple-tenant/multiple-use* building is occupied by more than one tenant, each of whom conducts business not necessarily related to the others' business. An example would be a commercial office building that includes law firms, public utilities or agencies, management consultants, and financial institutions.

There are two types of structures commonly associated with commercial office buildings that technically are classified as high-rise buildings, but usually are not required to conform to high-rise building laws, codes, and standards (particularly, the laws requiring the installation of approved automatic sprinkler systems). These structures are (1) buildings used solely as open parking structures, and (2) buildings where all floors above the high-rise height limit (variously set between 75 to 100 feet) are used for open parking.

For the purposes of this book, the high-rise buildings used as examples are stand-alone, steel-frame, multiple-tenant/multiple-use structures used primarily for commercial office purposes. For illustration, the hypothetical high-rise building in this book is located in a major downtown financial district and consists of a 36-story tower with a triple-level subterranean parking structure.

Summary

Since their first appearance over a hundred years ago, high-rise buildings have changed considerably in their design and construction and resistance to fire. These structures first emerged as a symbol of the United States' booming industry which was the foundation of her new wealth. From a security and fire life safety standpoint, they have unique requirements that distinguish them from low-rise buildings. When designing a security and fire life safety program for any high-rise building, the type of tenancy and pattern of use are essential factors to consider.

References

Abbott, Richard J., "Lesson 3," *Fire Science Institute Office Buildings Fire Safety Director's Course* (New York, 1994).

American Protective Services, Inc., "Introduction," *Commercial Building Security: The Notebook Lesson Series for Security Officers* (Oakland, CA, 1980).

Bathurst, Donald G., "Business occupancies," *Fire Protection Handbook*, 17th ed. Editor-in-Chief, Arthur E. Cote, Managing Editor, Jim L. Linville (All NFPA material in this chapter is used with permission from the National Fire Protection Association, Quincy, MA 02269. Copyright 1991).

Boyce, Roger, Sr., "Occupancies in special structures and high-rise buildings," *Fire Protection Handbook*, 17th ed. (National Fire Protection Association, Quincy, MA, 1991).

Brannigan, Francis L., *Building Construction for the Fire Service*, 3rd ed. (National Fire Protection Association, Quincy, MA. Copyright 1993).

Brannigan, Francis L., and Maurine Brannigan, *Building Construction for the Fire Service* (letter to the author from Francis Brannigan, March 16, 1995).

Clarke, Frederick, B., "Fire hazards of materials: An overview," *Fire Protection Handbook*, 17th ed. (National Fire Protection Association, Quincy, MA, 1991).

Concrete and Masonry Industry, "Fundamentals of fire safety," *Fire Protection Planning Report* (Concrete and Masonry Firesafety Committee, Skokie, IL, November 1991).

Council on Tall Buildings and Urban Habitat, *The 100 Tallest Buildings in the World* (LeHigh University, Bethlehem, PA, 1995).

Dodge, F. W., National Information Services, as reported in the *Fire Protection Planning Report*, "Fundamentals of firesafety in high rise buildings" (Concrete and Masonry Industry Firesafety Committee, Skokie, IL, November 1991).

Fleming, Russell P., "Automatic sprinklers," *Fire Protection Handbook*, 17th ed. (National Fire Protection Association, Quincy, MA, 1991).

Fortune, James W., "Wright to the top." Adapted from a paper presented at the International Association of Elevator Engineers' Elevcon '92 conference; first published in *Elevator Technology* (*The Construction Specifier*, September 1992).

Hall, John R., Ph.D., "U.S. high-rise fires: The big picture," *NFPA Journal* March/April 1994 (National Fire Protection Association, Quincy, MA. Copyright 1994).

Institute of Real Estate Management of the National Association of Realtors, "Office building industry: Past, present, and future," *Managing the Office Building*, revised ed. Revisions Author, Ronald A. Harris (IREM, Chicago, 1985).

Institute of Real Estate Management, "Fires," *Before Disaster Strikes: Developing an Emergency Procedures Manual* (IREM, Chicago, 1990).

International Fire Service Training Association, "Access problems," *Fire Problems in High-Rise Buildings* (published by Fire Protection Publications and Oklahoma State University, Stillwater, OK, 1976).

Merritt Company, The, "High-rise structures, section A, Life safety considerations," *Protection of Assets Manual*, vol. III, 9th printing. Editor, Timothy J. Walsh (Used with permission from The Merritt Company, Santa Monica, CA, 800/638-7597. Copyright 1991).

Moore, Wayne D., "Automatic fire detectors," *Fire Protection Handbook*, 17th ed. (National Fire Protection Association, Quincy, MA, 1991).

NFPA 101, *Life Safety Code*, Chapter 3 Definitions, Section 3-2 (National Fire Protection Association, Quincy, MA, 1994).

O'Hagan, John T., *High Rise/Fire and Life Safety*, 2nd printing (Fire Engineering, A PennWell Publication, Saddle Brook, NJ, 1977).

Salvadori, Mario, "Structures," *Why Buildings Stand Up: The Strength of Architecture* (W. W. Norton, New York, 1980).

3 Security Systems and Equipment

In high-rise commercial office buildings there are many types of security systems and equipment. Their purpose is to help ensure that a building is safe to use, and that protection is provided "for materials, equipment, information, personnel, physical facilities, and preventing influences that are undesirable, unauthorized, or detrimental to the goals of the particular organization being secured" (Post and Kingsbury 1991, p. 1).

This chapter outlines the various systems and equipment that may be found in public access or common areas, rented or assigned occupancies, and maintenance spaces in a typical modern high-rise building. Chapter 5, *Security and Fire Life Safety Surveys*, outlines these three types of interior spaces in detail.

The focal point for the security systems operations of the entire building may be either local annunciator and control panels built into an open-style desk arrangement, or a more complex and sophisticated Security Command Center, either of which often is located in the main lobby. There are two obvious drawbacks to the former system. The security staff monitoring the equipment may be required to monitor passing pedestrian traffic and assist building occupants and visitors with their inquiries and service requests. This detracts from the staff's effectiveness in monitoring annunciator and control panels. Secondly, the placement of the building security systems and equipment "out in the open" somewhat compromises overall security and makes it more susceptible to interference and (in a highly unusual but nonetheless possible situation) direct attack. However, equipment may have to be placed in this open-style arrangement because in many smaller high-rise buildings there may not be enough activity to justify having a separate Security Command Center, or because budgetary constraints may not support the extra security personnel required to both staff a Security Command Center and meet the needs of the lobby itself. If the Security Command Center is located in a separate room, access to it should be controlled at all times, and it should not be used for any other purpose than that for which it is designed. An example of a Security Command Center is shown in Figure 3.1.

Figure 3.1   A Security Command Center.   Photograph by Roger Flores.

The Security Command Center often contains the following equipment:

- Building and elevator keys
- Systems for remote locking and unlocking of emergency exit stairwell doors when doors are locked from the stairwell side, roller shutter doors and gates, etc.
- Control systems for card access and biometric readers
- Telephones, portable two-way radio systems, public address (PA) systems, megaphones, intercom systems, and speakers
- Monitoring and recording systems for closed-circuit television (CCTV) devices
- Monitoring and control systems for intrusion alarms
- Monitoring systems of fire detection, sprinkler control valve and water flow alarm devices, and other fire protection equipment (as discussed in Chapter 4, *Fire Life Safety Systems and Equipment*)
- Monitoring and control systems for elevators (also discussed in Chapter 4)
- An operator terminal and printer arrangement for security and fire life safety systems

All security systems should be listed as having met minimum standards by either the Underwriters Laboratories Inc. (UL), Factory Mutual Research Corporation (FMRC), Wernock Hersey International (WHI) , or Electronic Testing Labs (ETL).

Before examining lighting, communication, CCTV, and intrusion alarm systems, it is appropriate to review the types of physical barriers, locks, and locking systems that may be found in a modern high-rise commercial office building.

Physical Barriers

A *security barrier* is any boundary or obstacle that separates an area and is designed to deter, delay, or prevent access of persons or vehicles to that area. The barriers usually involved with high-rise buildings are described in the next sections.

Perimeter Landscaping, Walls, Fences, Sidewalks, Access Pathways

All perimeter landscaping—including plants, trees, and shrubs—should be chosen, located, and maintained so that it deters and delays an intruder, does not provide any concealing cover that can be used for surprise attacks on persons, cannot be used to gain entry to upper levels (such as promenades, walkways, etc.), and does not obstruct lines of sight, lighting, CCTV, or intrusion alarm systems. Earth berms, in conjunction with lights, may be useful to silhouette an intruder moving over the top of a berm.

Walls may be constructed of brick, masonry, stone, concrete block, or any other aesthetically pleasing materials. To discourage people from climbing over them, walls should be at least seven feet in height and may be topped, in areas where it is deemed fitting, with materials to prevent actual scaling of the wall. To deter graffiti, climbing ivy or prickly or thorny plants—cactus, boxwood, bougainvillea, quince, locust, or natal plum—can be planted at the base of the wall.

Fences may be of the wrought-iron type and should be constructed with as few openings as possible. (Chain link, barbed wire, barbed tape fences, and the like are usually not considered appropriate in the urban high-rise environment.) Barriers to vehicle entry and exit often consists of a railroad-crossing type of barrier with a wooden cross arm. The barrier may be manually operated by a parking attendant, electrically by the driver pressing a button and pulling a paper ticket, or by acquiring a right of passage by way of an access control card reader installed at the barrier. Because high-rise commercial office buildings usually are located in urban areas where real estate is at a premium, there may be little exterior landscaping and the perimeter may actually be the walls of the building itself. Pedestrian pathways should be well lighted and provide the most direct access possible to the building.

Building Exterior

Building Exterior Walls and Roof

The building's exterior walls should be of sufficient strength to make unauthorized entry difficult. Walls at least eight inches thick are difficult to penetrate using hand tools. However, hand tools in conjunction with small amounts of explosives can be used to penetrate barriers. The use of steel rebar (consisting of either a steel bar or rod) to reinforce concrete will substantially increase the strength of these walls.

Building Exterior Openings

Openings in the building exterior permit ingress and egress of pedestrians to lobbies and utility and delivery vehicles to building loading dock areas. If there is a parking structure, openings are provided for passenger vehicles to enter and leave. In addition, there may be openings in the roof and exterior walls of the parking structure for the purpose of providing natural light and ventilation; underground tunnels for utilities such as domestic water, electrical power, gas, and telephone; and drains, conduits, or sewers leading away from the building. Such openings, including windows and doors, should be properly secured as described in the following sections.

Doors

There are several types of *exterior* doors associated with high-rise buildings:

1. *Lobby Doors.* These doors are single or double, and can be constructed of tempered plate glass (at least ¼ inch thick) or stronger burglar-resistant glass or polycarbonate glazing material (both meeting UL standards). The glass often is secured in aluminum, stainless steel, or some other metal framework. These doors are designed to swing out and are fitted with a door closer. The Americans with Disabilities Act (ADA) requires the doors to be operable by a disabled person in a single effort, with no grasping motion; this requirement can be met by the provision of a low-energy powered door opener such as a push button or push plate switch, or by fully automatic operation with doors activated by motion detectors on the door transom or header bar, or floor pressure pads or mats.

For other pedestrian traffic, the door can open manually from the outside or inside. In some high-rises, turnstile-type or revolving doors are used to regulate the flow of pedestrian traffic into and out of the lobby. These doors are designed so that during a building emergency they can be collapsed to enable straight-through egress. With a revolving door, code regulations require an adjacent swing door to be provided. Door hinges should be designed as described in the next paragraph.

2. *Stairwell Exterior Fire Doors.* These doors can be single or double. In high-rise buildings they are of solid-core construction, often with heavy-gauge sheet metal or steel plating. Door hinges should be designed so that they are not accessible from the outside; however, if they are accessible, the hinges themselves should be of heavy-duty construction to resist destruction, and hinge pins made unremovable by being welded or flanged.

"Regardless of how the pin is protected, if the knuckle [the part of the hinge that holds the hinge pin] is exposed on the outside, it is generally possible to saw off or otherwise remove and/or destroy the assembly and thus gain entry by prying open the door from the hinge side" (Gigliotti and Jason 1989, p. 213). This statement is a compelling reason for never exposing door hinges in buildings, and its originators suggest a possible countermeasure to this vulnerability. This involves the use of a piano hinge that consists of a continuously interlocking hinge system running the full length of the door.

The actual frame in which the door is mounted should be secured to the wall in such a fashion that it resists penetration to at least the same degree as the door itself. Figure 3.2 shows common attack methods on doors and frames.

A. Jamb spreading by prying with two large screwdrivers.

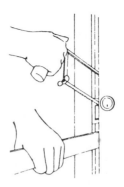

D. Sawing the bolt with a hacksaw.

B. Use of an automobile bumper jack to spread the door frame. Standard bumper jacks are rated to 2000 pounds. The force of the jack can be applied between the two jambs of a door to spread them and to overcome by deflection the length of the latch throw.

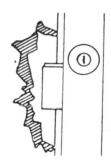

E. Jamb peeling to expose the bolt.

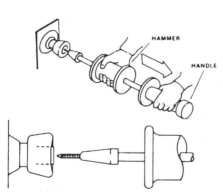

C. Cylinder pulling with a slam hammer.

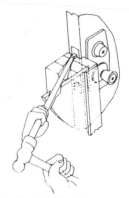

F. Forcing the deadbolt with a drift punch and hammer.

Figure 3.2   Common attack methods on doors and door frames.   Reprinted courtesy of the National Crime Prevention Institute, School of Justice Administration, University of Louisville, from Edgar et al., *The Use of Locks* (Butterworth–Heinemann, Boston, 1987), pp. 72–76.

Windows

Windows in modern high-rise buildings usually are permanently fixed in place and typically are constructed of annealed (plate), tempered, or laminated glass. The glass itself is often the weakest part of the window because it can be broken or a section of it can be removed using a glass cutter to gain access to a facility. Nevertheless, properly mounted plate glass is usually difficult to smash unless considerable force is applied. Synthetic materials, such as plastic or polyester film (e.g., Mylar™), can be applied to plate glass to increase its strength. Furthermore, if the glass breaks, the pieces adhere to the coating to reduce the potential lethal effects of broken glass. Such materials are inexpensive to install but may require replacement after 10 years.

Tempered glass is also found in modern high-rise buildings. If a tempered glass window breaks, it separates into small fragments. In most jurisdictions, building codes require tempered glass at the lobby level for the safety of persons if the glass should happen to break, and on upper floors for the purpose of mechanical smoke ventilation (when the window is broken out). For example, in Los Angeles high-rise buildings, tempered glass is required every fifty feet in upper-floor windows so that windows can be broken out for smoke ventilation. This alleviates the danger of large pieces of glass dropping from the upper floors and seriously injuring people below, or cutting fire hoses being used at a building during a fire emergency. The use of tempered glass also reduces the risk of injuries from falling glass during a major earthquake.

Laminated glass consists of a thin membrane, usually a resilient plastic material, sandwiched between two sheets of glass. It has considerable resistance to impact and the glass tends to hold together when cracked or broken. *Wired glass* also may be used in high-rise buildings, sometimes for narrow windows immediately adjacent to doors leading to tenant spaces. It resists shattering and fragmentation on impact but is not aesthetically appealing. In areas where the added expense could be justified by an insurance premium reduction or where unauthorized penetration is expected, stronger *burglar-resistant glass* or *polycarbonate glazing material* (both meeting UL standards) might be used.

Another weakness of window openings is that the glass itself can be removed and replaced, often with no telltale sign. Either putty or molding is removed and on replacing the glass the original molding is reused, or putty of a similar color to the adjoining windows is used. Such surreptitious removal and replacement of glass is much more difficult to achieve if the glass has been secured in grooves in the window frame using an elastic glazing compound.

Openings for Vehicles

Overhead gates protecting vehicle openings to parking structures tend to be either rolled, corrugated steel shutters or metal, open-grille roll-down gates. (Open-grille gates may be suitable for exterior openings because they can be seen through. They also allow ventilation of vehicle exhaust fumes and, in the case of a fire, smoke and other products of combustion.) After normal operating hours when the parking structure is closed, these gates may be operated:

- Manually using a chain
- By an electric motor manually activated at the gate

- Remotely from another location (often in conjunction with a CCTV system so that the gate operator can remotely observe the gate area)
- Automatically using an electric motor triggered to raise the gates when activated by an electronic card reader verifying the vehicle occupant's card, by a device affixed to the vehicle, or by a vehicle-sensing motion detector

One physical barrier used to protect openings for vehicles consists of steel wedges installed in the ground across vehicle openings to a parking area. This barrier can be driven over safely when a vehicle is exiting a parking area, but will cause severe tire damage if a vehicle attempts to reverse direction or drive in through an exit. Prior to installing such a device, the building insurance carrier should be consulted.

Within multilevel parking structures, steel shutter roll-down doors are used as fire barriers. Each door is equipped with a *fusible link* in the chain used to hold the door open. During a fire, the fusible link is designed to melt at a predetermined temperature, causing the door to automatically descend, thereby limiting the spread of fire and restricting the movement of smoke.

Openings for Ventilation, Utilities, and Sewers

These openings may be protected by various methods using materials such as chain-link fabric, welded wire fabric, expanded metal, barbed wire, razor ribbon, metal grates, metal louvers, metal grilles, steel bars, or steel rods.

Building Floors, Ceilings, and Interior Walls

Modern high-rise buildings have floors that provide a substantial barrier to unauthorized physical access upward or downward through the floor or ceiling to an adjoining floor. Composite concrete floor slabs, resting on metal decks atop horizontal steel beams, constitute this barrier. Interior walls and ceilings may be constructed of lath and plaster or prefabricated sheets of material such as fire-rated drywall, plasterboard, plywood, or wooden paneling attached to wooden or metal studs or rafters. Ceilings also may be constructed of noncombustible acoustical ceiling tiles hung from metal hangers attached to the floor above.

The concealed space created above the ceiling often extends throughout an entire floor area (apart from mandatory fire walls extending from a base floor slab to the floor slab of the floor above) and provides a possible means of ingress to a tenant office. A person can remove the ceiling tiles on one side of a wall, climb up into the ceiling space, crawl over the wall partition, and again remove ceiling tiles to drop down into the tenant office. There are two obvious physical countermeasures to prevent this from happening: Use floor slab–to–floor slab partition walls for all sensitive areas or, if floor slab–to–floor slab partition walls surrounding these areas do not exist, install steel bars or rods above the partition walls to deter unauthorized entry.

Further, electronic security devices may be installed to detect any possible intrusion. This concealed space could also be used to hide unauthorized listening or viewing devices such as microphones or cameras.

The central heating, ventilating, and air-conditioning (HVAC) duct systems also provide a similar means for unauthorized listening and viewing. Counter-measures—steel bars or rods, electronic security devices, or providing a separate, stand-alone HVAC system for sensitive areas—are possible solutions to this potential security problem.

Building Interior Doors

Doors to Offices and Interior Areas

Doors leading to offices and other interior areas can be single or double. Perimeter doors to tenant offices and inner office doors usually are constructed of solid-core materials (any fire doors must, by code, be of solid-core construction). Doors to sensitive areas, depending on the degree of physical security required, may have heavy-gauge sheet metal or steel plating. Door hinge and frame construction requirements are the same as discussed earlier in the "Stairwell Exterior Fire Doors" section. These doors should be locked at all times, preferably with the locks being part of a master key system. Access control systems, CCTV systems, and intrusion alarm systems also may be incorporated into the total security system protecting these interior offices and sensitive areas.

Some doors within high-rise buildings may be equipped with door viewers of a minimum 180-degree angle of vision. The specific application will vary depending on the security or safety reason for installing such a device. From a security standpoint, a door viewer allows one to see the person requesting entry through a doorway before the access is granted or denied. From a safety standpoint, the door viewer may be used by the person about to exit a door that swings out into a public corridor. By looking out through the viewer before exiting, the potential safety hazard of the door swinging out and hitting a passerby may be avoided. In addition, door viewers are installed on conference room doors to allow a person to see in to the room. This helps prevent unnecessary interruptions of meetings.

Within tenant areas there may be doors leading to individual offices, conference rooms, libraries, computer rooms, storage areas, and break rooms. Also, there may be various files, safes, and vaults used to store and protect papers, files, documents, computer software, cash, checks, bonds, precious metals, and other items of high value or sensitivity. The protection afforded may not only be against security threats such as burglary, but also against safety threats such as fire and explosions. It is important to realize that burglar-resistant containers are not necessarily fire-resistant, and vice versa. On many occasions, irreplaceable documents have been stored in safes that offer strong resistance to a would-be thief, only to have the items perish in a fire. Similarly, valuable items such as cash and precious metals have been stored in safes that were designed to resist the high temperatures of a major fire, but that offered no resistance to an enterprising burglar. The ideal solution may be a container that is burglar-resistant and built into a fire-resistant receptacle. The degree of protection depends largely on the value of the planned contents of the files, safes, and vaults.

Stairwell Doors

These single doors are of solid-core construction and made of wood, heavy-gauge sheet metal, or steel plating. They always swing in the direction of egress travel and are required to be equipped with self-closing and self-latching devices. Because these doors constitute openings in fire barriers, they are required to have a fire protection rating to limit the spread of fire and restrict the movement of smoke. A label indicating the rating is required on both the door and the door frame. For example, NFPA 101, *Life Safety Code*, Section 6-2.3.5, requires that an opening in a 2-hour fire barrier has a 1½-hour fire protection rating (NFPA 101 1994, p. 101-50). These doors should be inspected after an area has been painted to ensure that the fire protection rating label has not been obscured.

As for the stairwells to which these doors lead, details on their construction are found outlined in the laws, codes, and standards adopted by the authority having jurisdiction. These details include the following: The requirement that each floor in a high-rise has two or more stairwells, exit capacity, fire resistance rating of the walls (usually 2-hour), interior finish of walls and ceilings, width of stairwell, types of stairs, tread construction, types of guards and handrails, access to the roof and ground level, natural ventilation, mechanical ventilation, stairwell pressurization, lighting, signage, and so on.

Figure 3.3 shows the inside of a typical emergency exit stairwell. In some high-rise buildings, stairwells are occasionally *interlocking-* or *scissor-type* stairs (i.e., two stairways are located close together in the same stairshaft).

Doors to Maintenance Spaces

Doors leading to maintenance spaces can be single or double, of solid-core construction. They usually are made of wood, heavy-gauge sheet metal, or steel plating. (For preferred hinge and frame construction, see the "Stairwell Exterior Fire Doors" section.) These doors should be locked at all times, with the locks preferably being part of a master-key system. They should be equipped with automatic door closers and self-latching mechanisms to prevent them being accidentally left unlocked.

Rest Room Doors

These single doors usually are of solid-core construction and made of wood, heavy-gauge sheet metal, or steel plating. They should be locked at all times. They should be equipped with automatic door closers and self-latching mechanisms to prevent them being accidentally left unlocked. Keys to rest rooms should not provide access to any other areas. The rest rooms intended for public use should be located on the ground floor lobby or as close as possible to this location; they should be distinctly marked, in public view, and usually remain unlocked.

If advice is required about doors in commercial office buildings, a certified door consultant or an architectural hardware consultant should be contacted. Both these individuals are members of the Door and Hardware Institute.

Figure 3.3 A typical emergency exit stairwell located in a modern high-rise building. Photograph by Stephen Lo.

Elevators, Escalators, Dumbwaiters, Rubbish Chutes, and Moving Walks

The operation of elevators, escalators, rubbish chutes, and moving walks varies from system to system and building to building. Chapter 4, *Fire Life Safety Systems and Equipment*, outlines the basic similarities of elevator features and controls in high-rise buildings. In terms of tenant security, the access the elevator affords to the tenant space is of critical importance. The ability to "lock out" certain floors or place certain floors "on security" is an essential security tool. For example, for unoccupied floors or floors under construction, the ability to prevent elevators from accessing these floors will not only avoid the problem of unwanted visitors to an unsupervised area, but also the negative impression an unoccupied floor may convey to building users such as tenants. To prevent this, these unoccupied floors can be placed "on security" at all times. Similarly, some tenants may require a higher degree of security for their floor, particularly as it pertains to deliveries via the service/freight elevator. In this case, the elevator for the floor concerned is placed "on security" at all times and the elevator programmer will only take it "off security" when directed to do so by the tenant.

The person responsible for programming may be a member of building management or security. Some elevators are fitted with card access control systems that enable additional security controls to be implemented. These access control systems are discussed in detail later in this chapter. In modern telecommunications one must be particularly careful when granting access to computers such as those controlling elevator functions. One incident in a modern high-rise comes to mind.

> For months this building had been experiencing thefts of computer systems from various tenants distributed throughout its 40-floor structure. The *modus operandi* was always the same. The computers would disappear from locked tenant spaces after normal business hours. There were never any visible signs of unauthorized entry. Every conceivable pathway the thief might have taken to remove the items from the building was examined. It was determined that the only possible pathway for removal of the items was through the service/freight elevator. However, after normal business hours this particular elevator was always programmed to be "on security." It was finally ascertained through a check of the elevator programming records that the elevator was being taken "off security" for a short time period that coincided with the time of the thefts. Further investigation revealed that a member of building staff had not only accessed the elevator computer but had done so via a modem. The thefts were carried out using a building master key to gain access to the tenant space, and the elevator was taken "off security" for a short time to enable the stolen items to be loaded into the elevator car and transported down to the loading dock (where no CCTV cameras were installed in positions to view the incident). The elevator was then placed back "on security" before the undetected thief left the site.

Locks and Locking Systems
Pin Tumbler Locks

The *pin tumbler lock* (or *mortise cylinder lock*) is the type of key-operated lock most widely used in architectural or builders (door) hardware (see Figure 3.4). In high-rise commercial office buildings, these locks may be found on various perimeter, stairwell, and maintenance areas, and on tenant doors. This type of lock is installed by hollowing out a portion of the door along the front or leading edge and inserting the mechanism into this cavity. The security afforded by the pin tumbler mechanism ranges from fair, in certain inexpensive cylinders with wide tolerances and a minimum of tumblers, to excellent in several makes of high-security cylinders. Locks listed by Underwriters Laboratories as manipulation- and pick-resistant are characterized by an irregularly shaped keyway and a key that is grooved on both sides. Pin tumbler locks can be master keyed and are extremely useful in high-rise commercial office buildings where large numbers of keys are required.

A tumbler mechanism is any lock mechanism having movable, variable elements (the *tumblers*) that depend on the proper key (or keys) to arrange them into a straight line permitting the lock to operate (see Figure 3.5). The pin tum-

---

Note: The pin tumbler locks section is adapted from "The use of locks in physical crime prevention" by James M. Edgar and William D. McInerney, appearing in the *Handbook of Loss Prevention and Crime Prevention* by Lawrence J. Fennelly. Permission obtained from the National Crime Prevention Institute, School of Justice Administration, University of Louisville.

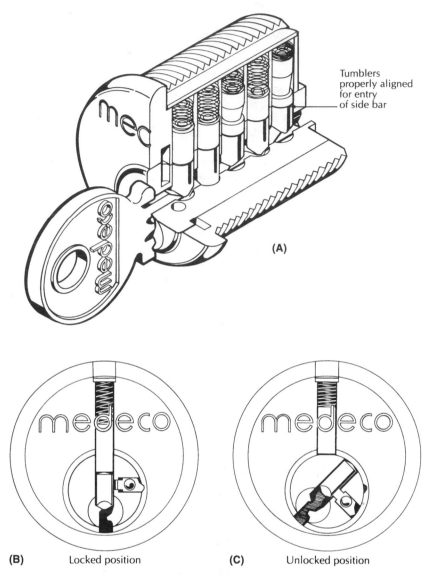

Tumblers
properly aligned
for entry
of side bar

(A)

(B)   Locked position   (C)   Unlocked position

Figure 3.4   (A) A cutaway of a pin tumbler lock showing the springs and
tumblers. (B) Locked position. (C) Unlocked position.   Courtesy of Medeco
Security Locks, Inc. Reprinted from *Introduction to Security* by Robert J. Fischer and
Gion Green (Butterworth–Heinemann, Boston, 1992), p. 217.

bler is the lock barrier element that provides security against improper keys or
manipulation. The specific key that operates the mechanism (which is called the
change key) has a particular combination of cuts or bittings that match the arrangement of the tumblers in the lock. The combination of tumblers usually can
be changed by inserting a new tumbler arrangement in the lock and cutting a
new key to fit this changed combination. This capability provides additional
security by protecting against lost or stolen keys. The different arrangements of

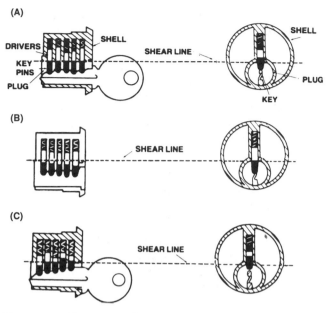

Figure 3.5 Operation of a pin tumbler cylinder mechanism. (A) When the correct key is inserted, the bittings in the key align the tops of the lower tumblers (*key pins*) with the top of the cylinder plug at the shear line. The plug may then be rotated in the shell to operate the lock. (B) When the key is withdrawn, the springs push the upper tumblers (*drivers*) into the cylinder plug. With the pins in this position, the plug obviously cannot be turned. (C) When an incorrect key is used, the bittings will not match the length of the key pins. The key will allow some of the drivers to extend into the plug, and some of the key pins will be pushed into the shell by high cuts. In either case, the plug cannot be rotated. With an improper key, some of the pins may align at the shear line, but only with the proper key will all five align so that the plug can turn. Reprinted from Edgar, James M., and William McInerney, "The use of locks in physical crime prevention," in L. Fennelly, *The Handbook of Loss Prevention* (Butterworth–Heinemann, Boston, 1989), p. 230.

the tumblers permitted in a lock series are its *combinations*. The total possible combinations available in a specific model or type of lock depends on the number of tumblers used and the number of depth intervals or steps possible for each tumbler. Master keying greatly reduces the number of useful combinations.

Pin tumbler mechanisms vary greatly in their resistance to manipulation. Poorly constructed, inexpensive cylinders with wide tolerances, a minimum number of pins, and poor pin chamber alignment may be manipulated quickly by persons of limited ability. Precision-made cylinders with close tolerances, a maximum number of pins, and accurate pin chamber alignment may resist picking attempts even by experts for a considerable time. (*Picking* a lock involves the use of metal picks to align the tumblers in the same manner as an authorized key would do, thus making it possible for the lock to operate.)

There are a number of variations of the pin tumbler cylinder on the market. The *removable core cylinder* (Figure 3.6) often is used in high-rise buildings. It was originally produced by the Best Universal Lock Company whose initial patents have now expired. This type of cylinder uses a special key called the control key to remove the entire pin tumbler mechanism (called the *core*) from the shell. This makes it possible to quickly replace one core with another having a different combination and requiring a different key to operate it.

Removable core cylinders provide only moderate security. Most systems operate on a common control key, and possession of this key will allow entry through any lock in the system. It is not difficult to have an unauthorized duplicate of the control key made. If this is not possible, any lock of the series (particularly a padlock) may be borrowed and an unauthorized control key may be made. Once the core is removed from a lock, a screwdriver or other flat tool is all that is necessary to operate the mechanism. Additionally, the added control pins increase the number of shear points in each chamber, thus increasing the mechanism's vulnerability to manipulation.

Bolts and Strikes

Before discussing the master keying of pin tumbler locks, it will be helpful to our understanding of locking systems to review two parts of locking mechanisms, namely *bolts* and *strikes*.

Bolts

There are two types of bolts used for most door applications: the *latch bolt* and the *deadbolt* (Figure 3.7). They are easily distinguished from each other. A latch bolt always has a beveled face, while the face on a standard deadbolt is square. (A *latch* is a device for holding a door closed and may incorporate a bar falling or sliding into a hole, catch, or groove.)

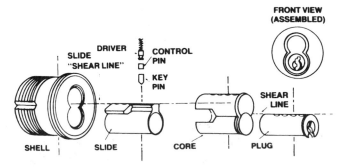

Figure 3.6 Removable core, pin tumbler, cylinder mechanism.   Reprinted from Edgar, James M., and William McInerney, "The use of locks in physical crime prevention," in L. Fennelly, *The Handbook of Loss Prevention* (Butterworth–Heinemann, Boston, 1989), p. 231.

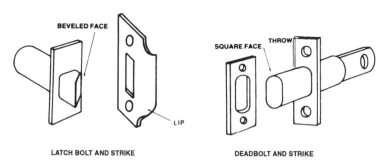

Figure 3.7 Basic types of bolts. Reprinted from Edgar, James M., and William McInerney, "The use of locks in physical crime prevention," in L. Fennelly, *The Handbook of Loss Prevention* (Butterworth–Heinemann, Boston, 1989), p. 236.

1. *Latch Bolt.* This bolt—which sometimes is called a *latch*, a *locking latch* (to distinguish it from nonlocking latches), or a *spring bolt*—is always spring-loaded. When the door on which it is mounted is closing, the latch bolt retracts automatically when its beveled face contacts the lip of the strike. Once the door is fully closed, the latch springs back to extend into the hole of the strike, securing the door.

A latch bolt has the single advantage of convenience. A door equipped with a locking latch will automatically lock when it is closed. No additional effort with a key is required. It does not, however, provide very much security.

The throw on a latch bolt is usually ⅜ inch, but seldom more than ⅝ inch. (*Throw* is the maximum distance that the bolt can extend.) Because it must be able to retract into the door on contact with the lip of the strike, it is difficult to make the throw much longer. However, because there is always some space between the door and the frame, a latch projects into the strike no more than ¼ inch (often as little as ⅛ inch on poorly hung doors). Most door jambs can be spread at least ½ inch with little effort, permitting an intruder to circumvent the lock quickly.

Another undesirable feature of the latch bolt is that it can easily be forced back by any thin shim (such as a plastic credit card or thin knife) inserted between the face plate of the lock and the strike. *Antishim* devices have been added to the basic latch bolt to defeat this type of attack (Figure 3.8A). They are designed to prevent the latch bolt from being depressed once the door closes. These often are called *deadlocking latches*, a term that is mildly deceptive because these latches do not actually deadlock and are not nearly as resistant to jimmying as deadlocks. Often a thin screwdriver blade can be inserted between the face plate and the strike, and pressure applied to break the antishim mechanism and force the latch to retract.

An *antifriction latch bolt* (Figure 3.8B) reduces the closing pressure required to force the latch bolt to retract, which permits a heavier spring to be used in the mechanism. Most modern antifriction latches also incorporate an antishim device. Without it, the antifriction latch is extremely simple to shim.

2. *Deadbolt.* The deadbolt is a square-faced solid bolt that is not spring loaded and must be turned by hand into either the locked or unlocked position. When a deadbolt is incorporated into a locking mechanism, the result usually is known as *deadlock*. The throw on a standard deadbolt is also about ½ inch, which

Figure 3.8
Modified latch bolts. (A) Latch bolt
with antishim device. (B) Antifriction
latch bolt with antishim device.
Reprinted from Edgar, James M., and
William McInerney, "The use of locks in
physical crime prevention," in L. Fennelly,
The Handbook of Loss Prevention (Butterworth–
Heinemann, Boston, 1989), p. 237.

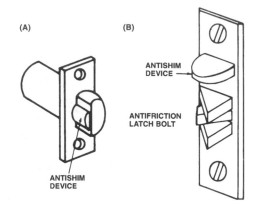

provides only minimal protection against jamb spreading. A *long-throw deadbolt*,
however, has a throw of one inch or longer. One inch is considered the minimum
for adequate protection. When properly installed in a good door using a secure
strike, this bolt provides reasonably good protection against efforts to spread or
peel the jamb.

The ordinary deadbolt is thrown horizontally. On some narrow-stile doors
(*stile* refers to the vertical uprights forming the frame around the glass panels),
such as aluminum-framed glass doors, the space provided for the lock is too narrow to permit a long horizontal throw. The *pivoting deadbolt* is used in this situation to get the needed longer throw (Figure 3.9). The pivoting movement of the
bolt allows it to project deeply into the frame—at least the recommended minimum of one inch, and usually more. When used with a reinforced strike, this
bolt can provide good protection against efforts to spread or peel the frame.

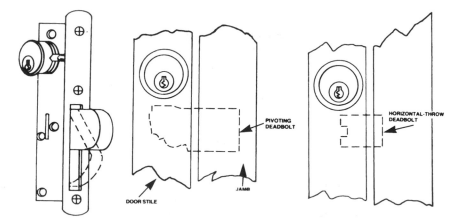

Figure 3.9   A modified deadbolt—the pivoting deadbolt. The deeper penetration into the door jamb afforded by the pivoting deadbolt increases protection
against door jamb spreading.   Reprinted from Edgar, James M., and William McInerney, "The use of locks in physical crime prevention," in L. Fennelly, *The Handbook of Loss
Prevention* (Butterworth–Heinemann, Boston, 1989), p. 238.

Strikes

Strikes are an often overlooked but essential part of a good lock. A deadbolt must engage a solid, correctly installed strike, or its effectiveness is reduced significantly (see Figure 3.10).

Master Keying of Pin Tumbler Locks

Master keying is a variation of pin tumbler locks that has been in widespread use for many years. Almost any pin tumbler cylinder can easily be master keyed. Additional tumblers called *master pins* are inserted between the drivers and key pins. These master pins enable a second key, the *master key*, to operate the same lock (see Figure 3.11).

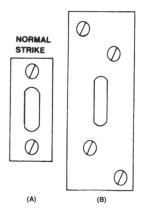

Figure 3.10
(A) Normal strike. (B) Security strike with offset screws.
Reprinted from Edgar, James M., and William McInerney, "The use of locks in physical crime prevention," in L. Fennelly, *The Handbook of Loss Prevention* (Butterworth–Heinemann, Boston, 1989), p. 243.

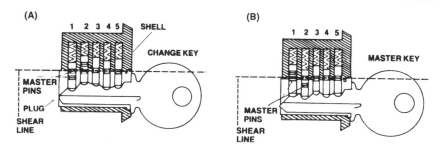

Figure 3.11 Master-keyed pin tumbler cylinder mechanism. (A) This is a simple master-keyed system using master pins in the first and second tumbler positions. When the change key is inserted, note that the top of the first master pin aligns with the top of the cylinder plug. The remaining positions show the key pins aligned with the top of the plug to turn. (B) With the master key inserted, the first position aligns the top of the key pin with the cylinder plug. The master pin is pushed further up the pin cylinder. The second position shows the master pin aligning at the top of the plug. The master pin has dropped further down the pin hole in the plug. The remaining three positions are unchanged. This arrangement also allows the plug to rotate.   Reprinted from Edgar, James M., and William McInerney, "The use of locks in physical crime prevention," in L. Fennelly, *The Handbook of Loss Prevention* (Butterworth–Heinemann, Boston, 1989), p. 232.

Generally, an entire series of locks is combined to be operated by the same master key. There may also be levels of master keys including submasters that open a portion, but not all, of a series; master keys that open a larger part; and grand masters that open the entire series. In very involved installations, there may even be a fourth level (grand grand master key). A description of the various keys in a typical high-rise commercial office building master key system follows:

1. The *change* key operates a single lock within the master key system. For example, individual occupants of a tenant space have a key that unlocks the door of their office but does not unlock perimeter doors leading to the tenant space.
2. The *submaster* key operates all locks within a particular area or group. For example, a tenant office manager has a key that unlocks all perimeter doors leading to his or her tenant space and all interior office doors within this space.
3. The *floor master* key operates one or more submaster systems. For example, a member of building management has a key that unlocks all perimeter doors leading to tenant spaces on a multiple-tenant floor, all interior office doors within these tenant spaces, and all maintenance spaces *on that floor.*
4. The *grand master* key operates one or more master systems. For example, a member of building management has a key that unlocks all perimeter doors leading to tenant spaces, all interior office doors within tenant spaces, and all maintenance spaces *within the building.*
5. The *grand grand master* key operates one or more grand master systems. For example, in a high-rise project where there are several high-rise buildings, a member of building management has a key that unlocks all perimeter doors leading to tenant spaces, all interior office doors within tenant spaces, and all maintenance spaces *on all floors of all buildings.*

An example of a master key arrangement is shown in Figure 3.12.

There are a number of security problems with master keys. The most obvious one is that an unauthorized master key will permit access through any lock of the series. A lost master key compromises the entire system and may necessitate the rekeying of the entire complex, sometimes at a cost of thousands of dollars. Finneran (1981) advises, "If rekeying becomes necessary, it can be accomplished most economically by installing new locking devices in the most critical points of the locking system and moving the locks removed from these points to less sensitive areas. Of course, eventually it will be necessary to replace all the locks in the system, but by using the method just described the cost can be spread out over several budgeting periods."

Another possible solution to mitigate the cost of rekeying is a high-security lock system developed in the 1980s. InstaKey™ is a unique system that allows locks to be rekeyed by simply inserting and turning a specially designed key (see Figure 3.13). According to InstaKey, their lock permits up to fifteen changes to be loaded into the lock cylinder distributed in any combination between grand master, master, and change key levels. It achieves this by a special key that removes wafers from different stacks within the lock cylinders. The lock also allows any level to be changed individually without affecting the operation or keying of any other level. Once all wafers have been removed, the cylinder can be reloaded and the cycle begun again.

An important feature of this system is that it allows locks to be changed immediately by the simple turn of a key. This is crucial from a security stand-

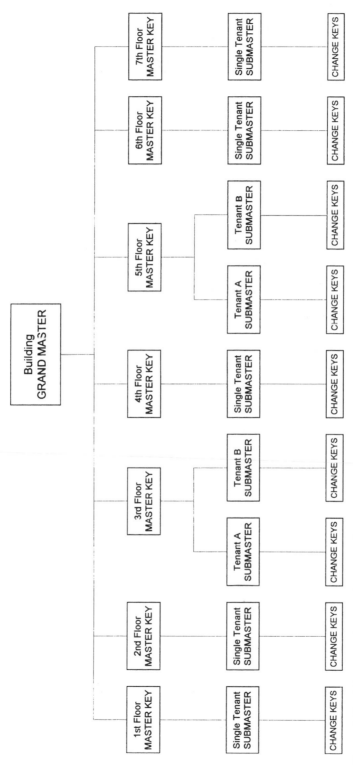

Figure 3.12 Diagram of a sample master key arrangement for a seven-story building.

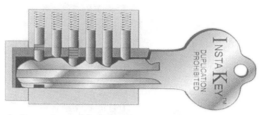

1. Step change key displaces wafer.

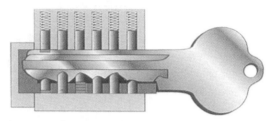

Figure 3.13
InstaKey™ four-step
key change.   Courtesy
of InstaKey Lock
Corporation.

2. Turning key disengages and captures wafer.

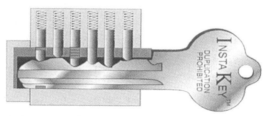

3. Returning key to original position leaves modified pin.

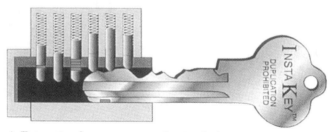

*4. Extracting key removes wafer, rendering previous
keys inoperative.*

point because a potential security breach can be addressed immediately. The expense of the lock change is restricted to the replacement keys for the affected level only. InstaKey is compatible with 90 percent of all locking systems, including Medeco, Corbin, and Falcon technologies. Converting locks to the InstaKey system is more expensive than a regular lock change. However, once the system is installed, subsequent lock changes are substantially cheaper and the system pays for itself within approximately three lock changes (InstaKey 1995). Another locking system, the Winfield Lock, performs a similar function to

InstaKey. Rather than removing wafers, this system operates using a mechanical adjustment.

A less obvious security problem with master key systems is the fact that master keying reduces the number of useful combinations because any combination used must not only be compatible with the change key, but also with the master key. If a submaster is used in the series, the number of combinations is reduced further to those compatible with all three keys. If four levels of master keys are used, the number of useful combinations becomes extremely small. If a large number of locks are involved, the number of locks may exceed the number of available combinations. When this occurs, it may be necessary to use the same combinations in several locks, which permits one change key to operate more than one lock (*cross keying*). This creates an additional security hazard.

One way of increasing the number of usable combinations and decreasing the risk of cross keying is to use a *master sleeve* or ring. This sleeve fits around the plug, providing an additional shear line similar to the slide shear line in a removable core system. Some of the keys can be cut to lift tumblers to sleeve shear line, and some to the plug shear line. This system, however, requires the use of more master pins. Any increase in master pins raises the susceptibility of the lock to manipulation, because the master pins create more than one shear point in each pin chamber, increasing the facility with which the lock can be picked.

The basic pin tumbler mechanism has been modified extensively by a number of manufacturers to improve its security. High-security pin tumbler cylinder mechanisms used in high-rise buildings commonly are produced with extremely close tolerances and provide a high number of usable combinations. Additional security features include the use of very hard metals in their construction to frustrate attacks by drilling and punching.

Perimeter Locking Devices

To meet life safety codes, perimeter legal exit doors require *panic hardware* such as panic bars or pads. This hardware is installed on building exterior doors normally located at the ground level, but excluding stairwell exit doors (the latter require *fire exit hardware*).

NFPA 101, *Life Safety Code*, Section 5-2.1.7.1, states: "Panic hardware and fire exit hardware consist of a door-latching assembly incorporating a device that releases the latch upon the application of a force in the direction of egress travel. Fire exit hardware additionally provides fire protection where used as part of a fire door assembly" (NFPA 101 1994, p. 101-30). The releasing device for the hardware must span not less than half of the width of the door and create a single motion operation to cause the door to open.

The different models of panic hardware and fire exit hardware include:

1. Latch at top and bottom of the door (called a *vertical rod device*): these can be surface-mounted (easier for installation) or concealed (aesthetically more pleasing)
2. Latch at one point in the door frame (referred to as a *rim exit device*)
3. *Mortised exit device* that also latches at a single point in the door frame

In more recent years, the push pad style has gained wide acceptance. One advantage to these push pads is that electric latching and electronic monitoring features can be added. Doors equipped with panic bars or pads may be locked on the exterior side, and at all times the inside of the door must be operable, providing uninhibited egress.

These devices function well but provide only a low level of security. A reason for this is that some doors can be compromised easily from the outside (using, for example, a simple device such as a coat hanger to pull a bar down to release the door). When these devices are installed on aluminum doors, particularly on large front entrance doors, the installation must be done in such a way as to make the device somewhat secure. One way to do this is to use an *electromagnetic lock*, which meets life safety requirements. "Devoid of moving parts—a characteristic that eliminates wear and binding—an electromagnetic lock possesses a holding power of from 1,500 to 2,700 lbs. and consumes six to nine watts of power at 24 volts" (Geringer 1991, p. 1).

Electromagnetic locks may be concealed (called *shear electromagnetic locks*) or exposed (called *direct hold electromagnetic locks*). They consist of an *electromagnet*, which is attached to the door frame header, and a metal *armature* or plate, which is mounted on the door itself. The *New Webster Dictionary* defines an *electromagnet* as "a bar of soft iron rendered temporarily magnetic by a current of electricity having been caused to pass through a wire coiled round it." When an electrical current is flowing through the electromagnet (usually at a low voltage of 12 or 24 volt DC), a magnetic field is created, and the armature is magnetically attracted to the magnet in the door frame, thereby holding the door closed.

Electromagnetic locks can be installed on perimeter legal exit doors and main entrance doors. Using a time clock, these doors can be locked automatically at the end of the day when the building closes. The times of opening and closing these perimeter doors can vary according to the building's needs. When

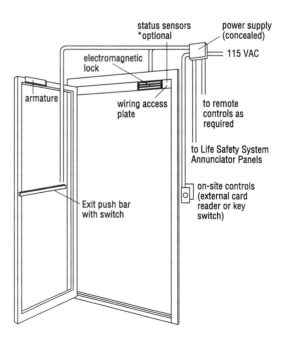

Figure 3.14
Typical installation of a direct hold electromagnetic lock for a single door with request to exit push bar. The electromagnet is attached to the door frame header, and a metal armature or plate is mounted on the door itself.   Courtesy of Security Door Controls of Westlake Village, CA (for the Series 1500 EMLock).

the doors are secured, access from the outside of the building can be obtained by hooking up a card reader (normal egress is permitted using panic hardware, or automatic unlocking devices such as motion detectors). Persons authorized to enter use their access card to open the door. In addition, the position of the door (whether it is open or closed) and its locking status (locked or unlocked) can be monitored at a remote location, such as the Security Command Center, by sensors included on the electromagnetic lock.

Life safety codes mandate that the power source to all locks restricting occupants' means of egress must be supervised by the building's fire life safety system. In the event of an emergency, such as a power failure or activation of a fire alarm, electrical current to the electromagnet ceases and the doors unlock. Occupants can freely exit the building and responding emergency agencies, such as the fire department, can enter.

"The benefits of electromagnetic locks are that fire safety requirements can be easily met, security is attained and access is provided for select personnel. Electromagnetic locks take the place of illegal or other unapproved methods of security by eliminating the need for chains, padlocks, and other mechanical devices" (Geringer 1991, p. 1). Also, electromagnetic locks require minimal maintenance and are well adapted to poorly fitted or poorly hung doors; however, a good flat connection of the electromagnet and the armature or plate must still be made. The invention of the electromagnetic lock has been a great asset to high-rise building owners and managers in satisfying the demands of both fire life safety codes and security requirements.

Stairwell Locking Devices

Stairwell door security is a lot more complicated than perimeter door security. The stringent code requirements and specifications for stairwell locks and locking systems are essential because stairwells are a critical means of egress for occupants during high-rise building emergencies. During a fire, elevators generally are not considered a safe means of general population evacuation (although under special circumstances, when the fire department directs, they may be used safely for evacuation of the disabled in some buildings). This leaves the stairwells as the primary means of egress.

Critical stairwell specifications of NFPA 101 *Life Safety Code* (which itself, or a modification thereof, has been adopted by many authorities having jurisdiction) are:

> Section 5-2.1.5.1 Doors shall be arranged to be opened readily from the egress side whenever the building is occupied. Locks, if provided, shall not require the use of a key, tool, special knowledge, or effort for operation from the inside of the building.
>
> Section 5-2.1.5.2 Every stair enclosure door shall allow reentry from the stair enclosure to the interior of the building, or an automatic release shall be provided to unlock all stair enclosure doors to allow reentry. Such automatic release shall be actuated with the initiation of the building fire alarm system. (NFPA 101 1994, pp. 101-28 and 101-29)

The Code allows for some exceptions to this, particularly in older high-rise buildings where automatic release systems are not installed. These exceptions may allow selected doors on stair enclosures to be equipped with hardware that prevents reentry into the interior of the building provided that, for example, there are:

- At least two levels where it is possible to leave the stair enclosure
- Not more than four floors intervening between floors where it is possible to leave the stair enclosure
- Possible reentry points on the top or next to top floor, permitting access to another exit
- Doors permitting reentry, identified as such on the stair side of the door

As Geringer (1991, p. 2) points out,

> The inherent problem is that building tenants may need to lock these exits on the stair side for obvious security concerns, such as transient pedestrian traffic. To ensure life safety, all stairwell doors require a locking mechanism that maintains a closed and latched door position, even when the door is unlocked, to prevent smoke and fire from entering the stairwell. . . . One solution is to install high-tower-function electrified mortise locksets on appropriate stairwell doors [see Figure 3.15]. These locks are equipped with door-position sensors as well as locked/unlocked status sensors. When energized, only the stair side is secured. . . . Generally, high-tower-function mortise locks are energized and locked at all times. Access control is accomplished by either a mechanical key, digital keypad, or a card reader. . . . The power source for these locks is controlled by the building life safety system so that in an emergency, doors immediately unlock yet remain closed and latched, protecting the stairwell from smoke and fire.
>
> The obvious benefits of this type of lock are that:
>
> - Life safety is provided.
> - Authorized personnel have controlled access.
> - Building tenants have supervised security.

Before leaving the discussion of stairwells, let us address the subject of *fire exit hardware*. Fire exit hardware is installed on fire doors within a high-rise building, including stairwell exit doors that normally exit at the ground level. These doors must remain closed and latched at all times for fire compartmentation purposes. Fire exit hardware may consist of panic bars or pads (see the previous section for the different models available).

Stairwell exit doors that normally exit at the ground level may be locked on the exterior side as long as, at all times, the inside of the door is operable, providing uninhibited egress. When an exiting occupant applies pressure to the fire exit hardware, the door will immediately unlock (although, as is discussed in Chapter 10, *Building Emergencies*, a delayed egress lock may be incorporated into the emergency exit system under special circumstances). One way of doing this is to use a powerful electromagnetic lock to deter unauthorized entry from the outside of the building.

Tenant Locking Devices

Office doors within tenant space create a different type of problem. Those not leading to a legal exit, such as a perimeter or stairwell door, are permitted to use a variety of electric and combination locks (in addition to key-, card-, token-, and biometric system-operated locks), depending on their application.

Figure 3.15 HiTower™ electrically controlled mortise lockset that installs in the stairwell door, with the electric controller that installs in the door frame.   Courtesy of Security Door Controls of Westlake Village, CA.

Electric Locks

The three main types of electric locks are electromagnetic locks, electric strikes, and electric bolt locks. They are available in two operating modes: *fail-safe*—unlocked when deenergized, locked when energized, and fails into safe (unlocked) mode; and *fail-secure*—locked when deenergized, unlocked when energized, and fails into secure (locked) mode. The exception to this is the electromagnetic lock described before, which is fail-safe only.

The following description of electric strikes and electric bolt locks was obtained from *Electronic Locking Devices* by John L. Schum (1988, pp. 23–69).

- *Electric strikes* (also called *electric door openers* or *electric releases*) use either an electromagnet or a solenoid to control a movable keeper (see Figure 3.16). The *New Webster Dictionary* defines a *solenoid* as: "a coil of wire wound in the form of a helix, which, when traversed by an electric current, acts like a magnet." The keeper interfaces with the bolt of the lock device on the door. Electrical actuation of the strike allows the door to open even though the bolt of the lock device still is extended. Electric strikes usually are installed in the door frame in place of the

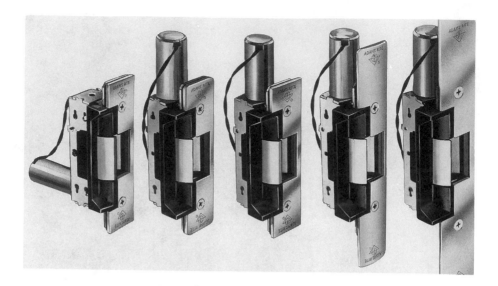

Figure 3.16   Electric strike releases for access control systems.   Courtesy of Adams Rite Manufacturing Company. Reprinted from *Security: A Guide to Security System Design and Equipment Selection and Installation* by Neil Cumming (1992), p. 231.

conventional lock strike plate. They also are available for mounting on the door frame. They are used in conjunction with various door locksets to provide additional security features, including convenience and remote operation to lock or unlock doors electrically to control the egress and ingress of persons. Tenant receptionists often use these devices to open entrance doors without the inconvenience of physically going to the door itself.

- *Electric bolt locks* (or *electric locks, electric deadbolts,* or *power bolts*) consist of a spring-loaded bolt that is activated by an electric solenoid and moves into or out of a mounting strike. These generally are mounted in or on the door frame (see Figure 3.17). They are not for use on doors used as points of egress. These devices can provide a range from low to high security. They are used in traffic control situations, especially interlock systems. An *interlock* is a system of multiple doors with controlled interaction. Interlocks also are commonly known as *mantraps* and *sally-ports*. Security interlocks are popular in high-security areas such as tenant computer rooms. Unlike electric strikes, electric bolt locks require no other mechanical lock device to provide security.

Combination Locks

These locks either operate mechanically or electrically (and are not to be confused with the dial-type combination locking mechanisms used on safes, etc.). A *mechanical* push-button combination lock has an alphanumeric keypad that is part of the locking mechanism. The keypad is used to enter a series of letters or numbers in a particular predetermined sequence. If the correct sequence of letters or numbers is entered, the bolt in the lock is released mechanically. Some mechanical push-button combination locks are combined with a key that will only operate when the correct sequence of letters or numbers has been entered (see Figure 3.18).

Figure 3.17
A mortise-mount right-angle electric bolt.
Courtesy of Security Door Controls of Westlake Village, CA.

An *electrical* push-button combination lock is different in that the alphanumeric keypad assembly is remote to the locking mechanism. When the correct sequence of letters or numbers is entered, an electrical signal is generated to operate the lock.

One problem with combination locks is that denying access to a person who has the lock combination requires erasing the codes from the lock itself. Also, someone can surreptitiously obtain the correct sequence of letters or numbers required to operate the lock by looking over the shoulder of a person as they enter the appropriate letters or numbers. A modern electronic numeric keypad manufactured by Hirsch Electronics Corporation has addressed this problem. The Hirsch ScramblePad™ Secure Electronic Keypad (see Figure 3.19) has a scrambler that automatically changes the position of the numbers on the keypad after each use, and can only be read by a person standing directly in front of the keypad. This makes it much more difficult for anyone other than the person using the device to observe the numbers being entered. A safety feature incor-

Figure 3.18 An example of a mechanical push-button lock.   Courtesy of Simplex Access Controls, Winston-Salem, NC.

Figure 3.19 Hirsch ScramblePad™ Secure Electronic Digital Keypad.   Courtesy of Hirsch Electronics Corporation, Irvine, CA.

porated into some combination locks is a *duress alarm* that is automatically initiated when a particular letter or number or sequence of letters or numbers is entered.

Push-button combination locks should never be installed on doors used as points of egress. Instead they are commonly installed within already-secured areas on doors leading to isolated areas such as a door leading to a computer room within an access-controlled tenant suite. Electrical push-button combination locks should be equipped with standby power so that in the event of the loss of normal power the lock will continue to operate. If locks are not equipped with this feature, they often are designed, for security reasons, to *fail-secure*. Also, combinations on push-button locks always should be able to be changed rapidly and without difficulty.

The code acceptance of electromagnetic locks, electric strikes, electric bolt locks, or combination locks always should be checked with the local authority having jurisdiction, a registered locksmith, a certified door consultant, or an architectural hardware consultant.

Note: The preceding treatment of perimeter, stairwell, and tenant locking devices was developed using an article that appeared in *Access Control Magazine* (June 1991), "High-Rises Look to Lock Out Problems," by Richard Geringer of Security Door Controls.

Before proceeding to card-operated locks, we will address the use of electromagnetic hold-open devices on elevator lobby doors. Elevator lobby doors normally are held in an open position. On activation of the building fire life safety system, electrical current to the electromagnetic hold-open device ceases and the device releases the lobby doors, which swing shut (see Figure 3.20). This causes compartmentation of the elevator lobby and assists in preventing the intrusion of fire and products of combustion into the lobby.

Card-Operated Locks

Card-operated locks are part of electronic access control systems commonly found in modern high-rise commercial office buildings. In general, access control systems consist of the following basic components:

- The access control device itself (whether it be a card, token, or biological characteristic of the person requesting access)
- The access control reader (whether it be a key pad, card reader, or biometric reader)
- The central processing unit (CPU) controlling the access control system
- The wiring or wireless communication systems from the access control reader to the microprocessor
- The locking device or, in elevator installations, the elevator control system itself
- The closing mechanism of the door and the barrier itself or, in the case of elevator installations, the elevator operating system itself
- The Security Command Center, or similar location, where the microprocessor, keyboard, monitor display screen, and printer is located

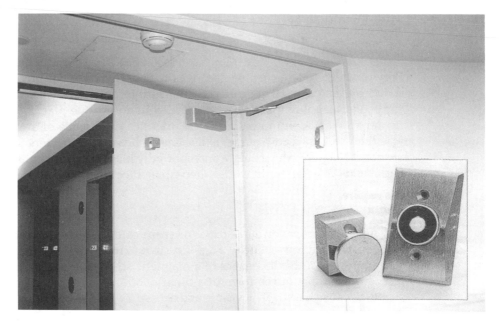

Figure 3.20 Elevator lobby doors closing on activation of the building fire life safety system. Insert, courtesy of Sentrol, Inc., Portland, OR, is a close-up of an electromagnetic door holder.

According to Cumming (1992, p. 238),

> The various categories of the system all act under the same principle—that recognition of a binary [or, in large systems, hexadecimal] code generated electronically, activates a checking procedure within the system. If, after checking, the code is verified, a second signal activates a locking device [or, in elevator installations, the elevator control system itself], allowing entry. The choice of a particular access system is a matter of trying to match the product to the environment in which it will operate, the level of security required, and the needs of the users.

In the case of the card-operated lock, the unique card of the building user is presented to a card reader at the location where access is being controlled. Within the card reader a sensor deduces information from the card. This information is translated by the card reader into a binary code that is transmitted electronically to the CPU controlling the system. The access information of the card holder has previously been programmed into the computer memory. This information, which will include the identification of the card holder and the time period in which to grant access, is then compared by the CPU with the code number it has received from the reader. The CPU will then communicate back to the locking device to unlock and facilitate access, or remain locked and thereby deny access. The time the card was used and the identity of the card holder will be recorded in the memory of the CPU and may also be printed out for future reference. If a communication failure occurs, some modern systems are designed to perform, at the card reader location, limited functions of the CPU such as allowing or denying access.

Card-operated locks use various types of cards. Because the card is the key to the system, the system is only as secure as the security afforded to the card itself. The following five sections describe cards that can be found in use with card-operated locks.

Magnetic Slug Cards

Previously the magnetic slug card was widely used but has now been superseded by magnetic stripe cards and barium ferrite cards. The magnetic slug card consisted of magnetic bits embedded in an opaque plastic card in a particular row-and-column pattern. The presence or absence of a magnetic slug was then read by a row of magnetic-sensing heads to determine the appropriate code. Magnetic slug cards were reportedly responsible for obliterating magnetic fields of other credit cards when carried together in wallets.

Magnetic Stripe Cards

The magnetic stripe, or mag-stripe (or strip) card is the most inexpensive and frequently used low-security access system card. It has the appearance of a standard credit card. It consists of a magnetic stripe fused onto the card's surface. Information, in the form of a binary code, is recorded on the magnetic stripe. Because the stripe is visible and accessible, and the technology involved is well known, the codes are susceptible to being duplicated, changed, or obliterated (low-strength magnetic fields may cause distortion of the coded information). To address this issue, some manufacturers have recorded on the magnetic stripe a unique code that cannot be changed or removed, and can be read only by using specialized equipment. The cards themselves are prone to normal wear and tear such as cracking and scratching. They are very reliable, producing few false readings, and have particular application where a large number of cards is required. Automatic Teller Machine (ATM) cards are an example of magnetic stripe cards. The level of security of the monetary transaction is raised by using a keypad in conjunction with the card reader. Not only is the correct card required for controlled access to the ATM machine, but also the correct four-digit identification number.

Magnetic Sandwich or Barium Ferrite Cards

In these cards a sheet of magnetic material, usually barium ferrite, is laminated in sandwich fashion between two plastic layers. Spots in the magnetic material are magnetized in a particular row-and-column pattern. The presence or absence of a magnetic spot is then read by a row of magnetic-sensing heads to determine the appropriate code. These cards stand up to normal wear and tear very well with the recorded code being protected by the two outer layers of plastic material.

Wiegand Effect Cards

These cards, also known as *embedded wire* cards, are used for high-security applications where a limited numbers of cards is required. The card has short lengths of special wire embedded within it. A magnetic field is generated within a card reader, causing the wires to carry electronic signals when the card is passed through the reader. These electronic signals determine whether or not a card user is authorized for access. These cards are relatively expensive, but are difficult to reproduce, and do stand up well to a considerable amount of wear and tear.

Before moving on to examine other types of cards, it is appropriate to mention that the cards described here usually are read by one of the following types of card readers:

- The *insertion type* where the card is held by its end and the entire card is inserted into a slot in the card reader (Figure 3.21). With this type, clips or chains attached to the card may interfere with the insertion of the card.
- The *swipe type* whereby magnetic stripe cards are held along the top edge of the card and are "swiped" through a slot in the card reader allowing the magnetic stripe to be read (Figure 3.22). This type of reader is preferred because clips or chains attached to the card are not a problem, it has no moving parts requiring maintenance, and its design makes it less susceptible to jamming and the effects of the weather.

Proximity Cards

These low-security cards are usually of the standard credit type with three laminated layers, the center layer containing the coding information. They operate locks in a similar fashion to the aforementioned cards but are not required to come into contact with the card reader.

Figure 3.21
Insertion-type electronic card
reader. The access card is
inserted into the horizontal
slot and then removed.
Photograph by Roger Flores.

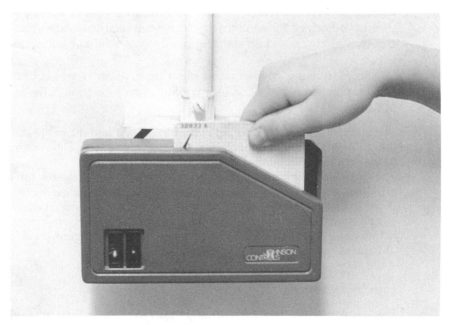

Figure 3.22   Swipe-type electronic card reader. An access card is "swiped"
through the slot in the card reader.   Photograph by Stephen Lo.

Proximity cards, when brought in close proximity, can communicate with the sensor by electromagnetic, ultrasound, or optical transmissions. Because these user-friendly cards do not need to be inserted into or swiped through the reader, there is less wear and tear on the cards themselves. Because the proximity card readers contain no moving parts, maintenance is seldom required. Also, persons carrying items such as books, manuals, a briefcase, umbrella, etc., can use proximity cards more conveniently than the previously mentioned insert- or swipe-type cards. Proximity cards may be more convenient for disabled persons to use and therefore new facilities may be required to utilize this technology for the sake of ADA compliance. A feature of proximity readers is that they can be mounted behind glass or otherwise made inaccessible to acts of vandalism.

In addition to these card access systems, one may find *optical* or *barcode* cards, where the code is embodied in infrared or ultraviolet light form; *induction* cards, where an electrical circuit contains the coded information; *tuned circuit cards*, where the code is sensed by radio-frequency waves emitted by the reader (because these cards do not have to come into contact with the reader, they are sometimes called proximity cards); and *smart* cards, where microprocessor-type integrated-circuit chips and memory are embedded in the plastic card itself. Smart cards can be used to store large amounts of information about the card holder and may be used more often in the future.

Card readers can be used for tenant spaces, and at the various ingress and egress points to a high-rise building (lobbies, loading dock, parking areas, stairwells, elevators, roofs, elevator machine rooms, fan rooms, central plant, mechanical and engineering facilities, and electrical closets). In some modern high-rise commercial office buildings, the tenants use the same access card to enter the parking structure, the building itself, the elevator, and their tenant space. Some card access systems that have both entry and exit card readers have an anti-passback feature. This prevents a card from being used again to authorize entry before the card has been used to exit a facility. The anti-passback feature often is used to control access to parking garages. As with all card readers, the designed level of security can be compromised when tailgating or piggybacking is permitted by the card user. This occurs when a person who is authorized to enter at the location where access is being controlled permits, willingly or unconsciously, another individual to enter without being subject to the verification procedure. This phenomenon is particularly prevalent at card readers located at building entrance doors and in elevator cars. After the card has granted access, the authorized tenant holds the building or elevator door ajar so that the person immediately behind can gain access.

Access Control Magazine reports that some modern parking garages are testing a new system, the SmartPass integrated reader system, developed by Amtech Corporation, that eliminates the need for vehicles to stop at garage entrances and exits. The system reads and identifies a tag located in the vehicle and enhances comfort and safety because the driver does not need to open the vehicle window at parking entrances and exits (Steenburg 1994, p. 1-21).

Cards, in addition to facilitating access, may also be used as company identification cards. In this case, a photograph of the card holder, a panel requiring the signature of the authorized card holder, and possibly a company logo, can be added to the card itself. The first two features help ensure that the card is being used by the person authorized to do so. To enhance security, the badges may be numbered and issued in sequence. These permanent badges are either the common, photographic-based, laminated identification badges, or those produced using the increasingly popular, computer-based, video imaging systems. As Goldfeld (1994, p. 22) says, the former

> are not capable of efficient badge verification or authentication, because photos and other ID information must be stored in hard copy form and are not readily retrievable. These types of systems also have no safeguards against fraudulent badge production. On the other hand, computer-based, video imaging systems store and retrieve all pertinent verification and authentication information electronically, keep track of IDs that have been produced, as well as who produced them, and often have a number of security features to combat fraud.

Biometric System–Operated Locks

In modern high-rise commercial office buildings biometric system–operated locks are part of electronic access control systems only in very specialized areas. Biometric system–operated locks work on the principle that people have certain biological characteristics unique to each individual. Such characteristics may include fingerprints, hand geometry, signatures, voice patterns, and eye retina patterns. The biometric system works by checking a physical characteristic. If, after checking, the personal characteristic is verified within the system, a second signal activates a locked device, allowing entry.

At present many of these types of systems are susceptible to errors such as rejecting a person authorized to have full access, and permitting access to a person whose access is not authorized. Part of the problem lies in the fact that over a given period of time human biological characteristics change. These changes may be due to weight loss and gain, physical injuries, extended periods of prolonged usage, tiredness, and stress. A possible solution to overcoming this problem of changes may be the development of biometric systems that operate on more than one personal characteristic. Also, biometric systems are presently more expensive than the conventional card access systems and do not have the ease of user operation that the simple inserting or swiping of a card affords. Hence, card-operated locks are a far more attractive vehicle for electronic access control in high-rise buildings.

Rapid Entry Systems

Before leaving the subject of locks and locking systems, it is important to discuss the availability of building and elevator keys for fire department use during an emergency situation. Forcible entry to locked buildings slows down emergency personnel response time, and doors may not be able to be relocked after the incident has been handled. Essential building keys should therefore be readily available to a responding unit when arriving on site. If building staff,

---

Note: A reference book that was essential in compiling the card-operated locks section (pages 49–54) is *Access Control and Personal Identification Systems* (Bowers 1988).

such as security or engineering personnel, are not available to meet the responding agency, it is necessary to provide an alternative means to access the site and structure and move freely through it. One possible solution is for the fire department to be in possession of the essential keys for high-rise buildings to which they may be required to respond. For most city fire departments, however, it is virtually impossible to manage and control effectively the thousands of keys that could be involved.

In thousands of buildings across the United States this critical issue of key control is accomplished by way of a fire department rapid entry system, namely a *Rapid Entry Key Vault* or *Fire Department Lock Box*. Suppliers of Rapid Entry Vault Systems in the United States are the Knox Company* of Irvine, California, and Supra Products, Inc., of Salem, Oregon. Selected building keys, access control cards, and, depending on the size of the selected container, the Building Emergency Procedures Manual, a list of key building personnel contacts, building floor plans, and Hazardous Material Safety Data Sheets may be stored in these specially designed, weatherproof, fixed steel encased boxes and vaults. They are usually installed in a conspicuous location on the exterior vertical wall of the building. The city of Houston even now has a fire depository box ordinance for all its city high-rises requiring fire information and equipment to be placed in such lock boxes.

To prevent tampering, the lock box usually will be situated more than six feet above the ground and securely mounted on the surface or recessed into the building wall. In some buildings, the rapid entry box or vault will be equipped with an alarm tamper switch connected to the building intrusion alarm system. These UL-listed boxes and vaults are all fitted with the same specially designed master key, supplied free ahead of time to the local fire department. The key is secured to fire department primary response vehicles and ambulance or paramedic units and its use is strictly controlled. Such an arrangement can also reduce liability on the part of building owners and managers because building keys that are only needed during a fire are well secured and do not need to be left in the custody of building personnel.

Lighting

Lighting serves the purposes of security by acting as a psychological barrier against criminal attacks and, if such an attack should occur, making identification and potential apprehension by security and law enforcement personnel more likely. It likewise serves the purposes of safety by illuminating slip and fall hazards such as puddles of water, potholes, and difficult-to-see steps. Yet it also serves to make areas more aesthetically pleasing. Security lighting can be used to complement and enhance other security measures such as physical barriers, stationary posts or patrols, and CCTV and intrusion alarm systems.

An unusual argument has been used in litigation regarding lighting providing people with a justifiable sense of security. It was brought before the Michigan Supreme Court and concerned the question of whether a property owner, by

---

* **Note:** Much of the information in this section was provided by Knox, the major U.S. supplier of rapid entry systems (Knox System 1991).

increasing lighting in a parking area and advertising this fact, was liable in an assault that later occurred in that area (*Scott* v. *Harper Recreation, Inc.*, No. 92995, reported in the *National Law Journal*, 12/13/93). The assaulted patron sued on the basis that an owner increases the risk of harm by causing area users to be less anxious when property is made visibly safer. The Michigan Supreme Court denied the litigation (The Merritt Company Bulletin 1994, pp. 3, 4).

The following factors need to be taken into consideration when selecting an appropriate lighting system:

1. The numbers and positions of light fixtures
2. The direction of light beams (often light will be directed toward walls, barriers, and the building itself)
3. The extent of illumination of particular areas (for example, security-risk locations such as parking areas will often require total rather than partial illumination)
4. The type of lighting sources—incandescent, mercury vapor, metal halide, fluorescent, and high- or low- pressure sodium vapor
5. The type of lighting equipment (*continuous* lighting is continuously applied to an outside area during periods of darkness; *standby* lighting is continuous lighting intended for reserve or for standby use, or to augment continuous lighting; *portable* lighting is movable and manually operated and can be used to augment continuous or standby lighting; and *emergency* lighting duplicates any or all of the previous three types and generally operates during power failures)
6. The method of activation of the light fixtures (manual, or automatic using a timer or photoelectric cell system)
7. The recommended minimum illumination levels for areas such as pedestrian walkways, building and vehicle entrances as may be required by local ordinances and the Illuminating Engineering Society (see the 1993 *IES Lighting Handbook*).

For exterior lighting, consideration also must be given to protecting the light fixture from weather and vandalism. When making recommendations regarding lighting, a qualified lighting engineer should be consulted.

The descriptions of the general types of lighting sources that follow were adapted from a chapter, "Security Lighting," in the *Handbook of Loss Prevention and Crime* (Girard 1989, pp. 281–283).

Incandescent

These common, relatively inexpensive, glass light bulbs become luminous (i.e., emit light) through the action of an electric current on a material called a filament. They produce very good to excellent *color rendition* (color rendition affects one's ability to discriminate, grade or select colors, and determine whether colors will appear natural), providing warm, white light. They are relatively short in rated life (500–4,000 hours) and low in lamp efficiency as compared with other lighting sources. These lights are generally for interior use and have largely been replaced by fluorescent lights in high-rise commercial office buildings.

Mercury Vapor

These lamps emit a purplish-white color because of the action of an electric current passing through a tube of conducting and luminous gas. They are considered more efficient than incandescent lamps of similar wattage, have widespread application for exterior lighting, and produce good color rendition. They are used in approximately 75 percent of street lighting and are commonly used as security lighting in parking lots. They have a long life (24,000+ hours) and are used where long burning hours are required. The time needed to light these lamps once they are switched on is considerable. However, once illuminated they can tolerate substantial dips in power.

Metal Halide

These lamps are similar in physical appearance to mercury vapor, but provide a light source of higher luminous efficiency and better color rendition. Therefore, fewer fixtures are required to light the same area as mercury vapor lamps. The rated life (6,000 hours) is short when compared with mercury vapor lamps. They are used where the burning hours per year are low and color rendition is of utmost importance. As with mercury vapor, the time to light these lamps once they are switched on is considerable. However, once illuminated they can tolerate substantial dips in power.

Fluorescent

These large, elongated bulbs have a long rated life (9,000–17,000 hours), a high lamp efficiency, and produce good color rendition. They cannot project light over large areas and may have a decreased efficiency at low ambient temperatures. Because of the latter they have limited value in colder climates for outdoor use. Compared with incandescent lamps, their initial cost is higher, but they have a lower operating cost because they require less electrical power to emit an equivalent amount of light. Fluorescent lights provide ample illumination for safe working conditions. They are commonly used as interior lights in modern high-rise buildings.

High Pressure Sodium Vapor

These discharge lamps are similar in construction to mercury vapor lamps but emit a golden-white to light pink color. The cost of the light fixture is high, but the cost of operation is low. They have a long life (up to 24,000 hours), produce relatively good color rendition, and are used for the exterior lighting of parking areas, roadways, and buildings.

Low Pressure Sodium Vapor

These discharge lamps are similar in operation to mercury vapor lamps but produce very poor color rendition. They emit a light yellow color and their maintenance of light output is good throughout their rated life. Their expected life is good (up to 20,000 hours) and they operate at a low cost. The cost of the light fixture is equivalent to high pressure sodium vapor lamps. Previously, they were widely used in urban centers. They are now most common on major highways.

Atlas (1993) emphasizes: "The important thing to remember is to make the light selected best fit the need or purpose. . . . If a parking lot is very large, and many fixtures are required, the priority should be a long lasting bulb with good maintenance (higher mean time between failures) and low replacement costs" (pp. 6–7). Also, if the light is to be used for CCTV cameras, the lower the available minimum ambient lighting level is, the more expensive will be the camera required to produce images of reasonable clarity and definition. The extra cost invested in the lighting system can result in an overall reduction of costs because a less expensive camera may be able to be used.

In some facilities the control of internal and external lighting systems may be provided remotely from the Security Command Center.

Communication Systems

There are various forms of verbal communication systems available for use in high-rise commercial office buildings and tenant spaces, as described in the following sections.

Telephones

Telephones are an essential communication tool within a high-rise complex. Telephones located in the Security Command Center should be sufficient to handle daily operations plus the extra demands placed on them when building emergencies are being handled. Important telephone numbers, particularly those of emergency services (fire department, police department, emergency medical services such as paramedics, etc.), may be programmed into many telephone systems so they can be speed-dialed to save time. In selecting telephone systems, an important feature to consider is whether the system can operate in the event of a power failure. Portable cellular telephones also have application in large high-rise complexes because they afford mobility to the user. Also, paging devices are an important adjunct to conventional telephone systems.

As with most systems, telephones can, at times, be subject to misuse. The primary misuse is by making unauthorized calls such as excessive personal ones, including those to pay-per-minute services. Arrangements can be made with the telephone company to screen out and block certain numbers so they cannot be dialed without an authorized code.

Portable Two-Way Radio Systems

Portable two-way radios (sometimes called *hand-held radios*) are another essential communication tool within a high-rise complex. All two-way radios have two major components: the *transmitter* that converts sound waves into inaudible radio frequency energy that is broadcast over the air, and the *receiver* that converts the inaudible radio frequency energy into sound that can be detected by the human ear. The following information was obtained from the American Protective Services *Tools for Security Training Course* (1980, p. 1) and Motorola (Worldwide Learning Services 1994, p. 2).

For *transmitter* control, most radios have a "Mic Key," or "Press-To-Talk Switch," used to turn off the receiver and activate the transmitter. *Receiver* controls are more diverse. A "Volume Knob" is used to adjust the level of sound that is heard but has no effect on the loudness of transmissions. The "Squelch Knob" is used to adjust the sensitivity of the receiver to incoming signals and acts like a filter. A common way of adjusting it is to turn it down until a rushing noise is audible and then to turn it up just until the noise stops. The "PL," or "Private Line Switch," is used to limit the signals heard to only those from radios that have the same crystal. The "Channel Selector" is used to select the frequency the radio will use to transmit and receive the radio frequency energy. In some high-rise buildings, radios with multiple channels are provided—one for the exclusive use of security staff, one for engineering staff, one for janitorial staff, one for parking staff, and one channel designated for use during emergencies only. A *base station*, located in the Security Command Center or the Building Management Office, should be able to broadcast to all frequencies.

The specific controls and their location on the radio will vary from manufacturer to manufacturer, and model to model. Because of the large amounts of concrete in high-rise structures, it is vital that the radio communication system selected have adequate power and quality to facilitate audible and clear communication to all normally occupied areas of a building. Usually in high-rise buildings a device called a *repeater* is added to the radio system to enhance radio coverage. A repeater receives radio transmissions and then retransmits them so that communication is maintained. The repeater consists of several basic components—a receiver, a transmitter, circuitry linking the transmitter and receiver, and either one *antenna* or two antennas and a *duplexer* (a duplexer permits a single antenna to transmit and receive at the same time). An antenna is a conductor used for transmitting or receiving electromagnetic radio waves. The repeater usually will have its antenna located on the roof of a high-rise building and will permit inexpensive, low-powered radios to communicate with each other over greater distances.

Public Address Systems

As described in Chapter 4, *Fire Life Safety Systems and Equipment*, this is a one-way system providing a means of communication from the Building Control Station to the occupants of the building. It should have adequate power and speaker quality so that, in all normally occupied areas of the building (including elevator cars), voice messages can be clearly and distinctly heard. Each PA system is different, depending on the manufacturer and system models. Usually, the system will function with the operator manually selecting the required zones (ordinarily separate paging zones will be designated for each floor and for stairways and elevators) and speaking loudly and clearly into a microphone that connects to these areas. The capability for communication to individual floors or the whole building at once is usually provided.

Megaphones or Bullhorns

These devices can be important communication tools, particularly if the public communication system in a high-rise building fails to operate. They can also be of great value in communicating with large groups of people inside, or congregated together outside, the building.

Intercom Systems

An intercom is a two-way communication device enabling communication between the Security Command Center, Building Control Station, or another constantly monitored location, and specified locations throughout the building. These locations may include elevators, stairwells (for the use of occupants who are inside the stairwell and need assistance), on the roof at the entrance to stairwells, passenger elevator lobbies, and various outside locations and parking structures. Intercoms in parking structures are primarily to assist lost persons and those requesting emergency assistance. They usually are mounted on walls, columns, or bollards and may be operated by the occupant simply pressing a button and speaking while the button is depressed, or speaking hands-free after the button has been pressed to activate communication (Figure 3.23 shows a simple intercom). This action will initiate a signal at the monitoring location and

Figure 3.23
A simple intercom station.
Photograph by Roger Flores.

should identify the station from which the call originated. If the button is pressed and no answer is received from the originating station, many security operations require staff to be dispatched immediately to that location. The intercoms should be clearly visible, particularly those in parking areas, and should have their number and location distinctly marked on them, along with written instructions as to how to operate them. Many facilities include phrases such as "SECURITY ASSISTANCE" or "EMERGENCY INTERCOM" printed in bold letters on signs at each intercom location. For safety and identification purposes, some intercom systems have distinctive flashing lights that activate at the station that is in use. Others are integrated with the CCTV system so that, on activation of an intercom station, the appropriate camera will be automatically called up for the operator who is monitoring the system.

Speakers and Microphones

A two-way voice communications system from the Security Command Center to speakers and microphones located at sensitive areas, such as stairwells, can be a valuable tool for security. If there is a problem in a remote area, it can be handled by security staff immediately communicating to that location. Used in conjunction with CCTV, speakers and microphones can become an effective part of the total security system. Figure 3.24 shows a speaker in conjunction with a CCTV camera. If, for example, security staff observe a crime in progress while monitoring camera images, they can use the speaker system to communicate to that area and possibly thwart the crime. This combination of CCTV and speaker systems has been very effective in exterior parking areas where potential car thieves have been successfully warned off before they have had the opportunity to carry out their intentions.

In addition to these communication systems there may be fire department voice communication systems, cellular telephones, pagers, scanners, fax machines, etc. All telephone, radio, public address, and intercom systems necessary for communication from the Security Command Center should be designed with a backup power system to make them operable during a power failure.

Closed-Circuit Television Systems

Closed-circuit television, sometimes called closed-circuit video, involves the transmission of scenes or moving pictures by conversion of light rays to electrical waves, which are reconverted to reproduce the original image on a video monitor. The camera image is transmitted, via a *closed-circuit* route, to a video display monitor, or the image is stored on a video-recording device, for possible later review.

CCTV and closed-circuit video recording systems are used extensively for surveillance in high-rise buildings and can be useful in solving security problems. The primary purpose of a properly designed CCTV system is to enhance existing security measures and amplify the range of observation of security staff. To improve security further, it may be useful to interface the CCTV sys-

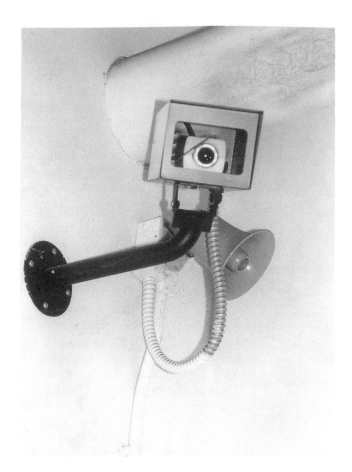

Figure 3.24
Speaker with CCTV
camera.   Photograph b
Roger Flores.

tem with intercom systems and intrusion alarm devices such as magnetic door
contacts, motion detectors, or video motion detectors. The primary purpose of
the video-recording system is to record the picture from a camera and provide
a permanent record that can easily be made available for review. As with other
security systems and technical equipment, such as physical barriers and lighting and locking systems, CCTV is part of the basic security measures that make
up the total security program.

Area Observed and Ambient Lighting Levels

Illumination is an important factor in the quality of the CCTV picture. For exte-
rior- and interior-mounted cameras it is essential that adequate levels of useful
light be available (whether it be sunlight, moonlight, starlight, or an artificial
source of illumination such as mercury, fluorescent, sodium, metal-arc, tung-
sten, or other lamps). For nighttime viewing, infrared lighting may be more
cost effective than traditional security lighting. For all cameras it is essential
that not only adequate levels of useful light be available, but also that the light
be compatible with the type of image sensor contained in the camera.

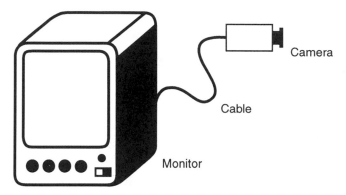

Figure 3.25   Three essential parts of a CCTV system—camera, cable, and video monitor.   Courtesy of Charlie Pierce, *Video Theory* (L.T.C. Training Center, Electronics Company, Davenport, IA, 1995), p. 1.4.

Camera and Lens

The camera is the device that facilitates the conversion of the optical image, produced by the lens, to an electrical signal for transmission via a coaxial cable, or other means, to the remote video monitor. The function of the lens is to collect the light from the area being observed and form an image of the scene on the imager contained within the camera (i.e., the lens focuses light onto a chip or tube within the camera). Lenses come in different sizes that allow choices for the area view. Each lens has a specified *focal length*. The focal length (FL) is "the distance from the lens center, or second principal plane to a location (plane) in space where the image of a distant scene or object is focused. FL is expressed in millimeters or inches" (Kruegle 1995, p. 435). For use in remote control applications, fixed FL lenses are usually obtainable in an auto or motorized *iris* form. By varying the diameter of the aperture, the iris controls the amount of light reaching the image sensor.

The various types of lenses available are as follows:

1. *Standard, wide-angle,* and *telephoto lenses* are lenses with a fixed focal length. A *standard lens* produces an image that is the same as what the eye sees at the same distance; a *wide-angle lens* is designed to view a wide area up close; and a *telephoto lens* is designed to view distant areas and produce images larger than what the naked eye sees.
2. A *zoom lens* has a variable focal length. It can be manually operated or motorized and can be used as a standard, wide-angle, or telephoto lens.
3. A *split lens* or *bifocal lens* is a system consisting of two separate lenses that view two scenes with identical or different magnifications and then combines them on the camera imager.
4. A *pinhole lens* and a *right angle lens* can be used for covert surveillance purposes. The pinhole lens can be used with the camera mounted behind a wall and the lens viewing through a small hole in the wall. The lens is designed to produce an image with a wide angle field of view (i.e., the angle of view encompasses the width and height of the scene being monitored). The right angle lens can be used with the camera mounted inside a thin wall or above the ceiling.

An essential key in properly designing any CCTV system is to select the most appropriate lens for the application at hand. Doing so will maximize the practical value of the resultant video images.

Today *chip cameras* (also called *CCD solid state cameras*) have replaced the more conventional tube cameras such as vidicon, Newvicon™, and Ultricon™. CCD solid state cameras "are integrated circuit devices which utilize an array of solid state, light sensitive elements (pixels) arranged on a silicon chip to sense light passed from the scene through the lens. The pixels are arrayed in horizontal rows and vertical columns of varying size" (The Merritt Company 1991, p. 38-15). As Pierce (1989, pp. 71, 72) writes,

> The strongest advantages of chip cameras are that they require less energy and take up less space (because of the lack of high-voltage image tubes), require less maintenance (average image chip life expectancy is five years, compared to the average image tube life of one to two years), and are more flexible, coming with more standard features than tube cameras . . . Vidicon cameras have a high propensity to burn or retain images, meaning the pickup tube shows the scene it has been staring at even after the lens is capped. . . . Chip cameras, on the other hand, cannot burn or retain images, and are even warranted against such problems.

Camera Mounting, Housing, Pan and Tilt Capabilities

A camera can be mounted in several ways: on a support bracket; recessed into a ceiling or wall; or housed in a dome, box, or custom-shaped protective container made of metal or strong plastic material.

Camera housings can be designed to look like track lighting. In interior locations such as reception areas, these cameras are inconspicuous. When mounting a camera, the power supply to it should not be a simple plug-in, as is often the case, but should have the greater degree of security afforded by hard wiring extending from the camera into conduit, plastic channels, or directly into the wall. The camera should be mounted so that it is out of the normal reach of people and cannot be approached without the person doing so being caught on film. If it is not mounted at a sufficient height, the camera may be sabotaged by a person who, undetected, reaches the camera and either pulls the plug or cuts the power supply or covers the camera lens with an object to obstruct its view.

In some high-rise buildings, particularly in areas such as parking structures, *dummy cameras* are installed. A dummy camera looks like a camera but is not one. It could consist of an opaque camera housing with an apparent power supply connected to it—the housing may contain a camera that is not hooked up to any monitor, or may not contain a camera at all. The use of such devices can provide people with a false sense of security because they believe they are in an area monitored by personnel or recorded by a CCTV system. In the case of a security-related incident, such as robbery or assault, the presence of such devices can result in considerable liability for the owner or manager of the facility.

Exterior-mounted cameras, in particular, need to be protected against weather, vandalism, and intentional interference with a camera to make it inoperative. An environmental housing can provide protection against wind, snow, rain, moisture, dirt, or, in some cases, explosions (see Figure 3.26). Some housings are equipped with windshield wipers and heaters.

Pan, or pan and tilt, mechanisms are peripheral devices that allow the camera or the weatherproof housing to move along a horizontal plane (*pan*) or vertical plane (*tilt*). Pan moves the camera mounted to it from side to side. Pan/tilt moves the camera mounted to it from side to side and up and down.

These mechanisms can be designed to operate automatically or manually. A *controller* is a device that controls the pan, pan/tilt, and/or automatic lens functions. Controller types include a lens controller; a pan or pan/tilt controller; or an operations controller, which is a combination of the first two in a single unit.

Transmission of Camera Image to Video Monitor

The most common systems for transmission of the video signal are coaxial cable or fiber optic cable. The maximum distance between the camera and the monitor over which the equipment will operate is generally specified by the CCTV camera manufacturer. Coaxial cable remains the preferred method for transmission over relatively short distances up to 3,000 feet. It is ordinarily reliable

Figure 3.26 Exterior-mounted camera with a weatherproof housing and equipped with a pan and tilt mechanism. Photograph by Roger Flores.

and often the up-front lowest-cost method. If there are difficulties with the installation of coaxial cable, the video signal can be transmitted via several other different transmission means: fiber-optic, two-wire, wireless, microwave, radio frequency, and infrared. "Fiber-optic cable is gaining acceptance because of its better picture quality (particularly with color) and lower risk factor with respect to ground loops and electrical interference" (Kruegle 1995, p. 183).

Video Monitor

The video monitor displays the image obtained from the camera. Sometimes the video monitor is called a television monitor. This is not a correct use of the term because a television and video monitor are, in fact, two different pieces of equipment.

The image can be displayed in black and white or color depending on the camera and monitor equipment. Black-and-white imaging is commonly used in security applications in the United States; however, color is becoming increasingly popular where enhanced imaging is vital to the scene being viewed. "In Europe the majority of CCTV systems are in color (estimated to be 10% black and white). In this country few systems are color (estimated to be 70% black and white). The reasons we resist color are cost and the requirement for a higher light level to obtain a usable picture" (The Merritt Company Bulletin 1994, pp. 6, 7).

In certain applications, particularly identification, it may be far better to have the camera image displayed in color. For example, a camera may be located in an area, with a dark-colored floor, that is being viewed to monitor property removal. If a person carrying property close to her or his body is wearing dark-colored clothing and walks across the area, the property itself may not be discernible on a black-and-white monitor. However, the same image displayed in color may clearly display the property being removed. Also, for covert surveillance purposes it may be more effective to use a color camera and color monitor. An incident to illustrate this involves theft in a high-rise building that contains a large number of occupants. If a surveillance has been set up in a particular area, it may be necessary to quickly apprehend the individual responsible for the theft while this person is still in possession of the stolen merchandise. If the image is displayed in black and white, it may be more difficult to identify the person in a group because his or her clothing will not be of a distinguishable color.

Before proceeding, it is appropriate to address a common belief—that CCTV video monitors are nothing more than overpriced television sets. "The video monitor is designed to work with the industrial closed-circuit video system, and will outlast—and out-perform—the consumer television at a lower overall cost, provided that it is installed in a proper environment" (Pierce 1993, pp. 29–32). Pierce further elaborates, "The average television is designed to operate eight hours a day for five years. The monitor is designed to run continuously for 24 hours per day for five years." In other words, the actual life of the CCTV video monitor is three times that of the consumer television. Pierce (1993, pp. 29–32) also states that the life of the monitor is reduced where:

1. Dust levels are high (dust gets inside the monitor and leads to heat buildup and premature breakdown of the solid state electronics)

2. Papers are stacked on top of and around the monitor (not permitting proper dissipation of heat and thereby resulting in premature failure of the cathode ray tube or CRT)
3. Brightness and contrast controls are turned to the maximum.

Controls

The controls on the monitor are similar to domestic television sets, with power on and off, contrast, brightness, horizontal, and vertical hold (and color controls, if the monitor is color).

Size

Video monitors can be procured with diagonal screen size of 5, 7, 9, 14, 17, 19, 21, or 23 inches, with the most common being 9 inches. Kruegle (1995, p. 189) gives several reasons for the popularity of the 9-inch screen:

1. The 9-inch diagonal screen provides the highest resolution from the monitor.
2. Using a 9-inch monitor, the optimum viewing distance of the operator from the monitor is approximately 3 feet, a convenient distance in many security console rooms.
3. The 9-inch monitor size is such that two 9-inch monitors fit side-by-side in the standard Electronic Industries Association (EIA) rack configuration. This is an important consideration, since space is generally at a premium in the security console room and optimum integration and placement of the monitors is important.

On-Screen Displays

Several types of displays and on-screen character generation can be used to assist the performance of an operator viewing a monitor. Displays using graphic floor plans and maps with flashing, colored icons symbolizing event locations and definitive text can be used to decrease the operator's response time and increase adherence to, for example, established procedures for responding to alarms.

On-screen character generation varies from camera system to camera system. It may show the camera number, camera title (brief description of camera location), date, and time. Also, if alarms are part of the CCTV system, it may show the alarm status of each camera being displayed at that time.

The date and time information is generated either by an exterior unit or the camera microprocessor unit. The unit producing this information should have battery backup to accommodate limited power outages.

Mounting

Monitors may be table-top or rack mounted depending on the number being viewed. "There have been several studies of operator effectiveness regarding the most effective angle of the monitors to the operator. . . . Design the console or viewing area in such a way that the monitors that will be viewed by the operator will be aimed straight at wherever the operator is sitting" (Pierce 1993, pp. 29–32). Figure 3.27 displays a two-guard security console configuration.

Rack mounting, particularly where large numbers of monitors are involved, permits the monitors to be mounted in a functional way that takes into

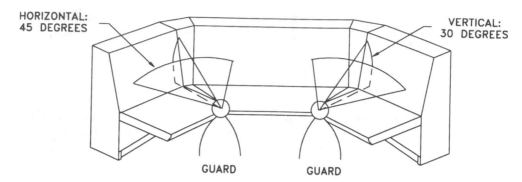

Figure 3.27 Two-operator security console configuration.   Courtesy of Herman Kruegle, *CCTV Surveillance: Video Practices and Technology* (Butterworth–Heinemann, Boston, 1995), p. 188.

account the camera scenes that are being monitored. For example, if there are a series of cameras in a corridor, the monitors displaying those images should be programmed together in a horizontal or vertical pattern where one monitored scene leads immediately to the adjacent monitored scene. Other examples in the high-rise setting may be a series of cameras monitoring the loading dock area, various levels of the parking structure, building lobbies, elevator cars, or ground floor exits from building stairwells. Rack mounting also saves space and the clutter that ensues when multiple monitors are mounted on a table top.

Video Switchers

The simplest CCTV system involves a single camera with its image displayed on a single video monitor. High-rise buildings often have an extensive camera system covering multiple locations, with the camera images being displayed on multiple monitors. A person viewing the monitors is restricted because he or she can comfortably view only a certain number of monitors at any given time. *Video switchers* are devices that allow multiple cameras to be monitored on a single monitor or multiple monitors, either in sequence or one at a time. "Video switchers enhance a video system, allowing it to save costs while remaining effective through multiple camera monitoring through a single source of view" (Pierce 1995, p. 1.4).*

Manual Switcher

This switcher can be operated manually and allows an operator to select one particular camera from a series of cameras and display the image from this single camera on a single monitor. This can be particularly useful when the operator viewing the monitors sees something of interest from a particular camera; by using the manual switcher the camera image can be switched to a monitor

---

* **Note:** The information in the following sections on basic types of video switchers is from *CCTV Surveillance: Video Practices and Technology* (Kruegle 1995, pp. 228–231).

in the operator's direct field of view for closer observation. Video switchers are available to handle from 4 to 32 cameras.

Homing Sequential Switcher

There are three modes of operation of homing sequential switchers: the *automatic sequencing* mode that involves the automatic selection of each of a series of cameras, sequentially displaying the image from each camera on a single monitor—the length of time each camera image is displayed on the monitor (*dwell time*) is variable and can be changed by the operator; the *bypass* mode whereby any particular camera can be bypassed and will not be displayed; and the *homing* or *select* mode in which the automatic sequencing function is over-ridden and one particular camera can be selected to display continuously.

Bridging Sequential Switcher

This switcher operates in a similar fashion to the homing sequential switcher, but the series of cameras can be sequentially displayed on two monitors, in-stead of one. The first, or sequential, monitor operates with all the same fea-tures as the homing sequential switcher; the second, or bridging, monitor views whichever camera is in the homing or select mode.

Homing and bridging sequential switchers can be interfaced with a camera motion detector or other type of alarm so that, when an alarm signal is acti-vated, the camera in question is automatically selected to display continuously on one monitor.

Looping-Homing Sequential Switcher

The looping-homing sequential switcher operates in an identical manner to a homing sequential switcher, with the additional feature that all camera inputs can be transferred to a second switcher or other device at another location.

Looping-Bridging Sequential Switcher

The looping-bridging sequential switcher operates in an identical manner to a bridging sequential switcher, with the additional feature that all camera inputs can be transferred to a second switcher or other device at another location.

Looping-homing and looping-bridging sequential switchers enable the es-tablishment of two independently controlled locations. Any camera may be selected at either location for viewing without interfering with the operation of the other location. This looping feature can be adapted to a high-rise building where, for example, part of the Security Command Center's CCTV system may be independently operated in the Director of Security's office.

Alarming Switcher

Each time a camera is activated to operate by an intrusion alarm device—a magnetic door contact, a motion detector, or a video motion detector—the alarming switcher displays the image of the camera on a monitor and/or activates a video-recorder to record the image. The video-recorder can be set up ahead of time to record in either real time or time lapse mode. (These recording features are discussed in a later section.) Alarming switchers are available in homing, bridging, looping-homing, and looping-bridging configurations.

Matrix Switcher

Mega-high-rise buildings may contain vast numbers of CCTV cameras and large numbers of monitors that require monitoring. As The Merritt Company puts it,

> Matrix switching uses microcomputer control circuits and permits the display of any camera in the network on any monitor. Available systems can include hundreds of cameras and scores of monitors. The cameras are all inputs to the central processor which can match camera to monitor manually via an operator keyboard, automatically through video motion detection or alarm activation, or in accordance with programmed sequence patterns developed via the keyboard and central processing unit or developed off-line and loaded into the central processing unit. (The Merritt Company 1991, p. 38-46)

Operator Viewing Effectiveness

Before proceeding, it is appropriate to mention a problem that occurs with monitoring large numbers of cameras. Sequential switching amplifies a person's ability to view many video monitors but there does come a point when the person cannot keep pace with the demands of the viewing operation. "There have been several studies of operator effectiveness regarding the number of monitors an operator can watch effectively. . . . The average person cannot watch more than four pictures simultaneously with any comprehension of what is happening" (Pierce 1993, pp. 29–32). The operator will view multiple monitors by repeatedly scanning back and forth across them. To monitor effectively, additional operators may need to be added. However, because of the financial impact such a move would have, this issue in many cases is not addressed. As a result, the effectiveness of the security operation suffers and the operators themselves are subjected to stress and fatigue.

Possible solutions to monitoring large CCTV installations are to continuously display a few cameras that have security importance, continuously record all cameras, and call up cameras on alarm (using alarm devices such as a video motion detector, switch, or infrared detector). Another technique employed to view many scenes on a single monitor is to use a split-screen monitor display whereby 2, 4, 9, 16, or 32 scenes are simultaneously displayed. The problem with this technique is that the resolution of the scenes is decreased proportionately and it becomes more difficult for the operator to distinguish what is being viewed. As previously mentioned, matrix switching does allow multiple operators to monitor a CCTV system effectively, each having total access to the camera system.

Another important factor in the monitoring of CCTV systems is the total time an operator is able to stay alert and work effectively while viewing single or multiple monitors. The studies mentioned earlier have addressed this vital, but often neglected, factor. "After approximately one hour (less time for people of below average intelligence) the average operator's mind has mentally shut off the monitor to the point that an object or objects of identifiable size can be moved into and consequently through the scene at a rate of six inches per minute" (Pierce 1993, pp. 29–32). One obvious solution to this problem is to rotate the video operators. However, in many high-rise building operations, training multiple operators and frequently rotating them may not be a viable option because of the limited size of the staff. Providing color monitors and alarm interfacing can assist by breaking the monotony of black-and-white images where little change is occurring. The more that is happening, the more likely it is that the operator will stay active and alert and thereby make monitoring of the CCTV system more effective.

Image Recording and Reproduction Devices

The camera image may be recorded on a video-recording device for later review. Such tapes may be used in investigations and as evidence in incidents that result in civil litigation or criminal proceedings. Previously in the security field the use of reel-to-reel video tape recorders was the standard. Today videocassette recorders (VCRs) of the VHS type are in widespread use. Videorecorders can record in either *real time* or *time lapse* mode. Real time means that all images the camera captures are recorded by the video recorder. Time lapse means that only some of the images the camera captures are recorded. "Present real time recording systems record 2, 4, or 6 hours continuous black and white or color with more than 300 line resolution. Time lapse recorders have total recording time up to 200 hours and an alarming mode in which the recorder reverts to real time when an alarm condition exists" (Kruegle 1989, p. 345). (The alarm condition may be generated by an electronic motion sensing device built into the camera, a motion detector, or another intrusion alarm device installed in the area being viewed by the camera.)

One of the problems involved in reviewing video recordings is related to when multiple camera images are sequentially displayed on a single monitor and then recorded on a VCR. When the video is played back, the images from all the cameras are sequentially displayed. The frequent image switching makes it very difficult for the reviewer to follow clearly what is occurring on any one particular camera. The situation becomes chaotic when up to 16 camera images are being viewed. The development of *multiplex* recording has addressed this issue.

Multiplexing (putting two or more signals into a single channel) permits up to 16 cameras to be linked to a single VCR. The Merritt Company (1991, pp. 38-54 and 38-55) explains,

> Instead of switching from camera to camera to select the image, the multiplexer merely selects or "grabs" a frame from each camera in series, processes or enhances the signal and passes it to the VCR, until all cameras have been selected . . . when grabbing frames the multiplexer electronically identifies each with its source camera. When the tape is played back, utilizing the multiplexer unit as a playback control, only the successive images from the selected camera are displayed. The net effect is as though the tape was made from a single camera.

Because there is a small time lapse between camera images, when the tape is played back motion may appear slightly "jumpy." Despite this, the quality of the tape will be acceptable for most applications in the high-rise setting.

Videotapes can be used over and over. It is a sound practice to establish a library of videotapes—between one day's and three months' supply, depending on the needs of the building. Videotapes should be replaced frequently, according to the manufacturer's specifications. Providing a library of tapes will incur more initial expense. However, the extended life of the tapes, due to less usage, compensates for this. The tapes should be clearly and accurately labeled so that there is no confusion as to which tape corresponds to which period.

As with other security systems and equipment, rapid changes are occurring in the technology that supports CCTV systems.* Computer technological developments make it possible to store monochrome video frames on hard disk magnetic systems, while photoimaging technology can produce high-quality color identification badges quickly and easily, complete with company logos and text.

Meanwhile, microcomputer-based systems are being used for controlling lens, pan and tilt, alarm, and automatic switching functions. CCTV specialists, consultants, manufacturers, dealers, and suppliers can be an invaluable source of information for determining what state-of-the-art systems and equipment are available in this ever-changing and developing field. However, one needs to be aware that advice may be given with the specific intention of promoting one particular product or system. Cumming (1992, p. 178) says,

> Systems may be simple or complex, but the fundamental principles are the same: The viewed scene must have sufficient light reflected back from it, toward the camera, for the camera to generate a good, clear picture; the picture signal transmission must be fast, efficient, and without loss of strength or quality; the signal should arrive at the monitor in as good a condition as when it left the camera; the monitor should faithfully convert the signal into a high-quality picture of the viewed scene and, when necessary, enhance what was actually "seen" to improve guard recognition of any potential trouble.

Camera Locations

There are various types of CCTV systems available to enhance the quality of security provided for the building perimeter, the building, public access or common areas, maintenance spaces, and tenant areas. Entrances, exits, corridors, elevators and elevator lobbies, parking lots, and other sensitive areas can be monitored and kept under surveillance. CCTV cameras are recommended for the following locations in a high-rise commercial office building:

- *Access points where occupants enter on foot.* If an entrance door is remotely controlled, it is vital that persons be viewed on camera to determine whether they are to be afforded access. If the door is equipped with an electronic card reader, a camera is useful to ensure that tailgating or piggybacking does not occur.

---

* **Note:** An excellent reference for more detailed information on CCTV systems is *CCTV Surveillance: Video Practices and Technology* by Herman Kruegle (1995).

- *Access points for vehicles to parking structures.* If a vehicle gate or traffic arm is remotely controlled, it is vital that vehicles, and possibly drivers, be viewed on camera to determine if they are to be given access. Some high-rise parking structure ingress/egress points have cameras installed that, in conjunction with a video-recording device, record the license plates of all vehicles entering and exiting the property, as well as images of the drivers.
- *Crucial entry and exit points.* These include crossover floors between elevator banks (for example, crossover floors between the passenger elevators that serve the building tower and the passenger elevators that serve a subterranean parking structure, or between low- and mid-rise elevator banks, or between the mid- and high-rise elevator banks), strategic locations on mechanical floors or floors that have restricted access, and critical reception areas.
- *Crucial egress points* such as ground floor exits from stairwells. A camera in conjunction with a motion detector alarm that, when movement is detected in the stairwell, trips a video-recorder to record the camera images in real time, can be an invaluable tool for detecting unauthorized removal of property from the building via the stairwells. The provision of a two-way voice communications system with a speaker and microphone at the camera location can be effective for communications between the Security Command Center and these stairwells.
- *Sensitive areas.* These include parking structures, passenger and service/freight elevator lobbies, stairwell exits leading to the roof of the building, dumpster and trash compactor areas, entrances to main utility areas such as the power transformer room and central plant, and high-value item storage areas, including safe and vault areas.
- *Inside passenger and service/freight elevator cars.* Cameras within elevator cars can be an effective deterrent to threats against persons (such as lewd behavior, assault, robbery) and threats against property (such as vandalism of the elevator car) (see Figure 3.28). In recent years vandalism, particularly graffiti, has caused considerable concern to high-rise building owners and managers (see the beginning of Chapter 1, *What Is Security and Fire Life Safety?*). If no action is taken against this type of activity, it tends to escalate. A possible solution for deterring or identifying the persons responsible for graffiti is to install a CCTV camera, either openly or covertly, in the affected elevator car.

Figure 3.28
Elevator car CCTV picture: A man trying to hide in the corner under the camera. Courtesy of Herman Kruegle, *CCTV Surveillance: Video Practices and Technology* (1995), p. 395.

- *Locations where covert surveillance is required.* Concealed cameras can be a tremendously important tool for observing activities, particularly illegal ones such as theft. A hidden camera can be used to observe events where it would be impossible to conceal the presence of a person. Modern technology has led to a reduction in the size of surveillance equipment and to aids such as pinhole devices. Many operators have ingeniously concealed cameras in emergency lighting systems, in emergency exit signs, behind clocks, behind works of art, behind one-way mirrors, in ceiling-mounted sprinkler heads, in portable radios, in air fresheners, and in other items openly displayed in the office setting. In conjunction with a video-recording device, concealed cameras can be used to view areas for extended periods of time and provide a permanent record of the taped events. In some applications, the portable unit of CCTV and VCR may need to be equipped with a self-contained power source—for example, on top of elevator cars where the camera, equipped with a pinhole lens, and the VCR may be installed as a self-contained unit. Note that such installations must always be carried out in conjunction with certified elevator technicians.

Of course, not all public access or common areas may be monitored by any CCTV system, covert or not. Usage is not permitted in rest rooms, or in any other area where users have a reasonable expectation of privacy. The question of whether employers can use CCTV cameras and other surveillance equipment for security purposes continues to be the subject of legislation, including federal legislation before the U.S. House of Representatives (H.R. 1900) and Senate as of the writing of this book. The latter bill includes a proposal to permit covert surveillance of employees if they are notified at the point of hire that such surveillance may occur.

The actual design, configuration, and location of any CCTV system in a high-rise building will depend largely on the particular security and life safety requirements of the building or the specific areas being addressed.

Intrusion Alarm Systems

There are various types of intrusion alarm systems available to enhance the quality of security provided for the building perimeter, public access or common areas, maintenance spaces, and tenant areas. The purpose of an intrusion alarm system is to detect when an unauthorized intrusion has occurred in an area and to transmit a signal. The signal may be transmitted to sound a local alarm—a bell, horn, siren, whooper, etc.—at or near the protected area. It may be transmitted to an on-site monitoring location staffed with operators trained to carry out a predetermined alarm response procedure, or to an off-site central station likewise staffed with personnel trained to notify the appropriate agencies.

In the high-rise building, the on-site monitoring location may be the local annunciator and control panels built into an open-style desk arrangement, or the more complex and sophisticated Security Command Center, both of which usually will be located in the main lobby. In the case of on-site monitoring, when an intrusion alarm is activated, security staff will either investigate the alarm themselves or notify the appropriate law enforcement agencies. If the intrusion alarm involves a tenant space, a prearranged tenant notification procedure will be carried out.

In the case of off-site monitoring, once the monitoring staff at the central station are notified of an intrusion alarm, they will either notify any security staff at the building, dispatch a responding agent such as a patrol officer, or notify the appropriate law enforcement agency and request a response to investigate the alarm. In addition, the central station staff may also directly notify the building management, or a tenant representative if the incident involves a tenant area. The specific response procedures will be preplanned and should be in writing or stored on a computer. An intrusion alarm system consists of three basic components: a sensor, a control unit, and an annunciation device.*

Sensors

Sensors are installed in the area being protected and are designed to detect intrusion. The types of sensors that may be found in high-rise buildings are described in the following sections.

Pressure Mat or Pad Detector

These detectors are, in effect, simple switches that either react to pressure when it is applied to them, or react when normally applied pressure is released. They may be in the form of a strip or a mat. In some locations—for example, inside tenant offices—they may be secreted under carpeting with the associated electrical wiring concealed from view.

Magnetic Contact Switch

These reliable, simple devices consist of a permanent magnet attached to a door (and in some applications, to a window), and a magnetically operated switch attached to the frame. The magnet may be surface-mounted and visible, or flush-mounted and concealed. The switch operates by means of a magnetic field generated when the door is closed. If the door is opened, the magnetic field is interrupted and an alarm is initiated. Magnetic contact switches are effective devices but surface-mounted ones can be defeated by bridging or jumping the circuit; they are commonly used in high-rise buildings for exterior doors (particularly stairwell exterior fire doors), interior doors (particularly stairwell doors and doors leading to maintenance spaces), and interior doors leading to offices and sensitive areas within tenant spaces. These devices can be an invaluable tool for security staff to monitor intrusions into stairwells.

Electrical Switch

These devices are installed in a similar fashion to magnetic contact switches. However, in this case, they consist of electrical contacts. They operate on the principle that an electrical circuit is completed when the door is closed and the contacts come together. If the door is opened, the electrical current is interrupted and an alarm is initiated. As with magnetic contacts, electrical switches can be defeated by bridging or jumping the circuit.

---

* **Note:** The information in the following sections was compiled with the assistance of "Intrusion Alarms: Sensing Principles" (Purpura 1991).

Break-Wire System

Very fine, electrically conductive wire configured in the form of a screen or a criss-cross arrangement across an opening can be used to detect intrusion. When the wire is broken, the electrical circuit is severed and an alarm is initiated. Such an arrangement can be useful in protecting building exterior openings such as those leading to HVAC air intakes. The wiring system also may be modified by using magnetic contact switches to detect movement of the wiring assembly without the wire actually breaking. Accordingly, an alarm will be initiated to notify security personnel of the intrusion.

Vibration Detector

This device utilizes microphones to detect audio noise. The sensitivity of the detector can be adjusted to initiate an alarm when it detects vibrations such as those resulting from forced entry. It can be installed on surfaces—walls, ceilings, floors, and doors—and objects such as works of art, files, safes, cabinets, and vaults. Although vibrations of the building and equipment contained within it can lead to false alarms, by adjusting the sensitivity of the vibration detector system, these false alarms can be reduced.

Capacitance Detector

These detectors operate using an electromagnetic "barrier." On application of a small electrical charge to a metal object, an invisible electromagnetic field is set up around the object such as a file, safe, cabinet or vault. If something intrudes into the field, an alarm will be initiated. When this device is in use, it is vital to properly ground the object being protected.

Passive Infrared Detector

Instead of emitting a signal or field that can be disturbed by an intruder, passive infrared (PIR) devices are passive or inert and operate on the principle that human beings emit heat, in the form of infrared radiation, from their bodies. When an intruder moves within the range of the detector, an alarm is triggered by the very small, but detectable, variations in heat caused by the intruder's presence (see Figure 3.29). Because false alarms can be caused by sunlight and HVAC systems, the proper location of the passive infrared detector is critical. In high-rise buildings, PIR detectors are also commonly used as automatic door openers, particularly in heavily traveled public access or common areas such as building lobbies.

Ultrasonic Motion Detector

These detectors operate on the principle that a space can be filled with inaudible sound waves. Using a transmitter, the device both sends and receives ultrasonic waves. If an intruder enters the protected space, the standing-wave pattern is disturbed and an alarm is initiated (see Figure 3.30). Ultrasonic motion detectors can false-alarm because HVAC systems discharge air into the protected space. In addition, noises (such as telephones ringing) within or outside the protected area can cause false alarms by disturbing the wave patterns.

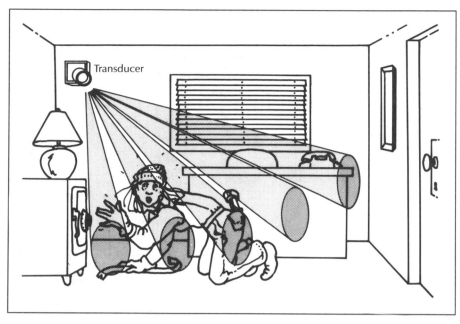

Figure 3.29 Infrared motion detector. Courtesy of Robert Barnard, *Intrusion Detection Systems* (Butterworths, Stoneham, MA, 1981), p. 152.

Microwave Motion Detector

These detectors have an operating principle similar to ultrasonic motion detectors, with the exception that high-frequency electromagnetic microwaves are transmitted into an area. If an intruder enters the protected space, the standing-wave pattern is disturbed and an alarm is initiated. Because microwaves can penetrate building walls they may be used to detect movement outside of areas where the device is operating, but this feature can also lead to movements being detected that are not of consequence to the space being protected. Some tuning devices can circumvent these problems by restricting the area covered by the detector. False alarms can be caused by electric motors, fluorescent lights, or other devices that interfere with the detector by emitting electromagnetic waves.

Closed-Circuit Television Camera Motion Detector

These devices result in the image from the camera becoming the alarm sensor. This is achieved by means of an electronic motion sensing device that can be built into the camera but is nearly always an add-on device. The underlying principle of operation is that the contrast change in a specific area of the image causes an alarm output. If motion occurs and the particular scene changes, the sensing device will initiate an alarm to draw the viewer's attention to this fact, or will switch on a video-recording device to record the activity.

Figure 3.30   Ultrasonic motion detector.   Courtesy of Robert Barnard, *Intrusion Detection Systems* (Butterworths, Stoneham, MA, 1981), p. 125.

Acoustic Detector

These detectors use a very sensitive and accurate hi-fi microphone to detect noise created by an intruder attempting to gain entry to a particular area or moving within the protected space. Their use is usually restricted to vaults and other high-security applications.

Photoelectric Detector

When an invisible beam of light projected from this device's transmitter to its receiver is interrupted, an alarm is initiated. Various patterns of the photoelectric beam can be devised, and mirrors can be used to deflect the beam around corners. An obvious method an intruder can use to circumvent the system is to climb over the beam or crawl under it. Photoelectric detectors tend to be more frequently used in outdoor applications.

Duress Alarm Switches and Kick Bars

These devices are simple, electrical switches manually operated by people to summon assistance. They may be mounted underneath or on the side of a desk or counter, or on the floor. The assistance may be requested for security reasons such as when the person feels threatened, is under attack, or has just been attacked; or for safety reasons such as a medical emergency. The switches operate through an electric current continuously running through a circuit. When the duress alarm switch is activated, the current stops, resulting in the initiation of an alarm at a remote location. The remote location may be another area within the facility, the Security Command Center, an off-site central station, or some other location that is constantly monitored when the switch is operational.

In the security application, it is generally considered safer to transmit a signal that does not sound a local alarm (such as a bell, horn, or whooper) at or near the protected area. Sudden noise around a person committing a robbery, for example, may lead that individual to react violently.

As with all security systems and equipment, the operation of duress alarms should be regularly tested and this activity documented. Duress alarms are particularly important because their activation usually indicates an emergency situation. It is critical that they operate as designed. Their construction should always include protective guards or other design features to avoid accidental activation.

Control Unit

The sensors are linked, usually electrically, to the control unit. The control unit normally will consist of circuitry installed in a metal enclosure. The cover of the unit often contains a key-operated switch that permits one to alter the signal(s) sent to the annunciation device and deactivate the sensor, thus permitting access to the protected area without an alarm signal being activated. A standby battery source normally will be provided to furnish power in case the primary power source fails. Also, a tamper switch usually will be provided so that if the unit is interfered with a signal is sent to the annunciation device.

Annunciation Device

On activation of a sensor a signal will be sent to the control unit, which in turn will transmit a signal to sound a local, audible alarm (such as a bell, horn, or siren) at or near the protected area; transmit a signal to an on-site monitoring location; or transmit to an off-site central station. A combination of these signals is also possible.

Often in high-rise commercial office buildings, tenants will have their own intrusion alarm systems, separate from the building's systems. Usually the tenant systems are monitored by private security company central stations. Sometimes, building owners and managers are approached to monitor tenant alarm systems within the building. This is not recommended. It can lead to many operational problems associated with the alarm response itself and result in substantial liability risks for the building.

The security equipment this chapter describes will produce heat and so it is essential that adequate ventilation and air conditioning, as well as heating, be provided for the area where it is monitored. If the Security Command Center is located in a separate room, it should be highly secure and access doors to it kept locked at all times. Interior windows should be constructed using burglar-resistant glass, and windows facing the exterior of the building should be kept to a minimum. Other security elements to be considered include providing dip trays, if a window that is accessible to the public exists. A *dip tray* is a small opening at the base of a window through which keys, access cards, and other small items can be passed. Also, high-security doors should have peep-holes and possibly mantraps. Some buildings, for security purposes, prefer to house the Security Command Center in a windowless room so that outsiders are not even aware of its presence.

Summary

The security systems and equipment for individual high-rise buildings vary according to the specific security needs of each facility and any requirements specified in local building codes. Buildings utilize a combination of various barriers, locks and locking systems, lighting, communication and CCTV, and intrusion alarm systems integrated into a total security system that is both functional and adequate in meeting the protection requirements of the site.

As mentioned at the beginning of this chapter, the focal point for the whole building's security operations may be local annunciator and control panels built into an open-style desk arrangement, or a complex and sophisticated Security Command Center. In either case, their design should configure the security systems and equipment in a user-friendly manner that takes into consideration the operator's intelligence and educational level. The systems should be readily accessible to the operator and positioned in such a way that monitoring does not contribute to operator stress and fatigue. The design should bear in mind the comfort of the operators who will be spending considerable periods of time performing routine and, at times, monotonous tasks within its confines.

A vital reminder: the organization and appearance of the open-style desk arrangement or the Security Command Center often will reflect the building's commitment to security. If the area is attractive and well laid out, if equipment is up-to-date, well maintained, and sufficient for the needs of the security staff to carry out their duties and responsibilities, and if the work surface of the operators is clean and free of clutter, then it is a fair indication that building security is taken seriously, and that the program is being professionally managed.

Comprehensive listings of the manufacturers and installers of the security systems and equipment detailed in this chapter may be found in three publications—*Security Industry Buyers Guide* (1994), *Sweet's Accessible Building Products* (1994), and *Controls and Security Systems* (1994).

References

American Protective Services, *Tools for Security: Two-Way Portable Radios* (American Protective Services, Inc., Oakland, CA, 1980).

Atlas, Randall I., "Security design: Lighting for security," *Protection of Assets Manual*, 9th printing. Timothy J. Walsh, Editor (Used with permission from The Merritt Company, Santa Monica, CA, 800/638-7597. Copyright October 1993), Bulletin.

Bowers, Dan M., *Access Control and Personal Identification Systems* (Butterworths, Stoneham, MA, 1988).

Controls and Security Systems, 1994 Edition (Hutton Publishing, Indianapolis, 1994).

Cumming, Neil, *Security: A Guide to Security System Design and Equipment Selection and Installation*, 2nd ed. (Butterworth–Heinemann, Stoneham, MA, 1992).

Fennelly, Lawrence J., Editor, *Handbook of Loss Prevention and Crime Prevention*, 2nd ed. (Butterworth–Heinemann, Stoneham, MA, 1989).

Finneran, Eugene D., *Security Supervision: A Handbook for Supervisors and Managers* (Butterworths, Stoneham, MA, 1981).

Geringer, Richard G., "High-rises look to lock out problems," *Access Control Magazine* Reprint (Atlanta, June 1991).

Gigliotti, Richard, and Ronald Jason, "Physical barriers," *Handbook of Loss Prevention and Crime Prevention*, 2nd ed. Lawrence J. Fennelly, Editor (Butterworth–Heinemann, Stoneham, MA, 1989). Adapted from *Security Design for Maximum Protection* by Richard Gigliotti and Ronald Jason (Butterworths, Stoneham, MA, 1984).

Girard, Charles M., "Security lighting," *Handbook of Loss Prevention and Crime Prevention*, 2nd ed. Lawrence J. Fennelly, Editor (Butterworth–Heinemann, Stoneham, MA, 1989). Adapted in part from *An Introduction to the Principles and Practices of Crime Prevention* by Koepsell-Girard and Associates, Inc. Also adapted in part from the revised edition of *An Introduction to the Principles and Practices of Crime Prevention* (1975), and *Principles and Practices of Crime Prevention for Police Officers* (Texas Crime Prevention Institute, San Marcos, TX).

Goldfeld, Doron, "Badging technology offering new options," *Access Control Magazine* (Atlanta, December 1994).

IES Lighting Handbook, 8th ed. (Illuminating Engineering Society of North America, New York, 1993).

InstaKey material obtained from *InstaKey: Re-Key Your Own Lock in Seconds* and conversations with Scott Serani and Harvey Hlista (Englewood, CO, 1995).

Knox System, *A Guide to Professional Rapid Entry* (The Knox Company, Newport Beach, CA, 1991).

Kruegle, Herman, *CCTV Surveillance: Video Practices and Technology* (Butterworth–Heinemann, Boston, MA, 1995).

Kruegle, Herman, "Closed circuit television security," *Handbook of Loss Prevention and Crime Prevention*, 2nd ed. Lawrence J. Fennelly, Editor (Butterworth–Heinemann, Stoneham, MA, 1989).

Merritt Company, The, "Television in security," *Protection of Assets Manual*, vol. IV (Used with permission of The Merritt Company, Santa Monica, CA, 800/638-7597. Copyright 1991).

Merritt Company, The, "Added lighting does not increase liability," *Protection of Assets Manual* (Used with permission of The Merritt Company, Santa Monica, CA, 800/638-7597. Copyright February 1994), Bulletin.

Merritt Company, The, "Security technology: Color TV," *Protection of Assets Manual* (Used with permission of The Merritt Company, Santa Monica, CA, 800/638-7597. Copyright January 1994), Bulletin.

New Webster Encyclopedic Dictionary of the English Language, 1980 Edition, Editor-in-Chief Virginia S. Thatcher (Consolidated Book Publishers, Chicago, 1980).

NFPA 101, *Life Safety Code*, 1994, Chapter 5: "Means of Egress," Section 5-2: "Means of Egress Components," Sections 5-2.1.5.1, 5-2.1.5.2, and 5-2.1.7.1 (All NFPA material in this chapter is used with the permission of the National Fire Protection Association, Quincy, MA. Copyright 1994), pp. 101-28, 101-29, 101-30.

NFPA 101, *Life Safety Code*, 1994, Chapter 6: "Features of Fire Protection," Section 6-2.3.5 (a) (National Fire Protection Association, Quincy, MA, 1994), p. 101-50.

Pierce, Charlie R., "CCTV: Kiss and choose," *Security Management* (Copyright L.T.C. Training Center, November 1989).

Pierce, Charlie R., "CCTV: Monitor overview," *Access Control Magazine* (Atlanta, June 1993).

Pierce, Charlie R., "CCTV: Video theory." Paper presented to the International Security Conference, Anaheim, CA. (L.T.C. Training Center, Davenport, IA, February 1995).

Post, Richard S., and Arthur A. Kingsbury, "What is security?" *Security Administration: An Introduction to the Protective Services*, 4th ed. (Butterworth–Heinemann, Boston, MA, 1991).

Purpura, P. P., *Security and Loss Prevention*, 2nd ed. (Butterworth–Heinemann, Boston, 1991); "Intrusion Alarms: Sensing Principles" as it appeared in *Encyclopedia of Security Management* by John Fay (Butterworth–Heinemann, Stoneham, MA, 1993), pp. 432–433.

Schum, John L., "The load," *Electronic Locking Devices* (Butterworths, Stoneham, MA, 1988).

Security Industry Buyers Guide, 1994 Edition (Phillips Business Information, Inc., Potomac, MD, and ASIS, Arlington, VA, 1994).

Steenburg, E.V., "LSU parking entry goes non-stop," *Access Control Magazine* (Atlanta, December 1994).

Sweet's Accessible Building Products, 1994 Catalog File (McGraw-Hill, Inc., New York, 1994).

Worldwide Learning Services, *Motorola Radius GR300 and GR500 Reference Guide* (Motorola Schaumburg, IL, 1994).

4 *Fire Life Safety Systems and Equipment*

In high-rise commercial office buildings there are many types of fire life safety systems and equipment. Their primary purpose is to help ensure that a building is safe to use, that occupants are able to escape safely and quickly in the event of a fire, and that appropriate control measures are rapidly initiated. This chapter outlines the systems and equipment that may be found in a typical modern high-rise building. It is stressed here that this outline is generic in nature. Because of the number of different model codes and standards, the following does not focus on the statutory requirements of any one code or standard; however, reference is made to National Fire Protection Association (NFPA) National Fire Codes®, a registered trademark of NFPA. To determine what is actually required at a specific site, one must review the laws, codes, and standards that have been specifically adopted by the authority having jurisdiction.

The focal point for the fire life safety operations and communications network of the entire building may be either a simple local annunciator and control panel, or a more complex and sophisticated *Building Control Station*, both of which may be located in the main floor lobby. The latter may be called the Central Control Station, Command Center, Control Center, Fire Control Center, Fire Command Station, Fire Command Center, or the Fire Control Room (see Figure 4.1). In the event of a fire, the fire department will usually designate this area as its command post. If the Building Control Station is located in a separate room, it should be identified as such by a conspicuous sign on its door. (Some authorities discourage this for security reasons—in that case, the local fire department must be consulted and a nonpublic identifier established.) The door should be kept locked at all times. The Building Control Station (or the local annunciator and control panel) will usually be located near or adjacent to the main entrance to the building; its actual location and accessibility is determined by the fire authority that has jurisdiction in the area.

The Building Control Station is separated from the remainder of the building by fire-resistive construction, with all openings protected by assemblies with a fire-resistive rating specified by the local authority having jurisdiction. The Building Control Station should not be used for any other purpose than that for which it is designed. It usually will contain the following as a minimum:

Figure 4.1
Example of a Building
Control Station (in this
case, a Fire Control
Center).   Photograph
by Roger Flores.

- Voice communication and building public address (PA) system
- Fire department voice communication systems
- Public telephone for fire department use
- Stairwell intercom systems
- Fire detection and alarm system annunciator and control panels
- Sprinkler control valve, water-flow detector, and fire pump status panels
- Other fire protection equipment and system annunciator or status indicators
- Air-handling system controls and status indicators
- Elevator status panel displaying elevator operations
- Emergency and standby power systems status indicators
- Controls for simultaneously unlocking stairwell doors locked from stairwell side
- Building and elevator keys
- A copy of the Building Emergency Procedures Manual (as described in Chapter 11, *Building Emergency Planning*)
- A computer terminal and printer arrangement is often included for the fire life safety systems.

All fire life safety systems should be Underwriters Laboratories (UL), Factory Mutual Research Corporation (FMRC), Wernock Hersey International (WHI), or Electronic Testing Labs (ETL) listed as having met minimum standards.

Voice Communication and Building Public Address System

The voice communication and building PA system is a one-way system providing a means of communication from the Building Control Station to the occupants of the building. It should have adequate power and speaker quality so that, in all normally occupied areas of the building (including elevator cars), voice messages can be clearly and distinctly heard.

Each system is different depending on the manufacturer and system models. Usually, the operator manually selects the required zones (ordinarily separate paging zones will be designated for each floor and for stairways and elevators) and speaks loudly and clearly into a microphone that connects to these areas (see Figure 4.2).

The system almost always allows communication to individual floors or the whole building at once. (This feature has sometimes led to problems in high-rise buildings. By mistake, operators have activated the "ALL CALL" feature of the panel, thereby causing the audible fire signal to sound on all floors of a build-

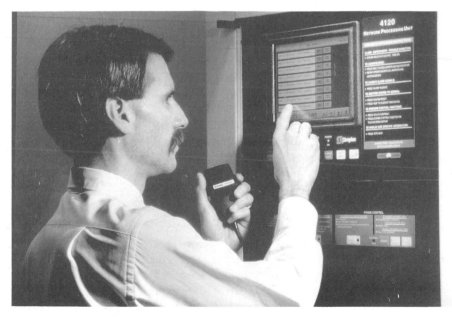

Figure 4.2 A Building Fire Safety Director identifies the type of fire detection device in alarm and its location, prior to making a public address announcement to the occupants of a modern high-rise building.   Courtesy of Simplex Building Systems.

ing. To reduce the chance of accidentally activating this feature, some buildings, with the approval of the local fire authority having jurisdiction, install a molded polycarbonate cover over the "ALL CALL" button or switch. This cover is hinged to the panel and if the "ALL CALL" feature needs to be used, the operator swings the cover open to access the appropriate button or switch.) Systems usually are designed so that the sounding of a fire alarm signal in any particular area or floor will not prevent voice communication to other floors or areas; also, when the voice communication system is selected for a zone in which a fire alarm is already sounding, the audible fire alarm will automatically discontinue while the microphone is activated for the operator to speak.

Fire Department Voice Communication Systems

This emergency communication system is provided for fire department use. It enables two-way telephone communication between the Building Control Station and specified locations throughout the building where telephone jacks (refer to Figure 4.3) or handsets are installed. These locations include entries into stairwells on each floor, standby and emergency electrical power rooms, elevator cars, elevator machine rooms, and passenger and service/freight elevator lobbies. In Los Angeles, for example, the systems permit simultaneous voice communication between six locations. If phone jacks rather than fixed handsets are installed, the handheld phone sets normally will be kept in the Building Control Station, one being permanently installed with a cord long enough to reach all areas of the Building Control Station. Some authorities having jurisdiction permit the use of an approved fire department radio communication system operable to all locations within the structure.

Public Telephone for Fire Department Use

This telephone allows controlled access to the public telephone system. Its call-back number should be clearly marked on the handset. Often this telephone is red in color to indicate that it is to be used for emergency purposes only.

Stairwell Intercom Systems

An intercom is a two-way device enabling communication between the Building Control Station, or another constantly monitored location, and specified locations throughout the building. From a life safety standpoint, intercoms are often installed in stairwells for the use of occupants who are inside the stairwell and need assistance. They are usually mounted on the wall just inside the stairwell entrance and may be operated by simply pressing a button and speaking while the button is depressed (see example of an intercom in Figure 3.23).

The intercom should have its floor number and location marked on it, along with written instructions on how to operate it. Some jurisdictions require that older high-rise buildings, which do not have stairwell door automatic unlocking systems that activate when a fire alarm occurs, provide two-way intercoms inside the stairwells at every fifth floor. This is to ensure that any occupant trapped inside the stairwell would have a means of communicating with building staff to notify them of the situation. Someone could then come and open a stairwell door near the location, thus eliminating the need for the occupant to walk down the entire height of the structure to exit the building safely.

Fire Detection and Alarm System Annunciator and Control Panels

Annunciator and control panels monitor and control the fire detection and fire alarm system devices located throughout the building. According to Wilson (1991, p. 4-15),

> Fire protective signaling systems are classified according to the functions they are expected to perform. The basic features of each system are:
>
> 1. A system control unit.
> 2. A primary, or main, power supply that usually is a connection to the local public electric utility.
> 3. A secondary power supply.
> 4. A "trouble" power supply.
> 5. One or more initiating device circuits to which manual fire alarm boxes, sprinkler waterflow alarm devices, automatic fire detectors, and other fire alarm initiating devices are connected.
> 6. One or more alarm indicating appliance circuits to which alarm indicating appliances, such as bells, horns, [sirens, whoopers], and speakers, are connected, or to which an off premises alarm is connected, or both.

The secondary supply is an emergency power system from which power is automatically transferred. Examples of emergency power supplies include a storage battery or group of batteries, a generator driven by a fuel-supplied prime mover, or an *uninterruptible power supply* (UPS); also, there may be other means authorized by the authority having jurisdiction. (Emergency power systems will be elaborated on later in this chapter.) The secondary power supply may also energize trouble signals in the fire detection and fire alarm system. A trouble signal initiated by the system will be because of either a problem with the fire protective signaling system equipment itself (such as a device or the wiring associated with the system) or the failure of the system's primary power supply.

According to Bryan (1982, p. 320), "The primary purpose of a fire detection system is to respond to a fire, and to transform this response into a visual-audible signal which should alert the building's occupants and the fire department that a fire has been initiated. The fire detection system is intended to respond to the initial signs, signals, or stimuli which indicates that a fire has begun." When a fire detection device is activated, a signal immediately will be sent to the Building Control Station. The signal may also be sent to the Security Command Center, depending on the on-site monitoring arrangements, or to an off-site central monitoring station.

In some modern high-rises, alarm signals may be graphically displayed on a video monitor with operator input using touchscreen, mouse, or keyboard commands. (Some systems use the popular Microsoft Windows* operating platform.) Screen information, such as floor plans and maps with flashing icons symbolizing event locations and programmable step-by-step emergency instructions, can be customized for a specific building. Using graphic systems can help train operators quickly and thoroughly, decrease an operator's response time, and increase adherence to established alarm response procedures.

Manual Fire Alarm Stations

Manual fire alarm stations are sometimes called *manual fire alarm boxes, manual pull stations,* or *manual pull alarms.* According to the NFPA 101 *Life Safety Code* (NFPA 101 1994, p. 101-58), this station

> shall be provided in the natural path of escape near each required exit from an area, unless modified by another section of this *Code.* . . . Additional manual fire alarm stations shall be located so that, from any part of the building, not more than 200 feet (60 m.) horizontal distance on the same floor shall be traversed in order to reach a manual fire alarm station. . . . Each manual fire alarm station on a system shall be accessible, unobstructed, visible, and of the same general type.

However, according to Bill Webb, Chief Engineer of Rolf Jensen and Associates, some authorities discourage or prohibit the use of manual fire alarm stations (Webb 1994).

In a typical modern high-rise, manual fire alarm stations (see Figure 4.3) will be mounted on walls located in the common area corridors adjacent to the stairwells, in passenger and service/freight elevator lobbies, and at the roof adjacent to the exterior door of each stairwell.

A manual fire alarm station may be activated by depressing, lifting, or pulling a lever or switch, or by breaking a thin glass plate and pulling a lever or switch. In modern high-rise buildings, this usually will cause the following sequence of operations:

- An audible and (as recently required by the ADA for new or modified construction) a visual signal—usually flashing lights—on the floor on which it is initiated. (In some high-rises a signal will simultaneously occur on the floor where the alarm initiated, on one or two floors above, and on one or two floors below.) (See Figure 4.4.)
- An audible and visual signal at the Building Control Station, and possibly the Security Command Center
- An audible and visual signal at an off-site central monitoring station
- A live voice or prerecorded evacuation or relocation message to the occupants (some fire departments do not allow a prerecorded message, because a prerecorded message may not be appropriate for every alarm situation)
- Shutdown of the air-handling—HVAC—system on the floor in alarm, and in other areas as designated by the building
- Activation of the smoke control system on the floor in alarm

---

* Windows™ is a registered trademark of Microsoft Corporation.

Figure 4.3 Example of a manual fire alarm station on the left-hand side and a fire department voice communication system jack on the right-hand side. Photograph by Roger Flores.

- Activation of building stairwell and elevator shaft pressurization fans
- Release of hold-open devices for doors on the floor in alarm
- Release of all stairwell door locks in the building

In addition, some municipalities provide a means for an alarm to be manually sent directly to the local fire department from a street fire alarm box located outside of the building. Some fire departments are eliminating these city boxes to reduce nuisance alarms. The need for these public reporting stations has been largely eliminated by the widespread use of "911" emergency telephone services.

Automatic Detection Systems

As Bryan states, "The automatic fire detector is designed to respond and transmit a signal via a pneumatic, electric, hydraulic, or mechanical communications system. The automatic fire detector is programmed to respond when the appropriate physical-chemical condition exceeds certain response thresholds" (Bryan 1982, p. 320). A variety of detectors exist to sense the presence of smoke, heat, flame, and gas. The selection of the appropriate detector will depend on such factors as the type of combustion or gaseous build-up that may be anticipated, intended location and purpose of the detector, architectural configuration, and the presence of air currents caused by heating and air-conditioning systems. The selection, installation, and maintenance of the appropriate detector are all

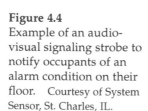

Figure 4.4
Example of an audio-visual signaling strobe to notify occupants of an alarm condition on their floor.   Courtesy of System Sensor, St. Charles, IL.

critical factors in avoiding false alarms. A *false alarm* occurs when a detector indicates that there is a fire but in reality there is none. Causes of false alarms include a lack of detector maintenance, short-term electrical interferences in the communications systems sending the signal back to the Building Control Station (these interferences typically can be eliminated by initiating an alarm verification feature), and—to a much lesser degree—faults in the detector itself. The false alarm also may be caused by conditions that appear to indicate a fire but actually are caused by the occupants themselves, such as an occupant smoking a pipe or cigarette and blowing the smoke towards a smoke detector.

Smoke Detectors

Smoke is often the first sign that a fire is occurring; therefore, an automatic detection system based on smoke detectors is a valuable tool in the early detection of fire. "Smoke is defined as the total airborne effluent from heating or burning a material" (Clarke 1991, p. 3-19). Smoke detectors are commonly classified by their mode of operation.

Ionization smoke detectors (see Figure 4.5) employ a radioactive material to convert the air contained within an ionization chamber into positive and negative charges. This allows the air to conduct a certain amount of electrical current. When smoke particles are present in the chamber, they attach themselves to the ions and cause the air to become less conductive. The detector initiates an alarm when the conductivity of the air falls below a certain predetermined level (see Figure 4.6).

Photoelectric smoke detectors (see Figure 4.7) use light to detect visible smoke particles produced by burning material. They are designed to detect when

Figure 4.5
An ionization smoke
detector.   Courtesy of
System Sensor.

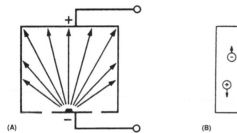 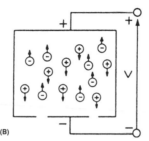 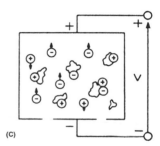

Figure 4.6   Diagrams of how an ionization smoke detector works. (A) Particle radiation pattern.
(B) Ion distribution. (C) Ion and smoke distribution.   Courtesy of System Sensor: *Guide for Proper Use of*
System Smoke Detectors.

smoke either obscures a light beam, thereby reducing the amount of light received by a photosensitive device (see Figure 4.8), or scatters a light beam,
thereby causing the light to fall on a photosensitive device that would not receive light when smoke was not present (see Figure 4.9). When this occurs, the
detector initiates an alarm.

According to Moore (1991, p. 4-46),

> As a class, smoke detectors using the ionization principle provide somewhat
> faster response to high-energy (open-flaming) fires, because these fires produce
> large numbers of smaller smoke particles. As a class, smoke detectors operating
> on the photoelectric principle respond faster to the smoke generated by low-
> energy (smoldering) fires, as these fires generally produce more of the larger
> smoke particles.

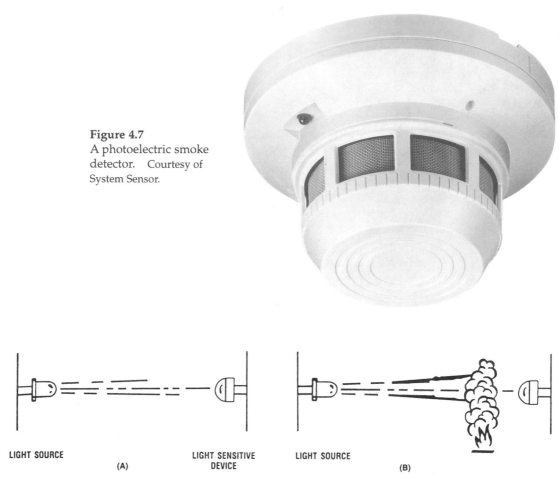

Figure 4.7
A photoelectric smoke
detector.   Courtesy of
System Sensor.

LIGHT SOURCE   LIGHT SENSITIVE   LIGHT SOURCE
                (A)   DEVICE   (B)

Figure 4.8   Diagrams of how a photoelectric light obscuration smoke detector works. (A) Light
obscuration detector. (B) Light obscuration detector with smoke.   Courtesy of System Sensor: *Guide for
Proper Use of System Smoke Detectors.*

Smoke detectors generally are located in open areas, in spaces above suspended ceilings, in spaces under raised floors (particularly in computer rooms),
in cafeteria areas, in air duct systems, in passenger and service/freight elevator
lobbies, in elevator shafts, in elevator machine rooms, in enclosed stairways,
in dumbwaiter shafts, in chutes, and in electrical and mechanical equipment
rooms. The specific locations and spacing of smoke detectors are determined by
an assessment of the guidelines set forth in the local fire code and by engineering considerations. Factors to consider include "ceiling shape and surfaces, ceiling height, configuration of contents, burning characteristics of combustible
material present, ventilation, and the ambient environment" (NFPA 72 1993, p.
185). For example, in reviewing ventilation it must be taken into account that at
times, particularly after normal business hours, the HVAC systems in the building may be shut down. Hence, duct smoke detectors must not be used as an
alternative to area smoke detectors because, during the times the HVAC system

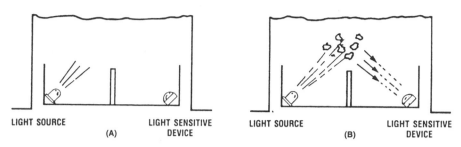

LIGHT SOURCE   **LIGHT SENSITIVE**   **LIGHT SOURCE**   **LIGHT SENSITIVE**
                      (A)   **DEVICE**   **(B)**   **DEVICE**

Figure 4.9   Diagrams of how a photoelectric light scattering smoke detector works. (A) Light scattering device. (B) Light scattering detector with smoke.   Courtesy of System Sensor: *Guide for Proper Use of System Smoke Detectors.*

is shut down, smoke may not be drawn from open areas to the duct detectors. Also, dilution of the smoke makes them inappropriate for area detection.

> In spaces served by air-handling systems, detectors shall not be located where air from supply diffusers could dilute smoke before it reaches the detectors. Detectors shall be located to intercept the air flow toward the return air opening(s). This may require additional detectors, since placing detectors only near return air openings may leave the balance of the area with inadequate protection when the air-handling system is shut down. (NFPA 72 1993, p. 192)

Of course, all locations chosen for the installation of smoke detectors must be accessible for periodic device testing and maintenance. If the detectors are located in areas where they may be subject to mechanical damage, they should also be adequately protected; for example, some smoke detectors may have a protective wire-frame covering.

The use of multiple smoke detectors in high-rise buildings has been made practicable by the development of the *addressable* system. That is, when an alarm occurs, this system can determine which individual device, at which address or location, is in alarm. This permits new systems to be zoned by device, rather than by floor. For instance, if an elevator lobby smoke detector is activated, all elevators are recalled in the manner described under "Controls in Elevator Lobbies" later in this chapter. The sequence of smoke detector operation in a typical modern high-rise building is detailed in Table 4-1.

Heat Detectors

Heat detectors are automatic fire detection devices that initiate an alarm when a certain temperature or rapid change in temperature causes a variance in the physical nature or electrical conductivity of a sensing material. Heat detectors are classified by their mode of operation:

- *Fixed-temperature detectors* initiate an alarm when a detecting metal or metals, heat-sensitive cable, or expanding liquid attains a predetermined temperature. The metal may be a fusible alloy such as that commonly used in automatic sprinklers.
- *Rate compensation detectors* initiate an alarm when the air surrounding the detector attains a predetermined temperature, irrespective of the rate at which the temperature rose.

Table 4.1   Sequence and Operation of Fire Life Safety Systems in a Typical High-Rise Building

	MANUAL FIRE ALARM STATION	AREA SMOKE DETECTOR	DUCT SMOKE DETECTOR	ELEVATOR LOBBY SMOKE DETECTORS	ELEVATOR SHAFT SMOKE DETECTOR	HEAT DETECTOR	SPRINKLER WATER-FLOW DEVICE	SPRINKLER VALVE TAMPER DEVICE	SPECIAL EXTINGUISHING AGENTS
AUDIBLE AND VISUAL SIGNAL AT BUILDING CONTROL STATION	YES	YES	YES	YES	YES	YES	YES	YES	DEPENDS ON THE SYSTEM
SIGNAL AT OFF-SITE MONITORING STATION	DEPENDS ON THE SYSTEM	DEPENDS ON THE SYSTEM	DEPENDS ON THE SYSTEM	DEPENDS ON THE SYSTEM	DEPENDS ON THE SYSTEM	DEPENDS ON THE SYSTEM	DEPENDS ON THE SYSTEM	DEPENDS ON THE SYSTEM	DEPENDS ON THE SYSTEM
AUDIBLE (& POSSIBLY VISUAL) SIGNAL ON FLOOR IN ALARM	YES	YES	YES	YES	NO	YES	YES	NO	DEPENDS ON THE SYSTEM
SHUTDOWN AIR-HANDLING SYSTEMS ON FLOOR IN ALARM	YES	YES	YES	YES	NO	YES	YES	NO	DEPENDS ON THE SYSTEM
ACTIVATE MECHANICAL SMOKE REMOVAL SYSTEMS ON FLOOR IN ALARM	YES	YES	YES	YES	NO	YES	YES	NO	DEPENDS ON THE SYSTEM
ACTIVATE PRESSURIZATION FANS IN BUILDING STAIRWELLS	YES	YES	YES	YES	NO	YES	YES	NO	DEPENDS ON THE SYSTEM
RELEASE HOLD-OPEN DEVICES ON FLOOR IN ALARM	YES	YES	YES	YES	NO	YES	YES	NO	DEPENDS ON THE SYSTEM
RELEASE STAIRWELL DOOR LOCKS IN BUILDING	YES	YES	YES	YES	NO	YES	YES	NO	DEPENDS ON THE SYSTEM
RECALL ALL ELEVATORS SERVING FLOOR IN ALARM	NO	NO	NO	YES	NO	NO	NO	NO	DEPENDS ON THE SYSTEM

- *Rate-of-rise detectors* initiate an alarm when the rate of increase in temperature exceeds a predetermined amount.

In addition, there are combination detectors that, for example, combine the features of both fixed-temperature and rate-of-rise devices. The fixed-temperature element will sense a slow developing fire when a predetermined temperature has been attained; the rate-of-rise element will sense a rapidly developing fire. (See Figure 4.10 for an example of a fixed-temperature/rate-of-rise thermal sensor.)

The selection of an automatic fire detection device, such as a heat detector, is important if it is to be effective in detecting the type of fires expected in the area concerned, and not be subject to frequent false alarms.

> Although [heat detectors] are the least expensive fire detectors, and have the lowest false alarm rate of all automatic fire detector devices, they also are the slowest in detecting fires. A heat detector is best suited for fire detection in a small confined space where rapidly building high-heat-output fires are expected, in areas where ambient conditions would not allow the use of other fire protection devices, or where speed of detection is not a prime consideration. (Moore 1991, p. 4-42)

The sequence of heat detector system operation in a typical modern high-rise building is detailed in Table 4-1.

Gas Detectors

Gas detectors are automatic detection devices that monitor low-level concentrations of combustible gases such as methane, ethane, natural gas, and propane. When concentrations reach a predetermined level, an alarm will be triggered to advise building occupants of the possible hazard. Various Los Angeles

Figure 4.10   A fixed temperature/rate-of-rise thermal sensor.
Courtesy of System Sensor.

high-rise structures, for example, use this type of device. Methane gas seeps up out of the ground in some downtown Los Angeles areas; as a result, methane gas detection systems have been installed as part of some high-rise fire life safety systems. If a certain concentration of methane gas is detected, an initial automatic alarm will notify security and engineering staff that further investigation is required. If the concentration continues to increase and reaches a predetermined level, the system automatically initiates another alarm indicating that the fire department and building occupants should be notified immediately of the potential hazard.

Automatic Sprinkler Systems

An automatic sprinkler is "a device for automatically distributing water on a fire in sufficient quantity either to extinguish it entirely or to prevent its spread in the event that the initial fire is out of range, or is a type of fire that cannot be extinguished by water" (Abbott 1994, p. 2-1). Automatic sprinklers not only are required in new high-rise office buildings, but in many cities it is mandated by code that existing high-rises be retrofitted with automatic sprinkler systems.

The Building Owners and Managers Association (BOMA) International *1993 Fire Safety Survey for High-Rise Commercial Office Buildings in North America* shows that 12% of these buildings are not sprinklered, 24% are partially sprinklered, and 64% are fully sprinklered (Little 1993, p. 26). The prime motivating factor for the installation of sprinkler systems is that in the more than 100 years they have been in existence, they have proven to be a most effective means of controlling fires. There is a substantial reduction of the chances of death or extensive property damage in a fully sprinklered building. "The NFPA has no record of a fire killing more than two people in a fully sprinklered public assembly, educational, institutional, or residential building in which the sprinkler system was operating properly, except in the case of explosions and flash fires and in instances in which fire brigade members or employees were killed during fire suppression operations" (Hall 1993, p. 47).

Sprinkler Control Valve, Water-Flow Detector, and Fire Pump Status Panels

These annunciator panels monitor the sprinkler control valves and water-flow detection devices located throughout the building, and the status of the fire pump(s). NFPA 101 *Life Safety Code* requires that: "High rise buildings shall be protected throughout by an approved, supervised automatic sprinkler system installed in accordance with Section 7-7 [Automatic Sprinklers and other Extinguishing Equipment]. A sprinkler control valve and a water flow device shall be provided for each floor" (NFPA 101 1994, p. 101-225).

The following description of automatic sprinkler systems was compiled using NFPA 13 *Standard for the Installation of Sprinkler Systems* and the *Fire Protection Handbook* (Solomon 1991, pp. 5-127–152 and 5-164–173) as references.

Water Supply for Sprinklers

For automatic sprinklers to work, there must be a supply of water to the sprinkler that opens to extinguish or control fire and prevent it from spreading. This water may come from a variety of sources such as public water systems (usually considered the principal or primary water supply) and storage tanks of three types.

Gravity tanks are tower- or roof-mounted water reservoirs that are not likely to be used for modern high-rise buildings. *Pressure tanks* are pressurized water reservoirs used to supply a limited amount of water for building sprinkler systems. Each tank is located above the highest sprinkler heads. When the public water pressure is too low to supply water to sprinklers on upper high-rise floors, the pressure tanks are used until water can be pumped into the sprinkler system through fire department connections (these connections are explained later). *Suction tanks*, equipped with automatically operated fire pump(s), are increasingly used as a secondary water supply and sometimes, where the authority having jurisdiction permits, as a principal water supply. These tanks are normally constructed of concrete, steel, or fiberglass and may be located directly beneath fire pump(s).

The selection and location of these tanks and automatic fire pumps are based on the size and height of the building, its type of tenancy, and pattern of use. A *fire pump* is a mechanical device for improving the water supply pressure from public water systems and storage tanks. In modern high-rise buildings, centrifugal force is primarily responsible for developing fire pump pressure. The pumps are driven by electric motors (see Figure 4.11), or by internal combustion engines fueled by diesel oil. Fire pumps usually are housed in areas protected from the possible effects of fires, freezing temperatures, explosions, and natural disasters such as floods and earthquakes.

NFPA 20 (1993, p. 20-15) states that:

Where electric motors are used and the height of the structure is beyond the pumping capability of the fire department apparatus, a reliable emergency source of power shall be provided for the fire pump installation. The emergency source of power shall be permitted to be provided either by standby engine-driven fire pumps or by part of other established requirements for emergency power sources for services essential to the safety and welfare of high-rise building occupants.

Fire pumps usually are designed to start automatically when water pressure in the fire protection system drops to a predetermined level, and to be shut down manually when their services are no longer needed.

In addition to automatic fire pumps, there are pressure maintenance *jockey pumps*. These very small pumps automatically maintain the operating pressure in the fire protection system. To avoid starting the fire pump engine when there are small fluctuations in pressure, the jockey pump automatically activates, boosts the pressure to the correct level, and then shuts itself down.

Fire Department Connections

In addition to the aforementioned water sources, on the exterior of the building there are fire department connections that can be accessed by the fire depart-

Figure 4.11
Two electric fire pumps located alongside each other in the fire pump room of a modern high-rise building.
Photograph by Roger Flores.

ment to pump water into the sprinkler system. These connections are required by NFPA 13 *Standard for the Installation of Sprinkler Systems*. They are used when the building water supply system is unable to provide water at sufficient pressure for the sprinkler system to discharge and disperse water effectively. These fire department connections are easily accessed, usually being situated on the street side of the building, and are conspicuously marked with signs. Examples of the signs are "AUTOSPKR.," "OPENSPKR.," or "AUTOSPKR. and STANDPIPE." The connections often are fitted with protective caps that can be easily removed by the fire department to attach their hoses (see Figure 4.12).

The fire department obtains water for these connections from water hydrants using fire department pumpers. Fire hydrants generally are located close to intersections and along the street to meet the needs of adjoining structures. Today there are two basic types of fire hydrants in use. The dry barrel, base valve, or "frost-proof" hydrant is the one most common and is found in areas where temperatures sometimes go below freezing. The wet barrel or "California" hydrant is used in areas where temperatures do not go below freezing (see Figure 4.13).

Figure 4.12 Fire department connections serving high, mid, and low zones of a modern high-rise building. Photograph by Roger Flores.

In the typical modern high-rise, water is vertically transported upward in the building through a sprinkler system riser or vertical pipe located in each stairwell. A system of overhead piping on each floor horizontally connects the riser to the sprinklers that are located at regular intervals along the pipes. The horizontal pipes themselves are commonly located in the concealed space throughout the whole floor area. They are attached to the floor above using hangers and clamps (see Figure 4.14).

In high-rise commercial office buildings, sprinklers usually are the standard spray type. These sprinklers often visibly protrude through the suspended ceiling (see Figure 4.15) or are flush with it and hidden from view by a metal cap or disk (see Figure 4.16). In the latter case, when a predetermined temperature is attained the cap or disk drops away leaving the sprinkler exposed. The cap is marked "Do Not Paint" to avoid the problem of the cap being painted over and thereby possibly adhering to the ceiling. Sometimes sidewall sprinklers are used in high-rise buildings. They have the same parts as a standard sprinkler with the exception of a special deflector that discharges water toward one side.

Figure 4.13
"California" wet barrel
fire hydrant.   Photo-
graph by Roger Flores.

How Sprinklers Work

Sprinklers commonly contain a fusible metal that melts rapidly at a certain temperature and fuses, thereby permitting a cover over an opening in the sprinkler
to drop away, water to flow, and a waterflow indicator to initiate a fire alarm.
The waterflow device is recommended by the NFPA "to indicate the flow of
water in a sprinkler system by an alarm signal within 90 seconds after flow of
water at the alarm-initiating device equal to or greater than that from a single
sprinkler of the smallest orifice size installed in the system. Movement of water
due to waste, surges, or variable pressure shall not be indicated" (NFPA 72
1993, p. 211). The reason for the 90-second delay is to avoid false alarms by
allowing sufficient time to establish that a stable water flow has been achieved.
The fire alarm is automatically transmitted to the Building Control Station and
possibly to an off-site central monitoring station, sounds on the floor where the
sprinkler water flow has occurred (and possibly on one or two floors above and
below the alarm floor), and sounds a sprinkler fire-alarm bell located on the
exterior of the building near ground level.

Figure 4.14   Sprinkler pipes and sprinkler before the suspended ceiling is installed. Photograph by Roger Flores.

Types of Automatic Sprinkler Systems

Wet-Pipe System

This is the most common sprinkler system used in high-rise buildings. In the event of a fire, if the temperature exceeds a predetermined point, the fusible link in the sprinkler fuses, the sprinkler opens, and *water contained in the pipe*, that is connected to the water supply, is immediately discharged on the fire. A prerequisite of this system is that the area in which it is installed must be kept at temperatures above freezing.

Dry-Pipe System

In the event of a fire, if the temperature exceeds a predetermined point, the fusible link in the sprinkler head fuses, the sprinkler head opens, and *pressurized air* (or *nitrogen* for a small dry system) *contained in the pipe* escapes, permitting a dry-pipe valve to open; water then enters the sprinkler piping and flows out of the open sprinkler. This type of system is used in unheated areas. If water were contained in a sprinkler pipe at low temperatures, it could freeze, thereby rendering the system ineffective. Because most commercial high-rise buildings are temperature controlled, few of these more expensive dry-pipe systems are used in them, except possibly in garage or loading dock areas.

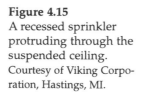

Figure 4.15
A recessed sprinkler
protruding through the
suspended ceiling.
Courtesy of Viking Corpo-
ration, Hastings, MI.

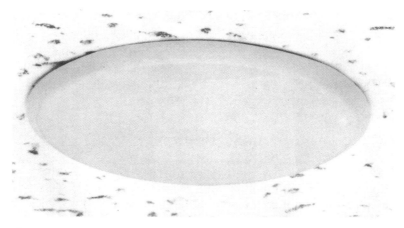

Figure 4.16   Cover plate for a concealed sprinkler.   Courtesy of Viking
Corporation.

Pre-Action System

This system works on the principal that, in the event of a fire, an automatic fire
detection device (such as a smoke or heat detector) located in the same area as
the sprinkler will be activated. This in turn will allow water to enter the piping
prior to the sprinkler being activated. Then, when the sprinkler is opened at a
predetermined high temperature, water can immediately flow out of it. This
system is used in areas such as tenant computer rooms and data processing
areas where there is great concern for the accidental discharge of water, which
could damage or destroy computers, or other valuable electronic equipment.

Supervision and Manual Operation of the Automatic Sprinkler System

A sprinkler control valve is provided on each floor in the stairwell(s) so that the automatic sprinkler system can be manually shut down for that floor. A *looped* sprinkler system means that the piping is continuous throughout a floor and a sprinkler control valve is located in each stairwell. To manually shut down the looped sprinkler system for a floor, the control valve in *each* stairwell must be shut down. Under normal conditions, the sprinkler control valve remains in the OPEN position. The sprinkler control valve is fitted with a supervisory signal-initiating device so that whenever the valve is moved from its normal position or moved back to its normal position, separate and distinct signals are initiated and immediately sent to the Building Control Station. The supervisory signal-initiating device that monitors a sprinkler control valve, the waterflow switch, and the hose connection and valve for a combined sprinkler and standpipe riser are shown in Figure 4.17.

Standpipe and Hose Systems

Before proceeding further, it is appropriate to discuss standpipe and hose systems. A *standpipe* system in a high-rise building is a pipe structure designed to vertically transfer water to upper floors of the building so that the water can be used to fight fires manually using fire hoses (see Figure 4.18). The standpipe system is another tool that can be used by trained building personnel or members of the fire department to combat fires. "Even in tall and large-area buildings that are protected by automatic sprinklers, standpipe systems play an essential role in building firesafety by serving as a backup for, and complement to, sprinklers" (Shapiro 1991, p. 5-198). There are three classes* of standpipe systems classified according to the service for which they are designed.

Class I Systems

Class I systems provide 2½ in. (63.5 mm) hose connections or hose stations supplied from a standpipe or combined riser for use by fire departments and those trained in handling heavy streams of water. A *hose connection* is the point where the fire hose connects to the standpipe system. A *hose station* is the location of the hose rack, hose nozzle, hose connection, and hose valve. The *hose valve* is the control valve to an individual hose connection. A *combined riser* is a vertical pipe that serves outlets for fire department use, and provides water for automatic sprinklers. Use of a Class I system reduces the time and number of fire department personnel needed to attack a fire because hoses can be run

---

* **Note:** The descriptions of these classes, and the ensuing description of the types of standpipe systems, were compiled using NFPA 14 *Standard for the Installation of Standpipe and Hose Systems*, the *Fire Protection Handbook* (Shapiro 1991, pp. 5-198–212), and *Fire Safety and Loss Prevention* (Cassidy 1992, pp. 167–172).

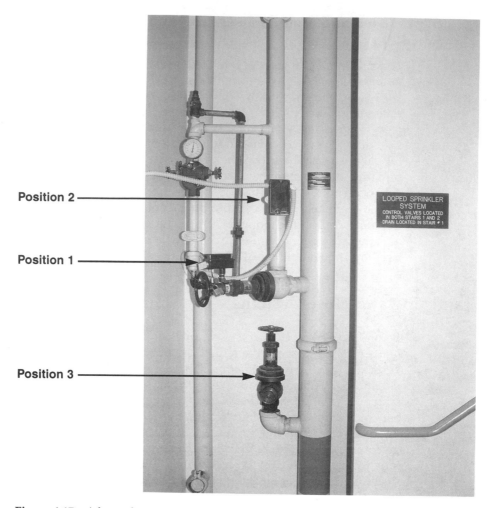

Figure 4.17   A looped wet-pipe sprinkler riser located in a stairwell. (The vertical pipe on the left-hand side is a drain and test pipe.) The supervisory signal-initiating device that monitors the open position of the OS & Y (outside screw & yoke) sprinkler control valve is located at position 1, and a waterflow switch is mounted at position 2. At position 3 is a hose connection and valve. (Note: The system displayed here is a combined sprinkler and standpipe riser.)   Photograph by Roger Flores.

within the building close to the fire rather than running extensive lines from exterior locations. Therefore, Class I systems are generally required in high-rise buildings.

Class II Systems

Class II systems provide 1½ in. (38.1 mm) hose stations supplied from a standpipe, combined riser, or sprinkler system for use by trained building staff, occasionally by the fire department on arrival, and perhaps by building occupants

Figure 4.18 A fire hose cabinet. (This cabinet is located on the roof of a high-rise building in Los Angeles, where such installations are required by code.)   Photograph by Roger Flores.

before the fire department arrives. The hose is connected to a ⅜ or ½ in. open nozzle. Usually the hose is kept permanently fixed to the shut-off valves at the outlets. Where the water for occupant-use hoses can be adequately supplied by connections to the risers of wet-pipe automatic sprinkler systems, separate standpipes to supply water to these hoses are not required. The use of Class II systems with hoses preconnected to standpipe systems is becoming less prevalent because of two main concerns: whether untrained occupants can safely use a 100-ft. (30.5 m) long hose providing water at a flow rate of 100 gal. per min. (378 liters per min.); and whether it is a sound practice for occupants to be involved in fighting a fire instead of immediately evacuating an area. Many jurisdictions have entirely removed the requirement for occupant-use hose systems in facilities that are fully sprinklered.

Class III Systems

Class III systems provide both Class I and Class II hose connections or hose stations supplied from a standpipe or combination riser for use by building occupants and a larger volume of water for use by fire departments and those trained in handling heavy streams of water. The use of Class III systems is becoming less prevalent because of the same concerns listed under "Class II Systems."

Types of Standpipe Systems

In the typical modern high-rise building, there are four main standpipe systems recognized by the NFPA. A *wet standpipe system* has its pipes filled with water at all times, an open supply valve, and a fixed water supply capable of sending water through the system on request. This means that a continuously sustained water pressure can be maintained by the system. A prerequisite of a wet standpipe system is that the area in which it is installed be kept at temperatures above freezing.

The first type of *dry standpipe system* has its pipes *filled with air* and is designed to allow water to flow through the *manual* operation of sanctioned remote-control apparatuses located at each hose station. This system is used when there is a fixed water supply capable of supplying water to the system on request and the area in which the system is installed is unheated and exposed to temperatures below freezing.

The second type of dry standpipe system is similar to the first type, and is used under the same conditions, but allows water to flow *automatically* via a dry pipe valve or other sanctioned apparatus.

The third type of dry standpipe system has pipes *filled with either air or water* and *does not have a fixed water supply* to provide water to the system on request. Instead, this type of system relies on the fire department supplying water to the standpipes. Even though the standpipe may be filled with water, it is still considered a dry standpipe. In an unheated building exposed to temperatures below freezing, the pipe would not be filled with water because it could freeze.

The wet standpipe system is most commonly installed in modern high-rise buildings with a fixed water supply, not exposed to freezing. It is considered more effective in fighting fires than any of the other three systems. Where there is not a permanent water supply but temperatures below freezing are not expected, the dry standpipe system filled with water is used. However, unheated buildings in which temperatures below freezing are expected use the dry standpipe system filled with air.

In high-rise buildings, to keep water pressures within a safety limit and, for example, to reduce the possibility of hoses attached to the standpipe system bursting or being too difficult to handle, standpipe systems are frequently separated into multiple zones that limit the maximum height of the water column. As Shapiro (1991, p. 5-203) points out,

> The goal of zoning systems is basically opposite to that of hydraulically sizing piping. When sizing piping for a standpipe system, the goal is to maintain high pressure to deliver a system's hydraulic demand without requiring large pumps. When zoning a standpipe system, the goal is to minimize the pressure that can

be developed at connections to, and within, system piping to reduce the need for high pressure fittings and pressure reducing valves.

As with automatic sprinkler systems, on the exterior of the building there are connections that can be accessed by the fire department to pump water into the standpipe system. This may be required if the building water supply system is unable to provide water at sufficient pressure for the standpipe system to disperse water effectively or if the standpipe system is a drypipe one without a permanent water supply capable of sending water to the system on demand. If the building has two or more zones, each pressure zone should have its own fire department connection. These fire department connections are easily accessed, usually on the street side of the building, and are conspicuously marked with a sign stating "STANDPIPE." If the hose connection also supplies an automatic sprinkler system, the sign or combination of signs will specify both services, for example, "AUTOSPKR. and STANDPIPE." The connections usually are fitted with protective caps that can be easily removed by the fire department to attach their hoses. The fire department obtains water for these connections from water hydrants using their pumpers. The sequence of automatic sprinkler and fire pump system operation in a typical modern high-rise building is detailed in Table 4-1.

Other Fire Protection Equipment and System Annunciator or Status Indicators

In addition to water, which is the primary extinguishing agent for building fires, there are other special extinguishing agents that may be employed in a high-rise commercial office building. Examples of these are carbon dioxide, halon, dry chemical, wet chemical, and foams. The authority having jurisdiction will require the Building Control Station to supervise any such special extinguishing systems located within the building.

Carbon Dioxide Systems

Carbon dioxide is one and a half times heavier than air; it is a colorless, odorless, noncombustible, electrically nonconductive inert gas found in the atmosphere. It comprises a significant percentage of air, and is a byproduct of the decay and burning of organic substances and respiration in humans and animals. Carbon dioxide can be used to extinguish fires because it reduces the amount of oxygen in the atmosphere to the point where combustion cannot be supported. Because it does not conduct electricity, it can be used on live electrical equipment. Also, it has the advantage that no cleanup is required after use because it does not leave behind a residue. One disadvantage, however, is that it produces solid dry ice particles on discharge that, because of their low temperature, may damage electrical equipment with which they come into contact. Carbon dioxide is not used in normally occupied areas and would require a predischarge alarm because discharge of it may cause suffocation.

NFPA 12 *Standard on Carbon Dioxide Extinguishing Systems* recognizes four basic types of systems for applying carbon dioxide to extinguish fires:

1. A *total flooding* system involves a fixed quantity of carbon dioxide that is stored in containers and, on activation of a manual control station (that is equipped with a manual override) or an automatic detector, is discharged through fixed nozzles attached to fixed pipes into a fixed enclosure surrounding the fire hazard. Because carbon dioxide is dangerous to human beings, the enclosed area must be evacuated of all occupants before the gas is discharged.
2. A *local application* system involves a fixed quantity of carbon dioxide stored in containers. On activation of a manual control station (equipped with a manual override) or an automatic detector, it is discharged directly onto the fire hazard through nozzles attached to fixed pipes.
3. A *hand hose line* system involves a fixed quantity of carbon dioxide that is stored in containers and has hand hose lines permanently attached and ready for immediate, usually manual, application to small fire hazards.
4. A *standpipe system and mobile supply* involves a mobile quantity of carbon dioxide that is stored in containers that in the event of a fire can be rapidly shifted into position and attached to a total flooding, local application, and hand hose line system.

Carbon dioxide can be used to suppress fires involving gas, flammable liquids, electrical equipment, and common combustible elements such as wood and paper.

Halon Systems

To extinguish fires involving expensive electrical office equipment like computers, halon, or a halon substitute, generally is used. Halons are colorless and odorless gases used in low concentrations to extinguish fires. Taylor (1991, p. 5-241) states that:

> Halogenated extinguishing agents are hydrocarbons in which one or more hydrogen atoms have been replaced by atoms from the halogen series: fluorine, chlorine, bromine, or iodine. This substitution confers not only nonflammability, but flame extinguishment properties, to many of the resulting compounds. Halogenated agents are used both in portable fire extinguishers and in extinguishing systems. Streaming agents, such as Halon 1211 and 2402, have most often been used in manually applied fire equipment and local application-type fixed systems. Halon 1301 has most often been used in total flooding-type fixed systems.

In high-rise buildings, the use of halon may be found in electrical switchgear rooms and in tenant computer rooms. It is preferred to water, which may cause irreversible damage to electrical equipment and computers.

The *total flooding* system application involves a fixed quantity of halon, usually Halon 1301 within the United States, that is stored in containers and, on activation of a manual control station (equipped with a manual override) or an automatic fire detector, is discharged through fixed nozzles attached to fixed pipes into a fixed enclosure surrounding the fire hazard. Because it is not dangerous to human beings at low concentrations, halon can be discharged first, and then occupants can safely evacuate the area.

The *local application* system involves a fixed quantity of halon, often Halon 1211 within the United States, that is stored in containers and, on activation of a manual control station (equipped with a manual override) or an automatic fire detector, is discharged directly onto the fire hazard through nozzles attached to fixed pipes.

"The exceptional firefighting effectiveness of the halons is only one of their virtues. They are also electrically nonconductive, dissipate quickly, leave no residue, and have proven remarkably safe for human exposure" (Grant 1990, p. 53). However, because of the evidence indicating the adverse effect of this man-made chemical on the earth's stratospheric ozone layer and the agreements of the Montreal Protocol, the United States and other countries (while reserving some for essential uses), have ceased halon production.

INERGEN™ is an alternative agent for Halon 1301 in total-flooding operations within spaces or areas where people work and may be exposed to the agent on discharge. Produced by Ansul Fire Protection of Marinette, Wisconsin, it is a mixture of three inert gases: nitrogen, argon, and carbon dioxide. Like halon, it is colorless, odorless, noncorrosive, and electrically nonconductive. It does not raise the carbon dioxide level enough to prevent respiration and the absorption of oxygen (occupants, therefore, are still able to breathe); but it lowers the oxygen content below the level required for combustion. Other agents approved by the Environmental Protection Agency (EPA) are FM-200™ by Great Lakes Chemical of West Lafayette, Indiana, and Triolide™ by Pacific Scientific, Duarte, California. These agents should never be used except with the approval of the authority having jurisdiction. A source for more specific information about halons and their substitutes is the EPA.

Dry Chemical Systems

A *dry chemical* is a powder composed of very small particles. "The principle base chemicals used in the production of currently available dry chemical extinguishing agents are sodium bicarbonate, potassium bicarbonate, potassium chloride, urea-potassium bicarbonate, and monoammonium phosphate. Various additives are mixed with these base materials to improve their storage, flow, and water repellency characteristics" (Haessler 1991, p. 5-257).

The exact way dry chemical agents extinguish fires is not yet fully understood. According to NFPA 17 (1994, p. 17-15):

> It is now generally accepted that the flame extinguishing properties of dry chemicals are because of the interaction of the particles, which stops the chain reaction that takes place in flame combustion. Dry chemicals vary in their flame extinguishing effectiveness. Multipurpose dry chemical owes its effectiveness in extinguishing fires in ordinary combustibles, such as wood and paper, to the formation of a glow-retarding coating over the combustible material.

Dry chemical is primarily used as an extinguishing agent for flammable liquid fires. The dry chemical system is "a means of applying dry chemical that can be automatically or manually activated to discharge through a distribution system onto or into the protected hazard. The system includes auxiliary equipment" (NFPA 17 1994, p. 17-5). Fixed nozzles or hand hose lines use expellant gas to discharge dry chemical.

In high-rise commercial office buildings, dry chemical systems are used mainly for restaurant hood, duct, and cooking appliance systems located in tenant kitchens and cafeterias. NFPA 17 *Standard for Dry Chemical Extinguishing Systems* outlines pre-engineered dry chemical systems used for such equipment, including deep-fat fryers. "A pre-engineered system, sometimes called a package system, is one in which the size of the system (i.e., the quantity of dry chemical, pipe sizes, maximum and minimum pipe lengths, number of fittings, and number and types of nozzles) is predetermined by fire tests for specific sizes and types of hazards" (Haessler 1991, p. 5-260). These systems are activated automatically by a fusible link or heat detector located, in some cases, above each cooking appliance or group of appliances protected by a single nozzle or, in other cases, at or within the entrance to the ducting system. "All cooking appliances protected by an extinguishing system shall be provided with an automatic means to ensure the shutdown of fuel or power to the protected appliances upon system actuation" (NFPA 17 1994, p. 17-11). This code even specifies which part of the duct system is the building owner's responsibility to protect and which is the tenant's responsibility.

Because of the fact that dry chemical is electrically nonconductive, it is also used for electrical equipment susceptible to flammable liquid fires. However, in telephone switching and computer rooms, where there are sensitive electrical contacts and relays, its use is not recommended. Application in these areas may cause the equipment to malfunction. Dry chemical should be removed as quickly as possible from the surfaces to which it has been applied because it may be corrosive.

Wet Chemical Systems

A *wet chemical* is defined by NFPA 17A *Standard for Wet Chemical Extinguishing Systems* as "normally a solution of water and potassium carbonate-based chemical, potassium acetate-based chemical, or a combination thereof that forms an extinguishing agent" (NFPA 17A 1994, p. 17A-5). The wet chemical solution extinguishes a fire on a flammable liquid surface by "rapid spreading of a vapor-suppressing foam on the fuel surface. The foam extinguishes and secures the flame by forming a barrier between the liquid fuel and oxygen. This barrier excludes oxygen from the fuel source and eliminates the release of flammable vapors from the fuel surface. The cooling effect of the solution also lowers the temperature of the flammable fuel, further decreasing fuel vapor release" (NFPA 17A 1994, p. 17A-10).

Wet chemical systems are similar in their application to dry chemical systems. The wet chemical can be activated automatically or manually to discharge through fixed nozzles and pipes by way of expellant gas.

In high-rise commercial office buildings, wet chemical systems are used mainly for restaurant hoods, plenums, ducts, and associated cooking appliances in tenant kitchens and cafeterias. NFPA 17A *Standard for Wet Chemical Extinguishing Systems* outlines pre-engineered wet chemical systems that are used for restaurant, commercial, and industrial hoods, plenums, ducts, and associated cooking appliances. Like dry chemical systems, these systems are activated automatically by a fusible link or heat detector located in some cases above each cooking appliance or group of appliances protected by a single nozzle or, in other cases, at or within the entrance to the ducting system. "Wet chemical extinguishing systems shall be provided with an automatic means to ensure the shutoff of fuel or power to the protected appliances, and other appliances located under ventilating equipment protected by the extinguishing system, upon system actuation" (NFPA 17A 1994, p. 17A-6). This code also specifies which part of the duct system is the building owner's responsibility to protect and which is the tenant's responsibility. As with dry chemicals, wet chemicals should be removed as quickly as possible from the surfaces to which they have been applied.

The annunciator and control panels that monitor and control the fire protection systems described here may take various forms depending on the designer and manufacturer of the equipment, and on the requirements of the authority having jurisdiction. Also, the procedures used to reset the systems after they have activated vary considerably from system to system.

Air-Handling System Controls and Status Indicators

Modern high-rise buildings are equipped with systems commonly called central heating, ventilating, and air conditioning (HVAC) systems, or air-conditioning and ventilating (ACV) systems. These systems allow the air within the building to be regularly exchanged, distributed, and maintained at certain levels of temperature, humidity, and cleanliness. The air within the building is thus rendered comfortable for the occupants, and the air temperature of certain areas, such as those containing sensitive equipment, is sustained at predetermined safe levels. "Air conditioning and ventilating systems, except for self-contained units, invariably involve the use of ducts for air distribution. The ducts, in turn, present the possibility of spreading fire, fire gases, and smoke throughout the building or area served" (Schmidt 1991, p. 6-172).

NFPA 90A *Standard for the Installation of Air Conditioning and Ventilating Systems* outlines the purpose of these systems and prescribes minimum requirements for safety to life and property from fire. According to NFPA 90A (1989, p. 90A-5), these systems must:

(a) Restrict the spread of smoke through air duct systems in a building or into a building from the outside.
(b) Restrict the spread of fire through air duct systems from the area of fire origin whether it be within the building or from outside.
(c) Maintain the fire-resistive integrity of building components and elements such as floors, partitions, roofs, walls, and floor/roof-ceiling assemblies affected by the installation of air duct systems.
(d) Minimize ignition sources and combustibility of the elements of the air duct systems.
(e) Permit the air duct systems in a building to be used for the additional purpose of emergency smoke control.

It is not within the scope of this book to describe in detail the HVAC systems that may be found in modern high-rise buildings. To determine what specific equipment should be installed in a building, consult the laws, codes, and standards that have been specifically adopted by the authority having jurisdiction, equipment manufacturer's operation and service manuals, architectural specifications, the building engineer of the site concerned, and possibly the local building or fire department. The *ASHRAE Handbook*, by the American Society of Heating, Refrigeration, and Air Conditioning Engineers, is a valuable source of information regarding such equipment.

In understanding these systems, it is helpful to know that HVAC equipment—heaters, fans, and filters—usually is located in service rooms separated from the remainder of the building by fire-resistive floors, walls, and floor-ceiling assemblies. These rooms generally are locked to deter unauthorized entry and may be equipped with automatic sprinklers for fire protection. They also contain smoke detectors that, on activation, will send a signal to the Building Control Station, automatically shut down the HVAC system, and close fire and smoke dampers serving that area. A *fire damper* is defined by NFPA 90A (1989, p. 90A-6) as: "a device, installed in an air distribution system, designed to close automatically upon detection of heat, to interrupt migratory airflow, and to restrict the passage of flame." A *smoke damper* is "a device within the air distribution system to control the movement of smoke. A smoke damper may also be a fire damper if its location lends itself to the multiple functions and it meets the requirements of both" (NFPA 90A 1989, p. 90A-7). The shutdown of the HVAC fans and the closing of fire and smoke dampers in the HVAC ductwork (a *duct* being a conduit through which air can be moved), in conjunction with the automatic closing of fire doors, such as stairwell and elevator vestibule doors, achieves compartmentation and the protection of occupant escape routes during the early stages of most fires.

In addition to this approach, there may be active use of the HVAC systems in some high-rise buildings "to create differential pressures to prevent smoke migration from the fire area, and to exhaust the products of combustion to the outside" (Schmidt 1991, p. 6-175). In modern high-rise buildings, on activation of the building fire life safety system, there will be automatic pressurization of stairwells using fans that keep smoke out of the stairwell. Status indicators for the HVAC systems and stairwell pressurization fans, and the controls that enable them to be operated manually, will be located in the Building Control Station.

Elevator Status Panel Displaying Elevator Operations

Elevator annunciator panels usually are located in the Building Control Station or at a designated location in the main building lobby. These panels visually display the location of passenger and freight/service elevators operating in the building. They indicate the number of the elevator car (sometimes called a cab) and the number of the floor on which the elevator is located at any particular time. Some elevator systems visually display on a computer monitor screen the floor that each elevator car is on, whether it is parked or traveling up or down, whether the elevator car door is opened or closed, and whether the elevator is empty or contains passengers.

Devices operated by key or by the computers controlling the elevators may also be provided so that elevator cars can be individually selected and their movement up and down manually controlled at the Building Control Station. As mentioned in Chapter 3, *Security Systems and Equipment*, some systems allow individual cars to be directed to a particular floor and then locked off with the elevator doors open, and individual floors to be locked off to prevent elevators from responding to those floors. These actions can be remotely performed at the computer terminal without the operator venturing near the elevators themselves.

Elevator Features and Controls

Elevator systems vary from building to building and even from model to model within the same manufacturer's line. Before proceeding further, it is appropriate to discuss the basic similarities of elevator features and controls.

In high-rise buildings, elevator cars are often separated into *banks* that serve different levels such as low-rise, mid-rise, and high-rise. For example, in the thirty-six floor high-rise tower described in Chapter 5, *Security and Fire Life Safety Surveys*, there may be seventeen passenger elevators, one service/freight elevator, and three parking shuttle elevators. The configuration of the elevators is as follows:

- Low-rise bank—six elevators (numbered 1–6), serve floors 2–12
- Mid-rise bank—six elevators (numbered 7–12), serve floors 13–23
- High-rise bank—five elevators (numbered 13–17), serve floors 23–36
- Freight/service elevator—one elevator (numbered 18), serves floors 1–36
- Parking shuttle elevators—three elevators serve floors P1–P3

A *cross-over* floor, or "sky lobby," where occupants can cross over from one elevator bank to the other, is provided at the twenty-third floor.

Freight/service elevators in a high-rise building usually are larger in size than the passenger elevators and are built to handle the demands of industrial applications. The larger size permits the transport of oversize items such as office furniture and equipment, and accommodates the use of gurneys used by personnel responding to medical emergencies within the building.

Controls Inside Elevator Cars

Inside the elevator car there is often an internal control panel that consists of two main parts:

1. The *passenger open control panel* or *main car station* consists of a floor selection panel (see Figure 4.19) that enables the passenger to select the desired floor by pressing the appropriately numbered button. The selected button then lights up, indicating that the selection has been registered. As required by code, Braille markings and raised numerals indicating the number of each floor are provided adjacent to the pushbuttons to assist people with disabilities. Some ultramodern elevators have incorporated high-fidelity synthesized voice systems for the visually disabled; these systems announce the floor, the direction of travel, and the next stop.

In elevator systems, manual floor selection can occur through completion of an electrical circuit either mechanically (like a door buzzer) or by heat being sensed from the passenger's finger (the latter does not meet ADA requirements). Other elevators use inductance of electricity (the application of the passenger's finger or other object causes a change in an electrical circuit).

In addition to the floor selection buttons, the following buttons usually are available to passengers:

- *OPEN DOOR.* Pushing and holding this button will extend normal door-opening time or re-open a closing elevator door so that the car doors can be kept open longer than the normally programmed time (e.g., to facilitate passenger loading).
- *CLOSE DOOR.* Pushing this button will close the elevator car door.
- *EMERGENCY CALL, EMERGENCY ALARM,* or *EMERGENCY ONLY.* Pushing this button (often red) will annunciate an audible and visual alarm in the Building Control Station, or similarly supervised location within the building, to indicate that there is a possible emergency situation in the elevator concerned. The alarm will be audible both within the car and outside the hoistway.
- *EMERGENCY PUSH TO STOP/PULL TO RUN.* Pushing this button (usually red) will stop the elevator car and annunciate an alarm similar to the one described earlier. Returning the button to its normal position will restore normal operation. In some jurisdictions this device is located in the locked control or service panel where it is not accessible to passengers. This prevents nuisance use and the associated unnecessary sudden stops.

There usually is a two-way emergency communication device, such as a telephone usually located in a compartment, that automatically connects to an elevator maintenance company or other answering service inside or outside the building, or an intercom that is connected to the Building Control Station or similarly supervised location within the building. If the call is directed offsite, the caller will need to communicate the name of the building and the number of the elevator car in which they are located. The ADA requires new or modified elevators to provide a form of communication that is not totally based on voice in case the caller is hearing or speech impaired.

2. The *locked control* or *service panel* consists of key-operated controls or controls located in a locked cabinet (see Figure 4.19). It usually is provided for the use of elevator maintenance, building security, building engineering, fire department, or other authorized personnel. Its control devices often include:

- A POWER OR MOTOR GENERATOR switch that is normally left in the ON position when the elevator car is in constant use. When moved to the OFF position, the elevator cannot be operated.
- An INDEPENDENT SERVICE device (or "manual operation" or "service switch") that permits the use of floor selector buttons to take the car directly to any floor, irrespective of any calls that have been registered inside or outside the elevator car. On independent service, if the car doors are open, the CLOSE DOOR button must be pushed continuously until the car starts to move. On arrival at the selected floor, the doors will open automatically and remain open until another floor selector button is pushed (this mode of operation may vary from system to system). If the operator wants to shut down the elevator while it is on independent service, the switch usually labeled POWER or MOTOR GENERATOR will need to be turned to the OFF or STOP position. Locking of the control panel door prevents any further use of the car without the appropriate key.

- An emergency door open switch that, irrespective of where the car is positioned in relation to the floor level, can be used to open the inner car door. Such a device may be useful if the car will not open normally because it is stalled above or below the floor level.
- An ON and OFF switch to control lighting inside the car. It must be in the ON position whenever the car is in use.
- An ON and OFF switch to control the car ventilation fan. It too should be in the ON position when the car is in use.
- An ON and OFF switch to control the electronic sensing devices (photoelectric or possibly infrared) that control automatic door opening when the elevator door-way is obstructed by a passenger or an object. This device will cause the elevator doors to remain open or to re-open if they have started to close.

Also, the operating and inspection license is posted inside each elevator car.

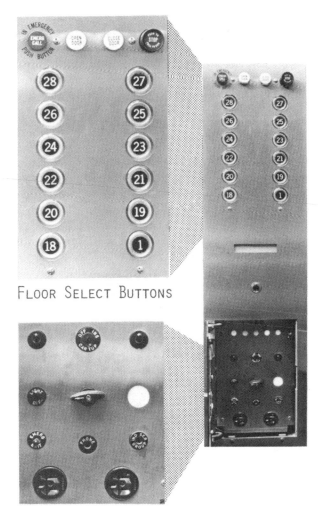

FLOOR SELECT BUTTONS

LOCKED CONTROL PANEL

Figure 4.19
An example of passenger open control and locked control panels located inside an elevator car. Courtesy of American Protective Services, Inc., "Elevators," *Commercial Building Security: The Notebook Lesson Series for Security Officers* (Oakland, CA, 1980), pp. 35 and 41.

Controls in Elevator Lobbies

In passenger elevator lobbies, there are two devices used to control the operation of elevators. *Elevator call stations* located on the wall outside the elevator shaft are pushed to summon a car to the floor. (The operating mechanism is similar to that described for operating floor selection buttons inside the elevator car.) The elevator call station will light up to indicate that the hall call has been registered by the elevator system. (Repeated pushing of the station has no effect on calling the elevator.) Some multiple-elevator installations have hall position indicators that visually inform waiting passengers of the location and direction of travel of elevators in the hoistways.

A *FIRE BYP OFF ON device* ("Fireman's Return Override," or "Fireman's By-Pass," or "Fireman's Service," or "Fire Service"), usually located on the wall near the car door on the recall floor only, allows fire fighters to use and control elevators by using a special key.

> At the main floor of a single elevator or for each of a group of elevators, there is a three-position (ON, OFF, BY-PASS) key-operated switch. During normal elevator operations, the switch is in the OFF position. When the switch is in the ON position, all elevators controlled by this switch and that are on automatic service will return nonstop to the main floor, and the doors will open and remain open. Any elevator moving away from the main floor will reverse at the next available floor without opening its doors. An elevator equipped with automatic power-operated doors and standing at a floor other than the main floor, with doors open, will have its doors close without delay, and then proceed to the main floor. (AIA 1974, p. 3-45)

If the main lobby key-operated switch is turned to the BYP position, the sensing devices will be bypassed and elevator operation will be in normal service during a fire alarm situation.

In modern high-rise buildings, the sequence of operation of fire life safety systems is usually designed so that when an elevator lobby smoke detector is activated it will cause all elevators serving the floor where the alarm is occurring to be recalled, nonstop, to a primary floor (generally the ground floor), the doors to open automatically to allow all passengers to exit, and the elevators to shut down automatically with doors open so that building occupants cannot use them; if the floor where the alarm is occurring is the primary floor, then the elevators will usually relocate to a secondary floor. Insertion of the key in the fire bypass switch, and turning it to BYP, will override the fire life safety system and cause the elevator car(s) concerned to be available for normal service.

Some elevators have fully integrated, state-of-the-art microcomputer-based systems that analyze calls, set priorities, dispatch cars on demand, and enable one to control every aspect of the elevator. For example, a simple stroke on the computer keyboard will enable one to program a particular elevator not to stop on a particular floor during certain time periods. Such controlled access is vital from a security standpoint.

The presence of emergency and standby electrical power systems (discussed in the next section) usually will allow for elevators to be operated under such power. The emergency power control panel for elevator operation may be located at a separate locked control panel or within the Building Control Station. Emergency power systems may vary but basically they provide power to emergency lighting within the elevator car; permit the operation of each elevator to allow passengers to exit the car; establish reduced service during the time of an emergency; and return the elevator system to normal service when electrical power has been restored. Section 30-8.4.21e) "High Rise Buildings" of NFPA 101 *Life Safety Code* (1994, p. 101-225), requires power to be available to at least one elevator serving all floors and this can be transferred to any elevator.

In high-rise buildings, in addition to elevators, there may be escalators, dumbwaiters, rubbish chutes, laundry chutes, and moving walks provided for the movement of people and property. The specific operation of these will vary from system to system and building to building.

Emergency and Standby Power Systems Status Indicators

In the event of an electrical power outage, modern high-rise buildings are equipped with private, permanently installed power supply systems to mitigate this threat to building operations. Indicators of these systems' operating status are found in the Building Control Station. NFPA 70 *The National Electrical Code* (NFPA 70 1990, pp. 7-272–277), outlines two such power systems—emergency and standby.

Emergency Power Systems

Emergency power systems are legally required by local, state, federal, or other codes, or by the authority having jurisdiction, to supply power and illumination automatically to areas that are essential for the life safety of building occupants. Typically these include voice communication and PA systems, means of egress lighting (*means of egress* is defined in Chapter 11) and other lighting specified as necessary, fire detection and alarm systems, fire pumps, elevators, and other facilities that could pose a threat to life safety when power is interrupted.

Usually, emergency power systems are designed to provide an automatic transfer to emergency power within 10 seconds after failure of normal electrical service to the building. This transfer can be powered by devices such as a storage battery or group of batteries, a generator driven by a fuel-supplied prime mover (see Figure 4.20), a UPS, or any other means authorized by the authority having jurisdiction. Lead-acid or nickel-cadmium batteries are dependable but must be located in well-ventilated areas because gases given off by them may be a fire hazard. They must also be recharged after each use. Batteries may also be used to power self-contained lighting assemblies. For generators driven by a prime mover, if the prime mover is an internal combustion engine, an on-site fuel supply, usually with a fuel supply sufficient for not less than two hours full-demand operation of the system, will need to be provided. A UPS is an invaluable system for tenant rooms containing sensitive computer equipment, because it automatically "upon loss of normal power, continues to supply power without waveform distortion, and the load is totally unaware of normal power loss" (DeLerno 1991, p. 2-105).

Standby Power Systems

Standby power systems are subdivided into two categories. *Legally required standby* systems are those mandated by local, state, federal, or other codes, or by the authority having jurisdiction, to automatically supply power to systems other than those classified as emergency power systems, the loss of which could create hazards or have an adverse effect on fire fighting and rescue operations. Typically these include communication systems, ventilation and smoke removal systems, heating and refrigeration systems, and lighting systems.

Legally required standby systems usually are designed to provide an automatic transfer to standby power within 60 seconds of failure of normal electrical service to the building. This transfer can be powered by devices such as a storage battery or group of batteries, a generator driven by a fuel-supplied prime mover, a UPS, or any other means authorized by the authority having jurisdiction.

Optional standby systems are designed to protect property when life safety is not involved. These systems may supply power, either automatically or manually, to data processing and communication systems, to heating and refrigeration systems, or to any other areas where a loss of power could cause discomfort to people, or serious disruption or damage to the systems involved.

Some high-rise buildings, in addition to emergency and standby power systems, provide the following:

- Back-up battery-pack lighting systems installed in elevators and on stairwell landings. These systems automatically activate in the event of disruption of primary and emergency electrical power.
- Luminescent, glow-in-the-dark signs in elevators and stairwells (in the former location these signs may indicate the elevator car number and the location of intercoms; in the latter, they may indicate re-entry points).
- Glow-in-the-dark tape or paint on stair treads and handrails, and on the perimeters of doors.

These improvements were made by the Port Authority operating the New York World Trade Center after the February 26, 1993, bombing.

Use of the Terms "Emergency Power System" and "Standby Power System"

The previous differentiation of Emergency Power Systems and Standby Power Systems was based on NFPA 70, *The National Electrical Code*. If, however, one considers NFPA 110, *Standard for Emergency and Standby Power Systems*, and NFPA 111, *Standard on Stored Electrical Energy Emergency and Standby Power Systems*, the meaning of these terms may overlap and lead to confusion. The reason for this is that NFPA 110 and NFPA 111 place all such systems into categories defined in terms of type, class, and level. "*Type* defines the maximum allowable time that the load is without acceptable electrical power. [For example, Type U refers to UPS systems, Type 10 refers to a maximum allowable time of 10 seconds, and Type 60 refers to a maximum allowable time of 60 seconds.] *Class* defines the minimum allowable time that the alternate source has the

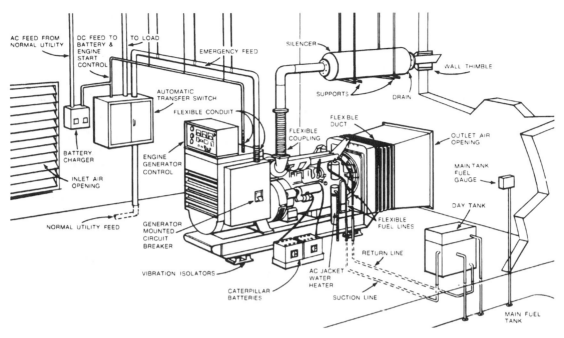

Figure 4.20   A typical package generator set installation used to supply emergency and standby power.   Courtesy of Caterpillar.

capability of providing its rated load without being refueled. *Level* defines the equipment performance stringency requirements" (DeLerno 1991, p. 2-104). For instance, in the case where 60 seconds is the maximum allowable time for the load to be without acceptable electrical power: according to NFPA 70, the correct term is "standby power system," while according to NFPA 110, the correct term is "emergency power system." These terms are different, but, in fact, refer to the same thing.

Controls for Simultaneously Unlocking Stairwell Doors Locked from Stairwell Side

In modern high-rise buildings, locking systems that automatically unlock during a fire emergency often are provided for stairwells located in the building tower. During normal building operations these locking systems, primarily for security reasons, permit doors to be locked from the stairwell side. However, during a fire emergency, these doors either automatically unlock on activation of the building fire alarm system (and remain unlocked until the fire protective signaling system has been manually reset), or else they are unlocked manually at the door or by pressing or turning a switch in the Building Control Station.

Refer to Table 4-1 which outlines the sequence of operation of fire life safety systems in a typical modern high-rise building. This is provided only as an illustration of how fire life safety systems may be designed to operate. The actual mode of operation will vary according to the building and what is required by the laws, codes, and standards that have been adopted by the authority having jurisdiction.

In addition, the Building Control Station may also contain other building and security systems and equipment as sanctioned by the authority having jurisdiction. There may be automatic dialing telephonic equipment to monitor the fire life safety systems at an off-site location and keys required by the fire department for access to elevators and all areas of the building. The provision of building and elevator keys in the Building Control Station is not to be confused with Rapid Entry Systems described in Chapter 3, *Security Systems and Equipment*. (Rapid Entry Systems, or Rapid Entry Key Vaults or Fire Department Lock Boxes, as they are commonly called, are designed for emergency access from the *exterior* of a locked building.)

Many jurisdictions require that the Building Control Station contain the Building Emergency Procedures Manual so that it is readily available for immediate reference by building emergency staff, fire departments, and other emergency responding personnel. Chapter 11, *Building Emergency Planning*, outlines in detail the content of a Building Emergency Procedures Manual. Also, the authority having jurisdiction may require various equipment operating licenses and permits to be displayed in the Building Control Station.

Before completing this description of fire life safety systems and equipment, with its particular reference to the Building Control Station, it is appropriate to describe another valuable piece of equipment to provide for the fire life safety of building occupants and property—the portable *fire extinguisher*.

Portable Fire Extinguishers

Today in the United States there are a number of portable fire extinguishers used in high-rise commercial office buildings. They can be used as a first line of defense in handling fires of limited size. The selection of the most appropriate fire extinguisher depends on the specific hazard it is designed to address, the effectiveness of the fire extinguisher on that type of hazard, and the ease with which the extinguisher can be used.

NFPA 10, *Standard for Portable Fire Extinguishers*, classifies fires, depending on the fuel type, as Class A, Class B, Class C, or Class D. Class D fires involve combustible metals such as magnesium, titanium, zirconium, sodium, lithium, and potassium. Because the occurrence of Class D fires is unusual if not nonexistent in high-rise commercial office buildings, neither they nor the dry powder that can be used to extinguish these types of fires will be discussed. The three classes of fire common in high-rise buildings are as follows:

1. *Class A*—fires in ordinary combustible materials, such as wood, cloth, paper, rubber, and many plastics. Water-based, multipurpose dry chemical, halon, or halon-substitute extinguishers are recommended for Class A fires.

2. *Class B*—fires in flammable liquids, gasoline, alcohol, lubricating oils, greases, tars, oil-base paints, lacquers, and flammable gases. Carbon dioxide, dry

chemical, halon, or halon-substitute extinguishers are recommended for Class B fires. Water should not be used on Class B fires except in the very rare case where the burning substance is known to be capable of being mixed with water. The water may then be applied in a spray form.

3. *Class C*—fires that involve energized electrical equipment, and which therefore require the extinguishing media to be nonconductive. Carbon dioxide, dry chemical, halon, or halon-substitute extinguishers are recommended for Class C fires. When the electrical equipment is de-energized, extinguishers for Class A or B fires may be safely used.

Figure 4.21 shows the marking recommended by the NFPA, in accordance with ANSI standards, to indicate the fire extinguishers suitable for use on each type of fire.

Most high-rise commercial office buildings have Class A fire hazards in public access or common areas and within tenant areas; Class B fire hazards in special areas such as kitchens and cafeterias; and Class C fire hazards in maintenance spaces such as electrical switch gear, generator, or elevator machine rooms, and tenant computer or data processing areas. Fire extinguishers in these areas should have sufficient extinguishing capacity and be immediately available in adequate numbers for persons trained in their operation.

The ensuing review of portable fire extinguishers has been compiled using a National Fire Protection Association article—"Selection, Operation, Distribution, Inspection, and Maintenance of Fire Extinguishers" (Demers 1991, pp. 5-294–312). The following sections describe the various types of extinguishers found in modern high-rise buildings.

Water Based

Water-based extinguishers use water or water solutions that have a cooling, heat-absorbing effect on fires, particularly those of Class A. These water solutions include antifreeze and wetting agents. Older, inverting types of water extinguishers, such as soda-acid and cartridge-operated water, are no longer manufactured.

Water extinguishers that contain water, stored under pressure, are still in use today for Class A fires (see Figure 4.22A). They can be used even in areas

(A)   (B)   (C)

Figure 4.21 Markings recommended by the NFPA for a fire extinguisher suitable for various types of fires. (A) Class A fire—trash, wood, and paper; (B) Class B fire—liquids and grease; (C) Class C fire—electrical equipment. Courtesy of NFPA 10, *Standard for Portable Fire Extinguishers* (1994), Table B-2.1, p. 10-31.

where temperatures may go below freezing, as long as they are charged appropriately, or if an antifreeze solution is added to the water. Wetting agents allow water discharged from the extinguisher to spread and penetrate more effectively by facilitating a reduction in the surface tension of the water.

When using a water extinguisher, the first step is to place the extinguisher on the ground, hold the handle in one hand and pull out the ring pin with the other hand. The ring pin normally keeps the operating lever locked and prevents accidental discharge of the extinguisher. Then take hold of the hose and squeeze the operating lever (usually located directly above the handle) with the other hand. "The stream should be directed at the base of the flames, and after extinguishment of the flames, directed generally at smoldering or glowing surfaces. Application should begin as close as possible to the fire. Deep-seated fires (i.e., smoldering fires such as those involving upholstered furniture) should be thoroughly soaked and may need to be 'broken apart' to effect complete extinguishment" (NFPA 10 1994, p. 10-36). NFPA 10, *Standard for Portable Fire Extinguishers* (1994, Table A-2-1, p. 10-20), states that a 2½ gallon water extinguisher has a solid stream range of approximately 30 to 40 feet horizontally and a continuous discharge time of about one minute. The person operating a water or water-based extinguisher may be injured, or the fire spread further, if the extinguisher is discharged on an electrical or flammable liquid fire.

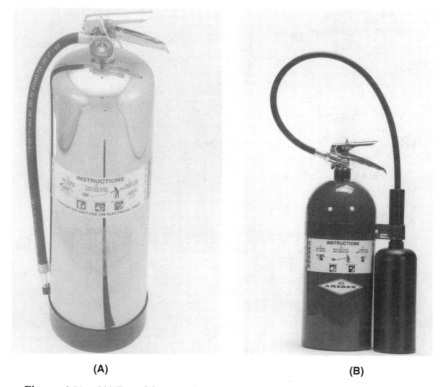

(A)   **(B)**

Figure 4.22   (A) Portable stored pressure water extinguisher. (B) Portable carbon dioxide extinguisher.   Courtesy of Amerex Corporation, Trussville, AL.

Carbon Dioxide

Carbon dioxide extinguishers stop fires by using carbon dioxide to reduce the amount of oxygen in the atmosphere to the point where combustion cannot be supported. For a description of the gas, and its advantages and disadvantages in fire life safety, see the "Carbon Dioxide Systems" section in this chapter. Carbon dioxide can be used to suppress fires involving gas, flammable liquids, electrical equipment, and, although less effectively, common combustible elements such as wood and paper. Figure 4.22B shows a portable carbon dioxide extinguisher.

When using a carbon dioxide extinguisher, the first step is to place it in an upright position using its carrying handle, hold the carrying handle in one hand and pull out the ring pin with the other hand. The ring pin normally keeps the operating lever locked and prevents accidental discharge of the extinguisher. Then direct the extinguisher as described below, taking care not to take hold of the discharge horn (because it may become very cold during discharge), and squeeze the operating lever (usually located directly above the carrying handle) with the other hand. When discharging it on flammable liquid fires, the extinguisher should be aimed at the near edge of the flames and swept from side to side toward the back of the fire, or aimed downward at a 45-degree angle toward the center of the area that is burning and the discharge horn kept stationary. The risk in discharging the extinguisher too close to oil and grease fires is that it may cause these substances to splash and thereby spread the fire. For fires involving electrical equipment, the extinguisher should be aimed at the base of the fire. To prevent reignition, the equipment should be switched off promptly. NFPA 10, *Standard for Portable Fire Extinguishers* (1994, Table A-2-1, p. 10-20), states that a 2½ to 5 lb. hand portable carbon dioxide extinguisher has a horizontal range of 3 to 8 feet and an approximate discharge time of 8 to 30 seconds.

Halon

To extinguish fires involving expensive electrical office equipment such as computers, halon generally is used. For a description of halons, their advantages, the environmental hazards associated with them, and their viable substitutes, see the "Halon Systems" section.

The technique for using a halon extinguisher is very similar to that employed for carbon dioxide extinguishers. NFPA 10, *Standard for Portable Fire Extinguishers* (1994, Table A-2-1, p. 10-21), states that a 2½ lb. Halon 1301 extinguisher has a horizontal range of 4 to 6 feet and an approximate discharge time of 8 to 10 seconds, while a 0.9 to 2 lb. Halon 1211 extinguisher has a horizontal range of 6 to 10 feet and a similar discharge time.

Dry Chemical

For a description of dry chemical agents, and an estimate of their function as fire extinguishers, see the preceding "Dry Chemical Systems" section. *Ordinary dry chemical extinguishers* (sodium bicarbonate, potassium bicarbonate, potassium bicarbonate urea base, bicarbonate urea base, or potassium chloride base) are primarily for use on Class B and Class C fires. *Multi-purpose (ABC) dry chemical* extinguishers (multi-purpose ammonium phosphate base) are used primarily on Class A, Class B, and Class C fires. When introduced in 1961, multi-purpose dry chemical "had the added advantage of being approximately 50 percent more effective than ordinary dry chemical on flammable liquid and electrical fires, and also was capable of extinguishing fires in ordinary combustibles" (Petersen 1991, p. 5-314).

A dry chemical agent can be discharged from an extinguisher in two ways. These ways depend on the basic extinguisher design. The *cartridge-operated* extinguisher uses an external pressurized gas cartridge to discharge the dry chemical, while the rechargeable *stored pressure* extinguisher pressurizes the dry chemical chamber to discharge the dry chemical itself. The operation of dry chemical extinguishers varies not only with extinguisher type, but also with fire type. Ordinary dry chemical extinguishers, when used on flammable liquid fires, should be aimed at the near edge of the flames and swept from side to side toward the back of the fire. There will be a sizable force generated by the initial discharge from the extinguisher; thus, it should not be used at a range closer than 5 to 8 feet for oil and grease fires, because it may cause these substances to splash and thereby spread the fire.

Multi-purpose dry chemical extinguishers are used in the same manner as ordinary dry chemical extinguishers on Class B fires. However, on Class A fires, it is important to attempt to coat all burning areas because the multi-purpose agent tends to soften and adhere to burning materials and creates a coating that smothers and isolates the fuel from air. NFPA 10, *Standard for Portable Fire Extinguishers* (1994, Table A-2-1, p. 10-20), states that a 1 to 2½ lb. dry chemical (sodium bicarbonate stored pressure) extinguisher has a horizontal range of 5 to 8 feet and an approximate discharge time of 8 to 12 seconds. These ranges and discharge times vary according to the type of dry chemical being used.

Because dry chemical is electrically nonconductive, it is also useful against Class C fires. However, in telephone switching and computer rooms, where there are sensitive electrical contacts and relays, its use is not recommended. Application in these areas may cause the equipment to malfunction. After any use of dry chemical, it should be removed as quickly as possible from the surfaces to which it has been applied, because it may be corrosive.

Positioning of Portable Fire Extinguishers

The distribution of the portable fire extinguishers throughout a building is determined by a physical survey of the areas that need to be protected. After the selection of the appropriate number and type of extinguishers is made, they should be located conspicuously in positions that make them readily available in the event of a fire. Often this will require that they be located in areas where there are specific hazards and along the normal paths of egress from a space to an exit. The NFPA states in its codes that 75 feet is the maximum travel distance a fire extinguisher can be from Class A hazards; the distance is 30 to 50 feet for Class B hazards (depending on whether the hazard is a flammable liquid of appreciable depth), and for Class C hazards the distance will depend on whether the electrical equipment is a Class A or Class B hazard (NFPA 10 1994, p. 10-9–10).

In high-rise commercial office buildings, portable fire extinguishers normally are located in public access or common areas such as freight/service elevator lobbies and outside entrances to stairwells; within tenant spaces in kitchens, cafeterias, photocopier rooms, computer or data processing areas; and in maintenance spaces such as electrical switch gear, generator, and elevator machine rooms. The extinguishers will be mounted on hangers or brackets, kept in unlocked cabinets (see Figure 4.23) or locked cabinets (provided the latter can be accessed in an emergency), or placed on shelves. They should be mounted in such a way that the operating instructions are immediately visible and the extinguisher is readily accessible to the user.

Figure 4.23
Portable stored pressure ABC multi-purpose extinguisher housed in a cabinet.   Photograph by Roger Flores.

Summary

This chapter discusses the many types of fire life safety systems and equipment found in typical high-rise commercial office buildings. It emphasizes that to determine what is actually required at a specific site, one must review the laws, codes, and standards specifically adopted by the authority having jurisdiction. To assist in determining what specific systems and equipment are installed and operating at the site, one should consult equipment manufacturer's operation and service manuals, architectural specifications, the Building Engineer of the site concerned, and the local building or fire department. If further expertise is required, a fire life safety consultant, such as a registered fire protection engineer, may be called in. Either the Building Engineer (particularly the Chief Engineer) or the Building Operations Manager is the key on-site person. This individual usually knows more about the building's operations, and about how the building is designed and configured, than anyone else.

To maintain a building's fire life safety systems and equipment in an operable condition, the authority having jurisdiction will require periodic inspection and maintenance according to specified guidelines. Buildings commonly employ a licensed contractor and support team specializing in life safety system maintenance to perform this work. Typically in large high-rise buildings, building engineers do not have the time to perform these labor-intensive inspections, and sometimes they do not possess all the skills necessary to perform the required maintenance services on the wide variety of equipment involved.

Comprehensive listings of the manufacturers and installers of the fire life safety systems and equipment detailed in this chapter may be found in the *NFPA Journal Buyer's Guide*. Further information on these systems and equipment may be found in the *NFPA Fire Protection Handbook* and the *ASHRAE Handbook and Product Directory*.

References

Abbott, Richard J., "Sprinkler systems, standpipe systems, detectors," *Fire Science Institute Office Buildings Fire Safety Directors Course*, New York, 1994).

A.I.A., "Elevator emergencies," *American Insurance Association Special Interest Bulletin*, No. 55 (February 1974).

ASHRAE Handbook and Product Directory (American Society of Heating, Refrigeration, and Air Conditioning Engineers, Inc., Atlanta).

Bryan, John L., "Fire detection systems," *Fire Suppression and Detection Systems* (Macmillan Publishing Co., Inc., New York, 1982).

Cassidy, Kevin A., "The overall importance of standpipes and hoses," *Fire Safety and Loss Prevention*, 5th ed. (Butterworth–Heinemann, Boston, 1992).

Clarke, Frederick B., "Fire hazards of materials: An overview," *Fire Protection Handbook*, 17th ed. Editor-in-Chief, Arthur E. Cote, Managing Editor, Jim L. Linville (All NFPA material in this chapter used with permission from National Fire Protection Association, Quincy, MA 02269. Copyright 1991).

DeLerno, Manuel J., "Emergency and standby power supplies," *Fire Protection Handbook*, 17th ed. (National Fire Protection Association, Quincy, MA, 1991).

Demers, David P., "Selection, operation, distribution, inspection, and maintenance of fire extinguishers," *Fire Protection Handbook*, 17th ed. (National Fire Protection Association, Quincy, MA, 1991).

Grant, C.C., "Halon design calculations," *SFPE Handbook of Fire Protection Engineering* (National Fire Protection Association, Quincy, MA), Section 3-4, p. 3-61, as reported in "Life beyond halon," *NFPA Fire Journal* May/June 1990.

Haessler, Walter M., "Dry chemical agents and application systems," *Fire Protection Handbook*, 17th ed. (National Fire Protection Association, Quincy, MA, 1991).

Hall, John R., Jr., Ph.D., "The U.S. experience with sprinklers," *NFPA Journal* (National Fire Protection Association, Quincy, MA, November/December 1993).

Little, Juanita, BOMA Research, "1993 Fire Safety Survey," *Skyline Magazine* (BOMA International, Washington, DC, October 1993).

Moore, Wayne D., "Automatic fire detectors," *Fire Protection Handbook*, 17th ed. (National Fire Protection Association, Quincy, MA, 1991).

NFPA *Journal Buyer's Guide, Fire Protection & Fire Service Reference Directory* (National Fire Protection Association, Quincy, MA. Copyright 1995).

NFPA 10, *Standard for Portable Fire Extinguishers*, Appendix D, Section D-4, "Fire Extinguisher Characteristics" (National Fire Protection Association, Quincy, MA. Copyright 1994), p. 10-36.

NFPA 10, *Standard for Portable Fire Extinguishers*, Chapter 3: "Distribution of Extinguishers" (National Fire Protection Association, Quincy, MA. Copyright 1994), pp. 10-9–10-10.

NFPA 12, *Standard for Carbon Dioxide Extinguishing Systems* (National Fire Protection Association, Quincy, MA. Copyright 1990).

NFPA 13, *Standard for the Installation of Sprinkler Systems* (National Fire Protection Association, Quincy, MA. Copyright 1990).

NFPA 14, *Standard for the Installation of Standpipe and Hose Systems* (National Fire Protection Association, Quincy, MA. Copyright 1990).

NFPA 17, *Standard for Dry Chemical Extinguishing Systems*, Appendix A: "Explanatory Material," Section A-2-1: "Extinguishing Mechanisms" (National Fire Protection Association, Quincy, MA. Copyright 1994), p. 17-15.

NFPA 17, *Standard for Dry Chemical Extinguishing Systems*, Chapter 1: "Administration," Section 1-4: "Definitions" (National Fire Protection Association, Quincy, MA, 1994), p. 17-5.

NFPA 17, *Standard for Dry Chemical Extinguishing Systems*, Chapter 7: "Pre-Engineered Systems," Section 7-3: "Restaurant Hood, Duct, and Cooking Appliance Systems," 7-3.2 (National Fire Protection Association, Quincy, MA, 1994), p. 17-11.

NFPA 17A, *Standard for Wet Chemical Extinguishing Systems*, 1994, Chapter 1: "General," Section 1-4: "Definitions" (National Fire Protection Association, Quincy, MA. Copyright 1994), p. 17A-5.

NFPA 17A, *Standard for Wet Chemical Extinguishing Systems*, Appendix A: "Explanatory Material," Section A-2-6.1: "Wet Chemical Solution Characteristics, Extinguishing Mechanisms" (National Fire Protection Association, Quincy, MA, 1994), p. 17A-10.

NFPA 17A, *Standard for Wet Chemical Extinguishing Systems*, 1994, Chapter 2: "Components," Section 2-4.2.2: "Shutoff Devices" (National Fire Protection Association, Quincy, MA, 1994), p. 17A-6.

NFPA 20, *Standard for the Installation of Centrifugal Fire Pumps*, Chapter 5: "Fire Pumps for High-Rise Buildings," Section 5-4: "Driver," 5-4.2.2—5-4.2.3 (National Fire Protection Association, Quincy, MA. Copyright 1993), p. 20-15.

NFPA 70, *National Electrical Code*, Chapter 7: "Special Conditions," Article 700: "Emergency Systems," Article 701: "Legally Required Standby Systems," Article 702: "Optional Standby Systems" (National Fire Protection Association, Quincy, MA. Copyright 1990), pp. 7-272 to 7-277.

NFPA 72, *National Fire Alarm Code*, Chapter 5: "Initiating Devices," Section 5-3: "Smoke-Sensing Fire Detectors," 5-3.5.1 (National Fire Protection Association, Quincy, MA. Copyright 1993), p. 185.

NFPA 72, *National Fire Alarm Code*, Chapter 5: "Initiating Devices," Section 5-3: "Smoke-Sensing Fire Detectors," 5-3.6.1 (National Fire Protection Association, Quincy, MA, 1993), p. 192.

NFPA 72, *National Fire Alarm Code*, Chapter 5: "Initiating Devices," Section 5-7: "Sprinkler Waterflow Alarm-Initiating Devices," 5-7.2 (National Fire Protection Association, Quincy, MA, 1993), p. 211.

NFPA 90A, *Standard for the Installation of Air Conditioning and Ventilating Systems*, Chapter 1: "General," Section 1-3: "Purpose," 1-3.1 (National Fire Protection Association, Quincy, MA. Copyright 1989), p. 90A-5.

NFPA 90A, *Standard for the Installation of Air Conditioning and Ventilating Systems*, Chapter 1: "General," Section 1-3: "Purpose," 1-3.1 (National Fire Protection Association, Quincy, MA, 1989), p. 90A-6.

NFPA 90A, *Standard for the Installation of Air Conditioning and Ventilating Systems*, Chapter 1: "General," Section 1-3: "Purpose," 1-3.1 (National Fire Protection Association, Quincy, MA, 1989), p. 90A-7.

NFPA 101, *Life Safety Code*, 1994, Chapter 7: "Building Service and Fire Protection Equipment," Section 7-6: "Fire Detection, Alarm, and Communication Systems," 7-6.2.3–7-6.2.5 (National Fire Protection Association, Quincy, MA. Copyright 1994), p. 101-58.

NFPA 101, *Life Safety Code*, Chapter 30: "Special Structures and High Rise Buildings," Section 30-8: "High Rise Buildings, Extinguishing Requirements," 30-8.2.1 (National Fire Protection Association, Quincy, MA, 1994), p. 101-225.

NFPA 101, *Life Safety Code*, Chapter 30: "Special Structures and High Rise Buildings," Section 30-8: "High Rise Buildings, Emergency Lighting and Standby Power," 30-8.4.2(e) (National Fire Protection Association, Quincy, MA, 1994), p. 101-225.

Petersen, Marshall E., "The role of extinguishers in fire protection," *Fire Protection Handbook*, 17th ed. (National Fire Protection Association, Quincy, MA, 1991).

Schmidt, William A., "Air conditioning and ventilating systems," *Fire Protection Handbook*, 17th ed. (National Fire Protection Association, Quincy, MA, 1991).

Shapiro, Jeffrey M., "Standpipe and hose systems," *Fire Protection Handbook*, 17th ed. (National Fire Protection Association, Quincy, MA, 1991).

Solomon, Robert, "Automatic sprinkler systems" and "Water supplies for sprinkler systems," *Fire Protection Handbook*, 17th ed. (National Fire Protection Association, Quincy, MA, 1991).

Taylor, Gary, "Halogenated agents and systems," *Fire Protection Handbook*, 17th ed. (National Fire Protection Association, Quincy, MA, 1991).

Webb, William, Review of Chapter 4 in *Fire Life Safety Systems & Equipment* (Rolf Jensen & Associates, Deerfield, IL, 1994).

Wilson, Dean K., "Protective signaling systems," *Fire Protection Handbook*, 17th ed. (National Fire Protection Association, Quincy, MA, 1991). This quote has been slightly modified. The original reads "a secondary, or standby, power supply." Also, "sirens, whoopers" has been added.

Appendix 4-1   Additional Information Sources

The following NFPA codes, standards, and recommended practices are suggested references to obtain additional information on fire life safety systems and equipment:

NFPA 10	*Portable Fire Extinguishers*
NFPA 12	*Carbon Dioxide Extinguishing Systems*
NFPA 12A	*Halon 1301 Fire Extinguishing Systems*
NFPA 12B	*Halon 1211 Fire Extinguishing Systems*
NFPA 13	*Installation of Sprinkler Systems*
NFPA 13A	*Inspection, Testing, and Maintenance of Sprinkler Systems*
NFPA 14	*Installation of Standpipe and Hose Systems*
NFPA 14A	*Testing, Inspection, and Maintenance of Standpipe and Hose Systems*
NFPA 15	*Water-Spray Fixed Systems for Fire Protection*
NFPA 17	*Dry Chemical Extinguishing Systems*
NFPA 17A	*Wet Chemical Extinguishing Systems*
NFPA 20	*Installation of Centrifugal Fire Pumps*
NFPA 22	*Water Tanks for Private Fire Protection*
NFPA 24	*Installation of Private Fire Service Mains and their Appurtenances*
NFPA 26	*Supervision of Valves Controlling Water Supplies for Fire Protection*
NFPA 70	*National Electrical Code*
NFPA 71	*Signaling Systems for Central Station Service*
NFPA 72	*National Fire Alarm Code*
NFPA 75	*Protection of Electronic Computer/Data Processing Equipment*
NFPA 80	*Fire Doors and Windows*
NFPA 90A	*Installation of Air Conditioning and Ventilating Systems*
NFPA 92	*Smoke Control Systems*
NFPA 96	*Ventilation Control and Fire Protection of Commercial Cooking Operations*
NFPA 101	*Life Safety Code*
NFPA 110	*Emergency and Standby Power Systems*
NFPA 111	*Stored Electrical Energy Emergency and Standby Power Systems*
NFPA 291	*Fire Flow Testing and Marking of Hydrants*

5 Security and Fire Life Safety Surveys

Security and fire life safety surveys can be important management tools by which building owners, managers, and security and safety professionals can operate high-rise buildings effectively and safely and reduce premises liability. Surveys are essential to identify the threats to security and life safety in a high-rise building.

A *security survey* is defined as "a critical on-site examination and analysis of an industrial plant, business, home, or public or private institution to ascertain the present security status, to identify deficiencies or excesses, to determine the protection needed, and to make recommendations to improve the overall security" (Momboisse 1968, p. 13). Fischer and Green (1992, p. 165) state:

> A security survey is essentially an exhaustive physical examination of the premises and a thorough inspection of all operational systems and procedures. . . . In the process of risk analysis that proceeds from threat assessment (identifying risk) to threat evaluation (determining the criticality and dollar cost of that risk) to the selection of security countermeasures designed to contain or prevent that risk, one of management's most valuable tools is the security survey.

Criticality is determined by the impact that a threat would have if it occurred at a facility. Also, as Post and Kingsbury write: "Security programs for business establishments are often built around the existing physical design features of the building. . . . Design characteristics of the building will either increase or decrease the ability and opportunity of employees and customers to steal. The integration of barrier systems, sensory devices, and access control points within the building ensures that opportunity and ability are reduced or eliminated" (1991, pp. 177, 178).

Before one can make the right management decisions to effectively carry out this integration, however, one must thoroughly understand how the present security program is operating. The security survey provides such a tool. A security survey may focus on different aspects of a high-rise facility. It may include the area and businesses surrounding the site, the facility itself, a tenant space within the facility, or defined aspects of the security operation such as policies, procedures, and equipment. It may also be used as a tool to investigate a particular incident or a security problem that has occurred. In addition, an opinion survey may be conducted among security staff to measure their morale or elicit their ideas regarding the effectiveness of the overall security program and their use of certain procedures and equipment; such an opinion survey also may be conducted among building staff (management, janitorial, parking, and engineering) or building tenants. An opinion survey of tenants is an important tool enabling building management to evaluate tenants'perception of the security program, to identify areas that may need to be changed or improved, or to evaluate the anticipated reaction of tenants if changes are to be made to the security program.

A *fire life safety survey* is very similar. Its objectives are to determine the present life safety status, to identify deficiencies or excesses, to ascertain the fire and life safety protection needed, and to make recommendations to improve the overall fire life safety of the facility under evaluation.

There is no real short cut in carrying out effective security and fire life safety surveys. Thomas Edison made the famous statement that "genius is 1 percent inspiration and 99 percent perspiration" (Israel, 1994, p. 13). It may not take a genius to conduct a survey—although technical expertise and experience are important aspects of the process—but there is no doubt that to make a thorough analysis of the security or fire life safety aspects of a facility, a considerable amount of work is required. To make the work as orderly as possible, it is helpful to use a standardized approach. Such an approach will make it more likely that vital areas are adequately covered, will maintain a uniform standard in surveys repeatedly conducted, and will assist the surveyor in efficiently carrying out the survey itself.

Security Survey

A physical security survey can be as extensive or as restricted as the surveyor determines. A formal documented survey basically will involve two major tasks, the fact-finding investigative process and writing the report that reflects the findings. The *fact-finding process* may include the following items:

1. Discussions with those commissioning the survey to define the reasons for and the scope of the survey, designate the time period in which the survey will be conducted, determine to whom the final survey report will be presented, and identify the individual(s) with authority to implement the survey recommendations.
2. Review of local laws and codes pertaining to required security measures.
3. Interviews with representatives of local law enforcement, such as police or sheriff's departments, to obtain crime statistics pertaining to the area encompassing the site (if possible, statistics should be obtained for the previous five years).
4. Interviews with the representatives of nearby businesses or visual observation of the immediate neighborhood and areas surrounding the site to determine what security precautions these businesses are taking.
5. Review of any previous surveys conducted at the site (such documents, if available, should provide background information and details of the follow-up on previously noted deficiencies).
6. Review of available documentation such as a description of the building and its construction features (sometimes this can be found in marketing material for the

site, or from architectural documents), site and floor plans, plans for changes at the site, records (particularly those detailing security-related incidents that have previously occurred), tenant leases, security services agreements, data, files, organizational charts, job descriptions, manuals, policies and operating procedures (including security instructions or post orders) that have relevance to the survey.

7. Conduct a profile of tenant businesses to ascertain which ones may constitute a high risk from a security perspective and be a strategic target for political terrorists, domestic activist groups, and criminals seeking high-value merchandise.

8. Interviews with persons having knowledge of the site: these individuals may include architects, building management, building engineers, janitors, security and parking staff, couriers, and possibly the vendors of the security equipment currently in place or planned for installation.

9. Visits to the site at different times during the day and night, business and non-business hours, to become familiar with:

   - Principal activities and usage
   - Physical layout and construction
   - Lighting
   - Landscaping
   - Electronic security systems
   - The security program in operation

   This may include testing of security systems. At times this testing may be carried out clandestinely by the surveyor to check the operation of the systems, particularly to determine whether certain procedures are being implemented as they were designed to be.

10. Review of insurance policies to determine whether present or planned security measures are of an acceptable level.

To approach the viewing of the site in an orderly fashion, it is helpful to consider that "the classical approach to perimeter security views a property in terms of rings. The property boundary is the first ring. The building is the second, and the specific interior spaces are the third" (Merritt Company 1991, p. 19-120). The *Protection of Assets Manual* further states that within the high-rise structure there are three classes or types of interior spaces.

1. *Public access or common areas* include street-level entrance lobbies, main elevator lobbies, access routes to retail sales spaces (and restaurants, etc.) in the structure, promenades, mezzanines, and—increasingly in new buildings—atria.

2. *Rented or assigned occupancies* (i.e., *tenant areas*) are leased or owner-occupied spaces on the various floors. Depending on the occupant, such spaces may be open to public access during building hours, or may be restricted to identified and authorized persons.

3. *Maintenance spaces* include mechanical rooms and floors, communications and utilities access points, elevator machine rooms, janitorial closets, paint rooms or paint storage rooms, and other spaces with strictly limited access.

To assist in the fact-finding process it is helpful to use a checklist of areas to be covered. Such a checklist for a physical security survey is provided in Appendix 5-1. The main sections in this checklist are: general information; site perimeter; building and building perimeter; maintenance spaces; loading dock/shipping and receiving areas; vehicular movement and parking areas; tenant offices; cafeteria, kitchen, and dining areas; security alarms, closed-circuit television (CCTV), and access control systems; key controls, locking devices, and containers; janitorial operation; security operation; security education; and insurance. (See Appendix 5-1 for complete details.)

Every facility, organization, and site, however, is different, and therefore no generic checklist can possibly cover all aspects of the facility being surveyed. In carrying out the fact-finding process for the particular area being surveyed, one may select as much, or as little, of the suggested checklist as one needs. The amount selected will be determined by the scope or extent of the survey being conducted. As Gleckman (1995, p. 4) summarizes,

> A checklist should be made up by the survey team (for extensive surveys there may need to be more than one surveyor) in preparation for the actual inspection. This checklist will be used to facilitate the gathering of pertinent information. The checklist is considered to be the backbone of the security survey or audit. This checklist will serve to systematically guide the survey team through the areas that must be examined.

The fact-finding process should include taking notes or using a small cassette recorder; also, it may be helpful to photograph various aspects of the site, particularly problem areas. Before taking photographs, permission should be obtained from the appropriate building representative. The fact-finding process, including planning the survey, will probably take 40 to 50% of the total time spent conducting the survey, while the other 50 to 60% will be spent writing the report.

Writing the report will involve assembling the ideas and information obtained in the fact-finding investigative process. Weaknesses in the security program should indeed be pointed out and accompanied by recommendations to address them, but security strengths also should be listed. If a word processor is used to create the report, changes, modifications, and additions can be carried out in a relatively effortless manner. A standardized approach like the following will help to properly organize this information into a logical and understandable format. Again, every facility, organization, and site is different, as is the scope of each survey, and individual surveyors will have their own specialized approaches. Hence, the suggested format is just that—a *suggested* one.

Title Pages

A typical title page indicates the confidentiality of the report, the name of the organization for whom the report is produced, the name of the site surveyed, the name of the person by whom the survey and report is compiled, the date, and a notation of the copy number. The next page should list the number of copies of the report and to whom each copy is distributed.

Cover Letter

The cover letter should be addressed to the individual who commissioned the report. It includes a brief statement of the report's scope, brief thanks to individuals who assisted with the report, a mention of anything pertinent to this particular report, and where to direct any inquiries regarding the report's content.

Table of Contents

The table of contents is a listing by page number of all pertinent sections of the report.

Introduction

The introduction briefly states who commissioned the survey, why it was performed, and its scope. An example is as follows:

> This survey and report were requested by Mrs. Shirley Thomas, Asset Manager, Pauley and Partners. The primary objective for conducting this survey was to review strengths and weaknesses in the security program at the Pacific Tower Plaza high-rise complex, with reference, in particular, to after-hours access control procedures of building occupants and the control of business and personal property leaving the site after normal business hours.

Method of Compilation

The method of compilation includes a description of how information was obtained for the survey, the names of individuals interviewed, a list of documents reviewed, and the time period in which the survey was conducted. For example:

> The survey was conducted on October 4–14, 1995, using information obtained from interviews with management personnel of Pauley and Partners; managers of the engineering, security, janitorial, and parking departments; individual security staff members; and a representative of Columbus Insurance Company. In addition, information was obtained by reviewing the Building Emergency Procedures Manual, a security survey previously conducted at Pacific Tower Plaza, current security instructions, security incidents reported since January 1, 1995, police crime statistics for the general area surrounding the site, a Tenant Information Manual (issued by building management to explain building policies and procedures), and crime coverage insurance policies in effect at the site.

Description of the Site, Building, and Surrounding Areas

The report should include a description of the site's size, zoning, boundaries, and landscaping; a description of the building, including any overpasses or subterranean passageways; the building's number of square feet, principal activities and usage, operating hours, and building population; nature of the surrounding area and occupancies, proximity to freeways, major roads, and the local police jurisdiction. Any available maps, floor plans, or site photographs may be noted at this point. The following is a sample description of a high-rise building and its surrounding area.

> Pacific Tower Plaza is a prestigious, multiple-tenant, multiple-use high-rise complex used primarily for commercial office purposes. It is typically operational from 7:00 AM to 7:00 PM, Monday to Friday, and 9:00 AM to 2:00 PM, on

Saturday. It has restricted access at all other times. It is located in Toluga Hills, a major downtown financial district. It occupies one half of the city block bounded by Mount Waverley, Poppyfields, and La Perouse Boulevards and is located close to the South Western Freeway. The Toluga Hills police department has a main station within two miles of the complex, and there is a fire station within three city blocks. It is surrounded by a high-rise residential building, a low-rise hotel, and a high-rise commercial office building.

Pacific Tower Plaza consists of a fully sprinklered thirty-six–story office tower with a three-level subterranean parking structure. The tower has 600,000 square feet of rentable office space, 7,000 square feet of rentable retail space, and 6,000 square feet of rentable storage space. The approximate size of each floor plate (the plate being the entire floor area including the public access or common areas, tenant areas, and maintenance spaces) is 18,500 square feet. The perimeter of the building consists of sculptures, fountains, an open-air restaurant and large planters containing flowers and small trees. The entrance to the building is through a large main lobby. The building has an approximate population of 2,400 occupants and 500 daily visitors. The on-site parking structure can accommodate up to 600 cars and connects to a subterranean pedestrian tunnel under Mount Waverley Boulevard.

The tower of Pacific Tower Plaza consists of steel-frame and concrete construction with metal stud partitions. It has a conventional curtain wall consisting of glass in aluminum frames. The structural steel frame supports lightweight concrete floor slabs resting on metal decks atop horizontal steel beams, which are welded to vertical steel columns. The building is supported on a foundation of structurally reinforced concrete. The tower is designed with a concrete-reinforced center core which houses the electrical, plumbing, and communications systems; the heating and air-conditioning (air supply and return) shafts; seventeen passenger elevators; one service/freight elevator; three parking shuttle elevators; and two major enclosed stairwells. Both stairwells provide egress to the street level, and access to the roof (the doors are locked at the roof). The stairwells are pressurized and protected by fire-rated doors and walls.

Vulnerability of Assets

The assets of the site should be identified with an estimation of their value and financial impact if they were to be lost, made inaccessible, or destroyed. For a high-rise commercial office building, these assets may be *tangible* (including the building itself, its fittings, its systems and equipment; tenant office equipment and furnishings; and vehicles in the parking structure) or *intangible* (including the livelihood of all building users, and proprietary information stored on site).

Review of Past Security Incidents

A review of previous security-related incidents that have occurred at the site over a designated period of time. Such information can be obtained from daily activity and incident reports generated by security staff. Crime statistics for the reporting district encompassing the area often can be obtained from local law enforcement and included here.

Description of Security Measures and Recommendations

This section reviews all security measures currently in place at the site. The areas that can be reviewed, depending on the scope of the survey, include perimeter barriers and fences, building construction and layout, lighting, intrusion and duress alarms, CCTV, security patrols, access control of vehicles, people, and property, identification badges, locking and key controls, trash removal procedures, personnel security, written procedures and policies, and communications. Again, strengths as well as weaknesses in the security measures should be pointed out to provide a balanced view of the security program. Recommendations should then be made for modifications or changes to the listed security measures (some surveyors include the cost of certain recommendations).

The following is an example of a security measure with associated recommendations for improvement.

Access control of building occupants after normal business hours is determined by visual recognition of the tenants by the lobby security officer who then asks individuals authorized to enter to print their names, the name of the tenant by whom they are employed, and the date and time, and to sign their names on the after-hours building register. If the officer does not recognize an individual, a file of tenant occupants authorized for after-hours access is checked. If the individual is not listed there, a call is made to the tenant suite to ask if anyone can authorize the entry of the individual. If no tenant is available, the individual is denied access. This procedure has caused continual problems because of the repeated denial of access to occupants who otherwise had permission from their employers to work in the building after hours. Two obvious reasons for this have been frequent changes of after-hours security personnel, who are not familiar with the building users, and the failure of tenants to provide up-to-date listings of employees authorized to work after normal business hours.
    Recommendations:

- Investigate why the turnover of security staff working after normal business hours is high.
- Have building management approach all tenants who are not providing up-to-date, after-hour authorization lists to reemphasize the need for such critical information.
- Have building management request that every tenant provide a list of key personnel who can be contacted after hours before any of their employees is denied after-hours access.
- Design an after-hours building access card and request that tenants issue the completed card to all their employees who need after-hours access.
- Obtain quotations from vendors to install a card access control system at the building.

Summary of Recommendations

This section is optional but may be included to summarize the findings of the survey. The recommendations for each security measure may be separately listed according to monetary cost, those planned for immediate attention, and those to be addressed at a future time. There could be a ranking of the recommendations, listing first those which, if implemented, would result in the greatest overall improvement in the performance and effectiveness of the security program. The recommendations also could be grouped into those providing low, medium, and high levels of security.

Executive Summary

This final section is a summary of the report itself. It provides the reader with a quick review of the survey and report by drawing attention to important items. A sample executive summary for Pacific Tower Plaza follows:

> The survey was conducted on October 4–14, 1995. The primary objective for conducting this survey was to review the strengths and weaknesses in the security program at the Pacific Tower Plaza high-rise complex; in particular, reference is made to after-hours access control procedures of building occupants and the control of business and personal property leaving the site after normal business hours.
>
> Interviews were conducted with management personnel of Pauley and Partners; managers of the security, engineering, janitorial, and parking departments; individual security staff members; and a representative of Columbus Insurance Company.
>
> The survey revealed that after-hours access control procedures of the building have been rigidly enforced by building security staff. This has resulted in very few unauthorized persons gaining after-hours access to tenant offices but has led to the repeated denial of access to occupants who otherwise had permission from their employers to work in the building after hours. The survey also revealed that there has been little control of business and personal property leaving the site after normal business hours. This factor is thought to have contributed considerably to the theft of personal computers and typewriters from secured tenant offices that has been occurring since the building was opened on January 1, 1995.
>
> These are some of the recommendations stemming from this survey for improving the effectiveness of the security program at Pacific Tower Plaza:
>
> - Investigate why the turnover of security staff is high
> - Have building management approach all tenants who are not providing up-to-date after-hour authorization lists to reemphasize the need for such critical information
> - Have building management request that every tenant provide a list of key personnel who can be contacted after hours before any of their employees is denied after-hours access
> - Design an after-hours building access card and request that tenants issue the completed card to all their employees who need after-hours access
> - Obtain quotations from vendors to install a card access control system at the building
> - Design a property removal system to control the movement of business and personal property from the building. This system should be implemented as soon as possible after all tenants have been thoroughly informed of the new policy and their cooperation has been solicited in supporting it
> - Encourage tenant representatives to inventory office equipment and to identify it clearly
> - Encourage tenants to anchor items—typewriters, fax machines, and personal computers—using devices such as metal plates or steel cables.

Building management representatives have indicated that they are very supportive of providing a sound security program for the tenants at Pacific Tower Plaza. They also appear willing, within reasonable cost constraints, to take whatever steps are necessary to achieve this goal.

Appendices

Any back-up documentation to which the survey refers, reference material that may help support the suggested recommendations, floor plans, maps, diagrams, forms, and photographs may be included here to substantiate the work of the surveyor.

Presentation of the Report

Once the report is written, it should be displayed in an understandable manner that reflects the professionalism that has gone into preparing it. Each major section of the report should be tabbed and any photographs and drawings neatly mounted and labeled. The report should then be placed in a three-ringed binder, bound, or encased between plastic covers.

If at all possible, the survey report should be personally presented to the parties requesting the project. Depending on the time allotted, one can be thorough or brief in presenting the material. For a formal presentation one may elect to use overheads, slides, or simply a page-by-page review of the report. Such presentations can be of immense value in making salient points clear and understandable. Also, the opportunity for questions and clarification of issues will increase the chance that the recommendations and suggestions will be successfully implemented.

Fire Life Safety Survey

A fire life safety survey also can be as extensive or as restricted as the surveyor determines. Like a formal security survey, a fire life safety survey will involve two major tasks: the fact-finding investigative process and the writing of the report that reflects the findings. Much of the work involved is the same as for a security survey; however, the security survey concentrates on security threats and tends to analyze the risks of crimes being deliberately committed by persons against people and property. The fire life safety survey, on the other hand, is predominantly concerned with life safety threats that may be deliberately or accidentally caused; it tends to analyze preventive measures to reduce the risk of such occurrences that, particularly if left unattended, may result in serious property damage, injury, or even death.

The *fact-finding process* for the fire life safety survey resembles that of a security survey, with the following exceptions:

1. The type of occupancy and classification of the facility, its principal activities, and the usage of the site are critical elements of any survey and are particularly important from a fire life safety perspective. For example, if the building has large

numbers of occupants with disabilities, it may not be practical to rapidly evacuate them using stairwells.

2. A review of state and local building and fire prevention laws and codes for mandated fire life safety requirements is necessary to determine if the facility is in full compliance.

3. In reviewing documentation, the testing records of fire life safety equipment and systems and the Building Emergency Procedures Manual (described in Chapter 11, *Building Emergency Planning*) should be reviewed. The testing records need to be checked to ensure that testing is adequate, according to accepted practices, and is being conducted in a timely manner by certified persons or companies. The Building Emergency Procedures Manual should be examined to ascertain if it is accurate, up-to-date, and adequately covers all emergencies that have occurred or are likely to occur at the site.

4. Insurance policies need to be reviewed to determine whether present or planned fire life safety measures are of an acceptable level and the fire life safety equipment meets the standards outlined in policies.

To assist in the fact-finding process it is helpful to use a checklist of areas to be covered. Such a checklist, emphasizing fire prevention, is provided in Appendix 5-2. The National Fire Protection Association's *Fire Protection Handbook* (Cote 1991, p. xiii) is organized around six major fire safety strategies in designing building fire safety: prevention of ignition, design to slow early fire growth, detection and alarm, suppression, confinement, and evacuation of occupants. The fire prevention survey checklist in Appendix 5-2 touches on these areas. However, it does not specifically address the design or fire-resistive construction aspects of a high-rise building nor does it purport to cover all branches of the *Firesafety Concepts Tree* used as a model by the National Fire Protection Association (NFPA 550 1993). If other fire life safety surveys are to be conducted, then the checklist will need to be modified to make it appropriate. The local fire department may require or recommend a particular fire inspection form.

The fire prevention survey checklist in Appendix 5-2 is intended for use by a fire safety director, risk manager, security director, or other member of building management who desires to evaluate the fire prevention program in place at their high-rise facility. It may be used for several reasons:

1. To assist in analyzing the fire prevention program with respect to certain incidents that have occurred at the site

2. In preparation for a visit by the city or state fire marshal, a fire prevention inspector of the fire department having authority over the building, or a representative of the insurance company providing coverage for the building owner

3. As part of a regular self-inspection program carried out by the building's Fire Safety Director to ensure that the building's fire prevention program is adequate and properly maintained

If a more extensive analysis of the building fire life safety program is required, an outside consultant or specialist, such as a registered fire protection engineer, should be considered. More will be said about consultants or specialists later in this chapter.

In the fact-finding process, a thorough building walkthrough should be conducted with individuals most knowledgeable of the building and its fire life safety systems. This person will probably be the Building Engineer and/or the Fire Safety Director. Start the walkthrough on the roof of the structure and proceed down through the stairwells and through every floor of the building. The reason for starting on the roof is that it is easier to walk down than to walk up through a high-rise building, particularly if one is surveying a 60-story skyscraper! In walking a floor, one usually will restrict the survey to public access or common areas such as the elevator lobbies and corridors, or maintenance spaces such as mechanical rooms, communications and utilities access points, elevator machine rooms, janitorial closets, paint rooms or paint storage rooms, and other spaces with strictly limited access. One will not tend to venture inside the tenant office space unless there is a particular reason to do so. Sufficient reasons would include past incidents of a fire life safety nature reported in the tenant space, a spot check of tenant housekeeping and storage of combustible materials, or a structural build-out or alteration of tenant space that has occurred. The primary emphasis of the walkthrough is to observe any obvious fire prevention problems or violations of fire life safety practices.

The main sections in this high-rise fire prevention survey checklist are general information; building information; building layout and exits; cafeteria/kitchen; building emergency exit and evacuation signage; fire protective signaling systems; smoke control systems; fire suppression systems; other fire suppression systems; portable fire extinguishers; emergency and standby power and lighting systems; testing and maintenance of fire life safety systems; surface finishes of interior ceilings, floors, and walls; general housekeeping, storage procedures, and adherence to safety; fire guard operations; building emergency procedures manual or fire life safety plan; fire life safety education; and insurance. (See Appendix 5-2 for complete details.)

Once again, every facility, organization, and site is different and therefore no generic checklist can possibly cover all aspects of the facility being surveyed. During the fact-finding process one may select as much, or as little, of the suggested checklist as one needs. Depending on the scope of the survey, the final checklist for it may even be a combination of both security and fire life safety checklists.

Writing the report will involve assembling the ideas and information obtained in the fact-finding investigative process. Weaknesses in the fire prevention program will be pointed out, with suggested recommendations to address them, but strengths also will be listed. The suggested format previously outlined for writing the security survey also can be adapted for writing the fire prevention survey.

A word of caution, learned through the bitter school of experience: the surveyor should reserve professional opinions as to the state of the overall security and fire life safety programs until the fact-finding process and the writing of the report is nearing completion. Of course, there are exceptions to the rule, but, particularly with major surveys, one needs to assimilate the mountains of information collected before one can thoroughly understand what is happening within the security and fire life safety programs. Often one aspect of the survey is closely interwoven with another. For example, in conducting a security survey primarily to investigate theft occurring at a building, one may immediately conclude that the solution to the problem is to implement a procedure in the building main lobby to control property removal. At the time this may appear to be the complete answer to the problem. However, at a later stage in the survey it may be discovered that building tenants can use passenger elevators at any time to exit their floor and travel directly down to the subterranean parking garage, thereby bypassing the building main lobby and walking unobserved to a vehicle. In this case, the presence of property removal controls in the building main lobby will be ineffective unless other measures are incorporated into the security program. Such measures may include reprogramming the elevators, particularly after normal business hours, to descend from the tower and terminate service in the main lobby. Other elevators can be programmed to serve the lower parking levels. This arrangement will cause occupants to pass through the building's main lobby and thereby permit an effective property removal control procedure to be instituted in that area.

Use of Consultants or Specialists

In carrying out security and fire life safety surveys it may be advisable at times to use a consultant or specialist to conduct the survey or to analyze specific areas of the security and fire life safety programs. The International Association of Professional Security Consultants defines a consultant as "a person who provides security advice, information, and recommendations to management" (Sennewald 1989, p. 6). A consultant or specialist is a person who, through some combination of study and experience, has acquired expertise in a particular discipline or area.

Possible reasons for hiring a consultant or specialist to conduct a survey or to analyze specific areas of the security and fire life safety programs are as follows:

1. The consultant or specialist is very knowledgeable in state-of-the-art security or fire life safety systems and is experienced in conducting surveys or analyses of the specific areas in which objective professional advice is required.

2. The consultant or specialist is already employed by the manufacturers or distributors of the security or fire life safety equipment installed or planned for installation, or is part of the management team of the contractor supplying security personnel at the building. This person may be well acquainted with the site and the issues that need to be addressed. Of course, if the consultant or specialist is employed by manufacturers or distributors of equipment, or the contract security provider, there is always a risk that the person may not be fully objective and will thereby present recommendations not fully geared to the client's needs.

3. At the time the survey or analysis is needed, there may be no person within the building operation who has the expertise or time to perform the task within the required period.

4. The individuals who have the authority to implement the recommendations of a survey or analysis have previously been made aware of what is needed but, for whatever reasons, do not want to accept the advice of the person(s) who brought these matters to their attention. Also, it may be that a particular security or fire life safety problem with several possible solutions has provoked disagreement within management as to what is the best course of action.

5. The consultant or specialist may have a well-established professional relationship with local law enforcement or the fire authority having jurisdiction and therefore is able to achieve certain objectives that others cannot.

6. The consultant or specialist may have certain professional qualifications or certifications which would qualify him or her to be called, in the event of future litigation, as an expert witness to testify on behalf of the building owner.

Those who hire a consultant or specialist* to conduct the survey or to analyze specific areas of the security and fire life safety programs should adhere to the following procedures:

1. Request a resume of the consultant or specialist and review his or her education, qualifications, professional experience, and professional affiliations. Examine any potential conflict of interest on the part of the consultant or specialist. Check client references.
2. Determine if the consultant or specialist has the necessary skills to carry out the project.
3. Be sure the scope of the project is clearly communicated to the consultant or specialist by the individual(s) requesting the project.
4. Have the consultant or specialist submit a written proposal of how the project is to be carried out, how long it is expected to take, and what form the final written report will take. This proposal should also address how costs of the project will be handled. (A total fixed cost may be proposed for the project, or hourly or daily costs quoted; in addition, transportation, accommodation, and administrative costs may be specified for separate billing. A retainer fee may be stipulated on acceptance of the proposal or commencement of the work, with additional regular payments scheduled during the project.)
5. When the terms of the agreement are accepted, draw up a written contract, including the above proposal and incidental items such as a confidentiality agreement. Once the contract is fully executed, the work should commence as outlined in the agreement.

A consultant or specialist may be selected from a number of sources. In the security and fire life safety fields there are a number of professional associations —the American Society for Industrial Security (ASIS), the National Fire Protection Association (NFPA), the Society of Fire Protection Engineers (SFPE), the International Association of Professional Security Consultants (IAPSC), the Society of Certified Fraud Examiners (SCFE), and the International Professional Security Association (IPSA) incorporating the International Institute of Industrial Security. With the exception of the last one, which primarily serves security interests outside of the United States, these associations can be contacted through local chapters. Other associations such as the Institute of Real Estate Management (IREM) and the Building Owners and Managers Association International (BOMA) are excellent sources within the high-rise building community.

Publications, such as ASIS *Security Management* and the *NFPA Fire Journal*, are filled with articles written by security and fire safety practitioners, many of whom will provide professional consulting services. The *Security Industry Buyer's Guide* provides a list of consulting services. Local, county, and state law enforcement and

---

* **Note:** An excellent reference for detailed information on consultant's fees, expenses, proposals, and contracts is *Security Consulting* by Charles A. Sennewald (1995).

crime prevention departments, local and county fire prevention departments, and the local fire marshal will be most amenable to providing information and possible lists of consultants and specialists.

References for consultants or specialists may also come from the manufacturers and distributors of security and fire life safety equipment, or from representatives of the contract security company providing services at the building. A careful screening process can drastically reduce the risk that such persons may not be fully objective and totally geared to the client's needs. Finally, personal recommendations of a consultant or specialist may come from other security directors, fire safety directors, risk managers, property or building managers, and insurance agents.

Summary

Security and fire life safety surveys are important tools in analyzing security and fire life safety threats in a high-rise commercial office building. Not only can a security and fire life safety program be evaluated, but sound recommendations to mitigate risks can result. As a consequence, the liability to the building owner or manager for injuries suffered by tenants and visitors on the premises because of the criminal acts of employees and third parties can be contained; also, the chance of accidents occurring at the site can be reduced. To conduct a thorough inspection, it is essential that it be carried out in a methodical fashion. If the expertise for such a task does not exist on site, the selection of a professional consultant or specialist is vital.

References

Cote, Arthur E., *Fire Protection Handbook*, 17th ed. Arthur E. Cote, Editor-in-Chief, Jim L. Linville, Managing Editor (All NFPA material in this chapter is used by permission. National Fire Protection Association, Quincy, MA. Copyright 1991).

Fischer, Robert J., and Gion Green, "Risk analysis and the security survey," *Introduction to Security*, 5th ed. (Butterworth–Heinemann, Stoneham, MA, 1992).

Gleckman, Mark, *The Security Survey* (Security Management Services, 800/494-3006, Acton, CA, 1995).

Israel, Paul, *Life Lessons from Thomas Alva Edison*. Interview of the associate editor of the Thomas A. Edison Papers at Rutgers University by *Bottom Line*. (Boulder, CO, April 15, 1994). (Volumes I and II of the Edison papers are available from the John Hopkins University Press, Baltimore.)

Merritt Company, The, "High-rise structures, Section B, Security considerations," *Protection of Assets Manual*, 9th printing. Editor Timothy J. Walsh (Used with permission from The Merritt Company, Santa Monica, CA, 800/638-7597. Copyright 1991), vol. III. Extracted from R. J. Healy, *Design for Security*, 2nd ed. (John Wiley & Sons, New York, 1983). See especially Chapter 3.

Momboisse, Raymond M., *Industrial Security for Strikes, Riots and Disasters* (Charles C Thomas, Springfield, IL, 1968).

NFPA 550, *Guide to the Firesafety Concepts Tree* (National Fire Protection Association, Quincy, MA. Copyright 1993).

Post, Richard S., and Arthur A. Kingsbury; revised by Richard S. Post with Arthur A. Kingsbury and David A. Schachtsiek, "Business security," *Security Administration: An Introduction to the Protective Services*, 4th ed. (Butterworth–Heinemann, Stoneham, MA, 1991).

Security Industry Buyers Guide, 1996 Edition (Phillips Business Information, Inc., 1201 Seven Locks Road, Suite 300, Potomac, MD 20854 and ASIS, 1655 North Fort Myer Drive, Suite 1200, Arlington, VA 22209).

Sennewald, Charles A., "Security consulting as a profession," *Security Consulting* (Butterworth–Heinemann, Stoneham, MA, 1989).

Sennewald, Charles A. *Security Consulting*, 2nd ed. (Butterworth–Heinemann, Boston, 1995).

Appendix 5-1   Security Survey Checklist

Facility name
Address (including zip code)
Client representatives and telephone
 numbers
Position and title of persons interviewed
Survey date

I. General Information

Name of building owner and/or management
 company (name and telephone number)
Name, job title, and telephone number of
 person in charge of security
Principal activities
Operating hours
Number of tenants and building occupants
Approximate number of daily visitors
Nature of surrounding area and occupancies
 (noting any particular security hazards)
Proximity to freeways and major roads
Address and telephone number of police
 jurisdiction
Name and rank of police contact
Number of police personnel
Are crime statistics available and for what
 period?
Is there a business-community–based crime
 prevention program in place?
Of what does it consist?
Is the facility in general compliance with
 ADA requirements?

Comments

II. Site Perimeter

1. Are there any close-by bus stops, train
   stations, bus stations?
2. Acreage of site
3. What is the landscaping?
   Are there natural barriers present?
   Is shrubbery kept well pruned so as not to
    provide concealed hiding places?
4. Is there a perimeter barrier?
   What sort?
   Height
   Condition
   Distance of barrier from building
   Are there clear areas on either side of the
    perimeter barrier?

Is there public parking and/or metered
 parking directly adjacent to the building?
Are signs posted to make the public aware
 of towing policies, and the planned
 removal of unauthorized vehicles?
5. What type of perimeter lights are used?
   Do they meet minimum requirements of
    local codes and ordinances?
   Are lights directed toward the perimeter?
   Are all exterior doorways, walkways, and
    entries properly illuminated?
   Are exterior guard posts properly
    illuminated?
   Are there dark areas where criminals may
    conceal themselves?
   What additional lighting is required to
    illuminate these areas?
   Is lighting on an automatic timer system?
   Are the lights in operation during all
    hours of darkness?
   Is exterior lighting protected against theft
    and vandalism?
   Are any obstructions, such as tree
    branches, blocking the lighting?
   Is the lighting system regularly checked?
    By whom?
   Is there an emergency lighting system for
    use in the event of a power failure?
6. Are there perimeter intrusion alarms?
   What type are they?
   Does the system function properly?
   Is it adequate?
   To what area do alarms report?
   What is the procedure on receipt of an
    alarm?
   Whose responsibility is it to switch the
    alarm system off and on?
7. Is CCTV used?
   Are the cameras black and white or color?
   List the camera positions
   Do any cameras need to be relocated?
   What cameras are equipped with auto iris
    and with pan, tilt, and zoom mechanisms?
   Are outside cameras enclosed in weather-
    proof casings?
   Are the cameras adequately secured to
    deter theft or interference?
   Is lighting adequate for the cameras?
   Who is responsible for monitoring the
    camera images?

Are cameras linked to recording equipment?

If a videocassette recorder is used, is there automatic notification when a videotape needs replacement?

What is the recording time of the VCR (Real Time—2, 4, 6 hours; or Time Lapse up to 200 hours)?

Is there an adequate library of videotapes? For how long are tapes kept?

8. Is there access control of vehicles and pedestrians?

Are sign-in and out logs, badging, or electronic access systems used?

If used, describe these logs, badges, or access control systems.

Are visitors, delivery persons, and contractors issued identification badges?

9. What patrols are conducted of the site perimeter?

During what hours?

What is their frequency?

Who conducts the patrols?

Are these personnel in uniform?

Are they equipped with portable two-way radios?

Do they require flashlights?

Are the patrols recorded?

How are the patrols recorded (notebooks, reports, guard tour systems)?

Who reviews the records of these patrols?

Are the objectives of the patrols clearly outlined in written instructions?

10. How is trash stored and removed from the site?

Are transparent trash bags used?

Are boxes and cartons flattened before being removed?

Is trash removal supervised and by whom?

11. Is a property removal pass system used?

How does it work?

Who issues property removal passes?

Who is authorized to sign passes?

Are the passes checked to ensure they are correctly filled out?

Who reviews the passes when property is being removed?

Is the pass system effective?

12. Is there a control system for property brought onto the site?

How does it work?

Is it effective?

13. Is there a package control system for packages brought onto the site?

14. How is lost and found property handled?

Where is found property stored for safekeeping?

How long is it stored for?

How is it disposed of?

Comments

III. Building and Building Perimeter

1. Height

Number of floors (above and below ground level)

2. Total square footage of building

Typical floor size in square feet

3. Class of construction

Type of frame

Central core construction?

4. Presence of atriums, mezzanines, etc.

5. Are "Right to Pass by Permission. Permission Revocable at Any Time"–type signs or sidewalk plates installed?

6. Description of perimeter entrances and exits (including tunnels or overhead walkways)

Construction of doors, door frames, and hinges

State of door locking mechanisms

Are they self-closing?

If they have automatic closing devices, do they function correctly?

7. Are outside power transformers and other utilities properly secured?

8. Are heating, ventilating, and air conditioning systems accessible from outside the building?

9. Are ground floor windows protected?

10. Number of stairwells and configuration

Roof access of each stairwell

11. Are stairwell doors self-closing and self-latching?

Are all stairwell doors on upper floors kept closed and locked from inside the stairwell?

Which doors are locked and which are permanently unlocked?

Are stairwell doors equipped with door position switches to indicate when doors are in the opened or closed position?

Are stairwell doors (particularly those at the ground or exit level) equipped with audible exit alarms?

Are these doors equipped with time-delayed lock release mechanisms at the ground or exit level?

What is the time delay?

Are these doors monitored by CCTV cameras with recording capabilities?

12. Is there a common interconnected locking system on the stairwell doors?

If so, does it automatically unlock during a fire alarm (i.e., is it a fail-safe system)?

Are there manual controls for unlocking all stairwell doors simultaneously?

Where are these manual controls located?

13. Are there emergency telephones or intercoms located inside the stairwells? On what floors?

14. Are public rest rooms kept locked at all times?

Who controls access to them?

Are doors equipped with self-closing and self-latching devices?

15. Is access to building windows possible from adjacent rooftops?

Is access from the roof possible?

Is there a helipad or heliport?

Is there notification of incoming flights?

What type of lighting is used?

16. What type of perimeter lights are used?

Do they meet minimum requirements of local codes and ordinances?

Are lights directed toward the perimeter?

Are all exterior doorways, walkways, entries, and elevator lobbies properly illuminated?

Are there any dark areas where criminals may conceal themselves?

What additional lighting is required to illuminate these areas?

Is lighting on an automatic timer system?

Are the lights in operation during all hours of darkness?

Is exterior lighting protected against theft and vandalism?

Are there any obstructions, such as tree branches, blocking the lighting?

Is the lighting system regularly inspected?

By whom?

17. Is interior lighting of the building adequate?

Is there adequate lighting in corridors, exits, and stairwells?

18. Is there an emergency lighting system for use in the event of a power failure?

19. Are all exits and entrances supervised (including shipping and receiving/loading dock and basement areas)?

If not, how are they controlled?

Are sign-in and sign-out logs, badging, or electronic access systems used?

If used, describe these logs, badges, or access control systems.

Are visitors, delivery persons, and contractors issued identification badges?

20. Are there intrusion alarms?

What type are they?

To what area do alarms report?

What is the procedure on receipt of an alarm?

21. Is CCTV used?

Are the cameras black and white or color?

List the camera positions.

Do any cameras need to be relocated?

What cameras are equipped with auto iris and with pan, tilt, and zoom mechanisms?

Are outside cameras enclosed in weatherproof casings?

Are the cameras adequately secured to deter theft or interference?

Is lighting adequate for the cameras?

Who is responsible for monitoring the camera images?

Are cameras linked to recording equipment?

If a videocassette recorder is used, is there automatic notification when a videotape needs replacement?

What is the recording time of the VCR (Real Time—2, 4, 6 hours; or Time Lapse up to 200 hours)?

Is there an adequate library of videotapes and for how long are tapes kept?

22. What patrols are conducted of the building perimeter?

During what hours?

What is their frequency?

Who conducts the patrols?

Are these personnel in uniform?

Are they equipped with portable two-way radios?

Do they require flashlights?

Are the patrols recorded?

How are the patrols recorded (notebooks, reports, guard tour systems)?

Who reviews the records of these patrols?

Are the objectives of the patrols clearly outlined in written instructions?

23. Presence of internal staircases, dumbwaiters, and rubbish/trash chutes?

24. Elevators and their configuration

Can elevators be placed "on security" to deny access to specific floors?

Are elevators equipped with electronic access control devices (such as card readers)?

25. How is trash stored and removed from the site?

Are transparent trash bags used?

Are boxes and cartons flattened before being removed?

Is its removal supervised and by whom?

26. Is a property removal pass system used?

How does it work?

Who issues property passes?

Who is authorized to sign passes?

Are the passes checked to ensure they are correctly filled out?

Who reviews the passes when property is being removed?

Is the pass system effective?

27. Is there a control system for property brought into the building?

How does it work?

Is it effective?

28. How is lost and found property handled?

Where is found property stored for safekeeping?

How long is it kept?

How is it disposed of?

Comments

IV. Maintenance Spaces

1. Is access to these areas controlled?

Are these doors self-closing and self-latching?

2. What sort of controls exist?

Are escorts provided for outside vendors accessing these areas?

Is a sign-in and sign-out procedure used?

3. Who controls this access?

4. Who periodically checks the adherence to these controls?

Comments

V. Loading Dock/Shipping and Receiving Areas

1. Are shipping and receiving areas physically separated?

2. Is the platform height sufficient (usually 48 inches) so the truck bed is closely parallel to the dock?

Is there an adjustable height (mechanically or electrically operated) dock leveler?

3. Is supervision present whenever the areas are open?

Are these staff rotated to deter possible collusion with or favoritism to delivery persons?

4. Are all vehicles logged in and out?

5. Who is permitted to move vehicles?

Are persons who move vehicles properly trained and licensed?

Are persons who move vehicles covered by adequate vehicle insurance?

6. Are keys left in vehicles?

If not, where are they secured?

7. Is the movement of vehicle drivers and delivery people restricted in this area?

Are pedestrians allowed to enter these areas?

8. Are rest areas, toilet facilities, pay phones, etc., provided?

Are rest rooms kept locked?

Who controls access to them?

Are doors equipped with self-closing and self-latching devices?

9. Are drivers and delivery persons allowed to enter the building to carry out deliveries?

Are these persons required to leave some identification such as a driver's license?

Are these persons required to wear special ID tags when in the building?

10. What vehicles, other than those for delivery and pick-up, are permitted to park in these areas?

11. Is the dock area properly secured after normal business hours?

12. Are vehicles or deliveries received after closing hours?
    If so, how is this achieved?
13. Is lighting provided for the dock areas?
    What type of lights are used?
    Are all exterior doorways, walkways, entries, and elevator lobbies properly illuminated?
    Is the dock area painted in light colors to enhance reflectiveness?
    Do dark areas need additional lighting?
    What additional lighting is required to illuminate these areas?
    Is lighting on an automatic timer system?
    Are the lights in operation during all hours of darkness?
    Is exterior lighting protected against theft and vandalism?
    Is the lighting system regularly inspected? By whom?
    Is there an emergency lighting system for use in the event of a power failure?
14. Is CCTV used?
    Are the cameras black and white or color?
    List the camera positions
    Do any cameras need to be relocated?
    Are there cameras located at ingress and egress points of the dock areas?
    If so, do these cameras provide images of vehicle license plates?
    What cameras are equipped with auto iris and with pan, tilt and zoom mechanisms?
    Are outside cameras enclosed in weatherproof casings?
    Are the cameras adequately secured to deter theft or interference?
    Is lighting adequate for the cameras?
    Who is responsible for monitoring the camera images?
    Are cameras linked to recording equipment?
    If a videocassette recorder is used, is there automatic notification when a videotape needs replacement?
    What is the recording time of the VCR (Real Time—2, 4, 6 hours; or Time Lapse up to 200 hours)?
    Is there an adequate library of videotapes and for how long are tapes kept?

Comments

VI. Vehicular Movement and Parking Areas

1. Is there a parking structure or parking area?
   Is it a public or private parking area?
   Who operates the facility (the building owner or manager or a parking contractor)?
2. Are entrances and exits limited in number as practicable and always attended when open?
   Are all exterior doors securely locked in compliance with local building and fire life safety codes?
   Is the ground floor, and, if accessible, the second floor, completely enclosed?
   Do trees allow access to upper levels?
   Is shrubbery kept well pruned so as not to provide concealed hiding places?
3. Are there designated parking areas for tenants, employees, visitors, contractors, couriers, and disabled persons ?
   Is correct use of these designated spaces enforced?
   Are there designated parking spaces for building executives with their names displayed (names should not be displayed)?
   Are parking areas well marked for easy recognition by drivers as to where their vehicles are parked?
   Estimated number of vehicles parked daily
4. How is vehicle access controlled?
   Is the parking operation self-parking, attendant or valet parking, or a blending of both?
   Is there any height or weight restriction?
   Are access cards, tickets, passes or decals used?
5. Are vehicles inspected on entry or exit?
6. Does the garage have automatic opening and closing doors?
   If so, within how many seconds of a vehicle passing through do the doors begin to close?
   Is this considered safe in restricting unauthorized vehicle or pedestrian access?
7. Are security officers or law enforcement officers involved in directing traffic?
8. Are there speed bumps?
   Are there speed dots to deter vehicles from straying into the path of oncoming

vehicles, particularly at corners and curves?

9. Are speed limit signs posted?
   What is the speed limit?

10. Are stairwell doors self-closing and self-latching?
    Are stairwell doors on upper levels kept locked from the stairshaft side?

11. Is lighting provided for the parking areas?
    Does it meet minimum requirements of local codes and ordinances?
    What type of lights are used?
    Are all exterior doorways, walkways, entries, and elevator lobbies properly illuminated?
    Is the interior of the structure painted in light colors to enhance reflectiveness?
    Are there dark areas where criminals may conceal themselves?
    What additional lighting is required to illuminate these areas?
    Is lighting on an automatic timer system?
    Are the lights in operation during all hours?
    Is exterior lighting protected against theft and vandalism?
    Is the lighting system regularly inspected?
    By whom?
    Is there an emergency lighting system for use in the event of a power failure?

12. Are security mirrors used for drivers to view vehicles around corners or obstacles?
    Are they in correct locations?

13. Is CCTV used?

14. Are the cameras black and white or color?
    List the camera positions
    Do any cameras need to be relocated?
    Are there cameras located at all ingress and egress points of the parking areas?
    If so, do these cameras provide images of drivers and vehicle license plates?
    What cameras are equipped with auto iris and with pan, tilt, and zoom mechanisms?
    Are outside cameras enclosed in weatherproof casings?
    Are the cameras adequately secured to deter theft or interference?
    Is lighting adequate for the cameras?

Who is responsible for monitoring the camera images?
Are cameras linked to recording equipment?
If a videocassette recorder is used, is there automatic notification when a videotape needs replacement?
What is the recording time of the VCR (Real Time—2, 4, 6 hours; or Time Lapse up to 200 hours)?
Is there an adequate library of videotapes and for how long are tapes kept?

15. Are there emergency intercoms or duress alarm stations in the parking structure or parking area?
    What are their locations? Are there sufficient numbers in strategic locations (including stairwells)?
    Are signs prominently posted to depict their locations?
    Are the intercoms or duress stations readily accessible to disabled persons?
    Are parking cashier's booths equipped with duress alarms?
    To what area do these intercoms or duress alarms report?
    Are they constantly monitored?
    How often is their operation checked and by whom?

16. What patrols are conducted of parking areas?
    Are they performed at irregular intervals?
    What is their frequency?
    If parking stalls are angled, are patrols in a direction that permits a maximum view between parked vehicles?
    Who conducts the patrols?
    Are these personnel in uniform?
    Are they equipped with portable two-way radios?
    Are the patrols recorded?
    How are the patrols recorded (written reports, guard tour systems, etc.)?
    Who reviews the records of these patrols?
    Are the objectives of the patrols clearly outlined in written instructions?

17. What is the policy for handling abandoned vehicles?

18. What is the policy for assisting persons who lock themselves out of their vehicles?

19. How is lost and found property handled?
20. If rest rooms are provided, are they kept locked at all times?
    Are doors self-closing and self-latching?
    Who is allowed to use them? Who controls access to them?

Comments

VII. Tenant Offices

1. At which areas are receptionists controlling access?
   Has the receptionist been trained in security procedures and awareness?
   Which entrances are not controlled and can be accessed?
   Is an after-hours sign-in register kept?
2. Is interior lighting adequate?
   Is there adequate lighting in corridors and exits?
3. Are duress alarms provided in reception and other sensitive areas?
   To what area do these alarms report?
   Who responds to these alarms?
   Are these alarms and response times regularly tested? By whom?
4. Is CCTV used?
   Are the cameras black and white or color?
   List the camera positions.
   Do any cameras need to be relocated?
   What cameras are equipped with auto iris and with pan, tilt, and zoom mechanisms?
   Are the cameras adequately secured to deter theft or interference?
   Is lighting adequate for the cameras?
   Who is responsible for monitoring the camera images?
   Are cameras linked to recording equipment?
   If a videocassette recorder is used, is there automatic notification when a videotape needs replacement?
   What is the recording time of the VCR (Real Time—2, 4, 6 hours; or Time Lapse up to 200 hours)?
   Is there an adequate library of videotapes and for how long are tapes kept?
5. Are tenant employees issued identification badges?
   Are they color-coded to denote authorized access to particular areas?

Are employees required to visibly display them at all times?
What is the procedure when employees forget to wear or lose their badges?

6. Are visitors, delivery persons, maintenance people, and contractors required to sign in?
   Are they required to wear identification badges?
   What type are they (clip-on or adhesive)?
   Are they escorted when inside the tenant space?
7. Are exterior, unsupervised doors kept closed during normal office hours?
   Is someone designated to ensure the exterior doors are all locked at the end of normal business hours?
8. Do perimeter walls, and interior walls leading to sensitive areas, extend from the floor to the ceiling?
   If not, is the space between the top of the wall and the floor above fitted with steel bars and/or intrusion alarms?
   If rods are used, is it required (and practical) to periodically inspect them, to ensure they are still in place?
9. Is it possible for an intruder to use heating, ventilating, and air conditioning ducts as a means of entering the tenant office or interior room?
   If so, are the ducts fitted with steel bars and/or intrusion alarms?
   If rods are used, is it required (and practical) to periodically inspect them, to ensure they are still in place?
10. For particularly sensitive areas, are heating, ventilating, and air conditioning ducts leading to the areas periodically checked for listening devices and surveillance cameras?
    Does the degree of security required justify fitting the area concerned with a separate heating, ventilating, and air conditioning system?
11. Is there a concealed space between the ceiling and the floor above?
    In particularly sensitive areas, is this space periodically checked for listening devices or surveillance cameras?
12. Is after-hours access to the tenant office controlled?

Who controls the issuance of keys, access cards, or electronic access codes?

When employees are terminated, are keys and cards retrieved and codes changed?

Are unused keys and access cards properly secured?

Are sign-in and sign-out logs, badging, or electronic access systems used?

If used, describe these logs, badges, or access control systems.

13. Does the freight/service elevator provide direct access to tenant offices?

14. Are individual interior offices kept locked when not in use?

What is the state of door-locking mechanisms?

15. Are equipment rooms kept locked at all times?

16. Are common area restrooms kept locked at all times?

17. Does the tenant office have intrusion alarms?

Of what do they consist?

To what area do these alarms report?

Who responds to these alarms?

18. Where is petty cash kept and how is its use controlled?

Are unsigned and any presigned checks properly secured?

At the end of daily business are petty cash and checks counted?

19. How and where is sensitive information stored and secured?

What type of file cabinets and safes are used?

Do they provide sufficient protection considering the sensitivity of the information stored within them?

Are file cabinets and safes kept locked?

Are safes located in areas where they can be easily observed?

Are they properly bolted to the floor?

Are there any intrusion alarms to protect safes, cabinets, etc.? Who monitors and responds to them?

How often is an inventory of sensitive information conducted and by whom?

20. Before leaving for the day, are employees required to clear desk and work surfaces?

21. Is there an awareness by management of the importance of safeguarding sensitive proprietary information?

Is there an established procedure for destroying sensitive information when it becomes trash?

Who oversees this?

22. After meetings or conferences involving sensitive information is the meeting area cleaned of all working material and the trash properly discarded?

23. Are all new hires required to complete a confidentiality of proprietary information agreement?

24. Are pre-employment background investigations carried out for all personnel (including temporary employees)?

What is the extent of these investigations?

Who conducts these investigations?

25. Is a security orientation given to all new employees (including temporaries)?

Who conducts this orientation?

Is ongoing security education provided for employees (particularly regarding any changes in the security program and any criminal incidents or security problems of which they should be aware)?

Are company security rules posted or distributed to all employees?

Are they easy to understand?

26. On termination of employment are exit interviews conducted?

Who conducts them?

Is a check carried out to ensure all keys, identification cards, credit cards, pagers, mobile telephones, and all other company property has been retrieved? Are access codes belonging to this person immediately changed?

Are other employees notified of the termination?

27. Are special security measures taken for tenant executives?

Is access to the executive offices controlled?

Are duress alarms installed in executive offices?

Who monitors and responds to these alarms?

Are these alarms and response times regularly tested? By whom?

Do executives have an emergency escape route or access to a safe room?

Are executives briefed on security precautions for home, travel, and business?

28. Does the office have a mainframe computer installation?

Is access to this area tightly controlled? How is it controlled?

Is a trusted, well-trained individual in charge of controlling access to programs and data?

How is processed information protected?

How is the removal of property and information controlled?

How is the destruction and disposal of material supervised?

Are back-up records made of sensitive information and copies stored on-site and off-site?

Is there a separation of staff working on system development and system operations?

Are changes to the computer system formally controlled and authorized?

Is there an Emergency Plan for the facility? Of what does it consist?

29. Is office equipment clearly and permanently identified and inventoried?

Are high-value items physically secured?

Are items such as typewriters and desktop personal computers anchored using devices such as metal plates or steel cables?

Are desktop personal computers, laptop, and notebook computers kept locked up when unattended?

Are passwords used to limit access?

Are data files backed up daily?

Are copies of data backups, program backups, and forms kept at an off-site location?

30. Does the office have Local Area Network (LAN) and Wide Area Network (WAN) systems?

Are there physical security measures to protect the workstations and the file server?

Is privacy of user-ID and passwords maintained?

Is a trusted, well-trained individual in charge of controlling access to programs and data?

Do networks have dial-up access?

Are compromises of the systems immediately and thoroughly investigated?

31. Are photocopiers and FAX machines equipped with recorders to monitor their usage?

Can these machines be used after normal business hours?

Are postage meters locked up after normal business hours?

32. Are telephone bills regularly reviewed for possible misuse?

33. Are after-hour escorts provided? Who conducts the escorts?

34. Is a property removal pass system used? How does it work?

Who issues property removal passes?

Who is authorized to sign passes?

Are the passes checked to ensure they are correctly filled out?

Who reviews the passes when property is being removed?

Is the pass system effective?

35. Is there a control system for property brought into the tenant space?

How does it work?

Is it effective?

36. Is there a separate mail room?

Is screening conducted of mail envelopes, packages, and parcels?

Are the screening procedures sufficient for the security risks involved?

Are the mail room staff properly trained in security procedures?

Who trains the mail room staff?

37. How is lost and found property handled?

Where is found property stored for safekeeping?

How long is it kept?

How is it disposed of?

38. If there are security problems within the office, who handles them?

Comments

VIII. Cafeteria, Kitchen, and Dining Areas

1. What are the cafeteria, kitchen, and dining area operating hours?

2. Who operates them and who has responsibility for their security?

3. How are cash, voucher tickets, etc., handled?
4. Are spot checks made of the cashiers?
5. If a safe is used to store cash and receipts, is it in an area where it can be observed easily?
   Is it bolted to the ground?
6. Are administrative offices locked after hours?
   Who has keys to them?
7. Are storage rooms and refrigerators properly secured, particularly after hours?
   How often is an inventory conducted and by whom?
8. Is anyone permitted to be in the dining area(s) after the cafeteria is closed?
9. How is the disposal of waste food, garbage and trash handled?
10. Are periodic checks made to ensure "good" food is not being removed as trash?
11. Are all vending machines properly secured and their use strictly monitored?
12. Is there any equipment that needs to be monitored after hours to prevent food spoilage?
    Who monitors this equipment?

Comments

IX. Security Alarms, Closed-Circuit Television, and Access Control Systems

1. Are alarm devices used?
   What are their types, locations, and manufacturers?
   Does leaving alarmed doors open defeat the security system (for example, magnetic contacts on stairwell doors)?
   How are these alarms monitored (local, central station type, etc.)?
   What is the established procedure when an alarm is received?
   Are up-to-date lists kept of personnel authorized to open and close alarmed areas?
2. Is CCTV used?
   Are the cameras black and white or color?
   What cameras are equipped with auto iris and with pan, tilt, and zoom mechanisms?

Are outside cameras enclosed in weatherproof housings?
Are the cameras adequately secured to deter theft or being interfered with?
Is lighting adequate for the cameras?
Who is responsible for monitoring the camera images?
Are cameras linked to recording equipment?
If a videocassette recorder is used, is there automatic notification when a videotape needs replacement?
What is the recording time of the VCR (Real Time—2, 4, 6 hours; or Time Lapse up to 200 hours)?
Is there an adequate library of videotapes and for how long are tapes kept?
3. Are mechanical and electronic access systems used?
   If so, describe these systems
   Where are the devices located?
   If cards are used, what type are they (Magnetic Stripe, Barium Ferrite, Weigand, Proximity, Smart)?
   Do the cards have photographs (is photo-imaging used)?
   Who is responsible for programming and deleting cards?
   What is the procedure for lost cards?
4. Are biometric access control systems used?
   If so, describe these systems
5. Are the security alarm, CCTV, and access control systems integrated?
6. Are the security alarm, CCTV, and access control systems inspected and tested on a monthly basis (and this procedure properly documented)?

Comments

X. Key Controls, Locking Devices, and Containers*

1. Is there a grand master, master and submaster system in use? Describe it.
2. Is there a common interconnected locking system on emergency exit stairwell doors?

---

* This list is from James F. Broder, *Risk Analysis and the Security Survey* (Butterworth–Heinemann, Stoneham, MA, 1984).

3. Are locks throughout the facility by the same manufacturer?
4. Is there a record of lock issuance?
5. Is there a record of key issuance and inspection?
6. How many grand master and master keys are in existence?
7. What is the security of grand master and master keys?
8. What is the security of the key cabinet or box?
9. Who is charged with handling key control?
   Describe the control system.
   Is the system adequate?
   What is the frequency of record and key inspections?
10. Are keys made at the site?
    Who makes them?
11. What is the type of lock used?
    Are all adequate in construction?
12. Would keys be difficult to duplicate?
    Are they marked "DO NOT DUPLICATE" to deter unauthorized duplication?
13. Are locks changed periodically at critical locations?
14. Are any "sesame" padlocks used for classified material storage areas or containers?
15. If a key cutting machine is used, is it properly secured?
16. Are key blanks adequately secured?
17. Are investigations made when master keys are lost?
18. Are locks immediately replaced when keys are lost?
19. Do locks have interchangeable cores?
    Are extra cores properly safeguarded?
20. Are combination locks the three-position type?
21. How many people possess combinations to safes and containers?
22. How often are combinations changed?
23. How are combinations chosen?
    Are lazy-man combinations used?
    Are birth dates, marriage dates, etc. used as combinations?
24. Are combinations recorded where they might be accessible to an intruder?
25. Have all faces of the container locked with a combination lock been examined to see if the combination is recorded?

26. Are combinations recorded and properly secured so that authorized persons can get them in an emergency?
27. Is the same or greater security afforded recorded combinations as that provided by the lock?

Comments

XI. Janitorial Operation

1. Who is responsible for the janitorial operation (name, job title, and telephone number)?
2. Are outside contract or building in-house employees used?
   Are their backgrounds checked (including, as a minimum, past employment and personal references)?
3. What are the hours of operation?
4. How are the janitorial staff supervised?
   Are janitorial staff required to wear a distinctive uniform?
   Is the supervision adequate considering the sensitivity of the area being cleaned?
   Are staff escorted when working in particular areas?
5. Do they possess keys?
6. How are keys controlled?
7. What method of cleaning is used (individual janitors assigned to particular areas or gang cleaning)?
8. Do the janitors lock exterior doors when they are working after hours in tenant offices?
9. Do the janitors lock interior doors when they have finished cleaning?
10. Are transparent trash bags used?
    Are spot checks made of trash bags?
11. How is trash removed from the floors?
    By whom?
12. Is trash temporarily stored at the site?
    How long is it stored?
13. Is the trash placed in a dumpster, compactor, etc.?
    Is an escort provided when trash is brought to the compactor?
14. How is trash removed from the site?
    Are boxes and cartons flattened before being removed?
    Is trash removal supervised and by whom?

If billing is based on number of loads removed, is this spot-checked against billings?

15. Are janitors permitted to use stairwells?
16. Where do they take meal breaks?
17. Are they permitted to go to their private vehicles during breaks?
    Do these vehicles provide unsupervised egress from the building or site?
18. Are janitorial supplies kept properly secured?
19. Does janitorial equipment being used always remain in the building?
20. Are the janitorial staff trained to be aware of security issues?
21. Are janitorial supervisors informed in a timely manner of theft activity occurring in tenant areas?
22. Are janitorial staff searched and/or their personal belongings checked when they leave the site?

Comments

XII. Security Operation

1. Are outside contract or building in-house employees used?
2. If a contract company is used, is it properly licensed?
   Does it carry adequate liability and fidelity insurance?
3. Are all security staff properly licensed (including required state licenses to operate as a guard, or to carry a weapon, baton, mace, pepper spray, etc.)?
   Do they wear uniforms?
4. Are the wages and benefits of security staff specified in the contract?
5. How are security staff selected?
6. What background checks are conducted?
7. What are the posts?
   What are the hours of operation?
   How many security staff per shift (day, swing, and graveyard)?
   What duties do they perform?
   Is the level of staffing adequate?
8. Are there written procedures, job descriptions, instructions, and reports?
   Do the instructions coincide with actual practices and accurately reflect building policy?

Are the instructions sufficient in content and accuracy?
Are the instructions current and subject to at least annual reviews?
Are emergency contact lists kept up to date?

9. Are security-related incidents documented and logged?
   Is a database system used?
   Are these reports regularly reviewed to ascertain any significant trends in activity?
10. How are the security staff supervised?
    Are patrol monitoring devices utilized?
    Who checks them?
11. If the security staff are contract employees, how much training do they receive before coming on-site?
    What type of initial training do the security staff receive at the site?
    What type of follow-up and ongoing training do the security staff receive?
    Does this training satisfy mandatory state requirements?
12. How is the effectiveness of training measured?
13. If radios are used for communications, how effective are they?
    Do other departments share frequencies?
    Is there a channel designated for emergency communications?

Comments

XIII. Security Education

1. Do new occupants receive security education from the building staff or is this a tenant responsibility?
   If so, of what does this training consist?
2. What training do building management, engineering, janitorial, and parking staff receive?
   Who conducts this training?
   How often is it provided?
3. Are building staff and tenants kept informed of changes in the security program and of criminal incidents or security problems of which they should be aware?

Comments

XIV. Insurance

1. Has the insurance policy for the applicable area been reviewed?
2. Is the policy in effect?
3. Is there satisfactory compliance with the conditions of the policy?
4. Is the insurance policy adequate in terms of the present risks?
5. What is the total coverage?
6. What is the deductible?
7. If the policy is a specified peril contract, are there any possible perils that have not been adequately covered?
8. What have been the claims over the past year?
9. Should the insurance policy be revised?

Comments.

Appendix 5-2   Fire Prevention Survey Checklist

Facility name
Address (including zip code)
Owner (name and telephone number)
Client representative (name and telephone
  number)
Position and title of persons interviewed
Survey date

I. General Information

Building operator and/or management com-
  pany (name and telephone number)
Fire Safety Director and alternate (names
  and telephone numbers)
When was the building constructed?
Principal activities
Operating hours
Number of tenants and building occupants
Approximate number of daily visitors
Special usage features (large numbers of
  occupants with disabilities, restaurant on
  top floor, etc.)
Nature of surrounding area and occupancies
  (noting any particular fire hazards)
Location of nearest street fire alarm box (if
  provided)
Location of fire hydrants in relation to the
  building
Address and telephone number of nearest
  fire department jurisdiction (first and second
  alarm responders)
Travel time for each fire department respon-
  der to the site
Is there a mutual aid agreement with other
  fire department jurisdictions?
Is site and building access both suitable and
  available for responding emergency personnel and vehicles?
Are address numbers adequate and plainly
  visible from the roadway the building faces?
Are building keys for fire department use
  kept in a locked container or rapid entry box?
When were the keys last inspected to ensure
  all keys are present and correctly tagged?
Where is the rapid entry box located?
Does the rapid entry box also contain building information?
What information?
Is a Building Emergency Procedures Manual
  readily available for fire department use?

Is the facility in general compliance with
  ADA requirements?

Comments

II. Building Information

1. Type of occupancy
2. Utilities (electricity, water, gas)
   Location of utility shut-offs
3. Heating, ventilating, and air conditioning
   system
   Type of heat (gas or oil)
4. Height
   Number of floors (above and below
   ground level)
5. Total square footage of building
   Typical floor size in square feet
6. Class of construction
   Type of frame
   Central core construction?
7. Presence of atriums, mezzanines,
   etc.
8. Type of building exterior (conventional
   curtain wall?)
   Fireproofing of structure
9. Certificate of occupancy
   Where is it posted?
   Certificates for places of assembly (list
   places and approved capacities)
   Fire department licenses or permits
   Are licenses and permits up-to-date?

Comments

III. Building Layout and Exits

1. Description of perimeter entrances and
   exits (including any tunnels or overhead
   walkways)
   Construction of doors and hinges
   Are all doors in good working condition?
   State of door locking mechanisms
   Do exits open out?
   Are they self-closing?
   If they have automatic closing devices, do
   they function correctly?
2. Are there exterior fire escapes with fire
   escape drop ladders, exterior fire towers,
   or enclosed stairwells?
   What are their locations?

List the floors they serve (including roof access)

3. Are there two means of egress from each floor?

4. Are the emergency exit doors leading to fire towers or enclosed stairs kept closed?

   Are any objects, such as pieces of metal, wood, or door stoppers, used to keep them open?

5. Fire-resistive rating of stairwell walls and doors? Hourly rating?

   Are stairwell doors in good working condition?

   Are stairwell doors self-closing and self-latching?

   Are there any obstructions of pathways leading to emergency exits?

   Inside the stairwells, are there any obstructions to egress or storage of any flammable materials?

6. Are all the emergency exit doors kept closed and locked from inside the stairwell?

   Which doors are locked and which are left permanently unlocked?

   Are emergency exit doors (particularly at the ground or exit level) equipped with audible exit alarms? How often are these alarms checked and by whom?

   Are these doors equipped with time-delayed lock release mechanisms at the ground or exit level?

   What is the time delay?

   Are these doors monitored by CCTV cameras with recording capabilities?

7. Is there a common interconnected locking system on emergency exit stairwell doors?

   If so, does it automatically unlock during a fire alarm (i.e., is it a fail-safe system)?

   Are there manual controls for unlocking all stairwell doors simultaneously?

   Where are these manual controls located?

8. Is there a helipad or heliport?

   What type of lighting is used?

   Is there notification of incoming flights?

9. Are there handrails in the stairwells? Are they secure and smooth?

   What is the condition of stair treads?

   Is there glow-in-the-dark tape or paint on stairtreads, handrails, or the perimeters of stairwell doors?

10. Are there telephones or another two-way emergency communications system located inside the stairwells?

    On what floors are they located?

    Who monitors these communication devices?

    Is their operation regularly tested?

11. What type of perimeter lights are used?

    Does it meet minimum requirements of local codes and ordinances?

    Are lights directed toward the perimeter?

    Are all exterior doorways, walkways, and entries properly illuminated?

    Do dark areas need additional lighting?

    What additional lighting is required to illuminate these areas?

    Is lighting on an automatic timer system?

    Are the lights in operation during all hours of darkness?

    Is exterior lighting protected against theft and vandalism?

    Are there any obstructions, such as tree branches, blocking the lighting?

    Is the lighting system regularly inspected?

    By whom?

12. Is interior lighting of the building adequate?

    Is there adequate lighting in corridors, exits, and stairwells?

13. Is there an emergency lighting system for use in the event of a power failure?

    Are there any battery-operated lighting units?

    Are these units in good working condition?

14. Are there any internal staircases, vents, dumbwaiters, etc.?

    Is their interior covering noncombustible?

    What is the condition of stairtreads?

15. Layout of elevators and the floors they serve

    Are elevator lobbies enclosed with self-closing doors?

    Where are elevator control devices located (inside or outside the cab, Building Control Station, etc.)?

Is the operation of elevator emergency telephones or intercoms regularly tested? How often? By whom?

Comments

IV. Cafeteria/Kitchen

1. Where is it located?
2. What sort of fuel is used?
3. Are ovens, stoves, and fryers properly maintained and kept free of built-up combustible residues?
4. What is the condition of cooking equipment, hoods, vents, ducts, etc.?
   Are kitchen exhaust hoods properly protected?
   Are they clean?
5. What type of fire protection equipment is supplied?
   Are the cafeteria/kitchen staff trained in its use?
   Is the kitchen fire suppression system inspected and serviced annually?
6. Is refrigerating equipment used?
   How is it housed?
   What refrigerant is used?
   What is the condition of the refrigerator motor?
   Is the area properly vented?
7. Is the cafeteria/kitchen area maintained according to local fire safety codes and regulations?

Comments

V. Building Emergency Exit and Evacuation Signage

1. Where are building emergency exit and evacuation signs located?
2. Are there sufficient directional exit signs?
   Are any damaged or missing?
   Are there low-level exit signs?
   How are they illuminated (natural or artificial lighting)?
   Can they be read easily?
   Are there any lighted signs that are not working?
3. Are evacuation routes adequately posted?
4. Does signage inside the elevator lobbies display adequate information (such as floor plan, exit routes, what stairwells

have roof access, building name and address, floor number, fire department and building emergency telephone numbers, fire alarm looks like and sounds like, symbols depicting locations of fire equipment and manual fire alarm stations, and a warning "IN CASE OF FIRE USE STAIRWAY FOR EXIT. DO NOT USE ELEVATOR")?
   Is signage correctly mounted?
   Are there any defaced or missing signs?
5. Does signage inside the stairwell display adequate information (including stairwell number, floor number, and the uppermost and lowest floors the stairwell serves)?
   Is it correctly mounted?
   Are there any signs defaced or missing?
   At which levels are signs inside stairwells located (every floor)?
   Is the signage inside the stairwell designed and positioned in accordance with local codes and regulations?

Comments

VI. Fire Protective Signaling Systems

1. Fire alarm system type and manufacturer? Location?
2. Off-site monitoring of the fire alarm system?
   How?
3. Types of initiation devices (smoke detectors, heat detectors, manual fire alarm stations, water flow, special systems)?
4. Types of smoke detectors (ionization and photoelectric)?
   Where are they located?
   Does activation of an elevator lobby smoke detector automatically cause elevators serving that floor to travel to a predetermined floor? Which floor?
   If the elevator detector is activated on the floor to which it is designed to relocate, is there a secondary relocation floor?
5. Types of heat detectors (fixed-temperature, rate compensation, rate-of-rise, combination, etc.)?
   Where are they located?
6. Types of gas detectors, if any?
7. Manual fire alarm sending stations (correct name—manual fire alarm stations, manual pull stations, etc.)?

Where are they located?
8. Types of waterflow alarms (mechanically or electrically operated)?
   Where are they located?
9. If there is a parking structure, are there roll-down gates and doors with fusible links located on each level?
10. Is there anything special about the fire protective signaling systems?
11. What is the sound of the local alarm (siren, slow whoop, gong, bells, horns, etc.)?
    Is there also a visual alarm signal such as flashing lights?
    On what floors does the alarm annunciate (example, on fire floor, one above and below, two above and below)?
12. Where do the building fire protective signaling systems annunciate (local, off-site central station)?
    Is there a Building Control Station, Central Control Station, Control Center, Fire Command Center, or Fire Control Room (correct name)?
    Where is it located? What equipment and systems does it contain?
    Is annunciation of the alarm achieved by means of an audible signal and visual display (which indicates the floor or other designated area and the type of device from which the signal originated)?
    Who monitors the alarms? Are they monitored 24 hours per day, seven days per week?
    What is the established procedure when an alarm is received (including when and how fire department is notified)?
13. How are system trouble alarms handled?
14. Is the emergency notification list of personnel up-to-date?
15. What building voice communication systems are available (public address system, intercom, phone, etc.)?
    If there is a public address system, does it reach all areas of the building (public access or common areas, elevators, stairwells, parking areas, maintenance spaces, tenant areas)?
    Are prerecorded tape messages used to notify occupants of building emergencies?
16. Do building management personnel have two-way radio communication, pagers, etc.?

17. What building communication system is available for responding fire departments (sound-powered phones, two-way electrically supervised phone system, radios)?

Comments

VII. Smoke Control Systems

1. Is there a heating, ventilating, and air conditioning (HVAC) or air conditioning and ventilating (ACV) system?
   Is it a complete system serving the entire building, or are there separate systems for zones or individual areas?
   Description of system
   Location of intakes
   What causes it to shut off?
   How are smoke and fire dampers controlled?
2. On a fire alarm, does the air handling system automatically shut down?
   On what floor(s)?
   In what areas?
   Is the smoke vented out?
3. Are the stairwells automatically pressurized when a fire alarm occurs?
4. Is there a mechanical smoke removal system?
5. Can windows installed in the exterior walls be manually opened?
6. Are windows installed in the exterior walls fitted with tempered glass?
   Which ones?
   How are these windows identified?
7. Are there automatic closing fire assemblies for all elevator lobbies?

Comments

VIII. Fire Suppression Systems

1. Is there an automatic sprinkler system (or more than one)?
   What floors and areas does it serve?
2. What causes activation of a sprinkler head?
   Is there any obstruction of sprinkler heads? (Material should be stored no closer than 18 inches from the ceiling.)
3. Is there anything special about this system (linkage to other systems which must activate before discharge occurs, etc.)?

Is the system supervised? How?

4. What class of standpipe and hose system is installed (Class I, II, or III)?
 Where are the hose connections for these systems?
 What is the condition of hoses and nozzles?

5. What type of standpipe and hose system is installed (wet standpipe or dry stand-pipe)?

6. Are standpipe and sprinkler system con-trol valves secured in the open position?
 Are these shut-off valves visible and accessible?

7. Location on building exterior of fire department connections to sprinkler sys-tems and/or standpipe systems?
 Are they accessible, clearly marked, and fitted with protective caps?

8. Where are the fire pumps located?
 What is the system pressure?
 What is the suction pressure?
 What engine drives the pump(s) (electric or internal combustion)?
 Is it in the automatic mode?
 If internal combustion, what type and quantity of on-site fuel supply is available?
 Is this supply acceptable to the fire authority having jurisdiction?

9. Are jockey pumps available to maintain system pressure?
 Where are they located?

10. What on-site water supply is available if the principal water supply fails?
 Is this supply acceptable to the fire authority having jurisdiction?

Comments

IX. Other Fire Suppression Systems

1. Are there other fire extinguishing systems (carbon dioxide, halon, dry and wet chemical, etc.)?

2. Where exactly are they located?

3. How are these systems monitored?

Comments

X. Portable Fire Extinguishers

1. What type of extinguishers are located in public access or common areas?

Where exactly are they located?
 Are they in sufficient numbers?

2. What type of extinguishers are located in maintenance spaces?
 Where exactly are they located?

3. What type of extinguishers are located inside tenant areas?
 Where exactly are they located?

4. Are these types of extinguishers applica-ble for the type of hazard for which they would be used?

5. Is their type of use clearly marked?

6. Are sufficient numbers provided?

7. What is the condition of the extinguishers?

8. Can they be accessed easily?
 Are they properly mounted?
 Is there adequate clearance for all fire extinguishers?
 Do those housed in recessed cabinets have approved breakable fronts to deter vandalism and theft?

9. Is there a procedure for visually checking them monthly (or more frequently, if required by local code)?
 Are they checked annually to ensure that they are fully charged and operational?
 When were they last checked?

10. Are building emergency staff and occu-pants properly trained to use them?

Comments

XI. Emergency and Standby Power and Lighting Systems

1. What type of emergency and standby power systems are available?
 Location?
 What is the size of the generator?
 What systems and areas does the power system serve?
 What causes this alternate power system to operate? (Does it automatically trans-fer to emergency power?)
 How long after a power failure is it placed into operation?
 How long can this alternate power source provide power to its rated load without being refueled?
 When was the alternate power system last submitted to a full load test?

2. Are there other separate battery-operated lighting units?

Are all these units in good working condition?

3. Does the emergency lighting adequately illuminate paths of egress?

Comments

XII. Testing and Maintenance of Fire Life Safety Systems

1. What are the current procedures for testing and maintenance of fire life safety systems?
   What systems are tested on a monthly basis?
   What systems are tested on a semiannual basis?
   What systems are tested on an annual basis?
2. Have the testing and maintenance procedures been approved by the fire authority having jurisdiction?
3. When were the fire life safety systems last tested?
4. Is testing carried out by a certified tester?
5. Are adequate records being kept of this testing and maintenance?
6. What contracts are in effect for cleaning cooking equipment and hoods, for testing and maintaining the fire protective systems, and for testing and recharging fire extinguishers?

Comments

XIII. Surface Finishes of Interior Ceilings, Floors, and Walls

1. Are walls, ceilings, and floor finishes of proper rating?
2. Is fire-resistant acoustical ceiling tile used? Where is it used?
   Were any samples taken for testing?
   When the plenum space is part of the heating, ventilating, and air conditioning system, have any of the tiles been displaced to increase the flow of air to a particular area?
   Have tiles been removed and replaced with non–fire-resistant tiles?
   Have any of the tiles been damaged?
3. What type of covering is on the floor?

4. Are the wall coverings safe (no non-rated paneling, carpet material, straw or matting, fabric, etc.)?
   Were any samples taken for testing?

Comments

XIV. General Housekeeping, Storage Procedures, and Adherence to Safety

1. Are "NO SMOKING" signs posted?
   Are smoking areas clearly marked? Are they equipped with nontip ashtrays, metal waste receptacles, and fire extinguishers?
   Are smoking rules and regulations being observed? (Are there telltale signs of cigarette butts in the stairwells?)
2. What is the general standard of housekeeping?
   Are areas kept neat and clean?
   What areas are not?
   Are accumulations of lint, dust, and grease removed?
   What areas have excessive amounts of combustibles?
3. Are flammable materials (including paints and oily rags) correctly labeled and safely stored in approved containers away from combustibles?
   Is combustible waste stored in proper/approved containers?
   Any materials stored on the exterior of the building?
   Any piles of refuse, waste paper, furniture, etc.?
   What locations were observed to have unsatisfactory housekeeping?
4. Are patrols conducted to inspect housekeeping?
   Are patrols conducted to inspect for electrical appliances such as coffee pots, portable heaters, cooking equipment, etc., left on?
   Are tenant spaces inspected at the end of each business day?
   What is their frequency?
   Who conducts the patrols?
   Are the patrols recorded?
   How are the patrols recorded (notebooks, reports, guard tour systems)?
   Are the objectives of the patrols clearly outlined in written instructions?

5. Are maintenance spaces (particularly telephone closets, electrical, and mechanical rooms), corridors, and stairwells checked to ensure these areas are not being used for storage or as temporary offices?

6. Are there any obstructions of pathways leading to emergency exits (no storage of files, furniture, etc.)?
Fire doors not wedged or blocked open, especially at stairwell?
Inside the stairwells are there any obstructions to egress (obstacles, storage, debris)?
Stairwells, corridors, and exits free of trip and slip hazards (no holes, loose tiles, torn carpeting, defective mats)?

7. Is there any obstruction of sprinkler heads (material should be stored no closer than 18 inches from the ceiling)?

8. Is there any poke-through construction in floors, ceilings, and walls which has not been properly sealed with fire-rated material?

9. Are there examples of worn insulation on cords, cords under carpets or mats or run across doorways, missing or cracked faceplates, too many electrical cords for outlets (octopus), temporary wiring, or the incorrect use of electrical equipment?
Are heat-producing appliances well ventilated?
Is electrical equipment turned off when not in use?
Is malfunctioning electrical equipment immediately reported or taken out of service?
Is there adequate clearance of electrical power switch panels and power closets?
Are electrical power panels, switch and fuse cabinets in common areas properly secured?
Are junction boxes covered?

10. How is rubbish/trash removed from tenant spaces?
With what frequency?
Are trash bags ever temporarily stored where they may obstruct elevator vestibule door closing devices?
Is combustible trash placed in proper/approved containers?

11. Are rubbish/trash chutes used?
Are the chutes properly vented?
Are they enclosed with self-closing doors?
Are they lined with noncombustible materials?
Are fire protection signaling systems located in the chutes?
Inside the chutes are there automatic sprinkler systems?

12. At the loading dock area are there covered metal containers provided for rubbish and other materials?

13. Is a trash compactor provided?
Is its operating mechanism kept locked when not in use?
Is a fire extinguisher located close to it?

14. Are materials stacked so as not to tip or fall?
Is there safe storage on top shelves (height, weight, and bulk restricted)?
Are aisles between shelves kept clear?

Comments

XV. Fire Guard Operations

1. Are fire guards required by the authority having jurisdiction?
What are their hours of operation?
How many staff per shift?

2. What fire protection duties do they perform?

3. Are patrols conducted and what is their frequency?
Describe the patrols.
How are the patrols recorded (written reports, guard tour systems, etc.)?

4. If a firewatch is required, how many floors need to be continuously patrolled over what period of time?

5. Are there written procedures, instructions, and reports?
Are the instructions current and sufficient in content and accuracy?

6. How are the staff supervised?
If radios are used for communications, how effective are they?
Is there a channel designated for emergency communications?

7. What type of training do the staff receive?

How is the effectiveness of this training measured?

8. If the staff are contract employees, how much fire protective training do they receive before coming on-site?

Comments

XVI. Building Emergency Procedures Manual or Fire Safety Plan

1. Does the building have a Building Emergency Procedures Manual?
2. If so, what material does it contain and is it sufficiently detailed?
3. Does it thoroughly describe building fire life systems and equipment?
4. Does it address each emergency that is most likely to occur at the site?
5. Does it outline the Building Emergency Organization?
6. Does it list the specific duties of each team member both during normal business hours and after normal business hours?
7. Is the manual up-to-date?
   Are floor warden positions fully staffed?
8. Has the manual been certified by the local authority having jurisdiction?
9. Where is it located for easy access by the responding fire department?
10. Who is responsible for implementing and maintaining the manual and plan?
    Is the plan regularly tested?
    Are training records maintained?
11. Whose responsibility is it to make emergency public address announcements to building occupants?
12. What is the established evacuation or relocation procedure?
    Which floors usually evacuate during a fire alarm?
    How many floors do occupants usually travel down?
    What are the designated safe refuge areas inside and outside the building?

Comments

XVII. Fire Life Safety Education

1. Are all new building occupants given fire life safety training?

Of what does this training consist?
Does it include instruction in the use of portable fire extinguishers?
How soon after the occupant commences work at the building is this training available?
Does it include instruction about the safe use of electrical appliances such as coffee pots, portable heaters, toasters, etc., and the need to comply with smoking regulations?
Do the occupants received printed instruction?
What ongoing fire life safety training education is available for these occupants?

2. Is a tenant floor warden program in place?
   Are floor warden positions fully staffed?
   Are there alternate floor wardens?
   Do the floor wardens receive printed instruction such as a Floor Warden Manual?
   Are they provided with distinguishing attire (armbands, vests, hard hats, etc.)?
3. How often are fire life safety records updated?
   How regularly is the list of floor wardens and alternates updated?
   How regularly are lists of non-ambulatory or disabled persons updated?
4. Are fire drills for all building occupants regularly conducted in accordance with local laws and codes?
   How often?
   When was the last drill conducted?
   Who conducts the drills?
   Are records maintained of these drills?
5. What training do building management, engineering, security, parking, and janitorial staff receive?
   Does it include instruction in the use of portable fire extinguishers?
   Do staff on all shifts receive training?
   Is it conducted in any foreign languages?
   How often is it provided?
   Who conducts this training?
6. Are the records of fire life safety training kept in a protected area?

Comments

XVIII. Insurance

1. Has the fire insurance policy been reviewed and is it still in effect?
2. Is there satisfactory compliance with the conditions of the policy?
3. Is the insurance policy adequate in terms of the present risks?
4. What is the total coverage?
5. What is the deductible?
6. Is insurance for business interruption included?
7. What have been the claims over the past year?
8. Should the policy be revised?

Comments

6 *Computer Security*

Computers, computer systems, and the entire spectrum of electronic data processing (EDP) have become an essential part of daily business life in the United States and most developed nations. Computers and peripheral equipment—printers, data terminals, software, and the information contained within these systems—are subject to security and safety threats. In high-rise buildings these threats include theft, sabotage, fire, explosion, bomb threats, natural disasters, water leaks, power failure, riots and civil disorder, strikes and labor disturbances, hardware and software problems, and operator error and misuse of the systems and equipment.

As with all security and safety threats, it is necessary to conduct a survey of systems, equipment, and the areas where they are housed. This survey will consist of "a critical on-site examination and analysis to ascertain the present security [and safety] status, to identify deficiencies or excesses, to determine the protection needed, and to make recommendations to improve the overall security [and safety]" (Momboisse 1968, p.13). To conduct the survey, a similar approach is used to that outlined in Chapter 5, *Security and Fire Life Safety Surveys*, but the focus is on data processing systems.

An article used as a reference for the following review of computer systems was *Electronic Data Processing Security—An Overview* by Robert V. Jacobson, CPP (Merritt Company 1993, pp. 12-1–12-6).

Currently there are four common types of computer systems:

1. *Mainframe/Miniframe Computer Systems.* These expensive, large-scale computers and their peripherals usually are installed in a separate room called a computer data center (see Figure 6.1) and are connected through telephone or satellite circuits to remote terminals that may be located thousands of miles away. Miniframe computers are similar to mainframe ones, but are on a smaller scale and usually not housed in a special computer room. In high-rise commercial office buildings, major tenants may have mainframe or miniframe computer systems.

2. *Personal Computer (PC) Systems.* These microcomputer-based systems consist of a central processing unit (CPU) that processes information or data using computer software programs. Personal computer systems come in the form of desktop PCs, or highly portable and compact laptop or notebook versions. Data is entered manually into the systems via a keyboard or mouse, or automatically using either modems connected to telephone lines or scanners that read paper documents. A monitor produces a visual display of data for the operator. Information may be stored internally on a fixed hard drive or hard disk, or stored on a

Figure 6.1   A computer data center.   Photograph by Roger Flores.

diskette or backup tape system. It also may be printed out in paper form. In high-rise commercial office buildings, most tenants and many building staff have PCs.

   3. *Local Area Network (LAN) Systems.* These systems consist of several PCs (called *workstations*) linked in a network to a powerful, high-memory PC (called a *file server*). Network interface cards are installed in the PCs and are connected by cables to the file server. Network software installed on the workstations and the file server allows workstations to communicate with the file server and to use certain segments of the file server hard drive as if those segments were on the workstation hard drive. In high-rise commercial office buildings, some tenants and possibly the building management office will have a LAN.

   4. *Wide Area Network (WAN) Systems.* These systems are similar to LANs, but the file server is located at a remote location (possibly hundreds of miles away) and connected to the workstations through telephone or satellite circuits. The network interface cards are connected by cables to other workstations, and allow workstations to communicate not only with the file server, but also with each other via the file server. WAN networks connect multiple LAN networks together. This allows data to flow between distant LAN networks when needed. In high-rise commercial office buildings, some major tenants and possibly the building management office will have a WAN.

   In high-rise commercial office buildings, computer systems may be found in tenant areas or, possibly, as part of building automation and control systems. These systems must be protected by certain security and safety controls known as *computer security*. Computer security encompasses measures that can be taken to mitigate or reduce the impact of security and safety threats to a computer system.

Mainframe/Miniframe Computer Systems

The material in Appendix 6-1 is offered as a sample version of appropriate policy and procedures applicable to a computer security system. Although every computer operation is considered unique unto itself, this material should, nonetheless, provide ample food for thought. Because miniframe computers are often scattered throughout an office area, they do not require a separate data center to house them. Also, the operational impact of the loss of one will be far less damaging than the loss of a mainframe computer.*

Personal Computer Systems

Desktop, laptop, and notebook computers can be used to store large amounts of information. They themselves, as well as the tape backups and floppy disks on which information can be stored, are highly portable. The Merritt Company reports that Safeware™ The Insurance Agency, Inc., estimates that it insures one in every 1,000 personal computers in the United States and that there are over 60 million such computers in this nation alone. Extrapolating from its own claims data, it estimates that for 1992 the causes of PC losses in the United States ranked as follows:

Power surges	1.1 million losses	Lightning	243,000 losses
Theft	730,000 losses	Other, classified	141,000 losses
Natural disasters	283,000 losses	Fire	95,000 losses

The Agency notes that 62 percent of 1992 claims' dollars were paid as a direct result of theft, an increase of about 12 percent from prior years (Merritt Dec. 1993, p. 2).

The damage caused by power surges and lightning can be reduced by using surge protectors and software programs with automatic save features, which cause information to be saved automatically at regular times to the hard drive or diskettes. Keeping magnets, beverages, and other items that could harm equipment away from PC systems is another way of avoiding potential losses.

Theft of desktop PCs can be reduced by, if possible, keeping them in areas that can be locked when unattended. If desktop PC systems are located in open areas, unauthorized removal can be made more difficult by anchoring the computers to work surfaces using metal plates that screw in place. High-security steel cables and locks also can be used either to link the equipment securely to difficult-to-remove fixtures, or to initiate an audible alarm if removed (see Figure 6.2).

An accurate and up-to-date inventory of computer equipment should be maintained so that in the event of theft and subsequent recovery of the system, it can be returned to its rightful owner. The inventory may include a listing of the equipment, its model number, serial number, and possibly an asset tag number assigned to each item. Identifying marks also may be engraved on the equip-

---

* **Note:** This section and Appendix 6-1 are from "Computer Security" in *Security Managers Desk Reference* by Richard S. Post and David A. Schachtsiek (Butterworth–Heinemann, Stoneham, MA, 1986), pp. 348–356.

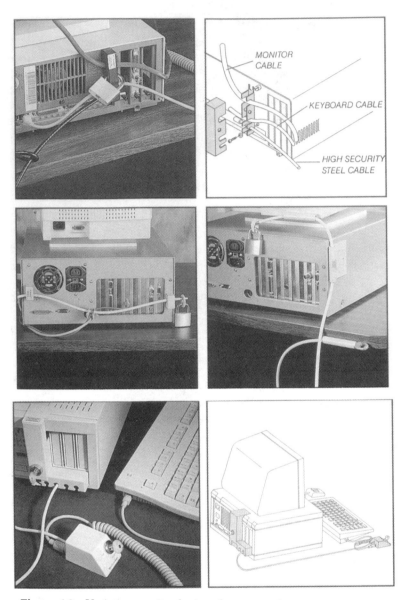

Figure 6.2   Various security devices for personal computer systems.
Courtesy of PC Guardian Micro Security Devices, Inc., San Rafael, CA
(800/288-8216).

ment to assist in recovery. Within an office, computers sometimes are moved
around or "borrowed" by enterprising employees. In such situations, identification marks can help facilitate the return of items to their authorized users.

     Unauthorized removal of desktop, laptop, and notebook computers from
high-rise buildings can be controlled to a degree by requiring property removal

passes for each item taken through an egress point that is controlled by well-trained security staff. Some buildings only permit the checking of property being removed after normal business hours. The problem, however, is that some laptop and notebook computers are small enough to fit inside a briefcase and can be carried out unobserved. Removal of diskettes and tape backups cannot be controlled by building security staff because these items are small enough to be easily secreted inside a briefcase, handbag, purse, billfold, or clothing for undetected removal.

Whatever security measures are taken to protect PC systems, the equipment should be adequately insured against loss or damage. Also, an adequate maintenance program should be designed for the computer system equipment. Spare parts may be maintained on site so that failure of certain components does not cause substantial downtime, or a maintenance contract may be negotiated with an outside vendor to ensure continuity of operations and control of computer system operating costs.

Part of the answer to controlling sensitive computer information is to permit access only to persons who have a "need-to-know," and by hiring honest and trustworthy individuals for positions of responsibility. The latter sometimes is difficult because "surveys have shown that the greatest threat to the security of information systems stems from disgruntled but trusted employees" (Keough Feb. 1988, p. 33). In other words, an employee previously considered to be honest and trusted may, because of events at home or at work, become dissatisfied and vent frustrations at perceived mistreatment by stealing sensitive information or maliciously tampering with the employer's computer system. Key locks and PC card readers on the computer will deter unauthorized use (although access keys are often left unlocked in drawers in close proximity to the computer). Password features can be used to deter unauthorized entry and limit access to computer information, but they cannot guarantee it because computer programs can be written to discover password codes.

A recent development in protecting information stored in notebook computers is the adoption of a new industry standard, the Personal Computer Memory Card International Association (PCMCIA). "This standard allows the notebook to use the same type of optional equipment as a desktop, such as modems, local area network (LAN) adapters, and memory expansion cards" (Patterson 1993, p. 94). It also allows the use of security devices to protect the information stored in a notebook computer. "The PCMCIA card encrypts the hard disk, turning it into gibberish for anyone who tries to read it without the card. The encryption is generated with a combination of the owner's card and his or her encryption key. Both are required. Even if the notebook and card are both lost or stolen, the data is still secure. Of course, it is more secure if the owner's card is kept separate from the notebook" (Patterson 1993, p. 94). The protected notebook is operated by inserting the credit card into the computer and typing in the appropriate password to gain full access to data, just like any other equivalent, but unprotected, computer.

The speed of computer operations is unaltered because "all reads and writes to the hard drive are passed through the independent processor and memory on the card, which quickly encrypts and decrypts the data" (Patterson

1993, p. 94). The PCMCIA slot is located on the exterior of the notebook. The PCMCIA standard is moving into desktop applications, as well. A recently developed encryption device, known as the *Clipper Chip*, "would allow legally authorized federal authorities to tap into encrypted communications sent or received by individuals suspected of being involved in criminal activity" (Keough, Oct. 1994, p. 9).

Malfunctions of computer hardware and inadvertent keystrokes have potentially damaging effects on computer operations. Many computer users, including the author of this book, can vividly remember accidentally hitting the wrong key, deleting an entire document, and then spending hours painfully recreating it. In *Office and Office Building Security* (San Luis et al. 1994, pp. 139, 140), Dennis M. Devlin defines *data security* as "the prevention of accidental or intentional disclosure, modification, or destruction of computerized data" and outlines four prudent steps that can be taken to ensure continued operations:

1.   All data files should be backed up daily. This single procedure will provide more data security than any other possible measure. Hardware can be readily replaced, but the data maintained on the computer cannot unless it is backed up. A single hard disk contains hundreds of million characters of data, and one hardware malfunction can render it all useless. Every PC system has software available in its operating system to provide daily backups either totally, or on an incremental basis.

2.   Maintain copies of data backups, program backups, and forms in an off-site location. If a catastrophe, such as a fire or flood, occurs, backups kept in the same area may be destroyed. In addition, special custom-made forms often require a long lead time to replace. If off-site, archived copies are available, operations can easily be restored using other computer hardware.

3.   Limit use of PCs to authorized persons. User authentication can only be carried out by limiting access to the computer. Often, adequate physical security is all that is necessary. Turn off and/or lock the computer when it is not in use. If the PC is in public area, use passwords to limit access. And use separate directories or libraries for individuals if multiple people share a PC. In this way multiple users cannot inadvertently disrupt another's work.

4.   Finally, exercise software testing controls and verify results. "GIGO," or "Garbage In, Garbage Out" is an old expression often used to describe computer programs. Today, unfortunately, the term has come to stand for "Garbage In, Gospel Out" as people become more dependent on personal computers. Results should never be trusted or relied on simply because they were produced by a computer without verifying the accuracy of programs with test data.

Fire is an ever-present risk with potentially disastrous consequences to computer systems. The fire protection of PC systems in high-rise buildings is closely aligned with the adequacy of building fire life safety systems, fire prevention and safety practices, and fire life safety training programs. Basic housekeeping measures, such as keeping the computer clean and free of dust and debris, not stacking paper files on top of and around the computer, and observing no-smoking rules, will go a long way toward reducing the risk of fire.

Local Area Network and Wide Area Network Systems

LAN and WAN systems, like PC systems, need basic physical security measures to protect the workstation PCs and the powerful, high-memory file server PC. In addition, the security of data usually requires particular user-identification and passwords to be used with the network software, and designated levels of access of workstation users to access file server programs and data. Users of the system should maintain privacy of their user-ID and password so that the confidentiality and integrity of information available to them is maintained. In originally selecting a password, often initials, backward initials, first or last name, business telephone extension, address names and numbers, driver's license and vehicle license number, social security number, date of birth, and place of birth are used. Anyone with access to this information generally can crack a person's password. Depending on the sensitivity of the information the password affords, one should be careful about the password selected.

It is essential to appoint a trusted, well-trained individual or group to control who accesses the various levels of programs and data. For example, some users may be permitted to create, modify, and delete certain programs and files, although others may only view data. The identification name and password security appointees use to access the system should be maintained under strict privacy. Compromise of this information could have dire consequences on the overall system integrity. To enhance data security, identification names and passwords should be periodically changed.

Electronic mail systems (commonly known as *e-mail*) are not secure, so information of a proprietary or sensitive nature should not be sent this way. When an e-mail message is sent, *all* workstations receive the message. Although software at each workstation is designed to disregard all messages except for those addressed specifically to it, the potential exists for someone to electronically eavesdrop. It is also a sound security practice to limit the number of saved e-mail messages on workstation PCs and the file server.

Dial-up access should not be provided to networks meant to be secure. If the system is known to be compromised, security personnel should conduct an immediate and thorough investigation to determine the cause and the perpetrators.

Computer Crimes

Computer crime is defined as a crime that: "requires the use of a computer system for its commission and makes significant use of a computer system in the conduct of a traditional crime" (Merritt 1993, p. 12-27). According to Jagger (1994),

The common thread in the commission of computer crimes is the intent to:

- Steal money
- Steal data for commercial purposes
- Use computer systems for private, unauthorized use

- Maliciously commit harm by altering or destroying data or applications
- Expose information that is considered confidential or potentially harmful if released to unauthorized persons.

An example of the last would be the obtaining of information pertaining to confidential investigations or the unauthorized release of financial or medical records.

The following sections describe the types of computer crimes that have occurred over the past several years. An article used as a reference is *Computer Crime Detection and Prevention* by Robert V. Jacobson, CPP (Merritt Company 1993, pp. 12-27–12-32).

Data Manipulation

Tremendous dollar losses have been caused by company employees and *hackers*—individuals who remotely access a computer system via telephone lines—who have altered payroll records so that certain employees receive a higher salary, altered pension fund data so that fictitious employees were created to receive benefits, altered credit bureau files to reflect favorably on otherwise risky individuals, and downloaded highly confidential records and classified information for sale to competitors and foreign nations. In addition, some have altered computer programs to accrue and electronically divert funds to their own bank accounts. The latter scam is commonly called the *Salami Swindle*, a sobriquet coined by Jacobson in 1971: "This descriptive term implies trimming off very small amounts of money from large numbers of sources and diverting the slices into one's own or into an accomplice's account" (Fischer and Green 1992, p. 406). The Salami Swindle is most prevalent in banking and financial institutions.

Sabotage of Software

Extensive disruptions of business have been caused by hackers and disgruntled company employees who have programmed a code into the computer software so that at a predetermined time or under certain conditions it will execute specific functions. For example, the entire payroll file may be erased if the name of the individual concerned is removed from the records (as it would be in the event of their termination).

Computer Virus and Trojan Horse

Computer viruses are another culprit of extensive business disruptions. Once one of these viruses is introduced into a computer, it copies itself onto the computer's operating system programs or onto other user files. The virus then passes from these infected programs or files onto any other programs with which they come in contact. Such replication has led to destruction of a computer's entire memory and files. With the advent of LANs and WANs, the potential danger that a virus could infect all of a company's PCs and then destroy all the data contained therein has greatly escalated. Certain software programs are commercially available to detect the presence of many known viruses and need to be updated when new viruses are created.

The term "Trojan Horse" comes from Greek mythology, which tells of a large, hollow, wooden horse that was used to hide Greek soldiers. The unsuspecting Trojans took the horse inside their city, only to have the soldiers emerge from it at night and open the city gates. The Greek army then invaded and sacked the city of Troy. In the computer world, the Trojan Horse is the crime of hiding an illegal computer code designed to execute an unauthorized function inside a legitimate computer program. The legitimate program performs normally, hiding the renegade code from view. Most computer viruses use the Trojan Horse method to wreak havoc with PCs, LANs, and WANs.

Electronic Eavesdropping

Electronic eavesdropping involves unauthorized tapping into telecommunications networks to access voice telephone calls or computer data that is not encoded for transmission. Access to sensitive data can be damaging to an organization. Telephone lines, including those used for LANs and WANs, and also microwave and satellite transmission networks, are all potentially susceptible.

Piracy of Software

Software piracy is the unauthorized copying of copyrighted computer software programs. This violates the vendor's software licensing agreement (usually software programs are sold on the understanding that they will be used on a single computer at any one time and duplicated only for backup purposes) and federal copyright laws; also, the pirated software may contain viruses. "It has been estimated that for each legitimate copy of software that is sold, between four and thirty additional copies are made illegally. One extravagant case reported a company that legally purchased a word-processing package and copied it for its 142 secretaries" (Fischer and Green 1992, p. 407). Individuals can report software violations to groups such as the Software Publishers Association (SPA).

Time Stealing

Time stealing is the unauthorized use of a computer and its services. Computer programs and services are expensive to develop and run, and an individual who gains access to them without paying is in effect committing a theft. Time stealing, however, is often difficult to detect.

Use of a Computer to Commit Traditional Theft

Computers have been used as tools to commit traditional theft in high-rise commercial office buildings. In one case (also described in Chapter 3), computer terminals located in a building's Security Command Center and engineering office could alter elevator service, placing certain building floors "on security." Neither the passenger nor freight/service elevators could respond to secured floors until building security staff reauthorized access. One day, after normal business hours, security staff duly placed the floors in question "on security." However, a building engineer had access to the engineering office computer by a modem in his home PC, and used it to take a certain floor "off security." He then drove to the site, used his parking card to enter the subterranean parking structure, parked his truck, and walked undetected to the ground level freight/service elevator lobby (no CCTV cameras were located either at the lobby or in the elevator car itself). He traveled in the elevator to the floor in question, used his grand master key to open tenant doors, stole several PC systems, and wheeled them to the elevator using a collapsible baggage trolley. He loaded the equipment into his truck, drove home, and placed the floor he had burglarized back "on security." Such thefts occurred repeatedly over several months, and an investigation narrowed suspects down to the building engineer. On his removal from the building the thefts stopped.

For more detailed information pertaining to computer crime refer to *Investigation and Resolution of Computer Crimes* by Robert V. Jacobson (Merritt Company 1993, pp. 12-33–12-47).

Summary

Rapid technological developments occurring in the computer field need to be matched by updated computer security measures. Computer security measures and controls should prevent or deter computer crime and, when it does occur, detect it as early as possible for thorough investigation by trained computer security professionals. Toward this end, a formal security review should be conducted by professional computer security consultants every two to three years.

References

Fischer, Robert J., and Gion Green, "Classic computer crime methods," *Introduction to Security*, 5th ed. (Butterworth–Heinemann, Boston, 1992).

Jagger, Hugh G., Partner in Management Consultants, Coopers and Lybrand, London, 1994. Comments to the author.

Keough, Howard, "Safety pins," *Security Management* (Arlington, VA, February 1988).

Keough, Howard, "Computer Security," *Security Management* (Arlington, VA, October 1994).

Merritt Company, The, "Computer theft and other losses," *Protection of Assets Manual*, 9th printing. Editor, Timothy J. Walsh (Used by permission from The Merritt Company, Santa Monica, CA, 800/638-7597. Copyright December 1993), Bulletin.

Merritt Company, The, "Electronic data processing security—an overview," by Robert V. Jacobson, CPP, *Protection of Assets Manual*, vol. II (The Merritt Company, Santa Monica, CA 1993).

Merritt Company, The, "Computer crime detection and prevention," by Robert V. Jacobson, CPP, *Protection of Assets Manual*, vol. II (The Merritt Company, Santa Monica, CA 1993).

Merritt Company, The, "Investigation and resolution of computer crimes," by Robert V. Jacobson, CPP, *Protection of Assets Manual*, vol. II (The Merritt Company, Santa Monica, CA 1993).

Momboisse, Raymond, M., *Industrial Security for Strikes, Riots and Disasters* (Charles C Thomas, Springfield, IL, 1968).

Patterson, Tom, "Notebook security in a nutshell," *Security Management* (Arlington, VA, September 1993).

San Luis, Ed, Louis A. Tyska, and Lawrence J. Fennelly, Appendix 1, "Ten steps toward increased computing and data security." Reprinted in *Office and Office Building Security*, 2nd ed. by permission of Dennis M. Devlin (Butterworth–Heinemann, Stoneham, MA, 1994).

Appendix 6-1   Sample of an Appropriate Computer Security Program

I. Physical Protection

A. *Responsibilities.* The manager of the facility in which a computer data center will be installed should be responsible for advising on construction of the computer data center, including environmental security support systems. The manager of the computer data center also should be responsible for proper maintenance of all security support systems.

B. *Standard Practices*

1. *Location.* A computer data center should be located away from outside walls, clear of any piping and in areas of the building not subject to rising or falling water. If it is not possible to avoid locations containing such hazards, special precautions must be taken to protect the equipment.

2. *Construction.* A computer data center should be constructed in accordance with applicable building codes and the applicable NFPA standards. Partition walls and ceilings should be constructed of fire-retardant material. The primary access to the machine room should be from an anteroom under environmental control, rather than from a public corridor.

   If the machine room floor is constructed of raised metal panels, the panels should form a National Electrical Manufacturers Association (NEMA)–rated enclosure for electrical power cables and interconnection cables between computer system components. Machine rooms containing raised floors also should include a ramp to provide a means of installing and removing equipment and to meet Americans with Disabilities (ADA) requirements.

3. *Air Conditioning.* Air temperature, humidity, and flow for the enclosed area should be designed to conform with local codes for basic room office environments, as well as with the manufacturer's cooling/heat dissipation requirements for major components. If a vendor's requirements for temperature, humidity, or air flow are more stringent than the local codes, the vendor's specifications should apply.

4. *Electrical Service.* Electrical service should be provided from a central distribution panel dedicated to the computer room area. This panel should be located within the controlled access area. The sizes and locations of incoming service, panel, and breakers should conform with national and local electrical codes and the hardware vendor's specifications. Emergency Power Off (EPO) switches that can cause immediate power-down of the mainframe computer operation should be well labeled and equipped with protective covers to reduce the chance of accidental activation.

5. *Telecommunications.* Telecommunications service should be provided by a dedicated cable direct from the building distribution frame. No service for any telephones or equipment, other than those in the machine room, should be connected to this cable. In complex teleprocessing installations, a NEMA-rated metal enclosure should be provided to house the modems and interconnecting and access equipment.

6. *Fire Suppression.* The manager of a computer data center should evaluate the need for permanent fire suppression equipment over and above local code requirements. However, acquisition of such equipment should be approved by the Director of Security

Source: From "Computer Security" in *Security Managers Desk Reference* by Richard S. Post and David A. Schachtsiek (Butterworth–Heinemann, Stoneham, MA, 1986), pp. 348–356. Minor revisions and/or additions have been made to enhance or make the material more readable.

and the Building Fire Safety Director. In addition to any permanent suppression equipment, a data center also should have portable extinguishers of the proper size and type according to NFPA guidelines.

7. *Fire and Smoke Detection.* Computer data centers also should be equipped with UL-listed smoke detectors installed in sufficient numbers to provide proper coverage based on local codes or manufacturers' recommendations, or one for each room smaller than the minimum protection area. The detection system must be connected to the building fire life safety system. Fire detection and automatic suppression equipment must be interconnected as well.

8. *Water Detection.* Any raised floor areas and any machine room areas must be equipped with UL-listed water detectors (water damage is a high risk).

9. *Housekeeping.* The equipment rooms should be cleaned on a regular basis to prevent the accumulation of dust and debris that could harm the equipment. Further, any and all filters should be cleaned in accordance with the manufacturer's instructions. Waste materials must be discarded into fire-safe containers that should be emptied daily. No more than a two-day supply of paper should be stored within the equipment room. Any paper that must be stored there should be in metal cabinets.

II. Access Control

A. *Responsibilities.* The manager responsible for the operation of a computer data center also should implement a security support system designed to control access to the computer room, data entry areas, off-site storage areas and supporting equipment areas. The security support system should include the necessary controls and procedures to achieve required minimum levels of protection and to implement the required standard practices described in this section.

B. *Standard Practices.*
1. *Required Minimum Levels of Protection.*
   a. A computer data center should be located and equipped so that entry of unauthorized persons can be detected during both operating and nonoperating hours.
   b. Access to a computer data center should be restricted to the following authorized personnel:
      1) Employees having job assignments within the computer data center
      2) Employees having job assignments that require regular access to the computer data center
      3) Nonemployees, such as vendor maintenance personnel and couriers, who require entry to the computer data center on a regular basis
   c. Authorization for access should be effective only during those periods when a person legitimately requires access to the computer data center.
   d. Access to the computer data center by unauthorized persons should be approved on a visit-by-visit basis. Visitors should be recorded on a register and should be escorted by an authorized person at all times while in the data center.
2. *Restricted Area.* The computer data center (including computer room, data entry areas, off-site storage areas, and supporting equipment areas) should be designated as a restricted area.
3. *Access Authorization Procedure.* A formal procedure should be established for authorizing individuals to have access to the computer data center.
4. *Access Authorization Identification.* A method also should be devised so that persons controlling access know who has been authorized access and can positively identify these individuals.

C. *Guidelines.*
1. *Construction.* The location and construction of a computer data center should be such that some degree of destructive force is necessary for unauthorized, undetected entry. Conse-

quently, avoid locating the data center adjacent to building windows, and avoid the use of glass in data center walls. Care also should be taken to ensure that the data center walls extend from the structural floor to the structural ceiling (i.e., from the base floor slab to the floor slab of the floor above). These issues should be addressed in the preconstruction phase.

2. *Detection Measures.* Measures that can be taken to detect intrusion into the data center restricted areas should typically include use of CCTV cameras, motion detection devices, and/or scheduled checks by security officers.

3. *Restriction Methods.* Access to the computer data center must be restricted to authorized persons. Choice of an access control method should be based on cost and appropriateness to the local situation. Some possibilities are:

   a. Visual recognition of authorized persons by an employee controlling computer data center entrances.

   b. Assignment of special ID badges to authorized persons.

   c. Installation of door locks opened only by keys, cards, or combinations issued under control to authorized personnel.

   d. Use of mantraps (especially where access is highly restricted). A *mantrap* or *portal* is a small holding area to which an authorized person is admitted, prior to being asked to submit to another form of access control before they are allowed to proceed further. For example, a mantrap may take the form of a small cubicle located at the entrance to the computer center. To enter the mantrap a person will, via a CCTV and two-way voice communication system, identify himself or herself to an operator located inside the computer center. If the person is authorized to enter the mantrap, the operator will remotely operate a door to admit them (the door closes behind them once they have entered, thereby isolating them inside the mantrap). The person then will be required to submit to further verification before being allowed to proceed into the computer center. Such an arrangement reduces the chance of unauthorized persons *tailgating* into the computer center. Tailgating or *piggybacking* occurs when a person who is authorized to enter an area is accompanied by another person who has not submitted to the access verification process.

III. Program Control

A. *Responsibilities.* The manager responsible for the operation of a computer data center must implement a security support system to protect computer programs from destruction, unauthorized use, and unauthorized revision. All programs (purchased, leased, or developed) that are used or controlled by the computer data center must be protected.

B. *Standard Practices.*

   1. *Required Minimum Levels of Protection*

      a. A current executable copy of all production programs, including systems software, must be maintained at a location remote from the computer data center.

      b. Source programs in machine-readable form or current copies of program documentation also must be maintained elsewhere.

      c. Use (execution) of programs must be restricted to authorized purposes (i.e., for company business, for production processing according to documentation, or for testing during maintenance or modification).

   2. *Documentation.* Program revisions must be documented according to predetermined and standard practices.

   3. *Computer Usage.* A record of all computer use must be maintained for verification of authorized execution. It should not be possible to interfere with the audit log that provides a record of all computer activity. The

printout of the audit log should be done in a secure location.

IV. Information Protection

A. *Responsibilities.* The manager responsible for the operation of a computer data center must develop and implement an information security support system to protect all computer-readable information processed in the center.
B. *Standard Practices.*
1. *Information to Be Protected*
   a. *Computer Input/Output.* Computer-generated information on paper, carbon paper, microfilm, or other permanent visual media should be subject to special security standards. This includes all system documentation, procedures, and forms used for the application.
   b. *Systems Operations.* Information regarding the operation of systems in a computer data center must be restricted on a need-to-know basis.
2. *Information Classification.* All information processed or to be processed in a computer data center must be reviewed to determine the applicability of information classifications defined by security standards. This review will be performed in concert with EDP or Automated Information Services (AIS) support groups and the organizations owning the information.
3. *Stored Computer Information.* All removable computer storage media containing restricted information must be externally labeled with the appropriate classification. Therefore, physical access controls also must be established to prevent removal of the storage medium.
4. *Restricted Information.*
   a. *Processing.* Restricted information must be processed on employee-controlled computers unless a contractor providing the service signs a legal proprietary agreement.
   b. *Transmission.* Transmission of restricted information must be controlled to limit access to authorized individuals.
   c. *Destruction.* Controls must be implemented for monitoring the destruction (including shredding, carting, etc.) of restricted information to ensure compliance with predetermined policy.
   d. *Access Approval.* Nonemployees must be denied access to all restricted information unless prior approval is obtained from the owner of the information.
   e. *Access Records.* A record of access to restricted information must be maintained so that authorized access can be tracked and verified.
5. *Strictly Private Information.* Information of this classification must be controlled according to requirements determined by its originator.
6. *Information Sharing.* Sharing information between systems controlled by different organizational units must be approved by the owner of the data.
7. *Access Control.* Access codes used to restrict access to protected information must not be printed or displayed on a terminal. If appropriate access controls are not available in operating software, they must be incorporated into appropriate, written application programs.
8. *Separation of Duties.* To prevent collusion separate staff should work on system development and system operations. The system development staff should work on a system separate from the main "live" system.
9. *Formal Change Control.* Changes to the system, such as, for example, updates and patches—adding information—should be formally controlled and authorized.
10. *Security Systems.* Obviously, computer data centers that have equipment or operating systems with security capabilities must utilize those features in their security support systems.

V. Contingency Planning

A. *General Information.* Interruption of computer processing operations can be caused by a variety of conditions that result in interruptions lasting from a few hours to an extremely long period of time. Efficient recovery of the computer processing facility can only be accomplished by having established contingency plans. The degree of advanced preparedness has a significant impact on the efforts expended and on the cost, length of disruption, and security exposure incurred recovering from service disruptions. Consequently, standard operating procedures must be designed to respond to day-to-day minor operating problems as well as major disruptions and disasters.

B. *Standard Practices.*

   1. *Responsibilities.* The manager responsible for the computer data center should be responsible for developing a contingency plan that details emergency measures covering all likely disruptions or disasters.

   2. *Contingency Plan Contents.* The contingency plan should include:

      a. *Emergency Response Plan.* This details steps to be taken to protect life and property and to minimize the impact of any emergency threats such as sabotage, fire, explosion, bomb threats, natural disasters, power failure, water leaks, riots and civil disorder, and strikes or labor disturbances.

         1) Emergency procedures
         2) Emergency equipment
         3) Facility layout
         4) Responsibility and authority

      b. *Administrative Action Plan.* This details steps to be taken in case of a disaster. These plans should cover damage assessment, activation of disaster contingency plans (items c and d below), disaster organization structure, and a notification system.

         1) Emergency notification procedure
            a) Notification contact list
            b) Order of contact regarding decisions
         2) Damage assessment procedures
            a) Notify assessment team members from a predetermined contact list
            b) Specify place of assembly
            c) Assess site damage
         3) Backups and recovery implementation decision criteria
            a) Discuss decision-making process
            b) Criteria to attempt normal recovery
            c) Criteria to implement backup/recovery plan
         4) Responsibility and authority
            a) Decision-making authority
            b) Approval requirements
            c) Proposed action documentation

      c. *Backup Processing Plan.* In the event of a disaster, this plan should provide for alternate processing capabilities for all affected EDP and AIS applications at service levels commensurate with their predesignated criticality classification.

         1) Application criticality—processing priorities
         2) Configuration requirements
         3) Relocation procedures and schedule
         4) Starting procedures and schedule
         5) Organizational responsibility and authority
         6) Manning requirements/assignments
         7) Application recovery instructions
         8) Backup data file inventory
         9) Data recovery instructions
         10) Network recovery/reconnection.

      d. *Recovery Plan.* This provides for smooth and rapid restoration of an AIS database or EDP site following a disaster.

         1) Situation assessment
         2) Immediate protective/security measures
         3) Vendor contact list
         4) Recovery team members
         5) Organizational responsibility and authority
         6) Planning and implementation

      e. Copies of routine pre-emergency procedures implemented in support of, and necessary for the initiation of, the contingency plan.

         1) Off-site file backup protection

2) Operating and program documentation

f. Information required to execute the contingency plan, such as contact names and phone numbers, location and inventory of backup supplies, and so forth.

C. *Classification of Service Disruptions.* In a high-rise commercial office building each tenant company, and the building itself, may have their own policies regarding service disruptions.

1. *Major Disruption.* The disruption is classified as major when conditions exist that interrupt or disable critical demand processing but do not require physical recovery of equipment, media, and facilities.

2. *Disaster.* The disruption is classified as a disaster when conditions exist that totally disable computer processing services and require physical recovery of equipment, media and facilities. Conditions constituting a disaster include, but are not limited to, fires, explosions, water leaks, natural disasters, and riots or civil disorders.

D. *Preparing a Contingency Plan.*

1. *General.* A plan should be of a general enough nature to allow the interface of detailed plans during and after the disruption/disaster. It should specify actions to be taken, individuals or organizational functions responsible for those actions, and respective time relationships of the actions. Of major importance is the preidentification of the recovery teams that will relocate application production and those who will recover the data center facility. Remember that this contingency plan also must satisfy the current requirements of both the user and the computer operations department.

2. *Elements of the contingency plan for major disruptions.* The following documentation in the contingency plan is provided primarily to ensure continued processing or resumption of processing in the event of a major disruption:

a. *Operational procedures.* Establish written procedures to be followed when responding to major disruptions. Specify actions to be taken by operations management, vendors, and supporting functions such as power and air conditioning. Provide contact phone numbers (both office and home) and equipment lists that identify vendors and vendor maintenance personnel.

b. *Backup processing procedures.* Under certain circumstances, the need for service level continuation in support of critical and semicritical systems will require initiating backup processing procedures during a major disruption. A procedure for backup processing must be established.

3. *Elements of the contingency plan for disasters.* The following documentation in the contingency plan is provided primarily to ensure personnel safety, continued processing capability, and physical recovery after a disaster:

a. *Emergency procedures.* The safety of EDP and AIS personnel is foremost during the initial phase of a disaster. Formal emergency procedures are required to ensure a safe and proper evacuation of personnel.

b. *Interim production planning procedures.* An interim production plan must be implemented immediately after a disaster to resolve disposition of processing load and minimize the impact on critical applications. The procedures for production demand planning must be predeveloped as an element of contingency planning.

c. *Data center recovery planning procedure.* Recovery of the data center must address equipment, software, and physical facilities. Because the initial concern will be continuity of computer processing, this plan normally will be implemented after the initiation of the processing demand plan. The procedure for data center recovery planning must be predeveloped as an element of the contingency plan.

4. *Storage and distribution.* Once developed, the plan should be maintained in a Contingency Plan Manual divided into two major sections: "Major Disruption" and "Disaster." Further division of each section should be made as needed to address the subelements defined in this appendix. Copies of the manual should be distributed to members of the recovery team as well as maintained in off-site storage.

E. *Data Center Recovery Team.* The data center recovery team should comprise personnel from functional areas both within and outside the company who can assist in the efficient and timely recovery of the facility. Team members should be selected jointly by the Director of Security, the manager of the computer data center, and appropriate top management administrators.

7 *Security Rules and Procedures*

Security programs for high-rise buildings, and for their individual tenants, involve procedures, rules, and regulations needed "to prevent unauthorized persons from entering, to prevent the unauthorized removal of property, and to prevent crime, violence, and other disruptive behavior" (American Protective Services 1990, p. 17). Security's main purpose is to protect life and property.

Access Control of Building Users

There are many different people who may, at any one time, attempt to enter a high-rise facility. They include building management staff, building contractors (such as elevator technicians, engineering, security, janitorial or maintenance, and parking personnel), tenants, visitors, salespersons, tradespeople (including construction workers, electricians, plumbers, carpenters, gardeners, telephone repair persons, persons replenishing vending machines, and others who service equipment within the building), couriers, messengers, solicitors, building inspectors, vagrants, panhandlers, sightseers, teenagers on a lark, people lost, and mentally disturbed individuals. There also may be others who enter the building—or an individual tenant space—with the sole purpose of committing a crime against people or property. The access control measures for this wide spectrum of persons are determined largely by building owners and managers, and individual tenants.

These measures aim to sift out unwanted persons or intruders and at the same time provide a minimum of inconvenience to legitimate building users. Factors such as the type of building tenancy, pattern of building use, and the time and day (normal business hours or after hours, weekends, and holidays) need to be considered when the security program is designed and implemented.

As explained in Chapter 2, *High-Rise Development and Utilization*, a building can be single-tenant/single-use, single-tenant/multiple-use, multiple-tenant/single-use, or multiple-tenant/multiple-use. A single-tenant/single-use building is more conducive to stricter access control of employees and members of the public at the building's entrance: standard security rules and procedures can be communicated and enforced more easily with employees of one tenant only. "Access control may be tight and involve a badging system for regular employees and a careful monitoring of visitors through direct observation, or video displays and other devices" (Geiger and Craighead 1991, p. 11B).

Implementation of strict access control in a multiple-tenant/multiple-use building, however, is more difficult because each tenant will have different expectations of the degree of security the building should have. "In multiple tenant buildings, access controls will generally be relaxed, although they usually tighten up after business hours. Sometimes the main deterrent that security provides is a psychological one—the presence of uniformed officers may persuade a potential thief or vandal to go elsewhere" (Geiger and Craighead 1991, p. 11B).

Once building management formulates access control measures, management and the security staff must communicate these rules and procedures and obtain the support of tenants. Each tenant, in turn, will need to decide what additional access control measures should be implemented for its own space. The tenant must then communicate both its own and the building's rules and procedures to employees. The high-rise buildings used as examples in this book are multiple-tenant/multiple-use structures used primarily for commercial office purposes.

Building Access Controls

Building access controls include vehicle access to parking lots, structures, and loading dock/shipping and receiving areas; pedestrian access to building lobbies, elevator lobbies, passenger and freight/service elevators; and access routes to retail sales spaces, restaurants, promenades, mezzanines, atria, and maintenance areas. Measures for controlling access to these areas vary from site to site, depending on building management's policy, but generally will incorporate some or all of those described in the following sections.

Vehicle Access to Parking Lots or Structures

Access to parking lots or structures may be gained by:

1. Entering at will and parking at whatever parking stalls are available
2. Driving up to a motion detector or pressure pad, which detects the presence of the vehicle and automatically opens a parking gate or traffic arm
3. Being admitted by a parking attendant or valet stationed either at the point of entry or at a remote location linked to the point of entry by an intercom and CCTV system that permits visual recognition of the vehicle or the driver
4. Pulling a ticket, imprinted with the time and date of entry, from a machine that also automatically opens the parking gate or raises the traffic barrier
5. Using a remote control device or access card to open gates or raise a traffic barrier

When exiting the parking lot or structure, the driver usually will be required to submit to a similar procedure to that encountered on entry, including possibly making payment at a parking booth. If an access card has been used, many modern card access systems have both entry and exit card readers that have incorporated an *anti-passback* feature. This prevents a card from being used again to authorize entry of a second vehicle before the first vehicle has exited the parking lot or structure.

Vehicle Access to Loading Dock/Shipping and Receiving Areas

Vehicles entering loading dock/shipping and receiving areas either may do so at will and park at whatever loading bays are available, or they may be permitted to enter and be directed to park in certain areas by a loading dock attendant who will then supervise the subsequent loading or unloading activity. Some higher-security buildings require vehicles, particularly vans and trucks, and especially those that will proceed to underground loading dock/shipping and receiving areas, to undergo an on-street inspection before being permitted to enter. Loading docks that are normally unattended may have an intercom or buzzer system available, possibly in conjunction with a CCTV system, that allows the driver to summon building staff for assistance. For security purposes, the dock attendant normally will maintain a log or record of the vehicle license plate number, the driver's name and company, the time in, and the time out. Depending on building policy, the vehicle keys may remain in the vehicle, or be given to the dock attendant for safekeeping and to allow the vehicle to be moved if necessary.

Movement of drivers and delivery persons usually will be confined to the loading dock/shipping and receiving areas. For this reason, rest areas, toilet facilities, and pay phones often are provided. If drivers and delivery persons must enter the building for drop off or pick up, they may be required to notify the dock attendant of the specific building area they will be visiting and the approximate duration of their stay. They may also be issued special identification badges and required to leave some form of personal identification (such as a driver's license) with the attendant to ensure that they come back to the dock area to return any identification issued to them.

Pedestrian Access to Buildings

Pedestrians entering multiple-tenant/multiple-use buildings during normal business hours usually may simply enter at will and proceed to whatever area they desire. In other types of occupancies they may be asked to submit to some form of verification procedure before they are permitted to enter the facility and proceed to various areas. The procedure usually depends on the time (normal business hours or after hours) and the day (standard working days or weekends and holidays) that access is requested.

During normal business hours, access control to buildings and their common areas usually is relaxed and may consist solely of a security staff member or receptionist trained to observe both ingoing and outgoing pedestrian traffic. Any persons who do not appear to belong may be challenged with a simple "May I help you?" Specific questions can then determine the particulars; for example, whether the person is a tenant, is visiting a tenant (if so, which one?), is delivering or picking up items (if so, to whom? from whom?), is servicing or inspecting equipment in the building (if so, where? at whose request?). These questions not only help screen out intruders with no legitimate reason for entering, but also assist persons who genuinely need directions to their destination. The degree of access control permitted by building policy will determine the percentage of unwanted persons successfully screened out. "The security program should be designed just tight enough to screen out as many intruders as it takes to reduce problems to the level that can be accepted. This means that a useful security program will rarely screen out *all* intruders" (American Protective Services 1980, p. 11). If all intruders were screened out, it would undoubtedly result in what could be considered unacceptable delays or inconvenience to the legitimate occupants and visitors of the building.

Access control to building maintenance spaces—mechanical rooms and floors, communications and utilities access points, elevator machine rooms, janitorial closets—and areas under construction or renovation usually will be tight, even during normal business hours. Depending on building policy, persons accessing these areas may be logged in and out, required to wear special identification badges, given keys to a particular area (although issuing any keys to vendors or visitors is considered a security risk), or accompanied by a building escort. Some contractors servicing certain types of equipment in specific building areas may be permitted to install their own locking devices at access points leading to this equipment. Some building owners and managers consider the main electrical switchgear and power transformer room such a life safety risk that not even building personnel are issued keys to it.

After normal business hours, access control to all areas should be stricter. One way to provide off-hours access to a high-rise facility would be to furnish keys to all building occupants or to those who need to enter after hours. This approach, however, can have disastrous consequences proportional to the size of the building and the number of occupants. A gigantic workload and expense can be created by lost keys, keys not returned by departing tenant employees, and the necessity of rekeying building entrances and reissuing keys to building key holders every time a key has gone astray. In addition, there may be the problem of unauthorized duplication of keys. To avoid all this, most high-rise buildings do not issue any building access keys to tenants but rely on some way of verifying a person's right to enter the building. This verification may involve the following procedures.

Visual Recognition

Building security staff or a receptionist may verify a person's right to enter on sight. Several problems may result, however, from this form of verification. For example, someone who closely resembles a person authorized to enter may be admitted in error. Also, particularly if the building is large with a dense population, it will be difficult for security staff or the receptionist to learn to recognize all persons authorized to enter. If there is a change or substitution of the security staff or receptionist, the new person will not be familiar with the persons authorized to enter through this area. Questioning persons who normally are never challenged can lead to complaints by tenants to building management. Finally, if the security staff is distracted by another duty, an unauthorized person may gain entry without being observed.

After-Hours Authorization Documents

A document listing those authorized for after-hours access may be provided in advance to security staff at the building entrance. Persons requesting access will then identify themselves to building security staff, who will check their name (which should be confirmed by a driver's license or another form of legal identification) with the names listed in the document. In many buildings, tenants will provide management with a written request on their own stationery listing the names of the persons involved and the period of time after-hours access is permitted. Building security staff or the receptionist often will set up a file sorted alphabetically by tenant name, or by the last name of the person to be granted access, to minimize time spent searching for the appropriate authorization.

Building security staff must thoroughly check all documents authorizing access to ensure that the decision to grant access is valid. An unusual example illustrates the point. Recently in a major Los Angeles high-rise, management gave the building security staff a memorandum to permit access for a pest control company to a specific tenant suite on a particular Friday night. The pest control company failed to appear on the night authorized but did arrive the following Monday evening. Building security staff did not thoroughly check the paperwork and permitted the pest control company to enter and carry out their work. The next business day several of the tenant employees became ill from the lingering effects of the pest treatment. The reason for authorizing entry on Friday evening had been to allow two days for any residual pesticide to dissipate. This safety goal was frustrated by permitting the work to occur on a Monday evening.

Once the person's right to enter is verified, he or she may already have a tenant key to use, or one may have been left ahead of time with the document authorizing entry—although the latter practice is not recommended because it can lead to misplaced or lost keys. Alternatively, if someone is present in the tenant space, they may be telephoned and asked to come to the building entrance with a key to provide admittance and escort the person. (After normal business hours most tenant areas are locked.) A building security or engineering staff member may be required to escort the individual to maintenance areas or other areas with limited access. Some buildings have a permanent list of local and state agencies whose inspectors have authorized entry, but it is absolutely critical to thoroughly verify these persons' identification, and to make building management aware (if possible) of these persons' presence before they are granted entry. It is also important to escort anyone claiming to be an inspector while he or she is in the facility. On occasion, professional burglars posing as local or state inspectors have been granted entry to high-rise buildings.

Building Identification Cards, Passes, and Badges

Sometimes a building identification card, pass, or badge is used to verify the bearer's identity and privilege to enter after hours. The identification should be numbered sequentially, list the person's name and the company's name, and contain the person's signature, a color photograph, and in some instances an expiration date. It should be laminated for durability, and be tamper-resistive (although this will not necessarily eliminate the potential for the plastic envelope being cut and the card, pass, or badge being modified and then relaminated). The recent development of laser technology to create holograms (three-dimensional images) may lead to their use for building identification cards, passes, or badges, but the present high cost does not currently justify it. In case it is lost, the card, pass, or badge can include a note such as, "IF FOUND DROP IN ANY MAILBOX. P.O. BOX NO. ___, CITY & STATE. POSTAGE IS GUAR-ANTEED." This can be presented by the bearer to security staff for entry to the building or used to verify identification within the building. However, if the card, pass, or badge is not thoroughly checked for details, this form of access control will soon lose its effectiveness. Also, it must be retrieved from holders whose employment is terminated, or else it can remain in use after the person no longer has a legitimate reason for gaining after-hours access to the building.

Building Access Cards

Building access cards provide after-hours access by operating an entry door to the building. An intercom, telephone, or CCTV camera also may be provided at the point of entry. If there is a problem using the card, the person requesting access may use the intercom or telephone to communicate with building staff or an off-site central monitoring station. If the person's right of entry is confirmed, the monitoring staff can grant access remotely. Some high-rise buildings have a card reader installed at the main lobby security desk. Tenants entering the building are asked to insert, swipe, or bring their building card into close proximity to the card reader (depending on the type of reader). If a green light is displayed the tenant is permitted to proceed into the building and the event is recorded in the system database. This system can be used to generate its own after-hours access register or log (described later). In some buildings, when the tenant card is validated, elevators are automatically released for travel to floors that the card holder has a right to access.

If this system is installed in elevator cars, the same card may be used to provide controlled access to building floors using passenger and freight/service elevators. Some systems can be programmed so that within certain time periods the elevator car will only respond to a particular floor if an authorized access card is used. The person will enter the elevator, insert, swipe, or bring the card into close proximity to the card reader, and select the desired floor by pressing the appropriate button on the floor selection panel.

Building access cards can feature the same data, tamper-resistive protection, and lost-card notice as identification cards, passes, or badges. However, some buildings, for security reasons, prefer to have no details listed on the card apart from its sequential number and, if it is used with an insertion or swipe-type card reader, an arrow depicting the correct way to insert or swipe the card. Then if the card is found by an outsider, no identifying marks indicate where it may be used. One advantage of a building access card is that if the employment of the card holder is terminated, the card can be deactivated immediately by computer.

Whatever access control procedures are used, many high-rise buildings maintain an *after-hours access register* or *log* to record after-hours access activity. This log records details such as the person's name (printed for legibility) and signature, the name of the company they represent or tenant they are visiting, the date, and time in and out. In case of an after-hours building emergency, such a log can be used to help ascertain who is in the building. However, the register or log does not provide a record of *all* persons in the building after hours, because some persons will have accessed the building when it was open, before the documented access control procedure was in place. To determine exactly which tenants are in the building after hours, it would be necessary either to telephone or to personally visit every tenant. Such a procedure, particularly in large high-rises, is not considered practical.

Signs or sidewalk plates, generally located outside the property, may clearly state: "RIGHT TO PASS BY PERMISSION, AND SUBJECT TO CONTROL, OF OWNERS" or "PERMISSION TO PASS REVOCABLE AT ANY TIME," and they may include a reference to the code that states this right (see Figure 7.1).

If a person is discovered who does not have a legitimate reason for being in the building, then the right to remain may be revoked by the owner, manager, or agent acting on behalf of the building. After being told to depart the premises, those who refuse to leave may be arrested for trespassing. Also, anyone reentering a building after having been warned that he or she is not authorized to enter may be treated as a trespasser and asked to leave.

Tenant Access Controls

Tenant access control involves *rented* or *assigned occupancies*. These are leased or owner-occupied spaces on various floors, and are either open to public access during normal building hours, or restricted to identified and authorized persons. The access control measures for tenant areas will vary from tenant to tenant, depending on their type of business activity, the design of the tenant space, and the individual tenant's management policy.

In some cases, visitors entering tenant space may simply enter at will and, in some instances, may proceed to any area in the tenant space. However, in

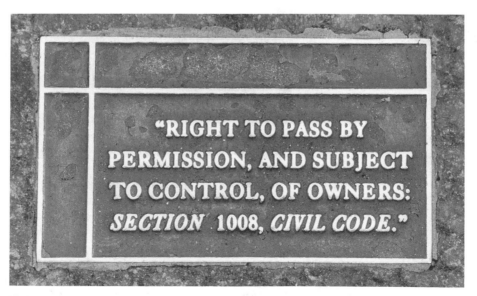

Figure 7.1   Example of a sidewalk plate.   Photograph by Roger Flores.

today's security-conscious world, it is more likely that the visitor will be greeted by a receptionist and asked to submit to some form of verification procedure before being permitted to enter the tenant space. As with building access control, the dominant factor in tenant access control is the time and day access is requested.

Tenant Space Access during Normal Business Hours

Tenants in most high-rise commercial office buildings practice some form of access control to their space. A receptionist often is present at the main point of entry to a tenant area, acting as the tenant's first line of defense.

Tenant space layout varies from tenant to tenant; however, if possible, it is helpful to channel incoming persons through one area and keep all other access points properly secured. Some tenants establish a staffed reception area that is separated by physical barriers from interior tenant space. Once a person has been cleared for admittance, the receptionist can remotely signal another person behind the protective barriers to allow admittance (without the screened individual even being aware that passage was previously blocked).

Large companies that occupy several full floors served by one elevator bank can establish access control to their elevator bank at the street level. If there is no elevator bank serving the tenant floors exclusively, the elevators can be programmed to stop at only one floor of that particular tenant. A reception area at this point can be used to control access to that tenant's other floors by way of an internal staircase or card-controlled access to the elevator. It is the responsibility of the receptionist often, in addition to answering telephones and handling other duties, to monitor both incoming and outgoing pedestrian traffic for the tenant space. Only if the receptionist is properly trained to screen and direct incoming persons will the security of the space be considerably enhanced.

The receptionist must question incoming persons of all types to determine whether they are authorized to enter the tenant space. Over the years a common ploy in high-rise buildings has been for a person to pose as a photocopier or telephone repair person and, after gaining entry, proceed to steal purses, billfolds, petty cash, credit cards, and other small valuable items left unattended in the tenant space. These criminals are aided by two common practices: Businessmen often leave their suitcoat, containing their billfold, hung on a clothes stand or behind their office door; businesswomen, similarly, often hang a handbag on a chair or leave it under their desk. Another trick has been for an intruder, having gained access to a tenant space, to memorize a name from a desk or a directory board. If challenged by an occupant, the intruder simply states the name to avoid detection: "Oh, I'm looking for Mr. Searcy!" Unfortunately, on hearing such a reply, many an unknowing occupant has escorted the person to Mr. Searcy's desk, and left them there to continue with their deception and possible theft. This type of criminal behavior can occur more easily on *open* floors, where elevator lobbies open into corridors which, in turn, open without any form of barrier into the main floor areas (see Figure 7.2).

Once it is established that a person is permitted to enter tenant space, the receptionist should arrange for it to take place in a manner that does not compromise security. The person may be issued a temporary "visitor" or "contrac-

Figure 7.2   An example of an open floor viewed from the open passenger elevator lobby.   Photograph by Roger Flores.

tor" identification badge for the day and asked to fill in and sign the appropriate register. Commonly, the receptionist telephones the employee expecting the visitor to come to the reception area to escort the guest. Also, with some large companies there can be a mailroom with a separate entrance where all couriers, messengers, or others dropping off or picking up merchandise from the tenant space can be directed. This eliminates the need to escort these individuals.

Receptionists also can play an important role in building security by reporting solicitors they encounter. As defined by the high-rise community in the United States, *solicitors* are persons who come into high-rises and attempt to sell their wares to tenants. They often come to buildings with items for sale secreted in a container such as a bag or briefcase. Once past the lobby, they will open up the container, take out their product, and proceed from floor to floor, tenant to tenant, touting their merchandise. Even though many solicitors may be legitimate, their presence can be disruptive to tenant business; furthermore, many criminals pose as solicitors. If a tenant receptionist detects an unwanted person such as a solicitor or someone who is behaving suspiciously, it is helpful to security staff if the receptionist who telephoned and requested their assistance delays the person as long as possible on the floor until security assistance arrives. It is generally better to have a co-worker call for security personnel out of the hearing of the solicitor. A signal or code phrase ("Sarah, could you watch the phones for me? I'm going to be busy with the flower seller for a few minutes.") that will not alert the solicitor could be used. If the solicitor is successfully delayed, security staff will not have to chase all over the building looking for the individual.

One way to detain a solicitor is to feign interest in the product, call other "interested" employees to look at the merchandise, and thereby preoccupy the solicitor. Suspicious persons may be detained by carrying on a friendly conversation, offering an employment application, or using some other ruse to give sufficient time for building security staff to arrive. Simply telling the solicitor that soliciting is not permitted generally is not enough. For the protection of all tenants, it is best to have security personnel escort the solicitor out of the building. The tenant should never buy anything the solicitor is selling. To do so provides an excuse for the solicitor to attempt to reenter the building. If it is not possible to delay the solicitor, it is helpful if the receptionist can at least notify security staff as soon as possible and supply a good description of the person involved, including physical characteristics as well as clothing.

Some tenants have installed their own access control systems—electric locks, mechanical or electrical push-button combination locks, card-operated locks, or biometric system-operated locks—that control the operation of entry door(s) to tenant areas. Sometimes, CCTV systems, intercoms, and intrusion detection systems are used in conjunction with these devices. Before a system can be considered, the local fire authority having jurisdiction should be consulted to determine whether such an installation is permitted by local and state codes—this is particularly important when the access control devices are to be installed on doors leading directly from elevator lobbies to the tenant space. These doors involve paths of egress during emergency evacuation and therefore require special locking arrangements permitted by the local codes.

Tenant Space Access after Normal Business Hours

After normal business hours in most high-rise commercial office buildings, access control to all areas is stricter. Perimeter doors to the tenant space usually are locked when normal business is completed. Each tenant needs to establish a specific policy and procedure for access after this time. One possible solution is to furnish keys to all employees who require access. This approach, however, can lead to the same problems discussed earlier, under "Pedestrian Access to Buildings." Instead, some tenants issue access keys only to a few select individuals. This alleviates some key control problems but creates the need for one of these persons to be present when special after-hours access is required. In some instances, building management has permitted some tenants to leave keys with security staff for special after-hours access. The tenant's employees must then return the keys to their representative on the next business day.

There is no clear-cut answer to the issue—factors such as the number of employees requiring after-hours access, the frequency of after-hours access, and tenant management's attitude toward its employees, as well as building management policies, all need to be taken into consideration before a well-defined key policy is formulated. As noted earlier, some tenants have installed their own access control systems to operate entry doors to the tenant area, possibly in conjunction with CCTV systems, intercoms, and intrusion detection systems. Some large companies who have around-the-clock operations provide a security staff member or receptionist to control after-hours employee access. Some maintain an after-hours access register or log similar to that required for the building itself (as described earlier in this chapter). If the tenant is a theater or restaurant that is open after normal business hours and on weekends and holidays, there will be a need to provide easy access for the patrons but additional security measures to ensure these persons do not stray into other building areas.

Despite the access control measures implemented, there still exists the possibility that a "building creeper" may slip through the net. The "building creeper" dresses in conservative business attire. Late in the afternoon on a normal business day, the creeper confidently enters through the main lobby and nonchalantly passes the building security staff. Taking an elevator to an upper floor, this "businessperson" enters a rest room and quietly sits in a cubicle until the tenants on the floor are about to close business for the day. He or she then exits the rest room and systematically walks the corridors checking doors to see if they have been secured. On finding one unlocked, the creeper enters the tenant space and proceeds through it looking for small items such as calculators, dictating machines, cash, checks, credit cards, and other things that can be easily placed in a jacket or briefcase. On being challenged in one suite by building janitorial staff, a tenant business card (which moments before was lifted from an executive's desk) is politely presented with the statement of gratitude, "I'm so glad to see that even the janitorial staff in our building are so security conscious!" After fifteen minutes of work, the creeper descends to the lobby, using a passenger elevator, and warmly waves to the security staff as he or she exits the building. To prevent this from happening, tenants should ensure that all perimeter doors not supervised by their staff are kept locked at all times.

It is important that tenants *never* open their doors after normal business hours for anyone not personally known to them. In a Los Angeles high-rise commercial office building, a temporary female employee working alone after hours one night opened the door to a man claiming to be the window washer. The intruder raped the woman, then even had the nerve to say good-night to the security officer posted in the lobby. Tenants should be instructed that if someone belongs in their space, either building management or tenant management will have already provided the means of obtaining access. Otherwise, the person should be kept locked out and building security staff (or the police) should be called immediately for assistance.

Escorts of Building Users

Escorting is accompanying individuals either for the purpose of protecting them, protecting the property they may be carrying, and, as a courtesy, showing them where to go, or to ensure that they do not remove property illegally. In the high-rise setting, building users can be escorted to and from the building and within the tenant space.

Escorts to and from the Building

Escorts to and from a building usually occur after the building's normal business hours and generally are conducted by members of the security staff. When tenants finish business, their employees, often females, may request building security staff to escort them from the building to unsupervised areas of the property such as parking structures. Building policy should dictate how, when, and where the escorts are to be conducted. For liability reasons, escorting building users across streets or off the grounds is not encouraged.

Escorts within the Building

Building policy may require that persons needing access to certain maintenance spaces and areas under construction or renovation be provided with an escort to accompany them whenever they are in these areas. Such escorts may be provided by building engineering or security staff.

Janitorial staff may require escorts when they are removing trash material from building floors and transporting it to areas such as trash compactors and dumpsters. The escort is provided to reduce the possibility of the janitorial staff transporting stolen items, along with the trash from tenant floors, and depositing them in places where they can be picked up at a later time.

Escorts within Tenant Space

It is usual for visitors, such as salespersons, tradespeople, couriers, and messengers, to be escorted within tenant space. Depending on the type of business the tenant conducts, tenant policy, and staff availability, an employee may be summoned to the main reception area to accompany the individuals at all times while they are inside the tenant area, or just accompany them to particular areas and leave them to carry out the tasks they have been authorized to perform. On completion of these tasks, an escort back to the reception area may be required, or the individuals may be permitted to leave on their own accord.

Property Control

There are various property acceptance and removal systems that can be implemented by building management and tenants to provide some control over the property that on a daily basis moves in and out of commercial office buildings and tenant areas. The degree of control will vary from building to building and tenant to tenant, and will depend largely on the policies established by building management and the tenants themselves. The effectiveness of these policies depends on how thoroughly they are communicated to building staff, tenants, and occupants, how strictly they are enforced, and on the support afforded the program. Just as with access control measures, it is often difficult to implement strict property control measures in a multiple-tenant/multiple-use commercial office building, primarily because each tenant may expect a different degree of security.

According to American Protective Services (1980, p. 24),

The objectives of a property control system are threefold:

- *To prevent stolen property and other unauthorized items from leaving.* Stolen property may include computers (personal computers, notebooks, and laptops), typewriters, fax machines, calculators, and office equipment. An unauthorized item might be something like a sensitive or classified document which is not to be removed from a certain area or from the building.
- *To prevent dangerous items entering.* Bombs are the usual concern, but other items such as cameras or firearms might be prohibited.
- *To prevent unnecessary or disruptive delivery traffic.* By keeping out misdirected deliveries, unnecessary traffic is avoided. By routing deliveries through proper entrances, such as loading docks and freight/service elevators, disruptive traffic is avoided and, in some cases, the building and passenger elevators are protected against damage from handtrucks and bulky crates. By intercepting deliveries at these entrances to the building it may be possible to detect intruders posing as delivery persons.

Property Removal Pass System

Unauthorized removal of property from high-rise buildings can be controlled to a degree by requiring *property removal passes* for business and personal items taken through an egress point controlled by building security staff. The time period when the property removal pass system is to be in effect is set by building management and communicated to the tenants. (Some buildings only permit the checking of property removal after normal business hours.) Property removal passes are often supplied by building management to key tenant representatives who then supervise their distribution to tenant employees and visitors on an as-needed basis. The passes may vary both in design and in the information recorded on them. For the property pass to be of value in the security program, it should address at least the following areas of information:

- Name and signature of the person authorized to remove the property
- Name and room or suite number of the tenant or company from whom the property is being removed
- Printed name and signature of the tenant representative who has authorized the property removal
- Brief description of the property, including any model, serial, or asset tag numbers
- Date the property will be removed
- Date and time of removal of the property
- Signature of the person (usually a member of the building security staff or a receptionist) collecting the pass and permitting removal of the property
- Property passes should be sequentially numbered and a record kept of which tenants received which numbered passes
- Property passes should be in duplicate (following the removal of the property, the original is returned by the building security staff to the tenant representative and a copy is kept on file by the building security department)

A sample *Property Removal Pass* for a high-rise commercial office building is shown in Figure 7.3. After the authorized tenant representative has signed the form, any blank lines on the pass should be crossed out to prevent unauthorized entries.

Pass No: 000001

PACIFIC TOWER PLAZA

PROPERTY REMOVAL PASS

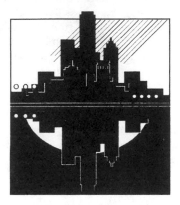

Name of Person Removing Property: _____

Signature of Person Removing Property: _____

The following material/items are authorized for removal from Pacific Tower Plaza on: (Date)_____

_____

_____

_____

(Brief description of the property, including any model, serial, or asset tag numbers)

Person Authorizing Removal

Signature: _____

Printed Name: _____

Tenant or Company Name: _____

Room/Suite Number: _____

Person Allowing Removal and Collecting Pass

Signature of Building Security Staff: _____

Date of Removal: _____   Time of Removal: _____

White Original--Tenant Copy   Yellow Copy--Building Security

Figure 7.3   Sample Property Removal Pass

Whenever building security staff receives property removal passes, they should always scrutinize the pass to ensure that it is complete and contains all the necessary information. The identity of the person actually removing the property should be confirmed by means of a valid driver's license or another legal identification.

It is best if each tenant has already provided an authorization letter containing sample signatures of each representative authorized to sign a property removal pass. Building security staff can then compare the signature on the pass with the signature on the letter. If it matches, security will sign the pass, keep it for distribution, and permit removal of the property. If it does not match, security personnel will keep the pass and can make an attempt to contact either an authorized tenant representative or building management to resolve the matter. Such a system can be effective in controlling the removal of some business and personal property. However, many computer-related items are small enough to be carried out unobserved, as detailed in Chapter 6, *Computer Security*.

Some high-rise buildings permit the use of a *permanent property pass*. This pass eliminates the need to continually issue property passes for personal or company property that is being removed from the building on a regular basis. The permanent property pass is similar both in design and recorded information to a regular property pass, except that it can be used repeatedly for the period of time stipulated on the pass. The card is often laminated to prevent damage and affixed at all times to the item being brought in and out of the facility. Building security staff should keep a log that shows all permanent property passes in use. This log should include the serial number of the pass, a brief description of the property, the period of time the pass is in effect, the identity of the person authorized to use the pass, the name of the tenant involved, and (in case the permanent property pass is lost or the tenant cancels its usage) the date when the pass is no longer to be honored by security.

Dangerous or Illicit Items

To prevent someone from entering the building with dangerous or illicit items is not as easy a task as it would at first appear. Bombs are the usual concern. As was demonstrated by the New York World Trade Center 1993 bombing incident, explosives can be carried by vehicles into parking areas and structures. More will be said about this subject in Chapter 10, *Building Emergencies*. Other items such as illegal drugs, cameras, or firearms, might be prohibited in a multiple-tenant/multiple-use structure used primarily for commercial office purposes, but in fact the transportation of these into such a facility can be accomplished easily without detection. Searching persons entering the facility and their briefcases, handbags, carryalls, and so on, is not an acceptable practice in today's high-rise commercial office buildings, although, as is discussed later in this chapter, many buildings do permit visual inspections of items carried by janitorial staff. Of course, building security or management staff can immediately address persons visibly carrying in prohibited items.

Messengers and Couriers

There are several alternatives open to building owners and managers who desire to prevent unnecessary, disruptive, or undesirable delivery traffic in high-rise buildings. Some management companies have instituted special programs whereby outside messengers and couriers, on arrival at the building, are directed to a central location such as the loading dock or building mailroom. At that location, in-house couriers, who are part of the building security staff, sign for the items and deliver them within the building by way of the freight/service elevators. When items are to leave the building, the building couriers pick up the articles from the tenants, bring them to the central location, and then outside messengers and couriers sign for them before taking them for delivery to their destinations. As a rule, regular courier services such as Federal Express, UPS, DHL, and so on, performing regular, multiple deliveries in a building, are permitted to perform their own pick ups and deliveries. Special deliveries, including those requiring signatures, can be facilitated by temporary badges for outside couriers or messengers, or by providing an escort for them while they are in the building.

This program has been very successful. When building security staff perform multiple deliveries and pick ups from tenants, the number of couriers and messengers roaming throughout the building can be diminished significantly: a valuable security advance when a million square foot high-rise commercial office building may have 300 or more individual deliveries per normal business day. In addition, the number of couriers and messengers using passenger elevators is reduced. It enhances security because it provides an added presence in the building, and because these building couriers have already been "security-vetted" (i.e., a background investigation of these individuals has been conducted) there should be less chance of theft or vandalism than when using outside couriers and messengers. Delivery to secured or normally "locked off" floors is also easier because building couriers can more readily be entrusted with the access codes or cards that allow them to enter these areas.

Like any well-run operation, such programs need to be meticulously documented to provide an audit trail to track deliveries and pick ups and ensure that these tasks are conducted in a timely manner. If there is a question about the time property was picked up or delivered, or about the individual who signed for it, accurate records should be available for review. Some individual tenants, particularly larger ones that occupy full floors and multiple floors, have addressed the issue of outside messengers and couriers roaming within their space by establishing mailrooms from which all deliveries within the tenant space are performed by in-house or proprietary messengers only.

Package Acceptance Policy

During normal business hours, the acceptance of packages for delivery to tenants is handled by the tenants themselves. After normal business hours, packages sometimes are delivered to high-rise buildings and the acceptance or rejection of them will depend on the policy established by the building owner or manager. For various security and safety reasons, most commercial office buildings do *not* permit after-hours acceptance of packages by security staff. The building would not want to accept the responsibility and ensuing liability from accepting packages the tenant may not want to have accepted; also, these packages may contain dangerous or illicit items such as bombs. Some buildings do permit the acceptance of after-hours packages on certain occasions and under special circumstances. This will usually entail a request in writing by the tenant, and an explicit understanding that the building and its agents are absolved from any potential liability resulting from accepting packages.

Lost and Found Property

Handling lost and found property is an often-neglected but critical part of an effective security program. Most people do not have to think too far back to recall the anguish they felt on discovering that a valuable personal possession or business item was missing. Likewise, one can remember the exhilaration at being contacted and informed that the missing property had been found and was available for pick up.

If property is lost in a high-rise building and is subsequently found and handed to building security staff, the item(s) must be kept in a secure place, and, if possible, expeditiously returned to its rightful owner. Such action can considerably enhance the trust and confidence that occupants and visitors in high-rise buildings will have in the building security operation. Just the opposite will be true if a tenant learns that the found item was handed to building security staff and was then lost or classified as "missing."

Building security staff should maintain a list of lost and found items in a *lost and found property log*. The log should contain details such as the following:

- A brief description of the property, including any serial or asset tag numbers
- The date, time, and place the property was lost or found
- The identity of, and means to contact, the person who lost or found the property
- If the property is claimed, the identity of, and means to contact, the claimant and the signature of the person who received the property
- The name of the security staff member who took the report of the lost property, logged in the found items, or handled the return of the property to the rightful owner

If the lost property is particularly valuable or sensitive, it may be necessary for the local law enforcement agency to be contacted; if the property is later handed over to them, this fact, including the identity of the receiving law enforcement officer, should be noted. A receipt for the property should be obtained. How to handle found property often will be determined by local and state laws.

> In California, for example, Section 2080 of the California Civil Code does not require a person to take charge of found property, but if they do, they can be sued for the negligent handling of it. The law provides further that if the owner of lost property is known, the property must be returned to that owner. If the owner is not known, and the property has a value above ten dollars, the property, within a reasonable period of time, must be turned over to the local police. (American Protective Services 1993, p. 4)

The handling of found property will be determined by the authority having jurisdiction. Some localities allow found property, when its owner is unknown and its value is below a certain amount, to be distributed to local charitable organizations. Others, after a certain waiting period, auction the property or allow the finder to assume ownership of it.

Trash Removal Control

There are a number of controls that can be placed on trash removal from tenant space and from a building. The design and implementation of controls will depend largely on the specific cleaning operations in effect at the building. Some operations "gang clean" using a team (including dusters, cleaners, waxers, polishers, and trash removers) to clean tenant spaces and rest rooms on a series of floors. Others assign janitorial staff on a regular basis to perform all functions on particular floors. This method is preferable because the regular janitorial staff are more likely to detect unauthorized persons who do not belong in a particular tenant space, and because security investigations are easier when the same janitors regularly work in a particular tenant space.

Depending on the sensitivity of their business, tenants may shred certain proprietary documents themselves, or employ contract shredding agencies who will come to the building on a scheduled basis to remove and destroy documents. These documents may include sensitive business data, client lists and billing information, documents that are confidential within the company, and any proprietary information that would be useful to competitors if it fell into their hands. Depending on the sensitivity of the data, it may be passed through a standard shredder or through a crosscut shredder, which more severely deters reassemblage of the shredded material.

Routine removal of trash from a tenant floor should be carried out under constant supervision by janitorial supervisors or building security staff. No interruption should take place in supervision during the janitors' passage from the tenant floor to a service or freight elevator, or to designated receptacles such as dumpsters, compactors, or holding areas, usually located at the building loading dock. Such supervision will deter janitorial staff from possibly secreting stolen articles in trash bags, and then dropping the articles in locations within the building where they can be retrieved at a later stage by themselves or an accomplice. To make scrutiny of trash easier, the bags should be made of transparent plastic. If, because of staffing limitations, direct supervision is not possible, then CCTV cameras in the dock areas are recommended to deter the removal of items from trash bags before they are placed in the dumpsters, compactors, or holding areas, or removed from the receptacles themselves.

Trash holding areas are common in multiple-tenant high-rise buildings where refuse from financial institutions is being handled. To avoid accidentally discarding important documents such as negotiable instruments (checks, bank drafts, savings bonds, securities, etc.), the trash from financial business tenants often is separated and held in a secured area for a period of time as determined by the financial institution concerned. The holding time permits losses to surface before the trash has been removed from the site for destruction.

The janitorial staff in many high-rise buildings are subject to certain property screening procedures on arrival and departure from work. The object of the screening procedure is to observe any prohibited items being brought into the building, and to detect any stolen property being removed from the building. As part of an agreement communicated to them before they commence employment, they may be asked to submit to a visual inspection of any items they are carrying to and from work—lunch pails, bags, packages, and so on. The frequency of the inspections can be established as part of the agreement: inspections may be conducted every time the employee enters or leaves the building for work, at random, or only with cause. Inspections usually are conducted by janitorial supervisors or building security staff. They are visual only, and employees are requested to open the appropriate items themselves. Under no circumstances does the inspecting person touch the items being inspected or attempt to inspect any part of the employee's person or clothing. All persons have a legal right and expectation of privacy, so purses will be subject to inspection only under special circumstances, the nature of which should be established in writing beforehand.

The success or failure of any property control system will depend largely on whether there are "controlled" exits or entries to the high-rise facility for use by building occupants and visitors. For example, if building users need to pass through one particular point to enter or leave the building, and if this point sometimes is not supervised, then the property control system can be circumvented. Similarly, if there are other unsupervised exits or entry points, persons can defeat the property control system by using these areas when they want to bring in or take out property. An example of the latter is in the high-rise building described in Chapter 5, *Security and Fire Life Safety Surveys*. If elevator systems allow anyone to leave the building undetected, building management should consider positioning CCTV cameras inside all elevators, or at the elevator lobbies in the parking structure. The latter arrangement is not ideal, but if the cameras are constantly monitored or the images constantly recorded, the unauthorized movement of property might be observed either at the time it occurs, or at a later stage when videotapes are reviewed.

Key Control

In high-rise commercial office buildings, keys to access the facility often remain under the control of building management, security, and engineering personnel. Building management personnel obviously need to have keys to gain entry to all areas of the facility they manage. Engineering staff, because of the nature of their work, also need access to virtually all areas, including tenant spaces. Depending on how the building is managed, security staff also will have access to most areas. Some buildings do make it a practice to keep tenant office keys out of the normal possession of security staff but provide a controlled, documented means for these keys to be obtained when necessary. During incidents such as building emergencies, the security staff can obtain these keys quickly. After the situation has been resolved, the keys are again placed under supervision, perhaps in a locked or sealed key cabinet with the cabinet's key or replacement seal in strict custody.

Basically, keys should only be issued to those persons who can be entrusted with them and who have an *absolute* need for them. The status a key holder may feel by possessing certain keys should not enter into the decision-making process. The following points are important to consider:

- Building tenants should be issued keys that pertain to their particular area only.
- Building tenants should never be issued building entrance keys. (If issuing entrance keys is unavoidable, the locks should be changed periodically and new keys issued to the tenants authorized to have them.)
- Building tenants should not be allowed to duplicate keys. (Keys duplicated by building management should be distinctively marked to ensure that any unauthorized keys may be easily identified.)
- When an employee ceases to work for a tenant, all the employee's keys should be returned to the tenant representative. Depending on the situation, locks may need to be changed.
- When tenants move into a new space, all locks should be changed and new keys issued.
- Janitorial staff should be issued keys only for the period of time they require them and for the particular areas to which they will require access. Depending on the size of the janitorial staff, designated supervisors within the janitorial operation may be issued master keys that, for instance, may provide access to tenant spaces on an entire floor. In this way, the general cleaning staff do not need to be issued keys. In some buildings no janitorial staff are issued keys, and security staff must unlock the appropriate doors and relock them after the work is completed. Procedures will vary from building to building depending on size, complexity, and the manner in which the cleaning is conducted and trash is removed.
- Elevator, escalator, dumbwaiter, rubbish chute, and moving walk technicians may be permitted to carry keys that provide access to their equipment, or the building may retain possession and issue them only as needed.

In some buildings maintenance personnel (telephone technicians, water and power utility workers, etc.) are permitted to attach their own locking devices to areas containing their equipment. This practice is convenient because no building staff are required to open these areas, but it compromises security because control of keys and the areas themselves has been lost. These areas can be used to store unauthorized or stolen items, and general housekeeping may become a problem. If this practice is permitted, no one should be allowed to place a lock on a door without Building Security or Building Operations Departments having a key. In an emergency, keys must be available for access. A possible alternative is for contractors to be permitted to stow their equipment in gang boxes that can be stored in a room.

In the event of a lost key, the circumstances surrounding the loss should be fully investigated and thoroughly documented. The following information regarding key control has been obtained (with slight modifications) from *Security Supervision: A Handbook for Supervisors and Managers* by Eugene D. Finneran.

Before an effective key control system can be established, every key to every lock used to protect the facility and property must be accounted for. Chances are good that it will not even be possible to account for the most critical keys or to be certain that they have not been copied or compromised. If this is the case, there is only one alternative—to rekey the entire facility.

Once an effective locking system has been installed, positive control of all keys must be gained and maintained. This can be accomplished only if an effective key record is kept. When not issued or in use, keys must be adequately secured. A good, effective key control system is simple to initiate, particularly if it is established in conjunction with the installation of new locking devices. One of the methods that can be used to gain and maintain effective key control follows:

Key Cabinet

A well-constructed cabinet for keys is essential (see Figure 7.4). The cabinet must be of sufficient size to hold the original key to every lock in the system. It also should be capable of holding any additional keys that are in use in the facility but are not a part of the security locking system. Of course, high-rise tenants will have files, safes, and locks whose keys are not supplied to building management. The cabinet should be well installed to make it difficult, if not impossible, to remove from the property. It should be locked at all times when the person designated to control the keys is not actually issuing or replacing a key. The key to the cabinet itself must receive special handling, and when not in use, it should be placed in a locked compartment inside a combination-type safe.

Key Record

Some administrative means must be set up to record key code numbers and indicate to whom keys to specific locks have been issued. This record may take the form of a ledger book or a card file. Many buildings now use computerized key control records.

Figure 7.4
Key cabinet containing
individually labeled keys.
Courtesy of Telkee, Dover, DE.

Key Blanks

Blanks to be used to cut keys for issue to authorized personnel must be distinctively marked for identification to ensure that no employees have cut their own keys. Blanks must be kept within a combination-type safe and issued only to the person authorized to cut keys and then only in the amount authorized by the person responsible for key control. Such authorization should always be in writing, and records should be made of each issue which will be matched with the returned key. Keys damaged in the cutting process must be returned.

Inventories

Periodic inventories must be made of all key blanks, original keys, and duplicate keys issued to employees. This cannot be done merely by phoning employees, supervisors, or executives and asking them if they still have their keys. Each key must be inspected personally by key control personnel.

Audits

In addition to the periodic inventory, a member of management should perform an unannounced audit of all key control records and procedures. During the course of this audit, a joint inventory of all keys should be conducted.

Master Key Control

Master keys and control keys for removable core cylinders should be kept under strict control by building management. Keys should be issued only to those who have a critical need for them. Whether master keys should be issued to building security staff will vary from building to building. (If they are not issued master keys, they will often be issued a ring of keys permitting them to enter various parts of the facility.) Keys issued to the security staff should never be permitted to leave the facility. They should be passed from shift to shift and a receipt should be recorded each time they change hands. The supervisor must ensure that all security personnel understand the importance of not permitting keys to be compromised.

Tenant Security Education

There are many ways to educate building users and tenants about the security program in place. All building users, particularly tenants and their visitors, must understand the program and how the various rules and procedures impact them. If people are aware of the logic behind security regulations, they usually will be more willing to comply with them. This communication can be achieved in the following ways:

1.   Explain the regulations on an informal, as-needed basis. For example, building security staff may explain the purpose of the after-hours access register or log to a tenant when asking him to sign it; or may inform a visitor leaving the

building that she must have a property removal pass signed by the tenant she just visited before the computer she is carrying can be permitted to leave the building.

2.   Use posted signs, written policies and procedures in the Tenant Information Manual, pamphlets, leaflets, flyers, newsletters, video training materials, and public address messages supplied by building management to the tenant or by tenant management to their employees. Appendix 7-1 is a sample *Tenant Security and Safety Awareness Checklist* that could be revised and sent to tenants at appropriate times during the year. Early to mid-November is often an opportune time to disseminate such information. During this month, tenants may be leaving the building in the dark, and the approaching festive season often brings a higher incidence of theft in high-rise commercial office buildings.

3.   Have building management or the tenants conduct security orientation lectures, classes, workshops, and seminars. Such events can be an effective medium, not only for communicating to tenants what is required of them in the building security program, but also as an opportunity to educate employees about basic security measures they can adopt at work, home, and on their way to and from their place of work. Such tips could include not leaving valuable items in view in parked vehicles; securing all vehicle doors and windows; securing desks, filing cabinets, business and personal property; and observing a "clean tabletop" policy. If practiced by tenants, these would contribute substantially to reducing theft at the building.

The length of security briefings will vary, but 45 minutes to an hour is probably the maximum busy tenants will permit. As with all effective teaching, the use of audio-visual aids—films, videotapes, overheads, and slide programs—can help gain the attention of participants and assist in effectively communicating the required message. The frequency of classes, meetings, conferences, seminars, and workshops will vary from building to building; they may be regularly scheduled or conducted when a specific need arises. Security training can be incorporated effectively into occupants' fire life safety training classes. More will be said about the training of occupants, floor wardens, and building emergency staff in Chapter 11, *Building Emergency Planning*.

The tenants themselves are an important part of any building security program. They must be educated to know that they are the "eyes" and "ears" of the building. If they see anyone who does not appear to belong, particularly someone within their own tenant space, a "May I help you?"–type of approach will reveal much about the person. Specific questions can determine if the person is an employee, or a visitor (if so, who are they visiting?), or is delivering or picking up items (if so, where? at whose request?), and so on. Although the tenants are not expected to be trained security professionals, they are expected to be active participants in the building security program by being aware of their surroundings and promptly reporting potential security problems to tenant management, building management, and building security staff.

Summary

From the time a vehicle enters the parking structure and pedestrians proceed to the building, travel in the tower elevators, and enter an individual tenant space, there is a need for access control measures that sift out unwanted persons and intruders and yet constitute a minimum of inconvenience to legitimate building users. In multiple-tenant commercial office buildings, the three lines of defense—the main lobby, the elevators and lobbies on each floor, and the entrances to tenant space—provide points at which access control can be effected. The degree of control is impacted by the time and day (since during normal business hours, access control is usually more relaxed), the type of tenant and their business activities, the configuration of lobbies and tenant areas, and the individual policies of the building owner and manager.

An essential part of the building security program is to provide strict control of all keys used at the facility. Also, personal and business property, which is moved in and out of commercial office buildings and tenant areas on a daily basis, must be controlled. To establish a successful property removal control system, there must be supervised egress points through which all property and trash must pass. As just mentioned, tenants are a vital part of security and must be educated in security awareness.

References

American Protective Services, *Commercial Building Security: The Notebook Lesson Series for Security Officers* (American Protective Services, Inc., Oakland, CA, 1980).

American Protective Services, "Objectives of a security program," *High-Rise Training Course* (American Protective Services, Inc., Oakland, CA, 1990).

American Protective Services, *Administrative News* (American Protective Services, Inc., Oakland, CA, 1993).

Finneran, Eugene D., *Security Supervision: A Handbook for Supervisors and Managers* (Butterworths, Stoneham, MA, 1981), as reported in *Handbook of Loss Prevention and Crime Prevention* by Lawrence S. Fennelly (Butterworth–Heinemann, Stoneham, MA, 1989, pp. 254, 255).

Geiger, Geoff, and Geoff Craighead, "Minding the store: Office security is big business," *Los Angeles Business Journal* (Los Angeles, July 1991).

Appendix 7-1   Sample Tenant Security and Safety Awareness Checklist

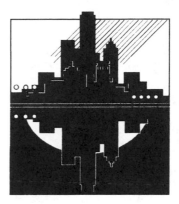

TENANT SECURITY AND SAFETY AWARENESS

The following security and safety tips may assist you and us during the upcoming holiday season.

Safety in the Parking Structure

- On leaving your vehicle, always lock its doors. If you possess a parking access card, do not leave it in your vehicle when you go to your office.

- Secure any belongings in the trunk or out of sight. Do not leave any valuables or possessions in plain view.

- Be alert to your surroundings and any people around you. Avoid using stairwells, alley ways, and areas that are out of the way or isolated.

- If you observe any suspicious activity, immediately report it to building security by using a parking intercom or dialing 555-8395.

- When approaching your vehicle, be aware of your surroundings and any people around you. Have the keys ready in your hand and, on reaching your vehicle, check the back seat before entering. Once you enter, immediately lock your doors.

- Observe speed limits and drive safely at all times.

Safety in the Building and Your Office

- Do not assist outsiders or strangers to enter the building or your tenant office.

- Challenge any strangers with a simple "May I help you?" Call building security, by telephoning 555-8395, if any unauthorized persons are detected in your office.

- Notify building security if any solicitors visit your office.

- Physically secure desktop PCs, laptop and notebook computers, and floppy disks, or other valuable equipment, or lock these items up when not in use.

- Record serial numbers and engrave identifying marks on equipment to assist in its recovery if it is "borrowed" by a fellow employee or is stolen.

- Never leave valuable items such as billfolds, purses, wallets, blank checks, petty cash, and keys unattended. If necessary, lock them in a desk drawer or cabinet.

- Keep a "clean desk" policy and secure all confidential files and information before leaving your office.

- When working alone in the office, lock all perimeter doors and activate any security systems.

- When working late, notify your supervisor or a friend or relative. When you are ready to leave, notify building security and request an escort.

- If you are in an elevator with a suspicious person, stand near the elevator control panel. If emergency assistance is required, press the EMERGENCY CALL, EMERGENCY ALARM, or EMERGENCY ONLY button.

- Use Building Property Removal Passes when removing equipment from the building.

Christmas Tree Safety

- All "live" cut trees must be fireproofed. The signed fireproof certification tag must be given to building management before any tree can be brought into your office.

- Lights may not be placed on "live" cut trees.

- Artificial trees may have lights but these must be turned off during non-business hours.

**The Building Management of Pacific Tower Plaza
Wishes You a Happy and Safe Holiday Season!**

8 *Management of the Security Function*

The security function encompasses the security-related activities and duties performed in a facility. Within a high-rise commercial office building these activities and responsibilities usually are performed by a security department acting on behalf of the building owner or manager. The size and makeup of the security department varies depending on the complexity of the facility and requirements of its security and fire life safety program. The head of the department may have one of various titles—*Director of Security, Security Director, Security Manager, Security Supervisor, Head of Security*, or, in a smaller building, *Post Commander*. For our purposes, this person will be called the Director of Security. Whether the security department is made up of contract or proprietary staff, the Director of Security has a key role in determining the quality and performance of the department. According to Keating (1994, p. 9), the Director of Security

> must have security experience, leadership ability, be an excellent communicator both verbally and in writing, be organized and a strong time manager, enjoy and interface well with all kinds of people, be intelligent and able to understand and teach complex systems, be patient, upbeat, positive, outgoing, self-disciplined, caring, energetic . . .

The remainder of the security department consists of supervisors and staff with job titles determined by the functions they perform; for example: *Lobby Director, Lobby Ambassador, Lobby Officer, Console Operator, Command Center Operator, Patrol Officer, Rover, Dockmaster*, and *Security Officer*. Just as the term *night watchman* was replaced years ago by security guard, *security guard* now has been largely replaced by *security officer* in most areas of the United States.

The Security Budget

In today's business world, the costs of security in a high-rise building need to be justified to the building owner and manager before the security department will be adequately funded. *Webster's College Dictionary* defines *budget* as "an estimate, often itemized, of expected income and expenses for a given period of time in the future. . . . A plan of operations based on such an estimate." When the budget is reviewed, it is often difficult to quantify the value of the services

211

that the security department provides and convince management that the security function does in fact generate income for the facility, if only indirectly. How does one, for example, place a monetary value on the security benefit CCTV cameras installed in all elevators have on building operations? Other departments, such as parking, can justify their activities based on the real income produced, measured in dollars and cents. The Director of Security needs to demonstrate that the security function's activities and duties performed within a particular period of time (usually the past twelve months) have produced value commensurate with the funds allotted to it. This will allow the budget for the ensuing fiscal period to be presented in a manner that elicits the support of management. For instance, it would be helpful to cite the expenses incurred in repairing damage caused by vandalism in the elevators for the period of time before and after CCTV installation. If the incidence of reported vandalism is lower after the installation, the monetary value of the security measure can be demonstrated for the period in question.

Not all aspects of the security function, however, can be assessed in dollars and cents. For instance, how would one evaluate in monetary terms the absence of crimes of opportunity, such as thefts by intruders in tenant areas, which may result from an effective security education program the building security department provides for tenants?

For building owners and managers, a key budget issue is whether costs are escalatable or not. The term *escalatable* refers to costs the building itself incurs that may then be charged proportionately to tenants based on lease provisions. For example, costs associated with the building parking operation may be *nonescalatable* if parking operations are considered to be a separate profit center; whereas, costs associated with the security operation are escalatable because they are typically part of the building's routine operating expenses.

A security budget may include as line items the estimated cost of the following:

- The itemized capital cost of security systems, equipment, and fixtures (e.g., physical barriers, lighting, locks and locking systems, communication systems, CCTV systems, intrusion alarm systems, equipment used by security staff), including installation and maintenance costs. Security budgets also may include costs pertaining to fire life safety systems, equipment, and fixtures, if these costs are not part of a separate safety budget.
- Insurance charges for systems and equipment (adding systems and equipment may reduce insurance premiums for other areas of coverage such as theft, liability, and fire)
- Legal, professional, and consulting charges
- Permits and licenses
- Security staff, including (1) wages and benefits, payroll taxes, worker's compensation claims and insurance, costs of uniforms, hiring, training, supervision, administration, liability claims and insurance; (2) sundry items such as office and stationary supplies, secretarial help, and so on; (3) utilities such as lighting, electricity, and telephones; (4) maintenance of equipment used by security staff (If contract staff are employed, the preceding costs may be either itemized or summarized.)

Depending on the building owner or manager, certain of these line items may be amortized over a period of time, equipment may be leased, or other arrangements made to suit the building operation. It must be kept in mind that "one does not plan or budget for the unknown or the unpredictable; one budgets for intelligently anticipated and predictable conditions" (Sennewald 1985, pp. 163, 164). Natural disasters and other catastrophic events are not predictable; budgeting, therefore, usually will not take them into consideration. However, some buildings provide various supplies and equipment in case of a major emergency. Of these items, food, water, and some medical supplies have a predetermined shelf life, and their replacement costs should be included in annual budgets.

Contract versus Proprietary Security Staff

Security staff that make up a security department in a high-rise building can be either employed directly by the building owner or manager (i.e., proprietary or in-house), or employed by a contract security company. In the United States today, most high-rise commercial office buildings employ contract security personnel. The Hallcrest Report on Private Security and Police in America states that contract guards now represent 61% of all employed guards in the United States (up from 55% in 1978) (Cunningham and Taylor 1985, p. 114). Building managers usually do not have large human resource departments to handle the many facets of recruiting, hiring, and training security staff to work in their buildings.

The use of proprietary security staff has certain advantages to building owners and managers; the use of contract security staff has others:

Advantages of Using Proprietary Security Staff
- Staff are recruited, screened, and selected using procedures and methods stipulated and controlled by the client.
- Staff can share the same benefit programs as other building employees.
- Staff are under the direct "employer–employee" control of the building owner, or manager.
- Staff, as employees of the building, usually have an undivided loyalty to the building.
- Building management does not need to communicate with a contractor to supply their security staffing needs and provide direction to their security staff.

Advantages of Using Contract Security Staff
- Staff employed at the building are recruited, screened, selected, uniformed, equipped, trained, supervised, insured, and paid by the contractor; building management does not need to be involved in the process.
- Because security staff are employees of the contractor, considerable liability burdens and responsibilities reside with the contractor, not the building owner or manager.
- A contractor, particularly a large one, has access to a large labor pool of employees and can provide additional personnel and supervision during emergencies and special events.
- Building management can request, under the terms of the contract, that unsuitable staff working at the building be removed quickly.
- Replacements for employees who are away from work because of sickness, holidays, vacations, and so on are the responsibility of the contractor.

- The security department can be downsized and employees reassigned by the contractor rather than being terminated.
- The contractor will supply forms, records, reports, office supplies, and auxiliary equipment (e.g., flashlights) required to carry out the security operation.
- The security contractor, if properly selected, will have staff within their company to provide professional expertise to building management. A professional security contractor can conduct surveys, formulate and document policies and procedures for the security staff, conduct investigations, provide advice and knowledge regarding developments in the security and safety field, and assist building management in developing relationships with local law enforcement and the fire department.

Selection of a Contract Security Service

Building owners or managers who decide to employ a contract service to staff their security department and operate their security program must take special care to select a *professional* contractor. A professional security contractor does business based on the highest ethical and industry standards, providing properly selected, screened, trained, and supervised staff. The building owner or manager also must ensure that fundamental provisions of the security services agreement between their facility and the contractor constitute an attainable goal—that the contractor reasonably can be expected to provide the requested quality of service. Good wages and benefits for staff, adequate working conditions and amenities, and a reasonable profit margin for the contractor providing the services are prerequisites for a successful security program. In addition to these factors, the client–contractor relationship must be clearly delineated and an essential element of trust established. One does not have to go far to ascertain the root cause of high turnover of unsuitable, poorly trained, poorly supervised, poorly motivated, and unkempt security personnel—a predicament that, if it persists, will have devastating effects on any building security program. If this happens, the chances are that a professional contractor has not been selected, or that the provisions of the security service agreement are not adequate for quality service.

According to Allied Security (1983, p. 2), "the traditional contracting process for security guards involves few, if any, performance specifications. The user relies on the assumption that he [or she] is requesting and receiving proposals on a service with generally accepted performance standards." Such assumptions, however, can be problematic, for performance varies dramatically from one contractor to another. The following issues, therefore, need to be addressed:

- The state and local business licenses of the contractor should be examined.
- The history, ownership, and financial stability of the contractor should be reviewed.
- The liability insurance coverage to be provided by the contractor should be specified and proof of such insurance furnished.
- The requirements for each position that needs a contract security staff member (including a job description of the basic work to be performed, specific qualifica-

tions, and the expected hours of coverage) should be outlined in the proposal specifications.
- The wages and (especially) the benefits of the security staff need to be specified. These factors will not only impact the quality of service to be provided but will also permit the building owner and manager to make an "apples to apples" comparison. It should not be enough for a contractor to say, "Yes, we provide vacations, holidays, and health insurance benefits to our security officers"; further information should be ascertained: How many days of vacation? What holidays are recognized? What is the name of the health plan? What benefits does the health plan provide? Does the employee contribute to its premiums? How much? What is the qualifying period before the plan is in effect? What is the deductible? What is the maximum allowable claim?
- A contractor's management approach and depth of organizational staffing also need to be examined. Who are the managers and supervisors? How will they interface with the client and the site operation? What are their security qualifications, background, and experience both within the security industry and with the present contractor? How would they handle the start-up and transition of contract security staff at the client site? Are they able to conduct security surveys? How do they formulate and document policies and procedures for security staff working at client sites? How do they conduct training at client sites? How will they audit and evaluate performance at the job site? How are incidents reported and tracked? How do they conduct investigations? How do they relate to local law enforcement?

  To evaluate operational capabilities, it is best to visit the contractor's office and meet with the administrative staff who would support the security staff if the contractor were chosen. A guided tour of the operation should be included, with a demonstration of essential tasks such as recruiting, screening, selecting, uniforming, cleaning of uniforms, issuing equipment, training, scheduling, supervising, administering the payroll, and billing. One should also request sample personnel files to see whether the contractor has kept employment applications and records and has both conducted and documented background checks. If time permits, one should attend a training session to examine the quality of training and materials provided.
- To determine whether the contractor has the necessary proven expertise, examine references of comparable clients to which the contractor is currently providing service. Such references should reveal whether the contractor has fulfilled the security services agreement and performed at the level of service originally agreed on, and also show the contractor's responsiveness to problem solving and other requests. One might then visit and inspect other client sites where the contractor provides a similar type of service and wages and benefits of a similar standard to those being requested.

Contractors usually base their charges on an hourly billing rate for security staff working on a client site, commonly using the terms spread and spreadsheet. The *spreadsheet* details each hourly pay rate and its associated billing rate (or provides a weighted average or composite billing rate for all hours worked). The difference between pay and billing rates is the *spread*. The spread may include costs of background checks; uniforms; training; estimated overtime; paid holidays; sick leave and vacation; payroll taxes; health, life, and accidental death and dismemberment insurance; miscellaneous benefits; worker's compensation and liability insurance; administrative overhead; and profit. The administrative overhead can include branch management, operations management, account management, human resources, scheduling, field supervision, legal expenses, training and communications, information systems, risk management, accounting (payroll, billing, accounts payable, and general ledger), credit and collections, purchasing, sales and marketing, quality assurance, and executive costs. The costs of purchasing and maintaining equipment—vehicles, portable radios, and patrol management systems—usually are itemized separately.

Only after an exhaustive investigative proposal process can a client make a thoroughly informed and sound selection of a contract security provider. Once this is accomplished, a security services agreement outlining the general and specific terms of the contract, including terms of payment, should be fully executed, with client and contractor agreeing on its contents. If the selection process is pursued thoroughly, the client will not only be completely familiar with the selected company's policies, procedures, and operations, but also will have established a working relationship with key members of the contractor's management team.

Determining Adequate Levels of Security Staffing

The level of security staffing needed to provide an adequate security and fire life safety program for any facility requires a two-step analysis, according to Colling (1982, p. 85): "It is necessary first to determine the security [and fire life safety] vulnerabilities and services to be performed. The next step is to design a program that will properly manage these vulnerabilities and provide the intended services. Only then can the number of persons required to operate the program be determined."

In the high-rise setting, building management will first need to conduct a security and life safety survey. After that, a security and fire life safety program needs to be designed; only then can the adequate levels of staffing be determined for the building. The required levels of staffing for most high-rise commercial office buildings are higher during normal business hours, when the building is open with access to lobby entrances, passenger elevators, loading dock and parking areas, than after normal business hours, when the building is closed and access to interior areas is limited. During normal business hours most tenants are open for business and there is an increased building population of tenant employees, visitors, salespersons, tradespeople, building management staff, building contractors, couriers and messengers or companies delivering or picking up merchandise from the building, solicitors, building inspectors, and others who may require the attention of building security staff. After normal business hours, traffic usually lessens; only the number of janitorial and cleaning staff will increase.

Although levels of staffing, hours of coverage, and specific functions vary, the following supervisory and nonsupervisory positions (with actual job titles varying from building to building and region to region) often are found in larger high-rise buildings:

- *Director of Security.* He or she oversees and coordinates the activities of the security department.
- *Fire Safety Director.* This is the person who establishes, implements, and maintains the Building Emergency Plan. In some buildings the Director of Security and the Fire Safety Director are the same person.
- *Shift Supervisors.* These persons are assigned to the various shifts—usually designated as day, swing or mid, graveyard; or perhaps 1st (grave), 2nd, and 3rd. They oversee and coordinate the activities of security staff assigned to their shift. Shift supervisors report to the Director of Security.
- *Lobby Director, Lobby Ambassador, Lobby Officer.* These persons, assigned to lobby areas, control access to the building, provide information to building users and visitors, and perform other duties as specified by the facility.
- *Concierge.* A person often assigned to building lobby areas who performs a similar function to a hotel concierge, providing information and services to building tenants and visitors, and performing other duties as specified by the facility. In some buildings, for instance, the concierge prepares a regular newsletter for tenants.
- *Console Operator, Command Center Operator.* These are the persons assigned to the Security Command Center who monitor and operate building security and fire life safety systems and equipment.
- *Dockmaster.* This individual supervises the loading dock, including all loading and unloading operations.
- *Freight/Service Elevator Operator.* This person operates the freight/service elevator and screens all elevator users for authorization to travel to various floors of the building.
- *Security Officer.* This officer performs security and fire life safety functions as determined by the building operation.
- *Patrol Officer, Parking Patrol, Rover.* These persons patrol various parts of the building and parking areas and perform other duties as specified by the facility.
- *Training Officer.* Particularly in larger high-rise projects, the training officer is responsible for training and testing all building security staff regarding their security and fire life safety duties and responsibilities.

The functions required for each of these positions should be specified in a *job description.* This description also should mention the abilities and skills necessary to carry out these functions effectively. Job descriptions can be used for training, and they establish a basis for employee performance reviews and appropriate wage and salary ranges.

Security Staff Duties and Written Instructions

The primary role of security staff in a high-rise building is to help implement the security and fire life safety program. Some buildings may have a separate safety department; in others, the security department may assume safety responsibilities. Duties of the security staff vary from building to building, and depend largely on the policies and procedures determined by management.

Security staff duties should be written clearly, concisely, and accurately, and kept readily accessible for training and for reference during an emergency. These *security instructions* (commonly called *post orders*) should be periodically reviewed, regularly updated, and contain at least the following information:

- Statement of purpose and a notice of confidentiality.
- An overview of the building and a profile of the tenants doing business there.
- List of emergency telephone numbers for police and fire departments, paramedics or ambulance services, utility companies, and other agencies.
- List of after-hours telephone contact numbers for building management, engineering, security, janitorial and parking staff, elevator company representatives, security and fire alarm companies, haz-mat contractors, window board-up contractors, and so on.
- Description of the building and its operation, including up-to-date floor plans and maps, and security and fire life safety systems and equipment. This should include an overview and description of each system, an account of how the systems operate under normal and emergency conditions, and an explanation of how system components are related and connected. Photographs and diagrams will make the descriptions much more effective.
- Review of subjects such as building access control, handling trespassers, tenant access, handling service of process (writs, complaints, summonses, etc.), key and equipment control, property removal, escorts of building users, patrolling, arrests, and other policies and procedures.
- Specific instructions on handling emergency situations such as fires, fire alarms, explosions, bombs, bomb threats, violence in the workplace (including assaults or other criminally-threatening behavior), aberrant behavior (such as that caused by substance abuse), medical emergencies, power failure, elevator stoppages, natural disasters, water leaks, chemical/hazardous material incidents, strike and labor disturbances, demonstrations, riots and civil disorders, aircraft collisions, hostage taking and barricade situations, and assaults or other criminal activities.
- List of security staffing levels, their hours of coverage, and their specific functions and job duties. Wherever possible the duties should be described by shift, day of the week, and specific time.
- Instructions on public relations, including how to handle hostile situations, telephone and radio communications techniques, and how to conduct interviews and write reports. (These subjects either may be included in the instructions or may be communicated to security staff through other means.)
- A Code of Ethics and official Standards of Conduct. These should be established to help foster a strong ethical climate throughout the security organization and to provide clear and specific guidance to employees. Adherence to professional ethics is critical in any organization, but particularly so in one entrusted with the security of a high-rise building. *Webster's College Dictionary* defines *ethics* as "a system or set of moral principles . . . the rules of conduct recognized in respect to a particular class of human actions or governing a particular group." According to Ferrell and Gardiner (1991, p. 2), an ethical act or decision is "something judged as proper or acceptable based on some standard of right or wrong. Although people often have different morals and standards of right and wrong, many are shared by most members of our society." The shared mores or customs of "Western society" are largely those fundamental Judeo-Christian principles that are the foundation of its culture.

  Professional ethics are very much a matter of *conscience*, which is defined by *Webster's College Dictionary* as "the inner sense of what is right or wrong in one's conduct or motives." Because ethics require this inner sense, there is no guarantee that the existence of a Code of Ethics will prevent undesirable actions by a security employee. However, such a code does clarify to security staff what is expected of them. Appendix 8-1 reproduces the *Security Officer Code of Ethics* established by the National Association of Security Companies (NASCO).

- Standards of Conduct specify actions that may be subject to disciplinary action: unexcused absences or excessive tardiness, unacceptable appearance or attire, use of profane language, making racial or ethnic slurs, engaging in sexual or other forms of harassment, disorderly conduct, sleeping or dozing on the job, being insubordinate, unauthorized disclosure of confidential information, making false statements, unauthorized use of company property, unauthorized acceptance of gifts, failure to observe security and safety rules and regulations, and so on.
- A signature and acknowledgment page for individuals to acknowledge in writing that they have read the instructions and any specific additions or deletions.

These instructions may be housed in one binder (preferably a ringed one that permits easy removal and replacement of pages), or in separate binders or folders. The binders or folders should be clearly labeled for easy reference. All copies should include the date the instructions were established or last revised, by whose authority the instructions were made, and which individuals have the authority to change or modify them. Changes and modifications made to operating procedures should be dated and incorporated into all existing copies of written instructions as soon as possible. Outdated instructions should be retained by the security department for a period varying from five to seven years (as determined by the building's document retention policy or legal advisor), because they may be needed later as evidence for legal action.

Instructions for complex procedures and systems must be written in easy-to-understand, action-oriented terms, keeping in mind that, according to Bennet H. Berman (1980) of the University of Michigan Institute for the Study of Mental Retardation and Related Disabilities,

> One of every four Americans in the work force is functionally illiterate, that is, unable to comprehend at least 50% of reading material beyond the fourth grade level.
>
> A significant number of work errors result not from an inability to do the job, but from a misunderstanding of what the job is. Many employees can't read the memos from the boss, the company's rule book, the training manual, or other written instructions.
>
> And the problem is not limited to school dropouts. A federal survey in the middle 1960s showed that 55% of the country's high school seniors could not understand stories in *Reader's Digest*, 75% could not comprehend *Time* magazine, and 96% could not read *Saturday Review*.
>
> However, 90% of all meaning can be conveyed with a vocabulary of 600 words. For maximum readability, company manuals should follow this average guideline per 100 words: 7 to 9 sentences, 12 to 14 words per sentence, and 140 to 160 syllables.

Those who write these instructions should avoid cumbersome writing and overuse of the passive voice. For example, "Building console operators while away from the Security Command Center are required to maintain a two-way radio on their persons at all times" can be understood more easily if written, "When away from the Security Command Center, always carry a two-way radio with you."

Like any extensive document, the instructions should have a clearly labeled table of contents and numbered pages and, for ease of reference, each subject should be separately tabbed and there should be an index. Photographs, diagrams, checklists, summary sheets, and flow charts should be included to make the material more interesting and easier to comprehend.

Written Records and Reports

Security staff in a high-rise building must make observations and provide thorough and accurate recording and reporting of security and safety operations, activities, and incidents. Observation may involve any or all of the senses—sight, hearing, smell, touch, or (possibly) taste—and requires the capacity to understand the meaning of what has been observed. "In security work it is important to determine whether what has been observed is significant for security or safety and is routine or unusual" (American Protective Services 1990, p. 33). After observation and appropriate action, security personnel must furnish an accurate record and report of important observations.

Forms, records, and reports used by security staff may vary from building to building, but all aim to provide a thorough, accurate, and permanent account of events that have occurred. Such documentation can be used to generate statistical data that may be useful to justify existing or future expenditures for security and fire life safety systems and equipment. Some common forms, records, and reports found in high-rise facilities are as follows:

- *Daily or Shift Activity Report*—includes date and time of duty; name, badge or employee number (if appropriate), and signature of the reporting officer; position or post to which the officer is assigned; equipment the officer has received (including keys, patrol monitoring devices, radio, pager, etc.); and a chronological narrative of events and incidents that have occurred while the officer was on duty. They generally do not contain detailed descriptions of unusual events and incidents such as crimes and accidents. The report should be in duplicate so that an original is available to building management, with a copy retained by the security department.
- *Incident Report*—elaborates on unusual events and incidents in the Daily or Shift Activity Report and may include name, badge number (if appropriate), and signature of the reporting officer; the incident's date, time, type, and location; a full description of the incident; names and contact details of any victims, suspects, and witnesses; action taken (including who was notified of the situation); and follow-up action that may be required. Any photographs, sketches, or exhibits should be noted on the report and clearly labeled. The report should be in duplicate or triplicate, so that the original can be supplied to building management, and the security department can keep at least one copy.
- *Safety Hazard Report*—similar to the Incident Report but reports a hazard rather than an incident.
- *Vehicle Accident Report*—includes name, badge or employee number (if appropriate), and signature of the reporting officer; date, time, and precise location of the accident; description of the accident (including a sketch of the accident scene) and property damage; posted speed limits, stop signs, traffic lights and signals; license number of vehicle(s); estimated speed of vehicle(s); weather and light conditions; indication of whether seat belts were in use; any evidence of substance abuse; name, driver's license number, and contact details of driver(s); details of insurance companies of driver(s); name(s) and contact details of injured person(s) and wit-

nesses; the action taken (including who was notified of the situation and whether a traffic citation was issued); and follow-up action that may be required. Any photographs, sketches, or exhibits should be noted on the report and clearly labeled. The report should be in duplicate or triplicate, as in the case of an Incident Report.

- *Tenant and Visitor Log*—includes the names (printed for legibility) and signatures of persons entering or leaving the building, the names of the companies they represent or tenants they are visiting, the dates, and times in and out.
- *Courtesy Notices*—vary in format depending on designated purpose. The security or parking department may use special parking courtesy notices to inform a driver that his or her vehicle was found parked (1) illegally (with a reminder to park in designated areas only); (2) incorrectly (with a reminder to park correctly in a designated parking stall); (3) in a space reserved for the physically disabled; (4) with the vehicle unlocked, with windows open, or with personal property in view; or (5) some other vehicle-related matter that needs to be brought to the driver's attention. These notices should be designed so that an original can be left on the vehicle windscreen and a duplicate copy retained by the issuing department.
- *Tenant Security Notice*—used by security staff to notify a tenant, for example, that a door to their area was found unsecured and subsequently locked by security at a specific time. The notice could be designed to hang on a door and a copy or stub of the original should be retained by the security department. The building security department also should notify the designated tenant contact person of the security violation on the next business day.

There also may be contractor sign-in logs; personnel escort logs; elevator malfunction reports; security and fire life safety systems and equipment checklists; fire alarm report logs; stairwell inspection reports; lost and found property reports; and various other forms, records, and reports designed for use in the building. The individual needs of the security and safety program will determine their content and usage.

Security staff often will use notebooks to record details that, at a later stage, may be used as legal evidence. These books should be small enough to fit snugly in a pocket, equipped with hard covers to protect the pages, bound, and sequentially numbered to make the removal of any pages immediately evident. The pages should be lined and entries written legibly and in chronological order as soon as possible after an observation is made. Any changes to entries should be lined out and initialed, rather than erased or obliterated. Entries should address the six essential components of any successful report—who, what, when, where, why, and how; the *Protection Officer Training Manual* (Fawcett 1992, pp. 42, 43) outlines them as follows:

- *Who*—relates to who was involved in the event, the name of the complainant, client, witnesses, suspects, accused parties, or officers.
- *What*—relates to the type of incident or event, what actually occurred.
- *When*—this is the time and date that the incident occurred.
- *Where*—this is the location that the event took place, with subsequent locations depending on the type of incident.
- *Why*—this is the motive. It can frequently be determined by proper investigation. It may explain the reason for the occurrence, but cannot be officer speculation or unfounded opinion.
- *How*—how did the event come to your attention; how did it occur? This means the complete details on how the event happened from start to finish.

All six of these will be present in even the simplest event. Not recording some details because they seem unimportant at the time results in lost information that eventually may prove valuable; it also may lead to an embarrassed security staff member having to explain a sloppy report to an irate building manager or security supervisor, or investigator.

Legible, thorough, accurate, clear, concise, and prompt documentation of incidents has been of inestimable value to many building owners and managers, particularly when litigation occurs. Incidents, such as slips and falls, do occur in high-rise buildings, and much of the potential for liability can be mitigated substantially by handling, recording, and reporting these incidents in a thoroughly professional and competent manner. "For clarity's sake the author should write reports in the first person. The narrative should never make judgments regarding responsibility or blame for any loss or injury and should not refer to prior similar events (Bates 1995, p. 79). Reports of security staff should be reviewed by supervisors and "any spelling or structural errors should be noted, and the report rewritten by the original author. Substantive changes—normally made by the author—should only be made after discussion [by a supervisor] with the author. Otherwise, an opposing party in litigation might infer that an effort was made to hide something" (Bates 1995, p. 79).

The retention period for reports will depend on the type of report, the requirements of state law, and the building's policy. This period may vary from a few months for daily activity reports, to three to seven years for incident reports. It should be considered that "reports help identify future security needs and that a claim of inadequate security can be brought anytime during a state's statute of limitations for negligence (two or three years from the date of injury in most jurisdictions). With that in mind, reports should be kept at least until the local statute of limitations expires" (Bates 1995, p. 80).

In the past, all records and reports were recorded on paper. Today, because of technological developments, information can be managed using computer programs. The PPM 2000 Security Management Software InCase System, for instance, allows a personal computer to sort data contained in incident reports by time of day, day of week, month, year, type of incident, suspect, or any other user-defined field in the reports. This allows an incident reporting system to be tailor-made for a facility and the analyses it conducts. Trends in certain types of incidents can be discovered, weaknesses revealed, and loss prevention strategies devised. "Computers allow a security department to work smarter since vast amounts of information can be stored in a small space and retrieved at any time. Operations reports no longer have to be done manually. Budget figures can be obtained and expenses monitored at will" (Denekamp 1989, p. 43).

Selection, Training, Testing, and Supervision of Security Staff

Individuals employed as security staff at a high-rise facility must be properly selected, trained, tested, and supervised. All these processes must be thorough and well documented, especially in today's litigious society.

Selection

Selecting the right person to work in the high-rise environment begins at recruitment. A comprehensive employment application should be filled out by the applicant and a thorough background check conducted. A good background check should include the following: proof of identity and right to work; aliases; current address and previous addresses for the past ten years; educational background; current and past employers and supervisors (for the last five years), with explanations of any breaks in employment greater than 30 days; details of any military service, criminal convictions, and records check; surety that the applicant can comply with all applicable state and local security personnel registration and licensing laws; a check of financial responsibility, character references, and interviews conducted by trained staff; drug screening; integrity testing; and if driving is a job requirement, proof of a valid driver's license and a driver's record check.

Honesty, trustworthiness, and loyalty are important character traits to look for in a candidate. Because certain security positions require specific physical prowess or mental ability, an applicant should be evaluated for meeting essential performance standards. According to Geiger and Craighead (1991, p. 11B),

> Today's security officer must successfully operate equipment that is at times highly technical, particularly that installed in high-rise towers. He or she must operate hand-held radios and monitor CCTV systems, elevator recall panels, fire annunciator panels, and card access and intrusion alarm systems. Most importantly, from the perspective of fire and life safety, the modern security officer must respond during building emergencies such as fire, earthquakes, bomb threats, medical emergencies, and power failures.

Individuals monitoring security and fire life safety systems and equipment in the Security Command Center require a certain level of intelligence to handle these complex tasks. The Americans with Disabilities Act prohibits employers from discriminating against qualified individuals with disabilities; however, if an applicant cannot perform an "essential job function" (in this case, carrying out complex monitoring duties) because of a physical or mental disability for which the employer cannot make a "reasonable accommodation," such an applicant can be rejected. Applicants also should be tested to determine if they are able to read, write, understand, and speak English effectively. Security staff often are required to understand complex verbal and written instructions and to write detailed reports. They must be able to maintain language comprehension and fluency not only during the performance of regular duties but also under the emotional duress of emergency or crisis situations.

Applicants should be evaluated for standards of personal appearance and hygiene, and they must possess public relations skills sufficient to allow them to interact in a positive manner with fellow security staff, building management, tenants and visitors, law enforcement and fire department personnel, the media, and the general public.

Training and Testing

Once appropriate individuals have been selected, they must receive sufficient training to perform all duties required of their positions. *Training* is defined as "the formal procedure which a company utilizes to facilitate learning so that the resultant behavior contributes to the attainment of the company's goals" (Yoder and Heneman 1979, p. 33-1). In our case, the company is the security department, and the company's goal is to administer the building's security and fire life safety program effectively. A high-rise building training program can be separated into three distinct areas:

1. *New Employee Orientation.* This basic training should be at least eight hours long and introduce basic security concepts as they relate to high-rise building security and fire life safety programs. Areas to include are:
   - What is security and fire life safety?
   - Building and assets protection
   - Security systems and equipment
   - Security rules and procedures
   - Patrol techniques
   - Fire life safety systems and equipment
   - Fire prevention
   - Standards of Conduct and Code of Ethics
   - Security and the law (including private security powers)
   - Role of law enforcement versus private security
   - Role of public relations
   - Effective communications
   - Interview techniques
   - Observation techniques and report writing
   - Uniform policies and grooming standards

   The training includes written materials, audiovisual aids, and classroom instruction from competent personnel. Testing should be used to motivate trainees to assimilate the course material and to evaluate the trainee's performance.

2. *On-the-Job Training.* This basic orientation training, referred to as OJT, will vary from 8 to 40 hours in length depending on the complexity of the building and the position for which the person is being trained. The training should orient the person to the building and its security and fire life safety program, equip the trainee with the necessary skills and job knowledge to carry out the responsibilities of the designated position, and help build confidence through hands-on experience. Activities to include are:
   - A tour of the building exterior, selected tenant floors, passenger and freight/service elevators, stairwells, parking areas, loading dock areas, roof areas, and maintenance spaces (including mechanical areas and elevator machine rooms)
   - Inspection of building fire life safety systems and equipment, including the types of devices found on tenant floors
   - Inspection of building security systems and equipment
   - Review of building security rules and procedures
   - Review of building occupant fire life safety instruction
   - Review of security instructions or post orders, including the complete job description for the trainee's position, and emergency response procedures
   - Explanation of the chain of command within building management and the security department
   - Orientation to the designated position
   - Any specialized training such as First Aid and CPR; this may be administered during the training session, or within an agreed-on time period following assignment

There are several problems associated with OJT. Its quality will depend largely on the competency of the trainer; if this person has performance deficiencies, they will be passed on to the trainee. What is learned will depend on what events occur during the training (some areas may be missed simply because on that particular day some routine events did not occur), and the training itself may interfere with the job that is being demonstrated. Testing and checklists should be used in OJT to evaluate comprehension and performance and help ensure that the trainee has acquired the necessary skills to assume the responsibilities of the position. These tests and lists should be developed by the security department itself— or, if the security staff is provided by a contractor, by representatives of the contractor's staff that support the account. The extent and complexity of these tests and checklists depend on the size, intricacy, and requirements of the security operation. Appendix 8-2 shows a sample Security Officer Training Test.

3. *Ongoing* or *In-Service Training.* After employees have been assigned to work, follow-up checks must be made on their performance. Employees should be kept constantly informed of changes in the security program and the security industry as a whole, and should receive ongoing instruction and testing in key areas. Nowhere is this better demonstrated than with security staff who handle building emergencies such as fires and fire alarms. Such events usually do not occur on a daily basis in high-rise commercial office buildings (if they do, an investigation should be conducted to determine the reason), but security staff should always be in a state of readiness to handle them correctly. This is only possible if staff periodically rehearses procedures that need to be carried out. Hands-on practice, drills, and written testing assist in this process.

Ongoing training can be facilitated by regular handouts of written policies and procedures, pamphlets, newsletters, films, videos, computer disks, meetings, briefings, conferences, panels, seminars, and workshops. Also, staff may be given a set period of time, usually on the job, to study self-instructional material and then satisfactorily pass a written test. Quality assurance checks by security supervisors likewise are essential to training. If certain procedures are not being performed correctly or with confidence, the supervisor can provide retraining in the areas of concern. Inconsistencies or perceived problems in security sometimes can be a prompt for ongoing training. For example, if tenants complain to building management that, after normal business hours, they sometimes are challenged to produce passes to remove property from the building, and sometimes are not, all security staff must be made more fully aware of the building property removal control policy and the applicable procedures.

The training program for each person should be thoroughly documented. Training files should be established for every member of the building security department. A *Security Officer Training and Testing Log* (see Appendix 8-3) can be used to summarize each individual's training and testing.

Supervision

If an individual is selected or promoted to a supervisory position, special comprehensive training should be provided to equip him or her with supervisory skills. *Webster's College Dictionary* defines supervise as: "to watch over and direct (a process, work, workers)." A *supervisor* is a person who watches over staff or the labor performed by others. In high-rise security, supervisors guide and direct their staff as they perform assigned responsibilities determined by the building's security and fire life safety program. Let us examine this further.

There are various ways to watch over staff employed in a high-rise facility. Managers and supervisors can visit each position or post staffed by security personnel to observe and evaluate individuals. Visits may include watching the officers carry out the duties and responsibilities of their positions, asking them to demonstrate the operation of equipment, reviewing their written reports, and posing hypothetical situations to evaluate officers' responses.

Patrol Monitoring Devices

In high-rise facilities, building security staff activities, such as roving patrols or rounds, can be supervised using portable patrol monitoring devices. These devices may consist of mechanical clocks fitted with a graduated paper roll or disk, or electronic guard tour systems. Both systems generate a record of patrol activity and can be used to evaluate and control the performance of the patrolling officer. "They provide the security manager with a consistent record of rounds and occurrences at a facility without the need for human supervision to ensure that rounds are completed as assigned" (Roughton 1989, p. 52). A description of these two patrol management devices follows.

Patrol officers may carry the *mechanical clock* (commonly called a *watchman's clock* or *watchclock*; see Figure 8.1) around on the patrol. At certain locations, preinstalled keys are inserted into an opening in the clock. This causes the date, time, and key number to be imprinted on the paper; with some clocks, the key number or location is imprinted adjacent to a correct preprinted time. The supervisor carries a master clock key that enables him or her to review records of tours, wind the clock or add batteries, reset the date and time, and replace the paper roll or disk (some clocks require this every 24 hours; others, every week).

Unfortunately, unscrupulous security staff working alone in an area can remove keys from designated stations at the beginning of their shift, take them (lined up in their original order) to a central location, and then turn them in the clock at the required times (for instance, every hour), thereby simulating the tour. The keys subsequently can be returned to their original locations at the end of the shift. Supervisors can defeat this scam by visiting a patrol officer at unannounced times during a shift and inspecting key stations, or by securing the keys to their stations using screw flanges and requisite screw head "seals" to prevent tampering. Patrol personnel must never be issued the master key to the clock. As an added precaution, the tape or disk is marked each time the clock is opened so supervisors can inspect for nonauthorized access.

The mechanical clock can sometimes be cumbersome to carry and made inoperable by being dropped or impacted with a heavy object. Since the 1980s, it has met with stiff competition from various electronic guard tour systems.

The *electronic guard tour system* (see Figure 8.2) functions either alone or with software packages. It includes a *reader* that may be of various shapes and sizes, consisting of either a contact wand or a noncontact laser scanner. The reader or data acquisition unit is carried around the patrol area by the officer and at certain locations preinstalled data strips are "read" by the reader, record-

Figure 8.1
A watchclock.
Courtesy of Detex Corpo-
ration, New Braunfels, TX.

ing information such as date, time, station number, and location. The data strips consist of barcodes, magnet strips, chips, or other such devices. Data can be transferred from the reader to a computer or printer by placing the reader in a cradle or data transfer unit, or by connecting the reader directly to a printer.

Some advantages of electronic guard tour systems over mechanical clocks are:

- Readers are smaller and lighter than traditional mechanical clocks.
- The data strips are small, unobtrusive, easy to install, and can be colored to match their surroundings.
- The printout of information is easier to read than that generated by traditional mechanical clocks. Some systems have the additional advantage of being able to print the data out in various ways, showing the name of the patrolling officer, the length of the tour, tour stations completed, and exceptions to the tour (including stations missed or duplicated). Data also can be saved to a computer file for later reference.
- Most systems are virtually tamper proof.

"Guard tour management systems not only provide the security officer with a sense of added responsibility and feeling of selfworth, but generate accurate reports that verify the effectiveness of each tour or patrol" (Minion 1992, p. 10).

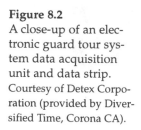

Figure 8.2
A close-up of an electronic guard tour system data acquisition unit and data strip.
Courtesy of Detex Corporation (provided by Diversified Time, Corona CA).

Patrol monitoring devices frequently are deployed in building towers, zigzagging from floor to floor at stairwells; mechanical equipment rooms, and other areas that may contain sensitive equipment that needs to be regularly monitored; exterior areas such as parks and gardens, and parking areas. These systems not only provide a documented means to monitor the patrol activity of security staff, but also can provide valuable evidence to explain why a given incident was slow to be observed (if the officer is documented to have been at another location), and can fix the approximate time of an occurrence.

In addition to the two systems just described, building card access systems can help monitor the patrol activities of security staff. Patrol officers are each issued an access control card that is used exclusively while on their rounds. The records obtained from the card access system can then be used to monitor the patrol.

Patrols in High-Rise Buildings

Patrols may be conducted in high-rise buildings for a variety of security and fire life safety purposes, but all attempt to note and quickly address anything significant or unusual affecting security or safety. The frequency and route of these patrols can be predetermined by building management and the security department and then documented. Some municipalities require *Fire Guards*, as they are commonly known. Starting from within a maximum of one-half hour from the time that operations in a facility normally cease, these persons must perform *hourly* rounds unless the authority having jurisdiction allows the rounds to be conducted at less frequent intervals. NFPA 601 *Guard Service in Fire Loss Prevention* outlines such guard service functions and duties.

A *fire watch* may be required when a building or premises presents a hazard to life or property as the result of a fire or other emergency, or when it is determined that any fire protection equipment or system is inoperable, defective, or has been taken out of service. In this case, patrols at appropriate intervals are conducted with the purpose of detecting fires and transmitting an immediate alarm to the building occupants and the fire department.

Unless otherwise specified by the authority having jurisdiction, periodic patrols in high-rise commercial office buildings may occur as follows:

- For approximately the first hour after opening the building on a regular business day, when there are not many occupants in the building tower, patrols may provide security presence throughout common areas and tenant floors.
- After the building is closed at the end of the business day, patrols may be conducted on tenant floors to check for suspicious persons and doors left unlocked.
- For all hours when the building is normally closed, periodic patrols may be conducted throughout all common and maintenance areas, including stairwells, to monitor certain equipment and to detect and report obstructions, fire hazards, water and/or gas leaks, wet floors, holes, defects in floor coverings, unsecured areas, signs of forced entry, and unauthorized or suspicious persons, etc.
- Patrols may be conducted continuously in parking structures to deter theft of vehicles and property within them; to note parking violations and issue warnings or citations; to observe vehicle lights or engines left on, leaks from vehicles, or other unusual conditions of parked vehicles; and to provide a security presence for the safety of tenants. Motorized vehicles, such as golf carts (see Figure 8.3), may be used for patrolling large parking areas with long travel distances.

Figure 8.3 Examples of golf carts used for patrol purposes.   Photograph by Roger Flores.

In some high-rise commercial office buildings, security staff perform periodic patrols within tenant space. Sometimes this practice places the patrol officer in "difficult and sensitive" situations, particularly after normal business hours. If it is necessary for security staff to enter tenant areas after normal business, several members should enter together or be accompanied by an engineer or other building staff. They should knock on the door before opening it, and call out loudly to identify themselves and their intentions. Such actions can help avoid embarrassing and awkward incidents and protect security staff from unfair accusations. Intrusions into tenant space should always be documented.

High-rise tenants can participate in watching over security staff by communicating difficulties with the program or staff to building management, or directly to the security department.

Guiding and Directing Security Staff

Various ways and means can be used to guide and direct security staff to perform responsibilities as determined by the building's security and fire life safety program. First, employees need the following basic tools to do their job:

- A well-defined security and fire life safety program with clearly documented and communicated building policies and procedures
- Security and fire life safety systems and equipment that are adequate for the building's program and maintained in good working order
- Up-to-date, thorough, accurate, concise, and clearly defined security and fire life safety instructions that can be easily obtained for reference
- Comprehensive and well–laid-out orientation, training, and testing programs for security staff

In addition, security staff need a working environment in concert with their required professional image. Building owners and managers often overlook amenities such as clean changing areas, adequate and secure storage areas for uniforms and personal belongings, restrooms, and break areas; but these are essential to the welfare and morale of security staff. Supervisors should, if possible, have access to a private area where counseling can be conducted in a professional setting with minimal distractions. If the security department is large enough to warrant a Director of Security, a private office should be provided where the director can work and safely store reports and confidential employee files. It is not uncommon to find high-rise security staff who are required to change uniforms in corridors or public restrooms, security uniforms stored in building fan rooms, nonexistent break areas, and the Director of Security housed "under the stairs" or in an area where no privacy or permanent work space is afforded. These conditions degrade the morale of the entire security department and can cause a less than professional attitude of security staff at work.

Much literature is available about motivating employees to perform better, work harder, and stay interested in what they are doing. McGregor's "Theory X" or "Theory Y," the Autocratic Theory, the Custodial Theory, the Supportive Theory, Herzberg's Work Motivation Theory, and Maslow's Theory of Needs will not be addressed here, but the following actions produce positive results when practiced by security supervisors.

- Take a genuine interest in employees and treat them with courtesy and respect.
- Know the strengths and limitations of employees and assign them to positions of responsibility that match those strengths and limitations.
- Adequately train and test employees so they know what is expected of them.
- Communicate clearly, concisely, and in a timely fashion so employees can adjust to any requested changes in duties and responsibilities.
- Actively listen to employees and encourage their ideas and input—"What do you think we can do about the recent vehicle break-ins?"
- Be decisive and avoid vacillation.
- View people as individuals and approach them in appropriate ways to obtain their cooperation.
- Make requests of employees rather than give direct orders—"Would you help Philip over at the Loading Dock?" The problem with direct orders is that people sometimes disobey them. If a person refuses to comply, then the supervisor's authority and ego are challenged. Of course, direct orders will need to be given under certain circumstances.
- Give positive feedback, compliments, and recognition to employees—"Barbara, thanks so much for the great job you did handling the special event today."
- Perform periodic employee performance reviews and evaluations.
- Assist employees in developing skills and self-confidence, and encourage them to accept responsibility.
- Assist employees' advancement and promotion within the organization.
- Support employees, particularly during difficult situations.
- Handle complaints from employees in a timely, fair, and equitable manner.
- Do not make promises or commitments that cannot be met.
- Admit a mistake when it has occurred, and apologize when necessary or appropriate.
- Maintain a professional Code of Ethics and Standards of Conduct and do not compromise personal standards.

Discipline, an effective and necessary tool of supervision, will be treated separately. The word *discipline* is derived from the Latin word *discipulus*, which means learning. *The Encyclopedia of Security Management* states that "the word conveys an important concept in supervision, i.e., that discipline is a mechanism for correcting and molding employees in the interests of the organization. Punishment, the negative aspect of discipline, is tangential to the larger purpose of fostering desirable behavior" (Fay 1993, p. 234). Fay adds that there are certain principles that need to be taken into consideration when an employee is being disciplined:

- *Principle 1—Assume Nothing.* Ensure that everyone knows the rules. Put the rules in writing; make them a regular item of discussion in formal and informal sessions; disseminate and display them prominently. An employee who does not know the rules cannot be expected to follow them, and a supervisor should not discipline an employee when there is doubt that the employee was aware of the rule.
- *Principle 2—Discipline in Privacy.* Receiving discipline is never a pleasant experience and can be particularly unpleasant in the presence of co-workers or others who have no legitimate role in the process. Embarrassment, anger, and resentment are the natural emotions that follow criticism given publicly. Discipline is a private matter to be handled behind closed doors or in a setting that ensures absolute privacy.
- *Principle 3—Be Objective.* Rely on the facts, not opinions and speculations. Consider all the facts and examine them with an open mind. Look for and eliminate

any biases, for or against the offender. Make sure there is in fact a violation and determine the relative severity of the violation. Was the offender's act aggravated or mitigated in any way?

- *Principle 4—Educate the Violator.* Administer discipline that is constructive. The purpose is to bring about a positive change in the violator's conduct or performance. Discipline should be a learning experience in which the violator gains new insights that contribute to personal improvement.
- *Principle 5—Be Consistent.* Inconsistent enforcement of policy and rules should be totally unacceptable. For example, if the policy of the department is to terminate officers who sleep on the job, then all officers so caught must be terminated. To fire one and not another will breed contempt for the rules and those who set the rules [and can result in U.S. Department of Labor complaints and/or lawsuits].
- *Principle 6—Do Not Humiliate.* The intended outcome is to correct, not hurt. When humiliation is made a part of the process, the offender will come away angry, resentful, and perhaps ready to fail again. Both the offender and the organization will suffer as a consequence.
- *Principle 7—Document Infractions, Counseling, Discipline, and Corrective Actions.* Make a record of violations. This is not to say that a negative dossier should be maintained on each employee, but it does mean that instances of unacceptable performance have to be recorded. The record of an employee's failures is valuable as substantiation for severe discipline, such as termination, or as a diagnostic aid to counseling professionals.
- *Principle 8—Discipline Promptly.* With the passage of time, an uncorrected violation fades into vagueness. The violator forgets details, discards any guilt he or she may have felt at the time of the violation, and rationalizes the violation as something of little importance. When opened for discussion, an uncorrected violation is likely to lead to disagreement about what "really happened" and any disciplinary action at that point can appear to be unreasonable (Fay 1993, pp. 234–235).

Generally speaking most employees want to do a good job. If they slip up, however, the supervisor must discipline in a professional manner and focus on the problem, not the personality of the offender. The intention is to train, develop, and improve performance, and, perhaps, to rescue a valuable employee from failure. In providing comprehensive training to new or experienced security supervisors, the following areas should be addressed:

- Responsibilities and duties
- Leadership skills
- Communication skills
- How to develop relationships
- How to avoid sexual harassment
- How to avoid favoritism
- How to handle complaints
- How to conduct inspections
- How to document inspections
- How to counsel and discipline
- How to conduct performance evaluations
- Organizational skills
- Time management
- Stress management

Sometimes when nonsupervisory employees are promoted to supervisory positions, they need to be taught to think and behave as supervisors rather than as line employees, and to alter their interactive relationships from "peer-to-peer" to "peer-to-subordinate." If they do not make this transition they will not become effective supervisors. As Vail (1993) states, "The best leaders know themselves, their strengths, their weaknesses, their skills, and their abilities. Most of all, they know how to control themselves and present a commanding image that will inspire subordinates. They commit themselves to continually developing leadership characteristics in themselves and their subordinates" (1993, p. 56).

Motivational and Incentive Programs

Employee recognition programs are an important tool in staff retention, boosting morale, raising the quality of service rendered by security staff, and reducing overall operational costs. It decreases staff turnover, thus reducing the amount of training and supervision required. Security staff who carry out responsibilities in a competent and professional manner may be recognized by an award for employee of the month, quarter, or year; or for an outstanding job performed in handling a particular situation; or for length of service. The recognition program may take the form of a letter of appreciation, newsletter write-up, certificate, plaque, personalized badge, tie tack, stick pin, or a cash award. Such recognition of security staff members often motivates others to excel.

Uniforms and Equipment

There are various types of uniforms and equipment that can be supplied to security staff working in a high-rise environment. Uniforms are an essential part of the appearance of security staff. If security staff are well groomed; outfitted in a well-tailored, clean, and pressed uniforms; and have clean and well-polished footwear, professional appearance and overall effectiveness will be much enhanced. The image building owners and managers desire security staff to project will determine the style and selection of uniforms. Because security staff currently are viewed as service providers and ambassadors of building management, uniforms follow the military-law enforcement image less, and the professional concierge image more. Instead of security patches and badges, staff usually are outfitted in a soft-look uniform consisting of tailored slacks, white dress shirt, business tie, and blazer, or, in some instances, a tailored business suit. Often a discreet name plate identifying the wearer, with possibly a monogram of the building's logo on the blazer or suitcoat pocket, are the only identifying marks on the uniform itself.

In the United States it is highly unusual for security staff assigned to high-rise commercial office buildings to be armed with weapons of any type. A national survey by *The Hallcrest Report on Private Security and Police in America* found that less than 10 percent of all contract and proprietary security officers were armed. The data, literature review, and field interviews of the survey revealed a dramatic *decrease* in the carrying of firearms by contract security personnel in the previous ten years as well as a lower incidence of armed proprietary security personnel (Cunningham and Taylor 1985, p. 94).

The type of business usually conducted in high-rise commercial office buildings and the large number of people who frequent most of these facilities on a daily basis make it not only undesirable but potentially dangerous for building security staff to be equipped with weapons such as nightsticks, firearms, chemical agents, or aerosol propelled agents. The chances of a building tenant, visitor or innocent bystander being injured in a situation involving a weapon are high. However, some high-rise building tenants (such as retail banking institutions) do employ armed security personnel within their premises, and some corporate executives retain armed executive protection staff. During the 1992 Los Angeles riots, some high-rise commercial office buildings in the city used civilians trained and certified to carry concealed weapons to supplement unarmed security staff during that difficult period of civil unrest. However, such deployment is unusual in the high-rise setting and is reserved for special and unusual circumstances.

The Role of Public Relations

Public relations plays a vital role in the administration of the security function in a high-rise building. Security staff are exposed to all users, from tenants to visitors to those persons servicing and operating the facility. They are expected not only to provide directions and information about the building and its locale, but also to persuade people to cooperate willingly with the security program. In carrying out these responsibilities they are required to represent the security department in a professional manner under all circumstances. How effectively they interact with people will directly influence the image of security in the building and will indirectly reflect on the building owner or manager, and even the tenants. Currently, high-rise building owners are striving to attract and retain tenants. Building security especially can contribute to the achievement of these goals.

Public relations entails creating kindly feelings and positive interaction between an organization and the public. It should not be identified with the image of a slick sales person promoting a product. Rather, in the security context, it implies a professional and well-trained staff interfacing with the public in a manner that favorably reflects their department and the building. Good public relations allows staff to carry out the roles and objectives of the building security program effectively, and can be an invaluable tool in getting people to comply willingly with security rules and procedures. To create the positive impression so essential in human relations, security staff should:

- Be well groomed with good personal hygiene
- Be outfitted in clean, well-tailored, and pressed uniforms with clean, well-polished footwear
- Have what is best described as a "military bearing," whether they be sitting or standing

- Have a smile on their faces at the appropriate time
- Maintain good eye contact with people, particularly when they are talking to them
- Use hands, arms, or head in a nonthreatening way
- Practice good listening skills and speak politely and courteously, using key phrases and words such as "May I help you?", "Please," and "Thank you"
- Remain calm, avoiding outward displays of emotion when confronted with a hostile or hazardous situation
- Carry out their duties and responsibilities with decisiveness and consistency

As expressed by American Protective Services (1980, p. 2),

> Good human relations for the security officer begins with an interest in people and in their safety and welfare. When successful, it produces mutual good feelings and willing cooperation. Cooperation is the real meaning of good human relations at all levels. . . . It is only through cooperation of all concerned that security officers can carry out the mission of protecting people and property. Good human relations is the basis of good security.

Summary

In carrying out a successful security program in a high-rise commercial office building, it is essential that it be adequately funded. The security staff that oversee and implement many aspects of this program may be directly employed by the building owner or manager (i.e., proprietary in-house) or by a contract security firm (i.e., contract). If the latter, it is critical that special care be taken to select a professional contractor. Building security staff need to be of sufficient numbers to adequately carry out their responsibilities as determined by the building security and fire life safety program. These duties should be documented in comprehensive security instructions that are clear, concise, accurate, periodically reviewed, and regularly updated. All security staff must be properly selected, trained, tested, supervised, uniformed, and equipped in order to perform their job in a professional manner.

References

Allied Security, Inc., *A Guide to Contracting for Security Guard Services* (Copyright Allied Security, Inc., Pittsburgh, PA, 1983).

American Protective Services, Inc., "The meaning of human relations," *Human Relations: The Notebook Lesson Series for Security Officers* (American Protective Services, Inc., Oakland, CA, 1980).

American Protective Services, Inc., "Skills of the security officer," *High-Rise Training Course* (American Protective Services, Inc., Oakland, CA, 1990).

Bates, Norman D., "The power of paperwork" (*Security Management*, Arlington, VA, May 1995).

Berman, Bennet H., as quoted in the *Nation's Business*, January 1980, page 30B, and reported in The Merritt Company, "Training," Part I, *Protection of Assets Manual*, vol. IV, 9th printing. Editor, Timothy J. Walsh (Used with permission from The Merritt Company, Santa Monica, CA, 800/638-7597. Copyright 1991).

Colling, Russell L., "Security staff organization," *Hospital Security* (Butterworth–Heinemann, Stoneham, MA, 1982).

Cunningham, William C., and Todd H. Taylor, "The growth of private security," *The Hallcrest Report I: Private Security and Police in America* (Butterworth–Heinemann, Stoneham, MA, 1985).

Denekamp, Mark L., "PCs and security: A perfect match," *Security Management* (Arlington, VA, January 1989).

Fawcett, Martin A., International Foundation for Protection Officers (IFPO), "Field notes and report writing," *Protection Officer Training Manual*, 5th ed. (Butterworth–Heinemann, Stoneham, MA, 1992).

Fay, John, ed., *Encyclopedia of Security Management: Techniques and Technology* (Butterworth–Heinemann, Stoneham, MA, 1993).

Ferrell, O. C., and Gareth Gardiner, "Honesty may be the best policy but some days it's tough," *In Pursuit of Ethics: Tough Choices in the World of Work* (Smith Collins Company, Springfield, IL, 800/345-0096, 1991).

Geiger, Geoff, and Geoff Craighead, "Minding the store: Office security is big business," *Los Angeles Business Journal* (Los Angeles, July 1991).

Keating, Thomas K., "Site supervisors—A critical link," *The Vigilant* (American Protective Services, Inc., Oakland, CA, December 1994).

Minion, Ronald R., *High Rise Building Security* (International Foundation for Protection Officers, Bellingham, WA, 1992).

NFPA 601, *Guard Service in Fire Loss Prevention,* Chapter 3, "Guard service functions and duties" (Used with permission of the National Fire Protection Association, Quincy, MA. Copyright 1992).

PPM 2000 Security Management Software InCase System (PPM 2000 Inc., Edmonton, Alberta, Canada, 1990–93).

Roughton, Jim, "Scanning the lines for security," *Security Management* (Arlington, VA, January 1989).

Sennewald, Charles A., "Planning and budgeting," *Effective Security Management*, 2nd ed. (Butterworth–Heinemann, Stoneham, MA, 1985).

Vail, Christopher L., "What good supervisors are made of," ASIS Reprint Series, *Security Management* (Arlington, VA, 1993).

Webster's College Dictionary, 1992 Edition (From *Random House Webster's College Dictionary* by Random House, Inc. Copyright © 1995, 1992, 1991 by Random House, Inc. Reprinted by permission of Random House, Inc., New York, 1992).

Yoder D., and H. Heneman, eds., *American Society of Personnel Administrators' "Handbook of Personnel and Industrial Relations"* (Bureau of National Affairs, Washington, DC, 1979), as reported in The Merritt Company, "Training," Part I, Protection of Assets Manual, vol. IV (The Merritt Company, Santa Monica, CA, 1991).

Appendix 8-1 NASCO Security Officer Code of Ethics

As a private security officer, I fulfill a vital function in the preservation and well-being of those whom I serve. In doing so, I pledge:

- To serve my employer and clients with loyalty and faithfulness, respecting the confidentiality of my job.
- To fulfill my duties in full compliance with the laws of the land.
- To conduct myself professionally at all times, and to perform my duties in a manner that reflects credit upon myself, my employer, and private security.
- To be fair and impartial in discharging my duties without prejudice or favoritism.
- To render reports that are complete, accurate, and honest.
- To remain alert to the interests of the client and the safety of those whom I serve.
- To earn the respect of my employer, clients, and fellow officers through my personal integrity and professionalism.
- To strive continually to improve my performance through training and education which will better prepare me for my private security duties.
- To recognize my role as that of a private security officer.

Reprinted with permission of the National Association of Security Companies (NASCO), 1995.

Appendix 8-2   Sample Security Officer Basic Training Test

NAME: _____

POSITION/POST: LOBBY OFFICER _____

DATE: _____

1. What is the address of the building?
2. On what floor is the Office of the Building located?
3. What are the normal operating hours of the building? (Circle the correct one)
   6:00 A.M. to 7:00 P.M., Monday to Friday
   7:00 A.M. to 6:00 P.M., Monday to Friday.
4. What time do you secure the lobby doors?
5. When do building elevators go into the security mode?
6. If a visitor to the building asks an important question about the building operation that you cannot answer, what do you do? (Circle the correct one)
   Tell the person you don't know the answer and you cannot help them
   Tell the person that you do not know the answer but that you will call your supervisor to assist
   Tell the person they have no business asking questions about the building
7. As a private security officer you have the same rights as a police officer. (Circle the correct one)
   True
   False
8. If a person enters the lobby and asks you how to get to the roof of the building, what do you do? (Circle the correct one)
   Direct the person to the service elevator
   Politely tell the person that under no circumstances is anyone permitted to travel to the roof
   Direct the person to the Office of the Chief Engineer
9. If the person becomes upset, starts yelling obscenities, and refuses to comply with your wishes, what do you do? (Circle the correct one)
   Try to calm the person. Call for the assistance of your supervisor
   Yell back at the person.
10. If a person carrying a weapon enters the lobby, what do you? (Circle the correct one)
    Inquire as to what floor they want to find
    Carry out the procedures as outlined in your security instructions
    Run screaming out of the lobby
11. In the situation just mentioned, describe what you would initially do.
12. If a delivery person enters the lobby with a cart, where do you direct this person to go?
13. If a fire alarm sounds in the lobby, whom do you immediately notify? (Circle the correct one)
    The fire department
    All occupants in the lobby
    Building Management
14. If an earthquake occurs while you are in the lobby, what is your first action? (Circle the correct one)
    Run out of the building lobby
    Take an elevator to an upper floor
    Move near an interior wall away from light fixtures, tuck your head to your knees, and cover your head with your arms to protect against falling objects
15. List six essential ingredients of any successful report of an incident.
16. After normal business hours, if a building occupant exits the passenger elevator carrying a personal computer

and several large boxes, what do you do? (Circle the correct one)

Ask if you can help carry the items to their vehicle

Tell the person they cannot remove anything from the building and request that they return the property to their office

Politely request a Building Property Removal Pass

17. If the person carrying the property has a Building Property Removal Pass but it is not filled out, what do you do? (Circle the correct one)

Take the pass and tell the occupant you will fill it out for them

Politely request that the occupant return to their office to have the pass completed before the property leaves the building

Let the person leave with the property and tell them to return the completed pass the next business day

18. What is the building policy for handling solicitors?

19. When the building is closed, a person dressed in coveralls asks to be allowed admittance to service a vending machine on a tenant floor. What do you do? (Circle the correct one)

Allow this person to do so on the understanding that they return to the lobby as soon as their work is completed

Request identification and allow the person to proceed to the tenant floor

Politely tell the person that the building is closed and that Building Management does not allow after-hours work to be conducted without prior authorization

20. If there is a smell of burning material in the lobby, what do you do? (Circle the correct one)

Ignore this observation

Immediately notify the Security Control Center and Building Fire Safety Director

Tell no one and leave your post to investigate the odor

21. If an occupant spills a soft drink on the lobby floor, what do you do? (Circle the correct one)

Go to the loading dock to get a cloth to clean up the spill

Leave it because it is a hot day and it will soon dry up

Cordon off the area and call for the assistance of a building janitor

Signature of the person being tested: _____

Signature of the supervisor conducting the test: _____

Appendix 8-3 Sample Security Officer Training and Testing Log

NAME: _____

POSITION/POST: _____

Program/Procedure/Test	Date(s) Trained				Date(s) Tested			
Employee Orientation								
Building Tour and Familiarization								
Inspect Building Security Systems and Equipment								
Review Building Security Program								
Review Security Instructions or Post Orders								
Inspect Building Fire Life Safety Systems and Equipment								
Review Building Fire Life Safety Program								
Review Building Emergency Procedures Manual								
Review Specific Post Duties and Responsibilities								
Specialized Training (CPR, First Aid, etc.)								

Note: Each training and testing should be initialed by the Security Supervisor conducting the training.

9 *Security Investigations*

An *investigation* is an objective, fact-finding, systematic inquiry into particular incidents, conditions, subjects, or behavior with a specific, predetermined purpose in mind. A *fact* is an event that has actually occurred or is known to be true. The inquiry not only involves gathering relevant information, but also involves making assumptions and logical conclusions based on that evidence.

> *Evidence* is anything that tends to prove a fact or support a conclusion. There are three kinds of evidence:
>
> 1. Physical evidence—objects, materials, documents
> 2. Stated evidence—what people such as victims, witnesses, suspects, and technical experts say.
> 3. Circumstantial evidence—facts that lead to a logical or at least likely conclusion. (American Protective Services 1980, p. 14)

Owners and managers of high-rise commercial office buildings may become involved in many types of investigations pertaining to security and fire life safety matters: analysis of specific events or certain conditions; examination of complaints about a particular building policy, procedure, or person; investigation of a crime, suspected crime, or some other infraction (criminal or civil actions); and physical or electronic surveillance of someone or something.

This chapter not only addresses the methodologies of conducting these specific investigations, but concentrates on the general principles involved in gathering, organizing, and evaluating information to properly establish the facts of an investigation. It does not address background investigations—employment histories of job candidates or financial and life-style inquiries of present employees.

Nature of Investigations

Investigations may be informal or casual in nature, with something unusual or important being observed and then questions being asked or further observations made regarding the matter. For example, a member of a building's security staff, while patrolling a parking structure that has recently been the site of several vehicle break-ins, discovers a person loitering in the vicinity of an expensive automobile. On questioning this person it is discovered that the individual is in fact the owner of the vehicle, has locked the vehicle with the keys inside, and is unsure how to handle the dilemma.

Investigations also may be formal in nature. "A formal investigation may be conducted in response to a major incident or threat, or in response to a complaint. It is more organized than the casual investigation and proceeds through fairly well-defined stages" (American Protective Services 1980, p. 2). To illustrate a major event that might cause an investigation, suppose a fire occurs after normal business hours in the office of a building tenant. Analysis by a trained investigator reveals that the fire was started by a lighted cigarette butt found in the wastepaper receptacle underneath a desk in the gutted office. A check of the building's after-hours access register reveals that the tenant whose office was involved had signed out of the building 20 minutes before a fire sprinkler alarm for the floor in question was received on the fire detection and alarm system annunciator panel located in the Building Control Station. A subsequent interview of the tenant by a fire department arson investigator reveals that the tenant did in fact throw a lighted cigarette butt in the trash bin minutes before leaving the building on the night of the fire.

Likewise, to illustrate a complaint that would prompt an investigation:

> Suppose several occupants in a tenant space complain that over the past two months business items, such as calculators, dictating equipment, laptop computers, computer diskettes, and personal things—cash, small mementos, and valuable pens, have been stolen from their offices. Building management, in conjunction with the office manager of the tenant concerned, arranges for a hidden surveillance camera to be placed in one of the areas where the thefts have occurred. This camera is connected to a videotape recorder that requires replacement by building security every 24 hours. The tape from the third day of recording shows a tenant employee who walks into the office at 7:00 P.M. after most workers have left, and proceeds to rifle through desk drawers and place petty cash, a calculator, and a small travel clock in a briefcase and leave the area. The next day, the tenant's head of human resources conducts an interview with the employee. At the interview the employee, who happens to be a trusted worker who has been with company for 10 years, admits to the offenses and subsequently resigns.

Private Sector and Public Law Enforcement Investigations

Investigations in high-rise buildings may be carried out by tenants; building owners and managers; building security staff; licensed private investigators; local law enforcement or the fire department; and various other local, state, and federal agencies. The types of actual or suspected crimes that require investigation in commercial buildings include trespass, burglary and unauthorized entry, larceny, vandalism, fraud, and, to a lesser degree, crimes of violence such as murder, manslaughter, robbery, assault, rape, and terrorism. The primary objective of a criminal investigation by law enforcement is to serve the best interests of society by identifying and prosecuting offenders, whereas in the private sector the primary objective is to serve the best interests of the organization concerned. As Sennewald explains,

It is interesting to note that what serves the best interests of society may not necessarily serve the best interests of the organization, and vice-versa. For example, the society's interests are protected when an embezzler is prosecuted and sentenced to prison. There are occasions, however, when the embezzler, having banked all his thefts, would be happy to return the stolen funds in order to avoid prosecution. Such an agreement would be unacceptable in the public sector. A seasoned private investigator, on the other hand, is not primarily concerned with prosecution and sentencing. Recovery of the loss might be a more important achievement, better serving the interests of the private organization. (Sennewald 1981, p. 11)

Other factors that influence whether the investigation is carried out in the private or public sector are the nature of the crime and the resources available to conduct the investigation. Merritt (1991, pp. 16-69–70) explains,

Although the crime is of interest to law enforcement (and hence a matter for police investigation), there may be considerable preliminary effort required [by tenants, building owners or managers . . ., the building security department, and licensed private investigators] even to establish the existence of a crime. The police, generally overworked in criminal investigations, will not undertake preliminary inquiries in most situations unless there is a clear threat to public order or the general welfare.

An incident that illustrates this point recently occurred in a large California high-rise building.

Over a period of six months a number of thefts of blank checks from the middle or back of tenants' checkbooks occurred throughout the building. These checks were then filled out and cashed at a local bank with individual amounts ranging from $500 to $3,000. The thefts often were not discovered for months, because tenants did not realize that certain checks were missing until then. The bank, when notified of the fraud, refunded the full amount of each forged check to the tenant concerned. The tenants, after receiving full restitution, were unwilling to cooperate with building management by making police reports of the stolen checks. After six months of these thefts the total money involved in these forged checks amounted to $50,000! Local law enforcement representatives were reluctant to begin an investigation because they were already overwhelmed with work and no official police reports had been made. After considerable efforts by building management, the private contractor who supplied security staff at the building, and a private investigator who was hired by building management, a suspect was identified and the case was handed over to local law enforcement.

The authority of a public investigator is based on constitutional and statutory law, while the authority of a private investigator is similar to that of a private citizen. As a private citizen the private investigator has no right to detain people against their will for questioning. The authority to conduct a private investigation and request cooperation from tenants and visitors of a high-rise building comes from the rights of a building owner or manager, and tenants themselves within their own tenant areas, to maintain order on their property. Private investigators do not have the same right of access as public investigators to information such as criminal records that are available at municipal, county, state, and federal levels. Also, charges of *entrapment* (solicitation by police officers for crimes to be committed) may be leveled against private investigators. Fischer and Green (1992, p. 151) caution,

> While entrapment does not generally apply to private citizens (the case of *State* v. *Farns* [542 P.2d 725 Kan. 1975] is frequently cited to prove that entrapment does not apply to private citizens), several states have passed legislation that extends entrapment statutes to cover private persons as well as police officers. Until the issue is resolved in the courts in the next few years, security officers [and private investigators] involved in undercover operations should be careful to avoid actions that might lead to entrapment charges.

Private investigators also are more susceptible than public investigators to civil actions resulting from their work. The private investigator acting on behalf of a private company or individual is a far more attractive target for a lawsuit than the public investigator acting on behalf of a government entity. It is therefore essential to fully evaluate any private investigator hired to conduct an investigation to ensure that he or she is professional, well trained, highly skilled, and trustworthy.

Skills of the Investigator

To effectively conduct an investigation, the investigator must possess certain qualities or attributes. Charles Sennewald outlines 21 characteristics an investigator should possess, in varying degrees, either as innate or learned qualities (Sennewald 1981, pp. 20–31). He or she should be observant, resourceful, patient, people-oriented, understanding of human behavior, knowledgeable about legal implications of the work, a skilled communicator, receptive, possessed of a sense of well-being, dedicated to the work, a self-starter, skeptical, intuitive, energetic, a good actor, capable of good judgment, logical, intelligent, creatively imaginative, of good character, and professional.

It is essential to assign each case to an investigator who has the necessary expertise to conduct it. For example, if the investigation involves computer fraud, it would be wise to use an investigator who has expertise in this area. An investigator who is not trained in computer operations would require the technical assistance of a computer consultant to conduct the investigation.

In addition, an investigator must always be thorough. A thorough investigation is one in which all possible leads have been pursued; key leads have been rechecked several times to make sure they provide accurate results; crucial evidence has been corroborated, wherever possible, from more than one source; and the investigation has been continued until all information relevant to the case has been obtained.

To demonstrate in a constructive fashion why this thoroughness is so critical to supplying building owners and managers with accurate information on which to base management decisions, consider this example.

> One evening a concierge finished work at her desk, located in the lobby of a high-rise commercial office building. Before leaving, she secured the desk and placed the telephone handset underneath it. When she arrived at work the

next morning, she discovered the telephone was missing. She immediately notified building security staff, who began an investigation by reviewing videotape obtained from the building's closed-circuit television (CCTV) system. A camera located in the lobby directly viewed the desk. The tape was reviewed from the time the concierge reportedly left the desk until an incident thought relevant to the case was viewed. The recorded image showed a building janitor come up to the desk in question, go behind the desk and stoop for a brief period, and walk away concealing something under his arm. The "something" could not be clearly observed, even when video prints were taken from the tape and the image enlarged. Building security staff interviewed the janitor involved, who denied any wrongdoing and said that he had passed by the desk but had not gone behind it. Because of the apparent inconsistency in the janitor's story and his suspicious behavior as depicted on the tape, the janitorial contractor was shown the videotape and asked to remove the janitor from working at the building. This was done, despite the janitor's objections that he had done nothing wrong.

For several weeks after the incident the janitor, through the contractor, continued to protest his innocence. Building security decided to further review the videotape of the incident. This showed that an hour after the janitor went behind the desk, the same janitor came up to the desk, momentarily looked at it, then turned and went away. It was then discovered that the janitor had in fact gone to the desk on two separate occasions but had failed to mention this in the interview. The second incident corresponded to the janitor's story about his actions near the desk. A subsequent interview with the janitor revealed that he had forgotten to mention that he had gone behind the desk to pick up a small trash bag from the trash bin located underneath the desk and had walked away with it tucked under his arm.

Further review of the videotape showed a third incident relevant to the case—two hours after the janitor walked away from the desk with the trash bag, an unidentified suspect walked up to the desk, went behind it, emerged with the telephone handset in his hand, and walked away toward an emergency exit. Building management, after being given this new information, made a full apology to the janitor involved and reinstated him.

Interviewing Techniques

"The most common way to get information and gather evidence, or at least identify it, is through people. Any time someone is spoken to for these purposes, an interview is conducted. Like the investigation itself, it can be casual or formal" (American Protective Services 1980, p. 17). The reason for conducting an interview is to obtain information or evidence relevant to the investigation.

The interviewing techniques in the following sections are taken (with minor modifications) from the *Protection Officer Training Manual* (Brennan 1992, pp. 153–155).

Preliminaries

It is important for the interviewer to go into an interview with a game plan in mind and with all the available facts ready at hand. The success or failure of an interview depends on many factors, some beyond the control of the interviewer. The more factors that can be controlled by the interviewer, the greater the chances are for a successful interview.

The first approach to the subject is very important. Many people will be emotionally upset, angry, hostile, physically injured, and so on. It may be necessary to tend to the subject's needs first before attempting to conduct a meaningful interview. Try to calm the subject, make him or her more comfortable, and enlist his or her active cooperation. Do not be rushed into an interview by the subject. Take your time, obtain all the facts, and get as much background information as possible before taking any action.

At times this approach will upset the subject, who feels that you should be taking swift action on his or her behalf; however, it is important to remember you are in charge and you are responsible for actions you take. Make sure you have all the information before committing yourself to a course of action. If at all possible, the location of the interview should be chosen by the interviewer and should be free of distractions.

Conducting the Interview

Getting Acquainted

Your greeting should be cordial and sincere. Identify yourself, and if you are not in uniform, produce your identification. Your initial approach can be formal or informal, depending on the circumstances.

Attempt to set the subject at ease by entering into a general conversation with him or her before getting to the matter at hand. People like to talk about themselves and their interests and this is a useful tool in obtaining information about your subject and locating a common ground for communication. At this stage, allow the subject to become accustomed to your presence and to the surroundings by setting the pace.

Developing Rapport

Your immediate objective is to establish common ground on which you can communicate with the subject. By following the preliminaries, you should have a good idea of what the subject's educational background is and at what level it is best to talk with him or her. If you are dealing with a laborer, do not speak down to him or her, or use terminology and words that he or she is not accustomed to hearing.

By the same token, you would not speak to an executive as you would a laborer. Find common ground and speak to the subject at his or her level. By finding areas of common interest, such as sports or hobbies, you can establish a rapport with the subject that will lead to easier communication. In developing a rapport with another person, you must be able to put aside your personal feelings, respect the subject as a person and show your understanding of the subject and the circumstances that have brought you together. If you are unable to establish a rapport with the subject, an unbridgeable gap will be created that may make further communication difficult, if not impossible.

Motivating the Subject

Most people you interview will be in a strange and stressed situation that makes them uncomfortable. It will be necessary for you to remove any fears they may have. Many people are afraid of "authority" as shown by a uniform; they also are afraid of appearing as witnesses, incriminating themselves or others, or may simply be unsure of what they are to do. If you have developed a rapport with the subject, it is a simple matter to convince the subject of the need to tell the truth and to enlist his or her active cooperation.

Keeping the Subject Talking

Once rapport has been established and the subject is motivated, turn the conversation toward the topic you wish to discuss. Allow the subject to give a complete account of his or her involvement without interruptions, but be alert for inconsistencies or omissions. At times, you may have to interrupt to guide the subject back in the direction you wish the conversation to go. You must control the conversation so that the subject keeps talking until you have all the information you require.

Listening to What Is Said and How It Is Said

The interviewer must not only induce the subject to freely relate information she or he may possess, but must also evaluate the person and the conversation. In many instances, it is not what the subject says that is important, but the manner in which she or he says it, or what a subject does not say. The interviewer must be constantly alert for signals that indicate she or he is telling the truth, lying, or merely withholding information. Your interviewing abilities can be advanced considerably by learning how to interpret body language.

Obstacles to Conversation

In most instances, the content of an incident will be covered in more than one conversation. The subject will be asked to repeat his or her story again to properly fill in gaps and correct previous statements. Again, it is important not to interrupt the subject during the initial stages and to allow the subject to recount his or her version in full. After the initial story has been told, the interviewer may then ask the subject to repeat it, this time taking notes and stopping the subject from time to time to get the "full" story "straight." Note, most people will never include all the details in the first attempt because they usually blurt out the information in rapid succession. After the initial telling, they will relax a bit, become more specific, and provide greater detail.

Specific Questions

By asking specific questions, the interviewer diverts and limits the interview rather than letting the subject give a narrative of the whole or part of the story. Direct questions also may lead the subject into a false line of thinking as to what you consider to be important areas of the story; as a result, the subject may omit some details in an effort to supply the information he or she thinks you consider important.

Direct questions do have a place in an interview, but they should not be asked until the subject has given a complete narration. Direct questions can then be used to clear up various areas within the narrative. If the subject hits a block and stops talking, a direct question can be used to lead him or her back into the conversation.

Yes/No Questions

For the interviewer to obtain full and detailed facts, the subject must respond with an explanation detailing the events. If a question is asked that requires only a yes or no answer, the subject will normally respond with a yes or no, and information that may have been gained will be lost. By avoiding yes/no questions, you also reduce problems of subjects not understanding your question, agreeing or disagreeing based solely on what they perceive you want to hear, or what they want to tell you.

Leading Questions

Leading questions have the same effect as yes/no questions. They may cause the subject to give false or misleading information to the interviewer. This may be done either mistakenly or on purpose.

Rapid-fire Questions

Rapid-fire questions may seem appropriate to the inexperienced investigator, but they only lead to confusion, emotional tenseness, and resistance to the rapport that may have been developed. They also stop the cooperative witness from completing his or her statement, thereby possibly losing information.

Encouraging Conversation

Open-ended Questions

By asking a series of questions in the early stages of an interview, you may be conditioning the subject to believe that if you want to know any information, he or she will be asked—that no spontaneous information is expected. On the other hand, asking relatively few questions leading into a conversation will give the subject the feeling that everything he or she tells has significance.

Typical open-ended questions are general queries: "Tell me what you saw," "Can you tell me more about that?" or "What happened next?" These types of questions do not permit yes/no answers and allow for no misunderstanding of what the interviewer wants. The subject is forced to give a narrative to answer the question.

The Use of the Long Pause

Sometimes during an interview, the subject will stop talking and a silence will descend on the room. To the inexperienced interviewer, this can be unnerving and cause the interviewer to lose control of the interview and start talking. Pauses in conversation are normal and are never as long in duration as they seem to be. The subject is as ill at ease as you are during these silences, and the experienced interviewer will use them to advantage. Be patient and wait— many times the subject will resume talking and frequently will volunteer additional information just to break the silence.

Nondirective Approach

The nondirective approach is a technique that turns the subject's statements into questions calling for more information. In using this method, simply repeat the subject's last phrase, but with a rising inflection on the last word so that it becomes a question.

During such an interview, control your emotions, do not register surprise or anxiety, but merely restate the subject's statement. The effect of this technique is that further information is drawn out without giving direction or restricting the thinking as in direct questioning.

Ending the Interview

No interview should be abruptly terminated with a curt dismissal of "Thank you," "O.K.," and so on. When it is apparent the interview is ending, close the conversation in a courteous and friendly manner. You may wish to summarize what has been said and ask the subject if there is anything else he or she wishes to add.

Let subjects know you appreciate what they have done, and that they have performed a valuable service. Thank subjects for their time and assistance. Treating subjects with concern and good manners will help ensure that, if you or another interviewer needs to speak with them in the future, they will be more cooperative and ready to assist instead of resist.

An *interrogation* is different from an interview in that it is "an interview which focuses upon a person as a suspect. It is conducted after a substantial amount of information from other sources indicates guilt of an individual. Interrogations are not conversations with the purpose of acquiring information, but with the obtaining of a confession from the subject in mind" (Hertig 1992, p. 177).

Managing Investigations

If a high-rise building owner, manager, or tenant hires a private investigator to conduct an investigation, it is essential to establish certain criteria clearly before the investigation commences. The following issues should be addressed:

- What is the exact purpose of the investigation and what do you expect from the investigator?
- What is the scope of the investigation, and how far can the investigator go in conducting it? For example, are there certain individuals who are not to be approached? Are there certain areas that cannot be entered?

- What are the time or financial limits on the investigation?
- How frequently or under what circumstances should the investigator provide progress reports to the building owner, manager, or tenant?
- If the investigation will necessitate calling in outside agencies, such as law enforcement, will the building owner, manager, or tenant be notified if and when this is to occur?
- How will final investigative results be handled?

These considerations do not imply that the building owner, manager, or tenant is at liberty to interfere and try to conduct the investigation. If a professional, well-trained, highly skilled, and trustworthy investigator has been selected, that individual will ensure the investigation is properly controlled and managed. However, as Hertig (1992, p. 180) warns: "If the investigative effort is not properly controlled, man-hours will be wasted, confidentiality may be compromised, and objectives will not be met." There also is the possibility that court action may ensue if the investigation is not properly conducted within the law and according to ethical guidelines. Thus, in selecting the investigator, it is imperative to follow these guidelines:

1.   Request the investigator's résumé and review his or her education, qualifications, licensing, and professional experience and affiliations. Most states license investigators through a state board, so the investigator's license can be verified. "A state board can also tell a prospective client how long a firm has been in business, whether it has branch offices, who the company's principals are, whether complaints have been filed against the company, and the nature and disposition of those complaints" (Kimmons 1993, p. 60). Any potential conflict of interest the investigator may have should be examined at this point.

2.   Ask how long the investigative company has been in business. "A firm should consider looking for agencies that have been in business for at least two years. It is best to work with a stable agency because a company may need testimony later or require an additional follow-up investigation on the case" (Kimmons 1993, p. 60).

3.   Determine if the investigator has the necessary skills to carry out the particular investigation required. Request corporate references (business names, addresses, and telephone numbers) of clients for which similar investigations have been conducted. Call these businesses and ask them detailed questions about "the quality of work performed by the investigator, timeliness, as well as confidentiality, results obtained, and the cost of the investigation. An organization should also ask references whether they received a full and detailed report of the agency's investigative efforts" (Kimmons 1993, p. 60).

4.   Request a certificate of insurance to verify that the investigator's company has adequate liability insurance coverage. "Most state boards require agencies to carry $3 million in liability coverage. However, many insurance carriers require that investigative companies carry $1 million in liability coverage with errors and omissions included" (Kimmons 1993, p. 60). The certificate of insurance should be requested directly from the insurance carrier.

5.   Have the investigator submit a written proposal detailing the purpose of the investigation; how it is to be carried out (depending on the circumstances, a general statement may only be possible); assurance that the investigation will be

conducted in an ethical manner within the boundaries of local, state, or federal laws; how long it is expected to take (if known); what form the final written report will take; and how costing the project will be handled. A total fixed cost may be proposed for the project, or hourly or daily costs quoted; in addition, transportation, accommodation, and administrative costs may be specified for separate billing. A retainer fee may be stipulated on acceptance of the proposal or commencement of the investigation, with additional regular payments scheduled during the investigation.

6.   When the terms of the agreement are accepted by both parties, a written contract should be drawn up to include the above proposal, and incidental items such as a confidentiality agreement and acknowledgment that the results of the investigation are the property of the client and the investigator. Once the contract is fully executed, the investigation should commence as outlined in the agreement, and all known facts should be revealed to the investigator.

An investigator may be selected from a number of sources. The *Security Industry Buyer's Guide* provides a list of investigative services. In the security and fire life safety fields there are a number of professional associations—the American Society of Industrial Security (ASIS), the National Fire Protection Association (NFPA), the Society of Fire Protection Engineers (SFPE), the International Association of Arson Investigators (IAAI), the International Association for Professional Security Consultants (IAPSC), the National Association of Certified Fraud Examiners, the Society of Certified Fraud Examiners (SCFE), the Society of Professional Investigators, the Association of Federal Investigators, the Council of International Investigators, the International Association of Computer Crime Investigators, the International Association of Credit Card Investigators, and the International Professional Security Association (IPSA)—incorporating the International Institute of Industrial Security. With the exception of the last one, which primarily serves security interests outside the United States, these associations can be contacted through local chapters. Local, county, and state law enforcement, local and county fire prevention departments, and the local fire marshal often will be most amenable to providing information and possible lists of investigators, consultants, and specialists. Finally, an investigator may be personally recommended by other security directors, fire safety directors, risk managers, property or building managers, and insurance agents.

Summary

Investigations can be an invaluable tool in managing high-rise building security and fire life safety programs. They may be casual or formal in nature. Investigations carried out by tenants, building owners and managers, building security staff, or licensed private investigators differ from those conducted by public law enforcement. The authority of a private investigator is very similar to that of a private citizen, while that of a public investigator is based on constitutional and statutory law. Investigators must possess certain qualities or attributes to successfully conduct effective and thorough investigations. For the building owner and manager, or tenant, there are specific basic criteria that should be adhered to when selecting a private investigator.

References

American Protective Services, *Investigations and Reports: The Notebook Lesson Series for Security Officers* (American Protective Services, Inc., Oakland, CA, 1980).

Brennan, R. Lorne, "Interviewing techniques," *The Protection Officer Training Manual*, 5th ed., International Foundation for Security Officers (Butterworth–Heinemann, Stoneham, MA, 1992). This reference recognized the assistance of Sgt. Steve Cloonan, Michigan State Police (Ret.).

Fischer, Robert J., and Gion Green, "Security and the law," *Introduction to Security*, 5th ed. (Butterworth–Heinemann, Stoneham, MA, 1992).

Hertig, Christopher A., "Security investigations," *The Protection Officer Training Manual*, 5th ed., International Foundation for Protection Officers (Butterworth–Heinemann, Stoneham, MA, 1992).

Kimmons, Rob L., "Investigate your investigator," *Security Management* (Arlington, VA, December 1993).

Merritt Company, The, "Incident type investigations," *Protection of Assets Manual*, 9th printing. Editor, Timothy J. Walsh (Used by permission of The Merritt Company, Santa Monica, CA, 800/638-7597. Copyright 1991).

Security Industry Buyer's Guide, 1994 Edition (Phillips Business Information, Inc., 1201 Seven Locks Road, Suite 300, Potomac, MD 20854 and ASIS, 1655 North Fort Myer Drive, Suite 1200, Arlington, VA 22209.

Sennewald, Charles, A., *The Process of Investigation: Concepts and Strategies for the Security Professional* (Butterworth Publishers, Woburn, MA, 1981).

10 *Building Emergencies*

Modern technology has permitted us to build structures higher and higher. The more people in a high-rise, the greater the potential for "something to happen" and for a disaster to occur.
 —CITY OF LOS ANGELES, EMERGENCY PREPAREDNESS UNIT

There are any number of emergencies that can occur in or affect a high-rise facility at any point in time. An *emergency* is defined by the *New Webster Dictionary* as "any event or combination of circumstances calling for immediate action." In the high-rise setting an emergency will pose a threat to both people and property: The people being occupants of the facility, whether tenants or visitors, and the property encompassing not only personal and business assets, but the physical structure itself. The emergency may be caused by people or may be a natural disaster. Usually a *disaster* is a more widespread event that affects the surrounding community. Besides disasters, one may hear of *contingencies*, *crises*, and *catastrophes*. These terms often are interchangeable, referring to events more serious than emergencies but usually less serious than disasters.

The location of a structure both geographically and topographically, the building design and type of construction, the type and location of building security and life safety systems and equipment, type of emergency, and location of the emergency incident itself, are all factors that may affect the impact of emergencies on the day-to-day operation of buildings. The following sections describe emergencies that may affect a high-rise building, and ways they may be handled.

Fires and Fire Alarms

Fire

The threat of fire is always present in high-rise commercial office buildings. According to Kruse (1993): "A fireproof building will minimize the destruction of fire, whenever it strikes. In order to be termed *fireproof*, a building must offer 100% fire protection. Fireproof does not mean the absence of fire. It simply refers to proper building design and detail that effectively checks the spread of fire, while allowing access for occupants to escape" (p. 12). Despite the fact that fires are rare occurrences, everyone working in a high-rise must be ready to act quickly if one should occur. In some other emergencies, such as a winter storm or civil disturbance/labor disturbance, the first three to four minutes of receiving warning of the incident will not necessarily determine its impact on the building. In a fire emergency, however, the first three to four minutes are crucial. The timely handling of a fire emergency, according to sound procedures established well before the incident ever occurs, can prevent the emergency from becoming a catastrophe. Before proceeding, it is helpful to understand the makeup of fire.

Fire is the combustion of fuels (whether solids, liquids, or gases) in which heat and light are produced. *Combustion* is a chemical reaction between a substance and oxygen that needs three factors to occur. These factors—fuel, oxygen, and heat—are commonly depicted in a triangle (see Figure 10.1). The removal of any one of these factors usually will result in the fire being extinguished.

Within a high-rise structure there is an abundance of fuel, much equipment and furnishings being made from highly combustible synthetic materials. The centralized heating, ventilating, and air-conditioning (HVAC) systems ensure that there is a plentiful supply of oxygen within interior spaces. An accidental or deliberate application of heat to this scenario may have dire consequences for the life safety of occupants. When combustion occurs, heat can travel by moving from areas of high temperature to areas of lower temperature. This transfer is accomplished by either conduction, convection, radiation, or direct contact with a flame (see Figure 10.2).

Conduction is the movement of heat by direct contact of one piece of matter (whether solid, liquid, or gas, but most often a solid) with another. This heat transfer is crucial to the spread of a fire in a high-rise. For example, when heat is conducted along a steel beam that passes through a fireproof barrier, its other end can ignite materials.

Convection involves the movement of heat when a liquid or gas is heated, expands, becomes less dense, rises, and is displaced by lower temperature and, hence, denser liquid or gas. This denser liquid or gas is then heated and the process continues. Heat transfer by circulating air is important in high-rises because when a fire occurs, convection currents can carry hot gases produced by combustion upward through floor-to-floor air-conditioning systems, elevator shafts, open stairshafts, dumbwaiters, mail chutes, the exterior skin of a building, and unsealed poke-through construction—thereby spreading the fire to upper floors. *Poke-through construction* occurs when holes are cut through

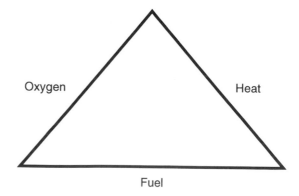

Figure 10.1
Triangle showing the relationship of fuel, heat, and oxygen.

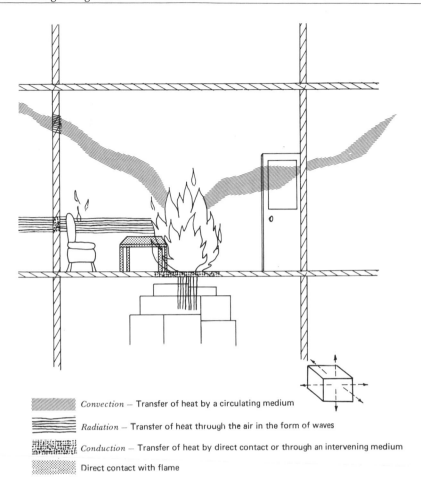

Convection – Transfer of heat by a circulating medium

Radiation – Transfer of heat through the air in the form of waves

Conduction – Transfer of heat by direct contact or through an intervening medium

Direct contact with flame

Figure 10.2   Kinds of heat transfer.   Courtesy of *Fire Problems in High-Rise Buildings* (Fire Protection Publications, Oklahoma State University, Stillwater, OK, 1976), p. 12.

concrete floors to allow the passage of conduit or ducts, primarily used for service utilities. Problems arise when the space between the conduit or duct and the surrounding floor is not properly sealed with a fire-resistant material. Figure 10.3 shows a diagram of the stack effect, as described by Boyce (1991, pp. 8-186, 187):

> The *stack effect* is the result of the temperature differential between two areas, which creates a pressure differential that results in natural air movements within a building. In high-rise buildings, this effect is increased due to the height of the building. Many high-rise buildings have a significant stack effect, capable of moving large volumes of heat and smoke uncontrolled through the building.

Smoke, which is usually the principal threat to building occupants' life safety, is the "total airborne effluent from heating or burning a material" (Clarke 1991, p. 3-19). It may spread not only vertically between floors but also horizontally

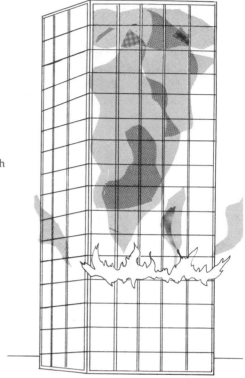

Figure 10.3
Diagram of "stack effect."   Reprinted with
permission from *Fire Problems in High-Rise
Buildings* (Fire Protection Publications, Oklahoma State University, Stillwater, OK, 1976),
p. 24.

through a floor's corridors, open spaces, conduits and ducts, and HVAC systems.
Smoke may also spread rapidly through the concealed space that extends throughout the entire floor area (located above the suspended ceiling floor of many modern high-rises), especially if this space is used as a return plenum for the HVAC
systems. *Radiation* is the movement of heat across a space or through material
by waves.

Hartzell (1991, p. 3-3) states:

> Exposure to the products of combustion presents numerous hazards to humans.
> Predominant among these hazards are effects from heat, impaired vision due to
> smoke density or eye irritation, narcosis from inhalation of asphyxiants, and irri-
> tation of the upper and/or lower respiratory tracts. These effects, often occurring
> simultaneously in a fire, contribute to physical incapacitation, loss of motor coor-
> dination, faulty judgment, disorientation, restricted vision, and panic.

The *New Webster Dictionary* defines *panic* as "sudden fear arising among people
without visible cause; terror inspired by a trifling cause." A common belief is
that people tend to panic. "Researchers who study human behavior in fires,
however, believe that the experience of panic is rare" (Keating and Loftus 1981,
p. 1). If a person does panic, though, security personnel should reassure the
person by exhibiting strong leadership and direction, dispelling rumors, and
giving the person something constructive to do.

Three major high-rise commercial office building fires have occurred since 1988:

May 4, 1988, Los Angeles—The First Interstate Tower fire resulted in the death of a building engineer, smoke inhalation by many of the 40 people located inside the building at the time of the fire, and more than $100 million in direct property damage and business loss (see Figure 10.4). The fire started on the 12th floor of this 62-floor high-rise building and the Los Angeles City Fire Department was first notified of it at 10:37 P.M. It was extinguished 3 hours and 42 minutes later on the 16th floor by the fire department, using over 300 fire fighters.

June 30, 1989, Atlanta—The Peachtree 25th Building fire resulted in the death of 5 occupants, the injury of 20 building occupants and 6 fire fighters, and direct property damage estimated at two million dollars. The fire began on the sixth floor of this 10-story building at 10:30 A.M. and was extinguished by the Atlanta City Fire Department only after it had caused heavy damage to the sixth floor and to electrical rooms on the fourth and fifth floors.

February 23, 1991, Philadelphia—The One Meridian Plaza fire resulted in the death of three fire fighters because of smoke inhalation and destroyed eight floors of this 38-story high-rise building. The fire reportedly started on the 22nd floor at 8:23 P.M. and was declared under control by the Philadelphia City Fire Department over 18 hours later on the 30th floor.

An investigation report by the NFPA, entitled *High-Rise Office Building Fires*, indicated that both the First Interstate Tower and One Meridian Plaza lacked automatic fire sprinklers on the floors where fires started. In the First Interstate Tower fire, there was a delay in notifying the fire department after an automatic fire alarm sounded inside the building, and the cause of the fire was never positively determined. The One Meridian Plaza building's automatic early-detection systems failed to sense the fire in its incipient stage; this fire was reportedly caused by spontaneous ignition of improperly stored linseed oil-soaked rags used for restoring and cleaning wood paneling. Both incidents involved rapid growth, development, and spread of the fire on the floor of origin, and significant floor-to-floor smoke spread. Both fires also occurred after normal business hours when there were not many occupants in the buildings.

During normal business hours in fully occupied high-rise commercial office buildings there usually are plenty of people in many areas of the building. As a result, if a fire occurs, it is more likely that either people or the building's automatic fire detection system will detect it quickly and cause notification of the fire department, and the fire will thus be suppressed before it has an opportunity to develop into a major conflagration. After normal business hours, including weekends and holidays, the number of people present in the building is severely reduced and so there is more dependence on the building's automatic fire detection and notification systems and on security staff.

High-rise fires can be particularly dangerous to building occupants. As The Merritt Company (1991) explains: "The most critical exposures in high-rise structures include fire, explosion, and contamination of life-support systems such as the air and potable water supply. These threats can be actuated accidentally or intentionally and can quickly develop into catastrophic pro-

Figure 10.4   TOWERING INFERNO—A fire department helicopter, at left, soars around First Interstate Tower early on Thursday morning, May 4, 1988, as flames shoot from the windows of the 62-story building. Fire officials described the 3½-hour blaze as the worst high-rise fire in the history of Los Angeles.   Used with permission from AP/WIDE WORLD PHOTOS.

portions because of the rapid propagation of fire, smoke, and contaminants" (p. 19-101).

Fire Alarms

Fire alarms are critical to high-rise buildings. As Bryan (1982, p. 320) explains, "The primary purpose of a fire detection system is to respond to a fire, and to transform this response into a visual-audible signal which should alert the building's occupants and the fire department that a fire has been initiated. The fire detection system is intended to respond to the initial signs, signals, or stimuli which indicates that a fire has begun." (See Chapter 4, *Fire Life Safety Systems and Equipment*, "Manual Fire Alarm Stations," for the sequence of events triggered by fire alarms in modern high-rise buildings.)

Whenever a fire or a fire alarm occurs, all building occupants need to be alerted to the existence (or possible existence) of fire to initiate emergency procedures. All occupants should be evacuated in a prompt, safe, and orderly fashion according to procedures established in the Building Emergency Procedures Plan. (More will be said about the plan in Chapter 11, *Building Emergency Planning*.) According to NFPA 101 (1994, p. 101-19), *Life Safety Code*, Section 2-8:

> Two means of egress, as a minimum, shall be provided in every building or structure, section, and area where size, occupancy, and arrangement endanger occupants attempting to use a single means of egress that is blocked by fire or smoke. The two means of egress shall be arranged to minimize the possibility that both might be rendered impassable by the same emergency condition.

Occupant Response to a Fire

When a fire occurs, occupants, floor wardens, and emergency staff have duties and responsibilities as outlined in the Building Emergency Procedures Plan. Occupants who discover a fire should know how to protect themselves, how to notify others who may be at risk, how to confine a fire, and how to notify those who will respond to the fire. The notification procedure may include telephoning the fire department and building management or security, and activating a manual fire alarm station on the floor where the fire is. Generally, if occupants discover a fire they should:

1. Notify anyone in the immediate area of danger.
2. Close doors to confine the fire/smoke, but not lock them.
3. Activate or request that someone else activate a manual fire alarm station.
4. Call the fire department by dialing 911, if this service is available (if another number is required, a sticker showing this number should be on all telephones), and give the following information:
   - Building name and address
   - Nearest cross street
   - Location of fire in the building (floor number, suite/room number)
   - Known information about the fire/smoke
   - Caller's call-back telephone number

The caller should not hang up until the emergency services operator does so.

5. If time allows, call the Building Management Office (or the Office of the Building) or security to notify them of the fire.
6. If time allows, contact floor wardens.
7. Operate a portable fire extinguisher if trained and if it is safe to do so, making sure to keep an unobstructed escape route in case the fire enlarges.
8. Listen for announcements over the public address (PA) system.

To evacuate a floor, occupants should proceed immediately to the nearest safe stairwell, and go down at least three* floors to reenter the building. If the fire floor is six or less floors from the ground level, many departments require occupants to evacuate the building entirely, relocating to a safe refuge area (see Chapter 11 for a definition). Occupants should *never* use elevators to evacuate, because of the following reasons, as reported in *Feasibility and Design Considerations of Emergency Evacuation by Elevators* (1992, pp. 1–19), prepared for the General Services Administration (published by the U.S. Department of Commerce):

1. There are "pressure disturbances caused by elevator car motion on smoke control"(Klote and Tamura 1987, 1986; Klote 1988). Such piston effect is a concern, because it can pull smoke into a normally pressurized elevator lobby.
2. Elevator doors may jam because of pressure differences caused by building fires. (This phenomenon, called the stack effect, is defined earlier in this chapter.)
3. Elevator doors may open into a fire. For example, when a building engineer in the First Interstate Tower fire rode an elevator to the fire floor, the elevator car doors buckled because of the intense heat and could not be closed. As a result, the engineer died.
4. Water from sprinklers and fire hoses can damage electronic, electrical, and mechanical components of an elevator evacuation system. This damage is most serious inside the elevator machinery room and inside the elevator shaft.

Evacuation is complicated by the tendency most people have to leave buildings by the same route they use to enter. Occupants should be taught the following evacuation guidelines:

• Try to stay as calm as possible.
• React immediately. Move quickly but do not run.
• Keep noise to a minimum and listen for instructions, particularly those over the PA system. Follow the directions of floor wardens.
• If there is smoke, crawl low, keeping the head above the floor. In its brochure *Fire Safety on the Job* (1993, p. 5), the NFPA recommends keeping the head 12 to 24 inches above the floor. The air near the floor is cleaner because heat and smoke rise. If necessary, place an article of clothing or a handkerchief over the mouth and nose to aid breathing. Do not wet the fabric as heat may result in steam being breathed into the lungs.
• Do not smoke.
• Feel each door with the back of your hand to ensure the door is not hot because of a fire behind it. If it is hot, do not go through it. If the door is cool, open it slowly.

---

* The exact number of floors will be specified in the Building Emergency Procedures Plan. The Los Angeles City Fire Department specifies a "five-move-five" plan: five floors—including the fire floor, two floors above it (for safety purposes), and two floors below it (so that the second floor below the fire floor can be used as a staging area for the fire department)—are evacuated to five floors below, or out of the building.

- Close doors behind you as you leave an area, but do not lock them. (If time permits, turn off electrical appliances, but leave lights on.)
- If trapped in a room, close all doors and seal the bottom of the door with clothing, towels, or the like. If the telephone is working, notify building management or the fire department of your predicament. If you can reach an exterior window, try to signal for outside assistance by placing a sign against the window or waving with something brightly colored. Windows should not be broken unless breathing becomes difficult (breaking them may allow smoke or fire lapping up from floors below to enter). In a modern high-rise, if a window has to be broken out, try to choose one with a decal marked "tempered" because its glass will shatter on impact.
- Stop, drop, and roll if your clothing catches fire. Do not attempt to run through a fire.
- If you encounter smoke on entering a stairwell, proceed to the secondary stairwell.
- If smoke is coming up in each stairwell, evacuate upward and enter a safe floor that is located at least three floors above the fire floor, or proceed to the building roof. Move away from the stairwell exit, and, if there is a helipad or heliport, proceed to the safe holding area's designated passenger pick up and make room for a helicopter to land to execute a rescue. (Evacuation upward is most unusual in modern high-rise buildings because the stairwells are designed to keep smoke out—also, evacuating to the roof is not encouraged because only a limited number of people can be accommodated and removed from the building there, possibly by way of helicopter.) If you have evacuated upward, try to notify building management or security of your actions.
- Always close stairwell doors after you enter them. (Occupants sometimes prop doors open, thereby allowing smoke to move into what should be a smoke-free zone.)
- Before entering the stairwell, remove high-heel or awkward shoes to avoid tripping injuries.
- Use the stairwell's continuous handrail and keep to one side in single file so that any responding building emergency staff or fire fighters are not obstructed.
- Do not use the stairwell to congregate with others.
- When you reach the relocation floor and reenter the building from the stairwell, remember to feel the stairwell door with the back of your hand to ensure the door is not hot because of a fire behind it.
- To descend a fire escape: face the rungs or steps, grasp both rails firmly, and look beneath your arms as you move down the escape. At the bottom there will be a "drop ladder" or "swing ladder." Another person should be at this location to assist descending occupants.
- When you exit the building, move away from it as soon as possible. Be careful of falling glass.
- Dispel rumors and false information. (Refrain from using the word "fire" because it may cause some people to panic.)

Building floor warden and alternate floor warden responsibilities include determining and coordinating emergency response actions for a particular floor or portion of a floor; ensuring that all occupants, including those with disabilities, are completely out of unsafe areas; making sure evacuees use stairwells and not building elevators; and keeping evacuated or relocated persons at the safe refuge area until building management or the fire department authorizes them to return to their workstations. For more information on floor wardens and the floor response personnel who assist them, please see the "Building Floor War-dens" section in Chapter 11.

Responsibilities of building emergency staff—such as building manage-ment, the building Fire Safety Director, engineers, and security staff—include ensuring that the fire department has been notified immediately, all occupants have been notified and advised, any necessary evacuation or relocation proce-dures for affected occupants have begun, building fire life safety systems are operating under emergency conditions, any investigation or initial suppression of the fire is carried out, and that the fire department and other responding emergency personnel are met when they arrive at the facility.

Occupant Response to a Fire Alarm

When a fire alarm occurs, duties and responsibilities will be similar to those carried out in a fire emergency, but will vary from building to building and city to city, depending on the requirements of the authority having jurisdic-tion. For instance, some fire departments require occupants whose fire alarm is activated to proceed to the nearest safe stairwell and descend at least three floors below (see footnote in preceding section), whereas other fire depart-ments require that when a fire alarm is activated, the occupants on the floor in alarm proceed immediately to the nearest safe stairwell and *wait* there for fur-ther instructions from building management (usually over the PA system) or from floor wardens. In a fire alarm situation, occupants should *never* use eleva-tors to evacuate because, if there is an actual fire, they may malfunction because of heat and cause entrapment of passengers. This point was addressed in the pre-vious section.

Fire alarms always should be taken as seriously as an actual fire. It has been the author's experience that the vast majority of building owners and managers take fire alarms seriously. Unfortunately, there are some who do not. Some, especially if there is a problem with the fire detection system triggering false alarms, even request that fire alarms be immediately silenced on alarm floors when they occur. Such a practice is not only illegal but can have dire conse-quences for the life safety of all building occupants. If there is a problem with the fire detection system, it should be treated as an engineering issue and appro-priately addressed—it should not be allowed to jeopardize lives.

Explosions, Bombs, and Bomb Threats

Explosions, bombs, and bomb threats are real possibilities in today's society. The Bureau of Alcohol, Tobacco and Firearms (ATF), Department of Treasury, reports that the number of bombings annually investigated has been gradually increasing since the mid-1970s; also from 1989 to 1993 there were a total of 1,468 bombing incidents involving commercial facilities in the United States (ATF 1993, p. 19). In these incidents, 13 people were killed, 1,290 people were injured, and $528,900,000 in property damage was incurred. A large percentage of these numbers is the result of the 1993 New York World Trade Center bombing. Figure 10.5 shows bombing and incendiary incidents by state (encompassing both actual and attempted incidents) for 1993 (ATF 1993, p. 17). Bombings involve either *explosives* or *incendiary devices*. *Webster's College Dictionary* defines the former as "devices designed to explode or expand with force and noise through rapid chemical change or decomposition"; the latter are "devices used or adapted for setting property on fire" and can be activated chemically, mechanically, or electrically.

Explosions, bombs, and bomb threats may be acts of *terrorism* used by a person or group of persons attempting to control others through coercive intimidation or by those who want to promote their views by claiming direct responsibility or causing other targeted groups to be blamed for an incident. Terrorism also may include taking hostages and other criminal acts.

The highly publicized 1993 terrorist bombing of the New York World Trade Center, the world's second tallest building and a symbol of corporate America and technological achievement, and the 1995 bombing of the Alfred P. Murrah Federal Building in Oklahoma City, a possible act of revenge against the government, have sent shock waves throughout the U.S. high-rise building community. Yet some still ask the question, "Could this happen in our building?" The sad but true answer is, "Yes, it could!"

> *February 26, 1993, New York City*—At 12:18 P.M. during lunchtime hours on a snowy Friday afternoon, a bomb containing over 1,000 pounds of explosives, located in a parked van, detonated and tore a 200 ft. by 100 ft. wide, five-stories-deep crater in the subterranean parking garage of the 110-story New York World Trade Center (NYWTC) located in lower Manhattan (see Figure 10.6). Of the estimated 100,000-plus occupants and visitors of this seven high-rise building complex, the explosion left 6 dead and 1,042 injured (including many who suffered from the effects of smoke inhalation). The explosion caused an estimated $500 million in property damage and severely damaged many of the complex's fire protection systems. The fire alarm communication system for the Twin Towers of the Trade Center, for example, was incapacitated, and there was an interruption of primary and emergency power systems.
>
> The bomb also resulted in a fire that rapidly disbursed thick, dark clouds of smoke to upper levels of the Twin Towers through horizontal openings—stairwell doors propped open while occupants were waiting to enter stairwells—and vertical openings—stairwells and elevator shafts. During this emergency, thousands of building occupants walked down darkened and smoke-filled stairwells to evacuate the building without the assistance of emergency lighting or of advisory emergency instructions delivered over the PA system. (Generators supplying emergency power to these systems started up but after 12 minutes they overheated and shut down because of damage from the explosion.) "Many persons were needlessly exposed to smoke inhalation and stress in premature evacuation from a structure in which upper floors were safer and more hospitable than the escape routes" (The Merritt Company 1995, p. 26-2).
>
> According to the ATF, a vehicle identification number from the van, which had been rented but reported stolen the day prior to the explosion, was uncovered after the explosion. The ensuing investigation ultimately led to the identi-

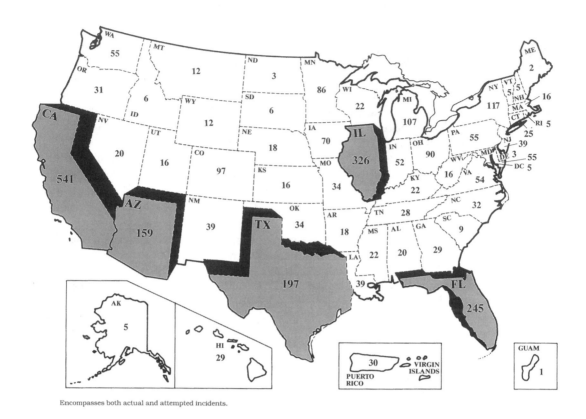

Encompasses both actual and attempted incidents.

Figure 10.5   Bombing and incendiary incidents[1] by state for 1993.
Courtesy of the U.S. Department of the Treasury, Bureau of Alcohol, Tobacco and Firearms,
Washington, DC.

fication and indictment of seven suspects, four of whom have been convicted
on conspiracy, assault, and various explosives charges. The evidence linked the
defendants to the purchase of chemicals and hydrogen tanks used to manufacture the bomb, to the rental of the shed to warehouse the chemicals and later
the bomb, and to the rental of the van that contained the bomb.

Considerable information relating to this bombing was obtained from ATF
and NFPA. After the incident, two ATF National Response Teams assisted the
New York City Police Department and the FBI in their investigation. A thorough *Fire Investigation Report on the World Trade Center Explosion and Fire*
can be obtained from the NFPA (Isner and Klem 1993).

April 19, 1995, Oklahoma City—At 9:02 A.M., when parents were dropping off
their youngsters at the Alfred P. Murrah Federal Office Building's day-care
center, a bomb containing more than four thousand pounds of a highly
deadly mixture of fuel oil and fertilizer, located in a large rented truck
parked in a no-parking, no-standing zone circular driveway outside the build-

Figure 10.6 DEVASTATION AT THE WORLD TRADE CENTER. Patient sifting through the debris of the severely damaged subterranean parking structure of the NYWTC led investigators to the discovery of a vehicle identification number from the van that contained the explosives used in this February 26, 1993, horrific bombing.   Courtesy of the Department of the Treasury, Bureau of Alcohol, Tobacco and Firearms, Washington, DC.

ing, detonated and blew away the facade and nearly half of this nine-story building located in downtown Oklahoma City (see Figure 10.7). The blast left a 30-ft.-wide, 8-ft. deep crater and shot a fireball and thick black smoke and debris high into the atmosphere. Shards of glass were propelled in every direction across several city blocks, office windows were shattered, several nearby buildings suffered major structural damage, and vehicles were damaged throughout the downtown business section. Of the estimated 500-plus occupants and visitors of this structure, the explosion left 162 dead, including 19 children in the demolished day-care center. In addition, there were four fatalities at an adjacent building and one outside, one in a parked vehicle, while a nurse running to the scene was killed by a falling piece of concrete. Over 400 people were injured. The explosion caused an estimated $650 million in property damage and resulted in the demolition of this reinforced concrete high-rise.

Immediately following the explosion, over 1300 federal buildings throughout the United States went on security alert with building perimeter patrols, inspection of packages, and heightened surveillance for persons and objects,

Figure 10.7   TERROR IN OKLAHOMA CITY. The Alfred P. Murrah Federal Building in downtown Oklahoma City sits in ruin after the April 19, 1995, devastating explosion that rocked the nation. Rescue workers using extension ladders work desperately to free survivors.   Used with permission from AP/ WIDE WORLD PHOTOS.

including vehicles, that were suspicious or looked out of place. Parking was restricted around some buildings and some have erected concrete barriers in front of the structures to protect against this type of threat. At the time of writing this book, two individuals have been charged with responsibility for this, the worst terrorist attack in U.S. history.

Prior to the Oklahoma bombing, there were no government-wide standards for security at federal facilities. After it, a security survey, entitled *Vulnerability Assessment of Federal Facilities* (June 28, 1995) conducted by the U.S. Department of Justice, including the Federal Bureau of Investigation (FBI), and the U.S. Secret Service, General Services Administration (GSA), State Department, Social Security Administration, and the Department of Defense, developed fifty-two recommended minimum security standards in light of the changed environment of heightened risk. These standards apply to what GSA describes as a "typical single- or multi-tenant federal office building" and cover the subjects of perimeter, entry, and interior security, and security planning. According to the *Los Angeles Times*, these standards, some of which are already in place, embody "new parking restrictions within buildings and in adjacent areas, use of X-rays and metal detectors at entrances for visitors and packages, erection of physical barriers, deployment of roving patrols outside the buildings, closed-circuit television monitoring, installation of shatterproof glass on lower floors, better alarm systems, locating new buildings farther from streets, grouping agencies with similar security needs, and tougher standards for visitor and employee identification" (Jackson 1995, p. A23).

Most of the information in the following section pertaining to bomb threats and physical security planning is, with some adaptations and additions, from an ATF publication of the same name (ATF 1987).

Bombs

Bombs can be constructed to look like almost anything and can be placed or delivered in any number of ways. The probability of finding a stereotypical-looking bomb is almost nonexistent. The only common denominator among bombs is that they are designed to explode. Most bombs are homemade. Their design is limited only by the imagination of, and resources available to, the bomber. Remember, when searching for a bomb, to suspect anything that looks unusual. Let the trained technician determine what is or is not a bomb.

Bombs can be received through the mail. The highly publicized California "Unabomber" incidents have involved the mail. This serial bomber was so named by the FBI because the targets of these letter and package bombs, that have been sent in the United States since 1978, had previously been universities and airlines. The record to date of the Unabomber is 16 bomb attacks, with 3 dead and 23 injured. To enhance letter and package bomb recognition, remember these are possible warning signs. One must be discerning since several of these characteristics (wrong addressee title, misspelling, etc.) apply to many letters from, for example, those applying for employment. The following general checklist was supplied by the ATF.

- Addressee unfamiliar with name and address of sender
- Package/letter has no return address
- Addressee is not expecting package/letter, or expects different size package
- Improper or incorrect title, address, or spelling of name of addressee
- Addressee title but no name given
- Wrong title with name
- Handwritten or poorly typed address
- Misspelling of common words
- Return address and postmark are not from same area
- Excessive postage or unusual stamps used versus metered postage
- Special handling instructions on package (SPECIAL DELIVERY, TO BE OPENED BY ADDRESSEE ONLY, FOREIGN MAIL, AIR MAIL, etc.)
- Restrictive markings (PERSONAL, CONFIDENTIAL, etc.)
- Excessive securing material such as wrapping, tape, or string
- Oddly shaped or unevenly weighted packages.
- Bulky, lumpy, or rigid envelopes
- Lopsided or uneven envelopes
- Oily stains or discolorations
- Strange odors
- Protruding wires or metal
- Visual distractions (drawings, statements, etc.)
- Mail arrives before or after a telephone call from an unknown person who asks whether the recipient has opened it or who requests that he or she open it.

This is only a general checklist. When an item is in question, your best protection is to make personal contact with the sender of the package or letter but not to open it.

Bomb Threats

Bomb threats are delivered in a variety of ways, but the majority are called in to the target. Occasionally these calls are through a third party. Sometimes a threat is communicated in writing or by a recording. There is more than one reason for making or reporting a bomb threat. For instance, a caller who has definite knowledge or believes an explosive or incendiary bomb has been or will be placed may want to minimize personal injury or property damage. This caller could be the person who placed the device or someone who has become aware of such information. On the other hand, a caller may simply want to create an atmosphere of anxiety and panic which will, in turn, result in a disruption of the normal activities at the facility where the device is purportedly placed. Whatever the reason for the report, there will certainly be a reaction to it. Through proper planning, the wide variety of potentially uncontrollable reactions can be greatly reduced.

Why Prepare?

Through proper preparation, you can foil the bomber or threat maker by reducing the accessibility of your business or building and identifying areas that can be "hardened" against potential bombers. This will limit the amount of time lost to any searching determined necessary. If a bomb incident occurs, proper planning will instill the notion that those in charge do care, and reduce the potential for personal injury and property loss.

Proper planning also can reduce the threat of panic, the most contagious of all human emotions. *Panic* is sudden, excessive, unreasoning terror that greatly increases the potential for injury and property damage. In the context of a bomb threat, panic is the ultimate goal of the caller.

Be prepared! There is no excuse for not taking every step necessary to meet any threat.

How to Prepare

To cope with a bomb incident, it is necessary to develop two separate but inter-dependent plans. The *bomb incident plan* provides the detailed procedures to be implemented when a bombing attack is executed or threatened. A *physical security plan*, which is covered in detail in the next section, provides protection of property, personnel, facilities, and material against unauthorized entry, trespass, damage, sabotage, or other illegal or criminal acts. In most instances, some form of physical security is already in existence, although not necessarily intended to prevent a bomb attack.

To carry out these plans, a definite chain of command must be established to instill confidence and avoid panic. This is easy if there is a simple office structure, or one business, in the building. However, in a multiple-tenant commercial office building a representative from each tenant should attend a planning conference. A leader—the Building Manager, Fire Safety Director, or Director of Security—should be appointed and a clear line of succession needs to be delineated. This chain of command should be printed and circulated to all concerned parties.

There should also be a command center to act as a focal point for telephone or radio communications. The management personnel assigned to operate the center should have the authority to decide what action is to be taken during the threat. Only those with assigned duties should be permitted in the center, and alternates need to be appointed in case someone is absent when a threat is received. In addition, obtain an updated blueprint or floor plan of the building and keep it in the command center.

Contact the police department, fire department, or local government agencies to determine if any assistance is available for developing a physical security plan or bomb incident plan. If possible, have police or fire department representatives and building and tenant staff inspect the building for areas where explosives are likely to be concealed; make a checklist of these areas for inclusion in command center materials. Determine whether there is a bomb disposal unit available, how to contact the unit, and under what conditions it will respond. You must also ascertain whether the bomb disposal unit, in addition to disarming and removing the explosives, will assist in searching the building if a threat occurs.

Training is essential to deal properly with a bomb threat incident. Instruct all personnel, especially those at any telephone switchboards, in what to do if a bomb threat is received. Be absolutely certain that all personnel assigned to the command center are aware of their duties. The positive aspects of planning will be lost if leadership is not apparent.

If possible, the command center should be located near the focal point for telephone or radio communications. In any case, the search or evacuation teams must be able to keep the center informed of their progress at all times. In a large facility, if the teams go beyond the communications network, the command center must have the mobility to maintain contact and track search or evacuation efforts.

Security against Bomb Threat Incidents

As mentioned earlier, although most high-rise commercial structures already have security measures and equipment in place (see Chapters 3 and 7 for details), the implementation of a specific physical security plan will prepare a facility against a potential bomb attack. Although there is no single security plan that is adaptable to all situations, the following recommendations are offered because they may help diminish vulnerability to bomb attacks.

The exterior configuration of a building or facility is very important. Unfortunately, in some instances, the architect has given little or no consideration to security, not to mention thwarting or discouraging a bomb attack. However, by adding physical barriers and lighting, by preventing vehicles from parking immediately adjacent to the building, and by controlling access, the vulnerability of a facility to a bomb attack can be reduced significantly.

Bombs delivered by a vehicle or left in a vehicle are a grave reality. Unfortunately, in high-rise commercial office buildings, checking passenger vehicles for suspected bombs as they enter a site is not practical. However, some higher-security buildings require vehicles, particularly vans and trucks, to undergo an on-street inspection particularly before they are permitted to enter underground loading dock/shipping and receiving areas. The 1993 New York World Trade Center bombing was an example of the damage that explosives transported into a subterranean parking structure can cause when detonated. One possible security and safety measure would be to direct visitor vehicles to a separate parking area located at least 300 feet from the building. However, this would be impractical in the majority of established high-rise facilities. If restricted parking is not feasible, it may be possible for tenant vehicles to be parked closest to a facility and visitor vehicles parked at a greater distance.

After the NYWTC bombing incident, many high-rise commercial office buildings in the United States installed CCTV systems at the entrance and exit points of subterranean garages. These cameras record close-up images of the driver and license plate number of every vehicle entering parking areas, and then the license plate number of all vehicles exiting these areas. If there were to be an incident, at least this would provide a way to identify vehicles that may have been involved.

Another result of the 1993 bombing is that system designers of mega-high-rise buildings are giving renewed attention to providing zoning and redundancy of life safety systems, so that if one portion of a building is destroyed, critical life safety systems do not fail in the entire building. A *mega-high-rise* building is defined in the NFPA Fire Investigation Report on the 1993 New York World Trade Center bombing (Isner and Klem 1993, p. 55) as:

> a large, tall (greater than 50 stories), densely populated structure where emergency evacuation is difficult or impractical. They are further characterized in that

the ordinary fuels which they contain may result in rapid fire growth, development, and spread because of their geometric arrangement, and in extensive smoke spread throughout the structure which threatens occupants in remote areas from the fire origin. Further, the time required for fire fighters to establish effective fire fighting operations can be extensive because of the vertical arrangement of the structure.

For example, emergency and standby electrical power, emergency lighting, fire suppression, and mechanical smoke evacuation systems could be zoned so that their controls are not isolated to one particular area of the building. NFPA 72 (1993, p. 63), *National Fire Alarm Code*, Section 3-2.4, already addresses this issue:

> The system shall be so designed and installed that attack by fire in an evacuation zone, causing loss of communications to this evacuation zone, shall not result in loss of communications to any other evacuation zone." "Evacuation zone" is not defined in the code but can be an area of a floor, an entire floor, or several floors that are always intended to be evacuated simultaneously.

Controls should be established for positively identifying personnel who have authorized access to critical areas and for denying access to unauthorized personnel. These controls should include inspection of all packages and materials being taken into critical areas, as well as the following:

- Security and maintenance personnel should be alert for people who act in a suspicious manner, as well as objects, items, or parcels that look out of place or suspicious. Surveillance should be established to include potential hiding places (e.g., stairwells, rest rooms, and any vacant office space) for unwanted individuals. Designated patrols of such areas will assist in this.
- Doors or access ways to certain areas—mechanical rooms, mail rooms, computer areas, switchboards, and elevator control rooms—should remain locked when not in use. It is important to establish a procedure to keep track of keys. If keys cannot be accounted for, locks should be changed.
- Good housekeeping also is vital. Trash or dumpster areas should remain free of debris. A bomb or device can easily be concealed in the trash. Combustible materials should be properly disposed of, or protected if further use is anticipated.
- Detection devices may be installed at entrances to high-risk tenant areas and CCTV in areas identified as likely places where a bomb may be placed. This, coupled with posting signs indicating that such measures are in place, is a good deterrent.
- Perhaps entrances and exits can be modified with a minimal expenditure to channel all visitors through someone at a reception desk. Individuals entering a building after normal business hours would be required to sign a register indicating the name and suite or floor number of the person they wish to visit. Employees at these reception desks could contact the person to be visited and advise him or her that a visitor, by name, is in the lobby. The person to be visited may decide to come to the lobby to ascertain the purpose of the visit. A system for signing out when the individual departs could be integrated into this procedure, although this may result in complaints from the public. If the reception desk clerk explains to the visitor that these procedures were implemented for the visitor's own best interest and safety, complaints may be reduced. A sign also could be placed at the reception desk informing visitors of the need for safety.

Chapter 7 elaborates on these controls suggested by the ATF.

Responding to Bomb Threats

Instruct all personnel, especially those at telephone switchboards, on what to do if a bomb threat call is received. It is always best if more than one person listens in on the call. To do this, a covert signaling system should be implemented, perhaps by using a predetermined signal to a second reception point.

A calm response to the bomb threat caller could result in obtaining additional information. This is especially true if the caller wishes to avoid injuries or deaths. If told that the building is occupied or cannot be evacuated in time, the bomber may be willing to give more specific information on the bomb's location, components, or method of initiation.

The person making the threat is the best source of information about the bomb. When a bomb threat is called in:

- Keep the caller on the line as long as possible. Ask him or her to repeat the message. Record every word spoken by the person. (Some building managers and individual tenants may provide tape recorders for this purpose; others by policy do not.)
- If the caller does not indicate the bomb's location or the time of possible detonation, ask for this information.
- Inform the caller that the building is occupied and that detonation of a bomb could result in death or serious injury to many innocent people.
- Pay particular attention to background noises such as motors running, music playing, and any other noise that may give a clue as to the location of the caller.
- Listen closely to the voice (male or female), voice quality (calm or excited), accent, and any speech impediment. Immediately after the caller hangs up, report the threat to the person(s) designated by management to receive such information.
- Report the information immediately to the police department, fire department, ATF, FBI, and other appropriate agencies. The sequence of notification should be established in the bomb incident plan.
- Remain available: law enforcement personnel will want to interview you.

When a written threat is received, save all materials, including any envelope or container. Once the message is recognized as a bomb threat, further unnecessary handling should be avoided. Every possible effort must be made to retain evidence such as fingerprints, handwriting or typewriting, paper, and postal marks. These will prove essential in tracing the threat and identifying the writer. Although written messages usually are associated with generalized threats and extortion attempts, a written warning about a specific device may occasionally be received. It should never be ignored. A *Bomb Threat Checklist* developed by the ATF can be found in Chapter 11, Appendix 11-1.

Decision Time

The most serious of all decisions to be made by management in the event of a bomb threat is whether to evacuate the entire building or only certain areas. In many cases, this decision may already have been made during the development of the bomb incident plan. Management may pronounce a carte blanche policy that, in the event of a bomb threat, evacuation of all affected areas will be effective immediately. This decision circumvents the calculated risk; however, such a decision can result in costly loss of time and may not be the best approach. In high-rise commercial office buildings, a decision to evacuate an entire building would be a most unusual step to take. If an evacuation or relocation of occupants is chosen, it usually will involve only the floor where the threat was received and possibly, as a safety precaution, two floors above and two floors below the affected floor. To evacuate an entire building would take considerable time and effort and is often an unnecessary step in handling this type of incident. The responsibility for deciding whether to evacuate a tenant space usually resides with the tenant's senior officer. Sometimes, however, depending on the circumstances surrounding the threat and considerations regarding the general safety of all building occupants, the building owner or manager will make the decision.

Essentially, there are three alternatives when faced with a bomb threat: (1) ignore the threat, (2) evacuate immediately, and (3) search and evacuate if warranted. *Ignoring the threat* completely can result in some serious problems. Although a statistical argument can be made that very few bomb threats are real, it cannot be overlooked that some bombs have been located in connection with threats. If employees learn that bomb threats have been received and ignored, it could result in morale problems and have a long-term adverse effect on business. Also, there is the possibility that if the bomb threat caller feels ignored, he or she may go beyond the threat and actually plant a bomb.

Evacuating immediately in response to every bomb threat is an alternative that on face value appears to be the preferred approach. However, the negative factors inherent in this approach must be considered. The obvious result of immediate evacuation is a disruptive effect on business and building operations. If the bomb threat caller knows that the building's policy is to evacuate each time a call is made, he or she can call continually and force tenants' business to come to a standstill. An employee who knows that the policy is to evacuate immediately may make a threat to get out of work. A student may use a bomb threat to avoid a class or miss a test. Also, a bomber wishing to cause personal injuries could place a bomb near an exit he or she knows is normally used to evacuate and then call in the threat.

To assess the credibility of a bomb threat, it is important to analyze the answers to the following questions:

1. What is the time of the threat?
2. How is the threat received (by telephone, by mail)?
3. How specific is the threat (type of bomb, place, time of explosion, etc.)?
4. What is the previous history of the company involved with regard to threats? (Is it presently involved in a labor dispute with its employees? Does it produce a controversial product?)
5. What is the identity of the person making the threat (if the threat is over the telephone, is the person a child, young or old, drunk, claiming to be a terrorist, etc.)?
6. What is the possibility of someone obtaining access to plant the device?

Initiating a search after a threat is received and *evacuating* a portion of a building after a suspicious package or device is found is the third, and perhaps most desirable, approach. It is certainly not as disruptive as an immediate evacuation and will satisfy the requirement to do something when a threat is received. If a device is found, occupants can be evacuated expeditiously, avoiding the potential danger areas near the bomb.

Evacuation

An evacuation team consisting of building management, the building Fire Safety Director, security, floor wardens, and floor response personnel should be organized and trained. This should be coordinated with all building tenants and designed in conjunction with developing the bomb incident plan. The team will be trained in how to evacuate the building during a bomb threat. You should establish the order in which to evacuate—for instance, by floor level. Evacuate the floor levels above and below the danger area to remove occupants from danger as quickly as possible. Training in this type of evacuation usually is made available by building management, with advice supplied by local law enforcement and the fire department.

The evacuation team also may be trained in search techniques, or there may be a separate search team. Volunteers should be sought for this function, but floor wardens, search monitors, and the like could be assigned to the task. To be proficient in searching the building, search personnel must be thoroughly familiar with all hallways, rest rooms, false ceiling areas, and other locations in the building where an explosive or incendiary device could be concealed. When police officers or fire fighters arrive at the building, its contents and floor plan will be unfamiliar to them if they have not previously reconnoitered the facility. Thus, it is extremely important for the evacuation or search team to be thoroughly trained and familiar with both the inside of the building and immediate outside areas. When a room or particular area has been searched, it should be marked or sealed with a piece of tape and reported as clear to the appropriate supervisor.

The team will be trained only in evacuation and search techniques and not in the techniques of neutralizing, removing, or otherwise having contact with the device. If a device is located, it should not be disturbed. However, its location should be well marked and the route to it noted.

Search Teams

It is advisable to use more than one individual to search any area or room, no matter how small. Searches can be conducted by supervisory personnel, area occupants, or trained explosive search teams. There are advantages and disadvantages to each method of staffing the search teams.

Using supervisory personnel to search is a rapid approach and causes little disturbance. There will be little loss of employee working time, but a morale problem may develop if it is discovered later that a bomb threat was received and occupants were not informed. Using a supervisor to search usually will not be as thorough because of her or his unfamiliarity with many areas and a possible desire to get on with business.

Using occupants to search their own areas is the best method for a rapid search. Concern for their own safety will contribute to a more thorough search. Furthermore, they are familiar with what does and does not belong in a particular place. Using occupants to search will result in a shorter loss of work time than if all were evacuated prior to search by trained teams; it also can have a positive effect on morale if a good training program is provided to develop confidence. Of course, this would require training an entire work force and, ideally, performing several practical training exercises. A drawback of this search method is the increased danger to unevacuated workers.

A search conducted by a trained team is the best option for safety, morale, and thoroughness, although it does result in a significant loss of productive time. It is a slow operation that requires comprehensive training and practice. The decision on search team personnel lies with senior management, and it should be considered with and incorporated into the bomb incident plan.

Search Technique

A common practice among security and law enforcement personnel involved in searching for a bomb is to maintain radio silence during the search out of concern that the radio transmissions of communication devices may cause a bomb device to accidentally detonate. The *Security Management Bulletin* reports that "the thinking of security professionals is shifting in regard to this rule . . . the new philosophy advocates sticking with the radios" (Stratton 1994, p.1). The logic behind this is that:

1. Searchers need the mobility of portable communication devices such as cellular phones and radios (using fixed-position phones is not practical).
2. The chances of detonation are low because the majority of bomb threats are hoaxes.
3. If there is a bomb, the bomber probably would not plant a device that is sensitive to radio waves. "What bomber planting an explosive device is going to takes a chance that a passing vehicle with a phone, CB, or other transmitting device could detonate the bomb with him [or her] standing next to it?" (Stratton 1994, p. 2).

These comments imply that a radio should not be used in the immediate vicinity of a suspected device, but may be considered for use in the general search. Larry Cornelison, Group Manager of the ATF's Los Angeles Arson and Explosives Task Force, made a similar suggestion in a presentation before the Los Angeles Chapter of ASIS on November 22, 1994. At this stage no further information is available on the subject of whether to use radios during searches.

Techniques for searching particular rooms vary in minor ways, but there are basic principles to be followed. (The procedures explained here are based on two-person search teams.) When the team enters the room to be searched, they should first move to various parts of the room, stand quietly with their eyes closed, and listen for a clockwork device (see Figure 10.8). Frequently this mechanism can be detected quickly without using special equipment. Even if none is detected, the team is now aware of the background noise level within the room itself.

Background noise or transferred sound is always disturbing during a building search. A ticking sound that is heard but cannot be located can be unnerving. The sound could come from an unbalanced air-conditioner fan several floors away or from a dripping sink down the hall. Sound will transfer through air-conditioning ducts, along water pipes, and through walls. A building that has steam or hot water heat is very difficult to search; it will constantly thump, crack, chatter, and tick because of the expansion and contraction of the pipes as steam or hot water moves through them. Background noise also may include outside traffic sounds, rain, and wind.

Figure 10.8 Room search—stop and listen.   Reprinted with permission from *Bomb Threats and Physical Security Planning* (ATF P 7550.2, July 1987), U.S. Department of the Treasury, Bureau of Alcohol, Tobacco and Firearms, Washington, DC.

The team's supervisor should look around the room and determine how to divide it for searching and to what height the first searching sweep should extend. This sweep usually covers all items resting on the floor up to the selected height. He or she determines the average height of most items, including table or desk tops and chair backs, which usually turns out to be about waist level (see Figure 10.9). Depending on its size, the room should be divided into two relatively equal parts, based on the number and type of objects to be searched and not on its floor area. An imaginary line is then drawn between two objects in the room; for example, from the edge of the window on the north wall to the floor lamp on the south wall.

First Room-Searching Sweep
After the room has been divided and a searching height, such as floor to waist level, has been selected, the two team members go to one end of the room division line and begin from a back-to-back position. This is the starting point and will be used on each successive searching sweep. Each person now starts thoroughly searching the perimeter of the room, working toward the other person. When the two individuals meet, they will have completed a "wall sweep." They

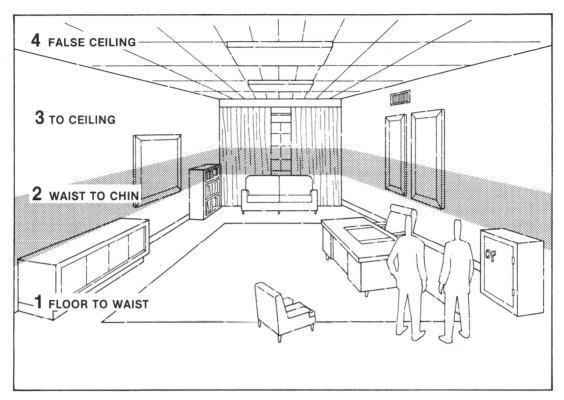

Figure 10.9 Divide room to search into sections by height.   Reprinted with permission from *Bomb Threats and Physical Security Planning* (ATF P 7550.2, July 1987), U.S. Department of the Treasury, Bureau of Alcohol, Tobacco and Firearms, Washington, DC.

should then work together and check all items in the middle of the room up to the selected height, including the floor under any loose rugs. This first searching sweep also should include any items below this height that are mounted on or in the walls such as air-conditioning ducts, baseboard heaters, and built-in cupboards. The first searching sweep usually takes the most time and effort.

Second Room-Searching Sweep
The team leader again looks at the furniture or objects in the room and determines the height of the second searching sweep—usually from waist level to the chin or top of the head. The two persons return to the starting point and repeat the searching technique at the second height. This sweep usually covers pictures hanging on the walls, built-in bookcases, and tall table lamps.

Third Room-Searching Sweep
When the second searching sweep is completed, the person in charge again determines the next searching height, usually from the chin or the top of the head up to the ceiling. The third sweep is then made. This sweep usually covers high-mounted air-conditioning ducts and hanging light fixtures.

Fourth Room-Searching Sweep

If the room has a false or suspended ceiling, the fourth sweep involves investigation of this area. Check flush or ceiling-mounted light fixtures, air-conditioning or ventilation ducts, sound or speaker systems, electrical wiring, and structural frame members. Post a conspicuous sign or marker indicating "Search Completed" in the area after this sweep. Place a piece of colored tape or a sticker across the door and door jamb approximately two feet above floor level if using signs is not practical.

The room search technique can be expanded, and can be applied to investigating any enclosed area. Encourage the use of common sense or logic in searching. If a guest speaker at a convention has been threatened, for instance, search the speaker platform and microphones first, but always return to the systematic searching technique. Do not rely on random or spot checking of only logical target areas. The bomber may not be a logical person.

To summarize, the following steps should be taken to search a room:

1. Divide the area and select a search height.
2. Start from the bottom and work up.
3. Start back-to-back and work toward each other.
4. Go around the walls and proceed toward the center of the room.

Suspicious Object Located

It is imperative that personnel involved in a search be instructed that their only mission is to search for and report suspicious objects. Under no circumstances should anyone move, jar, or touch a suspicious object or anything attached to it. The removal or disarming of a bomb must be left to explosive ordinance disposal professionals. When a suspicious object is discovered, follow these procedures:

1. Report the location and an accurate description of the object to the appropriate warden. This information should be relayed immediately to the command center, from which the police and fire departments, and rescue squad will be notified; they should be met and escorted to the scene.
2. If absolutely necessary, place sandbags, never metal shields, around the suspicious object. Do not attempt to cover the object.
3. Identify the danger area, and block it off with a clear zone of at least 300 feet, including floors below and above the object.
4. Check to see that all doors and windows are open (the latter will not be possible in modern high-rises) to minimize primary damage from blast and secondary damage from fragmentation.
5. Evacuate the building or selected floors as determined by the bomb incident plan.
6. Do not permit occupants to re-enter the building until the device has been removed/disarmed and the building is declared safe.

Summary

Develop a bomb incident plan like the one shown in Table 10.1. Draw on any expertise available to you from police departments, government agencies, and security and safety specialists; the local police bomb squad and the local field offices of the ATF can be invaluable sources of information. Don't leave anything to chance. Be prepared!

Table 10.1 Bomb Incident Plan

1. Designate a chain of command.
2. Establish a command center based on the recommendations below.
3. Decide what primary and alternate communications will be used.
4. Clearly establish how and by whom a bomb threat will be evaluated.
5. Decide what procedures will be followed when a bomb threat is received or a device discovered.
6. Determine to what extent the available bomb squad will assist and at what point the squad will respond.
7. Provide an evacuation plan with enough flexibility to avoid a suspected danger area.
8. Designate search teams.
9. Designate areas to be searched.
10. Establish search techniques.
11. Establish a procedure to report and track the progress of the search and a method to lead qualified bomb technicians to a suspicious package.
12. Have a contingency plan available if a bomb should go off.
13. Establish a simple-to-follow procedure for the person receiving the bomb threat.
14. Review your physical security plan in conjunction with developing a bomb incident plan

Command Center (or Emergency Operations Center) Recommendations

1. Designate a primary location and an alternate command center location.
2. Assign personnel and designate decision-making authority.
3. Establish a method for tracking search teams.
4. Maintain a list of likely target areas.
5. Maintain a blueprint of floor diagrams in the center.
6. Establish primary and alternate methods of communication.
7. Formulate a plan for establishing a command center if a threat is received after normal work hours.
8. Maintain a roster of all necessary telephone numbers.

The preceding information, including that in Table 10.1, is intended only as a guide. Building management ultimately must determine how to handle a bomb threat situation and assist tenants' management with incidents in specific tenant areas. Building owners and managers should also maintain a supply of up-to-date building plans offsite. These could be kept with the building architect, or even the commercial graphics firm that handles plan changes for the building. In the case of a major incident, like the 1995 Oklahoma bombing, such offsite plans could be invaluable.

Violence in the Workplace

Violence in the workplace has become a very real and present danger in today's society. The following incident in the high-rise environment vividly portrays the threat.

July 1, 1993, San Francisco—A solitary, heavily armed, disgruntled individual entered a 48-story commercial office building in San Francisco's financial district at midafternoon, during the time the high-rise was open to the public for normal business. He rode an elevator up to the 34th floor where the offices of Pettit and Martin, a major international law firm, were located. In a 15-minute rampage, he roamed through four floors, shooting to death eight people and injuring six others before being found dead himself in the stairwell.

The following observations underline the seriousness of violence in the workplace:

- National Institute for Occupational Safety and Health (NIOSH) statisticians report: "Homicide was the third leading cause of occupational injury death in the United States from 1980 to 1988; 12% of all occupational injury deaths in the period were homicides. Only motor vehicle (23%) and machine-related (13%) incidents accounted for more deaths. Of all occupational injury deaths of females from 1980 to 1988, 40% were homicides" (Jenkins et al. 1992, pp. 215, 218).
- The National Crime Victimization Survey data on crime and violence in the workplace from 1987 to 1992 was analyzed by the Bureau of Justice Statistics, which determined that "over 30% of workplace crime victimizations involved weapons, a third of them handguns, and that over half the workplace crime victimizations were not reported to police" (The Merritt Company Bulletin 1994, p. 2).
- NIOSH reports that "approximately 15 workplace murders occur each week in the United States" (Berry 1994, p. 4).
- In the *Wall Street Journal*, Rigdon (1994, p. B1) states: "Almost 25% of 311 U.S. companies surveyed by the American Management Association (AMA) report that at least one of their employees has been assaulted or murdered at work since 1990. An additional 31% of the respondents say employees have received violent threats while on the job."
- *Time Magazine* reports, "Murder has become the No. 1 cause of death of women in the workplace; for men it is the third, after machine-related mishaps and driving accidents" (Toufexis 1994, p. 35).

These shocking statistics do *not* necessarily mean there is a high incidence of such occurrences in U.S. high-rise commercial office buildings, because these numbers were obtained from workplaces that range from convenience stores to factories to high-rises.

If an armed and dangerous person is in a high-rise building, either at the main lobby level or on an upper floor, security staff *might* take the following actions:

1. Immediately notify local law enforcement, if safe to do so (using 911, if this service is available).
2. Notify building management.
3. Communicate with tenants, including floor wardens, over the building PA system, warning them of an emergency situation and directing them to seek a refuge area, lock doors to their offices (if possible), and stay put until further notice. Repeat the announcement periodically.
4. Limit access to the building, parking areas, and specific floors or areas.
5. Identify appropriate actions to isolate or contain the incident. These may include:
   - Recall and shut down building elevators to restrict the suspect's movement either from or to the main lobby.
   - Lock stairwell doors. (Panicked tenants may activate manual fire alarm stations in close proximity to the incident—in a modern high-rise building this activation will cause all stairwell doors to automatically unlock and thereby provide a possible route for the suspect to freely travel up or down between floors.)
6. Identify an area for responding emergency personnel to assemble. Provide them with radios, building floor plans, and maps of the facility.
7. Assist any tenants evacuating the site and direct them to a safe area.
8. If safe to do so, monitor the situation (using CCTV systems if possible) and keep law enforcement updated.

These are only suggestions; each set of circumstances is different, and nothing can be guaranteed to work in all these incidents. However, site-specific general procedures approved by building management and local emergency agencies should be developed for each facility's emergency staff, occupants, and floor wardens, then thoroughly documented in the Building Emergency Procedures Manual (described in Chapter 11).

The California Division of Occupational Safety and Health, in its *Guidelines for Workplace Security* (Cal/OSHA 1994, pp. 7, 8), divides workplace violence scenarios (committed by a person called a "hazardous agent") into three major types:

1. The agent has no legitimate relationship to the workplace and usually enters it to commit a robbery or other violent act.
2. The agent is either the recipient or the object of a service provided by the workplace or the victim—for instance, the assailant is a current or former client, patient, customer, passenger, criminal suspect, or prisoner.
3. The agent has an employment-related involvement with the workplace—she or he currently works or formerly worked there (employee, supervisor, manager), is or was related in some way to an employee (spouse, lover, relative, friend), or is any other person who has a dispute with someone who works there.

Bordes (1994, p. 20) summarizes some of the findings on these hazardous agents:

> The violent person profile which has been developed through several studies indicates that the middle-aged white male is the most common perpetrator. Other factors which can be considered as major contributors to the development of the perpetrator include, but are not limited to:
>
> - Frustrated employees, who in many instances are simply shuffled between jobs requiring only menial tasks with very little advancement opportunity open to them.
> - Professionals who are experiencing personal frustration and cannot handle emotional deflations such as workforce cutbacks or layoffs.
> - Individuals who are simply bitter, dissatisfied people and are unable to "shake" their negativity toward everything.
> - People unable to accept personal blame for their own problems.
> - Individuals with uncontrollable pent-up rage who operate on a "short fuse" when it comes to getting upset or mad over anything.
> - Persons who have little or no support systems such as family, friends, neighbors, and who are unable to vent their rage by either confiding in someone or having some other avenue of relief in which they can "blow off steam."
> - People who are prone to use firearms and have access to weaponry of any kind.
> - Individuals suffering from depression and who are potentially suicidal.

Alison Carper (1993) narrows the profile of the violent employee to: "male, white, 35–50 years of age, identifies closely with his job, and has multiple outside pressures, such as marital problems" (p. 5). The ideal solution would be to screen out, during the initial hiring process, those applicants who have an inclination for violence. However, this profile fits a large percentage of qualified individuals. Basic measures to take are to inquire about applicants' prior criminal convictions and to conduct a thorough background check with prior employers. Despite ethical questions and a degree of uncertainty about their predictive powers, psychological tests also are being used increasingly to screen prospective employees—and still it is often difficult to recognize potentially problematic employees.

The number of lawsuits related to the safety of employees in the workplace is growing as the frequency of these violent events continues to increase. "The rising incidence of workplace violence is an alarming trend that the total security program must address. . . . With each incident comes the prospect of litigation for inadequate security from both outside and inside the institution" (Chovanes 1994, p. 215). The onus is being placed on corporations, like those that often make up the tenant population in high-rise commercial office buildings, to do something about the problem. Some believe that many of these violent acts against employees are preventable and, as a consequence, constitute possible violations of the "General Duty" clause of the Occupational Safety and Health Act of 1970. This clause summarizes the act and states that each employer "shall furnish to each of his employees a place of employment free from recognized hazards that are causing or likely to cause death or serious physical harm to his employees" (OSHA 1974).

Tenant companies may take the following preventive measures, which have been adapted largely from the *Cal/OSHA Guidelines for Workplace Security* (1994), to address the problem:

- Control physical access through workplace design. This can include controlling access into and out of the workplace and freedom of movement within it, in addition to placing barriers between employees and those visiting. It may be appropriate, in certain situations, to use access cards or devices, a receptionist who can unlatch a door, the installation of duress alarms as a back-up measure (in conjunction with a CCTV camera system to monitor the duress alarm locations), or the presence of security personnel.
- Establish a clear antiviolence management policy and set boundaries as to what is considered acceptable behavior. Policies should be applied consistently and fairly to all employees, supervisors, and managers. Provide appropriate supervisory and employee training in workplace violence protection.
- Establish procedures for investigating occupational injury or illness arising from a workplace assault or threat of assault.
- Implement procedures to handle threats of violence by employees, including a policy on when to notify law enforcement agencies.
- Establish procedures to allow employees to confidentially report threats, and to protect them from physical retaliation for these reports.
- Provide training on how to recognize security hazards, how to prevent workplace assaults, and what to do when an assault occurs, including emergency action and postemergency procedures. Give employees instruction in crime awareness, assault and rape prevention, and hostile situations diffusion. For example, if you have employees working late at night, encourage them to keep their doors locked after normal business hours, and either to leave the building with a fellow employee or to call security for an escort to their vehicle if it is parked on-site.
- If a workplace assault occurs, reduce the short- and long-term physical and emotional effects of the incident by providing postevent trauma counseling to those who desire such intervention.

In addition, sound personnel practices, such as pre-employment screening and meaningful job performance evaluations, may help screen out and identify potential problem employees.

A large number of preventive measures can be accomplished without great expense to the employer. For example, if workforce reductions are anticipated, they should be thoroughly planned with dignity and respect afforded to affected employees. Workers who will be laid off need as much advance notice as possible. Giving severance benefits and offering placement counseling and assistance will help outgoing employees cope with their situation and nurture a supportive work environment for the remaining employees. It has the added benefit of lowering insurance premiums, because it avoids triggering an incident of violence in the workplace and the expensive litigation that could result.

Medical Emergencies

Medical emergencies that can occur in high-rise commercial office buildings range from choking to drug overdoses, from respiratory emergencies to seizures, and from serious injury to suicide. Because the building population is made up of people often working under pressure and stress, there is always the possibility of heart attacks. When an occupant or visitor needs urgent medical attention, this must be quickly communicated to medical emergency services or a personal physician (usually located outside the building), and to building emergency staff so they can prepare the building for medical responders' arrival. This is usually accomplished by dialing 911 if this service is available. If other numbers are required, a sticker indicating the numbers to call should be on all telephones in the building. The following information should be given:

Building name and address	Nature of the medical emergency
Nearest cross street	Victim's condition
Floor and room/suite number	Caller's call-back telephone number
Location and name of the victim	

The caller should not hang up until the emergency services operator does so. It is important to be sure the operator has all the information to dispatch the right help to the scene without delay.

Someone (preferably not the one tending the victim or making the first call) should then call the Building Management Office or security staff and Floor Warden to notify them of the situation. Another individual should be assigned to wait at the freight/service elevator lobby on the floor where the incident is occurring to direct medical responders to the victim's location. Building management or security will put a freight/service elevator on independent service (or "manual operation") to transport the medical responders directly from the building loading dock lobby to the victim's floor. If a physician has been notified, the procedure may vary because such a person usually will not park near the loading dock, and will therefore not require a freight/service elevator to reach the victim. If time permits, a building staff member trained in first aid and/or CPR should be sent to assist the victim. Unless an injured person is in danger of additional, more serious injury, he or she should not be moved or assisted by anyone who is not trained to do so—moving the person could cause further damage or injury.

Tenants should be encouraged to maintain records of the names of employees who are trained in first aid and CPR. Also, telephone numbers of all their employees' next of kin should be kept on file.

Power Failures

Failure of electrical power to a high-rise building will have a dramatic effect on its operations, particularly if the failure occurs during normal operating hours when the building is fully occupied. A power failure may consist of a *brownout* (a partial reduction in service) or a total *blackout*.

Power failure can be caused either by man-made or natural events. Man-made causes may include drivers who collide with utility poles or power transformers, or human error in operating equipment within the building or outside it (such as at the utility company supplying the power). Natural events include earthquakes, storms, and floods.

> *November 9, 1965, Northeastern United States*—The Northeast power failure of 1965 vividly demonstrated the necessity for the emergency availability of electrical power separate from that supplied by public utilities. Otis Elevator Company reported that the area affected by the blackout contained approximately 20,000 elevators serviced by their company, and that a total of 355 passengers were detained in 161 elevators located in 107 buildings. Most passengers were removed in less than one hour. However, in a few cases, passengers were not removed for several hours when the cars were stalled in express hoistways (Otis 5811, p. 1).

> *October 17, 1989, Loma Prieta, California*—At 5:04 P.M., the Oakland–San Francisco Bay Area was shaken by a 7.1-magnitude earthquake. The severe damage caused included fires, collapse of major freeways, and disruption of power and communications to many businesses that consequently, despite the relatively minor damage to buildings, could not reopen for a week.

Power failures also can cause computer memory loss and equipment damage. If the power loss is anticipated, computers and computer systems can be shut down before it occurs. If no prior notice is received, the equipment should still be turned off as quickly as possible to avoid potential serious damage to the electrical system from the sudden surge of power when it is first restored. Computer systems, particularly mainframes, often are equipped with an uninterruptible power supply (UPS); and personal computers often are equipped with surge protectors to reduce the chance of damage when power fluctuates, surges, or is lost.

High-rise buildings have emergency and standby power systems to provide safety and comfort to building occupants during interruptions in their normal power supply. See "Emergency Power Systems" and "Standby Power Systems" in Chapter 4 for a full description. These systems also provide power to operate building communication systems and to provide a minimum number of elevator functions, as described in Chapter 4's "Controls in Elevator Lobbies." Both functions are critical to high-rise buildings during power outages. The following example illustrates this point.

One day during normal business hours, a worker was operating a backhoe in downtown Los Angeles and, inadvertently, the machine severed an underground main power line. This resulted in the loss of electrical power to several high-rises, including the 62-story First Interstate Tower—at the time the tallest building west of the Mississippi River. The building was without primary power for several hours; this led to the evacuation of approximately 3,000 occupants, using the building's stairwells and elevators.

Operating on emergency power, the 26-passenger elevators serving the tower were brought down, one by one, to the mezzanine level to release any passengers. This was completed in less than 30 minutes. After this, the building maintenance and security staffs manually operated one elevator in each bank, plus one freight/service elevator, to evacuate building occupants from upper floors down to the mezzanine level, starting at the highest floor each elevator bank served. The building's PA system, also operating on emergency power, was used to notify building occupants of building management's decision to evacuate the building and how it would be done.

Despite the fact that power failures are not a regular occurrence in high-rise buildings, all occupants should be encouraged to keep a flashlight in their work area, and to make sure it is always in good working order. If a power failure occurs during the day, tenants should be encouraged to open window shades to let in daylight.

Elevator Malfunctions and Entrapments

Elevators have proven to be a very safe form of transportation in modern high-rise buildings. "According to the Elevator Escalator Safety Foundation, an estimated 85 billion people ride escalators and elevators every year. The fact that there is such a small number of injuries from elevator and escalator use is no accident" (Plenzler 1994, p. 27). Since the late 1970s elevators have been developed with fully integrated, state-of-the-art microcomputer-based systems that analyze calls, set priorities, and dispatch cars on demand, enabling operators to control every aspect of elevator function. However, not all elevator systems located in high-rise commercial office buildings are this modern and sophisticated. Sometimes, despite rigid continuing-maintenance schedules, they may malfunction or break down.

Elevator Safety Features

Before fully discussing elevator malfunctions and entrapments, it is helpful to examine the development of elevators, how they operate, and the reasons why, under normal operating or nonemergency conditions, they are such a safe form of transport. The following material, with some adaptations, is from the Otis Elevator Company booklet, *Tell Me About Elevators* (Otis 1982).

Elevators began with safety precautions: In 1878, Elisha Graves Otis not only developed the hydraulic elevator that was able to operate at speeds of 600 to 800 feet per minute, but also developed a governor-operated safety device to bring the high-speed car to a gradual stop in case of an emergency. A *governor* is a safety device that prevents an elevator car from falling, or from moving downward too fast.

In 1903 the Otis Elevator Company designed *gearless traction electric* elevators which today are used in office buildings over 10 stories high, for speeds varying from 400 to 1,800 feet per minute, or a maximum of about 20 miles per hour. Elevators could be designed to go faster but because it may take from 10 to 12 floors to bring the car up to speed and slow it down again, it is impractical to consider this. Also, some people may not feel comfortable traveling at high speeds. Examples of these elevators can be found in the John Hancock Building in Chicago (where express elevators are designed to move at speeds of up to 1800 feet per minute), the 110-floor twin towers of the World Trade Center in New York City (with express elevator speeds of up to 1600 feet per minute), and the Empire State Building (where the elevators move at speeds of up to 1200 feet per minute).

These elevators were followed by *geared traction* elevators, which operate similarly but are designed for lower speeds varying from 25 to 350 feet per minute, and for loads up to 30,000 pounds or more. As a result, geared systems are used for a wide range of passenger elevator, freight/service elevator, and dumbwaiter applications.

Both these types of elevators use six to eight lengths of wire cable, or "hoisting ropes" or "hoisting cables" as they are known in the industry, that are attached to the top of the elevator and looped around the *drive sheave*—a wheel with a grooved rim—in special grooves. The other ends of the hoist cables are attached to a counterweight that slides up and down in the elevator shaftway on its own guide rails. With the weight of the elevator car on one end of the hoisting ropes, and the total mass of the counterweight on the other, the cables are pressed down on the grooves of the drive sheave. Thus, when the motor turns the sheave, it moves the cables with almost no slippage. Actually, the electric hoisting motor does not have to lift the full weight of the elevator car and its passengers. The weight of the car and about half its passenger load is balanced out by the counterweight, which is sliding down as the car is going up (see Figure 10.10).

In 1921, the American Society of Mechanical Engineers established safety codes for elevators and escalators. They were developed from informal "laws" pertaining to the safety of passengers in elevators and became the American Standard Safety Code for elevators. This has been the model code ever since and is updated continually. Most elevators in the United States conform to its standards, which accounts in part for their excellent safety record. Over the years, safety developments for elevators have included:

- A self-leveling device that greatly reduces the tripping hazard for passengers as they step off elevators. (It is called the Microdrive and was developed in 1915 by Otis.)
- A door interlock system that prevents an elevator from operating unless the door at each floor is closed and locked.
- Enclosure of hoistways and the sides and backs of elevators.
- An electronic safety device, the *photoelectric eye*, that detects the presence of a person standing in the elevator's doorway, and causes the doors to return automatically to the fully open position.

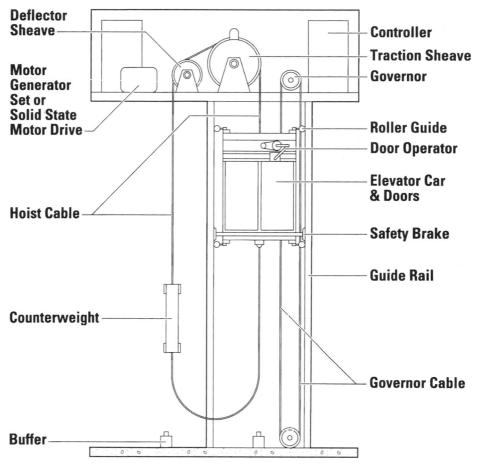

Figure 10.10 The working parts of a traction elevator.   Reprinted by permission from *Ups and Downs*, Schindler Elevator Corporation, Morristown, NJ.

- As mentioned earlier, six to eight hoisting ropes or steel cables are used to lower and raise the elevator. Any one of these cables is strong enough to support the weight of the car plus the maximum allowable weight of the passengers. (This serves as a safety feature, but the main purpose of the extra hoisting ropes actually is to increase the traction area on the drive sheave.)
- Weight sensors that stop an elevator car from operating if it is overloaded.
- The governor, a safety device that prevents an elevator car from falling, or from moving downward too fast. A steel rope or *governor cable* runs from the elevator car to the driving wheel of this device. If the elevator car exceeds its normal design speed for any reason, the driving wheel trips a safety switch that sets the brake on the elevator's driving machine. Usually this braking action is enough to stop the car. If for some reason it doesn't stop the car and its speed continues to increase, the governor causes safety clamps to be released against the elevator's guide rails, which are firmly secured to the building structure. This brings the car to a smooth, sliding stop.

- Seismic devices, designed to shut down elevators when the building itself moves, are incorporated into elevator systems in areas subject to earthquakes. On sensing movement, the device automatically sends a signal to the elevator control system and causes each affected elevator car to go to the nearest floor in its current direction of travel, makes its doors open automatically, and then shuts down the elevator. The elevator can only be restarted after the seismic device has been reset. After the probability of aftershocks has passed, a qualified individual—an elevator mechanic, building inspector, or possibly the building engineer—should inspect elevator shafts and elevator cars to check for any possible damage or safety hazards before resetting the seismic device. Possible damage could include loosening of counterweight guide shoes and counterweight rails, jammed hoistway doors, failure of hoisting ropes or supports, and dislocated control equipment in elevator machine rooms.

The emergency and standby power systems' effects on elevators (see Chapter 4) are important safety features as well.

Elevator Problems

The information on elevator malfunctions in this section was written with technical assistance from *How to Operate Elevators Under Emergency Situations* by Otis Elevator Company (Otis 5811).

Common problems associated with the operation of elevators in high-rise buildings include elevator cars that do not correctly align with the floor when they arrive there, elevator doors that do not close, and elevator cars that "slip" while in motion (possibly caused by stretching of the elevator cables) or stop between floors, entrapping occupants. If any of these conditions occurs, it must be reported promptly to management, engineering, or security staff, who in turn will notify the elevator company responsible for maintaining the equipment. The first three problems may result in temporary shutdown of the elevator for maintenance. The case of passenger entrapment, however, is a problem that requires immediate attention. The passengers can summon assistance by pushing the EMERGENCY CALL, EMERGENCY ALARM, or EMERGENCY ONLY button on the elevator car's floor selection panel, or by using the two-way emergency telephone that should be inside a compartment within the elevator car. (See "Controls Inside Elevator Cars" in Chapter 4 for a full explanation of both these communication devices.)

A certified elevator mechanic may be available on-site; if not, one should be summoned immediately by those who receive the signal or call from the trapped passengers. This person will be familiar with the operation of the equipment and the hazards involved in removing passengers from a stalled car. It may be possible to correct the problem that has disabled the elevator, restore normal operation, and release the passengers right away. The passengers may need to assist the process in some way; for instance, if they were instructed to push the EMERGENCY STOP button to the STOP position, they will need to be told to return it to the RUN position for service to be restored to the elevator.

While this is happening, constant contact should be maintained with the passengers to assure them that help is on its way. They should be told not to attempt to open the doors or do anything other than what they are instructed to do. If there is no direct communication system to the elevator car, it will be necessary to locate the position of the elevator in the hoistway, proceed to the nearest hoistway door, and speak to the passengers. Constant dialogue will help the passengers deal with the situation and reduce the chance of panic. If there is a delay in getting a trained mechanic to the site or if the problem cannot be corrected quickly, this communication will take on even greater importance. In situations such as needing to evacuate the passengers through a side emergency exit (if an adjacent elevator in the hoistway is running), through the hoistway door nearest the stalled car, or (as a last resort, because it is a difficult maneuver for aged, ill, or injured passengers) through the emergency exit in the top of the car, communication will be a vital component in relaying critical instructions that, if correctly carried out, will lead to the passengers' successful release from entrapment.

Removal of passengers from stalled elevators should be done only by qualified and trained personnel such as certified elevator mechanics and members of fire departments. Removal attempts by others could result in serious injury or fatalities.

Natural Disasters

Each natural disaster (earthquake, tsunami, volcano, winter storm, tornado, hurricane, or flood) requires a separate life safety approach and should be covered in the Building Emergency Procedures Manual (see Chapter 11).

Earthquakes

The foundations of the earth shake.
The earth is broken asunder,
The earth is split through,
The earth is shaken violently.
—Isaiah 24:18–19

Earthquakes obviously have been around for thousands of years. During the 100-plus years high-rise buildings have been in existence, the West Coast of the continental United States and Alaska has been subjected to numerous earthquakes ranging from an almost indiscernible tremble of the ground to the violent shaking of a major quake. This shaking sometimes has caused side-to-side motion, and other times caused up-and-down motion; it has lasted for a few seconds or for up to a minute. Reports from the 1964 Anchorage, Alaska, earthquake, estimated at an approximate magnitude of 9.1, indicated that some areas shook for up to seven minutes!

When earthquakes occur, the strength and duration of the shaking largely determines the potential for damage. Some earthquakes are preceded by smaller quakes called *foreshocks*, some occur suddenly with no forewarning, some occur in groups of approximately the same magnitude (called *swarms* or *clusters*), and some are followed by smaller quakes called *aftershocks*. Earthquake strength, or magnitude, can be measured on the *Richter Scale*—a logarithmic scale of increasing magnitude from 1 to 10 that was developed in 1935. Among scientists, it has been replaced of late by the *moment-magnitude scale*. The following are examples of earthquakes that have occurred this century in U.S. metropolitan areas.

> *April 18, 1906, San Francisco, California*—An estimated 8.3 magnitude earthquake on the San Andreas Fault near San Francisco, it was the largest one recorded in U.S history and resulted in urban fires that burned for three days afterward and caused property loss of about $350 million. More than 500 people lost their lives in the earthquake and the resultant fires.

> *March 10, 1933, Long Beach, California*—At 5:54 P.M., an estimated 6.3 magnitude earthquake took the lives of 120 people and caused considerable damage to the unreinforced masonry buildings prevalent at the time.

> *February 9, 1971, San Fernando, California*—At dawn the San Fernando community was shaken awake by an earthquake that measured 6.4 on the Richter scale. It caused the collapse of the San Fernando Veterans Administration Hospital and the resultant death of 44 people.

> *October 17, 1989, Loma Prieta, California*—At 5:04 P.M., the Oakland–San Francisco Bay Area was staggered by a 7.1 magnitude earthquake. According to the California Office of Emergency Services, 67 people were left dead, 3,757 were injured, and property damage exceeded $10 billion. The resulting fires added to the already severe damage. Power and communications were disrupted, a major freeway collapsed, and, despite the relatively minor damage to buildings, many businesses did not reopen for a week.

> *January 17, 1994, Northridge, California*—At 4.31 A.M. an earthquake measuring 6.6 on the moment-magnitude scale rocked the heavily populated San Fernando Valley (see Figures 10.11 and 10.12). It severely impaired the public transportation network and residential community; 57 people were killed and thousands were left homeless in the wake of this disaster that caused more than $20 billion in property damage.

California is in an earthquake zone because it lies on the boundary—marked by the infamous, 800-mile-long San Andreas Fault—between two tectonic plates, the Pacific and the North American. These two gigantic sections of the earth's crust float above a very thick layer of hot rocks called the mantle, which in turn floats atop the earth's core of molten rock. The Pacific Plate, to which Los Angeles is attached, is gradually inching its way north and west, past the North American Plate to its east, which is moving in the opposite direction. At most points, and at most times, these two plates obstruct each other's advancement, resulting in the buildup of intense pressure. An earthquake will occur at certain times when the blockage at a specific point along the fault line releases (*faults* are fractures in the earth's crust), the plates slide past one another, and the ground suddenly shifts. In California there are three known types of faults:

1. *Thrust faults.* These faults cause the ground to move vertically and break the earth's surface (see Figure 10.13A). They are the most common type.
2. *Hidden thrust faults.* These faults are located entirely underground and cause the ground to move vertically without breaking the earth's surface (see Figure 10.13B).

Figure 10.11 TOTAL DESTRUCTION. Some older concrete buildings lacked special reinforcements and were severely damaged during the 1994 Northridge earthquake. This high-rise medical office building in Santa Monica was so seriously harmed that it was deemed unsafe for entry, condemned, and completely demolished within days of the shaker. Tenants, because of the potential for serious injury, were not permitted to enter their offices to recover any business records, files, or personal belongings. Courtesy of Los Angeles City Fire Department, Disaster Preparedness Division.

3. *Strike-slip faults.* These faults cause the ground to move horizontally (see Figure 10.13C).

The concern in Southern California is that a magnitude 8.3 temblor, the so-called "Big One," could occur along the southern end of the San Andreas Fault, or that a less powerful earthquake could occur along the Newport–Inglewood Fault.

A *Los Angeles Times* (1994) article warned: "A landmark federal study prepared in 1981 at the request of the National Security Council estimated that [the former] quake would kill between 3,000 and 14,000 people, depending on the time of day it occurred, hospitalize up to 55,000 people and cause about $20 billion damage in property damage" (p. A-24).

In addition to the West Coast of the continental United States and Alaska, earthquakes can and do occur in every state. "Since 1700, more than a thousand earthquakes have been reported east of the Mississippi River. Earthquakes that caused widespread and severe damage have occurred in Charleston, South Carolina (1886–87); New Madrid, Missouri (1811); Hebgen Lake, Montana (1959); and Borah Peak, Idaho (1983)" (Kimball 1988, p. 5). In March 1993, a 3.1 earthquake occurred in western New York. A map indicating where earthquakes have

Figure 10.12 These tall, caster-mounted computer cabinets rolled across the floor of a second-story room without overturning. Unfortunately, the newly installed ceiling and lighting fixtures did not fare as well as a result of this earthquake.   Courtesy of Dames and Moore, *A Special Report on the January 17, 1994, Northridge Earthquake.*

occurred in the United States shows that few areas are considered low-risk for quakes (see Figure 10.14). Handling an earthquake can be approached in three distinct phases—before, during, and after the earthquake.

Before the Earthquake

Modern high-rise buildings in areas subject to earthquake activity have been constructed in accordance with strict building codes. Older buildings erected before seismic design considerations were mandated may be required to perform structural retrofits to bring the structures up to code.

The effect of earthquakes on a high-rise building depends on factors such as the building's location in relation to the quake's epicenter, type of soil or rock beneath the structure, magnitude of the quake, duration of the shaking, type of motion the structure is subjected to, and the building's design and quality of construction. The shaking of an earthquake may cause no structural damage, or it may cause destruction so severe that the building collapses. In areas like California, modern high-rise buildings are seismically designed to withstand certain magnitude earthquakes. "The idea of earthquake-proof construction is unrealistic, unless exceptionally expensive measures are taken. Any building will collapse if the ground under it shakes hard enough or becomes perma-

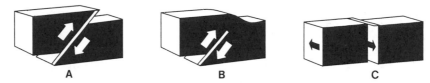

Figure 10.13   A, diagram of a thrust fault; B, diagram of a hidden thrust fault; C, diagram of a strike-slip fault.

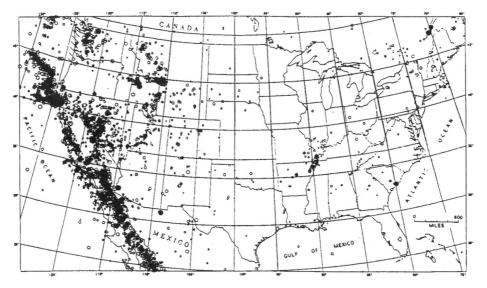

Figure 10.14   Earthquakes occur throughout the United States.   Courtesy of U.S. Geological Survey (National Earthquake Information Center, Denver, CO, 1990).

nently deformed. But structures can be designed and constructed to incorporate a high degree of earthquake resistance" (Kimball 1988, p. 42).

As Dames and Moore (1994) explain: "To resist seismic forces, steel buildings are either constructed with braced frames (such as X-bracing) or moment frames (rigid beam-column assembly)" (p. 21). Many structures, particularly seismically designed steel-framed buildings, have been constructed to flex and move without breaking. Lower floors may shake more rapidly, but movement of the building from side to side is greatest on uppermost floors. "To dissipate the force of the ground shaking through a tall structure, the building is designed to sway as a unit in a side-to-side motion" (Kimball 1988, p. 106).

It is of note that the January 17, 1994, Northridge earthquake has raised some serious safety concerns about the degree of earthquake resistance that high-rise buildings, in particular *steel moment frame* structures, afford. Unlike braced frames, these moment frames feature larger beams and columns, with additional welding or bolting of the connections. Prior to this earthquake, this structural system was thought to be among the safest seismically. As John Hall

(1994, pp. 1, 2), an associate professor of civil engineering at the California Institute of Technology, points out:

> During the 1994 Northridge earthquake, many modern steel buildings suffered unexpected fractures in welded beam-to-column connections. Although none of these buildings collapsed, fractured connections are a serious matter since they reduce the lateral strength of the structure, and, thereby, increase the risk of collapse. The problem is apparently widespread and, at this point, one must assume that any welded steel moment-frame is susceptible to this type of connection failure.

The following comments regarding this situation were written shortly after the quake in *The Northridge Earthquake, January 17, 1994, A Special Report* by Dames and Moore (1994, p. 21):

> Steel moment frame buildings have generally been considered very effective in resisting seismic forces. However, the high intensity of the Northridge earthquake pushed even steel moment frame buildings to their seismic limits, causing damage not experienced before. More than 50 relatively new 2- to 10-story structures that sustained brittle structural damage have been identified at the time of writing this report. Such damage raises troubling questions about the seismic resistance of this type of construction. Damage took the form of cracks in welds and rupture of steel sections at connections of beams to columns and columns to the base plate—both areas are critical for stability of the structure. Steel-framed buildings are designed to absorb energy by bending without breaking. However, the failure of welded connections would not allow the level of bending assumed in design and can cause brittle failures. Steel members in existing buildings are covered with fireproofing and are not readily available for inspection. Thus, damage caused by the quake may go unnoticed unless a detailed and costly inspection program is undertaken. The damage to steel moment frame buildings has potentially the highest structural significance of the Northridge earthquake and will probably result in substantial research and associated design code changes.

At the time of writing of this book, the City of Los Angeles is requiring by ordinance that owners of steel moment frame buildings inspect for damage, and the Federal Emergency Management Agency (FEMA) is preparing guidelines to address this potential hazard.

Even though issues raised about weld cracks in steel-framed construction were the most startling result of the quake, the failures of concrete-framed parking structures were among the most dramatic (see Figure 10.15). As the *Engineering News Record* (January 16, 1995, pp. 28–33) reported: "In response to such collapses, federal officials anticipate a new treatment of parking structures in the National Earthquake Hazard Reduction Program's 1997 provisions, to serve as a basis for model codes."

During a severe earthquake, occupants and building contents will move. Items not properly secured may fall; desks and furniture may slide; filing cabinets and bookcases may topple; ceiling tiles may be dislodged; windows may crack or shatter; sprinkler heads may shear off and result in water discharge; seismic devices may cause building elevators to go to the nearest floor in the direction of travel, stop, automatically open elevator car doors, and then cease operation; the automatic fire detection and reporting equipment may produce

Figure 10.15   TOTAL DESTRUCTION. Severe shaking of the ground during the 1994 Northridge earthquake led to the collapse of this recently constructed, precast four-level concrete parking structure at California State University.   Courtesy of Los Angeles City Fire Department, Disaster Preparedness Division.

multiple false alarms; electrical power may be disrupted; lights may go off; the telephone system may be damaged, or shortly after the shaking has stopped, be deluged with calls. Injuries often will be caused by falling objects.

Therefore, in earthquake-prone areas it wise to anchor PC systems to work-tables (also a security measure), attach unsecured bookcases and cabinets to walls, and place objects that may break close to the floor or in cabinets with latching doors. Do not store heavy objects on top of cabinets, credenzas, and bookcases, or place chairs with rollers close to floor-to-ceiling windows. The last precaution was the subject of a story once told by an emergency planner who worked in San Francisco.

> The individual was visiting his boss on the 50th floor of a major high-rise. The boss was sitting on a chair with recently lubricated rollers and suddenly a severe earthquake hit. The building swayed so violently that the boss started rolling rapidly toward the nearby window. The subordinate reached out and caught the chair before it went crashing into the window. The emergency planner said this incident had a profound impact on his career development within that organization!

Occupants should also identify safe areas in their office where they may take shelter if an earthquake hits; store items such as a flashlight, portable radio, extra batteries, walking shoes, food items, necessary medications, contact lens solution, and so on in a desk drawer; know ahead of time the location of emergency exits and stairwells; and have out-of-state telephone numbers for contacting family members. In a severe earthquake, regular telephone service may be disrupted. Public pay telephones often are the first services to be restored and can be used by family members to dial out-of-state and leave messages for each other.

Building management or individual tenants also may provide occupants with earthquake preparedness supplies, including bottled water, canned and dry food, first aid kits, sleeping bags, and other items detailed in the "Emergency Operations Center (EOC)" section in Chapter 11. All perishable items should be replaced every six months, or as needed, to ensure quality.

If a major earthquake occurs, occupants may have to remain in their building for several days because of the disruption of public transportation and communication systems, or widespread damage in the community. In California, emergency planners predict that after a severe earthquake, such as a magnitude 8.0 that is predicted along the San Andreas Fault, occupants may be without the assistance of outside emergency services for 72 hours or more.

During the Earthquake

An earthquake usually occurs without any warning other than possibly a roaring sound like a fast-approaching locomotive or airplane. Thus, occupants and building staff alike have only a few moments to act. During an earthquake, most actions of those inside a high-rise building are geared toward self-preservation, particularly on upper floors where the swaying may be the most extreme. The following are basic guidelines for these moments:

- Do not panic (easier said than done).
- If on an upper floor, do not attempt to rush for stairwells; if on the ground or street level, do not run outside. Occupants running out of high-rise buildings may be hit by falling glass and other materials, or by vehicles. If outside the building, do not attempt to re-enter the building but move, if possible, to an open area that is a safe distance away from the building, utility poles, fallen power lines, street light fixtures, trees, and objects that may be a hazard.
- If inside an elevator, remember that in earthquake-susceptible areas most building elevators are equipped with the seismic devices described in the previous section on "Elevator Malfunctions and Entrapments," which will take you to the nearest floor in the direction you were traveling, stop, and automatically open the doors. If the elevator stalls, do not attempt to force open the doors. Summon assistance by pushing the EMERGENCY CALL, EMERGENCY ALARM, or EMERGENCY ONLY button on the elevator car's floor selection panel. Then carry out the instructions of responding staff. Remember, power failures are commonly associated with severe earthquakes, and there may be some delay in freeing all passengers trapped in building elevators.
- If inside an office area, move away from exterior glass windows, interior temporary or glass partitions, hanging objects, free-standing bookcases or cabinets, and other objects that may fall. Get under a strong table or desk and hold onto it—it may move during a severe shaker.
- If in crowded interior areas such as conference rooms or auditoriums, try to keep others calm and take the same actions as for an office area.

- If in building corridors or lobbies, move to an interior wall away from light fixtures, tuck your head to your knees, and cover your head with your arms to protect against falling objects such as ceiling tiles. Do not attempt to use elevators.
- If inside a rest room, remain there and cover your head with your arms to protect yourself from falling objects.
- If in the parking area and it is safe to remain, tuck your head to your knees, and cover your head with your arms. In a severe earthquake there may be out-of-control vehicles.
- Stay in your protective position, unless it becomes unsafe to do so, until the shaking has ceased and it appears safe to move.
- Do not smoke or use a lighter or matches; if the building has gas lines, there may be leaks.

After the Earthquake

If the earthquake has caused damage, assist floor wardens and building emergency staff by checking for injured persons and providing assistance if you are trained to do so. If not, locate someone who is trained to assist. Do not attempt to move injured persons unless it is imperative or there is the risk of more severe injury occurring if they are not moved. If there are many injured occupants, it may be necessary to set up a triage (*triage* is the process of classifying victims according to medical treatment needs) and first aid area on each floor. There may be fatalities during a severe earthquake. One cause of death may be heart attacks suffered during such a traumatic event. Next, check your immediate area for damage and potential hazards if aftershocks should occur. Open doors cautiously because objects may fall. Check for telephone handsets that have been knocked off the hook. Use telephones for emergency communications only.

During this time, listen for announcements and instructions over the PA communication system if it is still operational. Follow the directions of building staff members, floor wardens, and responding public agencies. You could also listen to portable radios for public safety messages. Do not pass on anything to others that could be misinformation. Remain on your floor and do not use elevators until you are authorized to do so. Above all, *be prepared for aftershocks*. Depending on the severity of the event, building management will notify occupants if it is safe to return to work, if evacuation of the building or relocation within the building is required, or if occupants are to remain on their floor and await further instructions.

Soil liquefaction, landslides, and fires are frequent results of major earthquakes. *Liquefaction* occurs in areas where loose soils with a high water table are present. "As the earthquake causes water to percolate up through the loose soil, it creates quicksand. Heavy objects such as buildings and other structures may sink or tilt into the liquefied soil" (Kimball 1988, pp. 17–18). Fires can result from fuel spillages, rupturing of gas lines, and the many ignition sources available in urban areas. If the earthquake is a major one, public fire fighting capabilities will be severely strained because of extraordinary demands for service, difficulties in transporting equipment along damaged or blocked roadways and freeways, and possible disruption of the public water supply.

An earthquake that occurs after normal business hours during the week, or on weekends and holidays when most tenants are not in the building, may cause such serious damage to the building that for a period of time tenants cannot enter it at all, or can enter only under certain conditions. The building should be secured; a recorded message, informing tenants of the situation, can be placed on building telephones, particularly that of the Building Management Office.

Tsunamis

In coastal areas, vertical motion of the sea bed—which could be caused by an earthquake—may result in a tsunami or tidal wave. Japan has a history of tsunamis following major earthquakes; its government has developed a tsunami warning system similar to the U.S. Emergency Broadcast System, which broadcasts warnings over television and radio networks. Tsunamis also can occur at any point along the U.S coastline and may lead to waves over 50-feet high pounding the coastline. "The most destructive tsunamis have occurred along the coasts of California, Oregon, Washington, Alaska, and Hawaii" (BOMA 1994, p. 66).

If a tsunami warning is issued, television and radio networks should be monitored for information and instructions. If the building owner or manager deems it necessary to evacuate the building, it should be accomplished in an orderly fashion. Building elevators should be used, starting first with upper floors in each elevator bank.

Volcanoes

A volcano is defined as: "an opening in the earth's crust through which steam, gases, ashes, rocks, and frequently streams of molten material are or have been periodically ejected" (*Reader's Digest* 1979). If a volcano erupts and the volcanic ash travels to a high-rise building, all external doors should be kept closed and the HVAC system should be shut down, or outside air intakes closed off, to avoid contamination within the building. Occupants should be instructed to stay within the building while the ash is falling. Such an event is unlikely in the United States, but nonetheless possible, because there are active volcanoes in the Pacific Northwest, Alaska, and Hawaii.

Winter Storms

There are many types of storms (freezing rain, sleet, hail, snowstorms, blizzards) that may occur between autumn and spring. Depending on their severity, storms may hamper public transportation, cause power outages, and freeze building equipment. Critical high-rise building systems should be closely monitored, particularly equipment that is subject to freezing and is located in unheated areas, or areas that during a power failure would no longer be heated. Building staff also should be alert to exterior areas to ensure that pathways for building occupants and visitors are safe to use.

All building occupants should be kept informed, possibly by way of the building PA system, about the development of severe weather conditions that may affect their leaving the building. They should be advised to heed storm warnings issued by the National Weather Service (NWS). The NWS is a public service agency which aims to protect life and property from natural disasters such as flash floods, tornadoes, and severe thunderstorms. It is made up of a network of Weather Service Forecast Offices (WSFOs) and Weather Service Offices (WSOs).

Tornadoes

Tornadoes can "can occur in all fifty states, but the Midwest and Southeast parts of the country are the most vulnerable. Tornadoes can also strike at any time of the year, but occur most frequently during April, May, and June" (BOMA 1994, p. 66). A *tornado* is defined as "a violent storm, usually with heavy rain, in which wind rotates or constantly changes direction, especially in the Mississippi region of the United States" (*Reader's Digest* 1979). A tornado usually is characterized by a funnel-shaped cloud like a water spout.

If a threat of tornadoes is reported, tornado watch or tornado warning advisories may be issued by the NWS. A *tornado watch* means that tornadoes are possible; a *tornado warning* means that tornadoes actually have been sighted in the area.

Handling tornadoes, like handling earthquakes, can be approached in three distinct phases—before, during, and after the event. The following preventive measures were developed using *Before Disaster Strikes: Developing an Emergency Procedures Manual* by the Institute of Real Estate Management (IREM) as a resource.

Before the Tornado

National Weather Service advisories regarding the tornado should be monitored not only by tenants and their employees, but by building management, which may communicate updates of the situation over the building PA system or by telephone calls to office managers or other key tenant representatives. Preparations for the possibility of an incoming tornado may include the following:

- Secure or move outdoor objects such as trash containers, dumpsters, planters, signs, furniture, and vehicles that may blow away or cause damage to people or property.
- Prune trees of branches that may cause damage to the building, if time allows.
- Have occupants clear all objects from desks and working areas. All exposed paperwork should be stored in closed cabinets and other containers. Valuable equipment and documents should be moved from outer offices to interior rooms.
- To protect them from possible power surges, all office equipment, including computers, and appliances should be switched off and unplugged.
- All doors should be closed.
- Curtains and blinds should be shut.
- Personal possessions should be made ready in case of evacuation.
- Food, bottled water, and other supplies should be made ready in case they are needed.

The extent of preparation will depend on the time of day and day of the week that warning of the impending tornado is received. For example, if the warning is received after normal business hours when the majority of tenants have left the building, preparations within tenant space may not be possible or may be carried out on a restricted basis only. The extent of preparation also may be impacted by the behavior of the tornado. For example, if there is an abrupt change in the direction of the storm, preparatory actions may be curtailed substantially.

Depending on the expected nature of the tornado, building management may have engineering or janitorial staff board up or tape building windows, glass doors, and shopfronts on lower levels to reduce the possibility of pieces of broken glass becoming deadly missiles. Building engineering and security may be assigned to lock off building elevators at a level that is considered safe, or shut down HVAC systems and certain lighting. Walk-throughs of the building may be conducted (perhaps by floor wardens) to ensure that appropriate precautions are underway. It may be necessary to advise occupants to evacuate the building, or relocate to lower levels, including subterranean parking structures. If the building is evacuated, certain members of the building staff (usually engineering and security personnel) will often remain behind.

During the Tornado

Most actions of those inside a high-rise building are geared toward self-preservation during a tornado. The following are basic guidelines for this time:

- Do not panic.
- Take cover in interior areas or designated shelter areas. Interior areas may include building corridors that are well away from exterior glass windows, interior temporary or glass partitions, hanging objects, free-standing bookcases or cabinets, or other objects that may fall. Depending on the severity of the tornado, protect your head and face with your arms and get under a strong table or desk or shelter in areas such as interior offices or rest rooms.
- Stay in your protective position, unless it becomes unsafe to do so, until it appears safe to move.
- Do not attempt to use elevators because power may fail and passengers may become trapped.
- Do not attempt to leave the building.

After the Tornado

If there has been damage caused by the tornado, you can be most helpful by assisting building staff in the same ways as you would after an earthquake. Damage caused by a tornado may also have lasting effects on the building operations similar to the situation following an earthquake. (See "After the Earthquake" section earlier in this chapter.) The damage may not be finished either: in coastal areas, a tornado can be the forerunner of a hurricane.

Hurricanes

"Every Atlantic and Gulf coast area of the United States as well as the coastal areas of Hawaii and the Caribbean islands are threatened by hurricanes. Hurricane season extends from the beginning of June through November" (BOMA 1994, p. 67). A *hurricane*, which is also referred to as a *typhoon*, is defined as: "a violent windstorm . . . with air moving rapidly (up to 130 m.p.h.) around a central calm space, which with the whole system advances in a straight or curved track. Wind of 73 m.p.h. or more (force of 12 in the Beaufort Scale)" (*Reader's Digest* 1979). In addition to high winds, hurricanes are characterized by heavy rains. Although the winds can cause serious damage (see Figure 10.16), the majority of damage is a result of flooding during and after the hurricane. Remember, when weathering this kind of storm, that it has a central eye. When the hurricane passes over an area, the winds and rains will abate for a time period that may vary from a few minutes to half an hour or more. After this eye has passed, the storm will return with the full fury of its winds now gusting in the opposite direction. Hurricanes also may lead to the development of tornadoes.

> *1960, New York City*—"During Hurricane Donna, occupants of high-rise buildings were justifiably frightened when large glass panels of the curtain walls were blown *into* their offices by the wind pressure. They were probably even more frightened and amazed when the leeward wind action sucked the window panels *out* of their offices. These leeward panels fell into the street, creating an additional hazard to passersby. . . . The total wind force is the sum of the windward pressure and the leeward suction, but each of these two forces has its own local effects" (Salvadori 1980, pp. 50, 51).

> *August 24, 1992, South Florida*—In the predawn hours, Hurricane Andrew swept through southern Florida, leaving behind a 30-mile-wide swath of destruction. Houses and buildings were destroyed, thousands were left homeless, roads were blocked, telephone lines were downed, and power outages occurred.

If there is a threat of this kind of storm, hurricane watch or hurricane warning advisories may be issued by the NWS. A *hurricane watch* means that hurricane conditions constitute a threat to a coastal area; a *hurricane warning* means that sustained winds of 74 mph or higher are expected within 24 hours in a specific coastal area. Preparing for hurricanes requires similar methods to those employed in preparing for tornadoes, except that the flooding that often results from the heavy rains associated with them needs to be prepared for.

Before the Hurricane

National Weather Service advisories regarding the hurricane should be monitored in the same way as tornado advisories. Preparations for an incoming hurricane may include the following:

- Secure or move outdoor objects such as trash containers, dumpsters, planters, signs, furniture, and vehicles that may blow away or cause damage to people or property.
- Prune trees of branches that may cause damage to the building, if time allows.
- Have occupants clear all objects from desks and working areas. All exposed paperwork should be stored in closed cabinets and other containers. Valuable equipment and documents should be moved from outer offices to interior rooms. Heavy plastic can be used as a covering to lessen the chance of water damage.
- Valuable and water-sensitive equipment may be moved to upper levels to reduce the chance of damage by the flooding of lower levels.

Figure 10.16 ALICIA TAKES WINDOWS. On August 18, 1983, the high winds of Hurricane Alicia raked the downtown Houston, Texas, area and took a large toll on windows of the city's tall buildings. This is Allied Bank Plaza, which lost many windows. Used with permission from AP/WIDE WORLD PHOTOS.

- All doors should be closed.
- Curtains and blinds should be shut.
- To prepare for possible evacuation, personal possessions should be made ready.
- Food, bottled water, and other supplies should be made ready in case they are needed.

Building management, engineering or security staff, or floor wardens may conduct walk-throughs of the building to ensure that appropriate precautions are being undertaken.

The extent of preparation will depend on whether the hurricane is predicted to occur during business hours. "Because a hurricane's path is often tracked for days, there usually is time for preparation and preventive measures to be taken. At the minimum, a property manager should have at least one day's notice, inasmuch as hurricane watches will be upgraded to hurricane warnings when the hurricane is expected to strike an area within 24 hours" (IREM 1990, p. 138).

Depending on the expected nature of the hurricane, building management may have engineering, security, and janitorial staff take the following actions:

- Board up or tape building windows, glass doors, and shopfronts on lower levels to reduce the possibility of pieces of broken glass becoming deadly missiles.
- Lock off building elevators at an upper level that is considered safe from possible flooding.
- Shut down building HVAC systems and certain lighting.
- Lay down sandbags if flooding is expected.
- Advise occupants to evacuate the building, or relocate to lower levels of the building—but not subterranean areas, because of the potential for flooding. If the building is evacuated, certain members of the building staff (usually engineering and security personnel) will often remain behind.

During the Hurricane

It is of note that during a hurricane, horizontal swaying of the top of a high-rise may be caused by strong winds. Saladori (1980, p. 51) reports that:

> Under a strong wind the tops of the World Trade Center towers swing left and right of their vertical position by as much as three feet, and a hurricane can produce swings of six to seven feet on each side of the vertical. These horizontal swings are not structurally dangerous, but may be inconvenient for those who work at such great heights: occupants may become airsick.

Most actions of those inside a high-rise building are geared toward self-preservation during a hurricane. Follow the same basic guidelines as for during tornadoes.

After the Hurricane

If there has been damage caused by the hurricane, assist building staff in the same ways as you would after an earthquake. Damage caused by a hurricane also may have lasting effects on the building's operation similar to the situation following an earthquake. (See "After the Earthquake" section earlier in this chapter.)

Cyclones

A *cyclone* is defined as: "a system of winds rotating around a region of low barometric pressure (in the Northern hemisphere anti-clockwise, in the Southern hemisphere clockwise)" (*Reader's Digest* 1979). It is handled in a similar manner to a hurricane, except that flooding is usually not an anticipated problem.

Floods

Torrential rain, melting snow, a tsunami, or a hurricane may produce too much water for land, rivers, and flood control channels to handle and therefore result in serious flooding that will impact an entire area, including high-rise buildings. Floods also can occur as a result of a public water main breaking or a reservoir failing.

> *February 10, 1992, Los Angeles*—Within the space of two hours, eight inches of rain fell in the northwest portion of Los Angeles County and a torrent of rain entered the Los Angeles flood channel system. Storm water drains in several cities became clogged and could not handle the inundation of water. As a result, without warning, several subterranean parking facilities located beneath high-rise buildings became flooded with water up to two-feet deep. Substantial damage was caused to elevator systems because of water cascading into elevator shafts. Vehicles also sustained water damage, and a substantial cleanup of affected areas was required. The loss of elevator service for several days caused considerable inconvenience to building tenants who were forced to use stairwells to reach their place of work.

> *April 13, 1992, Chicago*—Floods of water inundated subterranean tunnels located beneath the downtown high-rise community. Almost 300 buildings were affected and many employees were unable to return to their place of work the next day. Some buildings reopened, but a massive cleanup of the impacted areas was required before business operations could fully return to normal.

If a *flash flood* occurs there usually will not be time for a building to prepare for the deluge. The first priority should be to provide for the safety of building occupants and visitors. Then efforts should concentrate on alleviating damage to the building and its contents. If advance warning of the flood is received, certain preparations can be taken, as the Building Owners and Managers Association (1994, p. 64) explains:

> Building contents can be removed or relocated to floor levels above the predicted flood level. Electricity can be turned off in areas likely to be flooded. Pumps and hoses can be readied. Sandbags or other protective devices can be put in place based on anticipated flood depths. If deep flooding is predicted, it may be advisable to allow floodwaters to enter basement areas or even to flood the basement intentionally in advance of the flood waters. This can reduce potential structural damage by lowering the hydrostatic [liquid] pressure on basement walls. Similarly, buried storage tanks may be flooded with clean water to prevent them from being crushed or pushed out of the ground by hydrostatic pressure.

The building owner or manager can decide whether to evacuate building occupants, depending on the expected seriousness of the flood and its time of arrival.

Water Leaks

A water leak in a high-rise building can result in considerable damage to the structure and its contents. Leaks may be caused by a broken water pipe, a severed fire system sprinkler head, leakage of water through subterranean walls, overflow of a toilet receptacle, a backed-up sewer line, a blocked drain, failure of a sump pump, or leakage of an artificial water fountain. It also may be caused by someone deliberately leaving a water tap running in an area such as a public rest room. The worse time for such an event to occur is after normal business operating hours when the number of building staff and occupants is greatly reduced, and when such a leak may go undetected for an extended period of time.

When a water leak is discovered, the first priority is to locate its source and attempt to shut off or control it as soon as possible. If there is difficulty in determining the exact location of the leak, it may be possible to shut down the entire system that is supplying water to the area. For safety reasons, electrical power to the affected area should be shut down, or electrical equipment turned off. This should be done *before* the leak is addressed if the electricity poses any danger. If possible, any building contents at risk of being damaged, or subjected to further damage, should be removed to a safe area or covered with plastic sheeting. Hand mopping or mechanical pumping can then be used to remove excess water. If not discovered quickly, serious water leaks—particularly those on upper floors of a high-rise—can have devastating effects. Water may drain down through multiple floors not only by way of stairwells, but also by poke-through construction (described earlier in this chapter under "Fire"), which can lead to water in concealed ceiling spaces, soaked acoustical ceiling tiles that may fall from their own weight, water-soaked walls, and malfunction and possible failure of electrical systems if water comes in contact with them.

Chemical/Hazardous Material Incidents

There are many different names and definitions of the term *hazardous materials*, depending on the nature of the problem being considered. The U.S. Department of Transportation (DOT) and the National Fire Protection Association (NFPA) use this term. OSHA and the Environmental Protection Agency (EPA) use the term *hazardous substances*, but their meaning is different. For our purposes, the NFPA's definition of a *hazardous material* will be used: "a substance (gas, liquid, or solid) capable of creating harm to people, property, and the environment" (NFPA 472 1989, p. 472-5). These substances may be corrosive, explosive, flammable, irritating, oxidizing, poisonous, radioactive, or toxic in effect.

A high-rise may be affected by hazardous materials generated within the building or from a source outside it. High-rise commercial office buildings, like any other facility, may contain such materials; these, by law, must be identified and Material Safety Data Sheets (MSDS) must be provided for each such chemical located on-site. As Fischer and Green (1992, p. 277) explain,

Each MSDS contains seven sections:

1. Product identification and emergency notification instructions.
2. Hazardous ingredients list and exposure limits.
3. Physical and chemical characteristics (vapor pressure, odor, etc.).
4. Physical hazards and how to handle them (that is, fire and explosion).
5. Reactivity data—what the product may react with and whether it is stable.
6. Health hazard information—how the product can enter the body, signs and symptoms of problems, and emergency first-aid steps.
7. Safe handling procedures.

The following hazardous materials, as mentioned in *Hazardous Materials in an Office Environment* (Bachman 1992, p. 6), may be present *within* a high-rise commercial office building:

- Photographic materials such as fixer solutions.
- Printing/reproduction/art materials such as inks, thinners, solvents, ammonia, and paint.
- Liquid office materials such as cleaners and pesticides.
- Maintenance supplies and materials such as oils, engine fluids, transformer dielectrics, lead acid batteries, paints, thinners, solvents, and fluorescent light tubes.
- Janitorial and cleaning materials such as cleaners containing solvents, acids, caustics, chlorine compounds, pesticides, and polishes.
- Renovation and construction materials such as varnishes, paints, coatings, glues, sealants, asbestos, and compressed gas.

The Code of Federal Regulations (CFR Section 40, part 761) has imposed a series of deadlines for protecting, retrofilling and reclassifying, or retrofitting polychlorinated biphenyl (PCB) transformers—noncompliance with any of these requirements can result in substantial fines, penalties, and possible imprisonment. All PCB transformers used in or near a commercial building are required by law to be registered with the building owner, who is responsible for maintaining records and adhering to reporting provisions. Building owners or managers should direct questions regarding the interpretation of the code to the EPA.

Tenants should be made aware of the fact that they are required to notify building management about hazardous materials within their offices. Tenants should instruct employees who may come in contact with hazardous materials on the location of the MSDS manual, how to interpret the information on MSDSs and labels, and how they can obtain additional information regarding hazards. This training should be documented.

February 15, 1992, Los Angeles—This fire occurred on the seventh floor of the 14-story County Health Building in downtown Los Angeles and was first reported at 10:06 A.M. As a result of the fire, smoke and heat damage occurred on the floor of origin and the floors above it, and water damaged floors below it. The fire suppression efforts of the 220 Los Angeles City Fire Department fire fighters assigned to this incident were hampered by (1) the fact that the building contained hazardous asbestos materials used in building construction, (2) a lack of automatic fire detection equipment near the origin of the fire to provide early warning, (3) a lack of automatic sprinklers to control the fire in its incipient stage, and (4) the failure of the building's HVAC system to automatically shut down when smoke was detected. Hence, the HVAC system distributed products of combustion to the eighth and ninth floors. The fire was controlled within one hour and 20 minutes of the initial alarm. According to the Los Angeles City Fire Department, its origin was probably accidental, caused by an arc/short of an undetermined electrical source.

The types of hazardous materials *outside* a high-rise commercial office building may include PCBs (as already mentioned), radioactive substances in a nearby nuclear reactor, potentially dangerous materials transported along an adjacent railway line, or flammable and potentially harmful chemicals contained in a petrochemical facility close to the building.

As mentioned at the start of this chapter, in high-rise structures the contamination of life-support systems, such as the air and potable water supply, are threats that can be actuated accidentally or intentionally and can develop quickly into catastrophic proportions because of the rapid propagation of contaminants. Therefore, to minimize or eliminate the hazards to people, property, or the environment, every chemical/hazardous material incident should be handled by building emergency staff trained according to standard operating procedures.

Procedures for Handling Incidents

Within the Building

These procedures are dictated largely by the type of chemical/hazardous material involved, the nature and scope of the incident, and the designated response specified by the appropriate MSDS. In addition, the following questions should be considered:

- What outside haz-mat (hazardous material) responding agencies should be immediately notified of the incident?
- Should the affected area be secured and entry to unauthorized persons denied? Should the floor involved be sealed and all elevators serving the floor shut down?
- Is it necessary to shut down HVAC systems serving the floor where the incident has occurred? Should this shutdown be expanded to include other areas or zones?
- Is it necessary to evacuate occupants from the area or floor where the incident has occurred? Will they be allowed to use elevators as well as stairwells? To what area will they be evacuated? Is it necessary to evacuate other floors?
- After the incident has been handled, what agencies must be notified?
- What documentation of the incident is required?

There are a number of agencies and regulations that govern the way hazardous materials are handled and the response to incidents involving these substances. The Superfund Amendments and Reauthorization Act (SARA) of 1986 established controls and requirements for reporting incidents and for emergency response by both industry and public safety agencies. The EPA administers the section of the SARA legislation that requires industry to report releases of hazardous substances to government agencies and the public. In addition, the NFPA has developed many standards relating to hazardous materials such as NFPA 471, *Responding to Hazardous Materials Incidents*, and NFPA 472, *Professional Competence of Responders to Hazardous Materials Incidents*.

If building owners or managers use employees on-site to clean up or work with hazardous materials because of the immediate cost savings involved, they must be very careful to comply with the applicable OSHA regulation, or they could incur substantial penalties and fines. As Giordano (1995, p. 31) details,

> During clean-up operations, the employer must periodically monitor employees who may be exposed to hazardous substances in excess of OSHA's regulations. Once the presence and concentration of specific hazardous substances and health hazards have been established, employees involved in the clean-up operations must be informed of any risks associated with their work. Under certain circumstances, regular ongoing medical surveillance of employees by a licensed physician, and without cost to the employees, may be required.

Outside the Building

These procedures, like those just described, will be determined largely by the type of chemical/hazardous material involved and the nature and scope of the incident, but there is one major consideration in handling such an incident: Are occupants to be evacuated from the building, or will they be able to remain in the building?

If they are to be evacuated, building management must decide when this will occur, whether evacuees will be allowed to use elevators as well as stairwells, and to what areas they will be evacuated. If occupants remain, it must be decided whether it is necessary to shut down the building HVAC systems, and whether doors and openings to the building should be sealed. These questions usually will be addressed by the responding agencies who assume control of the incident.

Labor Disputes, Demonstrations, Riots, and Civil Disorder

Events such as labor disputes, demonstrations, riots, and civil disorder can have a significant impact on the day-to-day operation of a high-rise building. Their effects will be influenced by the nature of the incident, the number of persons participating in it, the conduct of these persons, the response of building or tenant management and involved outside agencies, and the location of the incident in relation to the building.

Each type of activity needs to handled on its own merits, but it must be remembered that building and tenant managements have the right to conduct their daily business activities without disruption as a result of unlawful or unauthorized behavior. They also have the right to secure and protect their own property and assets. In particular, the owner or manager has the right to revoke permission for people to enter a building when it is open to the public ("Right to Pass by Permission. Permission Revocable at Any Time" signs or plates should already be installed on sidewalks outside the building); irrespective of this, the tenant always has the right to refuse persons entry to their premises.

Labor Disputes

Labor disputes may be peaceful affairs where orderly groups of persons assemble outside the building, quietly display placards and signs to passing motorists, pass out leaflets explaining their cause, and present petitions to the parties involved. They can, however, be violent events, where large groups of angry persons protesting a labor issue pertaining to the building, or one of its tenants, surround the building to prevent occupants and visitors from entering or leaving, and forcibly try to enter the building, throwing rocks and various other objects at it.

Before a Labor Dispute

If the potential exists for such a situation, building management should take these steps:

- Designate a representative of management, preferably one experienced in handling such incidents, to assume control of the building's response to the situation. If necessary, obtain legal counsel.
- Initiate liaison with local law enforcement agencies at a senior level.
- Explain the situation to representatives of the various departments within the building (engineering, janitorial, security, parking, etc.) and keep them informed of the status of the incident. These persons in turn should brief their staffs as to their responsibilities and provide any required additional training. Instruct all building personnel to avoid contact (particularly any type of confrontation) with those involved in the dispute, and to immediately report problems and direct all inquiries about the dispute (particularly those from the media) to building management. Security personnel, amongst their other duties, will be responsible for documenting events, particularly by investigating incidents that involve unlawful conduct (noting the date, time, location and possible identities of those involved, including any witnesses), and by photographing or video recording the events for possible later use as evidence. The overt use of a video or still camera can be an invaluable deterrent to illegal behavior—however, do note that conducting surveillance on and recording lawful picketing activities may infringe on the legal rights of employees and the union.
- Examine the building security program, including insurance policies pertaining to such incidents, in light of the potential threat. If the present deployment of security staff, plus the expected commitment of local law enforcement, is not sufficient to handle a labor dispute, make arrangements for additional personnel from a professional contract security provider. If appropriate, consult major tenants as to the status of their security preparations.
- Establish a command center including provisions for: adequate radio communications with all building personnel involved in handling the incident; still and video cameras for recording events involving mass picketing, blocking of entrances and exits, and other unlawful behavior (the building's CCTV system could also be used for this, if applicable); and a means to maintain a chronological log of events
- If the labor dispute involves unions, consider providing a separate entrance for workers involved in the dispute. Also, it may be necessary to consult other unions (including tenant unions), whose members work at the building but are not involved in the dispute, to ensure there is no disruption of their activities.

- Depending on the type of labor dispute and its expected impact on building operations, apprise all building tenants of the situation and instruct them to report problems to building management representatives or to the authorities.
- Make sure all oral and written communications regarding the event are cleared with a building management representative, its legal counsel, or designated representatives of building workers. Appoint one representative to handle media relations.

During labor disputes it is essential for all management and staff to remain neutral. Confrontations will only interfere with management's role of providing for the safety of all building users, protecting the assets of the building and its occupants, and minimizing any disruption of building operations.

During a Labor Dispute

If the dispute occurs *outside the building*, there are basic steps that may need to be taken to handle the situation:

- Call local law enforcement agencies to respond if it is a serious problem and their assistance is definitely required.
- Lock exterior doors to the building. Provide escorts for persons entering or leaving.
- Have building security or law enforcement authorities establish a perimeter around the building, or at entrances to it, or to any parking structures.
- If the participants outside the building want to enter it for the purposes of handing a petition to a representative within the building, permit this under mutually accepted conditions. These may include an agreement that the delegation consist of no greater than five persons, that there will be an established time constraint on the visit, and that an escort will be provided at all times.
- Depending on the seriousness of the situation, notify occupants on lower levels to close their window drapes or blinds. If any occupants should leave the building, they should avoid any confrontations with those involved in the situation.

If the dispute occurs *inside the building*, the way to handle it will depend on the nature of the situation, the number of persons involved, and their behavior. If there is an attempt to unlawfully enter a tenant space, the tenant should call for the assistance of security staff, and, if the situation warrants, local law enforcement. Further steps may need to be taken if the situation escalates. Participants in the dispute may be asked to leave if they are disrupting the authorized activities of the building; for example, if there are numerous protesters crowding lobbies, exits, and stairwell entrances, their presence may pose a life safety hazard to other building users. Elevators may be shut down to prevent access from the lobby to upper levels of the building. In addition, tenants may need to be notified of the situation and advised to lock doors to their offices.

Demonstrations

A *demonstration* is a gathering of people for the purposes of publicly displaying their attitude toward a particular cause, issue, or other matter. Such an activity, if carried out peacefully on public property, is permissible. However, such an activity may not obstruct, block, or in any way interfere with the ingress to and egress from private property such as a high-rise building. Prohibited interference includes any harassment or confrontation of building occupants and/or visitors. If demonstrators attempt to enter the building without permission, they may be arrested for trespassing.

As with a labor dispute, a demonstration may vary from a peaceful affair to a violent one (see Figure 10.17). The preparation for and handling of a demonstration is similar to that just outlined for a labor dispute.

Riots and Civil Disorder

Over the past 130 years there have been a number of major civil disturbances in large U.S. cities—New York (draft riots of July 1863), Detroit (riots of July 1967), Newark (riots of July 1967), Miami (riots of 1982), and Los Angeles (Watts riots of 1965 and the 1992 riots).

> *April 29, 1992, Los Angeles*—The so-called "Rodney King" riots erupted on this date after "not guilty" verdicts were handed down in the trial involving four white Los Angeles Police Department officers charged in the unlawful beating of a black civilian motorist named Rodney King. The three-day riot

Figure 10.17 BATTLE AT THE BARRICADES. New York City Police used their clubs in an effort to keep angry demonstrators behind barricades set up outside the Sydenham Hospital on September 20, 1980. The demonstrators were protesting the closing of the facility.   Used with permission from AP/ WIDE WORLD PHOTOS.

and civil disorder was the most destructive disturbance in the United States since the Civil War. For a time, the community watched helplessly as a swathe of destruction swept through: 53 people died, more than 2,400 were injured, and 862 buildings were set on fire, with a total fire loss of over $500 million.

The basic steps in handling a riot and civil disorder are similar to those outlined for dealing with a labor dispute or demonstration, but there are some major differences, largely determined by the nature of the riot, the behavior of the rioters, the area of the community affected by the riot, and the response of law enforcement in containing any civil disorder.

For example, the 1992 Los Angeles civil disturbance involved a large proportion of the community (many of whom were bent on committing criminal acts against people and property) and was widespread throughout Los Angeles County. It was initially met with passive resistance from the law enforcement agency primarily charged with maintaining law and order in the city. In fact, for much of the three-day event, local law enforcement agencies were overwhelmed by the immense proportion of the disturbance and were unable to contain the full-scale looting and burning that was occurring. Likewise, fire agencies had tremendous demands for their services and were unable, in the early stages, to respond to certain locations without being accompanied by protective police escorts. During this period many businesses were totally dependent on their own resources, including the utilization of private security staff, both proprietary and contract, to protect themselves and their assets.

Many high-rise commercial office buildings in Los Angeles took the following steps:

- A representative of building management assumed control of the building's response to the disturbance. A command center was established to maintain good radio communication with all building personnel.
- A chronological log of events was maintained.
- Wherever possible, CCTV cameras were used to monitor external areas of the building.
- Security staff, equipped with radio communications and binoculars, were posted on the roof or upper floors to observe activity outside.
- Exterior doors to the building and parking structures were locked. Escorts to parking areas were provided.
- Windows and shopfronts on lower levels were boarded up.
- Building management notified occupants, by telephone and announcements over the PA system, of the civil disturbance in the community. Some of these advisories recommended that tenants immediately leave the building or notify management of their plans.
- HVAC systems and certain lighting were shut down.
- Fire hoses were attached to standpipes and made ready in the building lobby.
- Elevators were moved to upper floors and were taken out of service. A freight/ service elevator remained at the ground floor lobby for the use of engineering and security personnel.
- A skeleton crew of building management, engineering, and security staff remained in the building; many worked 12-hour shifts and stayed even when not on duty.

As mentioned in Chapter 8, *Management of the Security Function*, some high-rise commercial office buildings contracted with civilians trained and certified to carry concealed weapons to supplement their unarmed security staffs during this difficult period of civil unrest. Fortunately, most office buildings were not subjected to the widespread looting, which centered mainly on retail businesses containing foodstuffs, liquor, cigarettes, electronic appliances, furniture, and clothing.

Aircraft Collisions

A high-rise building, like any other, is vulnerable to the remote possibility that an aircraft flying off-course could collide with it. Obviously, the additional height, as compared with other structures, makes them more susceptible.

> *July 28, 1945, New York City*—At approximately 10:00 A.M. on a rainy, foggy Saturday, a U.S. Army Air Corps B-25 bomber crashed into the north wall of the 102-story Empire State Building (see Figure 10.18). The impact tore a hole, approximately 20 feet by 18 feet, in the exterior wall of the building at the 78th and 79th floors, and a portion of the plane actually crossed one floor and exited through the south wall. The crash, along with several fires that resulted from flaming gasoline, resulted in the deaths of 3 crew members of the plane and 11 building occupants, injuries to 25 persons including several with severe burns, and property damage estimated at half a million dollars. A severed standpipe and damaged elevators caused by the crash restricted New York City Fire Department fire fighters' efforts; however, within an estimated 35 minutes they were able to control the fire. Despite the severity of the collision, the structural integrity of the building held.

Because the majority of today's airplanes travel at higher speeds and are much larger, heavier, and carry far greater fuel loads than the B-25 that collided with the Empire State Building, a similar incident involving a modern high-rise building would have far more devastating consequences.

The response to such an incident should be similar to that required for an explosion or fire. There would need to be an immediate call to the fire department to request assistance, and rapid evacuation of any building occupants from the affected area, including any injured persons, if remaining would subject them to more serious injury. Any fire would have to be contained and suppressed if safe to do so. Unauthorized persons would be restricted from entering the building or the actual incident scene, and a command center would be set up to oversee operations.

Hostage and Barricade Situations

In today's violent society, high-rise commercial office buildings have been subject to several hostage-taking and barricade situations.

> In 1982, a man entered a prominent Los Angeles high-rise, accosted the building's chief engineer in the main lobby, and demanded to be taken to the roof. On reaching it, he then tried to obtain publicity for a cause he was promoting—in this case, "smoking is bad for your health." Building management immediately called the police department, and after a tense standoff, the individual eventually surrendered without anyone being injured.

Figure 10.18   BOMBER STRIKES THE EMPIRE STATE BUILDING—A view from an upper floor of the building vividly shows the gaping hole at the 79th floor created by the impact of a B-25 bomber. Part of the wreckage of the plane, which crashed into the building on July 28, 1945, protrudes from the opening.   Used with permission from AP/WIDE WORLD PHOTOS.

In most hostage situations it is absolutely imperative to inform law enforcement as quickly as possible; these agencies have specialized training in handling such incidents. Before their arrival, the area where the incident is occurring must be contained to isolate the event from other individuals and, hopefully, to prevent the incident from moving beyond the area. Also, if safe to do so, anyone not involved in the incident should be evacuated from the location.

Some tenant companies, depending on the nature of their business and their potential for such incidents, have crisis management teams established in case such an incident occurs. These companies will be prepared to make decisions and, in conjunction with law enforcement, take the necessary actions to handle the scenario appropriately.

Impact of Building Emergencies on Security

Most, if not all, of the foregoing emergencies have some impact on the security of a high-rise building depending, once again, on the nature of both the incident and the facility. By assessing each of these emergencies and the impact they could have on the operation of the building, preventive measures can be designed to reduce either their likelihood or their projected effects. Yet as The Merritt Company (1991 p. 19-119) says:

> Some of the life-safety requirements [in a high-rise structure] actually pose unique security difficulties. The code provision which insists upon unimpeded exit during a building emergency means that if such an emergency can be faked, egress may be possible under little or no surveillance. Even if the emergency is genuine, it may occur at a time when the security forces are unprepared for the joint demands of emergency response and heightened security attention.

When a Building Emergency Is Faked

A few years ago, in a high-rise commercial office building, an individual set off a fire alarm by activating a manual fire alarm station on a tenant floor. This resulted in the evacuation of occupants from that floor and also two floors above and below it. An accomplice waiting on one of the evacuated floors, after all occupants had left, quickly roamed unchallenged through tenant offices and stole items from handbags and billfolds in coats that had been left behind in the hurry to evacuate. The thief then entered a stairwell, descended to the ground level, and walked out of the building.

Such an event could similarly be staged by two individuals to gain unauthorized entry to a floor that is normally always secured (i.e., the elevators only proceed to the floor if an authorized access card is used). One person could activate a manual fire alarm station on one floor, thereby causing the stairwell door locks to unlock automatically (if this feature is provided). An accomplice waiting in a stairwell on the targeted floor could then proceed into the tenant space (sometimes stairwells lead directly into tenant areas rather than into common corridors) and gain access to commit a crime. The thief could then board a passenger elevator—because during fire alarm situations in most high-rise buildings, the elevators remain in service unless an elevator lobby smoke detector has been activated—or re-enter the stairwell and proceed down to the ground level to rapidly exit the building. Some facilities have security staff manually recall all elevators serving floors in alarm to prevent occupants from using them during fire and fire alarm situations. This practice has the added advantage of securing the floor from unauthorized access using the elevators.

The following measures can be used to maintain a moderate level of building security during a fire or fire alarm emergency:

- If stairwells lead directly into tenant areas, consider redesigning the area to remove this security hazard.
- Train building occupants to always take personal valuables with them during evacuation and, if such actions do not place them in danger, to quickly secure other items.
- Position CCTV cameras with alarm-activated recording devices in tenant high-risk areas (particularly where valuables such as cash are found) to at least obtain a record of an incident.
- Install motion detector and CCTV cameras in building stairwells close to the ground-level exit. The system may be designed so that if a person comes down the stairwell, a motion detector will activate a video-recording device to record their presence.

The fact that security and fire life safety are different disciplines, and that their priorities are sometimes in conflict with each other, is nowhere better demonstrated than at the stairwell exit. "The conflict lies between the need to have immediate, unobstructed, one-step exit from a building that may be on fire and the need to prevent unauthorized ingress or egress" (Atlas 1993, p. 5).

As discussed in Chapter 3, *Security Systems and Equipment*, stairwell exterior fire doors may be secured with an electromagnetic lock to deter unauthorized entry from the *outside* of the building. This maintains a high degree of security and has no impact on life safety. However, only under specific conditions are doors designated as fire exits permitted to be locked from the *inside* of the stairwell at the point of exit from the building. The NFPA 101 *Life Safety Code* (1994, pp. 101-28, 29) states:

> Section 5-2.1.5.1. Doors shall be arranged to be opened readily from the egress side whenever the building is occupied. Locks, if provided, shall not require the use of a key, tool, special knowledge, or effort for operation from the inside of the building.
>
> Section 5-2.1.5.3. Doors shall be openable with no more than one releasing operation.
>
> Section 5-2.1.5.5. No lock, padlock, hasp, bar, chain, or other device, or combination thereof shall be installed or maintained on or in connection with any door on which panic hardware or fire exit hardware is required by this *Code* if such device prevents or is intended to prevent the free use of the door for purposes of egress.

These life safety requirements present a security problem—the need to maintain immediate, unobstructed, one-step exit from the stairwell at the ground level provides an opportunity for a person who has perpetrated a crime within the building to make a rapid exit.

The NFPA addresses the need to maintain a degree of security on these emergency exit doors in NFPA 101 *Life Safety Code*, Section 5-2.1.6 (1994, pp. 101-29): "Special Locking Arrangements." If adopted by the authority having jurisdiction, these arrangements permit the installation of delayed egress locks on stairwell doors.

> Section 5-2.1.6.1 In buildings protected throughout by an approved, supervised automatic fire detection system or approved, supervised automatic sprinkler system, and where specifically permitted by Chapters 8 through 29 [of NFPA 101 *Life Safety Code*], doors in low and ordinary hazard content areas as defined by 4-2.2 [i.e., those hazards most likely found in high-rise commercial office buildings] shall be permitted to be equipped with approved, listed, locking devices that shall:
>
> (a) Unlock upon actuation of an approved, supervised automatic sprinkler system installed in accordance with Section 7-7 ["Automatic Sprinklers and Other Extinguishing Equipment"], or upon the actuation of any heat detector or not more than two smoke detectors of an approved, supervised automatic fire detection system in accordance with Section 7-6 ["Fire Detection, Alarm, and Communication Systems"], and
> (b) Unlock upon loss of power controlling the lock or locking mechanism, and
> (c) Initiate an irreversible process that will release the lock within 15 seconds upon application to the release device required in 5-2.1.5.3 of a force that shall not be required to exceed 15 lbs (67 N) nor be required to be continuously applied for more than 3 seconds. The initiation of the release process shall activate a signal in the vicinity of the door to ensure those attempting to egress that the system is functional. Once the door lock has been released by the application of force to the releasing device, relocking shall be by manual means only. Exception to (c): The authority having jurisdiction shall be permitted to approve a delay not to exceed 30 seconds provided that reasonable life safety is ensured.
> (d) On the door adjacent to the release sign, a sign shall be provided that reads: "PUSH UNTIL ALARM SOUNDS. DOOR CAN BE OPENED IN 15 SECONDS." Sign letters shall be at least 1 in. (2.5 cm) high and of at least 1/8-in. (0.3 cm) stroke width.
> (e) Emergency lighting in accordance with Section 5-9 ["Emergency Lighting"] shall be provided at the door.

As Atlas (1993, p. 5) points out, "If the exit doors are designed as part of an integrated system, the time delay can be a substantial crime prevention tool" (see Figure 10.19).

If a person is using the stairwell to escape the building at the ground level after committing a crime on an upper floor, the following sequence of events could be designed to occur when he or she pushes on the emergency exit release bar: (1) An alarm on the door will sound but the door will not immediately open. (2) Activation of the door alarm will trigger an alarm signal at the Security Command Center to alert security staff to the situation. The person could be challenged by building security using an intercom that communicates with this area and staff members could be dispatched immediately to the location. If the suspect is attempting to flee the building, for example, security could go to the outside of the stairwell and possibly intercept him or her. (3) A CCTV camera at the emergency exit door could be activated to record the event.

Figure 10.19 Pair of emergency exit fire doors equipped with a delayed exit system. Note the rim-mounted push bar, the surface-mounted electromagnetic lock at the top of each door (close to the center divider), and the key switch that operates the electromagnetic lock immediately adjacent to the pair of doors on the right-hand side. (Each door is also equipped with surface-mounted automatic door-closing mechanisms.)   Courtesy of Von Duprin, Incorporated, Indianapolis, IN.

Thus, this 15- to 30-second egress delay may allow enough time for security staff to take action and to obtain a recorded image that may be helpful in identifying the individual and any property they may be carrying. The lock provides, then, an opportunity to implement basic security measures without a substantial impact on life safety. Some delayed egress locking systems are even designed with features such as verbal exiting instructions and a lighted digital countdown display to indicate how many seconds remain before the door will release (Security Door Controls 1995).

When an Emergency Overwhelms Security Staff

It is possible that a building emergency may be of such magnitude that security staff are unprepared to handle both the emergency response itself and the heightened security demands created by the incident. This may occur especially with fires (particularly if multiple ones simultaneously occur), explosions, violence in the workplace, civil disturbances, and some natural disasters.

The 1993 NYWTC bombing in New York (detailed in the "Explosions, Bombs, and Bomb Threats" section earlier in the chapter) illustrates this point. After the explosion, NYWTC security staff were involved in caring for the injured, assisting hundreds of fire fighters (the number of which constituted the greatest single response to a fire in the New York City Fire Department's history) and other emergency services in occupant evacuation, and assisting other agencies—the Port Authority Police and New York Transit Police among others—to control access to the complex. Because of the enormity of the incident, the thousands of people affected, and the disastrous effects the explosion had on building fire life safety systems, building security staff were inundated with demands for their services and were strained to the breaking point.

Dealing with the Media

Jack Popejoy, anchor/reporter for KFWB-AM in Los Angeles, talks about media relations from the media representatives' point of view:

> Our job, as dedicated journalists, is to attract an audience that can be sold to advertisers so that our paychecks will be good at the bank. That is neither cynical nor a joke. If we do not accomplish that, keeping our news organization financially viable, we will be out of a job. Our craft and our skill, then, is to take your emergency and make it audience-attracting: compelling, memorable, understandable, and important (Popejoy 1993, p. 8).

When an emergency draws the attention of the news media, the information released to them must be timely and accurate. Misinformation and news leaks of confidential information can be damaging to those involved. Information should be given only by persons authorized to do so and, if possible, only by persons who are experienced in dealing with the media.

It is essential to direct all inquiries from the news media to one individual appointed as spokesperson. All others, unless authorized otherwise, should be instructed not to discuss the situation with outsiders, especially the news media. It is important for the designated spokesperson to "understand that what they want from you is a quote (*soundbite*) that is understandable, memorable, speaks to the concerns of the audience, and projects emotion. If you accomplish that, you can be almost certain the media will transmit what you gave them in your words instead of theirs" (Popejoy 1993, p. 8).

The 1988 First Interstate Tower fire is an excellent example of how to successfully handle the media. Despite this tragedy that resulted in the loss of one life, multiple smoke inhalation–related injuries, and a financial loss of over $100 million, First Interstate Bank of California (whose corporate headquarters were located in the building) and the Los Angeles City Fire Department received very good press from the incident. Although few building owners or managers have the public relations resources of a major bank or a large city fire department, there are lessons to be learned from these organizations' techniques.

Beginning on the night of the fire, First Interstate Bank's Director of Public Affairs, John Popovich, and senior bank executives gave timely press releases to the media. These releases indicated that the bank had been prepared for such an emergency and would continue to provide for its customers by being open for business the very next day. Such actions avoided the financial impact of stock price falls and customer panic that could have resulted. Within hours of the fire, the bank set up a media center with 20 telephones and a customer "hot line" to deal with inquiries. Reporters and camera crews were permitted to take photographs of the damaged building and conduct interviews with key bank personnel. The bank also repeatedly publicized the fact that it had implemented a written Business Recovery Plan that, only weeks before the fire, had been tested by simulation of an earthquake disaster. First Interstate Tower representatives dealt with potential criticism for having no working sprinkler system by raising the point that the bank had made a voluntary decision to install such a system, and that it was 85 percent complete at the time of the fire.

The Los Angeles City Fire Department, through the fire suppression efforts of its highly trained members, achieved a tremendous operational feat in handling this incident—the largest fire involving a high-rise structure in the city's history. This was made clear to the general public by observing their efforts and through statements given to the media by fire department management, including Chief Donald O. Manning and Deputy Chief Doug Anthony. Accurate facts were released to indicate that 383 personnel (50 percent of the Los Angeles City Fire Department's resources), 64 fire suppression companies, 10 fire department ambulances, 17 private ambulances, 4 helicopters, plus support equipment were committed to bringing the situation under control. The department also used this opportunity to publicize the fact that many of the high-rises in the city were unsprinklered and that more stringent sprinkler retrofit laws were needed; it also released information that its fire fighters had communication difficulties during the fire because they had to use an antiquated radio system. Statements such as these helped influence the Los Angeles City Council to stiffen legislation regarding sprinkler retrofits for high-rise commercial office buildings, and also led to the Fire Department being given funding to obtain a new radio system.

Within weeks of the incident, First Interstate Bancorp, in conjunction with the Los Angeles City Fire Department, made a videotape available to the general public depicting the events, lauding the superb firefighting efforts of the Los Angeles City Fire Department, and explaining how the bank had pre-planned for such an emergency.

The following are some basic principles for effectively handling the media to advantage during and after a major emergency:

1. Preplan how the media will be handled. Consider these questions: What type of information will be released? Is it possible to give the media a marketable story? How can victims and their families be shielded? How can the image of the building or company be protected? Under what circumstances will photographs be permitted?

2. Designate a media spokesperson or public information person before an incident occurs. For various reasons, it is best if this person is a member of senior management: "The media will more readily accept that person who will have better access to the inside story and who will more quickly understand implications of legal issues, corporate recovery, and business" (Popejoy 1993, p. 8). Instruct building staff to courteously refer all requests for information or interviews to this designated media spokesperson.

3. Decide how media representatives will be accommodated and what access they will be granted to the facility. Will a staging area for their operations be designated? If attempts are made to keep them out and not deal with them, they will cover the story anyway, with or without the input of people who may know the real facts of the emergency in question.

4. Present timely and accurate information to the media.

An underlying reason for dealing with the media is so that the dissemination of information can be controlled and presented in a light that the organization involved wants it to be. Jack Popejoy (1993) sums it up this way: "You can control and manipulate the media if and only if you tell the truth. If you lie or withhold, you're dead meat. In the short term, we will quickly know it because we are always in private contact with our offices, which monitor each other, monitor all police and fire frequencies, and have access to wire services and telephone tipsters" (p. 9).

Summary

There are any number of emergency situations that can affect a high-rise commercial office building at any point in time. These include fires, fire alarms, explosions, bombs and bomb threats, violence in the workplace, medical emergencies, power failures, elevator malfunctions and entrapments, earthquakes, tsunamis, volcanoes, winter storms, tornadoes, hurricanes, cyclones, floods, water leaks, chemical/hazardous material incidents, labor disputes, demonstrations, riots and civil disorder, aircraft collisions, and hostage and barricade situations. Their impact on building operations and security may depend on the geographic and topographic location of the structure, its design and type of construction, the type and location of building security and fire life safety systems and equipment, and the location of the emergency incident itself. The need for an office building to maintain a predetermined level of security under normal operating conditions, while allowing immediate unimpeded exit under emergency conditions, is a dilemma that demands the attention of building owners, managers, tenants, security, and fire life safety professionals. Also, when an emergency attracts the attention of the news media, the way in which the building owner or manager handles the press will substantially impact the public's perception of the incident and the building itself.

References

ATF, *Bomb Threats and Physical Security Planning*, Bureau of Alcohol, Tobacco and Firearms, Department of the Treasury (ATF P 7550.2, Washington, DC, July 1987).

ATF, *1993 Explosives Incidents Reports*, Bureau of Alcohol, Tobacco and Firearms, Department of the Treasury, Washington, DC, 1993, pp. 19 and 21. Includes data from the Federal Bureau of Investigation, the United States Postal Service, and the Bureau of Alcohol, Tobacco and Firearms.

Atlas, Randall I., "Security design: Designing fire exits," *Protection of Assets Manual*, 9th printing. Editor Timothy J. Walsh (Used with permission from The Merritt Company, Santa Monica, CA, 800/638-7597. Copyright July 1993), Bulletin.

Bachman, James M., "Hazardous materials in an office environment," *BICEPP News* (Business and Industry Council for Emergency Planning and Preparedness, Spring 1992).

Berry, Kathleen N., "How to protect your company from office violence," *Investor's Business Daily*, March 28, 1994. As reported in "Violence in the workplace," *ASIS-NET Security Newsbriefs and Security News Database* (Bethesda, MD, copyright United Press International, Reuter's).

BOMA, "Considerations for specific types of emergencies," *Emergency Planning Guidebook* (Building Owners and Managers Association International, Washington, DC, 1994).

Bordes, Roy N., "Workplace violence," *Security Concepts* (Terra Publishing, Inc., Salamanca, NY, January 1994).

Boyce, Roger, Sr., "Occupancies in special structures and high-rise buildings," *Fire Protection Handbook*, 12th ed., Editor-in-Chief, Arthur E. Cote, Managing Editor, Jim L. Linville (All NFPA material in this chapter is used with permission of the National Fire Protection Association, Quincy, MA. Copyright 1991).

Bryan, John L., "Fire detection systems," *Fire Suppression and Detection Systems* (Macmillan Publishing Co., Inc., New York, 1982), p. 320.

Cal/OSHA, *Cal/OSHA Guidelines for Workplace Security* (California Division of Occupational Safety and Health, Department of Industrial Relations, San Francisco, August 15, 1994).

Carper, Alison, "Workplace violence becomes frightening trend," *Newsday*, September 1993, at 12, "Signs are there to read before workplace violence hits," *Business Wire*, May 1993. As reported in *Workplace Violence: Employer Obligations*, Thomas P. Burke, Esq., and Daniel Weisberg, Esq. (Pettit and Martin, San Francisco).

Chovanes, Michael H., "Does regulatory compliance provide serious security?" *Security Management* (Arlington, VA, May 1994).

City of Los Angeles, Department of General Services, Emergency Preparedness Unit, *High-Rise Fire Survival*.

Clarke, Frederick B., "Fire hazards of materials: An overview," *Fire Protection Handbook*, 17th ed. Editor-in-Chief, Arthur E. Cote, Managing Editor, Jim L. Linville (National Fire Protection Association, Quincy, MA, 1991).

Dames & Moore, "How buildings fared," *The Northridge Earthquake, January 17, 1994* (Dames and Moore, Los Angeles, 1994).

Engineering News Record (McGraw-Hill, Inc., New York, January 16, 1995).

Fischer, Robert J., and Gion Green, "Fire protection, safety, and emergency planning," *Introduction to Security*, 5th ed. (Butterworth–Heinemann, Stoneham, MA, 1992).

Giordano, Gerard M., Esq., "Property owners, clean-up and OSHA regulations," *Skyline Magazine* (BOMA International, Washington, DC, January 1995).

Hall, John F., *Response of Modern Steel Buildings*. Paper presented to the Seismological Society of America and the Earthquake Engineering Research Institute Joint Symposium, "Living with Earthquakes in Southern California" (Pasadena, CA, April 7, 1994).

Hartzel, Gordon E., "Combustion products and their effects on life safety," *Fire Protection Handbook*, 17th ed. (National Fire Protection Association, Quincy, MA, 1991).

High-Rise Office Building Fires, by Thomas J. Klem, as reported in the *NFPA Journal* (National Fire Protection Association, Quincy, MA, September/October 1992).

IREM, "Hurricanes," *Before Disaster Strikes: Developing an Emergency Procedures Manual* (Institute of Real Estate Management, Chicago, 1990).

Isaiah, Chapter 24, Verses 18–19, Old Testament, *New American Standard Version Bible, The Open Bible* (Thomas Nelson Publishers, The Lockman Foundation, New York, 1977).

Isner, Michael S., and Thomas J. Klem, "Discussion," *Fire Investigation Report, World Trade Center Explosion and Fire* (National Fire Protection Association, Quincy, MA. Copyright 1993).

Jackson, Robert, L., "Survey faults security at federal buildings" (*Los Angeles Times*, June 29, 1995). Adapted from *Vulnerability Assessment of Federal Facilities* (June 28, 1995)—for sale by the U.S. Government Printing Office, Superintendent of Documents, Mail Stop SSOP, Washington, DC 20402-9328, Stock #027-000-01362-7.

Jenkins, E. Lynn, Larry A. Layne, and Suzanne M. Kisner, "Homicide in the workplace: The U.S. experience, 1980–1988," *AAOHN Journal*, 40(5) May 1992). (Jenkins, Layne, and Kisner are with NIOSH.)

Keating, John P., and Elizabeth F. Loftus, "The logic of fire escape," *Psychology Today* Reprint (June 1981).

Kimball, Virginia, *Earthquake Ready*, 2nd ed. (Roundtable Publishing, Inc., Santa Monica, CA, 1988a), pp. 5, 17–18, and 42. (Kate Hutton, Technical Advisor, is a staff seismologist at the California Institute of Technology.)

Klote, John H., *An Analysis of the Influence of Piston Effect on Elevator Smoke Control* (U.S. National Bureau of Standards, NBSIR 88-3751, 1988). As reported in *Feasibility and Design Considerations of Emergency Evacuation by Elevators* (U.S. Department of Commerce Technology Administration and the General Services Administration, September 1992).

Klote, John H., and G. T. Tamura, "Elevator piston effect and the smoke problem" (*Fire Safety Journal*, 11(3), May 1986), pp. 227–233. As reported in *Feasibility and Design Considerations of Emergency Evacuation by Elevators* (U.S. Department of Commerce Technology Administration and the General Services Administration, September 1992).

Kruse, Tom, "Designing fireproof buildings," *Skylines Magazine* (BOMA International, Baltimore, March 1993).

Los Angeles Times, "Steel-frame building cracks spur wider damage fears" (The Times Mirror Company, Los Angeles, February 27, 1994).

Merritt Company, The, "NCVS data on workplace violence," *Protection of Assets Manual* (The Merritt Company, Santa Monica, CA, December 1994), Bulletin.

Merritt Company, The, "High-rise structures, Section A, Life safety considerations," *Protection of Assets Manual*, vol. III (Used with permission from The Merritt Company, Santa Monica, CA, 800/638-7597. Copyright 1991).

Merritt Company, The, "Bombs and bomb threats," *Protection of Assets Manual*, vol. IV (The Merritt Company, Santa Monica, CA. Copyright 1995).

Merritt Company, The, "High-rise structures, Section B, Security considerations," *Protection of Assets Manual*, vol. III (The Merritt Company, Santa Monica, CA, 1991).

New Webster Encyclopedic Dictionary of the English Language, 1980 Edition, Editor-in-Chief Virginia S. Thatcher (Consolidated Book Publishers, Chicago).

NFPA, *Fire Safety on the Job* (National Fire Protection Association, Quincy, MA, 1993).

NFPA 72, *National Fire Alarm Code*, Chapter 3: "Protected Premises Fire Alarm Systems," Section 3-2: "General," 3-2.4 (National Fire Protection Association, Quincy, MA, 1993), p. 63.

NFPA 101, *Life Safety Code*, Chapter 2: "Fundamental Requirements," Section 2-8 (National Fire Protection Association, Quincy, MA, 1994), p. 101-19.

NFPA 101, *Life Safety Code*, Chapter 5: "Means of Egress," Section 5-2: "Means of Egress Components," 5-2.1.5.1, 5-2.1.5.3, 5-2.1.5.5, 5-2.1.5.6 (National Fire Protection Association, Quincy, MA, 1994), pp. 101-28, 29.

NFPA 472, *Standard for Professional Competence of Responders to Hazardous Materials Incidents*, Chapter 1: "Administration," Section 1-3, "Definitions" (National Fire Protection Association, Quincy, MA, 1989), p. 472-5.

OSHA, *General Industry: Safety and Health Regulations*, Title 29 of the Code of Federal Regulations, Part 1910 (U.S. Department of Labor, OSHA, Washington, DC, 1974).

Otis Elevator Company, *Tell Me About Elevators*, 6th printing (United Technologies, Otis Elevator Company, Farmington, CT, 1982).

Otis 5811, *How to Operate Elevators Under Emergency Conditions* (United Technologies/Otis, SPF-513 [5811].

Plenzler, Jerry, "Elevator, escalator safety is no accident," *Skyline Magazine* (BOMA International, Washington, DC, November/December 1994).

Popejoy, Jack, "Emergency communications," *BICEPP News*, 2(1) (Business and Industry Council for Emergency Planning and Preparedness, Los Angeles, 1993).

Reader's Digest Great Encyclopedic Dictionary, 3rd ed. (The Reader's Digest Association, London, compiled by Oxford University Press, 1979).

Rigdon, Joan E., "Companies see more workplace violence," *Wall Street Journal* (April 12, 1994). As reported in "Violence in the workplace," *ASISNET Security Newsbriefs and Security News Database* (Bethesda, MD, copyright United Press International, Reuter's, 1994).

Salvadori, Mario, "Structures," *Why Buildings Stand Up: The Strength of Architecture* (W.W. Norton & Company, Inc., New York, 1980).

Security Door Controls, *SDC Exit Check* (Security Door Controls, Westlake Village, CA, 1995).

Stratton, David R., "New ideas about bomb searches," *Security Management Bulletin* (Bureau of Business Practice, Waterford, CT, 1994).

Toufexis, Anastasia, "Workers who fight firing with fire," *Time Magazine* (Washington, DC, April 25, 1994).

U.S. Geological Survey, "Earthquakes occur throughout the United States" (National Earthquake Information Center, Denver, 1990).

Webster's College Dictionary, 1992 Edition (From *Random House Webster's College Dictionary* by Random House, Inc. Copyright © 1995, 1992, 1991 by Random House, Inc. Reprinted by permission of Random House, Inc., New York, 1992.)

11 *Building Emergency Planning*

For a building owner or manager to effectively handle an emergency that may affect a high-rise commercial office building, it is necessary to plan ahead. During an emergency there may be chaotic conditions, particularly if there is a disruption in normal communications. A *plan* is defined by the *Webster's College Dictionary* as "a scheme or method of acting or proceeding developed in advance." The Building Owners and Managers Association International (BOMA) defines an *emergency plan* as "a set of actions intended to reduce the threat from emergencies that may affect a facility. A comprehensive plan reduces the threat from emergencies through prevention, early detection, notification, effective evacuation or relocation measures, control and mitigation, and recovery operations" (BOMA 1994, p. 1).

Fire Emergencies

Any building fire emergency plan should incorporate the features in the following sections.

Prevention

All building occupants should receive regular training in fire prevention practices. New occupants or employees should receive this training when they move into a building or at the start of their employment. Training should include what a fire alarm sounds like—and, in modern high-rise buildings (or older ones that have been retrofitted)—looks like, how to protect oneself if a fire occurs including the location of emergency exits, how to tell others who may be at risk, how to confine a fire, and how to notify those who will respond to the fire. Prevention also should include training in the following fire prevention practices to reduce the threat of fire before it occurs:

- Occupants should adhere to smoking rules and regulations. High-rise commercial office buildings have designated safe, supervised, and convenient smoking areas, with many prohibiting any smoking within the building because of health concerns related to second-hand smoke. Any smoking areas must be clearly marked and equipped with nontip ashtrays, metal waste receptacles, and fire extinguishers.
- Areas within tenant spaces, storage areas, and public corridors should be free of obstructions and of fire hazards such as empty cartons, dirty rags, trash, and

improperly stored materials. Good housekeeping practices should keep areas clean and as neat as possible. Violations should be reported promptly.

- Electrical equipment should be inspected regularly to ensure proper and safe functioning. Appliances and cords should be UL-listed; there should be limited use of extension cords; frayed or cracked cords, and broken connections should be replaced; cords should not be run across doorways or under carpets and mats where they may be stepped on; heat-producing appliances should have space around them for ventilation; all problems with electrical equipment should be immediately reported and/or the equipment should be taken out of service; and appliances such as cooking equipment, coffee makers, hot plates, and photo-copiers should be switched off when not in use, particularly at the end of each business day.

A sample *Fire Prevention Inspection Checklist* is included in Appendix 11-1.

Early Detection and Notification

During normal business hours in fully occupied high-rise commercial office buildings there are usually plenty of people—building management, engineering, security, parking, janitorial staff, contractors and repair personnel, or occupants and visitors—moving throughout many areas of the building. As a result, if a fire occurs, there will be early detection and notification of it by human means or by the building's automatic fire detection system, and the fire usually will be suppressed before it has an opportunity to develop into a major conflagration. However, after normal business hours and on weekends and holidays, the number of people present in the building is severely reduced, so there is more dependence on the building's automatic fire detection and notification systems and security staff. According to Klem (1992, p. 61):

> The reliability of such protection depends on the completeness of the fixed detection and suppression equipment and the emergency fire procedure training of security staff. If any of these are deficient, severe fires are more likely to occur. For these reasons, high-rise buildings where reliable fixed fire protection systems are not present simply are more vulnerable to the potential for large losses during nonbusiness hours.

Effective Evacuation or Relocation Measures

The size of high-rise buildings and the high number of people often contained in them makes it impractical to immediately and completely evacuate during a fire emergency. *Evacuation* or *relocation* is the movement of people during an emergency to a location, inside or outside the building, that is considered a safe refuge area. Evacuation involves leaving the building, whereas relocation involves moving to an area of relative safety within the building.

Control and Mitigation, and Recovery Operations

It is critical to apply appropriate control and mitigation measures rapidly during a fire emergency. Automatic fire detection and suppression systems found in modern high-rise commercial office buildings are essential in controlling a fire and mitigating its impact on operations. After the fire emergency has been handled successfully, recovery operations restore any affected areas of the building to their normal condition.

Emergency Planning Guidelines

A *Building Emergency Plan* incorporates the planning and preparation leading up to an emergency and shortly thereafter, while a *Business Resumption Plan* addresses issues that permit a business to resume operations as soon as possible after the incident. This chapter addresses the former but does not formally address the latter.

"The objective of a [Building Emergency Plan] should be to allow those responsible for the [facility] during an emergency to focus on the solution of major problems, not to attempt immediately to bring order out of chaos. If all predictable and routine items are considered in the plan, those responsible for actions during an emergency will be able to deal with the unpredictable or unusual situations that will surely develop" (The Merritt Company 1991, p. 10-3). A Building Emergency Plan consists of the following: (1) Building Emergency Procedures Manual, (2) occupant documentation and training, (3) Floor Warden Manual and training, (4) building emergency staff training, and (5) evacuation signage. The sections that follow address these areas in detail.

Building Emergency Procedures Manual

This manual is a written document that describes actions formulated to reduce the threat to life safety from emergencies that are most likely to occur in a specific building. The authority having jurisdiction, such as the local fire department, often will develop written criteria and guidelines on which plans may be based. The following *suggested* format for material that may be contained in the manual has been developed using the Los Angeles City Fire Department *Guideline Format for High-Rise Buildings: Emergency Procedures City of Los Angeles 1993*. For ease of explanation, some reference is made in this format to a hypothetical high-rise commercial office building, Pacific Tower Plaza, which also was mentioned in Chapter 5. Building owners and managers developing a Building Emergency Procedures Manual for their building should consult with the authorities having jurisdiction, including local officials, for precise criteria and guidelines on which their plan should be based.

Title Page

A typical title page indicates the name and address of the building, the name of the person by whom the manual is compiled, what authority having jurisdiction has approved the plan, who is authorized to change or modify the Building Emergency Procedures Manual, the authority having jurisdiction to which any future changes or updates of material should be sent, the date, and a notation of the copy number. The next page should list the number of copies of the manual and to whom each copy is to be distributed. Figure 11.1 shows a sample title page.

Copy No.: 001

Building Emergency Procedures Manual

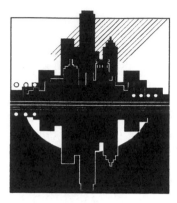

Pacific Tower Plaza

One Poppyfields Drive
Toluga Hills

The content of this manual has been approved by the City of Toluga Hills Fire Department. If changes in content, including either of the following, occur, it is the responsibility of the Building Owner or Manager to notify the City of Toluga Hills Fire Department:

1. Change of Building Owner or Manager
2. Change of building Fire Safety Director.

This revised information shall be communicated by telephone or mail to:

Toluga Hills City Fire Department
High-Rise Division
300 Main Street
Toluga Hills, SC 90000
Telephone (613) 726-0773

This manual is the property of Pacific Tower Plaza and was compiled by J. Smith.
January 1, 1995

Figure 11.1   Building Emergency Procedures Manual sample title page.

Table of Contents

The table of contents consists of a listing by page number for all pertinent sections of the manual.

Introduction

The introduction is a statement of the Building Emergency Procedures Manual's purpose, the name of the authority having jurisdiction with whose cooperation it was compiled, and which material in it is required by law. For example, the introduction may be as follows:

> Management of Pacific Tower Plaza, in cooperation with the City of Toluga Hills Fire Department, has produced this manual to help ensure the safety of occupants in the event of an emergency. The material pertaining to the State Fire Code and the Toluga Hills Fire Code is required by law. Owners, managers, and tenants of high-rise commercial office buildings in the City of Toluga Hills are required to comply with these requirements or be subject to prosecution and penalties, including fines as set forth in the State Fire Code. Additional procedures for explosions, bombs, bomb threats, violence in the workplace, medical emergency, power failure, elevator stoppage, natural disasters, water leaks, chemical and hazardous materials incidents, strike and labor disturbance/demonstration/riot and civil disorders, aircraft collisions, hostage taking, and barricade situations are provided by Pacific Towers Plaza Management for the life safety of building occupants. This manual, and its contents, remains the property of Pacific Tower Plaza, and should be readily available to the City of Toluga Hills Fire Department on request.

Legal Requirements

The legal requirements section is a statement of the applicable state and local laws pertaining to emergency planning and evacuation requirements for high-rise buildings.

Emergency Telephone Numbers

This section of the manual lists telephone numbers and ways to contact persons and agencies needed when a building emergency occurs. Because an emergency can occur at any time of day or night, on weekdays, or on weekends and holidays, it is essential to have a readily available current means of contacting appropriate individuals and agencies. Included in this section are:

1. Telephone numbers for outside emergency response agencies including fire and police departments, paramedic ambulances, local hospitals, poison control centers, hazardous material response agencies, and public utility companies.
2. Location and contact means (both during and after normal business hours) for building emergency staff such as the owner or manager, the building Fire Safety Director, the building Alternate Fire Safety Director, engineering, security, janitorial, parking, and other applicable departments. Management succession lists should be developed to include sufficient names to ensure that someone can be contacted during an emergency, no matter when it occurs. A notation should be made here about the confidentiality of this information and that it is only to be used for emergency purposes.

3. Locations and telephone numbers of floor wardens and their designated alternates. (A sample *Floor Wardens and Alternates Roster* is included in Appendix 11-1.)
4. Locations, telephone numbers, and type of disability of disabled and non-ambulatory persons and their assistance monitors. A confidentiality notation should be made here, as for building emergency staff. (A sample *Disabled or Non-Ambulatory Persons List* is included in Appendix 11-1.)

These emergency telephone numbers should be revised immediately when changes are received; also, all numbers should be verified, preferably monthly, or at least quarterly.

Building Emergency Staff Organization

This section outlines the Building Emergency Staff Organization that will carry out emergency response procedures until relieved by outside response agencies. Such a typical staff for a high-rise commercial office building is outlined in Figure 11.2.

Each unit of the Building Emergency Staff Organization will have duties and responsibilities developed and tailored to the specific needs of the building concerned and to each type of emergency they may be required to handle. These duties and responsibilities should be defined clearly so that there will be a coordinated and effective response to each emergency situation. For example, the duties and responsibilities of building management, the building Fire Safety Director, and the building engineering and security staff in handling a fire emergency will include ensuring that the fire department has been immediately notified, all occupants have been advised, any necessary evacuation or relocation procedures of affected occupants has begun, fire life safety systems are operating under emergency conditions, any investigation or initial suppression of the fire is carried out, and that the fire department and other responding personnel are met on arrival at the facility. In contrast, during a bomb threat incident, these personnel may be involved in supervising the evacuation or relocation of occupants or assisting in searching certain building areas. Building parking staff may be called on to assist in the evacuation of occupants from parking areas. Building janitorial staff may be required to clean up areas after water leaks; liquid spills; water discharged from sprinklers; or, in the case of a bomb threat, searching areas with which they are familiar.

The floor response personnel (floor wardens, stairwell monitors, elevator monitors, search monitors, and disabled assistance monitors) have specific duties and responsibilities that also will vary according to the type of emergency encountered. Primarily, they perform the safe and orderly evacuation or relocation of occupants from a building floor when a fire emergency exists. Their duties may vary as described in the next sections.

Building Floor Wardens
Usually each floor has a *floor warden* (in some localities these are called *fire wardens*) and a designated *alternate floor warden*; if the *floor plate*—the entire floor area including the public access or common areas, tenant areas, and maintenance spaces—is particularly large or there are many individual tenants, there may be additional floor wardens (some buildings refer to the floor warden of an individual suite as a *suite warden* or *deputy floor warden*). Some fire depart-

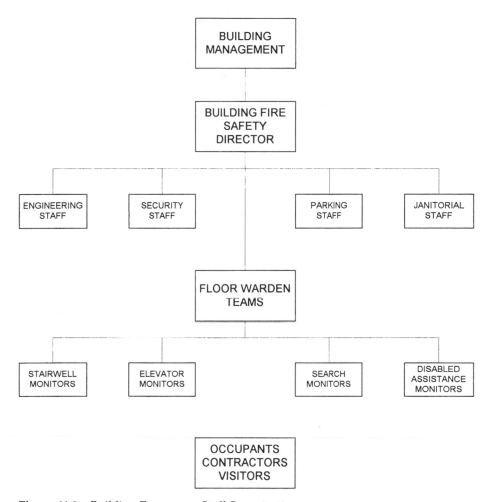

Figure 11.2 Building Emergency Staff Organization.

ments stipulate the number of floor wardens to be provided. For example, in New York City, "Each floor of a building shall be under the direction of a designated Fire Warden for the evacuation of occupants in the event of a fire. He shall be assisted in his duties by Deputy Fire Wardens. A Deputy Fire Warden shall be provided for each tenancy. When the floor area of a tenancy exceeds 7,500 square feet of occupiable space, a Deputy Warden shall be assigned for each 7,500 square feet or part thereof" (NYFD 1972, p. 5). Each of these persons may be identified by an armband, vest, or hard hat worn whenever they are called to duty. Floor wardens are selected for their ability to make sound decisions during emergency situations, provide direction, and maintain order. They should be thoroughly familiar with the Building Emergency Plan and, in cooperation with the building Fire Safety Director, should oversee and ensure safe and complete evacuation or relocation of occupants under their supervision during a fire or other emergency, or during a fire drill.

Duties of floor wardens and alternate floor wardens include:

1. Overseeing training and instruction of occupants.
2. Determining and coordinating appropriate emergency response actions for a particular floor or portion of a floor.
3. Ensuring a safe and complete evacuation of all occupants, including individuals with disabilities, from unsafe areas.
4. Ensuring that evacuated or relocated occupants are kept at a safe refuge area and prevented from reentering the building or returning to their workplace until proper authorization has been received from building management or the fire department. A *safe refuge area* inside and outside the building should be specifically designated. The authority having jurisdiction may need to be consulted to determine what areas are considered safe—the location of interior safe refuge areas will be largely determined by fire codes; outside safe refuge areas will depend on the site layout, adjacent streets, alleys, parking lots, and so on.

To carry out these responsibilities, as outlined by the Los Angeles City Fire Department *Guideline Format for High-Rise Buildings*, floor wardens should select and supervise floor response personnel, ensuring that these positions are always staffed. These personnel should be trained ahead of time for their respective duties, or, if designated on the spot by the floor warden or alternate floor wardens, quickly instructed on what to do. The following response personnel are needed:

- *Stairwell monitors*—one monitor per stairwell lines up occupants in an orderly fashion at the entrance to the stairwell, controls access, organizes an orderly flow of persons into the stairwell when evacuation begins, and closes the door when no one is moving through it.
- *Elevator monitors* direct all passengers who arrive at the floor to proceed to the nearest safe stairwell, and prevent any occupants from using the elevators for evacuation. (This can be a problem, particularly on heavily populated floors.)
- *Search monitors* systematically and thoroughly search all assigned floor areas to ensure that all occupants evacuate (this includes closed areas such as offices, photocopier rooms, restrooms, kitchens, rest areas, conference rooms, libraries, and computer rooms). After an area has been searched, doors leading to it are closed (but not locked) and each door is marked (for example, with a self-stick note or piece of tape) to identify the area within as having been searched and cleared of all occupants. This thereby avoids duplication of effort.
- *Disabled assistance monitors* locate disabled and nonambulatory persons and assist them to the nearest "area of rescue assistance" (a term defined in a later section, "Evacuation of Individuals with Disabilities"). Usually two monitors are assigned to each person.
- *Telephone monitors* provide telephone liaison between floor warden and floor response personnel, liaison between the floor warden and the Fire Safety Director or the fire department, and liaison between floors.
- *Runners/Messengers* provide physical liaison in the areas mentioned when there is a failure of telephone communications.

Because fire poses such a threat to people and property, and medical emergencies normally require rapid attention, some high-rise buildings provide training in the correct use of fire extinguishers, basic first aid, and cardiopulmonary resuscitation (CPR) for all floor wardens and alternates. In a building where stairwell doors are not equipped with locks that automatically unlock on activation of the fire life safety system, the floor warden and assistant floor wardens on the relocation floor will need to be notified, usually through the building public address (PA) system, to open the stairwell doors so that occupants can enter the relocation floor. As with building floor wardens, floor response personnel should have designated alternates who can assume their positions when necessary.

Building Fire Safety Director

The Fire Safety Director should be a responsible person who is employed on the premises, unless otherwise approved by the local fire department having jurisdiction. This person is a key component of any high-rise commercial office building fire life safety program. He or she represents the building owner and manager in all fire life safety issues—in particular, the building's response to on-site emergencies—and works closely with the fire department to establish, implement, and maintain the Building Emergency Plan. The Fire Safety Director should be an energetic self-starter with good organizational skills; have the ability and inquisitiveness to understand complex building systems; be able to communicate well both verbally and in writing; and be able to train and supervise others' activities. He or she must deal effectively at all levels with building management, emergency staff, tenants, occupants, and public agencies such as law enforcement and the fire department.

This individual is the driving force behind any successful building fire life safety program. If an experienced and highly motivated person occupies this position, the Building Emergency Plan will be up to date, effectively communicated to all building occupants, properly executed, and a valuable asset to building management in its relationship with its present tenants and its efforts to attract future tenants. Building emergency staff, floor wardens, and occupants will be well trained and in a state of readiness to successfully handle the types of emergencies the building is likely to experience.

The Los Angeles City Fire Department's *Guideline Format for High-Rise Buildings* outlines the responsibilities and duties of a Fire Safety Director. This staff member needs to do the following:

1. Implement the fire life safety program for the building as called for by state and local laws and the fire authority having jurisdiction
2. Establish and maintain an up-to-date Building Emergency Procedures Manual
3. Ensure that the building is maintained in a safe condition for occupants by conducting regular safety inspections of all areas, including tenant spaces, and documenting all efforts to correct hazards and problems
4. Maintain up-to-date lists of floor wardens and alternates
5. Maintain up-to-date lists of disabled and non-ambulatory persons
6. Distribute documentation and printed material to building occupants, floor wardens, and building emergency staff outlining procedures to be followed when an emergency occurs
7. Provide training that details the duties and responsibilities of these persons in an emergency situation, and maintain documentation of dates, subject, and attendance for each training session
8. Conduct fire evacuation drills as required by state and local fire codes.

See Appendix 11-1 for samples of a *Fire Prevention Inspection Checklist*, a *Floor Wardens and Alternates Roster*, and a *Disabled and Non-Ambulatory Persons List*.

In addition, during tenant buildouts, building interior construction, or up-grades of tenant and building systems and equipment, the Fire Safety Director should, as Studer (1992) points out, "verify that wall and floor slab openings around piping, conduit, and duct work are properly sealed with Underwriters Laboratories (UL)-listed fireproofing material to match the existing fire rating of the walls and slabs; ensure that new duct work passing through walls or floor slabs have been properly provided with fire dampers" (p. 8). Tenant storage areas should be a particular focus for inspections because they are often crammed full of material. Also, any loading docks and parking structures that have been converted for storage should be inspected. Studer (1992, p. 8) continues:

> To minimize the risk of fire in storage areas, building code requirements for these areas should be rigidly enforced, including:
>
> - Limit the size of storage areas and/or provide automatic sprinkler protection throughout the storage area.
> - When sprinklers are installed in a storage area, the height of the storage area should be kept at least 18 inches below the sprinklers' deflectors.
> - Storage should be prohibited [in] electrical rooms, mechanical rooms, elevator equipment rooms, electrical switchgear rooms, and other similar occupancies.

Whenever it is determined that a building or premises presents a hazard to life or property as a result of a fire or other emergency, or when it is determined that any fire protection equipment or system is inoperable, defective, or has been taken out of service, the Fire Safety Director needs to institute a fire watch. Patrols at appropriate intervals, as required by the authority having jurisdiction, are conducted with the purpose of detecting fires and transmitting an immediate alarm to the building occupants and the fire department.

The Fire Safety Director, alone or in conjunction with the engineering staff, generally is responsible for ensuring that fire life safety systems and equipment are inspected, tested, maintained, and repaired according to the specified guidelines of the authority having jurisdiction. Typically in large high-rises, building engineers do not have the time to perform these labor-intensive inspections, and sometimes they do not possess all the skills necessary to perform the required maintenance services on the wide variety of equipment. Most directors, therefore, hire a licensed life safety system maintenance contractor to perform this work using a support team. Further, the directors (or possibly the engineers) maintain the documentation of these activities so that it is readily available for review by the authority having jurisdiction.

During an emergency, a Fire Safety Director:

1. Ensures that the appropriate outside emergency agencies have been notified.
2. Coordinates the activities of all building emergency staff and floor wardens.
3. Coordinates all occupant notification and makes sure that any necessary evacuation or relocation begins.
4. Ensures adequate monitoring and control of all building life safety systems and equipment. During a fire emergency, some authorities having jurisdiction require that the building Fire Safety Director must ensure that all elevators serving the fire floor are recalled to the lobby level and taken out of service.
5. Confirms that any investigation or initial suppression of a fire emergency is performed.

6. Arranges for responding emergency personnel to be met at the designated entrance of the building and to be given an up-to-date report on the incident (including its location and any reported injuries), the status of security and building fire life safety systems, and the location and status of all evacuees and building emergency staff addressing the incident (building information forms, notification of specific hazards, floor plans, essential keys and access cards, etc. also should be readily available).

7. Ensures that every incident is thoroughly documented and that required notifications and reports to the appropriate authorities are carried out.

During a fire emergency, the Fire Safety Director should go to the Building Control Station to supervise the direction and execution of the Building Emergency Plan. Some authorities having jurisdiction specify this requirement in their local fire codes to ensure that it occurs—for instance, the City of New York Fire Department's Administrative Code, Section 27-4627, clearly states: "During fire emergencies, the primary responsibility of the fire safety director shall be the supervision and manning of the fire command station and the direction and execution of the evacuation as provided in the fire safety plan." To help facilitate this, the office of the Fire Safety Director should be located on lower floors of the building in reasonable proximity to the Building Control Station.

During normal business hours, if the Fire Safety Director is not on site at the time an emergency occurs, there should be an *Alternate* or *Deputy Fire Safety Director* who assumes the duties of the Fire Safety Director. Also, after normal business hours, when the Fire Safety Director is normally not on site, the plan should assign the duties and responsibilities to another individual. Sometimes —in New York City, for example—this after-hours individual is referred to as a *Building Evacuation Supervisor*.

Procedures for Handling Building Emergencies

This section outlines the procedures for handling emergencies that are most likely to occur in the building. Each emergency should be separately addressed, with the duties and responsibilities of each member of the Building Emergency Staff Organization documented in detail. It should be kept in mind that "no one individual can be expected to think of all the things necessary to a successful response to an emergency event. It is imperative that group interaction take place during planning so the multitude of things that must be considered are addressed. It is always smarter to have something and not need it than need something and not have it" (Gigliotti and Jason 1991, p. 53). Key members of the emergency staff should be consulted when a Building Emergency Plan is being formulated. The input of individuals such as the head of engineering (called the *Chief Engineer* in most large high-rises) is crucial to the success of any plan.

It is only through such a plan that training can be effectively conducted and much of the confusion frequently associated with emergencies can be reduced substantially. "All of the senses tune up and the adrenaline starts to flow. We react better in emergencies and in one like this, everything comes into play and starts to flow and people get into doing those types of things they are *trained* to do" (Anthony 1988). Chapter 10, *Building Emergencies*, contains a description of emergencies that may affect a high-rise building and ways they may be handled.

Evacuation and Relocation

This section of the Building Emergency Procedures Manual outlines the evacuation and relocation procedures formulated for the building during certain emergencies. Evacuation and relocation are defined earlier in this chapter, under "Effective Evacuation or Relocation Measures." The authority having jurisdiction over the building usually will establish the policy by which occupants will evacuate or relocate during a particular emergency. For example, in the city of New York, if a fire occurs in a high-rise building, the fire floor and floors immediately above are the most critical areas for rapid evacuation. In Los Angeles, however, if a fire occurs in a high-rise commercial office building and it is serious enough to evacuate one floor, five floors are evacuated (commonly referred to as the "Rule of 5"): the fire floor, two above for safety, and two below to be utilized as a base for the fire department to stage operations. Occupants on these five floors are relocated down five floors and are thus *at least three floors from the fire floor*; if the fire is on or below a floor that is six floors from street level, the occupants usually will be evacuated from the building. Figure 11.3 shows the floors from which occupants are usually evacuated or relocated during a fire situation in a Los Angeles high-rise commercial office building.

Once the occupants of the involved floors have been relocated, the decision whether to evacuate them further, using stairwells or elevators, or whether additional floors need to be evacuated, will be determined by building management, the Fire Safety Director, or the fire department if they have arrived. Total building evacuation usually is ordered only by the fire department. Such an evacuation would take a considerable period of time. Byrna Taubman, in *What Are Your Chances of Surviving a High-Rise Fire?*, estimates that it can take over an hour to evacuate a 50-story building (Taubman 1974). Of course, the time to evacuate any building will depend largely on the building population at the time of evacuation.

In the NFPA film *High-Rise Evacuation*, it is stated that it usually takes occupants, moving at a reasonable pace, a total of approximately 10 seconds to move down one floor in the stairwell of a high-rise building, allowing one second at each stairwell landing between floors. This means that for someone on the 36th floor of the theoretical high-rise, *Pacific Tower Plaza*, it would take about six minutes to descend down the stairwells to the ground level if the person did not slow down or stop for a rest when tired. It must be noted here that this statistic is for one occupant descending; a group of people will undoubtedly take longer.

It is advisable to go downward in a building during a fire; it is necessary or more desirable to go to an upper floor or to the roof only if the lower floors or stairwells are untenable because of heat or smoke. The problem with occupants relocating to the roof, particularly in substantial numbers, is that once there they may need to be evacuated from the roof itself. If the building has a helipad or heliport (see Figure 11.4), as many modern high-rise buildings do, there is not only the problem of obtaining a helicopter, but also of having it safely land to pick up occupants. During serious building fires, air turbulence and updrafts are caused by the presence of smoke and heated air. During the 1988 First Interstate Tower blaze, eight persons went to the roof and all were successfully transported to safety from the roof of this 62-story high-rise.

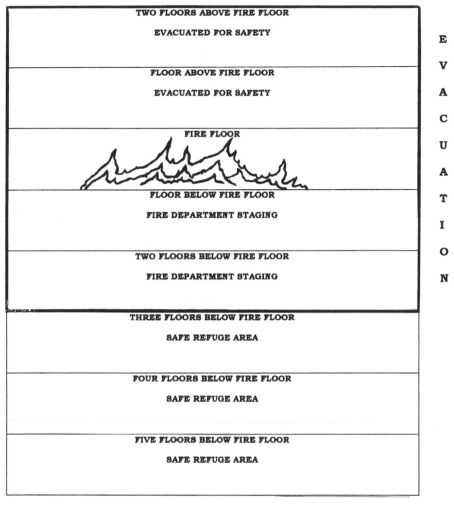

Figure 11.3 Floors from which occupants are usually evacuated or relocated during a fire situation in a Los Angeles high-rise commercial office building.

Evacuation of Individuals with Disabilities

Individuals with temporary or permanent disabilities, or other conditions that would require them to obtain assistance during an evacuation, require special consideration during evacuation or relocation. The Americans with Disabilities Act (ADA), Title 42, U.S. Code, Chapter 126, Section 12102, defines an individual's *disability* as "a physical or mental impairment that substantially limits one or more of the major life activities of such individual." (The previous term *handicapped* has been replaced.)

During an evacuation or relocation in a high-rise building, individuals who will require assistance from others may include persons confined to wheelchairs; persons dependent on crutches, canes, walkers, and so on; persons recovering from surgery; pregnant women; persons with significant hearing or sight

Figure 11.4   Helipad of a modern high-rise building.   Photograph by Roger Flores.

impairment; extremely obese persons; elderly persons; children; persons with mental impairments; and persons who may have become incapacitated as a result of the emergency incident. After the 1993 New York World Trade Center bombing, *Time Magazine* reported that a woman in a wheelchair was carried down 66 stories by two friends, and that a pregnant woman was airlifted from a tower roof (*Time Magazine* 1993, p. 17).

A listing of such individuals' names, locations within the building, telephone numbers, type of disability, and the names of assigned assistance monitors should be provided ahead of time to building management with the understanding that such information is confidential and is to be used only to facilitate safe and rapid evacuation or relocation during emergency conditions.

Title III of the ADA requires the establishment of "areas of rescue assistance" in all nonsprinklered buildings with occupied levels above or below the level of exit discharge. *Exit discharge* is defined by NFPA 101 *Life Safety Code*, Section 5-1.2, as: "that portion of a means of egress between the termination of an exit and a public way" (NFPA 1994, p. 101-26). An *area of rescue assistance* is defined by the ADA as: "an area that has direct access to an exit, where people who are unable to use stairs may remain temporarily in safety to await further instructions or assistance during emergency evacuation" (Cummings and Jaeger 1993, p. 46).

Wayne "Chip" Carson (1993, p. 2), in the NFPA *Fire News*, states:

These areas may include:

- A portion of a landing within a smokeproof stairway.
- A portion of an exterior exit balcony adjacent to an exit stairway. If there are

openings to the building within 20 feet of the area of rescue assistance, they must be protected by 45-minute opening protection.
- A portion of a one-hour fire resistance rated corridor located immediately adjacent to an exit enclosure.
- A vestibule located immediately adjacent to an exit enclosure.
- A portion of a stairway landing.
- An area separated by a smoke barrier when approved by the local authority having jurisdiction.
- A pressurized elevator lobby.
- A horizontal exit.

Once the "area of rescue assistance" has been reached, assistance monitors and the individual with the disability have two options: (1) dispatch someone to relate the situation to the building Fire Safety Director, building management, security, engineers, or—in the case of a fire emergency—the fire department, and await their assistance; or (2) once all occupants have been evacuated from the involved floors and moved past, the assistance monitors may move the individual with the disability to the designated safe refuge area inside or outside the building.

Information covering basic methods of manually evacuating individuals who require assistance during an emergency evacuation is provided in Figures 11.5 to 11.7.

Mel Harris (1995), Fire Protection Engineer of the General Services Administration (GSA), made the following comments regarding the emergency evacuation of disabled workers:

> The illustrated carries [in Figures 11.5 to 11.7] are not easy to perform. Not everyone has the physical strength to either carry another person or to participate with a partner in two-person carries. At best, going down stairs is difficult because of the ease with which one's grip can slip and allow the disabled person to be dropped. For many people it is very difficult to keep their balance while carrying the dead weight of a person.

The suggestions that follow, also from Harris (1995) with minor revisions, should be considered:

1. These carries should only be performed by trained personnel. Extensive initial training on how to safely perform them should be followed by retraining on a regular and periodic basis to ensure that personnel maintain their skills. Only in the most dire emergency should untrained co-workers attempt to evacuate the disabled. This is particularly critical in going down stairways.
2. The basic objective of evacuating a disabled person should be to have the disabled assistance monitors remove her or him to the nearest safe location. The monitors should stay with the disabled person, report their location to the floor warden, Building Fire Safety Director, or other designated member of the Building Emergency Staff Organization, and then wait for the fire department to accomplish the actual evacuation if they decide it is required.
3. If the building is equipped with automatic sprinklers, the disabled need only be moved to an adjacent safe area or floor, rather than being carried out of the building.
4. The evacuation procedures should be reviewed with disabled persons prior to an emergency so that they will know what assistance to expect during drills and actual emergencies.

Co-workers who are assigned to assist nonambulatory persons should discuss and work out the best way to lift and carry them to minimize the risk of physical injury. This is particularly true with paraplegia or quadriplegia persons who have lost sensation in their extremities and cannot receive warnings of pain.

There are generally four ways for one person to carry a nonambulatory person. None of the techniques is suitable for all persons. The increased weight of the disabled person increases the difficulty, unless he or she retains a moderate amount of arm strength.

The pack-strap technique, often preferred by health-care professionals, restricts the breathing of the person being rescued and may induce leg spasms where there is a history of prone-ness to this condition.

The cradle lift may be favored by both parties, but it is very risky if they are approximately the same size and weight; the rescuer is forced to assume a posture during the lift that can result in injury to the back.

The piggy-back technique causes less restriction of breathing. Lifting a person for the piggy-back technique can be made easier if done at the top of a flight of stairs where the rescuer can use the handrail for support in lifting.

The firefighter's lift re-quires considerable skill on the part of the rescuer to get a person being rescued into a position where breathing is not restricted.

Research indicates that the piggy-back technique is preferable. If, however, the handicapped person has no arm strength, or weighs less than half of the rescuer, then the cradle lift is preferable.

Figure 11.5 Lifting and carrying techniques.   Adapted from The Worksite Committee of The President's Committee on Employment of the Handicapped (1985), from "Employers are Asking . . . About the Safety of Handicapped Workers When Emergencies Occur." Illustrations by Adam Zimmer.

5. Although elevators are not used for general population evacuation, they may, when the fire department directs*, be safely used for evacuating the disabled in some buildings. There is much discussion on this concept in the fire protection field today. Research on it is being conducted by the National Institute of Standards and Technology (NIST) and sponsored by GSA. A discussion of this research is published in NISTIR 4870, *Feasibility and Design Considerations of Emergency Evacuation by Elevators*. This report can be ordered from the National Technical Information Service (NITS), Springfield, VA 22161. Using elevators for disabled evacuation would require training and close coordination between the local fire department and the Building Emergency Staff Organization.

---

* *Author's Note*: During some fire situations, fire fighters have been known to use elevators to move their equipment up in very tall buildings. Usually this has been restricted to elevator banks totally separate from the bank that serves a fire floor (i.e., the group of elevators not involved in the fire nor in the primary path of smoke flow). In the event that a fire was located in an elevator machine room, however, no elevator bank being operated by that machine room would be safe to use.

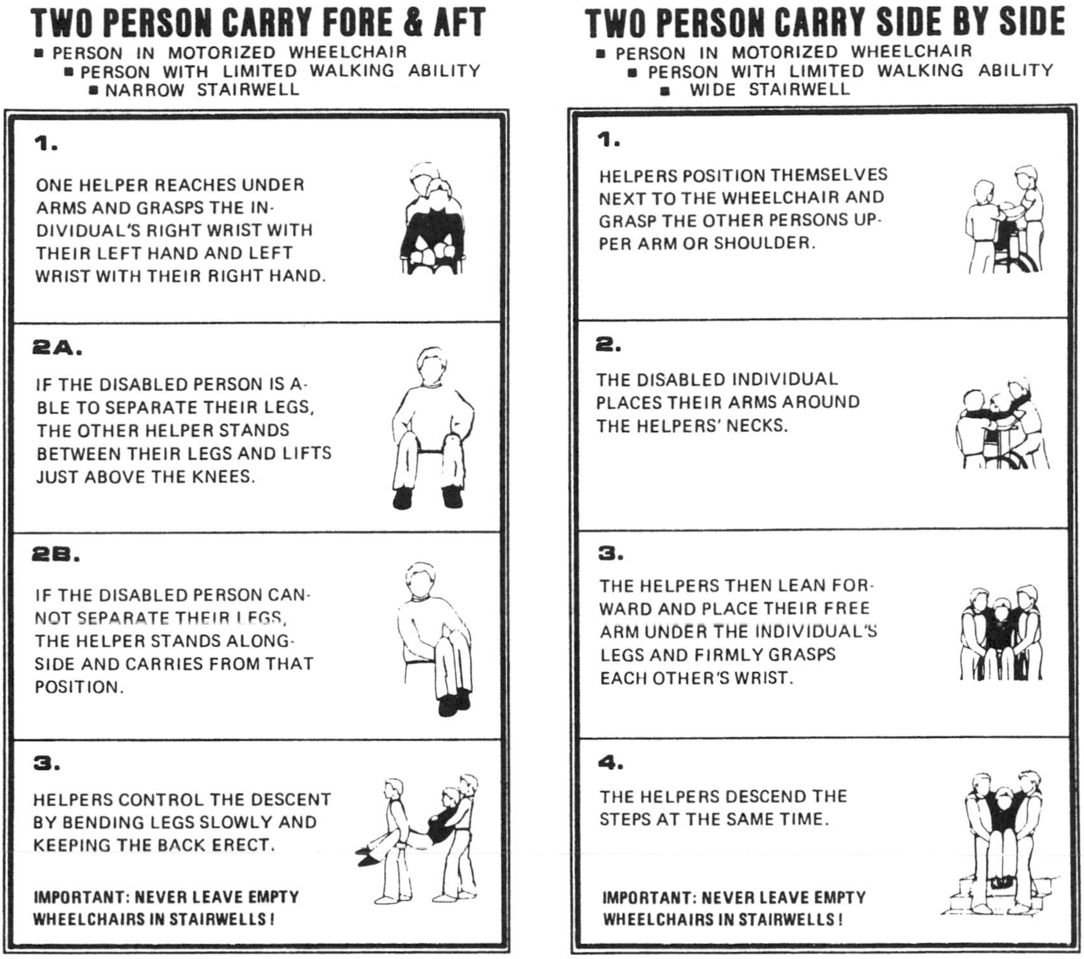

TWO PERSON CARRY FORE & AFT

- PERSON IN MOTORIZED WHEELCHAIR
- PERSON WITH LIMITED WALKING ABILITY
- NARROW STAIRWELL

1.
ONE HELPER REACHES UNDER ARMS AND GRASPS THE INDIVIDUAL'S RIGHT WRIST WITH THEIR LEFT HAND AND LEFT WRIST WITH THEIR RIGHT HAND.

2A.
IF THE DISABLED PERSON IS ABLE TO SEPARATE THEIR LEGS, THE OTHER HELPER STANDS BETWEEN THEIR LEGS AND LIFTS JUST ABOVE THE KNEES.

2B.
IF THE DISABLED PERSON CANNOT SEPARATE THEIR LEGS, THE HELPER STANDS ALONGSIDE AND CARRIES FROM THAT POSITION.

3.
HELPERS CONTROL THE DESCENT BY BENDING LEGS SLOWLY AND KEEPING THE BACK ERECT.

IMPORTANT: NEVER LEAVE EMPTY WHEELCHAIRS IN STAIRWELLS!

TWO PERSON CARRY SIDE BY SIDE

- PERSON IN MOTORIZED WHEELCHAIR
- PERSON WITH LIMITED WALKING ABILITY
- WIDE STAIRWELL

1.
HELPERS POSITION THEMSELVES NEXT TO THE WHEELCHAIR AND GRASP THE OTHER PERSONS UPPER ARM OR SHOULDER.

2.
THE DISABLED INDIVIDUAL PLACES THEIR ARMS AROUND THE HELPERS' NECKS.

3.
THE HELPERS THEN LEAN FORWARD AND PLACE THEIR FREE ARM UNDER THE INDIVIDUAL'S LEGS AND FIRMLY GRASPS EACH OTHER'S WRIST.

4.
THE HELPERS DESCEND THE STEPS AT THE SAME TIME.

IMPORTANT: NEVER LEAVE EMPTY WHEELCHAIRS IN STAIRWELLS!

Figure 11.6 Two-person carries. Reprinted with permission from "Emergency Evacuation Procedures for Disabled Individuals," developed through the cooperative efforts of the Los Angeles City Fire Department and Joni and Friends.

6. The AOK Medi-Chair is a convenient and safe device to evacuate the disabled down stairways. Although there are other evacuation chairs available, the AOK provides a unique belt mechanism to provide a controlled descent down steps. This chair is on the GSA Supply Schedule for ease in purchasing by government agencies.

Once all affected occupants have been evacuated or relocated, there needs to be a method to determine if the unsafe areas are truly vacated. This can be achieved by taking a "head count" of occupants at the safe refuge area, or by conducting a thorough search of all unsafe areas from which they have come.

The head count method usually is not a reliable technique. Workers may be out of their office for an outside appointment or away from work because of illness or vacation when the evacuation or relocation occurs—hence when a head count is taken, these individuals may be incorrectly listed as missing. Another

IN CHAIR EVACUATION

- PERSON IN NON-MOTORIZED WHEELCHAIR

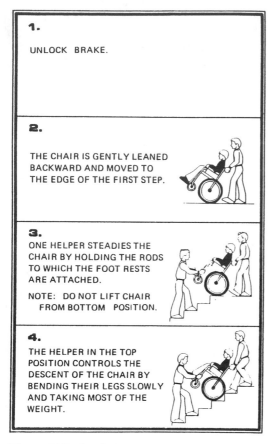

1.

UNLOCK BRAKE.

2.

THE CHAIR IS GENTLY LEANED BACKWARD AND MOVED TO THE EDGE OF THE FIRST STEP.

3.

ONE HELPER STEADIES THE CHAIR BY HOLDING THE RODS TO WHICH THE FOOT RESTS ARE ATTACHED.

NOTE: DO NOT LIFT CHAIR FROM BOTTOM POSITION.

4.

THE HELPER IN THE TOP POSITION CONTROLS THE DESCENT OF THE CHAIR BY BENDING THEIR LEGS SLOWLY AND TAKING MOST OF THE WEIGHT.

OFFICE CHAIR EVACUATION

- PERSON IN MOTORIZED WHEELCHAIR
- PERSON THAT APPEARS TO BE FRAGILE

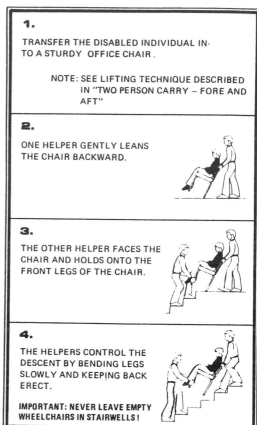

1.

TRANSFER THE DISABLED INDIVIDUAL IN-TO A STURDY OFFICE CHAIR.

NOTE: SEE LIFTING TECHNIQUE DESCRIBED IN "TWO PERSON CARRY — FORE AND AFT"

2.

ONE HELPER GENTLY LEANS THE CHAIR BACKWARD.

3.

THE OTHER HELPER FACES THE CHAIR AND HOLDS ONTO THE FRONT LEGS OF THE CHAIR.

4.

THE HELPERS CONTROL THE DESCENT BY BENDING LEGS SLOWLY AND KEEPING BACK ERECT.

IMPORTANT: NEVER LEAVE EMPTY WHEELCHAIRS IN STAIRWELLS!

Figure 11.7 In-chair evacuation carries.   Reprinted with permission from "Emergency Evacuation Procedures for Disabled Individuals," developed through the cooperative efforts of the Los Angeles City Fire Department and Joni and Friends.

problem with this approach is that visitors or temporary workers in the tenant space at the time of the evacuation may still be trapped inside but will not show up as missing during the head count. If the evacuation involves a large number of people, there also may be difficulty in physically grouping together all evacuees to perform a head count.

A thorough search of all areas is a more reliable technique for determining if all occupants have vacated an area in a multiple-tenant/multiple-use high-rise commercial office building. By focusing on the evacuated areas themselves, it can be positively determined if anyone has remained behind. Closed areas—computer rooms, conference rooms, libraries, rest rooms, and break areas—are some locations that may be overlooked in a hurried evacuation. The presence of well-prepared floor wardens, as described earlier, will alleviate much of the risk of someone being accidentally left behind in an evacuation.

Building Emergency Systems and Equipment

This section of the manual outlines the building emergency systems and equipment in the building. It should include an overview and description of each system, an account of how the systems operate under normal and emergency conditions, and how system components are related and connected. Photographs and diagrams are invaluable in effectively describing building fire life safety systems and equipment. The information should reflect the type of systems or equipment and their location within the building, the emergency function of systems and equipment, and the method of operating and resetting systems and equipment. The systems and equipment should include:

- Voice communication and building PA system
- Fire department voice communication systems
- Public telephone for fire department use
- Stairwell intercom systems
- Fire detection and alarm system annunciator and control panels
- Manual fire alarm stations (sometimes called manual fire alarm boxes, manual pull stations, or manual pull alarms)
- Automatic detection systems (smoke detectors, heat detectors, and gas detectors)
- Automatic sprinkler systems, sprinkler control valve and water-flow detector annunciator panels and fire pump status indicators, standpipe and hose systems
- Other fire protection equipment and system controls
- On-site and off-site monitoring arrangements of fire detection and suppression equipment
- Air-handling system controls and status indicators
- Elevator status panel displaying elevator operations
- Emergency and standby power systems
- Controls for simultaneous unlocking stairwell doors locked from the stairwell side
- Utility service (gas, electrical, water) shutdown locations, tools, etc.
- Fire department lock box or rapid entry key vault

Included in this section should be a description of the building—for example:

Pacific Tower Plaza is a prestigious, multiple-tenant, multiple-use high-rise complex used primarily for commercial office purposes. It is located in Toluga Hills, a major downtown financial district. It occupies one half of the city block bounded by Mount Waverley, Poppyfields, and La Perouse Boulevards and is located in close proximity to the South Western Freeway. It is surrounded by a high-rise residential building, a low-rise hotel, and a high-rise commercial office building. Pacific Tower Plaza consists of a fully sprinklered 36–story office tower with a triple-level subterranean parking structure. The tower has 600,000 square feet of rentable office space, 7,000 square feet of rentable retail space, and 6,000 square feet of rentable storage space. The approximate size of each floor plate is 18,500 square feet. The perimeter of the building consists of sculptures, fountains, an open-air restaurant, and large planters containing flowers and small trees. The entrance to the building is through a large main lobby. The building has an approximate population of 2,400 occupants and 5,000 daily visitors. The on-site parking structure can accommodate up to 600 cars and connects to a subterranean pedestrian tunnel under Mount Waverley Boulevard.

The tower of Pacific Tower Plaza consists of steel-frame and concrete construction with metal stud partitions. It has a conventional curtain wall consisting of glass in aluminum frames. The structural steel frame supports light-weight concrete floor slabs resting on metal decks atop horizontal steel beams, which are welded to vertical steel columns. The building is supported on a foundation of structurally reinforced concrete. The tower is designed with a concrete-reinforced center core which houses the electrical, plumbing, and communications systems, the heating and air-conditioning (air supply and return) shafts; 17 passenger elevators, one service/freight elevator, and three parking shuttle elevators; and two major enclosed stairwells. Both stairwells provide egress to the street level and access to the roof. The stairwells are pressurized and protected by fire-rated doors and walls.

The Plaza has 24-hour security staff, seven days per week, and engineering staff present during normal business hours, Monday to Friday.

The way systems and equipment operate in relation to each other also needs to be described. For example, see "Controls in Elevator Lobbies" in Chapter 4 for a description of how various systems usually are designed to respond to the activation of an elevator lobby smoke detector. A table detailing the operational sequence of life safety systems, like the one shown in Table 4.1, is an invaluable tool in outlining building systems and equipment and how systems interrelate.

This section also should include building drawings and plans detailing site plans, floor layouts, evacuation routes, stairwell and elevator configurations, and so on. Figures 11.8 through 11.15 show these diagrams for the hypothetical Pacific Tower Plaza.

Emergency Operations Center

There should be a designated area, or Emergency Operations Center (EOC), where building emergency staff can assemble to receive information, make decisions, and otherwise coordinate the handling of an emergency. For many buildings, depending on the incident, this area will be the Building Control Station, the Security Command Center (if appropriate), or other locations as considered necessary by the Fire Safety Director. The Building Control Station, described at the beginning of Chapter 4, is useful for most emergencies, particularly those that are fire-related, and those that require voice communication to the occupants of the building. However, in some situations, such as bomb threats and medical emergencies, the EOC is more likely to be the Security Command Center, or an area designated on a tenant floor at the time of the incident.

In a major emergency where there is likely to be a large congregation of building emergency staff, the Building Control Station may not be big enough to accommodate the EOC, so an alternate location should be found in advance. Some large high-rise buildings have a special room fully equipped and ready to be activated as the EOC. It may contain the following equipment:

- Communications equipment: multiple telephones, portable two-way radios, bullhorns or megaphones, cellular telephones, radio-telephones, pagers, radios including CB and other licensed bands, televisions, fax machines, etc. (Duplicate building PA, elevator communication, and intercom systems may also be provided.)
- Tools for documenting the emergency incident: word processors, logs, notepads, tape recorders, still cameras, videocameras, etc.

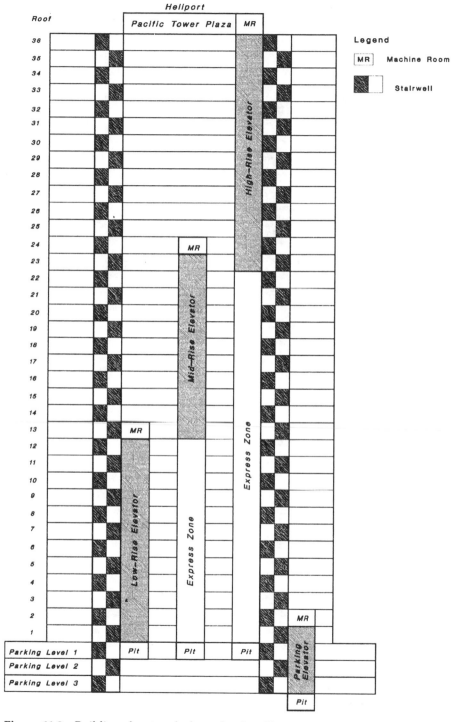

Figure 11.8 Building elevator shafts and stairwells.

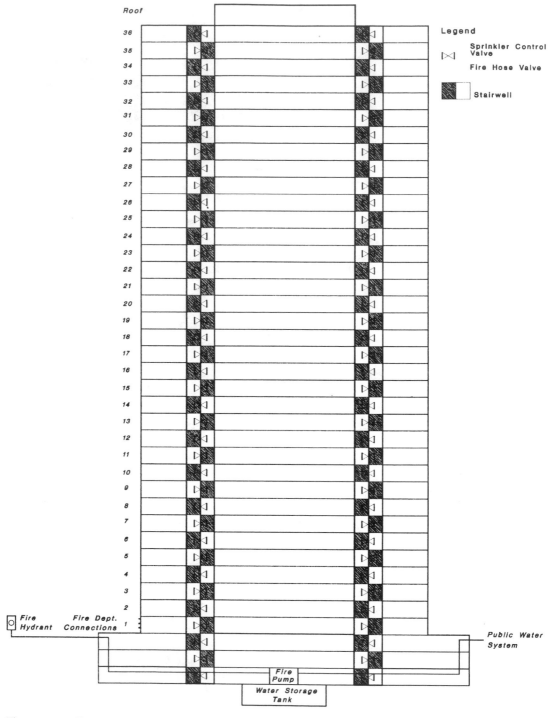

Figure 11.9   Fire protection riser diagram.

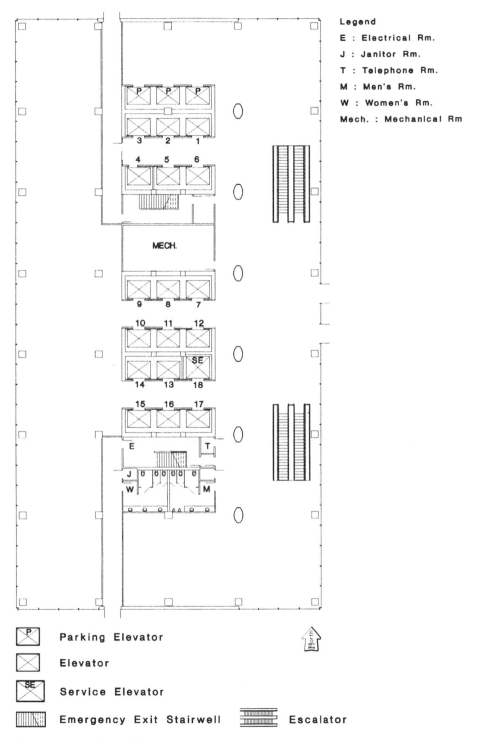

Figure 11.10   Ground floor plan.

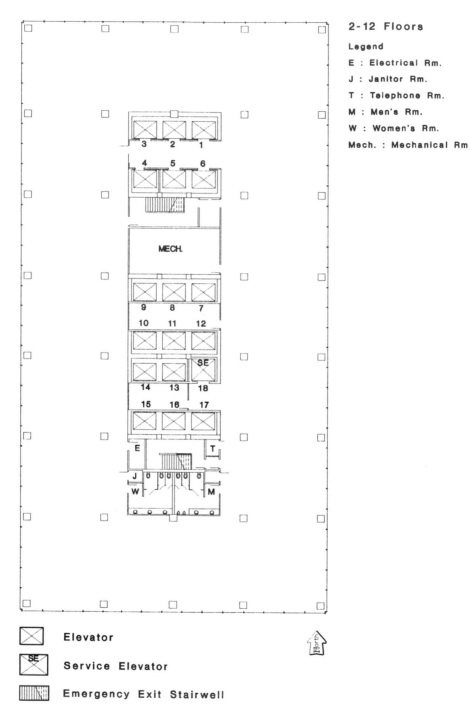

2-12 Floors

Legend
E : Electrical Rm.
J : Janitor Rm.
T : Telephone Rm.
M : Men's Rm.
W : Women's Rm.
Mech. : Mechanical Rm

Elevator

Service Elevator

Emergency Exit Stairwell

Figure 11.11   Low-rise floor plan.

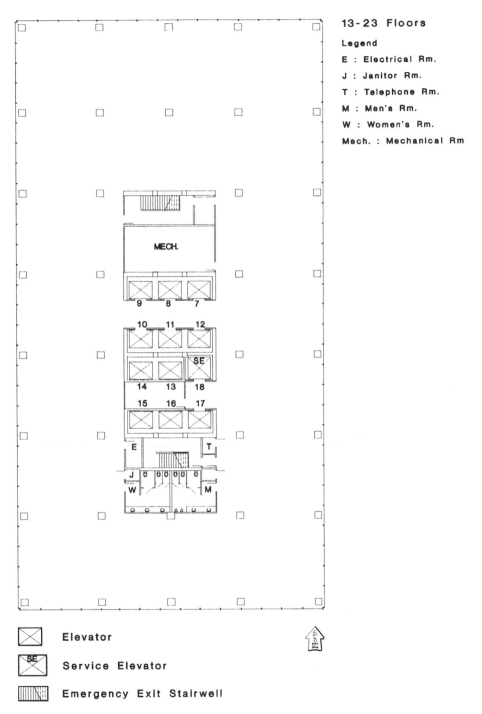

13-23 Floors

Legend

E : Electrical Rm.

J : Janitor Rm.

T : Telephone Rm.

M : Men's Rm.

W : Women's Rm.

Mech. : Mechanical Rm

Elevator

Service Elevator

Emergency Exit Stairwell

Figure 11.12   Mid-rise floor plan.

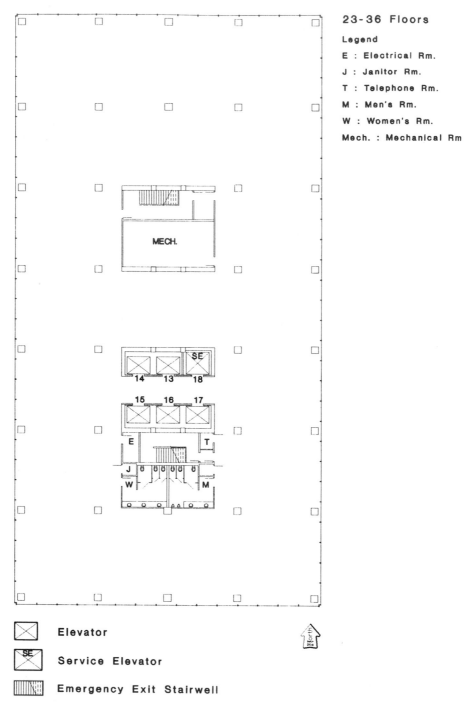

23-36 Floors

Legend

E : Electrical Rm.

J : Janitor Rm.

T : Telephone Rm.

M : Men's Rm.

W : Women's Rm.

Mech. : Mechanical Rm

Figure 11.13   High-rise floor plan.

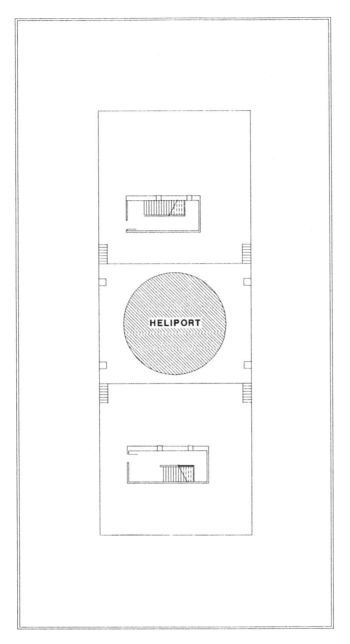

 **Emergency Exit Stairwell**

Figure 11.14 Roof floor plan.

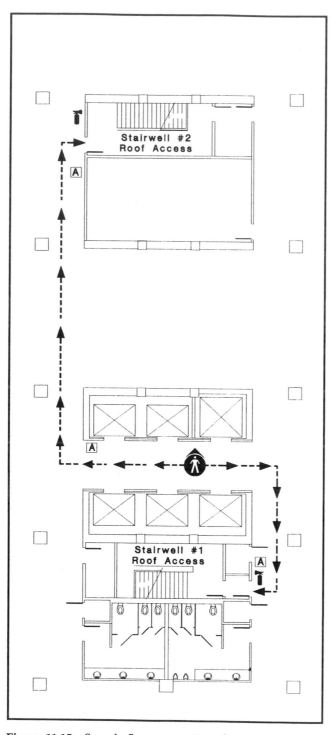

Fire Alarm A

You Are Here

Elevator

Fire Extinguisher

Emergency Exit
Stairwell

"Alarm sounds like" – Whoop
"Alarm looks like" – Strobe
(flashing light)

IN CASE OF FIRE
USE STAIRWAY
FOR EXIT.
DO NOT USE ELEVATOR

Building Security: 555-8395
Fire Department: 911

Figure 11.15   Sample floor evacuation plan.

- A copy of the Building Emergency Procedures Manual; site plans, and building floor plans that may, for convenience, be enlarged and displayed on walls
- Comprehensive contact lists for vendors and contractors who provide recovery services and materials, including general contractors; architects; plumbing, electrical, mechanical and fire sprinkler contractors; generator technicians; security providers; janitorial and waste disposal services; companies providing materials to board up windows, etc.
- Duplicate building security and fire life safety systems such as building and elevator keys, CCTV, and videocassette recorders
- An emergency generator that powers the Emergency Operations Center independent of building primary or emergency power systems
- Emergency supplies (or lists of emergency supply locations in the building)—bottled water, canned and dry food, first aid kits, sleeping bags, blankets, stretchers, portable emergency lighting, flashlights, batteries, safety gloves, heavy duty plastic trash bags (to line toilets if sewer services are interrupted), body bags, hard hats, protective goggles, dust masks, and light rescue equipment such as shovels, crow bars, and heavy-duty gloves

Drills

Drills are an invaluable tool to train, instruct, reinforce, and test the effectiveness of the emergency staff, occupants, and floor wardens to respond to the emergencies that are most likely to occur in the building. They also can be used to test the performance of building emergency systems and equipment.

Because fire safety is such a major concern of high-rise building owners, managers, and the local authority having jurisdiction, state and local laws specify intervals at which fire drills must be conducted. For example, fire codes in the city of New York require high-rise office buildings to perform fire drills every three months. Meanwhile, GSA buildings are required to conduct two fire drills a year, and the City of Los Angeles requires only annual drills.

To be successful, fire drills should be planned ahead of time and should be thoroughly documented. This documentation is used to analyze the training readiness of all persons involved and, like all documented life safety training, can be used as legal evidence (especially in the event of litigation following a major incident that results in injuries or loss of life) to prove that the building owner or manager has taken steps to ensure the safety of occupants. Tenants, emergency staff, and drill monitors all need to prepare adequately for fire drills as follows:

1. *Tenants.* Tenant representatives and floor wardens should be informed of the dates and times fire drills have been scheduled for their respective floors. All tenant employees should be told of the upcoming drill and asked to review occupant training material. Floor wardens should ensure that their floor response personnel are in place and prepared for fire drills—to assist in this preparation, meetings may be conducted to review evacuation procedures.
2. *Building Emergency Staff.* All staff participating in the drills should rehearse their duties, including performing special drill announcements. The local fire department should be telephoned before the drills start and immediately after the drills have been completed. These calls reduce the chance that the fire department will unnecessarily respond to a person mistaking the drill for an actual fire and making an emergency call to them.

3. *Drill Monitors.* There should be drill monitors stationed at strategic locations throughout the drill floors to observe and document on a *Fire Drill Checklist* the conduct of participants from the time the fire alarm first is activated.
4. After the evacuation or relocation has occurred, all evacuees should be grouped together at the safe refuge area and asked to sign a *Fire Drill Register*. The Fire Safety Director should verbally critique the performance of the drill before the participants are directed to return to their offices.

Appendix 11-1 includes samples of a *Fire Drill Notification* letter, fire drill announcements, a *Fire Drill Checklist*, a *Fire Drill Register*, and a *Bomb Threat Checklist*.

On completion of drills, a report should be produced by the Fire Safety Director. This report should include a brief goal statement; a description of how the drills were conducted; an overall review of how building fire life safety systems performed; an overall review of the how floor wardens, occupants, and building emergency staff performed; and recommendations on training improvements. Copies of all documentation should be included with the report. Some buildings, after these drills, determine which single-floor tenant and multiple-tenant floors performed the best and then present those involved with awards acknowledging their achievements.

A word of caution: Fire emergencies are not the only type of emergency for which drills should be conducted. To have an effective fire life safety program, staff and occupants should be kept ready to handle all types of emergencies that are likely to occur at their building.

Documentation and Recordkeeping

This section of the Building Emergency Procedures Manual contains documentation, records, and forms (see samples in Appendix 11-1) for all activities and training conducted under the Building Emergency Plan, including training for building emergency staff (building management, Fire Safety Director, Alternate Fire Safety Director, engineers, security, janitors, parking staff, etc.), building occupants, and floor wardens.

Handling the Media

This section contains guidelines for handling the media during and after a major emergency. It designates the spokesperson or public information person who will address the media, outlines how media representatives will be handled and accommodated, and specifies what access these representatives will be granted. See the section in Chapter 10, "Dealing with the Media," for guidelines for effectively handling the media to advantage during and after a major emergency.

Design of the Manual

The Building Emergency Procedures Manual should be in a three-ring binder so that outdated information can be removed easily and revised material can be added. Pages should be numbered and dated—this alleviates confusion when changes or revisions are made. Each section outlined in the table of contents and each emergency identified in the manual should be tabbed for easy identification and immediate reference. Use of colored tabs can aid reference—for example, a red tab for "Emergency Telephone Numbers."

The manual needs to be designed so that material from it can be broken out and used for the training and instruction of building management; the building Fire Safety Director; engineering, security, parking, and janitorial staff; floor wardens; floor response teams; and occupants. Copies of the Building Emergency Procedures Manual should be placed in the Main Office of the Building (or Building Management Office), the office of the Fire Safety Director, the Building Control Station, the Security Command Center (if appropriate), the office of building engineering, and other locations as deemed necessary by the Fire Safety Director. Copies of Floor Warden Manuals should be given to each tenant, floor warden, and alternate floor warden. Occupant documentation should be distributed to every person in the building. Of course, copies of all these items should be submitted for approval to the local fire authority having jurisdiction.

It cannot be stressed enough that the structure of the Building Emergency Procedures Manual just described is only an example. Every site and high-rise building is different, and plans vary according to state and local laws and the requirements of the authority having jurisdiction. Every emergency manual should be periodically reviewed and updated to incorporate any changes or modifications. When these changes are made, the authority having jurisdiction that approved the manual should be notified in writing, and all Building Emergency Procedures Manuals in existence should have the changes incorporated into them. The outdated material should be retained indefinitely as part of the building fire life safety records in case it is needed later as evidence for a legal action.

Occupant Documentation and Training

Occupant Documentation

Booklets, brochures, pamphlets, or leaflets are often used to train occupants. These materials are designed to contain the correct procedures to be followed in any emergency likely to happen in the building. Some buildings limit the documentation to a compact volume on fire, fire alarm, bomb threat, medical emergency, and natural disasters relevant to the location. Figure 11.16 is a sample occupant safety training brochure for Pacific Tower Plaza, the hypothetical high-rise, which is located in an area where earthquakes are likely to occur.

Many of these brochures include floor evacuation plans that show the building core, perimeter, stairwells, elevators, and every wall that faces every exit route; exit routes to the appropriate stairwells; symbols depicting the location of fire equipment and manual fire alarm devices; floor number; fire department and building emergency telephone numbers; what stairwells have roof access; and what the fire alarm looks and sounds like. (Refer to Figure 11.15 for a sample floor evacuation plan.) The brochure may also include a *Certificate of Occupant Training* (see Figure 11.17) to be filled out by the occupant receiving the training and returned to the floor warden or building Fire Safety Director for recordkeeping.

OCCUPANT SAFETY BROCHURE

Pacific Tower Plaza is a modern high-rise building with systems designed to address any emergencies that could take place anywhere in the structure at any point in time. Fire life safety systems are monitored 24 hours a day, seven days a week by a well-trained, on-site security staff. State-of-the-art automatic fire detection and suppression systems are designed to provide early detection and control of fires, permitting occupants to remain in the building for a period of time, safely isolated from a fire. The Toluga Hills City Fire Department is familiar with the building's emergency systems and usually will be on-site within minutes in the event of an emergency.

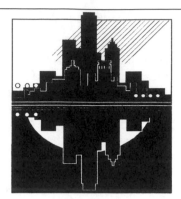

Pacific Tower Plaza
One Poppyfields Boulevard
Toluga Hills

Nearest Cross Street:
Mount Waverley Boulevard

The risk of a fire spreading at Pacific Tower Plaza is minimized, but if any emergency should occur, it is essential that you know what to do to protect yourself and warn others of any possible danger.

If a Fire Alarm Occurs:

1. Stay as calm as possible.
2. Immediately proceed to your nearest safe stairwell. Follow the directions on the public address system, or from Floor Wardens. DO NOT USE ELEVATORS.
3. In leaving an area, to confine the fire/smoke, close doors but do not lock them.

If You Discover Fire or Smoke:

1. Notify anyone in the immediate area of danger.
2. To confine the fire/smoke, close doors but do not lock them.
3. Activate a Manual Fire Alarm Station, if close by.
4. Call the Fire Department by dialing 911. Tell them:
   • Building name and address
   • Nearest cross street
   • Floor and room/suite number
   • Known information about the fire/smoke
   • Your call-back phone number
   DO NOT HANG UP UNTIL OPERATOR DOES SO.
5. If time allows, notify Building Management and/or Building Security by dialing 555-8395.
6. If time permits, notify the Floor Warden.
7. If you evacuate, use the nearest safe stairwell. DO NOT USE ELEVATORS.

If You Receive a Bomb Threat Call:

1. Keep the caller on the line and obtain as much information as possible:
   • When is bomb going to explode?
   • Where is the bomb?
   • What does it look like?
   • What will cause it to explode?
   • Did the caller place the bomb? Why?
   • What is the caller's name and address?
2. Record the time of call, words of the caller, and any background noises.
3. Notify Building Management and/or Building Security by dialing 555-8395. They will notify tenants and law enforcement.
4. If any suspicious object is found, DO NOT TOUCH IT. Move people away and notify Building Management.
5. The decision whether or not to evacuate usually is the responsibility of the senior officer of a tenant.

If There Is a Medical Emergency:

1. Call Paramedics by dialing 911. Tell them:
   • Building name and address
   • Nearest cross street
   • Floor and room/suite number
   • Location and name of victim
   • Nature of the emergency or victim's condition
   • Caller's call-back phone number
   DO NOT HANG UP UNTIL OPERATOR DOES SO.
2. Notify Building Management and/or Building Security by dialing 555-8395. (If a physician has been called, an escort should be arranged for him or her.)
3. If time permits, notify the Floor Warden.
4. Station someone at the service elevator lobby on the floor involved so paramedics can be escorted to the victim.
5. If properly trained, assist the victim, but do not move the victim unless there is danger of additional, more serious injury.

If There Is an Earthquake

1. Stay as calm as possible.
2. If in an office, move away from windows and interior glass partitions. Get under a strong desk or table and hold on to it.
3. If in a corridor or lobby, drop to the floor near an interior wall and take cover with your arms.
4. If inside an elevator, wait until it stops and the doors open, or summon emergency assistance.
5. Do not run outside the building. If outside, move to a clear area.
6. DO NOT USE ELEVATORS.
7. After the earthquake, if there is damage, assist Floor Wardens and Building Emergency Staff. BE PREPARED FOR AFTERSHOCKS.

Figure 11.16 Sample occupant training brochure.

Occupant Training

A class taught by a qualified person (preferably the building Fire Safety Director) is an invaluable way to inform high-rise building occupants of what to do in the event of a fire or other emergency. The City of Los Angeles Municipal Fire Code, for instance, requires all high-rise buildings to instruct occupants annually on the procedures to be followed in a fire, earthquake, or other emergency; instruction of all new occupants is required within 14 days of their assuming occupancy in the building. Documentation of this instruction needs to be maintained by the Fire Safety Director and be available for inspection by the Chief of the Los Angeles City Fire Department. To satisfy this legal requirement, many of the city's 750-plus high-rise buildings conduct one-hour occupant training classes every two weeks.

In such a class, it is important to explain legal fire life safety requirements, the building's emergency systems and equipment, and relevant emergency procedures. The instructor must be thoroughly familiar with the building in which the occupants work and with the Building Emergency Plan. Audiovisual aids and handout materials are extremely helpful; in fact, many high-rise commercial office building owners and managers throughout the United States have contracted with professional fire life safety consultants to produce films describing their emergency systems and equipment and vividly portraying the expected response actions of occupants to building emergencies.

A suggested outline for an occupant training class follows:

1. Sign in participants (or have them fill out a *Certificate of Occupant Training*).
2. Give a personal introduction—presenter's name, position, experience, and qualifications.
3. Explain legal requirements (state and local laws).
4. Give emergency telephone numbers, or explain where to find them.

CERTIFICATE OF OCCUPANT TRAINING

Name (PRINT): _____

Tenant Name (PRINT): _____   Floor and Room/Suite Number: _____

I acknowledge the following (mark box to certify):

[   ]   I have received training in building fire life safety.

[   ]   I have received a copy of the Occupant Safety Brochure.

[   ]   I will check the specific layout of my floor, including the location of my primary and secondary stairwells, location of manual fire alarm stations, and type and location of fire extinguishers.

[   ]   Presently I am non-ambulatory or a person with a disability.

Nature of Disability or Reason for Non-Ambulatory Condition: _____

Signature: _____   Date: _____

PLEASE FILL OUT AND RETURN TO FLOOR WARDEN OR BUILDING FIRE SAFETY DIRECTOR

Figure 11.17   Sample Certificate of Occupant Training.

5. Outline the Building Emergency Staff Organization—including an explanation of the concept of floor wardens and floor response personnel.
6. Explain building emergency systems and equipment, including a description of the fire detection and suppression systems, what the building's fire alarm sounds and looks like, and the configuration of a typical floor (the position of elevators, stairwells, which stairwells have roof access, etc.).
7. Describe procedures for handling building emergencies—what is expected of occupants in each type of emergency? For example, describe the occupant guidelines in Chapter 10's section on "Occupant Response to a Fire."
8. Familiarize class with the evacuation and relocation plan of the building, locked stairwell door procedures, safe refuge areas, and emergency evacuation procedures for individuals with disabilities.
9. Demonstrate or explain portable fire extinguisher usage. (Some high-rise building owners and managers, for liability reasons, do *not* train occupants—or even floor wardens—to use fire extinguishers.) The operation of each type of portable fire extinguisher varies depending on its type and the type of fire that it is being used to extinguish. (Chapter 4 includes a description of how to use the various types of extinguishers.) Thoroughly investigate the specific operating procedures for an extinguisher that a trained occupant may use. An excellent basic method to teach occupants how to correctly use portable fire extinguishers is the four-step P-A-S-S procedure approved by the NFPA (see Figure 11.18).
10. Give fire drill instructions.
11. Tour building floor to familiarize occupants with layout of a typical floor, including primary and secondary stairwells, location of manual fire alarm stations, and type and location of fire extinguishers.

Building owners and managers require all tenants to participate in the building fire life safety program, and some mandate these occupant training requirements in their leases.

Floor Warden Manual and Training

Floor Warden Manual

A Floor Warden Manual often is used to help train high-rise buildings' floor wardens, their alternates, and floor response personnel (including stairwell monitors, elevator monitors, search monitors, and disabled assistance monitors) in their duties and responsibilities. These manuals cover emergencies such as fires, fire alarms, explosions, bombs and bomb threats, violence in the workplace, medical emergencies, power failures, elevator malfunctions and entrapments, natural disasters, water leaks, chemical/hazardous material incidents, labor disputes, demonstrations, riots and civil disorder, aircraft collisions, and hostage and barricade situations. The general information and outline is taken directly from the Building Emergency Procedures Manual described in this chapter, but because the manual is meant for these specific persons, only their duties and responsibilities are emphasized.

Floor Warden Training

A floor warden training class, lasting from 1 to 2 hours, should be conducted by a qualified person, preferably the building Fire Safety Director, at least every

Pull the pin or ring: The pin normally keeps the operating lever locked and prevents accidental discharge of the extinguisher. (Depending on the type of extinguisher there may be different lever-release devices, and seals or devices to indicate whether it has been tampered with.)

Aim the extinguisher hose, nozzle, or discharge horn low at the base of the fire.

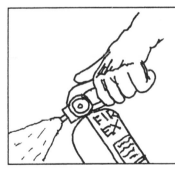

Squeeze or press the operating lever or button (usually located directly above the handle). Discharge will stop when the lever is released.

Sweep the discharge back and forth slowly across the fire. Keeping the extinguisher aimed at the base of the fire, move carefully toward it. Continue this sweeping motion until the flames appear to be extinguished. Repeat this action if the fire re-ignites.

Figure 11.18 Portable extinguisher operation using the P-A-S-S procedure. Artwork by Pip Craighead.

3 to 6 months. The class should include not only legal fire life safety require-ments and emergency systems and equipment, but also an outline of floor war-dens' duties and responsibilities in training occupants under their supervision, and a description of the emergency procedures addressed in the Floor Warden Manual. This class's outline and content should be similar to that described in the preceding "Occupant Training" section, but should naturally specify floor wardens' responsibilities in each area and should include a time at the begin-ning to hand out Floor Warden Manuals, floor warden identification material (vest, armband, hard hat, etc.), and any equipment (flashlights).

Some buildings vary the content of floor warden classes over the course of a year. This both stimulates interest and ensures that vital areas are adequately covered. For example, if four classes are provided in a year, the first one may address fire emergencies and preparations for building fire drills; the second one may address explosions, bombs, and bomb threats; the third one may address violence in the workplace; and the fourth one may address natural disasters. In addition, a hands-on "live fire" portable fire extinguisher class may be offered to floor wardens and conducted by representatives of the local fire department. This class could be scheduled to coincide with the annual recharging of build-ing fire extinguishers.

Guest speakers may be invited to give special presentations to aid in the education process. A uniformed member of the local law enforcement bomb squad, the local fire department, or representatives of organizations such as Alcohol, Tobacco and Firearms (ATF), the Federal Bureau of Investigation (FBI), and the Federal Emergency Management Agency (FEMA) can be great crowd drawers and in the process provide floor wardens and building management with up-to-date, interesting, and invaluable information.

Building Emergency Staff Training

Written Instructions

Building emergency staff procedures must be clearly and simply written. Each emergency should be addressed separately, and *each member's* duties and re-sponsibilities should be documented in detail. This point cannot be stressed enough. So many Building Emergency Procedures Manuals are written in a generic fashion and do not get to the heart of the matter. Yet if staff are to be ade-quately trained to handle emergencies, the emergency scenario must be thor-oughly analyzed and the best courses of action decided on, documented, and then used for training. This is not to say that everything can be written down or that every planned event can be explicitly defined. As defined by the *New Web-ster Dictionary*, an *emergency* is: "any event or combination of circumstances call-ing for immediate action" and sometimes these circumstances do vary. The geo-graphic and topographic location of a building, its design and construction, the type and location of security and life safety systems and equipment within it, the type of emergency and where in or outside the building it occurs are all fac-tors that may affect the impact a major emergency has on a building and its occupants. Despite this, the procedures for handling most emergencies can be planned and well documented.

All instructions for complex emergency procedures and systems material must be written in easy-to-understand, action-oriented terms, keeping in mind the principles in "Security Staff Duties and Written Instructions" in Chapter 8.

For example, if a fire alarm occurs on the 20th floor during normal business hours of the hypothetical Pacific Tower Plaza, the security officer whose responsibility it is to go to the Building Control Station may need to carry out the following tasks:

1. Identify the type of fire alarm and its location by checking the fire computer and the building fire detection and alarm system annunciator and control panels.
2. Acknowledge the alarm by pressing a button or flipping a switch on the control panel (this often also directs the panel to silence the audible signal sounding in the Building Control Station but does not affect in any way the operation of fire systems in the building).
3. Telephone the fire department by dialing 911 and notify them of the building name and address; nearest cross street; type of fire alarm and its location, and any other known details; and the security officer's call-back telephone number. The officer must not hang up until the emergency services operator does so.
4. Broadcast on all radio channels the type of alarm and its location. Direct appropriate engineering and security staff to report to the alarm location to investigate.
5. By radio, direct the lobby security officer to report to the main lobby and prepare for the arrival of the fire department.
6. Manually select the 18th, 19th, 21st, and 22nd floor paging zones on the PA system (the 20th floor is automatically activated because it is in alarm); key the microphone; and speak loudly, slowly, and clearly to make the following PA announcement to the floor in alarm, two floors above it, and two floors below it:

> May I have your attention, please. This is Building Security. There is an emergency on the 20th floor. All occupants on the 18th, 19th, 20th, 21st, and 22nd floors, please move to your nearest stairwell and stand by for further instructions.* (Repeat the message loudly, slowly, and clearly.)

If the order to evacuate is given, make the following announcement:

> May I have your attention, please. This is Building Security. All occupants on the 18th, 19th, 20th, 21st, and 22nd floors, please enter your nearest stairwell, descend five floors and reenter the building. (Repeat the message loudly, slowly, and clearly.)

7. Manually select the 13th, 14th, 15th, 16th, and 17th floor paging zones on the PA system, key the microphone and speak loudly, slowly, and clearly to make the following announcement to the relocation floors:

> May I have your attention, please. This is Building Security. In response to an emergency occurring on the 20th floor, all floor wardens on the 13th, 14th, 15th, 16th, and 17th floors, please proceed to your nearest stairwell to assist in relocating occupants. (Repeat the message loudly, slowly, and clearly.)

8. Broadcast on all radio channels any additional alarms that are received.

---

* Some fire departments allow building occupants to wait at the stairwell entrance, others mandate that occupants immediately move into the stairwell and evacuate from the floor in alarm.

9. When the all-clear verification has been given by the Fire Safety Director, Assistant Fire Safety Director, Chief Engineer, or the fire department, reset the alarm on the control panel.
10. Make the following announcement to the five relocation floors and stairwells:

> May I have your attention, please. This is Building Security. The emergency on the 20th floor is over. It is safe for all occupants to return to their floors. (Repeat the message loudly, slowly, and clearly.)

11. Manually deactivate the PA system on all floors where it was activated.
12. Broadcast on all radio channels that the alarm situation is over and that staff can return to their normal duties.
13. Document all actions on a Fire Alarm Report.

This procedure is designed for a fire alarm that occurs during normal business hours of the building. If the same alarm occurs after normal business hours, the procedure may need to be modified because at such a time the engineering staff may not be available and therefore security staff may need to assume additional duties.

From the preceding example, it is apparent that procedures for handling emergencies can become quite complicated for building emergency staff. Moreover, these procedures will vary according to the mandates of the authority having jurisdiction, the custom-designed policy for each building, and the actual operation of the fire detection and alarm system annunciator and control panels. Therefore, explanatory documentation should be provided for each building. Several documents can be kept in the Building Control Station. The first is the *Building Equipment Manual,* which should contain descriptions and photographs of systems and devices in the station itself, and specific explanations as to how the equipment operates under normal and emergency conditions. A *Normal Business Hours Fire/Fire Alarm Checklist* and an *After Hours Fire/Fire Alarm Checklist,* each outlining steps to handle these emergencies, should be conspicuously placed or posted near the control panel for easy reference. A *Building Emergency Announcement Book* should provide messages to give in case of emergencies such as fires, fire alarms, explosions, bombs and bomb threats, violence in the workplace, power failures, natural disasters, chemical/hazardous material incidents, labor disputes, and demonstrations/riots and civil disorder.

Fire and fire alarm announcements can be customized for when an alarm is activated on each individual floor of the building—this alleviates the need for the person reading them to work out which floors usually will be evacuated and relocated during such emergencies. In addition, the book should contain sample announcements for fire life safety system testing and drills. All messages must be short, to the point, and easy to understand. For example, this announcement should be made to the floor where testing will occur right before the testing starts:.

> May I have your attention, please. This is Building Security. Testing of the building fire life safety system on your floor will begin shortly and continue for approximately 15 minutes. During that time, please ignore all audible and visual fire alarms unless you are otherwise instructed by Building Security or your floor warden. Thank you for your assistance. (Repeat the message loudly, slowly, and clearly.)

After testing is completed, this announcement should be made to the floor where the testing occurred:

> May I have your attention, please. This is Building Security. Testing of the building fire life safety system on your floor has now been completed. Thank you for your assistance. (Repeat the message loudly, slowly, and clearly.)

Documentation not only helps train new staff and refresh the memory of established staff, but also boosts their confidence, particularly if they fear suddenly "blanking out" during a building emergency or announcement.

Training and Testing Methods

Emergency staff members must be properly trained and tested to carry out their duties in the event of a fire or other emergency. According to *Webster's College Dictionary*, to *train* an individual is "to give the discipline and instruction, drill, practice, designed to impart proficiency or efficiency"; *testing* is "a set of problems, questions, for evaluating abilities, aptitudes, skills, or performance. . . . The means by which the presence, quality, or genuineness of anything is determined."

Building management, the Fire Safety Director, the Alternate Fire Safety Director, building engineers, security officers, and janitorial and parking staff should be trained in emergency procedures for all shifts they work (including weekend and holiday shifts). (The question of "Who trains the Fire Safety Director?" has led to some larger city fire departments—such as New York, for example—requiring that individuals who assume this position attend certified training courses; see Chapter 14 for more details on this subject.) The Fire Safety Director generally determines the amount of time necessary to properly equip and prepare other staff members to competently handle their duties and responsibilities.

Some jurisdictional authorities, however, specify a minimum annual amount of training and testing. For example, in Los Angeles, all high-rise building emergency staff (except janitorial and parking staff who are exempted from certain technical aspects of the emergency procedures program) are required by code, and specific sections of the *Guideline Format for High-Rise Buildings: Emergency Procedures City of Los Angeles 1993*, to annually review the Building Emergency Procedures Manual and participate in at least three hours of instruction that includes:

1. A minimum of one hour dedicated to reviewing the building floor warden program, what occupants are trained to do in emergencies, evacuation and relocation procedures, how the building fire detection and control systems operate, what the building fire alarm sounds like (and, in some buildings, looks like), on what floors the alarm activates, and how the building fire life safety systems—including fire alarms—are monitored
2. A building walk-through and hands-on exercises to familiarize the appropriate staff with the operation of fire life safety systems and devices located in the Building Control Station, the operation of building fire life safety systems and equipment distributed throughout the building, and how to make voice communication PA announcements to selected floors of the building
3. A minimum of one hour dedicated to practical exercises designed to evaluate the staff's skills and performance in reacting to specific emergency scenarios pre-

sented to them. The building emergency staff should be sent to their normal working locations, at which point the simulated emergency is initiated. Afterward, the staff's performance is critiqued. Any deficiencies should be pointed out so that they learn from the experience.

All such instruction is documented and kept on file at the building. Copies also must be forwarded to the Los Angeles City Fire Department.

Some high-rise buildings set up monthly training for emergency staff. During these sessions, the staff review their duties and responsibilities, complete practical exercises, and take written tests to ensure that they are in a constant state of readiness.

Before leaving this subject, it is worth noting that building walk-throughs should be conducted systematically. A sample outline for touring the hypothetical building, Pacific Tower Plaza, and inspecting its fire life safety systems and equipment, follows:

1. Walk the site.
2. Walk the perimeter of the building and inspect all exits, including exits from the subterranean parking structure.
3. Walk the loading dock area and inspect its layout.
4. Enter the building at street level, inspect the main lobby, and note the configuration of passenger and freight/service elevators.
5. Take an elevator to the subterranean parking structure and walk all levels (take note of roll-down gates and doors with fusible links).
6. In the building tower, take an elevator to several individual floors (one in the low-rise elevator bank, one in the mid-rise elevator bank, and one in the high-rise elevator bank). On each floor, review the posted floor evacuation signs, walk through the common areas and public corridors to become familiar with each floor's configuration, and inspect each stairwell. Note the numbering sign within the stairwell. Inspect maintenance spaces, including mechanical areas and elevator machine rooms.
7. Access the roof and the heliport.
8. Proceed to the Building Control Station and inspect the following fire life safety systems and devices:
   - Voice communication and building PA system
   - Fire department voice communication systems
   - Public telephone for fire department use
   - Stairwell intercom systems
   - Fire detection and alarm system annunciator and control panels, including determining the types of devices and their locations
   - Sprinkler control valve, water-flow detector, and fire pump status panels
   - Other fire protection equipment and system annunciation or status indicators
   - Air-handling system controls and status indicators
   - Elevator status panel displaying elevator operations
   - Emergency and standby power systems status indicators
   - Controls for simultaneously unlocking stairwell doors locked from the stairwell side
   - Building and elevator keys
   - Fire computer terminal and printer
   - The Building Emergency Procedures Manual
9. On a typical floor, inspect the location of manual fire alarm stations and automatic detection devices (smoke, heat, or gas detectors).

10. Inspect the following systems and equipment distributed throughout the building:
    - Fire Pump Room
    - Domestic water valves
    - Emergency and standby power generator
    - Sprinkler control valves (main valve and those located in stairwells)
    - Main electrical panels (power transformer room)
    - Gas mains and shut-off valves
    - Fire department connections on the exterior of the building (for automatic sprinkler and standpipe systems)
    - Locations of elevator pits
    - Elevator car operation (including manual recall, independent service, and "Fireman's Return Override" or "Fireman's By-Pass")
    - Fire department lock box or rapid entry key vault
    - Any other fire life safety equipment
11. Inspect out-of-building safe refuge areas

Evacuation Signage

State and local laws require evacuation signs to be posted in high-rise buildings so that a means of egress is clearly visible at all times. The *means of egress* is defined by the NFPA 101 *Life Safety Code* (NFPA 101 1994, p. 101-26) as

> A continuous and unobstructed way of exit travel from any point in a building or structure to a public way consisting of three separate and distinct parts: (a) the exit access, (b) the exit, and (c) the exit discharge. A means of egress comprises the vertical and horizontal travel and shall include intervening room spaces, doorways, hallways, corridors, passageways, balconies, ramps, stairs, enclosures, lobbies, escalators, horizontal exits, courts, and yards.

NFPA 101 (1994, p. 48), Section 5-10, "Marking of Means of Egress," states the following concerning signs designating exits or ways of travel:

> Section 5-10.1.2. Exits shall be marked by an approved sign readily visible from any direction of exit access. Exception: Main exterior exit doors that obviously and clearly are identifiable as exits.
>
> Section 5-10.1.3. At each door into an exit stair enclosure, tactile signage stating and complying with CABO/ANSI A117.1, *American National Standard for Accessible and Usable Buildings and Facilities*, shall be installed adjacent to the latch side of the door 60in. (152 cm.) above the finished floor to the centerline of the sign.
>
> Section 5-10.1.4. Access to exits shall be marked by approved, readily visible signs in all cases where the exit or way to reach it is not readily apparent to all occupants. Sign placement shall be such that no point in the exit is more than 100 ft. (30 m.) from the nearest visible sign. Exception: Signs in existing buildings need not meet the 100-ft. (30 m.) distance requirements.

The Code goes on to address the size, color, design, mounting, and illumination of these signs (NFPA 101 1994, pp. 48, 49), yet this is a suggested standard—it is up to the individual authority having jurisdiction to specify what evacuation signage is required.

The ADA classifies exit signs, except for the one at the exit door, in two ways. *Directional* signs read "EXIT" with an indicator showing the direction of travel (see Figure 11.19). *Informational* signs are located on stairwell landings and usually indicate the stairwell number, what uppermost and lowermost floor the stairwell serves, including a notation whether the stairwell has or has not roof access. They are likewise in every elevator lobby above and below the ground floor, and in other conspicuous floor locations as required by the authority having jurisdiction such as inside all public entrances of the building. Those in elevator lobbies usually include the following information:

- A building floor plan that shows the building core and perimeter, stairwells, fire escapes, elevators, and every wall that faces every exit route.
- A "YOU ARE HERE" direction arrow.
- Exit routes to the appropriate stairwells.
- Symbols depicting locations of fire equipment and manual fire alarm stations.
- Information such as the building name and address, floor number, fire department and building emergency telephone numbers, what stairwells have roof access, and what the building fire alarm looks and sounds like.
- If incorporating language similar to: "IN CASE OF FIRE USE STAIRWAY FOR EXIT. DO NOT USE ELEVATOR," the sign should be installed adjacent to the elevator call station (see Figure 11.20).

Figure 11.19
Exit sign indicates the
stairwell entrance.

**In Case Of Fire
Do Not Use Elevators**

Use Stairways

Figure 11.20 Typical sign currently used to indicate that elevators should not be used during fire situations.

Signs inside stairwells also may include details regarding reentry of occupants from the stairwell onto the floor during a fire.

How to Communicate the Building Emergency Plan to Tenants

According to Lohr (1983): "In a well-planned firesafety education program, the all-important message must be *concise, positive, relevant and aimed at changing some-one's attitude and behavior* . . . making that message come alive and be meaningful is one of the vital aspects of the firesafety educator's program planning. . . . messages must be well-planned, realistic and relevant to particular needs" (p. 1).

Educational Materials

Fire life safety education can be achieved through a variety of means—lectures, classes, workshops, seminars, panel discussions, live demonstrations, and drills —using a variety of educational materials, both written (books, booklets, brochures, pamphlets, leaflets, flyers, and posters) and audiovisual (films, video-tapes, overheads, and slide programs). Adams (1983, p. 149) says that,

In spite of this overwhelming variety, they all have one focal point: firesafety education materials form a bond of communication between the "speaker" and the viewer. The mere presence of materials and a viewer doesn't mean there's always communication. Communication occurs when the viewer "listens" to the materials, hears and understands what they say, and remembers their message.

Also, as Joseph Sano (1994) of the New York State Public Employees Federation reminds us, "use audiovisual aids but don't overdo it! You do not want to compete for your audience's attention with your own props" (p. 48).

In addition to utilizing written and audiovisual materials to communicate information *to* building emergency staff, floor wardens, and occupants, certain information must be received back *from* building tenants. For example, tenants always must have trained persons assigned to the positions of floor warden and alternate floor warden, and must immediately inform building management and the building Fire Safety Director of any non-ambulatory individuals or individuals with a disability who may need help in an emergency.

Some buildings facilitate feedback of vital details by including requests for updates of fire life safety information from the tenants with Tenant Manuals and information packages given to new tenants. Others distribute a *Fire Life Safety Information Package* (see sample in Appendix 11-2) at least every quarter or six months to remind tenants of the building program and their responsibilities in it. This package could include an explanation of the building fire life safety program and the training available for occupants and floor wardens during the ensuing quarter or six-month period. It also could supply the current versions of building forms such as *Floor Wardens and Alternates Roster* and *Disabled and Non-Ambulatory Persons List*, with a request that tenants update any changes and return the forms to the building Fire Safety Director. (Samples of these forms appear in Appendix 11-1.)

A computer with a decent amount of memory can be of great assistance in maintaining fire life safety records. A database can be created with names and contact telephone numbers of tenants and building emergency staff, and training details of all participants in the program. Also, a word processor vastly simplifies the task of making procedural changes to the Building Emergency Procedures Manual.

Educational Methods

Lectures, classes, workshops, seminars, panel discussions, live demonstrations, and drills can all be used to communicate the Building Emergency Plan to tenants. The entire fire life safety education program, however, should be designed at least one year in advance. This ensures that the program is comprehensively planned, allows sufficient time to obtain guest speakers (perhaps from local law enforcement and the fire department), permits timely communication of the upcoming schedule to tenants and others for whom the education is intended, and allows the building Fire Safety Director to properly organize and prepare all the program's components. A sample yearly program for training building emergency staff, occupants, and floor wardens, and for updating fire life safety records, is shown in Appendix 11-3.

The actual training conducted may vary according to the requirements of state and local codes, the authority having jurisdiction, the historical and projected patterns of emergencies specific to the building, and the policy and support by the building owner and manager for the fire life safety program. Some buildings, on an annual basis, conduct a full-scale building mock disaster drill. A simulated emergency with "casualties" is planned in conjunction with local emergency response groups, such as fire department fire suppression crews and paramedics, local hospitals and health services, local law enforcement, the American Red Cross, utility company representatives, and other emergency organizations within the community. The media can be notified of the event and invited to participate in news briefings. The event itself may last two to three hours. During the mock disaster, drill monitors are stationed at strategic locations throughout the facility to observe and document the conduct of all participants from the time the simulated incident is first initiated. Afterward, all planners of the event meet to critique the execution of the plan and the overall performance of those participating. If thoroughly prepared and properly executed, the simulation can be of great educational value to high-rise building staff, tenants, and all outside agencies and groups who participate.

All fire life safety training is costly to a building in terms of participants' time commitment and the provision of educational materials. However, these financial costs are repaid many times over in terms of the emergency preparedness of the building and in the goodwill that can result among the building management, tenants, and local authorities.

Summary

The purpose of establishing, implementing, and maintaining a Building Emergency Plan is to promote a state of readiness within a building. In fact, the value is not just in the plan itself, but in the development process leading up to it and the education of the emergency organization that follows it. Communication with outside agencies—law enforcement, fire officials, and local government agencies responsible for emergency planning—is essential in both establishing the plan and coordinating planning efforts. Also, contact with other high-rise buildings in the area may lead to mutual aid arrangements that assist in addressing certain emergencies, particularly natural disasters (and in the case of incidents like the 1995 Oklahoma bombing), that tend to affect the entire community.

Planning does not end with a written document. A Building Emergency Procedures Manual is only a part of the planning process, and after it has been created it should not be placed on a shelf to gather dust. Because the Building Emergency Staff Organization is changing all the time, the plan must be systematically updated. Changes in personnel will occur, but if new personnel are not thoroughly familiar with the plan, it will not be long before the organization is a mere shell of formalities and the plan itself is no longer effective. Unfortunately, it will only take the next real emergency to reveal the true state of affairs in any high-rise building.

Plans must be maintained to be effective, indeed they must be "living" and dynamic.

—CALIFORNIA STATE OF EMERGENCY SERVICES (1993, p. 40)

References

Adams, Robert, "Materials," *Firesafety Educator's Handbook* (All NFPA material used with permission from the National Fire Protection Association, Quincy, MA. Copyright 1983).

Anthony, Doug, statement made on First Interstate Bancorp/Los Angeles City Fire Department Videotape regarding the May 4, 1988, First Interstate Tower Fire. May 5, 1988, was the day Anthony was interviewed and made this statement.

BOMA, "What is an emergency plan?" *Emergency Planning Guidebook* (Building Owners and Managers Association International, Washington, DC, 1994).

California State of Emergency Services, "Conclusion," *Business Resumption Planning Guidelines* (California State of Emergency Services Earthquake Program, June 1993).

Carson, Wayne "Chip," "Fire safety and the Americans with Disabilities Act," *NFPA Fire News* (National Fire Protection Association, Quincy, MA. Copyright December/January 1993).

Cummings, Robert B., and Thomas, W. Jaeger, "ADA sets a new standard for accessibility," *NFPA Journal* (National Fire Protection Association, Quincy, MA, May/June 1993).

"Employers are asking . . . about the safety of handicapped workers when emergencies occur." (Used with permission from Dale Brown of The Worksite Committee of The President's Committee on Employment of the Handicapped, Washington, DC, 1985).

Gigliotti, Richard, and Ronald Jason, "Emergency plan considerations," *Emergency Planning for Maximum Protection* (Butterworth–Heinemann, Stoneham, MA, 1991).

Harris, Mel, "Emergency evacuation of disabled workers," Letter to the author dated March 27, 1995 (General Services Administration, Washington, DC).

High-Rise Evacuation (National Fire Protection Association, Quincy, MA. Copyright 1993).

Klem, Thomas J., "Major high-rise fires reveal protection needs," *NFPA Journal* (National Fire Protection Association, Quincy, MA. Copyright September/October 1992).

Lohr, Cathy, "Message," *Firesafety Educator's Handbook* (National Fire Protection Association, Quincy, MA, 1983).

Los Angeles City Fire Department, *Guideline Format for High-Rise Buildings: Emergency Procedures City of Los Angeles 1993* (prepared by the Los Angeles City Fire Department Fire and Safety Education Unit, Disaster Preparedness Division, 1993).

Los Angeles City Fire Department and Joni and Friends, "Emergency Evacuation Procedures for Disabled Individuals" (obtained from the Los Angeles City Fire Department Fire and Safety Education Unit, Disaster Preparedness Division, 1994).

Merritt Company, The, "Disaster control," *Protection of Assets Manual*, vol. I (Used with permission. Copyright The Merritt Company, Santa Monica, CA, 800/638-7597, 1991).

New Webster Encyclopedic Dictionary of the English Language. Editor-in-Chief Virginia S. Thatcher, (Consolidated Book Publishers, Chicago, 1980).

NFPA 101, *Life Safety Code*, 1994, Chapter 5: "Means of Egress," Section 5-1.2: "Definitions, Means of Egress" (National Fire Protection Association, Quincy, MA. Copyright 1994), p. 101-26.

NFPA 101, *Life Safety Code*, 1994, Chapter 5: "Means of Egress," Section 5-10: "Marking of Means of Egress" (National Fire Protection Association, Quincy, MA, 1994), pp. 101-48–101-49.

NISTIR 4870, "Feasibility and design considerations of emergency evacuation by elevators," *National Technical Information Service* (Springfield, VA 22161, September 1992). Research conducted by the National Institute of Standards and Technology and sponsored by the General Services Administration.

NYFD, *Fire Safety Plan Format and Guidelines* (New York City Fire Department, 1972).

Sano, Joseph, "Speak well, and you'll be heard loudly and clearly," *The Firemen's Grapevine* (Los Angeles, March 1994). Reprinted from *The Communicator*, official publication of the New York State Public Employees Federation.

Studer, Craig, "Safeguarding against building fires," *Skylines* (Building Owners and Managers Association International, Washington, DC, March 1992).

Taubman, Byrna, "What are your chances of surviving a high-rise fire?" *New York Magazine* (New York, May 27, 1974).

Time Magazine, "Fire and smoke," *Time Magazine* (Washington, DC, March 8, 1993).

Webster's College Dictionary, 1992 Edition (From *Random House Webster's College Dictionary* by Random House, Inc. Copyright © 1995, 1992, 1991 by Random House, Inc. Reprinted by permission of Random House, Inc., New York, 1992.)

Appendix 11-1   Sample Documentation Forms

FIRE PREVENTION INSPECTION CHECKLIST

Housekeeping/Maintenance	No	OK
1. "NO SMOKING" signs posted.	[ ]	[ ]
2. Smoking areas clearly marked. Equipped with non-tip ashtrays, metal waste receptacles, and fire extinguishers.	[ ]	[ ]
3. "NO SMOKING" rules and regulations being observed.	[ ]	[ ]
4. Combustible waste stored in proper/approved containers.	[ ]	[ ]
5. Flammable liquids safely stored in approved containers away from combustibles.	[ ]	[ ]
6. Trash/rubbish removal done on a regular basis.	[ ]	[ ]
7. All electrical plugs, switches (no missing or cracked faceplates), and cords legal and in good repair. (Extension cords not to be used in place of permanent wiring).	[ ]	[ ]
8. Cords are not be run across doorways or under carpets or mats where they may be stepped upon.	[ ]	[ ]
9. No extensive use of cords from outlet (octopus).	[ ]	[ ]
10. Adequate clearance maintained at all switch and sub-panels (3 feet).	[ ]	[ ]
11. Heat-producing appliances well-ventilated.	[ ]	[ ]
12. Electrical equipment turned off when not in use.	[ ]	[ ]
13. Malfunctioning electrical equipment immediately reported or taken out of service.	[ ]	[ ]
14. Accumulations of lint, dust, and grease removed.	[ ]	[ ]
15. Areas kept as clean and neat as possible.	[ ]	[ ]
16. Materials stacked so as not to tip or fall.	[ ]	[ ]
17. Safe storage on top shelves (restrict height, weight, and bulk).	[ ]	[ ]
18. Aisles between shelves are clear.	[ ]	[ ]

Fire/Life Protection Systems	No	OK
1. Adequate lighting in corridors, exits, and stairwells.	[ ]	[ ]
2. EXIT signs illuminated as required (all lights working).	[ ]	[ ]
3. Evacuation routes adequately posted.	[ ]	[ ]
4. Evacuation signs maintained—none defaced or missing.	[ ]	[ ]
5. Fire doors not wedged or blocked open, especially at stairwell.	[ ]	[ ]
6. Stairwells free of obstacles, storage, debris, etc.	[ ]	[ ]
7. Corridors and exits unobstructed (no storage of files, furniture, etc.).	[ ]	[ ]
8. Stairwells, corridors, and exits free of trip and slip hazards (no holes, loose tiles, torn carpeting, defective mats, etc.).	[ ]	[ ]

Fire/Life Protection Systems *continued*	No	OK
9. Fire detection and alarm systems tested regularly.	[ ]	[ ]
10. Fire sprinkler connections and shutoff valves visible/ accessible.	[ ]	[ ]
11. Fire sprinkler heads clean and unobstructed (no material stored closer than 18 inches from the ceiling).	[ ]	[ ]
12. Adequate clearance (3 feet) for all fire extinguishers and hoses.	[ ]	[ ]
13. Fire equipment in proper locations and undamaged.	[ ]	[ ]
14. Floor wardens positions updated, fully staffed.	[ ]	[ ]
15. Tenants/new employees instructed on Building Emergency Plan.	[ ]	[ ]
16. Other observations: _____		

Report submitted by: _____

Date: _____

Suite/Room Number: _____

Checklist compiled with the assistance of the Los Angeles City Fire Department Fire and Safety Education Unit.

FLOOR WARDENS AND ALTERNATES ROSTER

FLOOR NUMBER	FLOOR WARDEN NAME	FLOOR WARDEN LOCATION AND PHONE NUMBER	ALTERNATE FLOOR WARDEN NAME	ALTERNATE FLOOR WARDEN LOCATION AND PHONE NUMBER

If any changes occur in the above information, immediately advise the building
Fire Safety Director or building management.

DISABLED OR NON-AMBULATORY PERSONS LIST

FLOOR NUMBER	INDIVIDUAL NAME	LOCATION AND PHONE NUMBER	NATURE OF DISABILITY	ASSISTANT MONITORS (2) NAMES

If any changes occur in the above information, immediately advise the building
Fire Safety Director or building management.

FIRE DRILL NOTIFICATION

Date: _____

Subject: **Required Building Evacuation Drills**

Dear Tenant:

State and local fire codes require that occupants of high-rise buildings participate in evacuation drills on individual floors. Building Management, in accordance with these requirements, has scheduled dates and times to conduct fire drills at Pacific Tower Plaza. The date and time for your floor is as follows:

Date: _____   Time: _____

The drill will start with the sounding of the building fire alarm on your floor, followed by an announcement by building security over the PA system directing occupants to proceed to the nearest stairwell. This will be followed by a second announcement directing occupants to enter the stairwell and proceed to their designated safe refuge area. When all occupants have arrived there, they will be asked to sign a *Fire Drill Register* that shows that they participated; also, building management will conduct a verbal review of the drill before directing participants back to their offices (at which point occupants may use elevators to return to their floor). If the drill is properly carried out, it is expected that the total time from the first sounding of the fire alarm to the return of your employees to their offices will be no longer than 15 minutes.

Drill monitors will be stationed at strategic locations to observe and document on a *Fire Drill Checklist* the conduct of drill participants from the time the fire alarm is first activated. This documentation will be forwarded to the City of Toluga Hills Fire Department. Any occupants who refuse to participate in these code-mandated drills may be cited by the fire authorities for noncompliance.

In preparation, all employees should be told of the upcoming drill and asked to review occupant training material. Floor wardens should be asked to ensure that their floor response personnel are in place. During the drill they should provide adequate control and direction for evacuating occupants and conduct a thorough search of the floor to ensure that all occupants have evacuated.

Both the City of Toluga Hills Fire Department and the Management of Pacific Tower Plaza thank you for your cooperation and continued support of the building fire life safety program.

Signed by Building Management _____

FIRE DRILL ANNOUNCEMENTS

May I have your attention, please. This is Building Security. This is a fire drill. All occupants please proceed to your nearest stairwell and stand by for further instructions.
Repeat the message loudly, slowly, and clearly.

May I have your attention, please. This is Building Security. All occupants please enter your nearest stairwell and relocate to your designated safe refuge area.
Repeat the message loudly, slowly, and clearly.

May I have your attention, please. This is Building Security. There is a fire drill being conducted on floors above your floor. Floor wardens, please proceed to your nearest stairwell to assist in relocating occupants.
Repeat the message loudly, slowly, and clearly.

Note: These announcements may also be required in a foreign language (for example, Spanish), depending on the proportion of non-English speakers in the building at the time of the drill.

FIRE DRILL CHECKLIST

Name of Building: Pacific Tower Plaza
Building Address: One Poppyfields Boulevard, Toluga Hills

Drill Monitor: _____

Title/Position: _____

Date of fire drill: _____

Time Fire Department notified of fire drill: _____

Name of Fire Department operator: _____

Fire drill floor: _____

Floor/location to which occupants relocated: _____

Method of activation of fire alarm: _____

Time fire alarm activated: _____

Time all occupants vacated fire drill floor: _____

	Check the appropriate box		
Floor Response Personnel	*yes*	*no*	*unobserved*
Floor Warden:	☐	☐	☐
Wearing distinctive marking (arm band, vest, or hard hat)?	☐	☐	☐
Assistant Floor Warden:	☐	☐	☐
Wearing distinctive marking (armband, vest, or hard hat)?	☐	☐	☐
Stairwell Monitors:	☐	☐	☐
Elevator Monitors:	☐	☐	☐
Search Monitors:	☐	☐	☐
Assistants to the Physically Disabled and Non-Ambulatory:	☐	☐	☐
Interior doors closed but not locked after searched?	☐	☐	☐
Interior doors tagged after searched?	☐	☐	☐
Search Monitors checked public rest rooms?	☐	☐	☐
If the drill involved simulation of a fire, was a portable extinguisher brought to the location of the fire?	☐	☐	☐

Overall response of floor response team: Satisfactory   Unsatisfactory

Occupant Response	Check the appropriate box		
	yes	no	unobserved
Occupant initial response on sounding of alarm:	Satisfactory	Unsatisfactory	
Occupant noise level:	Satisfactory	Unsatisfactory	
Occupants aware of location of stairwells?	☐	☐	☐
Did evacuation proceed in smooth and orderly manner?	☐	☐	☐
Did visitors to building participate in drill?	☐	☐	☐
Name and contact details of any occupants who would not participate: _____			
Overall response of occupants:	Satisfactory	Unsatisfactory	

Building Emergency Systems and Equipment

	yes	no	unobserved
Fire alarm clear in all areas?	☐	☐	☐
PA system announcement clearly heard in all areas?	☐	☐	☐
Did air conditioning systems shut down?	☐	☐	☐
Did pressurization of stairwells occur?	☐	☐	☐
Did stairwell doors automatically unlock?	☐	☐	☐
If no automatic unlock occurred, did floor wardens on relocation floors manually unlock the stairwell doors?	☐	☐	☐
Did door hold-open devices deactivate and the doors close?	☐	☐	☐
Were exits and corridors free of obstructions?	☐	☐	☐
Were any doors blocked or wedged open?	☐	☐	☐
Condition and accessibility of portable fire extinguishers: _____			
Portable electrical and gas appliances turned off?	☐	☐	☐

Total Performance of the Floor: Satisfactory   Unsatisfactory

Comments: _____

_____

_____

Deficiencies Noted and Actions to be Taken: _____

_____

_____

Signature of Drill Monitor: _____

FIRE DRILL CHECKLIST TO BE RETAINED IN BUILDING FIRE LIFE SAFETY FILES

FIRE DRILL REGISTER

Date: _____

Floor Number: _____

THE FOLLOWING PERSONS PARTICIPATED IN THE BUILDING FIRE DRILLS PERFORMED ON THE ABOVE DATE:

NAME OF PERSON (PRINTED)	NAME OF TENANT (PRINT)
1	
2	
3	
4	
5	
6	
7	
8	
9	
10	
11	
12	
13	
14	
15	
16	
17	
18	
19	
20	

FIRE DRILL REGISTER TO BE RETAINED IN BUILDING FIRE LIFE SAFETY FILES

BOMB THREAT CHECKLIST

Exact time of call: _____

Exact words of caller: _____

_____

_____

_____

Questions to Ask

1. When is bomb going to explode? _____

2. Where is the bomb? _____

3. What does it look like? _____

4. What kind of bomb is it? _____

5. What will cause it to explode? _____

6. Did you place the bomb? _____

7. Why? _____

8. Where are you calling from? _____

9. What is your address? _____

10. What is your name? _____

Caller's Voice (circle)

Calm	Stressed	Normal	Squeaky	Accent
Excited	Giggling	Slow	Nasal	Disguised
Angry	Crying	Rapid	Lisp	Slurred
Sincere	Loud	Deep	Stutter	Broken

If the voice is familiar, whom did it sound like? _____

Were there any background noises? _____

Remarks: _____

_____

Person receiving call: _____

Telephone number at which call received: _____

Date: _____

Reported call immediately to: _____

Reprinted with permission of Bureau of Alcohol, Tobacco and Firearms, an agency of the U.S. Department of the Treasury.

Appendix 11-2   Sample Fire Life Safety Information Package

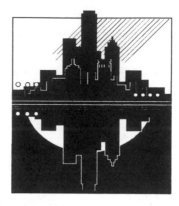

Date: _____

Subject: **PACIFIC TOWER PLAZA FIRE AND LIFE SAFETY PROGRAM**

Dear Tenant:

The Management of Pacific Tower Plaza, in cooperation with the City of Toluga Hills Fire Department, has developed a Building Emergency Plan to help ensure the safety of occupants in the event of a fire or other emergency that is likely to occur at this facility. The material in the plan pertaining to fires is required by the State Fire Code and the Toluga Hills Fire Code. Additional procedures are provided by management for the life safety of building occupants during explosions, bombs and bomb threats, violence in the workplace, medical emergencies, power failures, elevator malfunctions and entrapments, natural disasters, water leaks, chemical/hazardous materials incidents, labor disputes, demonstrations, riots and civil disorder, hostage and barricade situations.

Under the Building Emergency Plan, you, as an employer, and we, as building managers, equally share the responsibility for instructing building occupants in the emergency procedures, including evacuation or relocation procedures. The enclosed material explains the fire life safety program in place at Pacific Tower Plaza and provides the means for you to assist us in periodically updating the plan and records pertaining to it. We strongly urge prompt response to ensure compliance with regulations. Failure to comply subjects both you and us to potential prosecution and penalties, including monetary fines.

Both the Management of Pacific Tower Plaza and the City of Toluga Hills Fire Department thank you for your cooperation and continued support of the building fire life safety program.

Signed by Building Management _____

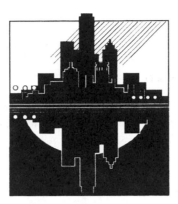

TENANT FIRE LIFE SAFETY PROGRAM
PACIFIC TOWER PLAZA

The fire life safety program for tenants consists of three major parts:

1. Occupant Documentation and Instruction

   The State Fire Code and the Toluga Hills Fire Code Emergency Planning and Evacuation requirements mandate that all high-rise building occupants be instructed annually on the procedures to be followed in the event of fire or other emergencies likely to occur in the building. All new occupants must be given this instruction within 14 days of assuming occupancy. Documentation of the instruction will be maintained by the building Fire Safety Director and available for inspection by the Chief of the Toluga Hills City Fire Department.

   To meet this requirement, Pacific Tower Plaza has the following publications available:

   • An *Occupant Safety Brochure* to be given to every occupant in your tenant space.
   • A *Certificate of Occupant Training* to be filled out by each occupant after each he or she has received fire life safety training. This certificate should then be returned to the Office of the Building or the building Fire Safety Director.

   The Building provides training classes twice each month for occupants, particularly new employees, to be trained in fire life safety. These classes are conducted from 2:00 P.M. to 3:00 P.M. on the scheduled days in the Office of the Building. The schedule of classes for the next quarter is as follows:

October 3	October 17	October 31
November 7	November 21	December 5
December 19		

   All occupants must receive fire life safety training. If necessary, additional classes can be conducted in your tenant space. Please communicate any requests for these classes to the building Fire Safety Director.

2. Floor Warden Manual and Training

   The State Fire Code and the Toluga Hills Fire Code Emergency Planning and Evacuation requirements mandate that a responsible person on each floor of every high-rise building be designated as a floor warden, with alternates. Floor wardens, in cooperation with the building Fire Safety Director, are to be thoroughly familiar with the Building Emergency Plan and oversee and ensure safe and complete evacuation or relocation of occupants during a fire or other emergency, or a fire drill.

   Usually each floor has a floor warden and a designated alternate floor warden; if a floor is particularly large or has many individual tenants, there may be several floor wardens (each individual suite having a suite warden). Each of these persons can be identified by an armband, vest, or hard hat that is worn whenever they are called to duty. Floor wardens should be selected for their ability to make sound decisions during emergency situations, provide direction, and maintain order. They also should be persons whose work responsibilities do not require extensive absences from the office.

The duties of floor wardens and alternate floor wardens, which include overseeing the training and instruction of occupants in their care, are outlined in the Floor Warden Manual that building management provides for every floor warden. Training for these persons is conducted using the manual, meetings, and fire drills. The schedule of activities for the next quarter are as follows:

- October 10: Floor Warden Training for Natural Disasters and Fire Drills. Classes are conducted in the Building Auditorium from 10:30 A.M. to noon and from 2:00 P.M. to 3:30 P.M. (floor wardens are required to attend one of these sessions).
- November 8, 9, 15, 16: Building Fire Drills. All floor wardens will be notified of the exact time and day on which their individual floor will be drilled.
- December 12 and 13: Fire Extinguisher Training. Classes are conducted on the roof of the Pardee Lane Parking Structure from 11:00 A.M. to noon and from 2:00 P.M. to 3:00 P.M.

3. Fire Drills

The State Fire Code and the Toluga Hills Fire Code Emergency Planning and Evacuation requirements mandate that occupants of high-rise buildings participate in evacuation drills on individual floors. A minimum of two fire drills on individual floors is required annually. Total evacuation of the building is not mandated. Documentation of all fire drills is maintained by the building Fire Safety Director.

Building management, in accordance with these requirements, has scheduled dates and times to conduct fire drills at Pacific Tower Plaza. The fire drills are scheduled for the next quarter on November 8, 9, 15, and 16. All floor wardens will be notified of the exact time and day on which their individual floor will be drilled.

The drill will commence with the sounding of the building fire alarm on your floor, followed by an announcement by building security over the PA system to direct occupants to proceed to their nearest stairwell. This will be followed by a second announcement to direct occupants to enter the stairwell and proceed to their designated safe refuge area. When all occupants arrive at the safe refuge area, they will be asked to sign a *Fire Drill Register* that shows that they participated. Also, building management will conduct a verbal review of the drill before directing participants back to their offices (at which point occupants may use building elevators to return to their floors). If the drill is properly carried out, it is expected that the total time from the first sounding of the fire alarm to the return of your employees to their offices will be no longer than 15 minutes.

Drill monitors will be stationed at strategic locations to observe and document the conduct of drill participants from the time the fire alarm is first activated. This documentation will be forwarded to the City of Toluga Hills Fire Department. Any occupants who refuse to participate in these code-mandated drills may be cited by the fire authorities for noncompliance.

In preparation, all employees should be told of the upcoming drill and asked to review occupant training material. Floor wardens should be asked to ensure that their floor response personnel are in place. During the drill they should provide adequate control and direction for evacuating occupants and conduct a search of the floor to ensure that everyone has left.

Attachments: Disabled or Non-Ambulatory Persons List
Floor Wardens and Alternates Roster
Fire Prevention Inspection Checklist

PLEASE RETURN THE COMPLETED LIST, ROSTER, AND CHECKLIST WITHIN TWO WEEKS TO THE OFFICE OF THE BUILDING OR THE BUILDING FIRE SAFETY DIRECTOR.

Appendix 11-3   Calendar of Annual Events

January

Building Emergency Staff—Training for Fires and Fire Alarms

Occupants—Building Fire Life Safety Training

Floor Wardens—Training for Fire Life Safety

All Building Occupants—"Safety Reminder of the Month" Bulletin

February

Building Emergency Staff—Power Failure and Elevator Safety Training

Occupants—Building Fire Life Safety Training

All Building Occupants—"Safety Reminder of the Month" Bulletin

March

Building Emergency Staff—Explosions, Bombs, and Bomb Threats Training

Occupants—Building Fire Life Safety Training

Floor Wardens—Update of *Floor Warden Rosters* and *Disabled and Non-Ambulatory Persons List*

All Building Occupants—"Safety Reminder of the Month" Bulletin

April

Building Emergency Staff—Training for Fires and Fire Alarms and May Fire Drills

Occupants—Building Fire Life Safety Training

Floor Wardens—Training for Explosions, Bombs, and Bomb Threats and May Fire Drills

All Building Occupants—"Fire Drills" Bulletin

May

Building Emergency Staff—Chemical/Hazardous Material Training

Occupants—Building Fire Life Safety Training

All Building Occupants—Fire Drills and "Safety Reminder of the Month" Bulletin

June

Building Emergency Staff—Violence in the Workplace and Hostage and Barricade Training

Occupants—Building Fire Life Safety Training

All Building Occupants—"Safety Reminder of the Month" Bulletin

July

Building Emergency Staff—Training for Fires, Fire Alarms, and Aircraft Collisions

Occupants—Building Fire Life Safety Training

Floor Wardens—Training for Violence in the Workplace Incidents

All Building Occupants—"Safety Reminder of the Month" Bulletin

August

Building Emergency Staff—Labor Disputes, Demonstrations, Riots and Civil Disorder Training

Occupants—Building Fire Life Safety Training

All Building Occupants—"Safety Reminder of the Month" Bulletin

September

Building Emergency Staff—Natural Disaster and Water Leak Training

Occupants—Building Fire Life Safety Training

Floor Wardens—Update of *Floor Warden Rosters* and *Disabled and Non-Ambulatory Persons List*

All Building Occupants—"Safety Reminder of the Month" Bulletin

October

Building Emergency Staff—Training for Fires and Fire Alarms and November Fire Drills

Occupants—Building Fire Life Safety Training

Floor Wardens—Training for Natural Disasters and November Fire Drills

All Building Occupants—"Fire Drills" Bulletin

November

Building Emergency Staff—Medical Emergency Training

Occupants—Building Fire Life Safety Training

All Building Occupants—Fire Drills and "Safety Reminder of the Month" Bulletin

December

Building Emergency Staff and Floor Wardens—Fire Extinguisher Training

Occupants—Building Fire Life Safety Training

All Building Occupants—"Safety Reminder of the Month" Bulletin

12 *Laws, Codes, and Standards*

As defined by *Black's Law Dictionary*, the *law,* "in its generic sense, is a body of rules or action or conduct prescribed by the controlling authority, and having binding legal force; that which must be obeyed and followed by citizens subject to sanctions or legal consequences is a law." A *code* is "a systematic collection; a private or official compilation of all permanent laws in force consolidated and classified according to subject matter." The Merritt Company defines a *standard* as: "a model, type, or gauge used to establish or verify what is commonly regarded as acceptable or correct. It is a means for defining minimum and maximum levels of quality, quantity, or performance" (The Merritt Company 1991, p. 1-41).

Laws, codes, and standards applicable to high-rise commercial office buildings aim to enhance public safety for the facility's users through guidelines established for the manufacture and use of various materials and equipment, the methods of construction, and the provision of various services for building operation. Building inspectors, fire marshals, testing laboratories, manufacturers, architects, builders, installers, consultants, owners, managers, risk managers, insurance agents, security directors, fire safety directors, maintenance departments, contract security firms, investigators, legal counsel, professional societies, trade associations, and tenants all have codes and standards to follow in their particular areas of expertise or responsibility. These regulations also provide a format for quality and standardization throughout the industry. There are two main types of standards relevant to the security and fire life safety operations of high-rise buildings.

    1. *Statutory or regulatory standards* are enacted under the law. Some come from federal sources such as the Occupational Safety and Health Act, the Americans with Disabilities Act (ADA), and the National Institute of Standards and Technology (NIST). Others, such as the licenses and regulations governing private security firms and certain building and fire codes, are adopted by state and local legislatures.

    2. *Consensus or private standards* are advisory recommendations applied by consent or agreement rather than required by law. Some of these standards have been developed or sponsored by the federal government, such as those created by

---

Acknowledgment: The Merritt Company's article "Standards in security" in the *Protection of Assets Manual* (The Merritt Company 1991, pp. 1-41–1-57) was invaluable in understanding laws, codes, and standards.

the Law Enforcement Assistance Administration (LEAA). Others were developed by private sources (professional societies, trade associations, insurance companies, equipment manufacturers, etc.); examples include the National Fire Protection Association (NFPA), Underwriters Laboratories Inc. (UL), the American Society for Testing Materials (ASTM), the American Institute of Architects (AIA), the American Society of Mechanical Engineers (ASME), the Security Industry Association (SIA), the National Association of Security Companies (NASCO), the National Burglar and Fire Alarm Association (NBFAA), the Illuminating Engineering Society (IES), the National Electrical Manufacturers Association (NEMA), the National Conference of States on Building Codes and Standards (NCSBCS), the Institute of Real Estate Management (IREM), and the Building Owners and Managers Association International (BOMA).

The American National Standards Institute (ANSI) is a private organization that does not develop or enforce standards, but reviews and validates the voluntary standards already prepared by private groups, designating the best of them as American National Standards. These standards represent a general agreement among manufacturers, distributors, and consumers on the best practices over a wide area of the building industry. ANSI reviews standards every five years to ensure they are up to date with current technology and practice.

The next sections review various organizations and their laws, codes, and standards. However, it is not within the scope of this book to list comprehensively all regulations applied in the United States. Even if such a list were provided, it would need to be customized for each facility, as Schum (1989, p. 205) points out:

> In your personal experience, you will be faced with codes and standards not listed therein, and you may never have to deal with many of those listed. Code use tends to be regional, and every state, county, and city must be dealt with individually for local approvals and restrictions. However, most codes are based on national code publications.

Laws

Occupational Safety and Health Act

The Occupational Safety and Health Act was passed by Congress to provide a legislative basis for safety activities. It was signed on December 29, 1970. As mentioned in "Violence in the Workplace" in Chapter 10, the "General Duty" clause summarizes the act and states that each employer "shall furnish to each of his [or her] employees a place of employment free from recognized hazards that are causing or likely to cause death or serious physical harm to his [or her] employees" (OSHA 1974).

On April 28, 1971, Public Law 91.596 became effective and the Occupational Safety and Health Administration (OSHA) was established within the Department of Labor. Each employer in the United States is now responsible for meeting the minimum requirements of the standards OSHA publishes. In addition, each employer must maintain injury and illness records. As The Merritt Company (1991, pp. 29-14–29-15) comments:

> The law also requires each employee to comply with safety and health standards as well as with all rules, regulations, and orders which are applicable to the employee's own actions and conduct. But no penalties are provided for employ-

ees who fail to do so. One way the language might be applied would be in mitigation of damages in any civil suit brought against an employer by an employee who had been non-complying. But most workplace accidents and injuries are dealt with under state Workers' Compensation law which, typically, doesn't recognize a "contributory" or "comparative negligence" type defense.

OSHA addresses safety issues and more recently is formally addressing security-related issues such as violence in the workplace incidents. As Fischer and Green (1992) summarize, it "speaks of free and accessible means of egress, of aisles and working areas free of debris, of floors free from hazards. It gives specific requirements for machines and equipment, materials, and power sources. It specifies fire protection by fixed or portable systems, clean lunch rooms, environmental health controls, and adequate sanitation facilities" (p. 276).

The means of egress requirements (sections .35 through .37 of OSHA's Title 29 of the Code of Federal Regulations, Part 1910, General Industry Standard) include standards on emergency plans and fire prevention plans. From 1970 to 1972, however, appropriate national consensus standards were adopted, including specific portions of NFPA 101 *Life Safety Code*™. Because "OSHA did not adopt all of the Life Safety Code, just specific portions of it, OSHA's standards on means of egress are incomplete at best" (Carson 1993, p. 48). OSHA has attempted to solve this problem by allowing one of the comprehensive and frequently updated NFPA standards to meet the requirements for a corresponding OSHA standard—not only in this area, but in many others. Fischer and Green (1992, p. 277) note:

> In 1988, OSHA issued the Hazard Communication Standard that states that all employees have the right to know what hazards exist in their place of employment and what to do to protect themselves from the hazards. Simple labels and warnings are not enough. Employers must have a program to communicate more detail on all hazards including a Material Safety Data Sheet (MSDS) that must be available for each chemical at the worksite. Each MSDS contains seven sections:
>
> 1. Product identification and emergency notification instructions.
> 2. Hazardous ingredients list and exposure limits.
> 3. Physical and chemical characteristics (vapor pressure, odor, etc.).
> 4. Physical hazards and how to handle them (that is, fire and explosion).
> 5. Reactivity data—what the product may react with and whether it is stable.
> 6. Health hazard information—how the product can enter the body, signs and symptoms of problems, and emergency first-aid steps.
> 7. Safe handling procedures.

At the federal level, the Department of Labor has the responsibility for enforcing the standards and regulations of OSHA. The standards also can be enforced at the state level using local laws, if they meet the minimum requirements of the federal legislation. Compliance officers inspect places of business to investigate adherence to OSHA standards. If a facility is not in compliance, these officers may issue citations, and penalties and fines may be levied against the employer.

Americans with Disabilities Act

The Americans with Disabilities Act (ADA) was signed into law in 1990. The protection it provides to specified classes of individuals is similar to that afforded by the Civil Rights Act of 1964, which prohibited discrimination on the basis of race, color, religion, sex, or national origin. The ADA provides comprehensive civil rights protection to "individuals with a disability" (the previous term "handicapped individual" has been replaced). The term *disability* (Title 42, United States Code, Chapter 126, Section 12102) means, with respect to an individual, "(A) a physical or mental impairment that substantially limits one or more of the major life activities of such individual; (B) a record of such an impairment; or (C) being regarded as having such an impairment." The term *reasonable accommodation* may include (Title 42, United States Code, Chapter 126, Subchapter 1, Section 12111): "(A) making existing facilities used by employees readily accessible to use and usable by individuals with disabilities; and (B) job restructuring, part-time or modified work schedules, reassignment to a vacant position, acquisition or modification of equipment or devices, appropriate adjustment or modifications of examinations, training materials or policies, the provision of qualified readers or interpreters, and other similar accommodations for individuals with disabilities."

The ADA has superseded the Architectural Barriers Act of 1968 and the Rehabilitation Act of 1973. Both these laws were directed toward assisting individuals with a disability. However, they were applied primarily to firms doing business with or receiving monetary assistance from the federal government. The ADA applies to almost every type of business. The Act is intended to ensure comprehensive civil rights protection to individuals with a disability with regard to employment, state and local government services, transportation, new and existing public accommodations, new commercial facilities, and telecommunications. It places certain obligations on employers and businesses and has a far-reaching impact on the security and fire life safety operations of buildings. Atlas (1992) notes, "ADA will affect architecture, life safety design, and building security technology dramatically. Some of the most critical impacts on building security will be building access, door hardware, fire egress, and system controls, including card readers used for entrance and exit access control, elevator controls" (p. 37), emergency intercoms, fire and life safety devices such as manual fire alarm stations, and evacuation signage. The government has published two technical manuals, *Uniform Federal Accessibility Standards and ADA Accessibility Guidelines*, which give detailed information regarding these issues.

The ADA consists of five parts or titles:

Title I: Employment—This title prohibits discrimination in employment against qualified individuals with disabilities. It went into effect July 26, 1992, for employers with 25 or more employees. On July 26, 1994, it became effective for employers with 15 or more employees.

Title II: Public Services—This title states that "no qualified individual with a disability shall, by reason of such disability, be excluded from participation in or be denied the benefits of the services, programs, or activities of a public entity, or be subject to discrimination by any such entity" (Title 42, United States Code, Chapter 126, Subchapter II, Section 12132). The term *public entity* includes any state or local government or their departments, agencies, special purpose districts or other instrumentalities, including public transportation.

Title III: Public Accommodations and Services Operated by Private Entities—This title deals with the accessibility requirements in public buildings and commercial facilities. "No individual shall be discriminated against on the basis of disability in the full and equal enjoyment of the goods, services, facilities, privileges, advantages, or accommodations of any place of public accommodation by any person who owns, leases (or leases to), or operates a place of public accommodation" (Title 42, United States Code, Chapter 126, Subchapter III, Section 12182).

This regulation applies to both the occupants of a building and any visitors to the facility. New buildings are required to comply fully with Title III. Existing buildings must comply to the extent that the changes required are *readily achievable*. This term means "easily accomplishable and able to be carried out without much difficulty or expense" (Title 42, United States Code, Chapter 126, Subchapter III, Section 12181). The Architectural Transportation Barriers Compliance Board (ATBCB) developed ADA Accessibility Guidelines for Buildings and Facilities (ADAAG) as specific Title III standards. Title III went into effect on January 26, 1992, for existing facilities, and on January 26, 1993, for all new construction.

Title IV: Telecommunications—This title requires all common carriers to provide a telephone service (Telecommunications Relay Service) that permits individuals with hearing or speech difficulties to use the telephone.

Title V: Miscellaneous Provisions—This title contains some of the technical information pertaining to the Act.

The ADA applies to new building construction and major alterations carried out in existing buildings. When a building owner or manager makes alterations in compliance with ADA, there are some financial and tax benefits to the building. OSHA does not enforce the ADA; instead, as Lindemann (1993) states: "The regulating government agencies—the Department of Justice (DOJ), the Architectural Transportation Compliance Board (ATCB), the Equal Employment Opportunity Commission (EEOC), and the Federal Communications Commission (FCC)—are responsible for enforcing various parts of the ADA" (p. 48A). Because the ADA is relatively new legislation containing broad definitions, the interpretations on how industry should implement it in the workplace have yet to be established by the legal system.

Codes and Regulatory Standards

National Institute of Standards and Technology

The National Institute of Standards and Technology, a unit within the U.S. Department of Commerce, was formerly called the National Bureau of Standards. NIST creates the Federal Information Processing Standards Publications (FIPS PUB), which are used both in the government and the private sector. It also produces standards and technical reports, which cover equipment such as control units for intruder alarm systems, and a Building Science Series, which "disseminates technical information developed at the Institute on building materials, components, systems, and whole structures. The series presents research results, test methods, and performance criteria related to the structural and environmental functions and the durability and safety characteristics of building elements and systems" (NIST 1991).

The NIST also houses the Building and Fire Research Laboratory (BFRL), which compiles data regarding the characteristics of materials and their behavior when subjected to fire. The objective of the research conducted by the BFRL is to improve fire life safety codes and standards.

Licensing and Regulation of Private Security Firms

State and local governments frequently license and regulate private security firms. To obtain a license to operate in some areas, both state and local requirements must be met. According to Cunningham et al. (1990, pp. 153–154),

> Approximately 75% of the states regulate some aspect of private security and its employees. In addition (or sometimes in place of state regulation), municipal or county governments often have ordinances regulating private security. Because laws pertaining to security licensing have changed often, it is nearly impossible to delineate the regulatory requirements of local and state governments. However, the table [Table 12.1] provides an overview of state regulatory activity. In addition to security business and personnel regulation, an estimated 2,000 local governments have enacted alarm ordinances.

Table 12.1   State Regulation of Private Security Firms*

	Number of States
Guard and Patrol	
Licensing of businesses	39
Registration	25[1]
Private Investigators	37
Alarm	25
Armored Car	9[2]

[1]Plus District of Columbia
[2]Does not include Public Utility Commissions or Interstate Commerce Commission

Sources: 1) "Security data bank," *Security*, June 1990, p. 55; 2) *Security Letter Source Book*, 1990–1991, Section H.H.6, Robert McCrie, Editor, Butterworths, Stoneham, MA, March 1990; 3) "Regulations vary by state," *Security Distributing and Marketing*, September 1989, p. 82; 4) Truett Ricks, Gill Tillett, Clifford Van Meter, *Principles of Security* (Second Edition), Anderson Publishing Co., 1988, pp. 168–171; 5) "Regulation of the Private Security Industry," National Institute of Justice, U.S. Department of Justice, (unpublished), January 1981.

State and Local Building and Fire Codes

According to Sanderson (1969, pp. 6-141, 142),

> A building code is a law that sets forth minimum requirements for design and construction of buildings and structures. These minimum requirements, established to protect the health and safety of society, generally represent a compro-

*Reprinted by permission from William C. Cunningham, John J. Strauchs, and Clifford W. Van Meter, *The Hallcrest Report II: Private Security Trends 1970–2000* (Butterworth–Heinemann, Stoneham, MA, 1990), p. 153.

mise between optimum safety and economic feasibility. Although builders and building owners often establish their own requirements, the minimum code requirements of a jurisdiction must be met. Features covered include structural design, fire protection, means of egress, light, sanitation, and interior finish. . . . The requirements contained in building codes are generally based upon the known properties of materials, the hazards presented by various occupancies, and the lessons learned from previous experiences, such as fire and natural disasters.

Building codes can be of two types, as Cote (1991, p. 6-141) notes:

Specification codes spell out in detail what materials can be used, the building size, and how components should be assembled. *Performance codes* detail the objective to be met and establish criteria for determining if the objective has been reached; thus, the designer and builder are free to select construction methods and materials as long as it can be shown that the performance criteria can be met.

There are a small number of model building code groups that have been largely responsible for building code development in the United States since the turn of the century. The American Insurance Association (AIA), then known as the National Board of Fire Underwriters (NBFU), first published the *National Building Code* (NBC) in 1905. The NBC was designed as an archetype for cities to adopt and as a means of grading the building regulations of cities and towns. "The NBFU began to emphasize safe building construction, control of fire hazards, and improvements in both water supplies and fire departments. As a result, the new tall buildings constructed of concrete and steel conformed to specifications that helped limit the risk of fire. These buildings were called Class A buildings" (Cote 1991, p. 6-141). The AIA last revised the code in 1976. Permission to use the term *National Building Code* was transferred to the Building Officials and Code Administrators in 1982. The AIA previously published a fire prevention code but no longer does so.

The Building Officials and Code Administrators International (BOCA) was first established in 1915 as the Building Officials Conference of America, and published the *Basic/Building Code* (BBC) in 1950. BOCA began publishing this code as the *National Building Code* (NBC) in 1987 (after acquiring rights to the term as explained above). The NBC is republished every three years. In addition, the BOCA publishes fire prevention, plumbing, and mechanical codes. Its membership primarily covers the northeastern United States and includes building officials, architects, engineers, and industry representatives. The BOCA is a service organization that provides its members with technical and educational information aimed toward developing safe and efficient building codes.

The International Conference of Building Officials (ICBO) first published the *Uniform Building Code* (UBC) in 1927. "The *Uniform Building Code* is the most widely adopted model building code in the world. Published every three years, it provides complete regulations covering all major aspects of building design and construction relating to life and fire safety and structural safety" (ICBO 1993, p. 1). The ICBO publishes a Handbook and an Application/Interpretation Manual for the UBC. With the International Fire Code Institute (IFCI), the ICBO co-publishes the *Uniform Fire Code*, which is a fire prevention code endorsed by the Western Fire Chiefs Association and the International Association of Fire Chiefs, and a *Uniform Mechanical Code*. The ICBO also co-publishes the *International Plumbing Code* (IPC) with its sister model code organizations, BOCA and

SBCCI. The ICBO membership primarily covers the western half of the United States and includes local government agencies, building professionals, and trade associations.

The Southern Building Code Congress International (SBCCI) first published the *Southern Standard Building Code* in 1945. It is now called the *Standard Building Code*™ (SBC) and provides minimum construction standards to safeguard life, health, and public welfare in all types of buildings and structures, including high-rises. The SBC "addresses life safety issues such as height and area requirements, fire protection, alarm systems, and means of egress. It provides design information such as minimum design loads, wind loads, snow loads, and earthquake loads. In addition, it gives information on specific construction materials such as masonry, steel, concrete, wood or gypsum" (SBCCI 1993, p. 2). The SBCCI publishes this code every three years and also provides a comprehensive commentary to assist in its interpretation. The SBCCI membership covers roughly the southeastern section of the country, as far west as Texas and Oklahoma; it consists mainly of building officials, with an associate membership of fire officials and industry representatives.

The BOCA, ICBO, and SBCCI have formed an organization called the Council of American Building Officials (CABO). Its Board for the Coordination of the Model Building Codes (BCMC) is attempting to coordinate the provisions of the NBC, UBC, and SBC, plus various NFPA codes and standards (mainly NFPA 101, the *Life Safety Code*).

Model building codes are not laws in themselves. They must be adopted into law by the appropriate state and local legislatures before they can be enforced. Figure 12.1 shows the general geographic areas where the three model building codes have been adopted.

As Cote (1991) explains, "Building code applicability usually ends with the issuance of an occupancy permit" (p. 6-145). In addition to building codes there are fire prevention codes. A building code generally deals with the construction of a building or with major alterations once it has been constructed (such as tenant build-out); a fire code or fire prevention code usually deals with fire hazards that exist in a building after occupancy has been granted. In the United States the model fire codes or fire prevention codes are:

1. The Fire Prevention Code of the AIA (this code has not been revised or published since 1976).
2. The BOCA *National Fire Prevention Code*.
3. The ICBO *Uniform Fire Code*.
4. The SBCCI *Standard Fire Prevention Code*.
5. The *Fire Prevention Code* of the NFPA. Often local authorities adopt the NFPA standards but do not update the standard when the NFPA does. Therefore, it is important to check the actual standard adopted rather than referring to the most up-to-date NFPA standard.

The building department having jurisdiction usually enforces building codes; a fire official such as the fire marshal usually enforces fire prevention codes. To determine the laws and codes that apply to a particular facility, one must determine exactly which ones have been adopted by the *authority having jurisdiction*. The following definition is contained in the definition section of every National Fire Code published by the NFPA:

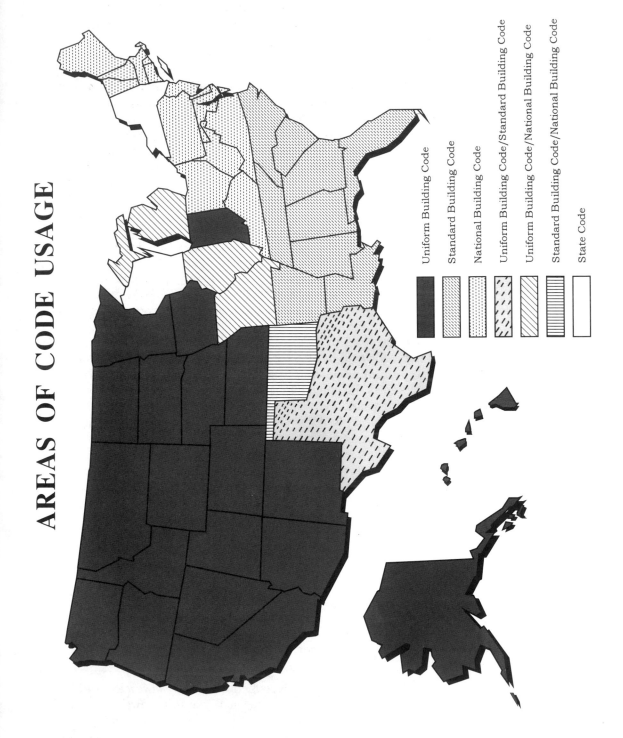

AREAS OF CODE USAGE

Uniform Building Code

Standard Building Code

National Building Code

Uniform Building Code/Standard Building Code

Uniform Building Code/National Building Code

Standard Building Code/National Building Code

State Code

The "authority having jurisdiction" is the organization, office or individual responsible for "approving" equipment, or an installation or a procedure.

NOTE: The phrase "authority having jurisdiction" is used in NFPA documents in a broad manner since jurisdictions and "approval" agencies vary, as do their responsibilities. Where public safety is primary, the "authority having jurisdiction" may be a federal, state, local or other regional department or individual such as fire chief, fire marshal, chief of a fire prevention bureau, labor department, health department, building official, electrical inspector, or others having statutory authority. For insurance purposes, an insurance inspection department, rating bureau, or other insurance company representative may be the "authority having jurisdiction." In many circumstances the property owner or his designated agent assumes the role of the "authority having jurisdiction."

Further, one should keep in mind that codes and standards are interpreted and enforced by human beings. As Cassidy (1992, p. 73) advises:

If you feel that an error has been made, contact the agency in writing and seek a clarification of that interpretation. Never assume that an agency official is correct. If a summons or a violation is issued to you, accept it, but advise the official that you are accepting it under protest. If the summons requires your signature, sign it, but also note that you are signing it under protest.

Arthur Cote's "Building and Fire Codes and Standards," written for the NFPA *Fire Protection Handbook*™ (Cote 1991, pp. 6-140–6-149), is an invaluable resource in understanding state and local building and fire codes.

Private Standards

Law Enforcement Assistance Administration

The former Law Enforcement Assistance Administration (LEAA), which was part of the U.S. Department of Justice, developed two sets of standards. The first was prepared by LEAA's Private Security Advisory Council (PSAC). As Cunningham, Strauchs, and Van Meter (1990, p. 3) summarize:

Among the publications prepared by the PSAC, and published by the LEAA, were model statutes for burglar alarms, and for state licensing of security guards; a code of ethics for security management and operating personnel; and standards for armored car and armed courier services. Additionally, the PSAC published documents outlining the scope of legal authority of security personnel and areas of conflict between law enforcement and private security.

The second set of standards, called the Report of the Task Force on Private Security (PSTF), was issued in 1976. According to Cunningham and colleagues (1990): "The Task Force suggested development of comprehensive standards in the following areas: selection of personnel, training, conduct and ethics, alarm systems, environmental security, law enforcement agencies, consumers of security services, higher education and research, and government regulation. In the 14 years since the release of that report, probably not more than 10 of the [83] standards have been universally implemented by the contract security industry, proprietary security, and law enforcement" (p. 151).

National Fire Protection Association

The NFPA was established near the turn of the century as an independent, voluntary-membership, nonprofit organization. Its mission, as stated in the *Fire Protection Handbook* (1991, p. C-1), is "the safeguarding of people, their property, and the environment from destructive fire, using scientific and engineering techniques and education." According to information obtained from *Building Life Safety with Codes* (Lathrop and Birk 1992, p. 46), in 1913, the NFPA formed the Committee on Safety to Life. This committee was responsible in 1927 for publishing the *Building Exits Code*, which addressed exits and fire life safety features in all occupancy classes. There were many revisions of and new additions to this code. In 1966, its name was changed to the *Code for Safety to Life from Fire in Buildings or Structures*, more commonly known as NFPA 101, the *Life Safety Code*.

As Cote (1991, p. 6-143) explains,

> The NFPA does not publish a model building code *per se*; however, NFPA 101, *Life Safety Code*, establishes minimum requirements necessary for providing a reasonable degree of safety from fire. The *Life Safety Code* addresses those construction, protection, and occupancy features to minimize danger to life from fire, smoke, fumes, or panic. It also identifies the minimum criteria for design of egress facilities to permit prompt escape of occupants from buildings or, where preferable, evacuation into safe areas within the building. The *Life Safety Code* does not attempt to address those general fire prevention or building construction features that normally are functions of fire prevention and building codes.

This code is revised and published by the NFPA every three years. "To date, approximately half the states in the United States have adopted the NFPA *Life Safety Code*, and many others use it as a model for local legislation dictating life safety standards for new construction, existing buildings, and renovations" (Garboden 1994, p. 35).

Presently the NFPA creates and updates over 270 standards and codes, including the *Life Safety Code*, that are published as the *National Fire Codes*® (NFC). They address virtually every aspect of fire protection, including prevention, detection, and suppression. These standards and codes are widely used and adopted as law by many state and local governments. They are used as a reference by many agencies of the federal government, such as OSHA, in their own regulations. Insurance agencies use them as a basis for risk evaluation and premium ratings. The NFPA also performs investigations of major fires; conducts research on important fire protection issues; collects and analyzes fire data and statistics; and produces educational brochures, videos, reference books and textbooks, training programs, and school curricula to assist people learning how to protect themselves from fire.

Underwriters Laboratories, Factory Mutual, Wernock Hersey

Organizations, such as Underwriters Laboratories Inc. (UL), Factory Mutual Research Corporation (FMRC), and Wernock Hersey International (WHI), conduct research, test products, and document the results, then create standards from this information. UL, established in 1894, is one of the most widely recognized and accepted testing laboratories in the United States. FMRC is a national testing laboratory that has been in existence for over 100 years. WHI was established in Canada in 1888 and provides fire testing and technical services to industry and government. These laboratories' testing consists of determining whether a particular product presents any safety hazard to the public and whether it performs as specified for its intended use. The actual areas of investigation may vary from laboratory to laboratory. Also, local codes may specify the laboratory by which a product must be tested. As with building codes, testing requirements tend to vary on a regional basis.

The major commercial insurance companies often require listing by these particular laboratories or conformity to their standards as a prerequisite for obtaining casualty insurance. In fact, two of these organizations were created for this purpose: Underwriters Laboratories Inc. was originally founded by the fire insurance industry, and the Factory Mutual System today is made up of three large mutual property insurance companies. The influence of these laboratories is considerable, then, because meeting their standards is of critical importance for businesses seeking to obtain adequate insurance.

American Society for Testing Materials

The ASTM Publications 1994 catalog states that "from the work of 131 technical standards-writing committees, the American Society for Testing Materials (ASTM) publishes standard specifications, tests, practices, guides, and definitions for materials, products, systems, and services. ASTM also publishes books containing reports on state-of-the-art testing techniques and their possible applications" (ASTM 1994).

The ASTM F-12 Committee on Security Standards and Equipment, according to Cumming (1992), is involved in "the harmonization, extension, codification, and production of new standards for the protection of people and property. It is probably the only organization in the security field that is taking a global view of minimum manufacturing, installation, and maintenance standards for systems. It is also involved in producing guidelines for the methods by which protection can be provided" (p. 25).

Other Building Institutes, Associations, and Societies

Groups whose quality criteria affect building standards include the American Institute of Architects (AIA); the Construction Specifiers Institute (CSI); the American Iron and Steel Institute (AISI); the American Institute of Steel Construction (AISC); the American Concrete Institute (ACI); the National Association of Architectural Metal Manufacturers; the Architectural Aluminum Manufacturers Association (AAMA); the American Plywood Association (APA); the Architectural Woodworking Institute (AWI); the Builders Hardware Manufacturers Association; the National Wood Window and Door Association (NWWDA); the Air Conditioning and Refrigeration Institute (ARI); the American Society of Heating, Refrigeration and Air Conditioning Engineers (ASHRAE); the National Association of Plumbing-Heating-Cooling Contractors (PHCC); the American Society of Mechanical Engineers (ASME); and the Steel Door Institute (SDI). The

SDI, for example, proposes that fire-rated openings specify an appropriate labeled fire door frame and fire door, an approved door closer, an approved latching device, and appropriate steel hinges. Chapter 10's "Elevator Safety Features" section explains how the ASME's safety codes have positively affected the nation's elevator and escalator safety records.

Security Associations

In the words of Nesse and Williams (1994),

> The Security Industry Association (SIA) is a national trade association comprised of manufacturers, distributors and service companies in the security industry. SIA works to further the growth, expansion and professionalism of the industry through various programs, including the development of standards. SIA operates an ANSI-approved Standards Program, which develops consensus standards directly through subcommittees and provides liaison to and from other standards-writing bodies. SIA develops product performance, application, and communication standards relating to the alarm industry.

The National Association of Security Companies (NASCO) was founded in 1972 as the Committee of National Security Companies (CONSCO). Currently, its 20 member firms collectively employ approximately a quarter million of the nation's most highly trained security personnel. "Today NASCO is at the forefront of efforts to set meaningful standards for the private security industry, and monitors state and federal legislation proposed for laws and regulations that might affect the quality and effectiveness of private security services" (NASCO 1994). The organization's goals clearly state its mission:

1. To maintain and upgrade standards within the industry.
2. To participate in the formulation and revision of legislation affecting the industry and the public.
3. To foster uniformity of regulation throughout the United States.
4. To increase public awareness of the distinction between private security and public law enforcement, as well as the complementary and cooperative functions they share.
5. To publicize the valuable services provided by hundreds of thousands of private security officers across the country.

The American Society for Industrial Security (ASIS), established in 1955, constitutes the largest body of security professionals in the world. It has a number of standing committees and councils concerned with "security problems affecting businesses such as banking and financial institutions, educational institutions, health care facilities, public utilities and retail establishments and general security problems such as fire prevention and safety, terrorism, white collar crime, computer security, physical security, privacy and information management and investigations" (ASIS 1994). ASIS attempted to encourage the development of standards in the security field through its Standards and Codes Committee; however, in 1981, ASIS abolished this committee. Through its sponsorship of a Professional Certification Program, ASIS sets high standards in security professionalism by testing and certifying the knowledge of security practitioners. To acquire the Certified Protection Professional (CPP) designation, each candidate must meet strict experience and/or education prerequisites, then pass a difficult battery of mandatory and specialty exams. To maintain the credential, he or she must pursue a program of continuing education and professional activity to earn required recertification credits every three years. The CPP is a widely accepted professional accreditation within the private security industry.

Fire Alarm and Burglar Alarm Trade Associations

The National Burglar and Fire Alarm Association (NBFAA) and the Automatic Fire Alarm Association (AFAA) represent fire alarm equipment installers and dealers; the NBFAA also represents burglar alarm installers.

Lighting and Electrical Associations

The Illuminating Engineering Society (IES) is concerned with lighting standards and practices. Electrical components and products are the focus of the Electronic Industries Association (EIA). The Institute of Electrical and Electronic Engineers (IEEE), the world's largest technical professional society, develops standards and directs its attention to advancing the theory and practice of electrical, electronics, and computer engineering. The National Electrical Contractors Association (NECA) is concerned with electrical standards for contractors.

The National Electrical Manufacturers Association (NEMA) has a division entitled Signaling, Protection and Communications, which maintains close liaison with related organizations, professional societies, trade associations, and approval and code writing agencies such as NFPA and NECA. It develops industry manufacturing standards on nomenclature ratings, performance and testing aimed at providing input to UL, FMRC, NFPA, WHI, authorities having jurisdiction, model building code organizations, and ANSI. It also has a continuing program for the definition and distribution of industry manufacturing standards and publications that address specific industry or user needs. Particular emphasis is placed on fire protective signaling systems and devices, security signaling systems and devices, and paging systems and devices (NEMA 1994).

National Conference of States on Building Codes and Standards, Inc.

The National Conference of States on Building Codes and Standards, Inc. (NCSBCS 1994, p. vii) states that it:

> promotes the development of an efficient, cooperative system of building regulation in order to ensure the public's safety in all residential and commercial buildings. The Conference also works for the acceptance of new building construction technologies; a uniform, national system of education and certification for building regulatory personnel; accountability in the design, construction, and inspection of buildings; public awareness of building regulatory personnel and the work they do; and interstate acceptance of modular and industrialized buildings. As a membership organization, NCSBCS provides state and local building officials,

architects and engineers, building contractors, manufacturers of building materials and equipment, national associations and corporations, federal government officials, consumers, and its governor-appointed delegate members with a forum for coordinating their building code and public safety interests and for discussing construction codes and regulations.

NCSBCS publishes the *State Directory of Building Codes and Regulations*. This directory "is a guide to the building codes and regulations that are adopted and enforced in the 50 United States and the District of Columbia for new construction and alterations" (NCSBCS 1994, p. 1). It lists building, mechanical, plumbing, electrical, energy, gas, fire prevention, life safety, and accessibility codes with their technical basis (the model code or standard on which the state code is based), their applicability—the types of buildings to which the code applies, their preemptive application—whether the code is mandatory or voluntary, and whether local amendments are allowed, the state agency responsible for administering the code, and the state agency responsible for enforcing the code. Also included is a brief summary of the state's code, the code change cycle, and a list of locations where state codes can be purchased.

Management-Related Associations

The Institute of Real Estate Management (IREM) of the National Association of Realtors is an organization, created in the 1940s, of professional property and asset managers in the United States and Canada. It produces books, courses, seminars, periodicals, audiovisuals, and other educational activities and materials. The Institute offers courses that teach a full range of property management duties, from carrying out basic functions to owning and operating a management company. Through its sponsorship of the Certified Property Manager® (CPM) program, IREM sets widely adopted standards of professional conduct and ethics for its members.

Founded at the turn of the century, BOMA is the oldest and largest trade association serving commercial real estate professionals. It is a federation of over 100 local associations in the United States, Canada, and the world. Its members include a wide cross-section of the building community including owners and managers of high-rise commercial office buildings. According to BOMA International, its members own and/or manage over five billion square feet of commercial office space in North America alone. Other members plan, develop, market and lease office buildings and provide the goods and services required to operate those properties. "The mission of BOMA is to actively and responsibly represent and promote the interests of the commercial real-estate industry through effective leadership and advocacy through the collection, analysis and dissemination of information, and through professional development" (BOMA International 1994). BOMA International sets strong national standards for commercial building professionals by sponsoring three separate property management education programs. Through these, it tests and certifies qualified individuals as Real Property Administrators® (RPA), Facilities Management Administrators® (FMA), and Systems Maintenance Administrators® (SMA). The Association publishes a monthly magazine, *Skylines*, and a number of books about the building industry. Combining such publications with its respected peer network, it is an invaluable resource for comprehensive industry research, education, and government representation.

Other Societies and Organizations

In addition to the professional societies and organizations already mentioned, there are various other groups in the United States that contribute to the development and maintenance of security and fire life safety standards. In the security field, these include the Academy of Security Educators and Trainers, the International Foundation for Protection Officers, the International Society of Crime Prevention Educators, the National Crisis Prevention Institute, the National Council of Investigation and Security Services, and the International Association of Chiefs of Police. In the fire life safety field, the National Fire Academy (NFA) and the United States Fire Administration (USFA) both report to the Federal Emergency Management Agency (FEMA) and make contributions to public fire safety. NFA, through its National Emergency Training Center, provides extensive training in fire-related disciplines and the application and enforcement of fire codes. The USFA, among other federal fire policy and coordination efforts, maintains an extensive fire data and analysis program.

The aim of the Society of Fire Protection Engineers (SFPE 1994) is "to advance the science of fire protection engineering and its allied fields, to maintain a high ethical standing among its members, and to foster fire protection engineering education. SFPE is the international clearing house for fire protection engineering state-of-the-art advances and information" (p. 1). The Society publishes a Bulletin, the *Journal of Fire Protection Engineering*, technology and other special reports, and also sponsors the *Handbook of Fire Protection Engineering*.

The National Institute for Certification in Engineering Technologies (NICET) is a nonprofit organization sponsored by the National Society of Professional Engineers. NICET is an examining body whose objective "is to provide nationally applicable, widely recognized certification programs by which engineering technicians and technologists can demonstrate competence and achievement in their areas of technical expertise" (NICET 1992). By doing this, it promotes high standards of safety and codes of responsibility for NICET-certified persons working in the engineering field.

The University of Maryland and the Worcester Polytechnic Institute are two other institutions that indirectly have made considerable contributions to the development of laws, codes, and standards by providing degree programs in fire protection engineering. In addition, organizations like the National Crime Prevention Institute, and various universities that offer security-related degree courses, have contributed greatly to the professionalism of the security industry.

Commentary

The laws, standards, and codes mentioned in this chapter can apply to both security and fire life safety in high-rise buildings; however, fire life safety operations are more strictly regulated than security operations. For example, building codes address security as well as fire life safety issues, but, in the United States, "more than 50 percent of a modern building code usually refers in some way or another to fire protection" (Cote 1991, p. 6-142). According to Rolf Jensen, founder of Rolf Jensen & Associates, Inc., "In the U.S. there is a greater emphasis on automatic suppression systems. Elsewhere in the world the emphasis is on fire resistive construction, detection, and manual suppression. But as more mega-high-rise* buildings are built world-wide, more countries are adopting laws requiring sprinklers, alarm-detection, smoke management and other fire safety regulations" (Jensen 1994, p. 2).

Through its laws, codes, and standards, the authority having jurisdiction specifies the type of fire protection equipment, how it should be installed, and how it should operate. As Knott (1994, p. 29) points out:

> For years, codes have been *specification-based*. In other words, codes cite specific requirements for the placement and the amount of equipment necessary. The result is codes that are easy to interpret and systems that are inflexible to design. However, there is a move toward the creation of *performance-based* codes. While these types of codes would focus on the same primary goal as a specification-based code—the saving of lives in fire situations—they would achieve that goal differently. Instead of listing exact specifications of equipment locations, performance-based codes would allow a fire technician to achieve a specific level of performance in almost any means possible.

Jensen (1994) adds that for several years there has been an increasing worldwide focus on using "performance-based codes as the fire safety approach of the future. Fire Protection Engineers and Fire Safety Scientists have made substantial improvement in fire modeling, and in our ability to assess the fire exposure or fire loading of a building. Far less progress has been made in our ability to develop a system by which we can objectively measure established performance goals. What is missing is an accepted risk assessment method; an objective way to set realistic goals and measure them" (p. 3).

The Occupational Health and Safety Act clearly holds building owners and managers responsible to ensure that adequate life safety precautions are taken to provide a safe and healthful working environment and to keep the premises reasonably safe for business visitors. Fire life safety operations are strictly regulated, as evidenced by local building codes; state building codes; the widely accepted NFPA codes and standards; and requirements (particularly by building insurers) to use equipment listed, recognized, or certified by Underwriters Laboratories Inc. and/or Factory Mutual.

---

*A mega-high-rise is defined in the *NFPA Fire Investigation Report on the 1993 New York World Trade Center Bombing* (Isner 1993) as:

> a large, tall (greater than 50 stories), densely populated structure where emergency evacuation is difficult or impractical. They are further characterized in that the ordinary fuels which they contain may result in rapid fire growth, development, and spread because of their geometric arrangement, and in extensive smoke spread throughout the structure which threatens occupants in remote areas from the fire origin. Further, the time required for fire fighters to establish effective fire fighting operations can be extensive because of the vertical arrangement of the structure.

The type and installation of security equipment is regulated to a degree by local and state building codes and UL, FMRC, WHI, or ASTM approval requirements. Also, private security firms—those providing guard and patrol services, private investigators, alarm services, and armored car services—are frequently regulated by state and local governments.

However, "America has very few national *mandatory* laws, statutes, or standards relating to security in the commercial, industrial, and private sectors" (Cumming 1992, p. 24). As Post and Kingsbury (1991) remind us, "It is also generally recognized that the security field does not have what might be classified as 'generally accepted security practices' comparable to the 'generally accepted accounting practices' that guide the accounting profession" (p. 222). There have been attempts to promote standards at the state and national levels but this has met with some resistance, particularly within the contract security industry.

The *Hallcrest Report II* states: "Many smaller security firms view standards and regulation as a means to promote increased market share for larger firms that are better able to meet the requirements" (Cunningham et al. 1990, p. 152).

This report further notes that in the United States only 14 of the 50 states require any training for unarmed security staff. (The vast majority of security personnel working in high-rise commercial office buildings is unarmed.) A law which went into effect January 1, 1994, in New York State now requires the state's approximately 150,000 security officers to receive an eight-hour basic training course and an additional sixteen hours of site-specific, on-the-job training (*Capitol District Business Review* 1994). This type of state legislation and federal legislation—the pending *Private Security Officers Quality Assurance Act* sponsored by Congressmen Barr and Martinez—may standardize minimum screening and training standards for private security officers who work throughout the 50 states. "We believe that it will contribute to the professionalism of our industry and streamline what had been a very laborious, costly and ineffective process in our previous efforts to achieve security officer standards state by state" (Keating 1994, p. 1). Also, the escalating problem of violence in the U.S. workplace is prompting agencies such as OSHA to develop models for applying security practices that would give businesses specific standards of security and safety.

An excellent review of the legal aspects of security and how the courts operate through trial and appeal can be found in *Introduction to Security* by Robert J. Fischer and Gion Green. Appendix 12-1 "Security and the Law" is also from that book, with some minor modifications and additions.

References

ASIS, promotional information (American Society for Industrial Security Membership Promotion Department, Washington, DC, 1994).

ASTM Publications 1994 Catalog (American Society for Testing and Materials, Philadelphia, 1994).

Atlas, Randall, "Will ADA handicap security?" *Security Management* (Arlington, VA, March 1992).

Black's Law Dictionary, 6th ed., by The Publisher's Editorial Staff. Co-authors Joseph R. Nolan and Jacqueline M. Nolan-Haley (West Publishing, St. Paul, 1990).

BOMA International, "Cornerstone of the commercial real estate industry," *Building Owners and Managers Association International* (BOMA International, Washington, DC, 1994).

Capitol District Business Review (Albany, NY, February 7, 1994); as reported in American Protective Services, Inc., *AdminNews* (Oakland, CA, February 1994).

Carson, Wayne G. "Chip," "Who sets means of egress standards?" *NFPA Journal* (All NFPA material in this chapter used with permission from the National Fire Protection Association, Quincy, MA. Copyright September/October 1993).

Cassidy, Kevin A., "Conflicting codes and how to deal with them," *Fire Safety and Loss Prevention* (Butterworth–Heinemann, Stoneham, MA, 1992).

Cote, Arthur E., "Building and fire codes and standards," *Fire Protection Handbook*, 17th ed. Arthur E. Cote, Editor-in-Chief, Jim L. Linville, Managing Editor (NFPA, Quincy, MA. Copyright 1991), pp. 6-140–6-149.

Cumming, Neil, "Stages of system design, selection, and installation," *Security: A Guide to Security System Design and Equipment Selection and Installation*, 2nd ed. (Butterworth–Heinemann, Stoneham, MA, 1992).

Cunningham, William, C., John J. Strauchs, and Clifford W. Van Meter, "Security personnel issues," *The Hallcrest Report II: Private Security Trends 1970–2000*, (Butterworth–Heinemann, Stoneham, MA, 1990).

Cunningham, William, C., John J. Strauchs, and Clifford W. Van Meter, "Introduction," *The Hallcrest Report II: Private Security Trends 1970–2000* (Butterworth–Heinemann, Stoneham, MA, 1990), p. 3. Information obtained from the Private Security Advisory Council to the Law Enforcement Assistance Administration, U.S. Department of Justice, 1973–1977.

Fire Protection Handbook, 17th ed. Arthur E. Cote, Editor-in-Chief, Jim L. Linville, Managing Editor (National Fire Protection Association, Quincy, MA. Copyright 1991), p. C-1.

Fischer, Robert J., and Gion Green, "Fire protection, safety, and emergency planning," *Introduction to Security*, 5th ed. (Butterworth–Heinemann, Stoneham, MA, 1992).

Garboden, Clif, "The life safety code: Responding to change," *NFPA Journal* (National Fire Protection Association, Quincy, MA. Copyright March/April 1994).

ICBO, *Publications List* (International Conference of Building Officials, Whittier, CA, 1993).

Isner, Michael S., and Thomas J. Klem, "Discussion," *Fire Investigation Report, World Trade Center Explosion and Fire* (NFPA, Quincy, MA. Copyright 1993).

Jensen, Rolf, *Design of Fire Protection and Life Safety Systems for Targeted Buildings* (Rolf Jensen & Associates, Inc., Deerfield, IL, 1994).

Keating, Thomas K., CPP, "Martinez bill update," *Vigilant* (American Protective Services, Inc., Oakland, CA, May 1994).

Knott, Jason, "Performance-based fire codes could improve protection, limit litigation," *Security Sales*, Vol. 16, No. 10 (Bobit Publishing Company, Redondo Beach, CA, October 1994).

Lathrop, James K., and David Birk, "Building life safety with codes," *NFPA Journal* (National Fire Protection Association, Quincy, MA 02169. Copyright May/June 1992).

Lindemann, Peter J., "What's up with the ADA?" *Security Management* (Arlington, VA, June 1993).

Merritt Company, The, "Standards in security," *Protection of Assets Manual*, vol. I, 9th printing. Editor Timothy J. Walsh (Used with permission from The Merritt Company, Santa Monica, CA, 800/638-7597. Copyright 1991).

NASCO, *Information Brochure* (National Association of Security Companies, Memphis, TN, 1994).

NCSBCS, *State Directory of Building Codes and Regulations* (National Conference of States on Building Codes and Standards, Inc., Herndon, VA, 1994).

NEMA, *Signaling, Protection and Communications Section Roster* (National Electrical Manufacturers Association, Washington, DC, 1994).

Nesse, Ted, and Virginia Williams, *Putting Security Product Standards to Work for You* (presentation by the Security Industry Association to the International Security Conference in Las Vegas, January 1994).

NICET, *General Information Booklet*, Engineering Technician and Technologist Certification Programs (National Institute for Certification in Engineering Technologies, Alexandria, VA, 1992).

NIST, *List of Publications by Subject Category*, SP305-22 Abridged (U.S. Department of Commerce, National Institute of Standards and Technology, Washington, DC, revised July 1991).

OSHA, *General Industry: Safety and Health Regulations*, Title 29 of the Code of Federal Regulations, Part 1910 (U.S. Department of Labor, Washington, DC, 1974).

Post, Richard S., and Arthur A. Kingsbury (revised by Richard S. Post with Arthur A. Kingsbury and David A. Schachtsiek), "Operational problems," *Security Administration: An Introduction to the Protective Services*, 4th ed. (Butterworth–Heinemann, Stoneham, MA, 1991).

Sanderson, R. L., "Codes and Code Administration" (Building Officials Conference of America, Inc., Chicago, 1969). As quoted in the *Fire Protection Handbook*, 17th ed. (National Fire Protection Association, Quincy, MA, 1991).

SBCCI, *1993 Products Catalog* (Southern Building Code Congress International, Birmingham, AL, 1993).

Schum, John L., "Codes and Standards," *Electronic Locking Devices: Toolbook Guides for Security Technicians* (Butterworth–Heinemann, Stoneham, MA, 1989).

SFPE, *An Invitation to Membership* (Society of Fire Protection Engineers, Boston, 1994).

Appendix 12-1   Security and the Law

The pursuit of security itself involves contact with others. In each such contact, there is a delicate consideration of conflicting rights. Whereas public police and protection services derive their authority to act from a variety of statutes, ordinances, and orders enacted at various levels of government, private police function essentially as private citizens. Their authority to so function is no more than the exercise of the rights of all citizens* to protect their own property. Every citizen has common law and statutory powers that include arrest, search, and seizure. The security officer has these same rights, both as a citizen, and as an extension of an employee's right to protect their employer's property. Similarly, this common law recognition of the right of defense of self and property is the legal underpinning for the right of every citizen to employ the services of others to protect property against any kind of incursion by others.

The broad statement of such rights, however, in no way suggests the full legal complexities that surround the question. In common law, case law, and state statutes, as well as in the basic authority of the U.S. Constitution, privileges and restrictions further defining these rights abound. The body of law covering the complex question of individual rights of defense of person and property contains many apparent contradictions and much ambiguity. In their efforts to create a perfect balance between the rights of individuals and the needs of society, the courts and the legislatures have had to walk a narrow path. As the perception of society's needs changed or as the need for the protection of the individual became more prominent, a swing in the attitudes of the courts and the legislatures became apparent. This led to some confusion especially among those with little or no knowledge of the law.

It is of enormous value, therefore, for everyone engaged in security to pursue the study of both criminal and civil law. Such a study is aimed neither at acquiring a law degree nor certainly at developing the skills to practice law. It is directed toward developing a background in those principles and rules of law that will be useful in the performance of the complex job of security. [*Author's Note:* The following study of criminal and civil law is purposely aimed at the private security officer. The reason for this approach is that, in a high-rise commercial building, the primary agent for implementing the security program, which provides for the protection of lives and property, is the building security staff. For simplicity, security staff are represented by the term *security officer*.]

Without some knowledge of the law, security officers frequently cannot serve their clients' interests. They may subject themselves or their employers to ruinous lawsuits through well-meaning but misguided conduct. In cases that must eventually go to court, handling of evidence, reports, and interrogations may be critical

---

Note: This entire appendix is reprinted, with some adaptations and additions, from Chapter 6 in *Introduction to Security* by Robert J. Fischer and Gion Green, 5th ed. (used with permission of Butterworth–Heinemann, Stoneham, MA, 1992). Definitions were largely obtained from *Black's Law Dictionary*, 6th ed., by The Publisher's Editorial Staff and co-authors Joseph R. Nolan and Jacqueline M. Nolan-Haley (West Publishing, St. Paul, 1990).

* In the high-rise setting such citizens may include building owners, managers, security directors, fire safety directors, building maintenance departments, security officers, and the individual tenants themselves. A *security officer* is a person who has been commissioned or authorized to perform duties primarily concerned with protection of the lives and property of people working within the private sector.

to the case; without an understanding of legal processes and how they operate, the cases would be lost.

Criminal law deals with offenses against society (corporations are of course part of society and can be either criminals or victims). Every state has its criminal [or penal] code that classifies and defines criminal offenses [and prescribes the punishment to be imposed for such conduct]. Criminal law is the result of a jurisdiction either using common law, which was adopted from English traditions, or passing specific legislation called statutory law. (In some jurisdictions both are used.) When criminal offenses are brought into court, the state takes an active part, considering itself to be the offended party.

Civil law, on the other hand, has more to do with the personal relations and conflicts between individuals, corporations, and government agencies. Broken agreements, sales that leave a customer dissatisfied, outstanding debts, disputes with a government agency, accidental injuries, and marital breakup all fall under the purview of civil law. In these cases, private citizens, companies, or government agencies are the offended parties, and the party found at fault is required to directly compensate the other party.

This review of *Security and the Law* is intended as a guide to some of the intricacies of criminal and civil law with primary emphasis on civil actions. It is aimed at those subjects with which a security officer would most likely be confronted. It will deal with substantive law (statutes and codes) or that portion of the law that concerns the rights, duties, and penalties of individuals in their relationships with each other.

Security, Public Police, and the U.S. Constitution

The framers of the U.S. Constitution with their grievances against England uppermost in mind when they were creating a new government were primarily concerned with the manner in which the powerless citizen was or could be abused by the enormous power of government. The document they created was concerned, therefore, not with the rights of citizens against each other but rather with those rights with respect to federal or state action.

Breaking and entering by one citizen on another may be criminal and subject to tort action (a civil wrong not involving a breach of contract), but it is not a violation of any constitutional right. Similar action by public police is a clear violation of Fourth Amendment rights and, as such, is expressly forbidden by the Constitution.

The public police have substantially greater powers than do security personnel to arrest, detain, search, and interrogate. Where security people are, as a rule, limited to the premises of their employer, public police operate in a much wider jurisdiction.

At the same time, the public police are limited by various restrictions imposed by the Constitution. Although the issue is not entirely clear, private police are not as a rule touched by these same restrictions.

Public police are limited by federal statutes that make it a crime for officials to deny others their constitutional rights. The Fourth and Fourteenth Amendments are most frequently invoked as the cornerstones of citizen protection against arbitrary police action. The exclusion of evidence from court action is one penalty paid by public police for violation of the search provision of the Fourth Amendment. For the most part private police are not affected by these restrictions.

Sources of Law

All law, whether civil or criminal, has its source in either common law, statutory law, or case law (judge-made). The following discussion can be applied to either civil or criminal law as it has developed over the past century. Although today's criminal law is primarily statutory, civil law, particularly tort law, is essentially judge-made and created in response to changing social conditions.

Common Law

At one time, the principal source of law in the United States was English common law. Although common law may also refer to judge-made (as opposed to legislature-made) law, to law that originated in England and grew from ever-changing custom, or to written Christian law, the term is most commonly used to refer to the English common law that has been changed to reflect specific U.S. customs.

Some states have preserved the status of common law offenses, while others have abolished common law and written most of the common law principles into statutes. Some states are still using both common and statutory law, whichever is appropriate.

Case Law

When a case goes to court, it is usually preceded by numerous cases of similar nature. Those preceding cases have usually been resolved in such a way as to put to rest any doubts as to the meaning of the governing statutes as well as to clarify the attitude of the courts regarding the violation involved. Each of these cases has established a precedent that will guide the court in subsequent cases based on the same essential facts. Since the facts in any two cases are rarely precisely the same, opposing attorneys cite prior cases whose facts more readily conform to their own theory or argument in the case at hand. They, too, build their case on precedents or case law already established. It is up to the court to choose one of the two sides or to establish its own theory. This is a very significant source of our law in addition to the common law.

Since society is in a constant state of change, it is essential that the law adapt to these changes. At the same time, there must be a stability in the law if it is to guide behavior. People must know that the law as it appears today will be the same tomorrow, that they will not be punished tomorrow for behavior that was permitted today. They need to know that each decision represents a settled statement of the law and they can conduct their affairs accordingly. So the published decisions of the appellate courts become guides to the meaning of the law and in effect become the law itself. Their judgments flesh out legislative enactments to give them clear outlines. Such interpretations based on precedents are never regarded lightly and in legal terms are "*stare decisis*" or "let the decision stand."

This does not mean that each decided case locks the courts forever into automatic compliance. Conditions that created the climate of the earlier decision may have changed, rendering the precedent invalid. And there are cases decided in such a narrow way that they cannot be applied beyond that case. Further, there is nothing that prevents review of a decision at the time of a later case. If the court agrees that the earlier case was in error, it will not be influenced by a faulty precedent.

So it can be seen that case law is an important source of the law; it provides a climate of legal stability without closing the law to responsiveness to changing needs.

Statutory Law

Federal and state legislatures are empowered to enact laws that describe additional crimes. The authority to do so emanates from the U.S. Constitution and from the individual state constitutions. These constitutions do not specifically establish a body of criminal law. In general, they are more concerned with setting forth the limitations of governmental power over the rights of individuals. But they do provide both for the authority of legislative action in establishing criminal law and for a court system to handle these as well as civil matters.

Much criminal law is, in fact, the creation of the legislatures. The legislatures are exclusively responsible for making and defining laws. The courts may find some laws unconstitutional or vague and thus set them aside, but they may not create laws. Only the legislatures are empowered to do that.

The Power of Security Personnel

Security personnel are generally limited to the exercise of powers possessed by every citizen. There is no legal area where the position of a security officer as such confers any greater rights, powers, or privileges than those possessed by every other citizen. A few states go contrary to this norm—for example, Michigan—and confer additional arrest powers for security personnel after the completion of a designated number of hours of training.[1] As a practical matter if officers are uniformed they will very likely find that in most cases people will comply with their requests. Many people are aware neither of their own rights nor of the limitations of the powers of a security officer. Thus security officers can obtain compliance to directives that may be, if not illegal, beyond their power to command. In cases where security officers have unwisely taken liberties with their authority, the officers and their employers may be subject to the penalties of civil action. The litigation involved in suing security officers and their employers for a tort is slow and expensive, which may make such recourse improbable for the poor and for those unfamiliar with their rights. But the judgments that have been awarded have had a generally sobering effect on security professionals and have probably served to reduce the number of such incidents. Criminal law also regulates security activities. Major crimes such as battery, manslaughter, kidnapping, and breaking and entering—any one of which might be encountered in the course of security activities—are substantially deterred by criminal sanctions.

Further limitations may be imposed on the authority of a security force by licensing laws, administrative regulations, and specific statutes directed at security activities. Operating contracts between employers and security firms may also specify limits on the activities of the contracted personnel.

Classes of Crimes

A crime has been defined as a voluntary and intentional violation by a legally competent person of a legal duty that commands or prohibits an act for the protection of society.[2]

Since such a definition encompasses violations from the most trivial to the most disruptive and repugnant, efforts have long been made to classify crimes in some way. In common law, crimes are classified according to seriousness from treason (the most serious) to misdemeanors (the least serious). Crimes in most states do not list treason separately and deal with felonies as the most serious crimes and misdemeanors as the next in seriousness, with different approaches to the least serious crimes, those known as infractions in some jurisdictions, less than misdemeanors in others, and petty offenses in still others. It will become apparent why security specialists should understand the nature of a given crime and its classification since such considerations will be important in determining their right to arrest, to use force in making the arrest, and to search and various other considerations that must be determined under possible difficult circumstances and without delay. Serious crimes like murder, rape, arson, armed robbery, and aggravated assault are felonies. Misdemeanors include charges such as disorderly conduct and criminal damage to property.

Felonies

From the time of Henry II of England, there has been a general understanding that felonies comprised the more serious crimes. This is true in modern U.S. law as far as it goes, but clearly the definition of felony must be pinned down more precisely than that if it is to be used as a classification of crime and if courts are to respond differently to felons than they would to another type of law breaker. The definition of a felony is by no means standard throughout the United States. In some jurisdictions, there is no distinction between felonies and misdemeanors.

The federal definition of a felony is an offense punishable by death or by imprisonment for a term exceeding one year. The test, then, for a felony is the length of time that punishment is imposed on the convicted person.

A number of states follow the federal definition. In those states, a felony is a crime punishable by more than a year's imprisonment. The act remains a felony whatever the ultimate sentence may actually be. The crime is classified as a felony because it could be punished by a sentence of more than a year. Other states provide that, "[a] felony is a crime punishable with death or by imprisonment in the state prison." This definition hinges on the place of confinement rather than, as in the federal description, the length of confinement.

Some states bestow broad discretionary powers on the judge by providing that certain acts may be considered either a felony or a misdemeanor depending on the sentence. The penalty clauses in the statutes thus involved specifically state that if the judge should sentence the defendant to a state prison, the act for which he was convicted shall be a felony (under the state definition of a felony) but if the sentence be less than such confinement the crime shall be a misdemeanor.

The distinction can be very important in that in most states where arrest by private citizens (for example, security personnel) is covered by statute, it is clear that arrests for crimes that are less than felonies may be made only where the offense is committed in the presence of the arrester. In the case of arrest for a felony, the felony must in fact have been committed (though not necessarily in the presence of the arrester), and there must be reasonable grounds to believe the person arrested committed it. In other words, security employees, unlike police officers, act at their own peril.

A police officer has the right to arrest without a warrant where he reasonably believes that a felony has been committed and that the person arrested is guilty even if, in fact, no felony occurred. A private citizen, on the other hand, is privileged to make an arrest only when he has reasonable grounds for believing in the guilt of the person arrested and a felony has in fact been committed.[3]

Some states, however, do allow for citizen arrest in public order misdemeanors. Making a citizen's arrest, which must be recognized as the only kind of arrest that can be made by a security officer, is a privilege not a right and as such is carefully limited by law. Such limitation is enforced by the ever-present potential for either criminal prosecution or tort action against the unwise or uninformed action of a security professional.

Private Security Powers

Arrest

Arresting a person is a legal step that should not be taken lightly. A citizen's power to arrest another is granted by common law and in many jurisdictions by statutory law. In most cases, it is best to make an arrest only after an arrest warrant* has been issued. Most citizen's arrests occur, however, when the immediacy of a situation requires arrest without a warrant. The exact extent of citizen's arrest power varies, depending on the type of crime, the jurisdiction (laws), whether the crime was committed in the presence of the arrester, or the status of the citizen (strictly a private citizen or a commissioned officer).

In most states warrantless arrests by private citizens are allowed when a felony has been committed and reasonable grounds exist for believing that the person arrested committed it. Reasonable grounds means that the arrester acted as would any average citizen who, having observed the same facts, would draw the same conclusion. In some jurisdictions, a private citizen may arrest without reasonable grounds as long as a felony was committed.

Most states allow citizen's arrest for misdemeanors committed in the arrester's presence. A minority of states, however, adhere closely to the common-law practice of allowing misdemeanor arrests only for offenses that constitute a breach of the peace and that occur in the arrester's presence [see table on next two pages].

Although the power of citizen's arrest is very significant in the private sector because it allows security officers to protect their employer's property, there is little room for errors of judgment. The public police officer is protected from civil liability for false arrest if the officer has probable cause to believe a crime was committed, but the private officer (citizen) is liable if a crime was not committed regardless of the reasonableness of the belief. This liability is because a citizen's arrest generally can be made only if a crime has definitely been committed.

This distinction is illustrated by the case *Cervantez v. J.C. Penney Company*.[4] In this case, an off-duty police officer, moonlighting as a store detective for J.C. Penney Company, made a warrantless arrest of two individuals for misdemeanor theft. Later they were released because of lack of evidence. The plaintiffs sued the company and the officer for false arrest, imprisonment, malicious prosecution, assault and battery, intentional infliction of emotional distress, and negligence in the selection of its employee. The primary issue in the Cervantez case was whether the officer could rely on the probable cause defense. The court's decision rested on whether the officer acted as a police officer in California or as a private citizen.

The store and officer argued that the probable cause defense was sound because the detective was an off-duty police officer and thus could arrest on the basis of probable cause. The plaintiffs argued that the store detective should be governed by the rules of arrest applied to private citizens and the officer was therefore liable for his actions because no crime had been proven. The plaintiffs contended that the officer was employed as a private security officer, and thus his arrest powers were only those of a private citizen.

The California Supreme Court ruled that the laws governing the type of arrest to be applied depend on the arrester's employer at the time of the arrest. Since the officer was acting as a store detective when he made the arrest, his arrest powers were no greater than those of a private citizen. Thus probable cause could not be used as a defense against false arrest.

---

* *Black's Law Dictionary* defines an *arrest warrant* as "a written order of the court which is made on behalf of the state, or United States, and is based upon a complaint issued pursuant to statute and/or court rule and which commands [a] law enforcement officer to arrest a person and bring him before [a] magistrate."

| | Minor Offense | | | | | | | | | |
| | Type of Minor Offense | | | | | | Type of Knowledge Required | | | |
	Crime	Misdemeanor Amounting to a Breach of the Peace	Breach of the Peace	Public Offense	Offense	Offense Other Than an Ordinance	Indictable Offense	Presence	Immediate Knowledge	View	Upon Reasonable Grounds That Is Being Committed
Alabama				•				•			
Alaska	•							•			
Arizona		•						•			
Arkansas											
California				•				•			
Colorado	•							•			
Georgia					•			•	•		
Hawaii	•							•			
Idaho				•				•			
Illinois							•				•
Iowa				•				•			
Kentucky											
Louisiana											
Michigan											
Minnesota				•				•			
Mississippi			•				•	•			
Montana					•			•			
Nebraska											
Nevada				•				•			
New York					•			•			
N. Carolina[a]			•								
N. Dakota				•				•			
Ohio											
Oklahoma				•				•			
Oregon		•						•			
S. Carolina											
S. Dakota				•				•			
Tennessee				•				•			
Texas			•					•		•	
Utah				•				•			
Wyoming											

[a] Statute eliminates use of word *arrest* and replaces it with *detention*.

Table 12.2 Statutory Arrest Authority of a Private Citizen.

| | Major Offense |||||||||||| | | |
| | Type of Major Offense |||||| Type of Knowledge Required ||||| Certainty of Correct Arrest |||| |
	Felony	Larceny	Petit Larceny	Crime Involving Physical Injury to Another	Crime	Crime Involving Theft or Destruction of Property	Committed in Presence	Information a Felony Has Been Committed	View	Reasonable Grounds to Believe Being Committed	That Felony Has Been Committed in Fact	In Escaping or Attempting	Summoned by Peace Officer to Assist in Arrest	Is In the Act of Committing	Reasonable Grounds to Believe Person Arrested Committed	Probable Cause
Alabama	•										•				•	
Alaska	•										•				•	
Arizona	•										•				•	
Arkansas	•									•					•	
California	•										•				•	
Colorado				•			•									
Georgia	•												•		•	
Hawaii				•			•							•		
Idaho	•										•				•	
Illinois	•									•						
Iowa	•										•				•	
Kentucky	•										•				•	
Louisiana	•										•					
Michigan	•						•				•			•		
Minnesota	•										•				•	
Mississippi	•										•				•	
Montana	•										•				•	
Nebraska	•	•									•				•	
Nevada	•										•				•	
New York	•										•					
N. Carolina[a]	•			•		•							•			•
N. Dakota	•										•				•	
Ohio	•									•					•	
Oklahoma	•										•				•	
Oregon					•		•									•
S. Carolina	•	•						•	•							
S. Dakota	•										•				•	
Tennessee	•										•				•	
Texas	•						•		•							
Utah	•										•				•	
Wyoming	•	•									•				•	

Table 12.2 *continued*

Source: Charles Schnabolk, *Physical Security: Practices and Technology* (Stoneham, MA: Butterworth Publishers, 1983), pp. 64–65.

Some states have avoided the problem of the Cervantez case by extending the probable cause defense to private citizens. The most common extension involves shoplifting arrests. Many states have a mercantile privilege rule that allows the probable cause defense for detentions but not for arrests. The law permits a private citizen or his employees to detain in a reasonable manner and for a reasonable time a person who is believed to have stolen merchandise so that the merchant can recover the merchandise or summon a police officer to make an arrest. Some states have extended this merchant clause to cover public employees in libraries, museums, or archival institutions.

The exact extent of the protection afforded to merchants and their employees or agents depends on the individual state's statutes. Some states offer protection against liability for false arrest, false imprisonment, and defamation; others offer protection against false imprisonment but not against false arrest. It is interesting to note that very few states allow a merchant to search a detainee. The private citizen's authority to search is unclear and will be discussed later in this section.

Detention

Detention is a concept that has grown largely in response to the difficulties faced by merchants in protecting their property from shoplifters and the problems and dangers they face when they make an arrest. Generally detention differs from arrest in that it permits a merchant to detain a suspected shoplifter briefly without turning the suspect over to the police. An arrest requires that the arrestee be turned over to the authorities as soon as practicable and in any event without unreasonable delay.

All the shoplifting statutes refer to "detain," not to "arrest," a terminology probably derived from the thought that a distinction could be made between the two. The distinction is based on the fact that an arrest is for the purpose of delivering the suspect to the authorities and of exercising strict physical control over that person until the authorities arrive. A detention, or temporary delay, would not be termed an arrest as commonly defined. The distinction is difficult to defend but the statutes are clear. In Illinois, for example:

Any merchant who has reasonable grounds to believe that a person has committed retail theft may detain such person, on or off the premises of a retail mercantile establishment, in a reasonable manner and for a reasonable length of time for all or any of the following purposes:

a. To request identification;
b. To verify such identification;
c. To make reasonable inquiry as to whether such person has in his possession unpurchased merchandise and, to make reasonable investigation of the ownership of such merchandise;
d. To inform a peace officer of the detention of the person and surrender that person to the custody of a peace officer.[5]

California was one of the first states to establish merchant immunity in a 1936 Supreme Court decision; in *Collyer v. S.H. Kress Co.*,[6] the court upheld the right of a department store official to detain a suspected shoplifter for 20 minutes.

Most statutes include the merchant, employee, agent, private police, and peace officer as authorized to detain suspects, but they do now include citizens at large, such as another shopper. Most of the statutes also describe the purposes of detention and the manner in which they may be conducted. These purposes are to search, to interrogate, to investigate suspicious behavior, to recover goods, and to await a peace officer.

The manner in which the detention is to be conducted is generally described as "reasonable" and for "a reasonable period of time."

The privilege of detention is, however, subject to some problems. There must be probable cause to believe theft already has taken place, or is about to take place, before a merchant may detain anyone. Probable cause is an elusive concept and one which has undergone many different interpretations by the courts. It is frequently difficult to predict how the court will rule on a given set of circumstances that may at the time clearly indicate probable cause to detain. Secondly, reasonableness must exist both in time and manner of the detention or the privilege will be lost.

Interrogation

No law prohibits a private person from engaging in conversation with a willing participant. Should the conversation become an interrogation, the information may not be admissible in a court of law. The standard is whether the statements were made voluntarily.

A statement made under duress is not regarded as trustworthy and is therefore inadmissible in court. This principle applies equally to police officers and private citizens. A confession obtained from an employee by threatening loss of job or physical harm would be inadmissible and would also make the interrogator liable for civil and criminal prosecution.

The classic cases involving interrogation, generally applied to only public law enforcement officers, are *Escobedo v. State of Illinois*[7] and *Miranda v. Arizona*.[8] Today the Miranda case has become the leading case recognized by most American citizens in reference to "their rights." On March 13, 1963, Ernesto Miranda was arrested at his home and taken to a Phoenix police station. There he was questioned by two police officers who during Miranda's trial admitted that they had not advised him that he could have a lawyer present. After two hours of interrogation, the officers emerged with a confession. According to the statement, Miranda had made the confession "with full knowledge of my legal right, understanding any statement I make may be used against me." His confession was admitted into evidence over defense objections during his trial. He was convicted of kidnapping and rape. On appeal, the Arizona Supreme Court upheld the conviction indicating that Miranda did not specifically request counsel. The U.S. Supreme Court reversed the decision based on the fact that Miranda had not been informed of his right to an attorney, nor was his right not to be compelled to incriminate himself effectively protected.

Although the principle behind the *Miranda v. Arizona* decision was the removal of compulsion from custodial questioning (questioning initiated by law enforcement officers after a person has been taken into custody or otherwise deprived of freedom), it generally only applies to public law enforcement officers. The police officer must show that statements made by the accused were given after the accused was informed of the facts that speaking was not necessary, that the statements might by used in court, that an attorney could be present, and that if the accused could not afford an attorney, one would be appointed for the accused prior to questioning. These Miranda warnings are not necessary unless the person is in custody or is deprived of freedom. Based on this distinction, most courts agree that private persons are not generally required to use Miranda warnings because they are not public law-enforcement officers.

In the case, *In re Deborah C.*,[9] the California Supreme Court upheld the principle that private citizens are not required to use Miranda warnings and that statements made by the accused in citizen's arrests are admissible in a court of law. The court felt that the Miranda rationale did not apply to the retail store environment because store detectives lack the psychological edge that police officers have when the latter are questioning someone at a police station.

A few states require citizens to use a modified form of Miranda before questioning, and some—a definite minority—prohibit questioning. Wisconsin law states, "[t]he detained person must be promptly informed of the purpose of the detention and be permitted to make phone calls, but shall not be interrogated or searched against his will before the arrival of a peace officer who may conduct a lawful interrogation of the accused person."[10]

In 1987, the case of *State of West Virginia v. William H. Muegge,*[11] expanded the Miranda concept to private citizens. In this case, Muegge was detained by a store security guard who observed Muegge place several items of merchandise in his pockets and proceed through the checkout aisle without paying for those items. The security guard approached Muegge, identified herself, and asked him to return to the store office the discuss the problem. The officer ordered Muegge to empty his pockets, which contained several unpaid-for items valued at a total of $10.65. The officer next read Muegge his "constitutional rights" and asked him to sign a waiver of rights. Muegge refused and asked for the assistance of a lawyer. The officer refused the request and indicated that she would call the state police. At some time either prior to the arrival or after the arrival of the state trooper, the defendant signed the waiver and completed a questionnaire that contained various incriminating statements. At the trial, the unpaid-for items were admitted without objection and the questionnaire was read aloud over the defendant's objection. Although the court felt that the specific Miranda warnings were not necessary, it ruled that whenever a person is in custodial control mandated by state statute (that is, merchant clauses) the safeguards protecting the constitutional right not to be compelled to be a witness against oneself in a criminal case apply.

Search and Seizure

A search may be defined as an examination of persons and/or their property for the purpose of discovering evidence of guilt in relation to some specific offense. The observation of items in plain view is not a search as long as the observer is legally entitled to be in the place where the observation is made. This includes public property and private property that is normally open to the public, for example, shopping malls, retail stores, hotel lobbies, and so on.

Common law says little about searches by private persons and is inconclusive. Searches by private persons, however, have been upheld by the courts where consent to search was given and where searches were made as part of a legal citizen's arrest. The best practice to follow is to contact police officials who can then ask for a search warrant* to search as part of an arrest. Since searches often need to be conducted on short notice without the aid of a police officer, however, it is important to understand several factors.

First, in a consent search, the searcher must be able to show that the consent was given voluntarily. Second, the search cannot extend beyond the area for which consent to search was given. It is advisable to secure a written agreement of the consent to search. Third, the consent must be given by the person who possesses the item. Possession, not ownership, is the criterion for determining whether a search was valid. Although many firms issue waivers to search lockers and other

---

* *Black's Law Dictionary* defines a *search warrant* as "an order in writing, issued by a justice or other magistrate, in the name of the state, directed to a sheriff, constable, or other officer, authorizing him to search for and seize any property that constitutes evidence of the commission of a crime, contraband, the fruits of a crime, or things, otherwise criminally possessed; or, property designed or intended for use or which is or has been used as a means of committing a crime."

work areas, an officer must remember that the consent to search may be withdrawn at any time. If the consent is withdrawn, continuing a search might make the officer and the company liable for invasion of privacy. Some companies have solved this problem by retaining control over lockers in work areas. In this situation, workers are told that the lockers are not private and may be searched at any time.

A search made as a part of an arrest is supported by case law. In general, the principle of searching the arrestee and the immediate surroundings, defined as the area within which one could lunge and reach a weapon or destroy evidence, has been repeatedly held as constitutional. The verdict on searches incident to arrest is still mixed. In *People v. Zelinski*,[12] the California court disapproved of searches made incident to an arrest but did approve of searches for weapons for protective reasons. New York courts tend to support searches, indicating that private officers, like their public counterparts, have a right to searches incident to an arrest. In general, it appears that unless the security officer fears that a weapon may be hidden on the arrestee, the officer should wait until the police arrive to conduct a search unless permission is given for such a search.

Even in the statutes governing retail shoplifting, the area of search is limited. Some states neither forbid nor condone searches; rather, they allow security personnel to investigate or make reasonable inquiries as to whether a person possesses unpurchased merchandise. In other states, searches are strictly forbidden, except looking for objects carried by the suspected shoplifter. Courts, however, generally favor protective searches where officers fear for their own safety.

Exclusionary Rule

In a historic decision, the Supreme Court ruled that any and all evidence uncovered by public law enforcement agents in violation of the Fourth Amendment will be excluded from consideration. That means all evidence, no matter how trustworthy or indicative of guilt, will be inadmissible if it is illegally obtained. This landmark case (*Mapp v. Ohio*),[13] was the most important case that contributed to the development of the "exclusionary rule," which states that illegally seized evidence (and its fruits) are inadmissible in any state or federal proceedings. *Weeks v. United States*[14] set the stage for the later, all-inclusive decision in Mapp by holding that evidence acquired by officials of the federal government in violation of the Fourth Amendment must be excluded in a federal prosecution.

The Mapp case is clear in its application of the exclusionary rule to state and federal prosecutions. The question is, does the exclusionary rule apply to private parties? The determining case in this area is *Burdeau v. McDowell*.[15]

Unlike illegal searches conducted by public law-enforcement officers, evidence secured by a private security officer conducting an illegal search is still admissible in either criminal or civil proceedings. In *Burdeau v. McDowell*, the U.S. Supreme Court said, "[i]t is manifest that there was no invasion of the security afforded by the Fourth Amendment against unreasonable searches and seizures, as whatever wrong was done was the act of individuals in taking property of another." If such evidence is admissible, why should private sector employees concern themselves with the legality of searches? Even though the evidence is admissible, security officers who conduct illegal searches may be subject to liability for other actions, including battery and invasion of privacy.

There is considerable controversy over the Burdeau case because some people fear that constitutional guarantees are threatened by the acceptance of evidence illegally obtained by private security personnel. It is clear that any involvement by government officials constitutes "state action" or an action "under color of law" and is limited by the constitutional restrictions that apply to public police actions.

In *State v. Scrotsky*,[16] the court excluded evidence obtained when a police detective accompanied a theft victim to the defendant's apartment to identify and recover stolen goods. The court held that "[t]he search and seizure by one served the purpose of both and must be deemed to have been participated in by both." The exclusionary rule is applied in this case, as in many others, to discourage government officials from conducting improper searches and from using private individuals to conduct them.[17]

In cases where private parties act independent of government involvement, the courts have not been so clear. In a significant case, *People v. Randazzo*,[18] the court admitted evidence obtained by a merchant in a shoplifting case. The court did not deal with any questions of Fourth Amendment violation since there was no state action involved. The court held that redress for the victim of an unreasonable search conducted by a private individual not under color of law is a tort action, and thus the exclusionary rule does not apply. In *Thacker v. Commonwealth*,[19] the court held that a private party acts for the state when that party makes an arrest in accordance with the state's arrest statute and thus would be subject to the exclusionary rule. On the other hand, following the Burdeau precedent, a federal district court found no state action in a case where the plaintiff alleged she was wrongfully detained, slapped, beaten, harassed, and searched by the manager and an employee of the store.[20] The plaintiff sued, alleging among other things that the employee, a security officer, was acting "under color of law" because he was licensed under the Pennsylvania Private Detective Act. The court rejected this argument and found that the Pennsylvania law "invests the licensee with no authority of state law."

In summary, although public police are clearly limited by constitutional restrictions, generally private security personnel are not so limited. Provided that they act as private parties and are in no way involved with public officials, they are limited by criminal and civil sanctions but are not bound at this time by most constitutional restrictions.

Use of Force
On occasion, security personnel must use force to protect someone or to accomplish legitimate purposes. In general, force may be used to protect oneself or others, to defend property, and to prevent the commission of a criminal act. The extent to which force may be used is restricted; no more force may be used than is reasonable under the circumstances. This means that deadly force or force likely to create great bodily harm will not be allowable unless the force being used by the assailant is also deadly force or force likely to create great bodily harm. If the force exceeds what is deemed reasonable, officers and their employers are liable for the use of excessive force, which can range from assault and battery to homicide. This is the same degree of power extended to the ordinary citizen.

Self-defense: In general people may use reasonable force to protect themselves. The amount of force may be equal to, but not greater than, the force being used against them. In most states, a person can protect herself, except when that person was the initial aggressor. Most states allow that self-defense is a defense against the criminal offense of battery.

Defense of Others: Security officers may protect others just as they protect themselves. However, two different approaches to defense of others are evident. In the first approach, the officer must try to identify with the attacked person. In this position, the officer is entitled to use whatever force would be appropriate if she were the person being attacked. If the officer happens to protect the wrong person—that is, the aggressor—the officer is liable regardless of her good intentions. In the second approach, the defender may use force when it is reasonable to believe that such force is necessary. In this case, the defender is protected from liability as long as she acted in a reasonable manner.

Defense of Property: In defense of property, force may be applied, but it must be short of deadly force, which is generally allowable only in cases involving felonious attacks on property during which loss of life is likely. As noted by Schnabolk, "one may use deadly force to protect a home against an arsonist but the use of deadly force against a mere trespasser would not be permitted."[21] Security officers acting in the place of their employers are empowered to use the same force that their employers are entitled to use.

Force Used during Arrest or Detention: Like the police, the private citizen security officer has the right to use reasonable force in detaining or arresting someone. Many states still follow the common-law principles that allow deadly force in the case of fleeing felons, but many others have restricted the use of deadly force. This restriction allows the use of deadly force only in cases where the felony is both violent *and* the felon is immediately fleeing.

Prevention of Crimes: To determine the amount of force a security officer may use to prevent crimes, the courts have considered the circumstances, the seriousness of the crime prevented, and the possibility of preventing the crime by other means. Under common law a person can use force to prevent a crime. The courts have ruled, however, that the use of force is limited to situations involving felonies or a breach of the peace and nonviolent misdemeanors do not warrant the use of force. Deadly force is justifiable in preventing a crime only if it is necessary to protect a person from harm. Some states have broadened this concept to permit the use of deadly force to prevent any felony.

Use of Firearms: Most states regulate the carrying of firearms by private citizens. Almost all states prohibit the carrying of concealed weapons while only half of them prohibit carrying an exposed handgun. Although all states excuse police officers from these restrictions, some states also exempt private security officers. Even in states that prohibit carrying concealed or exposed handguns, there are provisions for procuring a license to carry weapons in this manner.

Civil Law: The Controller for Private Security

Tort Law: Source of Power and Limits
A tort is a civil action based on the principle that one individual can expect certain behavior from another individual. When the actions of one of the parties do not meet reasonable expectations, a tort action may result. In security applications, a guard may take some action to interfere with the free movement of some person. There is a basis for a suit no matter whether the guard knows those actions are wrong or is unaware that the actions are wrong but acts in a negligent manner.

Thus tort law may be invoked for either an intentional or negligent act. In some cases, tort law may be imposed even though an individual is not directly at fault. Such a legal obligation is called "strict liability," and does not generally affect the security officer. Vicarious liability, however, is of concern to enterprises that contract or employ security services. Strict liability applies to the seller who is liable for any and all defective or hazardous products that unduly threaten a consumer's personal safety. [In the high-rise setting, strict liability may be applicable to the installation and maintenance of security and fire life safety systems and equipment.] Vicarious liability is an indirect legal responsibility; for example, the liability of an employer for the actions of an employee.

Negligence: The Restatement of Torts[22] states that "[it] is negligence to use an instrumentality, whether a human being or a thing, which the actor knows, or should know, to be incompetent, inappropriate or defective and that its use involves an unreasonable risk of harm to others." This statement has particular importance to security employers and supervisors in four areas: (1) negligent hiring, (2) negligent supervision of employees, (3) negligent training, and (4) supervisory negligence. Security officers have been held liable for negligent use of firearms and force.

In all cases of negligence, the plaintiff (the person who brings an action, the party who complains or sues) must prove the case by a preponderance of the evidence (more than 50 percent or "more likely than not") in all of the following areas:

1. An act or failure to act (an omission) by the defendant
2. A legal duty owed to the plaintiff by the defendant, the person defending or denying, and/or the party against whom relief or recovery is sought
3. A breach of duty by the defendant
4. A foreseeable injury to plaintiff
5. Harm or injury

A relatively new concept in the area of negligence is comparative fault. This concept accepts the fact that the plaintiff may have contributed to her own injury such as being in a restricted area or creating a disturbance or some hazard. In the past, the theory of contributory negligence prevented the plaintiff from collecting for injuries and so forth if she contributed somehow to her own injury. In comparative negligence, the relative negligence of the parties involved is compared, and the plaintiff who may have contributed to the injury may get some award for part of the injury for which she in not responsible. There are three types of comparative negligence statutes: (1) pure approach, (2) the 50/50 rule, and (3) the 51 percent rule. In the pure approach, the plaintiff may collect something for injuries even if she was primarily responsible for her injuries. In theory, the jury could award the plaintiff 1 percent of the damages if she is found to have contributed 99 percent to the injury. In the 50/50 rule situation the plaintiff can collect for damages if she was responsible for no more than 50 percent of the negligence. In the 51 percent situation, the plaintiff must not have contributed to more than 49 percent of the situation in order to collect damages. Regardless of the rule followed, the degree to which the plaintiff is responsible for the end result is considered before judgments are pronounced. One example of the 50/50 rule is the Illinois statute:

In all actions on account of bodily injury or death or physical damage to property, based on negligence . . . the plaintiff shall be barred from recovering damages if the trier of fact find that the contributory fault on the part of the plaintiff is more than 50% of the proximate cause of the injury or damage for which recovery is sought. The plaintiff shall not be barred from recovering damages if the trier of fact finds that the contributory fault on the part of the plaintiff is not more than 50% of the proximate cause of the injury or damage for which recovery is sought, but any damages allowed shall be diminished in the proportion to the amount of fault attributable to the plaintiff.[23]

Cases involving negligence in providing adequate security on the part of firms have been increasing. Recent cases have resulted in awards to plaintiffs in individual cases of over $1 million. More will be said about this issue later in the section entitled "Security and Liability."

Intentional Torts: An intentional tort occurs when the person who committed the act was able to foresee that the action would result in certain damages.

The actor intended the consequences of the actions or at least intended to commit the action that resulted in damages to the plaintiff. In general, the law punishes such acts by punitive measures that exceed those awarded in common negligence cases.

The most common intentional torts are:

Assault: Intentionally causing fear of harmful or offensive touching but without touching or physical contact. In most cases, courts have ruled that words alone are not sufficient to place a person in fear of harm and that the danger is imminent.

Battery: Intentionally harmful or otherwise offensive touching of another person. The touching does not have to be direct physical contact but may instead be through an instrument such as a cane or rock. In addition, the courts have found battery to exist if "something" closely connected to the body, but not actually a part of the body, is struck.[24] In this case (*Fisher v. Carrousel Motor Hotel, Inc.*), the plaintiff was attending a conference that included a luncheon. The luncheon was a buffet, and while Fisher was in line, one of the defendant's employees snatched the plate from his hand and shouted that no Negro [*sic*] could be served in the club. The court of appeals held that a battery can occur even though the subject is not struck. They ruled that, so long as there is contact with clothing or an object closely identified with the body, a battery can occur. From a security point of view, the contact must be nonconsensual and not privileged. Privileged contact is generally granted to merchants who need to recover merchandise; privilege is generally a defense against charges of battery if the merchant's actions were reasonable. If the touching were unreasonable, however, the plaintiff would have a case for battery. The same argument holds for searches: If a search is performed after consent has been given, no battery has occurred. If consent is not given, however, the search is illegal, and a battery has probably occurred.

False imprisonment or false arrest: Intentionally confining or restricting the movement or freedom of another. The confinement may be the result of physical restraint or intimidation. False imprisonment implies that the confinement is for personal advantage rather than to bring the plaintiff to court. This is one of the torts most frequently filed against security personnel.

Defamation: Injuring the reputation of another by publicly making untrue statements. Slander is oral defamation, while libel is defamation through the written word. The classic case of a security officer yelling "Stop thief!" in a crowded store has all the necessary elements for slander if the accused is not a thief. Although it is generally true that truth is an absolute defense in defamation issues, the courts may also look at the motivation. True statements published with malicious intent can be prosecuted in some jurisdictions. In this age of high technology, the courts have now included statements made on television or other broadcasts in the libel category. It is apparent that the courts view these types of statements as being more permanent and as reaching broad audiences.

Malicious prosecution: Groundlessly instituting criminal proceedings against another person. To prove malice, the plaintiff must show that the primary motive in bringing about criminal proceedings was not to bring the defendant to justice. Classic cases include proceedings brought about to extort money or to force performance on contracts. Although there is no liability for reporting facts to the police or other components of the criminal justice system if the prosecution resulted from biased statements of fact, incomplete reports, or the defendant's persuasion (political, sexual, religious, and so on), liability for malicious prosecution might be proved.

Invasion of privacy: Intruding on another person's physical solitude, disclosing private information about another person, or publicly placing someone in false light. Four distinct actions fall into this category: (1) misappropriation of the plaintiff's name or picture for commercial advantage, (2) placing the plaintiff in a false light, (3) public disclosure of private facts, and (4) intrusion into the seclusion of another. For security purposes, invasion of privacy generally occurs during a search or during observation of an individual. If signs outside fitting rooms advise customers that they may be observed, some legal observers believe that shoppers should not expect privacy and thus cannot legitimately complain of invasion of privacy. Concern over liability for invasion of privacy is increasing; this liability may be the result of reference checks, background investigations, or the use of truth detection devices.

Trespass and conversion: Trespass is the unauthorized physical invasion of property or remaining on property after permission has been rescinded. Conversion means taking personal property in such a way that the plaintiff's use or right of possession of chattel is restricted. In simpler terms, conversion is depriving someone of the use of personal property.

Intentional infliction of mental distress: Intentionally causing mental or emotional distress to another person. The distress may be either mental or physical and may result from highly aggravating words or conduct.

Security and Liability

In the past few years, the number of suits filed against security officers and companies has increased dramatically. Predictions for the next 10 years indicate that the increase will cease but that the number of suits will continue at the present levels. One possible reason for the leveling off of suits is that security management has a better understanding of the problems associated with liability situations today. The earlier increase may be partly attributed to the growth of the security industry and to the public's demand for accountability and professionalism in the security area. Most of the cases filed against private security officers and operations belong in the tort category as was mentioned earlier. The individual who commits a tort is called a tortfeasor, while the accuser is called the plaintiff. The plaintiff may be a person, a corporation, or an association. Torts are classified as either intentional, negligent, or strict liability. An intentional tort is a wrong perpetrated by someone who intends to break the law. In contrast, a negligent tort is a wrong perpetrated by someone who fails to exercise sufficient care in doing what is otherwise permissible. A strict, or willful, tort combines intentional and negligent torts; it involves elements of intent and malice or ill will. Malice of ill will may be attributed to someone who is aware of danger to others but who is indifferent to their safety or fails to use ordinary care to avoid injury.

In most cases of negligence, the jury considers awarding damages to compensate the plaintiff. The awards generally take into account the physical, mental, and emotional suffering of the plaintiff, and future medical payments may be allowed for.

Punitive damages are also possible but are more likely to be awarded in cases of intentional liability. Punitive damages are designed to punish the tortfeasor and to deter future inappropriate behavior. Punitive damages are also possible in negligence cases where the actions of the tortfeasor were in total disregard for the safety of others.

Foreseeability/Duty to Protect

The area of civil liability is of great importance to the security industry since the courts have been more willing to hold the industry legally responsible for protection in this area than in others. This trend is particularly noticeable in the hotel and motel industry where owners are liable for failure to adequately protect guests from foreseeable criminal activity. In some circumstances, a landlord or hotel or motel owner might be held accountable for failure to provide adequate protection from criminal actions. In *Klein v. 1500 Massachusetts Avenue Apartment Corporation*,[25] a tenant who was criminally assaulted sued the corporation. The decision centered on the issue that the landlord had prior notice of criminal activity (including burglary and assault) against his tenants and property. In addition, the landlord was aware of conditions that made it likely that criminal activities would continue. The court ruled that the landlord had failed in an obligation to provide adequate security and was thus liable. A similar case was made against Howard Johnson's by the actress, Connie Frances.[26] Frances alleged that the hotel had failed to provide adequate locks on the doors. The jury awarded Frances over $1 million.

Other decisions (*Philip Aaron Banks, et al. v. Hyatt Corporation* and *Refco Poydras Hotel Joint Venture and Allen B. Morrison, et al. v. MGM Grand Hotel, et al.*) have followed earlier landmark cases.[27] In the Banks case, the court held the hotel liable for foreseeable events that led to the murder of Banks by a third party. Banks was shot only four feet from the hotel door. The suit alleged that the hotel failed to provide adequate security and to warn Banks of the danger of criminal activity near the hotel entrance. The jury awarded the plaintiffs $975,000, even though evidence was introduced that showed that the hotel had made reasonable efforts to provide additional protection in the area. The court stated that "the owner or operator of a business owes a duty to invitees to exercise reasonable care to protect them from injury," noting that "the duty of a business to protect invitees can extend to adjacent property, particularly entrances to the business premises, if the business is aware of a dangerous condition on the adjacent property and fails to warn its invitees or to take some other reasonable preventive action." In the Morrison case, a robber followed Morrison from the hotel desk into the elevator after Morrison had cashed in his chips and withdrew his jewelry and cash from the hotel's safe. The robber took Morrison's property at gun point and then knocked him unconscious. Morrison brought suit against the hotel for failing to provide adequate security, noting that a similar robbery had recently occurred. The appellate court supported Morrison's contention saying, "a landowner must exercise ordinary care and prudence to render the premises reasonably safe for the visit of a person invited on his premises for business purposes." In *McCarty v. Pheasant Run, Inc.*,[28] however, the court recognized that invitees who fail to take basic security precautions may not have cause for action against the hotel.

In determining foreseeability, another factor to take into account is the nature and condition of the premises at the time the incident occurred. The following case was reported in *Premises Liability: Legal Considerations for the Industrial and Retail Manager.*

> In a case, *Gomez v. Ticor*,[29] involving a murder in a parking garage of a commercial office building the court commented that the very nature of a parking structure to be such that criminal activity was something that could be anticipated:
>
>> [W]e note the unique nature of a parking complex, which invites acts of theft and vandalism. In such structures, numerous tempting targets (car stereos, car contents, the cars themselves) are displayed for the thief; high walls, low ceilings and the absence of cars' owners allow the thief or vandal to work in privacy and give him time to complete his task. Such circumstances increase the likelihood of criminal misconduct. In addition, the deserted, labyrinthine nature of these structures, especially at night, makes them likely places for robbers and rapists to lie in wait. Robbery, rape, and violent consequences to anyone who interrupts these crimes, may thus also be foreseeable.

The foreseeability issue has been applied to other areas of business in recent years. In *Sharpe v. Peter Pan Bus Lines*,[30] the court awarded $550,000 for a wrong-

ful death attributed to negligent security in a bus terminal. The same basic concept of foreseeability was applied in *Nelson v. Church's Fried Chicken.*[31] In fact, the
concept of foreseeability has been expanded beyond the narrow opinion that
foreseeability is implied in failure to provide security for specific criminal behavior.
This concept implies that, since certain attacks have occurred in or near the company, the company should reasonably be expected to foresee potential security
problems and provide adequate security. In a recent Iowa Supreme Court decision,
the court abolished the need for prior violent acts to establish foreseeability. In
Galloway v. Bankers Trust Company and Trustee Midlands Mall,[32] the court ruled
foreseeability could be established by "all facts and circumstances," not just prior
violent acts. Therefore prior thefts may be sufficient to establish foreseeability
since these offenses could lead to violence. In another case, *Polly Suzanne Paterson
v. Kent C. Deeb, Transamerica Insurance Co., W. Fenton Langston, and Hartford
Accident & Indemnity Co.,*[33] a Florida court held that the plaintiff may recover for
a sexual assault without proof of prior similar incidents of the premises.

Nondelegable Duty

Another legal trend is to prevent corporations from divesting themselves of liability by assigning protection services to a contractor. Under the principle of agency
law, such an assignment transferred the liability for the service from the con-
tractee to the contractor. The courts, however, have held that some obligations
cannot be entirely transferred. This principle is called "nondelegable duty." Based
on this principle, contractual provisions that shift liability to the subcontractors
have not been recognized by the courts. These contractual provisions are commonly called "hold harmless" clauses.

Take for example, *Dupree v. Piggly Wiggly Shop Rite Foods Inc.* The court
decided that:

> [p]ublic policy requires [that] one may not employ or contract with a special agency or
> detective firm to ferret out the irregularities of his customers or employees and then
> escape liability for the malicious prosecution or false arrest on the ground that the
> agency and/or its employees are independent contractors.[34]

Imputed Negligence

Imputed negligence simply means that, "by reason of some relation existing
between A and B, the negligence of A is to be charged against B, although B has
played no part in it, has done nothing whatever to aid or encourage it, or indeed
has done all that he possibly can to prevent it. This is commonly called 'imputed
contributory negligence.'"[35]

Vicarious Liability

One form of imputed negligence is "vicarious liability." The concept of vicarious,
or imputed, liability arises from agency law in which one party has the power to
control the actions of another party involved in the contract or relationship. The
principal is thus responsible for the actions of a servant or agent. In legal terms,
this responsibility is called *respondeat superior*. In short, employers are liable for
the actions of their employees while they are employed on the firms' business.
Employers are liable for the actions of their agents even if the employers do
nothing to cause the actions directly. The master is held liable for any intentional
tort committed by the servant where its purpose, however misguided, is wholly or
partially to further the master's business. Employers may even be liable for some

of the actions of their employees when the employees are neither at work nor engaged in company business. For example, consider the position of an employer who issues a firearm to an employee. The employee, at home and therefore off duty, plays with the firearm, which discharges and injures a neighbor. The neighbor may sue the employer for negligently entrusting a dangerous instrument to an employee or for the negligence in selecting a careless employee. The principle or *respondeat superior* (let the master respond) is well established in common law. It is not in itself the subject of any substantial dispute, and at those times when it becomes an issue in a dispute, the area of contention is factual rather than the doctrine itself. As was noted earlier, in the doctrine of respondeat superior, "[a] servant is a person employed by a master to perform service in his affairs, whose physical conduct in the performance of the service is controlled or is subject to the right of control by the master. This court has stated that the right of control and not necessarily the exercise of that right is the test of the relationship of master and servant. Basically, it is distinction between a person who is subject to orders as to how he does his work and one who agrees only to do the work in his own way."[36] There is no question that an employer (master) is liable for injuries caused by employees (servants) who are acting within the scope of their employment. This is not to say that the employees are relieved of all liability. They are in fact the principal in any action, but since the employee rarely has the financial resources to satisfy a third-party suit, an injured person will look beyond the employee to the employer for compensation for damages.

Clearly the relationship between master and servant under *respondeat superior* needs definition. Under the terms of the *Graalum v. Radisson Ramp* ruling, in-house security officers are servants whereas contract security personnel may not be. In the latter case, as discussed previously, contract personnel are employees of the supplying agency, and in most cases, the hiring company will not be held liable for their acts. The relationship is a complex one, however.

If security officers are acting within the scope of their employment and commit a wrongful act, the employer is liable for the actions. The matter then turns on the scope of the officer's employment and the employer-employee relationship. One court described the scope of employment as depending on: "(1) The act being of the kind the offender is employed to perform; (2) it occurring substantially within the authorized time and space limits of the employment, and (3) the offender being motivated, at least in part, by a purpose to serve the master."[37]

. . . Liability then is a function of the control exercised or permitted in the relationship between the security officer and the hiring company. If the hiring company maintains a totally hands-off posture with respect to personnel supplied by the agency, it may well avoid liability for wrongful acts performed by such personnel. On the other hand, there is some precedent for considering the hiring company as sharing some liability simply by virtue of its underlying rights of control over its own premises, no matter how it wishes to exercise that control. Many hiring companies are, however, motivated to contractually reject any control of security personnel on their premises in order to avoid liability. This, as was pointed out in *The Private Police*, works to discourage hiring companies from regulating the activity of security employees and "the company that exercises controls, e.g., carefully examines the credentials of the guard, carefully determines the procedures the guard will follow, and pays close attention to all his activities, may still be substantially increasing its risk of liability to any third persons who are in fact, injured by an act of the guard."[38]

It is further suggested in this excellent study that there may be an expansion of certain nondelegable duty rules into consideration of the responsibilities for the actions of security personnel. As was discussed previously, the concept of the nondelegable duty provides that there are certain duties and responsibilities that are imposed on an individual and for which that individual remains responsible even though an independent contractor is hired to implement them. Such duties currently encompass keeping the workplace safe and the premises reasonably safe for business visitors. It is also possible that the courts may find negligence in cases where the hiring companies, in an effort to avoid liability, have neglected to exercise any control over the selection and training of personnel, and they may further find that such negligence on the part of the hiring company has led to injury to third-party victims.

Vicarious liability requires a direct employer-employee relationship; it does not apply to cases in which an independent contractor is working for a firm. This is because the employer has no way of controlling the way an independent contractor performs the work. There are many exceptions to this rule, however. For example, the employer may be liable for the negligent selection of the contractor, or the employer may have exercised some day-to-day control over the employee.

Criminal Liability

Criminal liability is most frequently used against private security personnel in cases of assault, battery, manslaughter, and murder. Other common charges include burglary, trespass, criminal defamation, false arrest, unlawful use of weapons, disorderly conduct, extortion, eavesdropping, theft, perjury, and kidnapping. Security officers charged with criminal liability have several options in defending their actions. First, they might try to show that they were entitled to use force in self-defense or that they made a reasonable mistake, which would negate criminal intent. Other defenses include entrapment, intoxication, insanity, consent (the parties involved concurred with the actions), and compulsion (the officer was forced or compelled to commit the act). As has been already noted in previous discussions, a corporation or an association could be charged with criminal liability as well as an individual officer.

The reporting of crime is an area in which security officers are liable for criminal prosecution. In general, private citizens are no longer obliged to report crime or to prevent it. But some jurisdictions still recognize the concept of misprision of felony—that is, concealing knowledge of a felony. Such legislation makes it a crime to not report a felony. To be guilty of misprision of felony, the prosecution must prove beyond a reasonable doubt that (1) the principal committed and completed the alleged felony, (2) the defendant had full knowledge of that fact, (3) the defendant failed to notify the authorities, and (4) the defendant took affirmative steps to conceal the crime of the principal.

Security officers may also be liable for failure to perform jobs they have been contracted or employed to perform. If guards fail to act in a situation in which they have the ability and obligation to act, the courts suggest that they could be criminally liable for failure to perform their duties. Another issue in security work involves undercover operations. Many times security operatives are accused of soliciting an illegal act. Where security officers clearly intended for crimes to be committed, they may be charged with solicitation of an illegal act or conspiracy in an illegal act. This is in contrast to the public sector, where most police officers are protected by statute from crimes they commit in the performance of their duty. Thus only the private citizen may be charged with such an offense, and the only issue that can be contested is the defendant's intent.

Entrapment, which is solicitation by police officers, is another charge that may be leveled against security officers. While entrapment does not generally apply to private citizens (the case of State v. Farns[39] is frequently cited to prove that entrapment does not apply to private citizens), several states have passed legislation that extends entrapment statutes to cover private persons as well as police officers. Until the issue is resolved in the courts in the next few years, security officers involved in undercover operations should be careful to avoid actions that might lead to entrapment charges.

Security and the Law References

1. Michigan Revised Statutes, Section 338.1051-338.1083.
2. Robert D. Pursley, *Introduction to Criminal Justice*, 5th ed. (Macmillan, New York, 1991), p. 35.
3. *U.S. v. Hillsman*, 522 F.2d 454, 461 (7 Cir. 1975).
4. *Cervantez v. J.C. Penney Company*, 156 Cal. Rptr. 198 (1978).
5. *Illinois Revised Statutes*, 1985, ch. 38, par. 16A-5.
6. 5 Cal. 2d 175, 54 p. 2d 20 (1936).
7. *Escobedo v. State of Illinois*, (378 U.S. 478, 32 Ohio Op 92d) 31, 84 S.Ct. 1758 12 L.Ed(2d)977 (1964).
8. *Miranda v. Arizona*, 384 U.S., 486 86 S.CT 1602, 16L.Ed.2d.691.
9. *In re Deborah C.*, 1977 Cal. Rptr. 852 (1981).
10. *Wisconsin Statutes Annotated*, Section 943.50.
11. *West Virginia v. William H. Muegge*, 360 SE, 2d 216 (1987).
12. *People vs. Zelinski*, 594 P 2d 1000 (1979).
13. *Mapp v. Ohio*, 367 U.S. 643 (1961).
14. *Weeks v. United States*, 232 U.S. 383 (1914).
15. *Burdeau v. McDowell*, 256 U.S. 465 (1921).
16. *State v. Scrotsky*, 39 NJ 410, 416 189 A.2d 23 (1963).
17. *People v. Jones*, 393 NE 2d. 443 (1979).
18. *People v. Randazzo*, 220 Cal. 2d 268, 34 Cal. Rptr. 65 (1963).
19. *Thacker v. Commonwealth*, 310 Ky. 701, 221 SW 2d 682 (1949).
20. *Weyandt v. Mason Stores*, Inc., 279 F. Supp. 283, 287 (W.D. Pa. 1968).
21. Charles Schnabolk, *Physical Security: Practices and Technology* (Butterworth Publishers, Stoneham, MA, 1983), p. 74.
22. Restatement of Torts, Second Edition 307.
23. *Illinois Revised Statutes*, ch. 110, sections 2-116.
24. *Fisher v. Carrousel Motor Hotel, Inc.*, 424 SW2d 627 (Texas 1976).
25. *Klein v. 1500 Massachusetts Avenue Apartment Corporation*, 439 F 2d 477 DC Cir (1970).
26. *Garzilli v. Howard Johnson's Motor Lodge, Inc.*, 419 F Supp. 1210 U.S. DCT EDNY (1976).
27. *Philip Aaron Banks, et al. v. Hyatt Corporation and Refco Poydras Hotel Joint Venture*, 722 F.2d 214 (1984); and *Allen B. Morrison, et al. v. MGM Grand Hotel, et al.*, 570 F. Supp. 1449 (1983).
28. *McCarty v. Pheasant Run, Inc.*, F.2d 1554 (1987).
29. *Gomez v. Ticor*, 145 Cal. App. 3d 622, 193 Cal. Rptr. 600, 1983 (as reported in "Premises Liability: Legal Considerations for the Industrial and Retail Manager," p. 6, Mary Ann Alsnauer, Laura D. Wolpow, Howarth and Smith, Los Angeles, California).
30. *Sharpe v. Peter Pan Bus Lines*, No. 49694, Suffolk County, MA.
31. *Nelson v. Church's Fried Chicken*, 31 ATLA L. Rep 84 (1987).
32. *Galloway v. Bankers Trust Company and Trustee Midlands Mall*, No. 63/86-1879 Iowa Supreme Court.
33. *Polly Suzanne Paterson v. Kent C. Deeb, Transamerica Insurance Co., W. Fenton Langston, and Hartford Accident & Indemnity Co.*, 472 S. 2d 1210.
34. *Dupree v. Piggly Wiggly Shop Rite Foods Inc.*, 542 S.W. 2d 882 (Texas, 1976).
35. William L. Prosser, *Handbook of the Law of Torts*, 4th ed., Hornbook Series (St. Paul, Minn.: West, 1970), p. 458.
36. *Graalum v. Radisson Ramp*, 245 Minn. 54, 71 NW 2d 904, 908 (1955).
37. *Fornier v. Churchill Downs-Latonia*, 292 Ky. 215, 166 SW 2d 38 (1942).
38. James S. Kakalik and Sorrel Wildhurn, *The Private Police* (New York: Crane, Russak & Co., 1977).
39. *State vs. Farns*, 542 P.2d 725 Kan. (1975).

13 *Liaison with Law Enforcement and Fire Authorities*

For a high-rise commercial office building to have a successful security and fire life safety program, it is essential for the building owner or manager to have liaisons with (i.e., develops and maintains a successful working relationship with) agencies in the public sector, including law enforcement and fire authorities who have jurisdiction over the building. *Webster's College Dictionary* defines *liaison* as "the contact or connection maintained by communications between units of the armed forces or of any other organization in order to ensure concerted action or cooperation."

Liaison with Law Enforcement

Law enforcement authorities are concerned primarily with crime prevention and control. This involves the protection of the lives, property, and general welfare of the public community. This protection is achieved largely through the enforcement of laws by police funded by public monies. High-rise building owners or managers may interact with public law authorities such as police and sheriff's departments and state or federal agencies.

Police and Sheriff's Departments

The *police department* is the primary law enforcement agency in a city. The *sheriff's department* serves a similar function outside city limits or if no municipal police department exists. Both departments are the point of origin for reporting all crimes. Although other agencies may have final jurisdiction over many classes of crime, initial authority almost always rests with the local police department. Police and sheriff's departments handle tasks such as taking reports and investigating crimes; maintaining arrest, missing persons, and identification records; keeping records of lost and stolen property; taking reports of vehicle accidents (but not those that occur on state roads); issuing gun permits; and transporting and maintaining custody of prisoners. Local police also may provide traffic control support for special events. A local marshal or constable may serve criminal and bench warrants and service of process.

State Law Enforcement Agencies

State agencies—the State Police, State Patrol, Department of Justice, Department of Public Safety, and so on—have authority that varies from state to state but may include enforcement of traffic laws, conducting investigations, gathering intelligence, and providing protection of public figures.

Federal Law Enforcement Agencies

Federal agencies have jurisdiction over areas as defined by their charters. The Department of Justice (DOJ) includes the following organizations:

- *Federal Bureau of Investigation* (FBI). The FBI has jurisdiction over federal crimes and offenses such as bank robbery, kidnapping, white collar crime, public corruption, and terrorism. It has concurrent jurisdiction with the Drug Enforcement Administration in drug enforcement.
- *Drug Enforcement Administration* (DEA). This administration has jurisdiction over federal narcotics offenses and provides special training and laboratory services to law enforcement.
- *U.S. Marshal's Office.* The U.S. Marshal's Office handles federal service of process.
- *Immigration and Naturalization Service* (INS). The INS handles immigration-related matters.

The DOJ, along with the Architectural Transportation Compliance Board (ATCB), the Equal Employment Opportunity Commission (EEOC), and the Federal Communications Commission (FCC), has responsibility for exacting compliance with various parts of the Americans with Disabilities Act (ADA).

The Treasury Department includes the Secret Service, which provides protection for the President and public figures and has jurisdiction over counterfeiting, credit card and wire frauds; the Bureau of Alcohol, Tobacco and Firearms (ATF) enforces laws pertaining to alcohol, tobacco, firearms, and explosives and conducts investigations (such as the 1992 New York World Trade Center bombing incident); the Customs Service enforces customs laws and regulations, including antismuggling; and the Internal Revenue Service (IRS) handles tax collection. The Department of Labor includes the Occupational Safety and Health Administration (OSHA), which regulates safety in the workplace. The Department of Defense includes the Defense Investigative Service, which regulates the protection of government contractors' classified information. The Federal Emergency Management Agency (FEMA) provides disaster relief and manages the civilian response to national security crises. Information obtained from *Liaison: Who's What in Law Enforcement and Regulatory Agencies* (Polek and Crowl 1994) was helpful in understanding law enforcement agencies.

The building security representative can foster relationships with law enforcement by formal and informal communication. Initially, the security representative most often successful at this is the former police officer now working in the private sector. There is already an established rapport, the individual knows how law enforcement operates, what departmental and legal constraints exist, and whom to call for a particular problem or request. The former law enforcement officer already has established the essential element in every successful human relationship—trust. Security representatives who do not have a law enforcement background need to develop this rapport and trust. Law enforcement people are pretty straightforward, and private security professionals can establish sound working relationships with them by approaching them in an open and honest fashion. There is a strong underlying reason such a relationship is of mutual benefit to both law enforcement and the private security representative: the common objective of crime prevention. During criminal investigations conducted within a high-rise building, for example, a successful working relationship with law enforcement can greatly improve the outcome. Such investigations commonly are conducted in conjunction with the local police or sheriff's department, or federal agency, and their support and assistance must be obtained to bring the effort to a satisfactory conclusion. It is important to remember that the authority of a private investigator is comparable only to that of a private citizen in areas such as detaining suspects and obtaining access to information. (See Chapter 9's "Private Sector and Public Law Enforcement Investigations" section for details on this subject.)

Liaison with Fire Authorities

Fire authorities are primarily concerned with the preservation of people's lives and property, including the enforcement of local and state fire codes. Municipal, county, and state fire marshals who enforce fire codes and conduct arson investigations may have police officer status to assist them in carrying out their duties and responsibilities.

Building fire life safety systems and fire prevention inspections, as well as investigations of building fires, commonly are conducted in conjunction with the local fire department inspector or the fire marshal who has jurisdiction over the building. Inspections and investigations related to occupant safety frequently are conducted by state or federal agencies such as OSHA. The building safety representative can foster relationships with these agencies and individuals by formal and informal communication.

As with the security discipline, the safety representative most often successful at this is the former fire department officer now working in the private sector. No matter what a person's background is, however, most experience shows that public agencies, such as fire departments, are only too anxious to assist high-rise buildings in establishing and maintaining sound fire life safety programs for building users. Fire departments in large cities—New York, Chicago, and Los Angeles—have even established specialized high-rise divisions and units.

For example, the Los Angeles Fire Department is tremendously supportive of fire life safety programs in the city's 750-plus high-rise buildings. Its fire safety specialists assist building owners and managers in:

1. Developing and maintaining up-to-date certified Building Emergency Procedures Manuals
2. Training building emergency staff, tenants, and occupants in high-rise fire life safety procedures
3. Conducting fire evacuation drills

4. Certifying private consultants who are authorized to write Building Emergency Procedures Manuals and conduct fire life safety training for staff and tenants of high-rise buildings
5. Offering professional expertise and advice on fire life safety matters
6. Inspecting and enforcing the requirements of the City Fire Code, as it relates to the installation and maintenance of fire life safety systems and equipment

Fostering Relationships with Law Enforcement and Fire Authorities

The following sections describe ways to initiate positive interaction with local law enforcement and the local fire authority having jurisdiction; these mostly have to do with mutual respect and planned coordination of efforts.

Communication

It is important to establish a clear line of communication with law enforcement and the fire department and, wherever possible, involve them in implementing the building's security and fire life safety program. Most city police agencies and some sheriff's departments have a community affairs manager or a contact officer—become familiar with that individual and learn of any services these agencies may offer and ways to support their efforts. Likewise, with the fire department, establish contact and learn ways to cooperate with each other. Any public service education programs appropriate to the building and offered by these agencies should be supported by the building.

Reporting Crimes

Whenever possible, provide law enforcement with statistics of criminal acts, particularly crimes of larceny, that have occurred at the building. Encourage tenants to report crimes to law enforcement. Public reports such as Uniform Crime Reports and the National Incident-Based Reporting Systems are based on data generated at the local level. By reporting crimes to law enforcement, the local criminal statistical data will more accurately indicate what types of crimes are being committed in the community. Such information will provide a clearer picture of crime and may assist law enforcement in justifying requests for additional law enforcement officers.

Complying with Laws, Regulations, and Codes

Always comply willingly with state and local laws, particularly as they pertain to maintaining a safe workplace for building occupants. Maintain up-to-date self-inspections and thorough maintenance of building fire life safety systems and equipment. Keep fire protection test records and log sheets current—including generator tests, sprinkler system water and air pressure gauge readings, tests of fire detection and suppression systems, portable fire extinguisher checks, and equipment service invoices. Maintain documentation according to the guidelines of the authority having jurisdiction. When inspections are conducted by state or local fire officials, escort the inspector on the tour of the building. The inspector will offer acceptable ways to correct deficiencies and will give advice that will be invaluable in preparing for the next inspection. Prompt correction of violations within established time frames and to the satisfaction of the inspector will assist in developing a good relationship with that individual.

Enlisting Public Agency Support

Consult the appropriate authority when problems exist that the building cannot satisfactorily handle. For example, if a tenant fails to respond to the constant warnings of the building Fire Safety Director regarding the storage of material that constitutes a fire hazard in public corridors, solicit the support of the local fire authority. The local fire inspector may decide to carry out an unannounced fire prevention inspection with particular emphasis on that tenant. The inspector thus takes building management out of what can be a sensitive and potentially confrontational situation. Also, consult with law enforcement regarding any serious theft problem within a building. When appropriate, involve law enforcement in security investigations.

Hospitality

Invite law enforcement agencies for a tour of the building to view the security program, and acquaint them with the role of the security staff. If law enforcement agencies wish to practice operations, such as hostage simulations, encourage these activities. Invite members of fire prevention groups to tour the building and view the fire life safety program. Invite the fire department to conduct familiarization drills of the building. If fire and law enforcement officials invite building representatives to tour their operations, such offers should always be graciously accepted. Taking local law enforcement and fire representatives to lunch, at least annually, is strongly encouraged.

Drills

Conduct a full-scale building mock disaster drill in conjunction with local emergency response groups—the local fire department's fire suppression crews and paramedics, local hospitals and health services, local law enforcement, the American Red Cross, and other emergency organizations within the community. If thoroughly prepared and properly executed, this drill can be of great educational value to high-rise building staff, tenants, and all outside agencies and groups who participate, and it can greatly assist in working effectively with the local fire authority having jurisdiction and local law enforcement.

Public Agency Presentations

Invite law enforcement and fire department representatives to give presentations to occupants and tenants. For example, representatives of police bomb squads and the ATF can provide very informative, interesting, and helpful information regarding bombs and bomb threats; likewise, the FBI, regarding white-collar crime and terrorism. Fire departments, particularly in larger cities where more staff generally are available, are willing to do special presentations on fire life safety. Some will even provide tabletop and live demonstrations and hands-on portable fire extinguisher training for building occupants. Fire department representatives always should be invited to attend building fire drills and evacuation exercises. Presentations by law enforcement and fire departments can benefit not only the building concerned but can also assist these public agencies in their efforts to control crime and promote public safety. For example, the local police may be experiencing considerable pressure from the business community at large because of a recent rash of vehicle burglaries and thefts in the city. An opportunity to present their *Protect Your Auto* message to building occupants should be welcomed.

Professional Security and Fire Life Safety Organizations

Support private organizations such as the American Society for Industrial Security (ASIS) and the National Fire Protection Association (NFPA). ASIS has local chapters and some law enforcement representatives attend these monthly meetings. It also has a Law Enforcement Liaison Council that provides guidelines and recommendations as to how private security can interact with law enforcement agencies. Annual events like "Law Enforcement Appreciation Day," when local members of law enforcement are invited by members of ASIS to a special luncheon, are opportunities to express gratitude to members of law enforcement. NFPA, among its myriad of activities, sponsors public fire safety education and awareness events such as the annual National Fire Prevention Week. In 1920, October 9—a significant date because the Great Chicago Fire occurred on that day in 1871—was declared National Fire Prevention Day by President Woodrow Wilson. In 1922, the observance was extended to one week by the NFPA when it assumed sponsorship of the event. In 1925, the entire week containing October 9 was officially proclaimed Fire Prevention Week by President Calvin Coolidge (*Security Sales* 1994, p. 127).

Community Service

It is a good practice to sponsor community service programs that are offered through local law enforcement or fire department agencies. Sponsoring youth sports teams and assisting in volunteer fund-raisers can help considerably in working effectively with local law enforcement and fire authorities.

Summary

In addressing security, the owner or manager of a high-rise building focuses on loss prevention, while public law enforcement agencies are primarily concerned with crime control and public safety. In addressing fire life safety, management must concentrate on the objectives of fire prevention, early detection and prompt suppression of fire, immediate notification of the fire department, and rapid notification and evacuation of occupants to safety.

Representatives of a high-rise commercial office building can find many opportunities to cooperate with public agencies. The result of this effort will be an enhanced building security and fire life safety program and a safer community at large.

References

Polek, Victor, and Larry Crowl, *Liaison: Who's What in Law Enforcement and Regulatory Agencies* (presentation for CPP Review Class, ASIS Los Angeles Chapter, October 15, 1994).

Security Sales, "Fire tech update," Vol. 16, No. 10 (Bobit Publishing Company, Redondo Beach, CA, October 1994).

Webster's College Dictionary, 1992 Edition (From *Random House Webster's College Dictionary* by Random House, Inc. Copyright © 1995, 1992, 1991 by Random House, Inc. Reprinted by permission of Random House, Inc., New York, 1992.)

14 *Trends in Security and Fire Life Safety Issues*

Security and fire life safety issues in today's high-rise commercial office buildings are of major concern to building owners and managers. A successful building program takes into consideration the security and fire life safety of existing tenants, serves as a means by which prospective tenants may be attracted to a facility, and can be used as a management tool to positively enhance ongoing tenant relations. In addition, such a program substantially mitigates the liability risk to which all businesses in modern high-rise buildings are exposed. The lack of adequate security and safety provisions for high-rise occupants combined with the increase in crime has led to much litigation, particularly over the past twenty years.

Adequate Security Measures

For security, increased litigation has not so much been due to the *lack* of adequate security measures, but, in many cases, a *perception of the lack* thereof. As Post and colleagues (1991) write, "It is difficult to protect against legal actions regardless of what measures of protection are taken unless there is a basic agreement about what constitutes *enough* security. . . . There has not, however, been a national effort developed to undertake the process of developing standards for the security industry as a whole because of the complexity of the issue" (p. 221). The security profession itself is divided over the question of whether developing additional standards will allow an objective determination of "adequate security."

Part of the problem lies in the fact that every high-rise facility is different and no two security professionals will consistently agree on what constitutes adequate security for a particular facility. So many recommendations are *subjective* determinations by individuals with varying opinions about the value of particular security measures. For example, one security professional may rely heavily on using closed-circuit television systems to observe security violations, while another may prefer the heavy deployment of security personnel; one may emphasize the use of electronic card systems to control access to a facility, while another may insist on the presence of a uniformed security officer to identify persons and control access. Even if security professionals were able to agree on what an adequate security level is for a particular facility,

435

inevitably budgetary considerations still must be taken into consideration. A fully occupied, financially sound building in a thriving business district probably will be more likely to invest money in its security program than a partially occupied building that can only charge lower-than-market rents because of the fact that the facility has deteriorated and is in a district many businesses have vacated. The dilemma for the building owner or manager is that the latter building may actually have a greater need for security than the former.

Adequate Fire Life Safety Measures

For fire life safety, the adequacy of safety provisions is somewhat clearer. Many of the requirements of high-rise buildings have been mandated by life safety codes. For example, modern high-rise buildings are required by code to install and maintain automatic fire detection and suppression systems and to establish and maintain a pre-fire plan that includes adequate training of occupants as to what they should do in case of a fire or other emergency. Any building owner and manager not complying with these codes and regulations is at considerable risk of sanctions and fines imposed by the local authority having jurisdiction and to significant liability risk if injuries, deaths, or property loss result from inadequate safety measures.

Security and Fire Life Safety Trends

In the future, we may see further development of security and fire life safety trends only beginning to emerge today:

1. "At 2 percent of the gross domestic product, economic crime is on the rise and seems to be out of control" (Cunningham and Strauchs 1992, p. 29). This tremendous drain on businesses may cause building management to implement stricter security controls on occupants and employees. As tenants become increasingly aware of the availability of cost-effective private security systems and devices, they will make more use of such products to enhance the security of their businesses.

2. If crime involving violence against persons further escalates in society, there will be increasing litigious pressure on building owners, managers, and tenants to take greater precautions to ensure the safety of building occupants and users. According to *USA Today*, between 1981 and 1991, the U.S. prison population more than doubled, while violent crime rose more than 40 percent. America [sic], in fact, has the most people in jail per capita in the world (Wolf 1994, p. 13). Cunningham and Strauchs (1992) state: "Tremendous increases in civil litigation and damage awards for security-related incidents have occurred over the past 20 years. By some estimates, experts agree that security- and crime-related lawsuits have risen 17 times higher than the inflation rate" (p. 29). Litigious pressures also are present in building emergency response areas; building staff are always, and will continue to be, under scrutiny at emergency scenes. To avoid liability, management will always need to ensure that their building has established, implemented, and maintained a sound Building Emergency Plan. Fire authorities in

each jurisdiction also will require more Building Emergency Procedures Manuals in generic format for easier use by responding fire departments. There will be a greater demand for increased security and fire life safety education of building occupants.

3.   The Americans with Disabilities Act, which became law in 1990, will continue to lead to modifications in high-rise building design and may result in a greater number of occupants with disabilities working in these facilities. The latter may cause increased problems involving the safe evacuation of occupants requiring assistance during building emergencies; also, the issue of whether dedicated elevators can be used to evacuate such individuals during emergencies will continue to be debated by fire safety specialists, mechanical engineers, and fire protection engineers.

4.   Security and fire life safety systems and equipment will continue to benefit from engineering and technological developments taking place in the field, and will become increasingly microcomputer-based and user-friendly. The electronic supervision of security and fire life safety systems will become further integrated into central monitoring systems. The benefits of such integration will include sharing of information and improved efficiency of system operations.

5.   Terrorist incidents, such as the 1993 New York World Trade Center and the 1995 Oklahoma City bombings, may lead to the threat of explosions being given more consideration in building design and construction. Previously, "[m]any government buildings have been designed for resistance to car bombs with vehicular barriers and adequate spatial separation of vehicles from buildings. However, commercial buildings like the World Trade Center have never taken explosion as a risk consideration. Buildings of the future will need to add new design criteria: explosion resistance, along with fire resistance and crime resistance" (Atlas 1993, p. 6).

The Oklahoma incident may also lead to greater cooperation of security professionals working with architects, builders, and structural engineers to identify and eliminate vulnerable points, which may provide for criminal opportunity, in facilities prior to incorporating them into the building design. Such an approach should embody the concept of *crime prevention through environmental design* (CPTED—pronounced *sep-ted*). According to Post (1995, p. 19):

> In its purest sense, CPTED is the passive use of the physical environment to reduce the opportunity for and fear of predatory stranger-to-stranger crime—burglary, robbery, assault, larceny, murder, rape, even bombing. CPTED relies on three main strategies: natural surveillance, natural access control, and territoriality—establishing boundaries and transitional spaces. CPTED looks at siting, landscaping, footprints, window schedules, facades, entrances, lobbies, layouts, lighting, materials, and traffic and circulation patterns.

"Security design asks, What kind of locks and electronics are required? CPTED asks, Why is there a door needed here? adds architect-criminologist Randall Atlas of Atlas Safety and Security Design Inc., Miami" (Post, 1995, p. 20).

The CPTED argument regarding the Oklahoma incident is that "if the Murrah Federal building had been set back from the street on four sides instead of three, would more of the children in the day care center above ground zero still be alive today?" (Post 1995, p. 26).

6.   Security and Fire Safety Directors will have increasing access to computer information services on security and fire life safety subjects. Also, computers will

become increasingly popular for report writing, security and safety incident tracking (sorting by time of day, day of week, month, year, type of incident, suspect, or
any other field in the incident report), spotting trends, reporting the activity of the
security department, conducting investigations, controlling building keys, monitoring savings in terms of recoveries and losses avoided, monitoring expenses,
and tracking the security budget.

7. Technological developments occurring in society at a blinding speed also
mean that "[d]uring the 1990s, public and private security practitioners will be
confronted with more sophisticated and technical crimes that will have a higher
dollar loss per incident than previously experienced" (Cunningham and Strauchs
1992, p. 29).

8. There will be a greater demand for improved recruitment, screening,
selection, and training of individuals who implement high-rise building security
and fire life safety programs. For these individuals, as staff are increasingly
required to interface with microcomputer-based systems, there will a greater
emphasis on computer literacy. Fire Safety Directors will be required to undergo
more formal training to ensure that they are competent to administer building fire
life safety programs. For example, the City of New York Fire Department's Local
Law No. 5 already requires Fire Safety Directors of high-rise office buildings to
satisfactorily complete a Certificate of Fitness. These individuals must possess
experience involving fire protection and fire prevention activity and must pass
both a Fire Safety Director test and an on-site test before being certified to work at
a particular facility.

As the *Hallcrest Report II* states: "During the period 1976 to 1990, a dramatic
rise in the number of security-oriented certificate and degree programs occurred.
In 1976, certificate and degree programs numbered 33, and by 1990 the total had
increased to 164" (Cunningham et al. 1990, p. 149). The demand for better-educated supervisory and management security staff in high-rise buildings will escalate. This trend will continue as higher demands are placed on these staff to efficiently plan, organize, and allocate the resources of building security programs.
Businesses will increasingly seek security managers with professional accredita-
tions such as a CPP certification. Also, greater professionalism in positions, such
as that of building Fire Safety Director, will occur as increasing demands are made
on them to produce better quality building fire life safety programs. "Companies
are demanding more qualifications from job candidates as the security [and fire
life safety] role takes on increased responsibility and importance" (Kerrigan 1985,
p. 42).

9. The quality of contract security companies providing service to high-rise
buildings will need to improve as building owners and managers rely more heavily on them to provide not only "bodies for the building" but also professional
security expertise in the form of consulting advice, audits and surveys, investigations, development of policies and procedures, and presentations for building staff
and tenants. This customer-driven demand for such expertise is already moving
into the fire life safety arena. Some savvy high-rise building managers, for example, make it clear to security contractor candidates from the start that the contractor hired will be required to develop the facility's Building Emergency Plan.

10. Less public spending for public protection by local and state governments will place a greater onus on building owners and managers to provide better protection for the tenants they serve, and develop more business community–

based crime prevention programs. In some downtown city areas in the United States, groups of high-rise building owners are forming a variation of traditional neighborhood watch programs to enhance public safety. These programs consist of private unarmed security officer patrol teams who patrol city block areas outside buildings in their neighborhood. These patrols are designed to act as a deterrent to crime and to observe crimes in progress and immediately report them to local police.

The trend of less public spending, plus the escalating costs of operating fire departments, may lead to more widespread legislation permitting fire departments to charge fees for certain services such as inspections, permits, and plan reviews that are provided for buildings. For example, Walter Smittle, West Virginia's state fire marshall, after losing half of his operating budget in three years, worked on legislation that allowed some of the lost money to be recouped in this manner in order to continue providing the same level of service (Teague 1992, p. 21).

Summary

Adequate security and fire life safety measures are essential to the safe operation of today's high-rise commercial office buildings. Building and life safety codes and standards specify what constitutes adequate fire life safety; however, there is some disagreement as to what constitutes adequate security.

Trends of rising economic crime, acts of violence, and litigation can be mitigated by factors such as modification of building design, technological sophistication of security and fire life safety systems and equipment, and the increasing use of computers to assist in documentation and operator interface with these systems. Better-educated, trained, and deployed security staff and more efficient utilization of building resources are essential in today's cost-conscious world.

References

Atlas, Randall I., "Security design," *Protection of Assets Manual*, 9th printing. Editor Timothy J. Walsh (Used with permission from The Merritt Company, Santa Monica, CA, 800/638-7597. Copyright September 1993), Bulletin.

Cunningham, William C., and John J. Strauchs, "Security industry trends: 1993 and beyond," *Security Management* (Copyright Hallcrest Systems, Inc., Arlington, VA, December 1992.)

Cunningham, William C., John J. Strauchs, and Clifford W. Van Meter, "Security personnel issues," *The Hallcrest II Report, Private Security Trends 1970–2000* (Butterworth–Heinemann, Stoneham, MA, 1990).

Kerrigan, Lydon, ed., "Job jumping in corporate security," *Security World* (September 1985).

Post, Nadine, M., "More than merely cops and robbers," *Engineering News-Record* (The McGraw-Hill Construction Weekly, May 1, 1995).

Post, Richard S., with Arthur A. Kingsbury and David A. Schachtsiek, *Security Admin- istration, An Introduction to the Protective Services* (Butterworth–Heinemann, Stone- ham, MA, 1991).

Teague, Paul E., "Profile: Walter Smittle, III, Fire Marshal scores points for fire safety," *NFPA Journal* (Used with permission from National Fire Protection Association, Quincy, MA 02169. Copyright November/December 1992), p. 21.

Wolf, Stephen M., "Harvest of tears," *Hemispheres* (Pace Communications, Inc., Nashville, January 1994).

Index